The Origins and History of the All-American
Girls Professional Baseball League

The Origins and History of the All-American Girls Professional Baseball League

Merrie A. Fidler

Foreword by Jean Cione

McFarland & Company, Inc., Publishers
Jefferson, North Carolina, and London

LIBRARY OF CONGRESS CATALOGUING-IN-PUBLICATION DATA

Fidler, Merrie A., 1943–
The origins and history of the all–American girls professional
baseball league / Merrie A. Fidler ; foreword by Jean Cione.
p.   cm.
Includes bibliographical references and index.

ISBN 0-7864-2243-2 (illustrated case binding : 50# alkaline paper) ∞

1. All-American Girls Professional Baseball League — History.
2.   Baseball for women — United States — History — 20th century.
I. Title.
GV875.A56F53   2006   796.357'64'0973 — dc22   2005029387

British Library cataloguing data are available

Cover photograph: Marie "Red" Mahoney and Marnie Danhauser *(courtesy Department of Special Collections at the University of Notre Dame)*

Manufactured in the United States of America

*McFarland & Company, Inc., Publishers
Box 611, Jefferson, North Carolina 28640
www.mcfarlandpub.com*

To the PLAYERS, PERSONNEL, AND FANS
of the
ALL-AMERICAN GIRLS BASEBALL LEAGUE
and to
ANITA M. LIBBEE,
guardian and friend,
who encouraged and enabled this endeavor beyond measure

"Now and forever, you are a part of me...."

List of Figures and Tables

Figures

1. League City Sites, 1943–1954   41
2. The Organizational Structure of the AAGSBL/AAGPBL, 1943–1944   43
3. The Organizational Structure of the AAGPBL/AAGBBL, 1945–1950   76
4. 1947 Pre-Season Tour Agenda for South Bend & Kenosha   97
5. The Organizational Structure of the AGBL, 1951–1954   126
6. The Organizational Structure of the South Bend Blue Sox, ca. 1951–1954   146
7. All-American World Champions' Tour Stops, 1955–1956   161

Tables

1. Optional Outdoor Baseball Regulations for Girls and Women, 1929   18
2. Baseball and Softball as Collegiate Sports for Women   18
3. Record of AAGBBL Equipment & Facility Changes   71
4. AAGBBL Teams, 1943–1954: Dates of Entry and Duration of Play   74
5. AAGBBL Team Operating Expenses, 1948   78
6. AAGBBL Expense-Sharing Plan, 1947   79
7. AAGBBL Expense-Sharing Plan, 1949   79
8. AAGBBL Commissioners, 1946   81
9. South American Tour Scorecard   117
10. Comparison of League Publicity and Promotion Budget with Seasonal Attendance, 1943–1954   137
11. AAGBBL Franchises Dropped and Reorganized, 1944–1954   151
12. AAGBBL Managers, 1943–1954   156
13. AAGBBL Chaperones, 1943–1954   168
14. Previous Softball Experience of 83 AAGBBL Players   183
15. Number of Players from Respective States/Provinces, 1943–1949 & 1951   186
16. Age of Selected AAGBBL Players Upon First Joining the League   187
17. Height and Weight for Selected AAGBBL Players   187
18. Occupations of Selected AAGBBL Players   188
19. Sport Interests of Selected AAGBBL Players   189
20. Number of Sport Interests of Selected AAGBBL Players   189
21. Evolution of Player Conduct Rules   196
22. AAGBBL Player Salaries, 1943–1954   199
23. AAGBBL All-Star Teams, 1943, 1946–1954   210
24. Sophie Kurys' Base Stealing Statistics   213

Table of Contents

List of Figures and Tables   vi

Acknowledgments   ix

Foreword by Jean Cione   1

Preface   5

PART I—HISTORICAL BACKGROUND

1: The Establishment of Softball as a Sport for American Women, 1900–1940   15

PART II—LEAGUE ADMINISTRATION

2: The Trustee Administration, 1943–1944   29

3: Establishing the Public Image: Publicity and Promotion, 1943–1944   50

4: The Management Corporation, 1945–1950   69

5: Expansion of Public Exposure: Publicity and Promotion, 1945–1950   86

6: Independent Team Owners, 1951–1954   125

7: Decentralization of Publicity and Promotion, 1951–1954   136

PART III—TEAM ADMINISTRATION

8: Team Administrative Structure and Personnel   145

9: Team Managers   154

10: Chaperones   166

PART IV—THE PLAYERS

11: Player Recruitment and Sociological Characteristics   181

12: AAGBBL Player Policies and Regulations   195

13: AAGBBL All-Stars   208

PART V—BEYOND THE PLAYING FIELD

14: The Newsletter and the First National Reunion   229

15: The Archives and the Baseball Hall of Fame   244

16: The Organization of the Players' Association and *A League of Their Own*   269

17: The Players' Association, 1990–2004   288

PART VI—SUMMATION

18: Summary and Conclusions   323

PART VII—APPENDICES

Appendix 1: AAGPBL Players' Association Offices and Committee
*   Positions Held, 1980–2004*   333

Appendix 2: AAGBBL Highlights   338

Appendix 3: The League Song   342

Appendix 4: AAGBBL Champions   343

Appendix 5: AAGBBL Point Rating Chart   344

Chapter Notes   347

Bibliography   369

Index   375

Acknowledgments

It is a privilege and a pleasure to acknowledge those who helped make this book a reality. First, the impetus behind this book must be credited to two UMass, Amherst, friends and colleagues from the 1970s. At that time, Dr. Ellen W. Gerber stimulated and encouraged my interest in women's sport history, and doctoral student (now Dr.) Jack W. Berryman assisted my research of the All-American Girls Baseball League.

The substance of the book was initially contributed by individuals who volunteered their personal time, materials, and information in response to inquiries and requests related to the writing of a master's thesis on the AAGBBL. Joe Boland, former *South Bend Tribune* sports editor, began the process in late 1971 when he responded to my inquiries about the AAGBBL and referred me to Jean Faut Winsch, former South Bend player, and ex-manager Chet Grant. Jean graciously loaned me the AAGBBL records Dr. Harold T. Dailey had bequeathed to her, and she also arranged interviews with other South Bend Blue Sox personnel, including players Lib Mahon and Betsy Jochum, chaperone Lucille Moore, business manager Ed Des Lauriers, and umpire Gadget Ward. Chet Grant, then director of Notre Dame's International Sports and Games Collection, loaned me some of his AAGBBL materials and suggested I contact former league owner Arthur E. Meyerhoff.

In early 1972, Mr. Meyerhoff devoted a day out of his busy schedule to be interviewed and welcomed me to examine the league files in his Chicago advertising agency office. He subsequently gave me complete freedom and every assistance in this endeavor. He also read the first draft of my master's thesis and offered valuable suggestions for its improvement. Dorothy Armington and Agnes Rhoten, members of his staff, contributed valuable assistance in examining and copying pertinent items from his files.

Throughout my thesis research in the 1970s, Philip K. Wrigley, founder of the AAGBBL, head of the Wrigley Chewing Gum Company, and owner of the Chicago Cubs, was most gracious in answering inquiries through correspondence.

Also in the 1970s, Marilyn Jenkins, of Grand Rapids, Michigan, arranged contacts with league personnel residing in the Grand Rapids area. These included Joyce Ricketts, Dorothy Hunter, Earlene "Beans" Risinger, and Carl Orwant. Mr. Orwant, former business manager of the Grand Rapids Chicks, contributed valuable AAGBBL records for 1951–1954. Other ex-players who shared their memories and loaned items from their personal scrapbooks at that time were Jean Cione, then of Ypsilanti, Michigan, and Nancy Mudge Cato from Elk River, Minnesota.

John Schultz at the University of Minnesota and Harold J. VanderZwaag at UMass, Amherst, contributed to my thesis research by sharing their memories as young fans of AAGBBL games. Harold VanderZwaag also served as a member of my thesis committee at UMass, Amherst, along with Dr. Guy M. Lewis and Dr. Betty Spears. These three ably guided my thesis research.

Other friends and colleagues to whom the master's thesis was indebted include Stephen D. Mosher, who shared in the struggles of research and writing; Belmar Gunderson, whose persistent prodding kept me at work; Sue Smith, Maryanne Schumm, and Mary Jo Haverbeck who helped with proofreading, editing, and typing the manuscript.

The author's recent research efforts are indebted to archivists George Rugg in Special Collections at Notre Dame's Library, Cheryl Taylor, and Joe Hughes at the Northern Indiana Center for History, and Jason White at the Grand Rapids Public Museum for assisting with photographs and information. Tim Wiles, Bill Burdick, Ted Spencer, Darci Harrington, and Becky Ashe from the Baseball Hall of Fame also contributed valuable assistance, materials, photographs, and suggestions.

Special thanks is extended to Janis Taylor and her students and Mary Moore for their oral history interviews. Janis began the effort in 1993. Mary Moore renewed the oral history project in 1996 and has continued interviews through the present. These were extremely valuable for updating the manuscript and exposing the author to new material.

Revision of the thesis for publication and provision of many photographs have been enabled and accomplished through the encouragement and generosity of many former players and a few league personnel presented here in alphabetical order: Isabel Alvarez, Lou Arnold, Dolores Bajda, Jackie Baumgart, Mary "Wimp" Baumgartner, Maybelle Blair, Wilma Briggs, Shirley Burkovich, Mary Lou Studnicka Caden, Helen Hannah Campbell (chaperone), Coralyn "Corky" Carl (bat girl), Nancy Mudge Cato, Jean Cione, Dottie Collins, Lavone "Pepper" Paire Davis, Ruth Davis (bat girl), Terry Donahue, Dorothy "Snookie" Doyle, Thelma "Tiby" Eisen, Jean Faut Fantry, Betty Francis, Eileen "Ginger" Gascon, Jean Geissinger Harding, Annabelle Lee Harmon, Jean Havlish, Alice "Lefty" Hohlmayer, Joan Holderness, Katie Horstman, Fran Janssen, Marilyn Jenkins, Betsy Jochum, Dorothy "Kammie" Kamenshek, Sue Kidd, Arlene Kotil, Karen Kunkel, Sophie Kurys, Jeneane Lesko, Lenora "Smokey" Mandella, Joyce McCoy, Jane Moffet, Mary Moore, Arleene Johnson Noga, June Peppas, Mary Pratt, Ruth Richard, Earlene "Beans" Risinger, Janet "Pee Wee" Wiley Sears, Helen Filarski Steffes, Marge Wenzell, Delores "Dolly" Brumfield White, Mary Wisham, Renae Youngberg, Leonard Zintak (manager).

Others who helped with materials, photographs, services, or suggestions toward the manuscript's completion include, in alphabetical order, Darrah Barnes, Diane Barts, Leigh and Diane Benson, Joanne Bickley, Pastor Mike Blaine and Joseph Blaine, Kelly Brown, Pat and Dale Bunselmeier, Sarah Campbell, Kelly Candaele, Andy Card, Ken and Dee Clark, Fran Cvitkovich, Geena Davis, Mary Dierstein, Gilbert Emralino, Marilyn and Marshall Fidler, Lorraine Fitzgerald, Murline Georgeson, Ellen W. Gerber, Millie Gerdom, Adrienne Graham, Tom Hanks, Jacqueline Heitmann, Carol Hendrich, Virginia Hunt, Yvonne Jacques, Susan Johnson, Kris Lipkowski, Sue Macy, Penny Marshall, Shelley McCann, Donna McLin, Ede Moody, Nan Nichols, Mary Renshaw, Jon Richards, Monica Rivera, Sharon Roepke, Chuck and Tressa (Fidler) Rosecrantz, Jnell Ruetz, Dona Schaefer, Erin Schmidt, Maria Sexton, Ronald Seymour, Joyce Smith, Ronald A. Smith, Carolyn Trombe, Tom E. Van Hyning, Judy Meyerhoff Yale, and Tracy Young.

The foregoing lists of contributors illustrate that the writing of a book is truly a team effort, as are most things in life; and that's why team sports are so important in young lives. My sincerest gratitude to all and my sincere apology to anyone who may have been inadvertently overlooked.

Foreword

by Jean Cione

WINTER, 1943, ROCKFORD, ILLINOIS

Bang! *The Rockford Register Republic* hit the storm door of our home on Seventh Avenue. Later in the evening, as my father sat reading the local paper, he called to me in an excited voice. The notice had arrived. Rockford, Illinois, would be the home city of the Rockford Peaches, one of the teams in the newly formed All-American Girls Softball League. At the time, I was a 15-year-old girl whose mother thought her daughter had an anatomical anomaly — a softball glove perpetually attached to her right hand. When the Rockford Peaches began to play in early May, my father and I were avid fans who attended many games. The AAGSBL players were my heroes.

WINTER, 1945, ROCKFORD, ILLINOIS

Bang! *The Rockford Register Republic* hit that same storm door. This time the paper announced that, early in the spring, the re-titled AAGPBL (All-American Girls Professional Ball League) would hold tryouts for those interested in playing in the league. Yes, yes, they were talking to me.

I attended the one-day tryout conducted by ex–major leaguer Max Carey, president of the AAGPBL. At the conclusion of the tryout, I was invited to the league spring training in Chicago, Illinois, in early May. At the end of the week-long spring training session, I was selected to be a member of the AAGPBL and assigned to the Rockford Peaches' roster. From that moment on, I was learning from and playing with the most talented women softball players in the United States, Canada, and Cuba. For two years, the Peaches had been my idols; now I was one of them.

For the next ten years, I enjoyed the fierce competitive nature, camaraderie, and humor of the players in the All-American Girls Baseball League (so named from the end of the 1945 season through 1950). Those ten years were unbelievably wonderful. Just think: In 1945, a young woman athlete was not only able to dream of competing at a very high level, but she was able to live her dream. It was incredible.

During the league's tenure, the game evolved from softball to baseball. The distances between the bases as well as between the pitching mound and home plate were extended; the pitching style changed from underhand to overhand; and the ball shrank (eventually to regulation baseball size). As previously noted, the league name changed several times during its twelve-year history (see chapters 2 and 6).

In the off-season, I earned a bachelor of science degree (1953) and subsequently taught high school physical education. I continued my education and, after earning a

1

Master of Science degree (1962), assumed the position of department chair of a newly opened high school in Rockford, Illinois. The following year, I received a call from my alma mater, Eastern Michigan University, to continue my contribution to education at the university level. In 1992, I retired as a professor in the Sports Medicine Program located in the School of Health Promotion and Human Performance at Eastern Michigan University. My years in education at both the high school and university levels were as enjoyable as those in the AAGBBL. The enthusiasm, energy, commitment, and humor of the students are unforgettable; these warm memories never fade.

To this day, I continue my close association with the women who played baseball during those wonderful years. In 1987, a small group of former players organized the All-American Girls Professional Baseball League Players' Association (AAGPBL-PA). Presently, I am the vice president and website liaison of this association. It is rewarding work that keeps me in very close touch with those former players as well as with associate members.

Jean Cione, 10 year AAGBBL veteran (courtesy of Jean Cione).

As the AAGPBL-PA website (AAGPBL.org) liaison, I receive hundreds of e-mail requests from all over the world. These messages come from researchers requesting additional information about the AAGPBL and from the players who played baseball professionally before Title IX was even a thought in Senator Birch Bayh's and Representative Patsy Mink's minds. The information contained on the website includes an extensive bibliography of reference materials. I emphasize the value of this bibliography and in particular the master of science thesis written by Merrie A. Fidler entitled "The Development and Decline of the All-American Girls Baseball League, 1943–1954." The thesis was completed in 1976 and submitted to the Graduate School of the University of Massachusetts, Amherst. From the time it was bound as a thesis and made available to libraries of institutions of higher education, it assumed the role of the most complete, accurate, informative, and clearly written publication about the AAGBBL.

At the Players' Association's 60th Anniversary Reunion in Syracuse, New York, in September of 2003, former AAGBBL players urged Merrie Fidler to publish her thesis. With this book, Merrie has not only accomplished the task, but she has done further research and has updated the information she presents through 2004. She has also added four chapters documenting the organization, operation, and accomplishments of the Players' Association from 1980 through 2004.

As Merrie traces the three administrative periods of the league in this work, from its founding by Philip K. Wrigley through the assumption of team ownership by individual city sponsors, her narrative is peppered with quotes from administrators and players. Her information is garnered from interviews with administrators and documents from their files. Former players graciously spent extensive interview hours with Merrie and provided her access to their memorabilia. In the 1970s, administrators and former players accommodated Merrie because she expressed a genuine interest in a significant aspect of their lives. Those she interviewed in 2003 and 2004 accommodated her because they respected the accuracy and quality of her original thesis and her thorough research methods.

This book is a must-read for researchers who wish to know the complete and accurate history of the AAGBBL as well as for those individuals who are just lovers of baseball.

Preface

"On October 22, 1924, Babe Ruth played an exhibition baseball game in Dunsmuir [CA] as part of his nationwide barn-storming tour. The Bambino was joined by Yankee teammate Bob Meusel and Manager Christy Walsh. The game was sponsored by the Dunsmuir Lions Club and drew 900 people in the stands."[1]

In keeping with the habit of the times, the people in the stands were dressed in their Sunday best on a Wednesday afternoon. The men wore suits, ties, and caps or hats, and the women's dresses were complemented by stylish hats. The existence of the grandstands, though small, testified to the mountain railroad town's absorption with the game of baseball. Attendance was impressive for the town's population of between 4,000 and 5,000.

Not so many years later, Jess "Dinger" Fidler, father of Jess William, Robert Griffith, Tressa Jean, and Merrie Ann, played baseball in front of the same Dunsmuir City grandstands. Fidler was a player from the mid–1930s through the late 1940s, except the years he served in the Navy during World War II. Sons Jess and Bob played there from the mid–1940s into the 1950s. Wife Jean, Tressa Jean, and baby of the family Merrie Ann sat in the grandstands and cheered for their men.

From my earliest conscious memories through my seventh year (1950), I spent many spring and summer Sunday afternoons in those grandstands, with my family, watching first my Dad and then my brothers, ten and eight years my senior, play the national game. Unlike many other children age seven and under, I was seldom bored by the game on the field. I preferred to sit under the roofed-over grandstands and watch the action. My dad would have allowed me to join other children seeking their own entertainment, but I just couldn't bear to miss seeing my Dad or my brothers— my heroes— play ball. I *wanted* to sit in those splintery, early 1900s bleachers beside my brothers or my Dad watching whoever was playing. One of them might make a good play in the field or hit a home run. I sat Sunday after Sunday listening to them talk baseball with each other and their friends. I couldn't help but absorb the game.

Too young to grasp the concept that I'd never be able to play baseball in that park because I was a girl, I pestered my brothers to play with me at home, and as much as possible, I played on the school playground with whoever was playing. When I was a first grader, fifth-grade sister, Tressa, allowed me to bat in a noon recess game with her friends; I remember how amazed they all were when I hit the ball as well as they did. From early childhood to adulthood, I was captivated by the game, and I played any form of it I could — even if it was just to play catch by the hour with a friend.

A move 50 miles south, to Redding, California, at the end of second grade, separated

5

me from the Dunsmuir City Baseball Park. Brother Jess went into the Army, and brother Bob went off to college. By this time Dad was no longer playing, but he frequently took me to watch Bob play basketball and baseball at Chico State College (now California State University at Chico).

The move to Redding broadened my opportunities for playing ball as I grew older. I was able to join playground baseball games with the boys and softball games with the girls in school and recreation programs throughout my grammar school years. I loved becoming a seventh grader in Redding, because there was a school softball team and competitive summer recreational softball for seventh graders and above. I played other sports, too, but softball was number one because I could play it in school during the spring and in a nearby park during the summer. Softball was as close to baseball as a girl could get in northern California in the 1950s; even there, it could be played five to six months out of the year.

I enjoyed softball in high school, also, but I was especially elated during the summer of my fifteenth year when I qualified for the Redding Comets, the city women's softball team. It afforded the opportunity to play with the best talent in the city against the best in the region and was oh, so much more challenging and satisfying than high school softball in those days. By this time, brother Bob, my baseball role model, was playing for a Boston Red Sox "A" League team on the east coast, and I continued to worship and emulate him.

The author as a Comet, Redding, California, ca. 1959.

Eating, drinking, and sleeping softball as a player, and baseball as a fan and spectator — from spring through fall, and from seventh grade through college — became routine. If I wasn't playing catcher, or first base, or third base, or shortstop, or left field, I was listening to a major league radio broadcast or watching a game on television. After college I sought out summer slow-pitch teams and played through my mid-thirties. The decision to quit playing summer ball didn't affect my love for the game — I can still be found glued to a radio or TV when there's a game on — especially a Giants or Cubs or Red Sox game!

In 1972, working as an assistant intramural sports director at the University of Massachusetts, Amherst, I took advantage of the opportunity to enroll in Umass's Sports Studies master's degree program. An assignment for the Women's Sport History class taught by Dr. Ellen W. Gerber required examination of the *Readers' Guide to Periodical Literature*. This exercise brought to my attention a 1943 *Time* magazine article touting the creation of the All-American Girls Softball League. It claimed to be a women's *professional* softball league! I knew of Amateur Softball Association leagues and industrial semi-pro leagues, but in my experience and knowledge, such a thing as a *professional women's softball league* did not exist — never existed! I was yet to discover that this women's professional softball league soon became a women's professional baseball league.

Captivated, and motivated to find out more, I wrote to the sports editors of the original four teams mentioned in the *Time* magazine article: Racine and Kenosha, Wisconsin; Rockford, Illinois; and South Bend, Indiana. It was my hope that one of them could shed greater light on this heretofore unknown league. Wonder of wonders, Joe Boland, *South Bend Tribune* sports editor and former South Bend Blue Sox director, responded and referred me to ex–South Bend Blue Sox manager Chet Grant and pitcher Jean Faut Winsch. Chet Grant, in turn, referred me to Mr. Arthur E. Meyerhoff, former owner of the All-American Girls Baseball League (AAGBBL*) and at that time still P. K. Wrigley's advertising agent.

I arranged a visit and interview with Mr. Meyerhoff at his Rancho Santa Fe, California, home during Christmas break, late December 1972. He graciously invited me to examine the AAGBBL files in his Wrigley Building office in Chicago. Two summers later, I spent a week there researching those files. He blessed me greatly by allowing me to make notes and copies of invaluable league documents. Unfortunately, by the time I began revising this thesis for publication, Mr. Meyerhoff had passed away, and his files could not be located for new research. However, the document copies that I obtained in the 1970s are in my thesis research files housed at the Northern Indiana Center for History in South Bend, Indiana.

On my return trip from California to Massachusetts during that 1972 Christmas break, I arranged to visit South Bend, Indiana, and interview Jean Faut Winsch. During the three days I was in South Bend, Jean arranged meetings with former Blue Sox manager Chet Grant, former players Lib Mahon and Betsy Jochum, chaperone Lucille Moore, umpire Gadget Ward, and business manager Ed Des Lauriers. They were all wonderfully gracious and contributed much to my early education of the league.

An unexpected and very important gift came my way from that visit to South Bend. Jean generously loaned me the equivalent of nine 3½ inch binders full of league records left in her keeping by former Blue Sox president Harold T. Dailey. These are referred to throughout this book as the Dailey Records. They include league and team board meeting minutes, newspaper clippings, pictures, financial records, and Dr. Dailey's personal comments about the league and the Blue Sox. These records are currently held in the Joyce Sports Research Collection in the University of Notre Dame Library's Special Collections Department in South Bend, Indiana.

Between 1972 and 1976 I continued to work full-time and complete master's degree courses. With little extra time or financial resources, and before the advent of the Internet, my contacts with other ex-players were accidental encounters. For instance, I took

The vision, industry, and accomplishments of the founders, officers, and members of the All-American Girls Professional Baseball League Players' Association (AAGPBLPA) changed the league's popular identity from that of the All-American Girls Baseball League (AAGBBL) to that of the more accurately descriptive All-American Girls Professional Baseball League (AAGPBL). Hence the use of the latter in the title of this book. Throughout the book, however, AAGBBL refers to the league's identity between 1946 and 1954, and AAGPBL refers primarily to the All-American Girls Professional Ball League, 1943–1945, and the Players' Association from 1987 to the present.

a position as an assistant intramural sports director at the University of Minnesota in 1973. Working on the Saint Paul Campus, my interaction with the staff at the Minneapolis campus was limited. However, in the spring of 1974, while discussing my still-unfinished thesis with a few University of Minnesota female physical education staff members, one of them, Nancy Mudge Cato, surprised me with the fact that she had played in the league. Nancy, in turn, put me in touch with Jean Cione. The following spring, I learned that one of my Minneapolis intramural colleagues, John Schultz, had been an AAGBBL fan as a youngster.

In the fall of 1975, I transferred to Penn State University as a doctoral candidate in sport history. About this time, Marilyn Jenkins, a former Grand Rapids Chicks team member, wrote to Mr. Meyerhoff inquiring about information related to the AAGBBL, and he forwarded her letter to me. This contact led to an interview session, organized by Marilyn, with Joyce Ricketts, Dottie Hunter, and Carl Orwant, all of whom still resided in Grand Rapids. Earlene "Beans" Risinger was unable to be present, but wrote a letter containing memories of her AAGBBL experiences shortly thereafter. This visit provided me with access to Carl Orwant's AAGBBL records, 1951–1954, currently held at the Grand Rapids, Michigan, Public Museum.

When meeting with my thesis committee upon completion of the first draft of my thesis in January 1976, I was delighted to learn that one of my committee members, Harold J. VanderZwaag, who was also the physical education department chairman, had been an avid Grand Rapids Chicks fan when he was a boy. Being a very busy man, he hadn't been aware of the content of my thesis research until he reviewed it for that first committee meeting.

The Dailey Records, the Meyerhoff Files, the Orwant Records, magazine articles, league city newspapers on microfilm, and the few player and league personnel interviews I'd conducted in the 1970s were finally drawn together into a master's thesis completed in September of 1976. As I read, researched and wrote, between studying and working, I constantly bemoaned the fact that I wasn't born in 1925 instead of the year the league was launched. How I would have loved the opportunity to become a professional ballplayer like my brother.

A family emergency required my return to California shortly after completion of my thesis in 1976. At that point, I embarked on a teaching and coaching career for the Anderson Union High School District (near Redding). When the AAGBBL's first national reunion was held in Chicago during the summer of 1982, I took advantage of my summer vacation to attend and mingle with ladies I knew to be professional baseball players, many of whom hadn't seen each other for 30 years or more.

What a special thrill it was to sit in the midst of that joyful group in the stands at Wrigley Field and watch the Cubbies play. It was exciting for a baseball-crazy California girl just to be in Wrigley Field, and it was overwhelming to be meeting, visiting with, and observing so many of the individual women professional baseball players I'd recently studied. I felt like the proverbial fly on the wall because although I "knew" them through league city sports pages, magazine articles, Meyerhoff's files and Dailey's and Orwant's records, they had no idea who I was. It was a joy to just listen, watch and absorb their interactions.

Privileged to address those present at the first reunion's closing banquet, I wanted to convey to them the importance of establishing a central archive where they could deposit their league memorabilia for future historical study. That was my dream for them at the time, but as it turned out, I dreamed small compared to what they accomplished in the following years (see chapters 14–17).

Returning to California after the reunion, I continued my career teaching English and physical education and coaching high school volleyball, basketball and softball. My career precluded attendance at succeeding league reunions held predominantly in the fall, except for the 1988 reunion in Cooperstown. The historian in me wouldn't let me miss that one! I managed to sneak it in between the end of volleyball season and the beginning of basketball season.

Talk about a thrill! To be at the National Baseball Hall of Fame—every baseball addict's dream! To be there with that wonderful group of joyful, happy, inspiring baseball women! Indescribable! My cup was full and running over—I frequently found myself wiping away tears of joy and awe at being associated with those women in that place. One of my favorite memories will always be presenting a copy of my thesis to Tom Heinz, then Hall of Fame Librarian, and having it accepted. My dad, deceased since 1971, would have been proud to know his daughter was, so to speak, "in" the Hall of Fame!

Then, in the summer of 1992, I was thrilled when *A League of Their Own* hit cinemas throughout the United States, informing and reminding Americans that once upon a time—during the volatile years of 1943–1954—*women played professional baseball.* THANK YOU, PENNY MARSHALL!

The film accurately represented some aspects of the league's history (the beauty training) and fictionalized others (the people who started the league), as is common for Hollywood productions. The best thing about the film is that it portrayed competitive young women playing the game of baseball in the uniforms of the All-American Girls Baseball League.

The film also accurately depicted the league's genesis during World War II. It revealed that some of its players came from remote, rural venues and that they experienced conflicts common to their time: husbands fighting a war on far-off continents; dreams of escaping small-town life; choices between the security of home and the risk of leaving for new adventures; and the challenge of living up to the reputation of an older sibling who did it all.

As the film showed, and as players, managers, chaperones, team and league administrators, and fans asserted, the players of the All-American Girls Baseball League played with the flair and competence of the highest caliber professional sports performers. The excellence of their play is the magic most clearly remembered about this "feminine phenomenon of sports Americana." As ex-manager Chet Grant confirmed, "You had to see it to believe it, and then you didn't."[2]

On one hand, *A League of Their Own* gave us a predominantly humorous vignette of owners, managers, players, and players' hi-jinks balanced by some tragic moments. On the other hand, it displayed the reluctance, joy, excitement, pride, grief, and awe reflected on the faces of ex-players and family members as they reunited in Cooperstown for the opening of the Baseball Hall of Fame's exhibit for "Women in Baseball." At the end of *A League of Their Own*, the scenes behind the credits show former AAGBBL players competing in a reunion game—providing ample evidence, forty to fifty years later, of the skill those players possessed.

Best of all, the film opened the eyes of the American public to a unique women's sport way ahead of its time. As a Hollywood film, however, it could not tell the whole story. It could not explain who really organized and administered the league or how it was operated. The film could not tell how the league's organization and operation was unique and how it changed over the years. It could not tell what team, league, and player policies predominated. It could not reveal the identity of the league's many outstanding players. Nor could it tell why the league folded when it did, or what nuggets of wisdom could be garnered from its day in the sun.

Nonetheless, I loved the film. I loved the humor of it. I loved recognizing a bit of Jimmie Foxx in Tom Hanks' character, and I envisioned Geena Davis' character as Grand Rapids catcher Ruth Lessing — though others would identify her with Bonnie Baker. I knew Walter Harvey was really P.K. Wrigley, and it seemed to me that Ira Lowenstein portrayed Arthur Meyerhoff. Just recently I learned that Ken Sells was the "Ira Lowenstein" who talked Mr. Wrigley into allowing him to run the league one more year at the conclusion of the 1943 season. Sells felt those "girls" deserved more than a one-year shot to prove their worth.[3] How right he was!

I loved the scenes of the 1988 reunion at the Hall of Fame. I loved recognizing some of the former players in the Hall of Fame scenes and the ball game played while the credits rolled. I loved knowing that when I mentioned the All-American Girls Baseball League from that point forward nearly everyone would be able to visualize it. Most importantly, no longer would the players, personnel, or the league remain an obscure historical fact to become more deeply buried with each passing year.

Prior to the film's production, other authors began investigating and writing books about the AAGBBL. Those who consulted me or requested a copy of my thesis for their research included Lois Browne, *Girls of Summer*; Diana Star Helmer, *Belles of the Ballpark*; and Sue Macy, *A Whole New Ball Game*. Susan Johnson didn't contact me directly but referenced my thesis in *When Women Played Hardball*. As a copy of each published book found its place on my bookshelf, I experienced a mixture of emotions: possessiveness — these were my research soulmates; pride — in having contributed a foundation on which these authors could build; and gratitude — that the league's story was appearing in bookstores and libraries. As each book materialized, any intentions I had to "publish my thesis someday" became less important.

Between 1988 and 2003, submerged in teaching and coaching, my contact with the All-Americans diminished. I maintained an associate membership in the Players' Association and read the newsletters, but geography and the daily demands of life distanced me from them. When I planned retirement in June of 2003, and learned that year's AAGPBL reunion would be the league's 60th anniversary, I was determined to attend. I would be free in the fall, unencumbered by teaching and coaching duties, and I wanted to see that group and visit the Hall of Fame again.

While attending the 60th AAGPBL reunion in Syracuse, New York, in early September 2003, I was impressed with the Players' Association's accomplishments since that first reunion in 1982. I was impressed with the association's leadership, and as I visited with players who had acquired a copy of my thesis along the way, I took heed when they urged me to publish it. They believed it was a well-documented history of the league and that it merited publication.

After considerable reflection, and after comparing my thesis with the books already in print, I decided to take their advice. The authors who preceded me utilized some of the same information my thesis supplied, but thanks to the development of the AAGPBL Players' Association between 1982 and 1990, they had access to many more players' stories than I'd enjoyed. They told those stories well and preserved those life experiences for generations to come. Meanwhile, they left the in-depth treatment of the organization and operation of the AAGBBL to my thesis — to this book.

My original thesis has been enriched by the recent addition of player anecdotes drawn from other writers' works, or acquired from oral history tapes or from player interviews conducted since September of 2003. This book includes a few new discoveries about the league along with a general updating of the thesis's contents. Also added are four chapters that illuminate the organization, operation, and accomplishments of the All-American Girls Professional Baseball League Players' Association from 1980 to 2004.

It is my hope that this book accomplishes three things: First, that it counterbalances the limitations of *A League of Their Own*—that it provides an in-depth look at the historical origins and operations of the All-American Girls Baseball League. Second, that it provides a foundation on which other authors can continue to build. There is still much of the AAGBBL story to be discovered and revealed.

Third, and most importantly, I hope it stands as a tribute to all the players, chaperones, managers, league and team administrators, umpires, sports writers, and fans of the All-American Girls Baseball League—the first completely professional women's *team* sport in the U.S.A.

Merrie A. Fidler
Fall 2005

PART I

Historical Background

Rogers Park Girls Indoor Baseball Team, Chicago, Illinois, 1902 — notice size of bat and ball. *Left to right, front*: Ruby Twamley, Ruth Lotz, Zella Frye, Dorothy Pratt. *Back*: Mary Stunach, Florence Hansen, Louise Lamphere, Carrie Stronack, Maude Lamphere (Chicago Historical Society, Glass Negative, SDN-007848).

1

The Establishment of Softball as a Sport for American Women, 1900–1940

The All-American Girls' Baseball League was initially established as the All-American Girls' Softball League, for good reason. The talent pool for the league consisted of thousands of amateur women's softball teams, not only throughout the United States, but also in Canada. The growth of the popularity of softball in Canada seems to have paralleled the popularity of its growth in America. While the women's leagues that flourished in Canada during the late 1930s were the schooling grounds for 64 AAGBBL players, the following discussion will focus on softball in the U.S.A.[1]

By 1942, approximately 200,000 men's and women's softball teams existed in the United States and softball was lauded as a sport for women.[2] The question is, how did softball, a team sport, become a participant sport for American women in the first half of the twentieth century when the most "acceptable" sports for women at that time were individual sports, such as tennis and golf? The answer lies in the historical development of softball for the masses, in the institutions and organizations that supported softball participation by girls and women, and in how the development of women's softball differed from the development of other women's team sports.

Indoor Baseball Became Outdoor Softball in Nineteenth Century Urban America

Essentially, softball is a standardized, modified form of regulation baseball. The modification of baseball to environmental conditions is probably as old as the game itself. The *standardization* of a modified form of baseball, however, could well be attributed to the chilly climate of Chicago on a November day. The promoters of softball pinpoint the source of its origin to an impromptu indoor baseball game first played and codified by members of Chicago's Farragut Boat Club in November of 1887.[3] The game became so popular that by 1892 there were "100 organized indoor ball clubs in Chicago" and their games attracted "thousands of spectators of the best classes. In fact, indoor baseball [was] particularly a sport of gentlemen, and especially of club members."[4] Like baseball during its early days, softball's origin was identified with the upper classes.

As with baseball, softball soon became a sport for all classes. It was not long before codified indoor baseball was played outdoors on playgrounds too small to accommodate regulation baseball.[5] As a mass participant sport, this modified form of baseball achieved its popularity from early industrial, urban conditions.

The nonexistence of zoning laws during the early industrial period, the construction of the greatest number of living units in the smallest amount of space by builders seeking to capitalize on housing shortages, and mass immigration which maintained a demand for housing far beyond the supply all contributed to the eradication of large open spaces in urban centers.[6]

Thus, regulation baseball became an impractical game in American cities in the late nineteenth and early twentieth centuries. Nevertheless, the enthusiasm of urban children for the game transcended their environmental limitations. They played whatever form of baseball they could in the streets despite the threat of arrest.[7] Indoor baseball played outdoors, therefore, became a viable, legal substitute for their urge to emulate participation in the national game.

Softball on Settlement House and School Playgrounds

The first institutions to support softball in its infancy were settlement houses and schools. Both institutions opened playgrounds for city children in response to social criticism levied by such reformers as Jane Addams and Jacob Riis. Jane Addams established Hull-House playground and lobbied for the opening of Chicago's school playgrounds during non-school hours to mitigate "the constant interruption to ... play which is inevitable on the streets...."[8] Riis in New York, Addams in Chicago, and other social reformers maintained a constant campaign for the establishment of small parks and open school playgrounds to provide children a healthy place to play, to force light and air into the slums, and to improve their living conditions.[9]

In 1910, Henry S. Curtis somewhat erroneously stated that "Indoor baseball was invented on the Hull-House Playground in 1894."[10] Curtis may have more accurately stated that indoor baseball was *first played outdoors by urban children* on the Hull-House playground. Joseph Lee, a Boston reformer, confirmed that indoor baseball was popular among midwestern settlement house playgrounds. In 1901 he observed that the popular games of the Hull-House playground were handball and indoor baseball,

> ...the latter being a most important adaptation of baseball for city conditions by the substitution for the regular ball of a soft ball five inches in diameter, which diminishes the diamond to about one-third of the usual size and dispenses with the out-field.[11]

Concrete evidence is not available to substantiate the hypothesis that girls first played softball, in the form of indoor baseball, on early 1900s settlement house and school playgrounds. In fact, early settlement house programs included little in the way of physical games for girls and women. Domestic education activities formed the core of settlements' female programs with dancing holding forth as the predominant form of physical activity for girls and women.[12] It is certainly conceivable, however, that to begin with, young girls, individually or in groups, played indoor baseball with their male peers on settlement and school playgrounds. In any event, it was reported that a girls' indoor baseball team was organized in Chicago's West Division High School as early as 1895. In 1899, a year after the supervised school park system was established in Chicago, the game "gained steadily in favor among girls of Chicago's various high schools."[13]

It should be noted that regulation baseball was not a fashionable sport for girls and women at the turn of the twentieth century. Part of the unpopularity of baseball as a sport for females had to do with the game's physical characteristics: "the hard ball, the heavy bat, the long-distance throws and ... the expensive equipment."[14] Another aspect of baseball's unpopularity as a feminine pastime was the social criticism levied against the pioneer Bloomer Girl teams. The evidence suggests that the members of these teams were selected more for their willingness to entertain male audiences in immodest uniforms than for their ability to play baseball.[15] They not only were accused of being prostitutes, but of prostituting the game.[16] Nevertheless, baseball seemed to capture the interest of significant numbers of girls and women and they played the game either because of, or in spite of, the physical and social taboos associated with it. In eastern women's colleges, for instance, young women played baseball, despite public criticism, as early as 1876: "The public so far as it knew of our playing [baseball], was shocked, but in our retired grounds and protected observation, we continued to play in spite of a censorious public."[17]

The emergence of a miniaturized and codified baseball game solved the perceived physical deterrents of the game for female participants in the early 1900s. Although it is impossible to determine whether or not the social criticism levied against Bloomer Girl teams transferred to those who played indoor baseball, it is reasonable to assume that the existence of such criticism was not vehement enough to eradicate female participation in the game. Most likely, those who promoted participation in indoor baseball for girls and women counterbalanced what criticism existed by lauding its physical, educational, ethical, and social values for both sexes.[18]

Assessing how rapidly schools and colleges adopted and promoted indoor baseball for girls and women after 1900 is difficult. However, it is known that baseball was one of the activities scheduled for girls in New York's Public School Athletic League by 1919.[19] A survey of Cleveland schools circa 1920 revealed that 91 percent of high school girls played baseball on the school grounds and many more played it elsewhere.[20] These references to girls and young women playing baseball may have referred to regulation baseball, but more likely were references to the more popular modified form of the game.

Before the mid–1930s, educators seemed to have a semantics problem when referring to the form of baseball played by girls and women. This undoubtedly occurred because the modified form of baseball played on the playgrounds between 1900 and 1930 was only in the formative stages of total standardization. Therefore, instead of referring to the females' modified baseball game by one of its various names—such as kittenball, or diamond ball, playground ball, or half a dozen other terms—educators merely referred to it as "baseball."

This theory was suggested in Helen Frost and Charles Wardlaw's book, *Basketball and Indoor Baseball for Women*. In this book, published in 1920, the authors pointed out:

> ...certain women's colleges have been playing baseball for years, and some under outdoor [regulation] rules with a regulation ball, gloves, masks, etc., [but] the game as a standard form of sport for girls is, as yet, only in its infancy.[21]

Frost and Wardlaw's focus on indoor baseball rather than regulation baseball was due to the greater popularity among girls at that time for indoor baseball, i.e., use of 12, 14, or even 17-inch ball and 35-foot base paths.

Gladys Palmer's book, *Baseball for Girls and Women*, published in 1929, illustrated the persistence of modified games for girls and women. In this book, rules for both indoor and regulation baseball were printed. The ball size and base path distance for indoor baseball were fixed at 17 inches and 27 feet respectively, but for outdoor play four official diamond sizes and accompanying rules were listed (see Table 1).

Table 1: Optional Outdoor Baseball Regulations
for Girls and Women, 1929

Regulation	Diamonds			
	1	2	3	4
Between Bases	35'	45'	60'	65'
To Pitcher's Plate	30'	35'	33–36'	40'
Number of Players	10	10	9	9
Size of Ball	14"	12"	12"	12 or 9"
Style of Pitching	UH*	UH	UH	OH*

SOURCE: Gladys E. Palmer, *Baseball for Girls and Women* (New York: A. S. Barnes and Company, 1929), p. 126.
*UH designates "underhand"; OH designates "overhand."

As can be seen in Table 1, most of the diamond sizes recommended for the various regulations more nearly approximated the soon-to-be standardized softball game than regulation baseball. These, therefore, were probably the most popular modifications played among girls and women in schools and colleges before standardized softball came into vogue.

The extent of softball's popularity as a school-sponsored sport after 1930 can partially be detected from periodic surveys conducted for college programs between 1930 and 1954. The frequency with which softball was sponsored in surveyed institutions is illustrated in Table 2.

From the data provided in the surveys itemized in Table 2, it was impossible to determine if the word "baseball" referred to regulation baseball or one of the modified forms of the game described by Gladys Palmer. In any case, "baseball" consistently declined and "softball" predominated as a sport for girls and women in schools and colleges. It seems very likely that the "baseball" referred to in these surveys was really a modified form of the game rather than regulation baseball. Regulation baseball was never vigorously advocated as a sport for girls and women in schools and colleges. On the other hand, modified baseball was openly supported as a female sport by at least 1908 and possibly earlier.[22]

Table 2: Baseball and Softball as Collegiate
Sports for Women, 1930–1954[23]

Date of Survey	No. of Instit.	% Sponsoring Extramural		% Sponsoring Intramural	
		Baseball	Softball	Baseball	Softball
1930	98	58.5	*	*	*
1937	77	*	*	82.9	*
1945	227	8.8	46.4	59.5	70.0
1954	230	*	42.1	*	*

*No statistics reported.

It can be noted from Table 2 that softball and/or baseball was considerably more popular when listed as an intramural sport in college women's programs. This dichotomy reflected educational policy for women's sport between 1900 and 1960: intramurals were diligently promoted and extramurals were diligently discouraged. This policy was consistent with the prevailing social philosophy that girls and women should not extend themselves in physical games. Doing so was a possible threat to their health; served no purpose toward preparing them to be better citizens, wives and mothers; and was unbecoming to their femininity. Socially, physical games were considered "masculine" pursuits. Therefore, those heading schools and colleges promulgated a restrictive philosophy for girls and women's sports. Girls and women were allowed and encouraged to participate, but not to the extent that boys and men enjoyed. In regard to girls' and women's games, educators mandated that publicity and spectators be discouraged, that only women should coach women, that charging admission or encouraging spectators to attend games was inadmissible, and that high level competition emphasizing winning was undesirable.[24] Some, if not most school physical education programs strictly enforced these values throughout the first half of the twentieth century.

A few All-American Baseball League (AAGBBL) players who joined the league as teenagers still in high school testified to strict treatment in their schools for those who stepped outside the bounds of the philosophy stated above. Delores "Dolly" Brumfield White, an Alabama native, acknowledged the fact that because she'd already played in the AAGBBL when she entered high school, she wasn't allowed to "even play intramurals because I was a professional athlete. That was intramurals in the P.E. classes."[25] Annabelle Lee Harmon, a Southern California native, experienced the same type of discrimination in high school before she joined the AAGBBL. Her teacher, however, wouldn't let her join the Girls' Athletic Association because "I was a pro, I was playing [softball] outside of school and I had a man manager. We weren't getting any money or anything like that. They did charge for our games in Hollywood. I think it was a quarter or something."[26] Dottie Wiltse Collins, also from Southern California, reported that she "started playing organized softball when she was 11 years old," but was not allowed to play any sports in high school. "They said we were professionals although all we ever got was a bag of peanuts."[27] Who knows how many more of the younger AAGBBL players encountered this type of repression in their high school settings.

In looking back, it's tempting to be overly critical of the conservatism of school and college administrators of girls' and women's sports. Nonetheless, it must be remembered that their prevailing concern was to promote the benefits of physical activity for all without offending the standards of social acceptability of the early and mid-twentieth century. Though they may be criticized for this stance, their patient and laborious efforts ultimately laid the firm foundation from which Title IX evolved. Their persistent promotion of the benefits of physical activity for all women was a necessary precondition for the wonderful athletic opportunities girls and women are afforded in schools and colleges in the twenty-first century.

Softball Promoted by Public Playgrounds and Industries

Although schools and colleges were, without question, instrumental in the promotion and development of softball as a game for girls and women, school and college softball were not what attracted national publicity in the late 1930s and early 1940s. Industrial and recreational softball were the strongest attractions. For the most part, industrial and recreational games were played on public playgrounds or private ball fields.

The number of playgrounds mushroomed as the popularity of settlement house and schoolyard playgrounds spread. Social reformers all across the nation lobbied municipal governments to create neighborhood playgrounds for children's welfare. Jane Addams in

Chicago, Jacob Riis in New York, and Joseph Lee in Boston were a few of the most vocal reformers to advocate and work for the establishment and support of neighborhood playgrounds by municipal governments.[28]

The organization of sport activities at the turn of the twentieth century was basically viewed as an educational tool for molding the social and ethical character of boys. This concept was emphasized in the development of school sports programs as well as in the development of park sports programs.[29] However, by 1910, similar concern was being voiced for the development of girls' sports programs in public parks. At this time, Joseph Lee observed:

> The girls are still a weak point everywhere. We give them baths [swimming pools], skating, sewing, and gymnastics, and on the playgrounds we are beginning to give them — besides the children's games and the manual occupations—basketball and a few other of the livelier games; but in these matters, the Spartan young woman is still far in the lead.[30]

This awareness of the lack of play opportunities for girls was a logical outgrowth of the general consciousness of women's status in society raised by the early feminist movement. Women were working toward the achievement of social justice and political identity during the first two decades of the twentieth century.[31] The possible enfranchisement of women required that they learn the same principles of cooperation and loyalty demanded of men in a democracy. Playground and education leaders viewed supervised sport activities as a viable means for molding the social and ethical character of growing boys toward these desired ends. It followed then that supervised sport activities should be viewed as offering the same character training possibilities for girls.[32]

Thus, it was not surprising that indoor baseball was among the "livelier games" organized for girls on American playgrounds. In 1908, Everett Mero observed:

> Indoor baseball is not baseball out of doors, but it is a good substitute. In the playground it can be used for the strenuously inclined girls who want to do as their brothers do, and has been so used with success.[33]

By 1917, the game had become a regular playground activity for girls. At that time, Henry Curtis described indoor baseball as a game "which at the present time is mostly played outdoors on a thirty-five foot diamond. This game is played by the girls nearly as much as by the boys."[34]

The growth of the playground movement and the organization of the National Playground Association, perhaps as nothing else, ensured the development of softball as a highly competitive sport for girls and women. The game could not have been played without a place to play and many of the small parks, where softball predominated, were carved out of crowded tenement districts.[35] Furthermore, playground administrators were not only instrumental in promoting modified baseball as a game for girls, they were also instrumental in establishing and promoting a set of standardized rules for the game.

Much confusion arose when interpark indoor baseball games were played because rules differed from playground to playground, from city to city, and from state to state. In 1923, Joseph Lee, then president of the Playground and Recreation Association, appointed a committee to standardize the rules of the modified game most popularly known at that time as playground ball.[36] This committee grew into the Joint Rules Committee on Softball by 1934 and enlisted representatives from such organizations as the National Collegiate Athletic Association, YMCA, Catholic Youth Organization (CYO), Young Men's Hebrew Association, National Recreation Association, Amateur Softball

Association, and National Softball Association.[37] Through these organizations, standardized softball was promoted throughout the nation. This standardization of a modified baseball game contributed to inter-city, district, regional, national and ultimately, international competition in softball for men and women.

The competitive opportunities available to women softball players through the standardization of rules was one of the factors that distinguished its development from other women's team sports. In no similar activity did a *team* of women players have the opportunity to play toward a national championship so early in the twentieth century. The basic reason for softball's uniqueness on this point may have been that its championship structure and tournament play were not administered by educators or circumscribed by educational policies governing sports for women. With the exception of basketball, other women's team sports, such as field hockey, volleyball, and lacrosse were largely conducted under an educational umbrella. In addition, these sport seasons coincided with the school year, whereas softball was regularly played in schools during the spring, but also in public parks during the summer. In the public parks, educators had little control over spectator attendance, publicity, coaches, or an emphasis on winning.

Another area where women's softball grew significantly was in the realm of industrial recreation. Industrial recreation, like the playground movement, was an outgrowth of the social reform movement. In the 1890s, industry was rife with human exploitation. Inadequate wages, miserable working conditions, and excessive hours of work threatened life, liberty, and the pursuit of happiness for the laboring classes.[38] As these inequities were exposed to public scrutiny by muckrakers and social reformers, employers began subsidizing facilities and programs to alleviate inhumane practices. This action was referred to as welfare work.

Welfare work for employees in industrial establishments consisted of provisions for medical services, sick leaves and vacations with pay, lunch rooms, disability funds, insurance, education, savings plans, personnel work, provision of community as well as employee needs, and indoor and outdoor recreation.[39] The development of industrially sponsored recreation as one phase of welfare work provided thousands of laborers with greater opportunities for participation in sports than would otherwise have been available to them.[40] Companies provided bowling alleys and billiard tables for employees at reduced costs and, as in the case of billiards, often at no cost. Industries subsidized YMCA and YWCA memberships for their employees in whole or in part. Some firms constructed swimming pools, tennis courts, baseball diamonds, gymnasiums, elaborate clubhouses, recreation parks, soccer and football fields, golf courses and summer camps.[41] In some cases, industries cooperated with other community organizations to provide recreational facilities and trained leadership to all members of the community.[42]

Of particular interest here, of course, was the matter of industrial sponsorship of women's baseball and diamond ball (playground baseball) teams. A report issued by the Bureau of Labor Statistics in 1926 noted that "regularly organized [baseball] teams among the women employees, while not common, were found in a number of instances."[43] This document also noted that "several girls' diamond ball teams were reported, in one case the company furnishing uniforms and equipment and paying the entrance fee in the municipal league."[44] By 1938, sponsorship of women's softball teams had been taken up by banks, bakeries, restaurants, ice creameries, truck lines, and businesses of all sorts.[45] It didn't take long for businesses to discover that sponsorship of men's and women's softball teams was a relatively cheap, effective advertising medium.

1926 World Softball Champions: Johnson's Wax Team of Racine, Wisconsin. *Left to right, front:* Gertrude Miller, Carolyn Kroupa, Polly Svec, Gertrude Kemman, Florence Kemman. *Back:* Gladys Reich, Stella Nelson, Ros Holsinger (coach), Christie Moritz (business manager), Jack Madden (team manager), Margaret Lamers, Myrtle Zeratsky (from 1944 Racine Belles Yearbook, courtesy Arthur Meyerhoff, 1974).

The Great Depression and the Establishment of National Softball Organizations

Between 1926 and 1938, two major events occurred that confirmed the future of softball as a distinct sport: (1) the Great Depression and (2) the establishment of softball organizations which actively promoted the sport on a nationwide scale. The Great Depression helped stimulate government subsidy of social reform measures, which reformers had labored to achieve since 1900. The Great Depression also clarified their demands to the general populace:

> As month followed month with no sign of recovery, despite reassurances that prosperity was on its way, the demand for action mounted. Public works, old-age assistance, and unemployment insurance won ever wider endorsement, from church groups, welfare associations, committees and leagues, conferences and clubs, and fraternal orders of all sorts. Even in the field of relief, where traditional beliefs in the virtue of voluntary aid and local responsibility persisted, community leaders slowly came to recognize that cash relief was better than relief in kind, that work relief was better than the dole, that work on constructive programs contributed more to morale than employment on made-work projects, that finally only the federal government had the revenue resources to carry through an effective relief effort.[46]

The Depression also accelerated the growth of softball. Widespread unemployment created enforced leisure for the laboring classes and instigated the establishment of government agencies to subsidize work projects to alleviate unemployment. The Works Progress Administration, for instance, was established to furnish "work that had value, and would not compete with private business, and was fitted to the endlessly varied abilities and experiences of millions of individuals."[47] Among the projects which conformed to these criteria was the construction of parks and playgrounds.[48] When the WPA terminated its activities in 1943, it had given work to more than eight million unemployed and among its accomplishments numbered the construction of 8,000 parks.[49] Like the playground movement at the turn of the century, the WPA contributed significantly to the establishment of areas where softball could be played. In addition, unemployment and shortened working hours gave a greater number of men and women the opportunity to play.

Other events that occurred during the Depression contributed to the rise of softball. Among these was a more general adherence to daylight savings time and utilization of lighted fields, which allowed longer periods of play in the evenings. In addition, softball didn't require expensive equipment, and people only had to go as far as the neighborhood park to see all the "dash and drama of the diamond."[50] During the Depression, sports participation was viewed and promoted as a morale-building activity as well as worthy use of leisure time.[51]

Jean Faut, an AAGBBL All-Star and MVP in the early 1950s, commented that during the Depression and the beginning of World War II, there wasn't much for kids to do in East Greenville, Pennsylvania. "In those days you either played ball or went swimming. There was nothing else to do. You couldn't go anywhere. You couldn't get any gas. So I played a lot of baseball."[52] In Jean's case, softball wasn't available, so she played baseball with the neighborhood boys, and she also joined in on practice sessions of a men's semipro team held two blocks from her home.[53] Many other AAGBBL players mentioned that in the late 1930s and early 1940s they played baseball with the neighborhood boys before joining organized women's softball leagues in their junior high or high school years.[54] Some, like Jean, Dolly Brumfield White, Shirley Burkovich, Wilma Briggs, and Sue Kidd, only played baseball before joining the league. Wilma, from East Greenwich, Rhode Island, observed that when she joined the league in 1948, "I was glad the league pitched overhand because I'd never played softball."[55]

The biggest selling point for softball, stressed by the Amateur Softball Association, was the fact that everyone could play the game — all ages and both sexes. And play they did. By 1935, there were "roughly 2,000,000 enthusiastic softball players in the United States, more than 60,000 organized amateur teams and 1,000 lighted parks, mostly in the Midwest."[56] The majority of teams were admittedly men's, but women were competing in numbers not to be disregarded. In 1938, for instance, it was reported that nearly 1,000 women's teams were playing in the Los Angeles area alone.[57]

Besides the Depression itself, the efforts of national organizations to standardize and promote softball contributed greatly to its popularization in the 1930s. In addition to the National Recreation Association mentioned earlier, the primary organizations concerned with standardizing softball were the National Softball Association and the Amateur Softball Association. The National Softball Association was semi-professional in nature, whereas the Amateur Softball Association claimed to conduct its tournaments for amateurs only.[58] Both of these groups were organized and administered by independent businessmen not primarily allied with education or bound by educational policies in the promotion of their girls and women's programs.

The promotion of women's softball leagues by these organizations was a logical extension of the prior participation of girls and women in playground ball and industrial leagues. The organizers of the Amateur Softball Association recruited teams from existent women's diamond ball or playground baseball leagues in the promotion of their first national tournament in 1933. The fifteen women's teams in that tournament represented playground champions, city teams, church league teams, industrial teams, and the Canadian national team.[59]

The administrators of the Amateur Softball Association and the National Softball Association did not adhere to the prevailing educational philosophy for the conduct of women's sport. They promoted their organizations by encouraging intercity, regional, and national championships for public display. They allowed admission charges, utilization of male managers, and encouraged publicity highlighting individual accomplishments. These practices were all contrary to principles for the conduct of women's sport espoused by professional physical educators and the National Amateur Athletic Federation.[60] Ultimately, softball emerged as the predominant form of modified baseball during the 1930s, and it did so without imposing different principles of tournament conduct or playing methods for men and women. This was a major difference between the development of softball as a sport for women and the development of other women's team sports.

1930s softball: Annabelle Lee playing first base for a Los Angeles area softball team (courtesy Annabelle Lee Harmon)

Summary

In the formative years of its development, softball was consistently identified with institutions and organizations promoting or reacting to social reform. The trend began with settlement house playground programs and social workers who lobbied for the opening of school and civic playgrounds. It gained momentum through the National Playground Association, also a product of reform movements. Those who promoted organized softball for park and school playgrounds emphasized its social and moral as well as its physical values.

Industrial sponsorship of men's and women's softball teams contributed to the popularization of the game among the laboring classes. The Depression, which stimulated general government support of social reform measures, helped crystallize the future of softball. People had the time and space to play and were encouraged to participate.

A significant aspect in the development of women's softball was the concept that it was a suitable game for girls and women. This concept was verbalized early in the sport's history and originated with the game's physical characteristics, including a large, soft ball and short base paths. Neither of these attributes threatened the possibility of physical harm or over-exertion for girls or women. The sport was also viewed as a viable means of building social and ethical character among girls during a period of time when such training was deemed desirable.

From 1900 to 1930, girls were encouraged to play modified baseball in schools and on playgrounds just as boys were encouraged to play baseball. When national softball organizations developed and promoted high level competition in the 1930s, it was logical for them to promote women's tournaments as well as men's. The fact that men's and women's games and tournaments were conducted in the same manner distinguished the development of women's softball from the development of other women's team sports. Other women's team sports operated almost exclusively under an educational umbrella and were largely circumscribed by a philosophy espousing participation for all, while suppressing elements considered excessive in high-level competition, such as charging admissions, employing male managers, publicizing contests, and emphasizing winning.

It must be remembered also, that during softball's developmental years, girls *wanted* to play the game just as their brothers and fathers did. They enjoyed the game, the skill development, the competition, the publicity, and the winning. As youngsters they learned to love the game. Many were afforded the opportunity to follow their love of the game into adulthood through the establishment of industrial and recreational programs and competitions held by national softball organizations. Those who developed their skills and were able to follow their passion for the game to city, state, and national championships in the 1930s and early 1940s were the pioneers Philip K. Wrigley recruited when he conceived of the All-American Girls Softball League.

PART II

League Administration

Safe at third. *Left to right:* Faye Dancer, unidentified umpire, and Marge Wenzell (courtesy Northern Indiana Center for History).

2

The Trustee Administration, 1943–1944

The development of softball as a popular sport for American women by 1940 was a major factor underlying the creation of the All-American Girls' Softball League (AAGSBL). The second major and catalytic factor for the establishment of the league in 1943 was America's near-total involvement in World War II. Military manpower demands created the very real possibility that Major League Baseball would be postponed for the war's duration. In response to this eventuality, Philip K. Wrigley, entrepreneur and owner of the Chicago Cubs, established the AAGSBL. Thus it was that the AAGSBL's beginnings germinated out of the potential wartime demise of Major League Baseball, and its early nature and development reflected its creator.

Baseball in Wartime America

In mid–January 1942, just a little more than a month after the United States officially entered World War II, President Franklin D. Roosevelt responded to a letter from Judge Kenesaw Mountain Landis, then the commissioner of baseball, concerning baseball's wartime future. In the face of massive military manpower mobilization, President Roosevelt supported the continuance of Major League Baseball as a national morale booster:

> I honestly feel that it would be best for the country to keep baseball going. There will be fewer people unemployed and everybody will work longer hours and harder than ever before.
> And that means that they ought to have a chance for recreation and for taking their minds off their work even more than before....
> Here is another way of looking at it — if 300 teams use 5,000 or 6,000 players, these players are a definite recreational asset to at least 20,000,000 of their fellow citizens—and that in my judgement is thoroughly worthwhile.
>
> With every best wish,
> Very sincerely yours,
> [Signed] Franklin D. Roosevelt[1]

The president's personal sanction and cooperative support of baseball in the face of military manpower mobilization efforts reassured major league team owners. The war's first manpower threat to Major League Baseball had been faced and resolved in the best interests of the sport. Less than a year later, however, government plans for increased military and industrial manpower mobilization posed a second, more pervasive threat to the maintenance of Major League Baseball during wartime.

In the fall of 1942, Ken Beirn, a representative from the Office of War Information, advised an assembly of Major League Baseball owners to expect a critical manpower shortage in the spring and summer of 1943. He explained that three to four million men would go into uniform, and millions more would be forced to "transfer from their non-essential occupations to war jobs." Non-war production was going to be cut "by more than one-third" in order to release men to double war production.[2] Mr. Beirn expressed concern over anticipated negative public reaction to exceptions made for baseball, an obviously non-essential occupation:

> ... This summer every baseball fan or potential baseball fan is going to be very conscious of the way their lives are affected by manpower needs— either because of their own experience or that of a brother, sister, father or maybe even a mother who has had to change jobs sometimes with a sacrifice of income.[3]

The baseball magnates were thereby alerted to the very real possibility that public sentiment would necessitate the postponement of Major League Baseball for the 1943 season. As it turned out, negative public opinion wasn't focused against the major leagues, probably because so many regular players either enlisted or were drafted into military service.[4] However, before the outcome of the effect of this new manpower mobilization on Major League Baseball could be determined for the 1943 season, Philip K. Wrigley took action. Corporate executive and owner of the Chicago Cubs baseball team, Wrigley didn't wait for the axe to fall; he organized the All-American Girls' Softball League to keep Wrigley Field operating if the men's game was curtailed.[5] Under Wrigley's direction, the AAGSBL became the first highly organized, totally professional women's softball league in the United States. As might be expected, the AAGSBL reflected the resources, character and philosophy of its creator.

PHILIP K. WRIGLEY, FATHER OF THE AAGSBL

Several factors help account for Phillip Wrigley's quick sponsorship of the AAGSBL. Primary among them were his considerable financial resources, his interest in sport, including an interest in promoting women's involvement in sport, and his desire to support the war effort in every way possible.

Born in December 1894, Philip Wrigley began his administrative career with the Australian Branch of the William Wrigley, Jr. [Chewing Gum] Company in 1915.[6] He became president of the parent company in 1925, and upon his father's death in 1932, Philip inherited "the Chicago Cubs ... Catalina Island ... and, more importantly about 400,000 of the two million shares of Wrigley stock outstanding, which ... paid $4 a share [1939–1942] and averaged nearly $4 throughout the depression."[7] The gum business was a very lucrative business "with an uncommonly low ratio of costs to prices and an uncommonly high ratio of profits to revenue."[8]

> In 1940, for instance, Wm. Wrigley Jr. Co. showed net sales of nearly $36 million. Manufacturing costs, including about $3 million for gum base, totaled barely $13 million. Administrative and sales costs were less than $11 million. Even after $4 million income and profit taxes, there was more than $8 million profit.[9]

At the beginning of 1943, Philip K. Wrigley had more than sufficient financial resources to appropriate the reported $100,000 required to create the AAGSBL.

In addition to being a wealthy man, Philip K. Wrigley was also a sportsman. Encouraged by his father, Philip began riding horses and sailing while still a young boy.[10] The sports organizations he maintained memberships in during his mature years reflected a continued interest in these and other activities. He belonged to the Arab Horse Society (England), the Arab Horse Registry of America, Saddle and Cycle, Yachtsmen's Association of America, Chicago Yacht Club, Catalina Island Yacht Club, Lake Geneva Yacht Club, a Racquet Club, and the Chicago Athletic Association. As president and director of the Chicago National League Ball Club, Wrigley was also a member of the National Professional Baseball Clubs Association.[11]

During his lifetime, many speculated that Philip Wrigley had no particular interest in baseball because he didn't attend as many Cubs' games as had his father before him. Wrigley disputed this image when he affirmed to an interviewer in 1936 that he "would be the most rabid sort of fan" if he didn't exert the greatest control over himself."[12] Wrigley justified his infrequent attendance at Cubs' games with the following rationale:

> ... I don't believe that the executive of a ball club should let himself become a fanatic. It is a handicap to his job. Several times when I have seen the team kick away a game, I have found myself wanting to fire everybody on the club. That sort of stuff won't do.
> Furthermore, ... I have too much other work to do to be at the ballpark every afternoon. As it is, I have to come back here to the office to catch up on my work in the evening when I take in a game.[13]

Wrigley was not what one would call a playboy sportsman; but he had participated in sport, he maintained membership in sport organizations, and he professed a keen interest in professional baseball.

One indication of Philip Wrigley's interest in promoting women's involvement in sport was his promotion of Ladies' Days at baseball games beginning in the early 1930s.[14] This was a continuation of a program begun by his father.[15] Paul Angle, Wrigley's biographer, suggested that his promotion of Ladies' Days was motivated more by a business interest in women as spectators than in an interest in promoting women's sports participation.[16] Nevertheless, Wrigley was among the first baseball owners to actively encourage women to be baseball spectators. Although it is impossible to objectively assess whether Ladies' Days at the ballpark had any effect on the growth of girls' participation in softball during the 1930s, it is not impossible to imagine a relationship between the two.

Indeed, some players recruited to play in the AAGSBL acknowledged that attendance at major league games influenced their playing. Dorothy "Kammie" Kamenshek, a 1943 recruit from Cincinnati, reflected that being able to attend major league games contributed to her development as a player.

> I lived in a neighborhood with mostly boys, and I played street ball and ... at the age of 14, I was recruited for [an industrial] softball team. I guess I had a lot of natural ability. I don't think anyone ever really taught me. I was a student of the game. I used to watch all of the big leaguers as much as I could. My mother used to take me on Ladies' Day at the ball park, and I just studied them — Stan Musial for one. He was one of the hitters I loved to watch. To play first base I taught myself on a pillow in front of a mirror — shifting my feet and stretching.[17]

Eileen "Ginger" Gascon, a Chicago native who played in the league from 1949 to 1951, also testified that being able to attend major league games encouraged her playing experience.

> I lived in a neighborhood of mostly all boys.... Whenever the teams were picked, I
> always was picked with the boys teams.... Also my uncle was a cop on the gate at Wrigley
> Field. When Cavaretta and Phil Nicholson and all those guys were playing, he used to
> stand by the gate and say, "Go on, get in there." So I was fortunate enough at that age to
> get in and watch baseball games. Between playing myself and watching those games, it
> really sparked my interest.[18]

From personal experience, young girls who love to play baseball or softball dream
of becoming professional ball players just as young boys do. Some do not realize, until
well into their high school years that, to date, only boys can grow up to become professionals in most team sports.

Considerable evidence points to the creation of the AAGSBL as being just one of
several programs Wrigley jumped into to support the war effort. His actions may have
been motivated by an acute business interest. However, the following items suggest his
motivations were more altruistic in nature.

> Shortly after December 7, 1941, and long before Broadway was dimmed, [Wrigley] dis-
> mantled the spectacular million-dollar electric sign on Times Square. The floodlights that
> had kept the Wrigley Building in Chicago looking like a big wedding cake all night long,
> he presented to the Navy. In March 1941, nine months before aluminum was prohibited
> to civilian manufacturers, he voluntarily surrendered to OPM his entire 500,000-pound
> inventory of aluminum ingots reserved for wrapping foil. Last spring [1941] he offered
> government agencies free use of his mailing list of nearly a million retailers.[19]

Another of Philip Wrigley's major war effort contributions on the home front included
assigning all of his radio time to selling the war, rather than gum. The extent of this contribution was considerable, involving "$2 million for two C.B.S. programs alone."[20] He
also loaned Catalina Island to the government for military training, which shut down
his tourist-based business ventures there.[21] In addition, Wrigley converted part of his gum
packing factory into an assembly line for packing the Army's "K" rations.[22] He also
directed his gum tappers in Central and South America to tap and harvest as many rubber trees as they could while they were working on gum trees.[23] These projects, it was
pointed out, were primarily designed to ensure that the gum business would remain an
essential industry during the war. They also reflected the public service orientation of
Wrigley's character.

Wrigley's wealth, his close association with sport, particularly baseball, his experience in promoting women's involvement as sport spectators, and his determination to
support the war effort at home and abroad were essential pre-conditions for his creation
of the AAGSBL. The event catalyzing Wrigley's inauguration of the league was the government's projected manpower shortage crisis for the spring and summer of 1943. As he
had in other instances, when the Cubs' immediate future was threatened, Wrigley wasted
no time in seeking a viable, war-friendly alternative. That alternative was women's softball.

Wrigley's awareness of the existence and popularity of men and women's softball
competitions occurred prior to 1943. In the late 1930s, softball was attracting more spectators than baseball in several cities, including Los Angeles and Chicago, where Wrigley
owned baseball parks. A survey conducted by one of Wrigley's Los Angeles employees
revealed the existence of 9,000 softball teams within a 100-mile radius of Wrigley Field
in Los Angeles in 1938. One thousand of these were women's teams. As a means of stimulating interest in baseball in Los Angeles, Wrigley Field there was offered "free each year

for the windup double-header to decide the championship in both men's and women's softball leagues."[24] These games drew up to 30,000 fans and netted as much as $7,000 at the gate. The Chicago Metropolitan Girls Major Softball League had similarly attracted Wrigley's attention by the rise in attendance at its games through the summer of 1942.[25]

Wrigley was an innovative, yet practical person with sufficient financial and organizational resources to create a women's professional softball league. The war, its manpower threat to Major League Baseball, and the popularity of women's softball as a spectator sport, all contributed to Wrigley's creation of the AAGSBL. Also he was obviously aware of the general change in expectations for women's position in society brought about by the contingencies of World War II.

Between April 1940 and August 1943, about three million women entered the labor force. Military manpower demands necessitated their employment outside the home.[26] More importantly, many of these women were employed in occupations hitherto reserved for men.

> Women were riveters, spot and torch welders, hydraulic press operators, crane operators, shell loaders, bus drivers, train conductors, bellhops, lifeguards, lumberjacks ... cowgirls, section hands, coal mine checkers, car washers, filling station operators, taxi drivers, barbers, policemen, [and] ferry command pilots....[27]

Like the workplace, the sporting world was also infiltrated by women during the war years. Here, too, women assumed positions traditionally occupied by men. They worked as jockeys, umpires, bowling pin setters, caddies, horse trainers, and even football coaches.[28] One of the AAGSBL's first press releases testified to Wrigley's consciousness of the increased activity and status of women in American society.

> World War One showed to the world for the first time on a large scale what women could and did do, and World War Two is going to carry this even further. American women have taken a very definite share of the load in the country's progress, and in the fields of science, business and sports they are now also working in ever increasing numbers....[29]

The establishment of a women's professional softball league, while novel, did not appear fatuous in relation to the prevailing social circumstances necessitated by war. It was logical, in the projected absence of men, for Wrigley to organize women to fill a spectator role for a war-weary public.

Once it became obvious that Major League Baseball would not be curtailed, Wrigley did not abandon his softball project. However, in light of the survival of men's baseball, he fashioned the league's objectives to compliment the war effort in the mid-sized industrial communities that supported its teams. The following objectives for the AAGSBL were outlined for the public:

1. To furnish additional means of healthful recreation to the public who are all in one way or another under severe pressure from war work during this critical war time.
2. To create the incentive on the part of girls and women employed in war work to get out and play softball themselves, thereby getting the exercise they need to carry on their jobs more efficiently.
3. To keep all workers better satisfied with living in the community in which they are now located by furnishing additional entertainment which may now be available to them only in large cities.[30]

The AAGSBL, like every other Wrigley enterprise initiated or modified during the war years, was justified by what it could contribute to the war effort. Nevertheless, Wrigley also envisioned long-term goals for the AAGSBL. He determined to "organize and develop girls professional softball on a sound and high standard as a national sport."[31]

> In two or three years time it's possible that girls softball may be recognized by the press and radio as of Major League possibilities and be treated as such. When that time arrives girl [softball players] will have the same opportunity to gain nationwide recognition and acclaim as feminine personalities in other sports— notably Helen Wills and Helen Jacobs in Tennis; Patty Berg and Helen Hicks in Golf; Gertrude Ederle, Gloria Callen and Eleanor Holm in Swimming.[32]

Wrigley had a personal interest in substituting women's softball for men's baseball in Wrigley Field, but as with his other wartime projects, his plans for the AAGSBL were designed to contribute something to the public, to improve the game and to raise the players' social standing. Ultimately, Wrigley believed the largest sector of the general public would embrace and support women's professional softball if it were based on the highest social standards of the day. A decade after Wrigley created the AAGSBL, Maria Sexton wrote the following in the concluding chapter of her Doctoral Dissertation:

> Since the instigation of the League, much effort has been made to convince the general public that participants are not only highly-skilled baseball players, but also excellent examples of good, clean American girlhood. Newspaper reports, as well as personal experience in sponsoring cities, assure the writer that members of League teams are well accepted and highly respected in the communities in which they play.[33]

Ms. Sexton lived and taught in Grand Rapids during the 1940s and attended Chicks games and observed for herself the caliber of skill and the quality of character the All-Americans displayed. Her exposure to the league contributed to her role in championing athletic opportunities for girls and women in colleges and universities and the AAU for the rest of her professional life.[34]

Organization of the AAGSBL, 1943

Wrigley was not one to approach the organization and administration of a new venture in a halfway manner.[35] Before committing himself to establishing the AAGSBL, he characteristically marshaled resource personnel to investigate the feasibility of the project. In the fall of 1942, his principal advertising agent Arthur E. Meyerhoff, the Chicago Cubs' lawyer Paul V. Harper, and the Cubs' chief scout Jim Hamilton were charged with establishing a preliminary plan for league operations and with investigating the softball situation in the country.[36] This committee was advised by one consultant:

> Without a doubt, softball, particularly among women, has the greatest potentialities from both competition and spectator standpoints of any of the growing sports.... The game itself should have a tremendous development in popularity due to the huge increase in the number of women war workers and the natural desire of industrial management to find some means of providing esprit de corps in their respective plants.[37]

The organizational structure Wrigley subsequently established for the AAGSBL reflected the influences of his association with baseball, his personal standards, the contemporary social climate, and necessities dictated by the venture itself.

Contrary to what might be expected, Wrigley did not organize the AAGSBL to be identical with the organizational structure of Major League Baseball. First of all, Wrigley determined that the AAGSBL would be a non-profit organization supervised by trustees rather than profit-motivated team owners. He felt it was "the only way to start during the war for the support of both the government and public psychology."[38] His experience with major league baseball had impressed upon him the exploitive nature of profit-oriented professional baseball men. He undoubtedly knew, for instance, that some ballpark operators were suspected of nickel snatching. The observation was made that few ballparks provided drinking fountains and that crowds were kept waiting outside so money could be saved on ushers' salaries. In one ballpark, the sale of gum was forbidden because of the belief that it quenched spectators' thirst and caused a reduction of soft drink sales.[39]

The management of the AAGSBL by trustees attempted to identify it as a beneficent rather than an exploitive organization. Trustee management was commonly identified with civic organizations such as colleges, churches, foundations, and hospitals. By association, the initial organizational structure of the AAGSBL was identified with the most reputable institutions in America's social tradition. The rationale for this structure rested on the concept that being a "non-profit organization [the AAGSBL] could control softball just as Landis [controlled] baseball, because its motives would be beyond reproach and not profit-minded."[40] This concept was considered a critical element in establishing the league as an honorable enterprise in the public mind.

A second major diversion from traditional Major League Baseball procedure, adopted for the AAGSBL, was the establishment of a unique player personnel system. Rather than each team "owning" its own players, all players were "owned" by the league. Players were pooled each year and allocated to the respective teams by an "allocation committee" composed of team managers and league administrative personnel. The theory behind this procedure was to equalize competition to prevent one team from dominating the league year after year as was common in the major leagues at that time.[41] One has only to recall the New York Yankee dynasty, which dominated major league baseball from 1920 to 1939, "including an unprecedented four straight Series titles in the years 1936–1939," to be reminded of the eventuality Wrigley tried to avoid.[42]

In yet another diversion from common baseball practice, player contracts were modeled after contracts in use by stage, screen and radio companies rather than those used by Major League Baseball. The contracts were identified as personal service contracts which granted players an "option to renew from year to year at a definite predetermined and agreed upon salary, which if not exercised by the league [left] the player a completely free agent."[43] Baseball's reserve clause was omitted from the original AAGSBL contracts, avoiding the buying and selling of players by individual team sponsors. In reflecting on the exclusion of the reserve clause, Wrigley noted:

> ... I'm probably the only one in professional baseball in the last 40 or more years who has never felt that the reserve clause as now written in the baseball contracts was really essential. I guess it is because I have sort of an old-fashioned idea that if a man likes his job he will give you his best. If he does not like it, no contract on earth can cause him to put forth his best efforts. The Girls' League was a good chance to try out a variation on something which had been long established and volubly supported by both professional baseball leagues.[44]

In addition to his efforts to structure the AAGSBL to avoid some of the pitfalls he felt were inherent in baseball, Wrigley initiated changes in the softball game then being played by women's teams to align it more closely with baseball. The pitching distance was lengthened from 35 to 40 feet; nine rather than ten players were used in the field;

base runners were allowed to lead off and steal; and pitchers were allowed to start with only one foot on the rubber instead of two.[45] League administrators concluded these changes would improve the spectator qualities of the sport and make it less of a pitcher's duel as was and is common of softball.[46]

These rule changes ultimately resulted in a revision of the league name. Midway through the 1943 season, sports writers were notified to replace "softball" with "baseball" in the league name. This change in identity from the All-American Girls' Softball League to the All-American Girls' Base Ball League (AAGBBL) was initiated "so that this pastime [would] not be confused with softball as it [was then] being played by amateurs."[47] This directive apparently stimulated some protest to the effect that even though the AAGSBL game was not strictly softball, neither was it strictly baseball as the underhand pitching style was still utilized. Thus, at the conclusion of the 1943 season, the league name was officially changed to the more descriptive All-American Girls' Professional Ball League (AAGPBL). This title was retained until the end of the 1945 season when All-American Girls' Baseball League (AAGBBL) was again officially adopted.[48]

The change in the league's name was one of the last steps Wrigley took toward establishing a distinct image for the All-American League. The first steps he emphasized to set the AAGSBL apart from existing amateur, industrial, and semi-pro women's softball included the establishment of strict off-the-field rules for player conduct, employment of team chaperones, charm school training for players, and the creation of a skirted uniform.[49] The capstone to these policies was an intensive publicity campaign to emphasize that AAGSBL players would not imitate male baseball stars as was commonly observed within amateur women's softball leagues.[50] Rather, the AAGSBL, local fans and magazine writers were advised, would, next to skill, emphasize "the highest ideals of womanhood" by requiring its players to "dress, act, and carry themselves as befits the feminine sex."[51] The image Wrigley wanted to establish, for public approval and support, was an image of socially acceptable athletic femininity. He certainly would not have wanted his name associated with the rough and tumble, "unladylike" image existing Chicago softball league players exhibited in bars like the one at 63rd and Halstead.[52] Thus, on one hand, Wrigley recruited the most skilled players he could find throughout the U.S. and Canada. On the other hand, he found it necessary, or at least wise, to publicize that he would indoctrinate his players in the principles of the prevailing concept of socially acceptable feminine charm and entertainment. As Annabelle Lee Harmon noted, "They wanted us to look like ladies and act like ladies, but play like men."[53] Some sport philosophers and sociologists might still argue that "athleticism" and "femininity" are contradictory terms, but Wrigley cannot be faulted for striving to establish the league on the highest standards of his contemporary upper class society.

Another indication of Wrigley's high aspirations for the AAGSBL was his intent to establish teams in cities like Chicago, Milwaukee, Detroit, Cincinnati, Cleveland, St. Louis, Louisville, and Gary, Indiana. His objective was to locate some teams in major league baseball cities and others in smaller war production cities like Gary. He reasoned that revenue generated from the larger cities would carry teams in the smaller cities and thereby demonstrate the league's sincere, patriotic service to war workers.[54] Despite Wrigley's preliminary plans, the original four AAGSBL teams were, in the end, all located in midsized war production cities within a 100-mile radius of Chicago. They included Racine and Kenosha, Wisconsin; Rockford, Illinois; and South Bend, Indiana.[55] These cities, incidentally, had been popular centers for men's and women's softball since the 1930s.[56]

AAGSBL models: The first four to sign contracts. *Left to right, back:* Clara Schillace, Ann Harnett, Edythe Perlick. *Seated:* Shirley Jameson (courtesy Northern Indiana Center for History; with permission of Ron Seymour, Chicago, Illinois).

A Chicago team was conspicuously absent from the league until 1948. This circumstance was likely linked to resistance the AAGSBL encountered from an established amateur softball organization in that city. When AAGSBL officials began offering contracts to the Chicago league's players, their managers accused Wrigley of "raiding" their teams. They hired a lawyer to see what could be done to stop Wrigley's "player raids." Since the players were amateurs and weren't under contract, no legal action could be taken against the AAGSBL. The only recourse the Chicago league had was to turn professional and place

1943 Kenosha Comets: *Left to right, front:* Clara Cook, Myrna Nearing, Mary Lou Lester, Shirley Jameson, Pauline Pirok. *Middle*: Phyllis "Sugar" Koehn, Kay Heim, Helen Westerman, Helen Nicol, Darlene Mickelsen. *Back:* Josh Billings (manager), Audrey Wagner, Ethel McCreary, Lee Harney, Ann Harnett, Janice O'Hara, Ada Ryan (chaperone) (reproduced from the original held by the Department of Special Collections of the University Libraries of Notre Dame).

all of its players under contract.[57] They did just that. In 1944, the Chicago National Girls' Baseball League was organized on a professional basis. Although this league was identified as a girls' baseball league from 1944 through the mid–1950s, it never abandoned use of the 12" softball or underhand pitching.[58] Wrigley, a believer in "live and let live,"[59] undoubtedly respected the Chicago league's territorial rights by refraining from establishing an AAGSBL team in the Windy City during the first years of play.

According to Maybelle Blair, who played in both leagues, after the National League turned professional, it was similar to the All-American in regard to number of games played, type of schedule, scouting all over the country, and contracts. She identified the main differences to be slightly higher salaries in the Chicago League; adherence to softball; and uniforms consisting of shirts, shorts, and long stockings.[60] Sophie Kury observed that the National League did not employ chaperones.[61]

Wrigley attempted to convince other baseball magnates to cooperate in his women's softball venture, but failed to do so. At a National League Club Owners' meeting in New York in February 1943, Wrigley approached the other baseball owners with a plan for scheduling AAGSBL games in major league parks when the men's teams were out of town.[62] Wrigley reasoned that the women's league would attract a somewhat different clientele than men's baseball and at the same time stimulate more interest for the men's

1943 Racine Belles: *Left to right, front:* Irene Hickson, Edythe Perlick, Clara Schillace, Annabelle Thompson, Madeline English. *Middle:* Eleanor Dapkus, Sophie Kurys, Dorothy Wind, Gloria Marks, Dorothy McGuire, Margaret Danhauser. *Back:* Charlotte Smith, Joanne Winter, Johnny Gottselig (manager), Mary Nesbitt, Dorothy Hunter, Marie Anderson (chaperone) (courtesy Northern Indiana Center for History).

game.[63] The other baseball owners viewed the situation differently. They weren't convinced that Major League Baseball was seriously endangered by the projected manpower shortage, and they considered the proposed women's league an unnecessary competitor to established men's teams. They reasoned that the sports dollar in every city was limited and whatever was spent on the women's league wouldn't be spent on the men's league.[64] (Would we have women's professional baseball as well as women's professional basketball now if Wrigley's peers had been more amenable to his plan?)

AAGSBL Administrators and Administration

At least one other baseball administrator demonstrated agreement with Philip Wrigley's AAGSBL venture. Branch Rickey, general manager for the Brooklyn Dodgers, agreed to lend his name and reputation to the AAGSBL by serving as one of its trustees. Wrigley asked Rickey to serve as a trustee because he believed, and he thought "practically everybody else in both leagues ... always considered [Branch Rickey] one of the outstanding baseball men in the country."[65]

Branch Rickey was in closer touch with the professional potential of women's soft-

1943 Rockford Peaches: *Left to right, front:* Eddie Stumpf (manager), Millie Warwick, Pauline Oravets, Helen Sawyer, Helen Nelson, Lorraine Wuethrich, Marjorie Peters, Olive Little. *Back:* Clara Cook, Dorothy "Kammie" Kamenshek, Terrie Davis, Eileen Burmeister, Josephine Skokan, Ethel McCreary, Rella Swamp, Lillian Jackson, Betty Fritz, Marie Timm (chaperone) (courtesy Arthur Meyerhoff, 1974).

1943 South Bend Blue Sox: *Left to right, front:* Doris Barr, Mary Baker, Lucella MacLean, Marge Stefani. *Middle:* Lois Florreich, Betsy Jochum, Jo D'Angelo, Margaret Berger, Dorothy Schroeder, Mary Holda. *Back:* Bert Niehoff (manager), Muriel Coben, Ellen Tronnier, Jo Hageman, Geraldine Shafranas, Betty McFadden, Rose Virginia Way (chaperone) (National Baseball Hall of Fame Library, Cooperstown, N.Y.).

Figure 1: League city sites, 1943–1954. Rockford, IL 1943–1954; South Bend, IL 1943–1954; Kenosha, WI 1943–1951; Racine, WI 1943–1950; Milwaukee, WI 1944; Minneapolis, MN 1944; Fort Wayne, IN 1945–1954; Grand Rapids, MI 1945–1954; Peoria, IL 1946–1951; Muskegon, MI 1946–1950; Chicago, IL 1948; Springfield, IL 1948; Kalamazoo, MI 1950–1954; Battle Creek, MI 1951–1952; Muskegon, MI 1953 (courtesy Jacqueline R. Heitmann, Women's Field of Dreams).

ball than other baseball administrators through his close friendship with George Sisler. Sisler, a retired major leaguer, owned and operated two softball parks in St. Louis, where men's and women's semi-pro softball flourished. He also owned the charter of the organization these teams belonged to, the American Softball Association.[66] George Sisler, therefore, was well aware of the popularity of women's softball as a spectator sport on a semi-pro level. Since he and Rickey maintained a close friendship throughout their lives, Sisler undoubtedly impressed Rickey with the favorable potential of developing a women's professional softball league. George Sisler, incidentally, was once a candidate for the AAGSBL presidency.[67]

Branch Rickey, like Wrigley, did not sit back idly when social forces impinged on the future of baseball. When the success of major league teams was threatened by the draft during World War I, Rickey signed "draft-proof Cubans as a hedge against the realities of military conscription."[68] He resorted to the same practice when the United States entered World War II.[69] When integration became an issue after World War II, he first toyed with the idea of organizing a black major league but finally signed the first black player, Jackie Robinson, to play on his National League team.[70] In the late 1950s and early 1960s, when baseball was threatened by the rising popularity of television, football, and an archaic tournament system, Rickey forced expansion of the major leagues by threatening to organize a third league.[71] His support of Philip Wrigley's plan to organize a women's professional softball league during wartime was therefore very much in character.

Although Branch Rickey did not take an active role in AAGSBL administration,[72] the association of his baseball and personal reputation with the league did influence the establishment of at least one AAGSBL team. Ernest Smith, President of Smith Oil and Refining Company in Rockford, Illinois, was the first person to sign as a local guarantor for the Rockford team. He testified that the reason he was willing to invest in the AAGSBL was because Rickey was a trustee. Rickey had rendered Smith a personal favor sometime before, and Smith disclosed that he subscribed as a supporter of the AAGSBL as a returned favor to Rickey.[73]

In addition to himself and Branch Rickey, the third trustee Wrigley recruited for the AAGSBL was Paul V. Harper. Harper was a longtime Wrigley friend, a prominent Chicago lawyer, a trustee for the University of Chicago, and an attorney for the Chicago

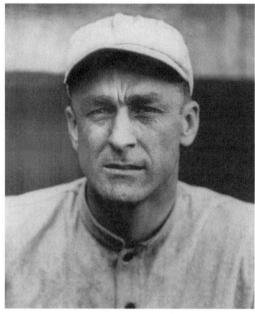

Philip K. Wrigley (reproduced from the original held by the Department of Special Collections of the University Libraries of Notre Dame).

Branch Rickey as a St. Louis Brown (National Baseball Hall of Fame Library, Cooperstown, N.Y.).

Cubs. Besides lending another sterling reputation to the AAGSBL's trustee triumvirate, Harper also served as its attorney.[74]

As nearly as could be determined, the AAGSBL's organizational structure during the 1943 season consisted of a simple administrative unit under the direction of the trustees (Figure 2). Ken Sells, former assistant to the Cubs' general manager, was chosen to serve as the AAGSBL's first president. He served in that capacity through the end of the 1944 season. Characterized as a "young and energetic executive, Sells was already well versed in baseball management and administration."[75]

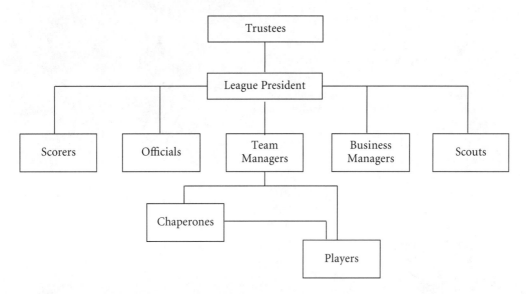

Figure 2: The Organizational Structure of the AAGSBL/AAGPBL, 1943–1944

> Born in Rockford, Illinois, he attended the University of Wisconsin, later joining the Wrigley Company organization on the west coast. In 1937, Ken was brought to the Chicago office of the Wrigley Company and became an active member of the Chicago Cubs management. In 1941, he became assistant to General Manager James Gallagher of the Cubs and the following year, when Mr. Philip Wrigley conceived the idea of the All-American Girls Professional Ball League, Sells was installed as President of the League. It was largely through his hard work, personal perseverance and enthusiastic pioneering that this new League was launched so successfully in 1943.[76]

Ken Sells testified that the initial organization of the AAGSBL could not have been accomplished without the services of Jimmy Hamilton, the Cubs' chief scout, who set up tryout camps throughout the country and selected the first players for the league. Hamilton's contributions to the AAGSBL grew out of an extensive baseball career.

> Vice-President James (Jimmy) Hamilton [was] one of the best-known baseball personalities in the country. He once played shortstop and third base for Richmond, Va., Brooklyn, St. Paul, Minn., and St. Joseph, Mo. He managed such teams as Charleston, S.C., Peoria, Ill., Vancouver, B.C., St. Joseph, Mo., and Nashville, Tenn. He was also vice-president and business manager of the latter club. For some years he served as scout for the Chicago Cubs and on the formation of the All-American, President Sells selected him as his right-hand man. He has been chief scout for the All-American, largely responsible for the fine

talent which has been culled from 26 States and 5 Provinces of Canada.[77]

Sells also affirmed that the myriad details of establishing the AAGSBL could not have been accomplished in the few months available "if it wasn't for the fact that the personnel of the Wrigley Company, its advertising agency, Arthur Meyerhoff Company, and the Chicago Cubs organization had not all been put at my disposal."[78]

During the 1943 season, President Sells and his assistants were responsible for the administrative details of the entire league, including the operation of all teams. Wrigley provided half of the financial base for league operations in 1943 ($100,000), and local business contributors provided the other half. Each of the four cities matched Wrigley's 22,500 subsidies to establish a $45,000 budget for individual team operations.[79] Available records indicate that local guarantors did not assume any administrative responsibilities during the 1943 season.[80] In essence, the All-American Girls' Softball League was conceived, organized, properly funded, and operated by Philip Wrigley and his staff during the 1943 season.

Ken Sells (reproduced from the original held by the Department of Special Collections of the University Libraries of Notre Dame).

AAGPBL Organization and Administration, 1944

The first modification in league structure for the newly named All-American Girls Professional Ball League (AAGPBL) occurred at the beginning of the 1944 season. Franchises "were granted to the four original clubs, and Mr. Wrigley operated Milwaukee and Minneapolis."[81] The restructuring of the league through the institution of franchises in 1944 took the burden of financial responsibility for the league off Wrigley and enabled "business and civic leaders in all participating cities [to] operate ... their clubs both financially and physically."[82] The franchise fee for 1944 was estimated at $25,000 with an immediate deposit of $17,200 required. Total minimum authorized capital established for each team for the season was estimated at $50,000.[83] In addition, the new structure stipulated that league administration would receive three cents on each attendance up to 90,000.[84] This income was established to support league administrative operations on a non-profit basis. League services rendered in return for the franchise fee included the acquisition, training and employment of players; the acquisition of uniforms and equipment; employment of scorers, officials, managers, and chaperones; purchase of personal property and public liability insurance; printing of tickets; provision of a complete season's advertising campaign in each league city; maintenance of a scouting organization; and finally, establishment of a financial reserve to handle emergency situations and enable the league to free itself from all financial obligations.[85]

On the local level, franchise fee contributors formed team boards of directors with

"A New Manpower Crisis, Ladies." Cartoon from the *Chicago Daily News*, 19 May 1944 (courtesy Arthur Meyerhoff, 1974).

elected administrators. Team directors retained the privilege of selecting their own business manager, team manager, and coach-chaperone. The latter two individuals, however, were actually employed through the league office rather than by individual clubs. It is assumed, however, that individual clubs had the right to approve or disapprove of managers and chaperones. Team organizations were also delegated the responsibility of ticket sales, some local advertising, game promotions, and related club business.[86] Although considerable responsibility for team operations was delegated to local directors in 1944, league affairs continued to be operated and administered by the league president under the direction of the original board of trustees.[87]

Two new teams were organized in 1944, one in Milwaukee and one in Minneapolis. Both teams played in American Association Baseball Club (men's minor league) parks, and the direct comparison with men's games was not favorable to AAGPBL teams.[88] A telephone poll in Milwaukee, though not extensive, revealed that some considered ticket prices for AAGPBL games too high, and others preferred to see the American Association team play. One respondent expressed the sentiments of the majority of spectators interviewed about the AAGPBL.

> I think it [AAGPBL] is O.K. and should be encouraged, but I think the management has made a mistake in setting up the present admission charge. Very few rabid baseball fans, of which there are many in Milwaukee, can see any logical reason for paying prices comparable, and, in some instances, higher than those they pay to see the Brewers perform, who at the present time are the leaders in the American Association.[89]

As might be expected from the foregoing comment, attendance figures for AAGPBL games were low in both Milwaukee and Minneapolis.

The Minneapolis Millerettes team was further handicapped by its geographical isolation from the rest of the league. Several other AAGPBL teams "objected to making the trip to Minneapolis because of the heavy traveling expenses with such small crowds attending the games."[90] By mid–July, 1944, it was deemed more profitable for the league to operate the Minneapolis team as a perpetual traveling team than to maintain home stands in the Twin Cities. The Millerettes were henceforth unofficially christened the Minneapolis Orphans.[91]

It is important to note that the Minneapolis and Milwaukee clubs did not seem to have the same enthusiastic local support that the other teams enjoyed. Marie Keenan, an AAGPBL publicist, noted that "Mr. Wrigley operated Milwaukee and Minneapolis." Max Carey, manager of the Milwaukee Chicks in 1944, reported that the "Milwaukee team had no local financial backing as did most of the other teams."[92] It is unclear if Mr. Wrigley was unable to solicit local businessmen in Milwaukee and Minneapolis to underwrite AAGPBL teams. If so, it would not have been out of character for him to subsidize teams in those cities as a personal experiment. It quickly became evident, however, that an absence of the vested interest of influential local businessmen doomed these AAGPBL teams. Without the support of influential businessmen, the teams also lacked the kind of wholehearted, unbiased support in the *Minneapolis Tribune* and the *Milwaukee Journal* that predominated in other league city newspapers. A comparison of all league city newspapers, from May to July 1944, revealed that the Minneapolis and Milwaukee papers printed shorter stories, less frequently, with a more marked chauvinistic attitude than the other papers.[93] Historical hindsight suggests it was fortuitous that Wrigley based league teams in cities where they received the unbridled support of leading citizens; obtained extensive and favorable newspaper coverage; and were, for the most part, free from direct comparison with men's semi-pro teams.

The possibility exists that men's baseball organizers in Minneapolis and Milwaukee undermined the AAGPBL in their cities because it constituted unwanted competition. This conjecture arises from an examination of a similar situation in Fort Wayne, Indi-

1944 Milwaukee Chicks (Schnitts): *Front, left to right:* Ernestine Petras, Josephine Figlio, Vicki Panos, Delores Klosowski, Merle Keagle. *Middle, left to right:* Chaperone Dorothy Hunter, Alma Ziegler, Clara Cook, Viola Thompson, Sylvia Wronski, Connie Wisniewski, Max Carey (Manager). *Back, left to right:* Doris Tetzlaff, Betty Whiting, Thelma "Tiby" Eisen, Dorothy Maguire, Emily Stevenson, Jo Kabick, Gladys Davis (courtesy Arthur Meyerhoff, 1974).

ana during the 1945 season. The AAGPBL Fort Wayne Daisies, who enjoyed the financial backing and support of Fort Wayne's leading businessmen, competed for spectators with a men's semi-pro team and a men's "World Championship Soft Ball Club."[94] Both the Daisies and the men's semi-pro teams were in contention for first place in their respective leagues toward the end of the season, but the AAGPBL team was averaging nearly 1300 in attendance per game while the men's semi-pro team was averaging only about 500 per game.[95] For the six weeks between July 7 and August 20, Fort Wayne newspapers were on strike, so advertising was restricted to radio promotions, store window cards, and announcements during games.[96] A few other interesting comparisons between these three teams included the following: (1) admission for adult tickets to AAGPBL games was 74 cents, whereas the men's semi-pro team charged 50 cents, and admission to the men's championship softball games was free; (2) teams did not play in the same park, thereby reducing direct comparison between the men's and women's teams and allowing the women's teams to play in the evenings; and (3) when the newspaper strike was over, the Daisies received more sports page coverage than the other two teams.[97]

The AAGPBL's Fort Wayne experience cannot categorically be compared to its Milwaukee and Minneapolis experiences because of the cities' diversity in size and population components. The Fort Wayne experience does, however, leave room for suggesting that failure of AAGPBL teams in Milwaukee and Minneapolis may well have stemmed from a lack of local support, an unfriendly press, and direct comparison with a men's

1944 Minneapolis Millerettes (Orphans): *Front, left to right:* Bubber Jonnard (Manager), Lillian Jackson, Betty Trezza, Helen Callaghan, Margaret Callaghan, Audrey Kissel, Faye Dancer, Lavone "Pepper" Paire, Ada Ryan (Chaperone). *Back, left to right:* Dorothy Wiltse, Kay Blumetta, Vivian Kellogg, Ruth "Tex" Lessing, Margaret Wigiser, Audrey Haine, Elizabeth Farrow, Annabelle Lee (courtesy Arthur Meyerhoff, 1974).

semi-pro team. The relative impact of these three factors cannot be directly measured, but logic suggests that lack of local businessmen's support and an unfriendly press critically affected the success of AAGPBL teams in those cities.

Advantages and Disadvantages of the Trustee Structure

The major advantages that the trustee structure held for the All-American Girls League included several elements. Primary among these was the sound financial base supplied by Wrigley. Also important was the public appeal of its non-profit, civic-oriented platform and the fact that initial league organization and operation were conducted by a well-established baseball organization with experienced administrative personnel who infused the league with high standards. The underlying source of all these attributes, of course, was none other than the league's creator, Philip K. Wrigley.

The major disadvantage of the trustee structure, especially during the first year of play, was the lack of representation for local guarantors in league affairs. Whether or not the league could have been inaugurated in 1943 with a more democratic administrative structure can only be conjectured now. However, the wartime emergency conditions

Wrigley faced left little leeway for employing other methods for launching the league immediately.

The problem of local representation in league administrative affairs was partially alleviated through the institutions of franchises and the organization of local administrations for the 1944 season, but it wasn't until the beginning of the 1945 season that local sponsors obtained an official voice in central league operations. In the meantime, the All-American Girls Professional Ball League had been auspiciously launched and firmly established as a spectator sport in the four Midwestern industrial centers of Kenosha and Racine, Wisconsin; Rockford, Illinois; and South Bend, Indiana. In all of these cities, AAGPBL teams had the financial backing of reputable local businessmen; they enjoyed positive, almost daily coverage in local newspapers; and they were free from direct comparison with men's minor league baseball.

3

Establishing the Public Image: Publicity and Promotion, 1943–1944

One of the hallmarks of the AAGBBL from its inception throughout the 1940s was the extensive publicity it received. Besides almost daily coverage in league city newspapers, the league was featured in nationally popular periodicals such as *Time, Life, Collier's, Deb, Liberty, American Magazine, Seventeen, Newsweek, Click, Holiday, Magazine Digest* and *McCall's*.[1] This publicity did not appear fortuitously or accidentally. It flooded the media through planning and hard work backed by a substantial budget. During 1943 and 1944, Philip K. Wrigley supplied the publicity budget.

Wrigley's Publicity Philosophy

Wrigley spent approximately $250,000 to establish and develop the AAGSBL. What specific percentage of this amount he designated for publicity and promotion is not known, but there is little question that it was a significant portion of the total because Philip Wrigley believed in the value of advertising.[2] He had grown up and worked intimately with his father, a man considered among the premiere advertisers of the early 20th century.[3] Advertising was William Wrigley, Jr.'s, specialty. Through advertising, his initial capital of $32 in 1891 grew to $13,000,000 by 1916.[4] When Philip Wrigley became heir to the William Wrigley, Jr. Company after his father's death in 1932, he adhered to his father's principles of business operation, including extensive advertising. In 1972, for instance, the William Wrigley, Jr. Company was assessed at "something in excess of $275 million."[5] More than $20 million was budgeted just for advertising gum in 1972.[6] Moreover, Philip Wrigley took a personal hand in the company's advertising.

> Phil Wrigley ... [held] with his father that anyone could make chewing gum; the trick was to sell it. And sales depended mostly on advertising. This part of the business he made his major concern. "How closely do I watch details?" he said in an interview published in *Printer's Ink* in the summer of 1938. "As closely as any advertising manager could. I know where every advertising dollar goes and why it is being spent. I select media, copy, and artwork. I even write copy and select whatever materials we may use. Nothing is initiated or changed without my knowledge and approval."[7]

Knowing this about Philip Wrigley, it is not surprising to discover that the establishment and development of the AAGSBL in 1943 was heralded by extensive publicity and promotional campaigns. The league began as a Wrigley enterprise and the Wrigley advertising influence remained until 1951, when team directors disassociated with Wrigley-affiliated personnel.

Arthur Meyerhoff's Role in League Publicity

Responsibility for carrying through with Wrigley's publicity plans for the AAGSBL was allocated to one of his principle advertising agents, Arthur E. Meyerhoff Associates, Inc. Meyerhoff's agency handled the league's publicity and promotional agenda from 1943 through 1950. From 1943 through 1944, Meyerhoff served the league under Wrigley's direction, and as previously mentioned, Meyerhoff purchased the league from Wrigley in the fall of 1944 and established a Management Corporation, which administered league affairs and was responsible for league publicity and promotion from 1945 to 1950. Meyerhoff had a vested interest in the league's success as well as an uninhibited faith in the value of constant advertising and promotion.[8]

The bulk of Meyerhoff's publicity and promotional efforts were understandably concentrated in Chicago and league cities, but his vision far exceeded local parameters. He recognized the value of national exposure to the league's popularization. Feature stories in nationally popular periodicals were viewed as a viable means of attracting new fans and new players to the league.[9] Meyerhoff's advertising agency not only solicited feature articles of the league in popular magazines but also in trade magazines such as *The Hotel Greeters Guide of Wisconsin*, *Dodge News*, *The Ashlar* (Massachusetts Mutual Life Insurance Company Publication), *Allsports* (U. S. Rubber Company Publication), *News of the Nation* (Quarterly Publication of the National Jewish Hospital), *The Torch* (Milwaukee advertising publication), *Once a Year* (Milwaukee Press Club Publication), *Forbes Magazine of Business* and *Moose Magazine*.[10] Nor were sport magazines neglected. At the end of the 1945 season, the league was renamed the All-American Girls Base Ball League (AAGBBL), and league feature stories appeared in such sporting periodicals as *Sport*, *Sports Graphic*, *Sportfolio*, *Sport Life*, and *Major League Baseball Facts and Figures*.[11] AAGBBL national newspaper feature stories materialized in the *New York Times Magazine* and *This Week Magazine*.[12]

League Publicity Themes

AAGBBL articles that appeared in popular periodicals and trade magazines listed in the preceding paragraphs spanned the years 1943–1950. The major publicity themes that characterized league publicity were developed during its infancy or during the Trustee years (1943–1944). One of the initial publicity themes, "Recreation for War Workers," was necessarily restricted to the war years, but the others, including "Femininity," "Community Welfare," and "Family Entertainment," had their genesis during the Trustee Administration and were repeated in somewhat different forms throughout Management's Administration (1945–1950).

The "Recreation for War Workers" publicity theme received considerable exposure under the era of the Trustees. It was a time of intense involvement in World War II by the American people, on the home front as well as on foreign battlefields. League cities were reportedly chosen "because of the large number of industrial plants nearby."[13] Many of the larger industries in league cities such as Studebaker and Bendix in South Bend, Indiana, and Nash-Kelvinator Corporation in Kenosha, Wisconsin, had converted to war production by the time the league was created, and there was an expressed need for recreation for war workers in these communities.[14] It follows that some of the top administrators in league city industrial plants were willing, on this basis, to contribute funds to help subsidize an AAGBBL team for their locales. Special nights for specific industries were set aside in league cities as a means of introducing the league to the working populace. Concomitantly, these special nights broadened the spectator base for home games. A Kenosha newspaper advertisement for the league admonished workers to attend AAG-BBL games to escape the pressures of war work:

> Come out and have the time of your life! See what a fast, exciting game these professional champions play. They're the top players of the country, keenly competing — upholding the best traditions of big-league play — boosting morale and providing the finest recreation on our home front! Forget your cares and worries — you'll go back to the job feeling better than ever.[15]

In an effort to stimulate attendance at the Kenosha Comets' games late in the 1943 season, four factories and the American Legion sponsored special nights during one week of play. The four factories, Frost, Tri-Clover, Specialty Brass, and Vincent-McCall, also cooperated in staging an 11:00 A.M. make-up game so "The second shift war workers ... who have been unable to see the night contests all year, are afforded a chance to enjoy a game...."[16] These special nights incorporated an incentive for each industry to outdo the others for an attendance record.[17]

Other war-related promotions included the league's policy of free admittance to service personnel and exhibition games at nearby military training bases and veterans' hospitals.[18] League administrators catered to military women as well as military men when it came to staging exhibition games.

Perhaps the most historic promotional effort of the Trustee Administration was a war-related, All-Star AAGSBL game featured at Wrigley Field the night of July 1, 1943. It was part of a large Women's Army Air Corps (WAAC) sports and recruiting rally attended by 7,000 fans free of charge. The preliminary to the AAGSBL game was a 6:00 P.M. softball contest between WAAC teams from Camp Grant and Fort Sheridan which Fort Sheridan won 11–5. The between-games program included "Calisthenics, precision drills, a dress parade led by the 28 piece Fort Sheridan band, and recruiting talks by members of the 6th service command, led by Gen. Aurand and Second Officer Orline M. Hall, commanding officer of WAAC recruiting in Illinois...."[19]

The All-American's only All-Star game prior to 1952 featured All-Stars from Racine and Kenosha, Wisconsin, versus All-Stars from Rockford, Illinois, and South Bend, Indiana. The Wisconsin All-Stars defeated the Illinois-Indiana All-Stars with a lopsided 16–0 victory.[20] According to researcher Jay Feldman, "Three banks of temporary lights, on poles, were situated behind home plate, first and third bases." Feldman recorded Shirley Jameson's recollection of the event: "The lights weren't all that great, but we were used to that — we had to play with whatever we had. Besides, just the fact that we were playing in Wrigley Field was enough. We'd have done it whether it was light or dark, because we were all on Cloud Nine."[21] Mildred Warwick echoed Jameson's sentiments about playing in Wrigley Field: "All of a sudden I'd landed in Wrigley Field. I was overwhelmed by the size of it, and I thought, 'Oh my goodness, I'm playing in Wrigley Field.' I was thrilled."[22]

Pitcher Helen Nicol noted that the lighting conditions challenged the outfielders: "The shadows would come up and all of a sudden you wouldn't be able to decipher where the ball was. It was pretty hard for the outfielders to see, especially if the ball got up high."[23] Betsy Jochum didn't realize she was part of an historic event: "I didn't realize at

Peaches play for "Our Boys": Rockford Peaches at Savanna Ordnance Camp, Savanna, Illinois, May 19, 1945. *Left to right, front*: Dorothy "Snookie" Harrell, Mildred Deegan, Helen Filarski, Dottie Green, Rose Gacioch. *Back*: Dorothy "Kammie" Kamenshek, Dot Ferguson, Irene Kotowicz, Bill Allington, Jo Lenard, Kay Rohrer, Carolyn Morris, Alva Jo Fischer, Jean Cione, Betty Carveth, Olive Little (courtesy Dorothy "Snookie" Harrell Doyle).

the time that they didn't have lights at Wrigley Field ... I just thought those lights were there all the time. We showed up for the game, the lights were on, and we played."[24]

The league also featured an AAGBBL night-time doubleheader in Wrigley Field a year later as part of a Red Cross "Thank You" program. This time, four league teams played. The express purpose of the event was to extend a tribute to blood donors and others who had contributed time, effort, or funds to the Red Cross. Admission was free to all service personnel and those who possessed a Red Cross button or identification card.[25] The games were played at Wrigley Field the night of July 18, 1944. These games were scheduled a bit later than those in 1943 as the first game didn't begin until 7:30 P.M. Since the AAGBBL game required a smaller playing area, portable lights were installed for the occasion, as they had been the year before, though not without difficulty. A memo dated July 12, 1944 explained:

> [There's] ... only a very remote possibility that they can have more light on [Wrigley] Field by next Tuesday. They are figuring on 300,000 watts. The cable necessary for conducting so powerful a current is hard to get, and since it is so heavy, it would probably

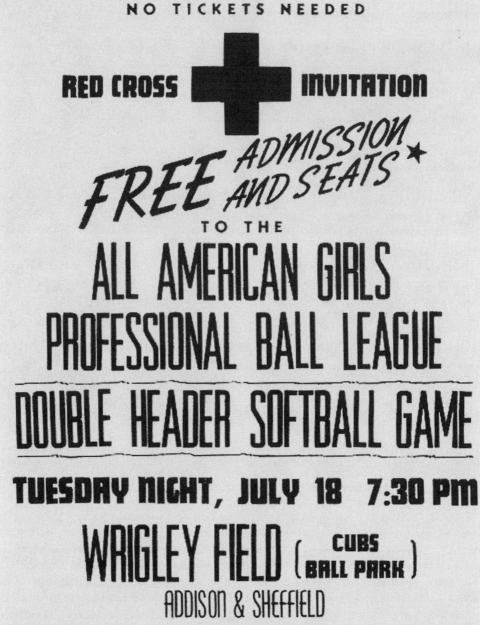

Flyer publicizing Red Cross Benefit Game at Wrigley Field the night of July 18, 1944. Approximately 25,000 of these flyers (with bright red print) were distributed to Chicago area Red Cross Chapters, U.S.O. Centers, Military Posts, and at Wrigley Field (courtesy Arthur Meyerhoff, 1974).

take too long to get it here and then get it installed by next Tuesday. They are, however, making some re-arrangements to increase the efficiency of the light they now have.[26]

The light wattage finally obtained for the games fell far short of the 300,000 ideal, totaling only 38,500.[27] Dorothy Hunter, a member of the Milwaukee team that played the first game of the doubleheader, described the lights as "little bitty flood lights on the grand stand."[28] Somewhere between 16,000 to 20,000 spectators appeared to witness these games in response to extensive radio spot announcements and newspaper lead-up stories.[29]

The first game of the evening featured a contest between the second place South Bend Blue Sox and the third place Milwaukee Chicks (dubbed Schnitts by the Milwaukee press). The game proved to be a marathon two-hour-and-25-minute contest with Milwaukee finally winning 20–11. One reporter noted, "Seven pitchers saw action — and lots of it — in the Blue Sox-Chicks contest. Kay Bennett of the Sox was the starter and loser, while Sylvia Wronski led off and got credit for the Milwaukee win."[30]

Standouts for Milwaukee were Pat Keagle, who collected four hits, including two triples, and Thelma "Tiby" Eisen, who drove in six runs with a single and a triple. The Chicks scored 11 runs in the sixth inning as 15 batters faced Sox pitcher Doris Barr. On the Blue Sox side, catcher Lucella MacLean drove in three runs on three hits. Third sacker Lois Florreich also had three hits. Outfielder Betsy Jochum led the team in hitting with three singles and a triple.

As it had the year before, inadequate lighting again plagued the outfielders and contributed to the lopsided score. The first game started at 7:30 and was nearly two-and-a-half hours long. Even in mid–July, by 9:00–9:30 P.M., dusk and darkness would have settled over the field. The artificial lighting made those long balls difficult to judge.

Between-game entertainment for the Red Cross Benefit featured an appearance by the concert band from Navy Pier and Chief Botswain's Mate Victor Mature of the Coast Guard "Tars and Spars" recruiting show. Mature, one of Hollywood's stars, didn't make a good impression on some spectators. He interrupted the progress of the first game and "had the over-long contest held up while he made an inconsequential series of wisecracks about himself, and was given a sound round of razzberries as he left."[31] Kenosha bat boy, Ed Ruetz, Jr., recalled picking up the bats and balls of the Comets/Racine game that night. He also recalled that pre-game promotion for the exhibition games "had included hyping the presence of movie star Victor Mature." His teenage ears picked up and locked in his memory "the public address announcer introducing [Mature] as 'Victor Mature and his lovely wife Imma.'" He appreciated the pun but was "not sure the crowd caught [it]."[32]

The second game of the evening was a closer contest between the first place Racine Belles and the fourth place Kenosha Comets. Unfortunately, because of the lateness of the first game and train reservations for a return to team home towns, the second game was called at 11:00 P.M. after three-and-a-half innings of play. Even so, each team managed to score six runs.

The highlight of the Racine-Kenosha game occurred when Sophie Kurys gave the Chicago fans a thrill by slamming the only home run of the evening into left field for the Belles' first run.[33] Four of those who performed notably on this historic night would later earn recognition as AAGBBL all-stars, namely Sophie Kurys, Pat Keagle, Tiby Eisen, and Lois Florreich.

Thus, the official "first professional baseball games under the lights in Wrigley Field," occurred July 1, 1943, and July 18, 1944, and were played by Wrigley's "Girls." His "Men"

Kenosha Bat Boys: Ed Ruetz, Jr. (*left*), and Charles "Cardo" Richards enjoy a seat on a Kenosha-built Pirsch fire engine with some of the team members (courtesy Jnell Ruetz).

wouldn't enjoy the privilege until forty-four years later. Their night-time play, however, would not be hindered by inadequate lighting.

If "Recreation for War Workers" was a transitory publicity theme for the AAGBBL, "Femininity" was one of its enduring themes. "Femininity" was an especially prominent publicity theme during the Trustee Administration (1943–1944). In fact, "Femininity" could be considered the prevailing theme of all league operations under Wrigley. He wanted to impress the public with the idea that the AAGSBL/AAGPBL was entirely a women's show and therefore a unique spectator sport separate from men's baseball.[34] Wrigley attempted to achieve this goal by soliciting the design of a special "feminine" uniform, by employing team chaperones, by establishing player conduct rules similar to those in vogue for women on college campuses, and by educating players in the finer points of "feminine" charm.[35] This emphasis on "femininity" issues comprised a novel tactic in the promotion of a woman's sport, which gave it a high publicity value.

Another goal of the "femininity" publicity was to distinguish the AAGSBL/AAGPBL from contemporary women's softball, which flourished in amateur and semi-professional forms. One news article suggested that the prevailing concept of women's softball was more "masculine" than "feminine."

> Softball as played by girls at the present time, has had a tendency to lean toward emulating their male brethren in the game of baseball. Their mode of dress, carriage and actions— even to the extent of being called nicknames like "Tiger," "Puggy," "Sonny," "Tommy," etc., have been annually moving toward the male side.[36]

The same article pointed out that the AAGSBL would emphasize femininity even to the extent of having a dress for a uniform.

The prevailing uniform styles of existing amateur and semi-professional women's softball teams consisted either of satin shirts, shorts, or long pants, or standard baseball uniforms.[37] Apparently these non-feminine modes of dress for that time period stimulated public controversy early in the 1930s. Frederick Cozens and Florence Stumpf (educators) reported that between 1929 and 1935 "There was ... much lively discussion of the propriety of participation by women in certain sports and the suitability of costume— the 'shorts' versus 'skirts' controversy."[38] Wrigley, undoubtedly aware of this controversy, enlisted his wife, his poster artist Otis Shepherd, and Ann Harnett, to design a "feminine" uniform. Ann Harnett was a prominent softball player in a Chicago league and, according to League President Ken Sells, was the first player signed to an AAGSBL contract.[39]

The AAGSBL uniforms designed by Mrs. Wrigley, Mr. Shepherd, and Miss Harnett consisted of a one-piece dress with a short, full, flared skirt. They were patterned after field hockey, tennis, and figure skating outfits then popular.[40] These sports were generally the most socially acceptable for girls and women at that time. The original AAGSBL uniforms were made from pastel shades of green, blue, yellow, and peach, complimented by accessories of a darker shade of the same color.[41] As time passed, the colors changed, and white as well as colored uniforms came into vogue. In addition, the skirts became shorter and less full to facilitate mobility, but the dress-style uniform remained an AAG-BBL trademark throughout the league's existence.

For the most part, players accepted and adjusted to the skirt-style uniform because, more than anything else, they wanted to play. As Madeline "Maddy" English professed, "I didn't care about the uniform. I just wanted to be on a team and in the league."[42] Joyce

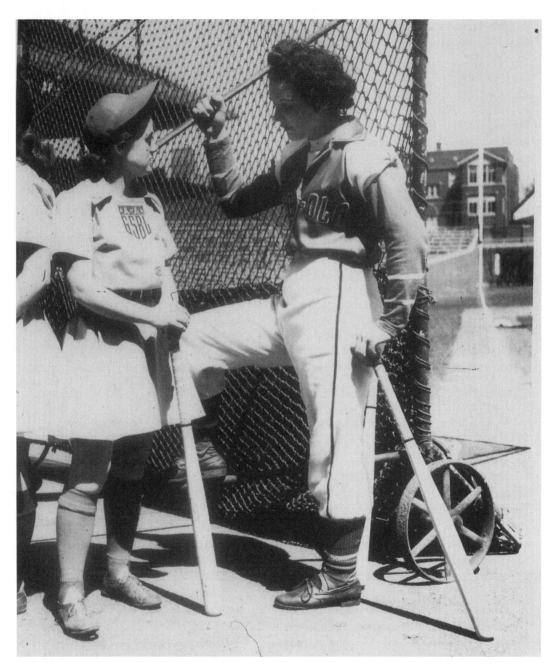

Contrasting uniform styles. *Left to right:* Shirley Jameson, Irene Ruhnke (courtesy Arthur Meyerhoff, 1974).

Hill Westerman admitted, " I was embarrassed [to play in skirts] to begin with. I just loved to play ball so much I told myself, 'It can't matter.' It didn't take me long to adjust."[43] Dorothy "Kammie" Kamenshek recalled:

> We kind of looked at [the uniforms] and realized if we were going to stay and play, we'd have to play in the skirts. The first year was very difficult because they were too

flaring and too long. You'd go to stoop for a ground ball and the skirt would be there. But we accepted it. We felt that if this [was] what we had to do to play professional baseball, we'd do it.

We'd shorten them up an inch or so every year, and we'd use safety pins to tie down the flare, so eventually they did sew them so they wouldn't be flaring.[44]

Another aspect of the "femininity" emphasis was the league's institution of chaperones to supervise players' off-the-field behavior. This added innovation set the AAGSBL/AAGPBL apart from existing women's softball leagues. Chaperones were necessitated as much by the nature of the league as by any desire on the part of league organizers to be different. Girls and women who played on existing amateur and semi-professional teams in metropolitan centers were basically part-time ball players who lived in or near the town or city they played for and did not spend extended periods of time away from home. The players in Wrigley's league, on the other hand, were full-time ball players for three-and-a-half to four months of the year. They were recruited from every section of the United States and Canada. Parents of single young women, particularly at that time in history, were disinclined to allow their daughters to move to strange towns many miles away and travel about supervised only by a male manager. Recruited from the Boston area in 1943, Madeline "Maddy" English explained:

My mother and father were reluctant [to let me go] at first because my brother and sister were in the Marines, but they were both sports minded. They followed me a week later and met Wrigley, the managers, and the chaperone. They saw that things were well conducted, and that we were well taken care of, and that they kept us busy.[45]

Dolly Brumfield White, Shirley Burkovich, Audrey Haine Daniels, and other AAGBBL players echoed Maddy's reference to her parents making the trip to Chicago or to a team city to examine things for themselves.[46] Terry Donahue noted that the presence of chaperones and living in private homes swayed her parents' decision to allow her to play in the league.[47] The AAGSBL chaperones served as itinerant housemothers and moral buffers for league teams. They reassured protective parents that their daughters would be taken care of as well as if they were living in a college dorm.[48] Their presence provided the opportunity to play professional baseball to many 15 to 20 year olds who otherwise would have been kept at home by concerned parents.

The concept of femininity in league publicity was not only emphasized in players' game apparel and supervision but, just as importantly, in a behavioral code to be complied with off the field. These conduct rules coincided with behavioral rules maintained by the AAU and by colleges for their female student residents. The following rules were frequently emphasized in AAGSBL/AAGPBL publicity:

1. ALWAYS appear in feminine attire when not actively engaged in practice or playing ball. This regulation continues thru (sic) the ... Play-offs. At no time may a player appear in the stands in her uniform.
2. Smoking and drinking are not permitted in public places.
3. All social engagements must be approved by the chaperones.
4. All living quarters and eating places must be approved by the chaperones.
5. For emergency purposes it is necessary that you leave notice of your whereabouts at your home phone.
6. Each club will establish a satisfactory place to eat and a time when all members must be in their individual rooms. In general the lapse of time will be two hours after the finish of the last game.[49]

League administrators maintained that "These general rules [were] necessary to build the organization and to maintain order in the clubs."[50] League administrators no doubt recognized the importance of these rules for public approval. They contributed an added dimension to the ideal concept of femininity the league attempted to project. In addition, they protected the players' moral reputations. Nearly all subsequent league publicity of an introductory nature highlighted these rules to educate the public of their existence and to promote social acceptance for the league.

League administrators not only established rules that would require players to conform to social expectations for women's behavior, but they went a step further and adopted advertising agent Arthur Meyerhoff's suggestion of offering the players training in the finer points of feminine charm.[51] In a sense, they offered a baseball finishing school for young women. At the beginning of the1943 season, the internationally famous beauty salon of Helena Rubinstein was engaged to educate and coach players in the finer points of make-up, posture, and carriage to benefit the AAGSBL as an entertainment spectacle.[52] This beauty training took place during spring training and tended to be ridiculed by sports writers[53] as a promotional gimmick. But some, like 1944 recruit, Tiby Eisen, responded positively:

> [Charm School] was only during spring training when everyone was together. I loved it. Being from Los Angeles, I was used to following the movie stars. I wanted to learn to walk and dress and talk, and to me it was the right thing. They were wonderful, beautiful teachers.[54]

Whether it was ridiculed or not, the beauty training was highly publicized and further promoted the identification of the league as a sports organization that stressed femininity. It must be assumed that the emphasis on femininity sat well with parents.

Player profiles were another avenue for emphasizing the concept of femininity in early pre-season publicity. Short biographical sketches of selected players appeared in local newspapers as a means of introducing players to the fans and stimulating interest in the league. Besides describing a player's family background, playing experience, and personal interests, the majority of these articles incorporated some mention of the player's domestic (feminine) skills. For instance, Ann Harnett, who assisted in 1943 pre-season league organization efforts, was portrayed not only as a member of several championship amateur teams, but also as an accomplished coffee-maker. Irene Ruhnke, a star shortstop, excelled in the techniques of cookie icing; outfielder Clara Schillace enjoyed cooking spaghetti and sewing; and utility player Dorothy Hunter's favorite domestic hobby was knitting.[55] The list could go on and on.

Highlighting attributes of the most feminine-looking players (attractive facial features, small, light physiques) was another technique of the femininity campaign. Star outfield Shirley Jameson was introduced as having "roguish eyes that refuse to behave; a saucy, turned-up little Irish pug nose, and enough concentrated personality to lend oomph to a carload of Hollywood starlets, all wrapped up in a 4 ft. 11 inch chassis!"[56] Catcher Helen "Pee Wee" Westerman was described as a "petite, blue-eyed blonde weighing only 95 pounds, fragilely built" with very small hands.[57] Catcher Bonnie Baker, perhaps the most publicized player during the league's twelve-year history, was a fashion model by profession and an excellent ball player besides:

> A gorgeous smile, dark eyes fringed by long lashes, dark hair that off the field she wears in a smart up-sweep, Mary [Bonnie] Baker has a truly regal bearing and knows how to wear clothes and set off her tall beauty.[58]

Publicizing "femininity." *Left to right:* Irene Ruhnke, Clara Schillace (courtesy Arthur Meyer-hoff, 1974).

Bonnie Baker epitomized the image of skilled performance combined with femininity the league attempted to convey to the public. Thus, she was often the center attraction in the league's national publicity features.[59]

The public was not trusted to *infer* that the league would emphasize femininity based on its player profiles, conduct rules, and beauty training. The public was *informed*, in no uncertain terms, that femininity would be emphasized. Sports page headlines announced "Femininity to be Featured in New Sport Unit"[60]; "Tom Boy Tactics Out-of Bounds in All-American Softball League"[61]; and "Girls Softball Loop Favors Beauty, Grace as Essential Factors."[62]

When it actually came down to selecting players, however, playing ability was given greater consideration than physical appearance.[63] League administrators conceded that it was easier to beautify a good ball player than to make a good ball player out of an attractive girl or woman. On the other hand, players who flagrantly violated the femininity image league administrators strove to project, were summarily dismissed, especially in the early years. In one case a player who reported to spring training with a too-short haircut was not allowed to unpack her suitcases before being sent home.[64]

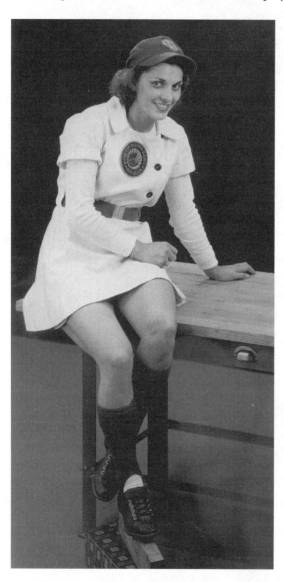

Mary "Bonnie" Baker. One of the AAGBBL's most publicized players (reproduced from the original held by the Department of Special Collections of the University Libraries of Notre Dame).

The league's publicity emphasis on femininity seemed incredible by the standards of sensitivity to sexual discrimination prominent as early as the 1970s. Yet during World War II and after, a double standard of "skill" and "femininity" was commonplace for women in other social contexts and therefore did not appear unreasonable or out of place when applied to the AAGSBL. For example, government propaganda and policy encouraged women to alleviate manpower shortages incurred by the war through employment in traditional male vocations. Yet the necessity of women's employment in "male" jobs did not alter social expectations for their continued traditional feminine roles of wife, mother, and homemaker. William Chafe pointed out that World War II significantly expanded women's employment opportunities, "yet traditional attitudes toward women's [social] place remained largely unchanged."[65]

The publication, in 1948, of Marynia Farnham and Ferdinand Lundberg's book *Modern Woman: The Lost Sex* may have reflected attitudes predominating during and after World War II. These attitudes may have contributed to the seeming overemphasis on femininity in AAGSBL/ AAGPBL publicity. The book warned:

... careers and higher education were leading to the "masculinization of women with enormously dangerous consequences to the home, the children dependent on it and to the ability of the woman, as well as her husband, to obtain sexual gratification."[66]

As previously noted, female softball players of the time were perceived to be more "masculine" than "feminine." Whether or not the AAGSBL/AAGPBL emphasis on femininity stemmed primarily from the Trustees' personal standards for female behavior or from their perceived concept of the public's standards can only be conjectured. Meyerhoff did mention a discussion with a psychiatrist about the "femininity" problem, but whether this discussion occurred before or after the inception of the AAGSBL was not clear.[67] Regardless of the source of the emphasis on femininity, it was consistent with prevailing social expectations and therefore could not help but contribute significantly to the league's initial and continued acceptance.

Another publicity theme emphasized throughout the league's history dealt with the concept that attendance at AAGSBL/AAGPBL games was the same as a contribution to community welfare. The basis of this idea was the fact that the league was chartered as a non-profit organization with the stipulation that any proceeds which might accrue would be devoted "to worthy community recreation and athletic activities for the youth of [the] community."[68] Another aspect of this publicity theme was the thought that team sponsors were performing a civic service by "providing [the] community with healthful and enjoyable sports relaxation and recreation, without any thought or possibility of personal gain or profit."[69] The thrust of the publicity was that everyone, from the team president down to the general admission fan was involved in promoting a community project for the welfare of all. In the succinct words of the Muskegon Lassie directors, "When you attend the Lassies games you are contributing to the Public Recreation Program of Greater Muskegon."[70]

As might be expected, "contributing to community welfare" was often invoked when attendance lagged. In Kenosha, Wisconsin, for example, league personnel found it necessary to appeal to the community for support at the gate during the first summer of play. In reaction to low attendance figures, two sports editorials appeared in the *Kenosha Evening News* entitled "Comets Proving Valuable Kenosha Asset: Need Help of Fans to Retain Franchise" and "Kenosha's 1944 Franchise in Girls' Softball League Goes on Trial Here for Next 11 Days: Fans Serve as Jury." Both editorials pointed out that the AAGSBL team brought favorable publicity to the city, that it provided "clean and wholesome entertainment and recreation" for the populace, and invoked civic pride by posing an attendance contest with nearby Racine.[71] The break-even goal for the attendance campaign was 37,500 and the "community welfare" publicity stint had its effect, because whereas attendance at the Comets' games through mid–July totaled only 12,000, the final season attendance figure added up to 38,724.[72]

The Rockford Peaches Board of Directors employed a similar fundraising campaign theme in 1950. A pamphlet issued to the public explaining the team's financial condition and soliciting ticket sales opened with the following statement:

> The Rockford Peaches Base Ball Team is a non-profit, civic enterprise that is a definite asset to the community, bringing recognition to Rockford, along with clean, friendly, top-quality entertainment.[73]

The last paragraph of the pamphlet urged: "...it is up to all of us who appreciate what the Peaches have done for Rockford to guarantee 96,000 Break-Even attendance this season."[74] Precise attendance figures for Rockford during the 1950 season were not available, but the team continued to operate the following year, indicating that community response to the fundraising campaign was positive.[75]

During the Trustee Administration, league administrators reinforced the concept of community beneficence by establishing "The Scholarship Series," which aimed at heightening community interest and attendance in the league's post-season tournament. A $1,000 scholarship was created and awarded to a resident of the city whose team won the tournament. The winning city selected a female recipient of the scholarship to cover tuition, fees, and other expenses for a four-year course in physical education at the respective state university. The purpose of the scholarship was to encourage "athletics among women for health and recreation."[76] The league office donated half of the funds for the scholarship and the other half came from gate receipts of the championship play-off games.[77] The league board of directors discontinued the scholarship series in the summer of 1945, probably because the play-off games did not generate enough funds to subsidize it.[78] The two individuals who benefited from this particular promotional tactic were Shirley Kappel of Racine, the 1943 recipient, and Muriel Healy of Milwaukee, the 1944 recipient.[79]

In succeeding years, league contributions to worthy community projects took the form of support for youth baseball and recreation programs. In addition to sponsoring boys' baseball teams, South Bend sponsored a girls' Bobbie Sox League in 1946, and other league cities were quick to follow its example. Racine, Kenosha, Rockford, Fort Wayne, and Muskegon supported similar programs within their cities' recreation programs. The 1947 Racine Belles' Yearbook featured an article about the Belles' contributions to their city's recreation projects.

> [The] Racine Belles [will] help to support the operation of as many as 24 different boys' baseball clubs playing under the direction of the Racine Recreational Department. In addition, newly organized junior girls' leagues will emulate the Belles by playing the same brand of baseball which was first devised by the All American Girls Baseball League.
> Thus, the Racine Belles are rendering a great community service to the youth of Racine and hope eventually to develop further plans, depending upon profitable operation, to the benefit of all the people of our City.

Not only was sponsorship of Bobbie Sox or Junior Leagues viewed as a worthwhile community endeavor, they were also perceived as viable and economically thrifty local training leagues for AAGBBL teams.[80] These Junior Girls' Baseball Leagues utilized AAGBBL rules, uniforms, and equipment.[81] In essence, they became part of an AAGBBL Minor League System, to be discussed in Chapter 5.

For the most part, Junior League competition was restricted to local city limits, but occasional intercity contests were scheduled. In 1952, for instance, two teams comprising members of Fort Wayne's Junior Daisy League and a similar group from South Bend took part in a five-inning preliminary to a Daisy-Blue Sox game.[82] A 1973 Fort Wayne Journal-Gazette article claimed that the "Fort Wayne Girls Baseball League [was] one of two organized baseball leagues for girls in the country..." and that it would celebrate its 25th anniversary that year. The article claimed the only other girls' baseball league was "in Bluffton which was started by a former Fort Wayne Coach."[83] If this claim was accurate, Junior League teams in other AAGBBL cities had faded from existence by 1973, if not earlier.

There is no doubt from the article, that the girls' baseball described in the article was "baseball" and not softball and that it was a continuation of the AAGBBL Junior League.

> The league started as an off-spring of the professional Fort Wayne Daisies, All-American Girls Baseball League and was used as a training ground for high school girls who aspired to the professional team. When the national league folded, the girls' baseball league here continued.
> Gerald Romary ... with the Fort Wayne league for 21 years ... in an interview explained..." There are too many girls who like to play baseball. We couldn't stop," [he said], emphasizing the word baseball as opposed to softball, often mistakenly referred to as "girls' baseball."

According to this report, 125 to 150 girls tried out for the Fort Wayne league each year and were placed on teams that played from the end of school to the day before the local Football Jamboree. Five games were played in the evenings every two weeks. The teams remained "the same each year, and the last place team [got] first choice of newcomers." Unmarried girls between the ages of 12 to 18 could play. Some of the older girls volunteered to coach the "Junior League for girls 8 to 12 years of age." In 1972, 175 girls played in this Junior League. Girls supplied their own shoes and gloves, but the Fort Wayne Girls Baseball League "carried on the style of the professional team with short skirts and the nine-inch baseball the Daisies used in the [1950s]." The league followed "official major league baseball rules and the baselines and bats [were] standard."[84]

The fate of Junior League teams in other league cities after the demise of the AAG-BBL in 1954 is not known. They may have continued as community recreation leagues as did Fort Wayne's Junior Girls' Baseball League, which continued to function at least through the 1973 season when it consisted of ten teams composed of more than 150 girls. Early on, at least, junior girl players had live role models to follow and the possibility of becoming professional baseball players. Indeed, some, like June Peppas, Mary Lee Douglas, and Joan Holderness graduated from Junior League teams to the AAGBBL.[85]

The concept of AAGBBL games as "family entertainment" was a publicity theme closely allied with the theme of "supporting the league for community welfare." Ed Des Lauriers, one time business manager for the South Bend Blue Sox, related that the league was actively promoted as family entertainment. "It was always under the lights so Pop could get home from work and have a bite and make it with his family to the ball game."[86] A 1943 newspaper advertisement for AAGSBL games concluded with the invitation to "Watch the girls play ball. Make it a date and bring the family."[87] One observer noted that one of the reasons league attendance continued to grow through 1945 was the fact that the game appealed to all members of the family, "...from youngsters to their grandparents, from housewives to clergy. The first timers upon viewing the game, invariably [expressed] amazement at the ability of the girls. Skeptics [became] dyed-in-the-wool fans."[88]

The family composition of AAGBBL crowds was not unique in sporting audiences in the postwar years. "In the years after the war, baseball crowds became predominantly family gatherings, united by the ethic of 'togetherness' in their fun-seeking."[89] Indeed, the ethic of family togetherness became an increasingly popular social theme in the postwar years, and rightly so, with husbands home from the war. As William Chafe pointed out, "...the joys of 'femininity' and 'togetherness' became staple motifs of periodicals like *McCall's* and the *Ladies Home Journal*."[90] The league's publicity emphasis on "family entertainment" reflected a prevailing social concept promulgated by the popular mass media.

One of the early league promotional efforts to include a "bring the family" theme was a combination outdoor concert — AAGPBL game program designed to stimulate attendance in Milwaukee in 1944. A radio spot announcement set the mood of the baseball-concert campaign, which lasted through July and August of 1944.

> Enjoy a new entertainment thrill! Something different, music and an unusual sports thrill at Borchert Field tonight at eight. There'll be tunes you've heard and loved all your life ... love songs and waltzes to stir your memories ... peppy marches that Dad and the youngsters enjoy. All this, combined with an interesting sports event everyone will enjoy. So come out to Borchert Field, Eighth and Chambers, at eight tonight ... it'll be a friendly outdoor get-together where you can sit around with your neighbors and family and have a good time ... a lot of healthful relaxation under the stars in the cool evening air. Don't miss it![91]

Advertising symphony and baseball (courtesy the Milwaukee *Journal*).

The intention behind this dual entertainment experiment was to attract non-baseball as well as regular baseball fans to the ballpark. The AAGPBL games were played in the same park as the Milwaukee Brewers for the same price, and the regular baseball clientele were reluctant to pay the same amount for a shorter show (11/4 hours vs. 21/2 to 3 hours).[92] Thus an hour of pre-game music was conceived as a means of attracting fans, offering them their money's worth, and offering the Brewers some competition. It was also hypothesized that symphony music prior to AAGPBL games would attract a "new audience who [would] judge girls' ball on its own merit and not in comparison with baseball."[93]

The original concept of a symphony concert, which played strictly classical music, was apparently not well received because the program changed to light opera, popular music, and semi-classics.[94]

> Symphony sounded too hush-hush.... We want people to come out and have a good time. They don't have to walk around on tip-toes and whisper. They can laugh and talk and chew peanuts if they want to.[95]

A typical concert program included selections such as "Pomp and Circumstance"; "Gypsy Baron Overture"; "Wine, Women and Song Waltz"; "Tales From the Vienna Woods" (Strauss); "Introduction to the Third Act of Lohengrin" (Wagner); and "Suite I from Carmen" (Bizet).[96]

Every promotional effort was exerted to make this entertainment package a success. Newsreel companies and periodical publishing houses were solicited to observe and feature the concert-ball game phenomena. Newsreel companies contacted by Meyerhoff included Paramount News, Movietone News, Universal Newsreel, Hearst Metronome News, and Pathé News.[97] These companies along with editors of the *Saturday Evening Post*, *This Week Magazine*, *Woman's Day*, *Cosmopolitan*, *Liberty*, *Look*, *Glamour*, *Coronet*, *Click*, *Charm*, *American Magazine* and *Picture Magazine* were informed:

> There's a new and very unusual type of entertainment opening in Milwaukee August 12th that will provide excellent material for a ... feature, especially one with a picture layout, and it offers a real news scoop besides. It combines glamour and human interest, athletics and family entertainment.
> To present to Milwaukee a new brand of enjoyable entertainment, the All-American Girls Professional Ball League will have Milwaukee's own top-flight team of nationally known girl stars play ball in conjunction with a very informal concert of music....[98]

Local newspapers and radio stations were utilized to disseminate essentially the same message to the community. A free Red Cross "Thank You" night was staged in conjunction with the orchestra-baseball program as part of the promotional effort.[99]

These promotional endeavors for the AAGPBL Milwaukee team were ultimately unsuccessful because the team was relocated to Grand Rapids, Michigan, in 1945, indicating that attendance didn't increase appreciably in response to the media blitz of the novel symphony-baseball experiment.

It was difficult to assess whether the orchestra-baseball combination did in fact attract a different type of audience, as Wrigley postulated it might. According to one sports writer, "Sporting and musical experts agreed that some ball fans might be converted to music lovers, but that the reverse possibilities were dubious."[100] Chick's player Sylvia Wronski recalled, "It was the same attendance, the same people."[101] The fact that a large number of AAGPBL games in Milwaukee had to be played in the afternoons rather than at night didn't help. The AA Brewers, it seems, reserved prime field times for themselves. This and a direct comparison between a struggling AAGPBL team and a men's AA championship team (playing in the same park during the same day) boded ill for the Chicks from the beginning.[102] In addition, two gentlemen who researched Chick's history in 1995 pointed out that the team suffered from the absence of local sponsorship, a recalcitrant press, an oversized field, and other big city diversionary activities such as the State Fair, concerts, and frequent Borchert Field boxing and wrestling matches.[103] The Chicks were a brand new team in an unfriendly environment, but they became the 1944 AAGPBL World Champions that year despite the odds. They just weren't blessed with a large following of dedicated fans.

Publicity and Promotion a Factor in the League's Success

The publicity and promotional efforts of the Trustee Administration focused on some compelling social themes: femininity, community welfare, family entertainment, and recreation for war workers. Without doubt, these advertising messages, consistent with prevailing social attitudes, were of primary importance. Just as, if not more important, was the application of William Wrigley, Jr.'s, philosophy of successful advertising articulated in 1920:

Advertising is pretty much like running a furnace. You've got to keep shoveling coal.
Once you stop stoking, the fire goes out. It's strange that some peoples' imaginations can't
compass this fact.[104]

In regard to the AAGSBL/AAGPBL, Philip Wrigley and Arthur Meyerhoff kept "shoveling coal." Local sports writers were hired as league scorekeepers,[105] and daily game reports appeared in local sports pages throughout the season along with special features on home town or visiting players. Radio announcements were utilized as well as posters and window displays to publicize home games. In short, every effort was made to make and keep the AAGSBL/AAGPBL visible to league city residents. Although the league was less successful in some sites, where it had to compete with established men's teams, overall attendance for 1943 totaled 176,612, and in 1944 it jumped to 259,658 with the addition of the Milwaukee and Minneapolis teams. This was an increase of approximately 49 percent.[106] Since Minneapolis became an orphan traveling team, and every possible technique was employed to improve attendance in Milwaukee, the bulk of the increase in attendance can't be attributed to only those two teams. Taken as a whole, the quality and quantity of advertising and promotion campaigns with which Wrigley and Meyerhoff flooded all league cities contributed greatly to the success the AAGSBL/AAGPBL enjoyed during the 1943 and 1944 seasons.

4

The Management Corporation, 1945–1950

After the 1944 season, John Black, an administrator in AAGPBL operations, observed that Wrigley wanted "to be free of the detail involved in the management of the league."[1] By this time the war was interfering less with business and baseball operations. Wrigley reportedly withdrew from the league "because of the pressure of other activities."[2] Yet, the 49 per cent increase in attendance at AAGPBL games by the end of the 1944 season showed promise of bigger and better things.[3] Arthur E. Meyerhoff, Wrigley's principle advertising agent, was interested enough in the AAGPBL's expansion potential to purchase league assets from Wrigley for $10,000.[4] At the end of the 1945 season, he changed the League name to the All-American Girls Base Ball League (AAGBBL). This became its identifying title through 1954.

AAGBBL Characteristics Under Meyerhoff's Direction

Arthur Meyerhoff, it should be recalled, had been closely associated with the AAGSBL/AAGPBL from its inception. He had worked closely with Wrigley in the league's developmental stages and had continued to work with administration throughout its first two years of operation.[5] Wrigley released the league to Meyerhoff for two reasons. First, because Meyerhoff demonstrated a sincere interest in developing the league's potential. Secondly, Wrigley was confident that Meyerhoff would maintain the ideals and professional standards on which the league had been established.[6]

True to expectations, Meyerhoff did adhere to the high professional standards Wrigley established for league operations. And, just as the inauguration of the AAGSBL reflected Wrigley's character and resources, so too, did the league reflect Meyerhoff's character and resources between 1945 and 1950.

Arthur Meyerhoff, born in 1895, survived childhood in a wretched Chicago neighborhood known as "back of the yards."[7] At 13 he became a traveling salesman and from there his intelligence and creativity led him in many directions. "A love of farming led him to develop a company called Myzon" and to experiment with "antibiotic food supplements for livestock and poultry." An interest in Saddlebred horses led to "a line of horse care products, including horse treats, first baked in the Meyerhoff Kitchen." One of his annual fall concoctions, to be called "Tom and Dill" became "the centerpiece for a company called Missouri Hickory." He was responsible for the success of Pam Cooking Spray, and he invented a canvas "Chill Shelter" to place over pool stairs when he climbed out of the pool. "The bedtime stories that he told his children became a book called *Ferlybutt*," and "his intense interest in world affairs [also] led to a book, *The Strategy of Persuasion*."[8] At 80 years of age he began taking flying lessons. He had a curiosity about things and a zest for life that enabled him to pursue his ideas to a workable, and often profitable end.

Arthur Meyerhoff's innate curiosity and inventiveness were balanced by a caring nature and a willingness to help. When he became a prestigious advertiser, he didn't divorce himself from his humble beginnings, but always "had a special place in his heart for children from disadvantaged neighborhoods.... [He] always had time to lend a hand and left a legacy of caring and sharing."[9] In the fall/winter of 1946, for instance, Meyerhoff invited a contingent of Southern California AAGBBL players to attend the Men's Major League Baseball Meetings on Catalina Island with all expenses paid. During this excursion, Meyerhoff learned that Thelma "Tiby" Eisen had sustained a seriously broken leg near the end of the season and couldn't return to her off-season job for an extended period. He took it upon himself to pay her a weekly salary until she was able to return to her regular job. He also offered her employment in his office during the off-season, but she preferred to remain in California. However, in her mind, "He was a good soul, that guy."[10]

Carolyn Morris, a pitcher from 1944 to 1946, was another player who benefited from Meyerhoff's largesse. Carolyn had some tumor-like growths on the back of her neck that bothered her. According to Dorothy "Snookie" Doyle, when the players returned for spring training in 1945, Carolyn revealed that the growths had been removed. Carolyn testified that Meyerhoff had arranged and paid for the surgery. As Snookie remarked, "That's just the kind of man he was. I really thought the world of him. I think all of us that really knew him did."[11] Meyerhoff's caring and generosity also became evident later in his administration of the 1949–1950 rookie tours. This will be discussed in detail in the next chapter.

In 1932, Meyerhoff embarked on a 60-year relationship with the Wrigley Company.

> [His] novel approach of advertising gum on the comic pages was the beginning of Arthur Meyerhoff Associates (to become BBDO Chicago in 1979). This association led to one of the most memorable advertising campaigns of this century, "Double your Pleasure, Double your Fun" and the Doublemint Twins. Arthur helped create the Girls' Baseball League during World War II and was the inspiration for a character [Ira Lowenstein] in the motion picture, *A League of Their Own*.[12]

Being a creative person of high intelligence and incessant activity, Meyerhoff experimented with and expanded the AAGBBL as he did his other ventures. Not surprisingly, the Management Corporation Administration was characterized by numerous game changes, growth of the league from six to ten teams, and proposals for the development

Carolyn Morris. Outstanding underhand pitcher (reproduced from the original held by the Department of Special Collections of the University Libraries of Notre Dame).

of AAGBBL affiliated leagues in other sections of the United States and even in other countries.

Table 3 illustrates the facility and equipment changes inaugurated during the AAGBBL's twelve-year history. Most of these changes occurred during the Management Corporation Administration, 1945–1950. The equipment and facility changes inaugurated between 1945 and 1950 evolved from the league administrators' philosophy of supplanting softball with baseball because they believed baseball held greater spectator appeal.[13]

Table 3: Record of AAGBBL Equipment & Facility Changes

Year	Ball Size	Length of Base Paths	Pitching Distance	Pitching Style
1943	12"	65'	40'	Underhand
1944	11½" (midseason)	68' (midseason)	"	"
1945	"	"	42' (midseason)	"
1946	11"	72'	43'	Underhand
				Limited Side-arm
1947	"	"	"	Full Side-arm
1948	10⅜"	"	50'	Overhand
1949	10" (red seam)	"	55' (midseason)	"
1950	10" (livelier)	"	"	"
1952	10" (livelier)	"	"	"
1953	"	75'	56'	"
1954	9" (midseason)	85'	60'	"

SOURCE: "Evolution of the Ball Size Used in All American Girls Base Ball League from 1943 to 1949, and Diamond Changes," Dailey Records, 1943–1946; "History During 1946–7," Dailey Records, 1943–1946; AAGBBL Board Meeting Minutes, 15 June 1946, Dailey Records; "All-American Girls Baseball League—1948," Dailey Records, 1947–1949; AAGBBL Board Meeting Minutes, 8 Jun, 11 July, 1949, 18 January 1950, 14 November 1951, 12 March 1952, 10 June 1954, Dailey Records; AAGBBL Board Meeting Minutes, 20 January 1953, Carl Orwant Records, McCammon Folder, Grand Rapids, Michigan.

"Fan appeal" constituted one of the league administrators' central concerns in their formulation of the league's very first playing rules. They observed that softball was essentially a pitcher's game, which lacked the fan appeal of baseball's hitting, base running, and spectacular fielding. To inject these qualities in the AAGSBL game, a committee was formed to modify the existing softball rules for AAGSBL play. The committee consisted of Jack Sheehan, a Chicago Cubs' employee; Vern Hernlund, Supervisor of Recreation in the Chicago Park District; and Miss Morgan, one of Hernlund's assistants. The changes they settled on included:

> ... the use of nine players instead of ten; the moving back of the pitchers' box to 40 feet from home plate [instead of 35 feet]; the use of gloves by all players; lead-off and stolen bases allowed; use of baseball bats; batters box ... increased in size to that of baseball; distance between bases moved from 60 feet to [65] feet.[14]

As Table 3 reveals, game changes begun during the Trustee Administration were increased during the Management Administration. Smaller and smaller balls were introduced, the pitching and base path distances were increased, and overhand pitching replaced underhand pitching.

Meyerhoff's willingness to experiment, coupled with the presence of baseball men such as Max Carey in administrative and management positions, made it almost inevitable that the AAGSBL game would become more and more like baseball. In addition, the

AAGBBL balls, 1943–1954. *Left to right:* 1943 12"; 1944 11½"; 1946 11"; 1948 10⅜"; 7/16/1949 10"; 7/1/1954 9¼" (reproduced from the original held by the Department of Special Collections of the University Libraries of Notre Dame).

players' ability to adapt to equipment and facility modifications encouraged change. According to Dr. Dailey, the limited side-arm pitching sanctioned in 1946 grew out of South Bend pitcher Sugar Koehn's style of delivery.[15] From then on, the progress toward overhand pitching took place rather rapidly because it was difficult for umpires to legislate the side-arm delivery.[16]

The main drawback caused by the evolution of the AAGBBL game from softball to baseball rested in the fact that fewer softball players could play the AAGBBL game immediately. For some it was the extension of the pitching distance. Canadian Betty Carveth Dunn, a slight built woman, testified that she only played the 1945 season because of the proposed extension of the pitching distance for 1946:

> "I was a pitcher and they put the pitching distance back six feet for that next year. I had a real fastball and I really didn't think I'd be as effective with that length of pitching distance. I sent my ticket back and said I was sorry but I didn't think I could make the team the next year."[17]

As it turned out, the pitching distance was extended a total of only three feet from what Betty was accustomed to; however, Betty did experience a two-foot extension of the pitching distance in mid-season 1945 which probably reduced her pitching effectiveness. This may have caused her to recognize that the even longer pitching distance proposed for 1946 would overtax her capabilities.

For others, the switch from underhand to overhand pitching curtailed their playing days in the AAGBBL. South Carolina native, Viola "Tommie" Thompson Griffin, acknowledged, "I pitched underhand for three years and tried sidearm. I couldn't handle overhand pitching. It was the end of my career."[18]

Former pitchers Jean Faut and Jeane Cione also commented that as the pitching and base path distances became longer, and overhand pitching predominated, the number of good softball players who could play the AAGBBL game decreased. Many weren't strong enough to adapt to the longer throwing distances.[19] Although the AAGBBL equipment and facility changes may have increased spectator appeal, they created a problem of player procurement, which was amplified with each successive change that lengthened the basepaths and pitching distance. Karen Violetta Kunkel, recruited as a rookie catcher in 1953, explained it this way:

I think probably the hardest thing to adjust to was the fact that ... I went from being the best to just another ball player having to work my way into the position, plus switching from softball as a catcher to catching baseball. We were playing regulation baseball at that time with [75 foot] base paths and [a 10"] ball. That was a real transition as a catcher.

I think the only thing that maybe saved someone like myself who came in very quickly from fast pitch softball and didn't come through the transition of the league was that it was a constant challenge every day.... It took absolute dedication and concentration in order to be able to do the job.[20]

As time progressed, league administrators became more and more aware of this problem, but the dye was cast. They apparently felt they could not revert to shorter distances because spectators had become accustomed to seeing players perform on the longer distances. The only direction left to go for promotional purposes was nearer to regulation baseball, which was all but achieved in mid–1954.

Viola Thompson. "One of the nicest girls in the league"— Dr. Harold T. Dailey, South Bend Blue Sox Director and President (reproduced from the original held by the Department of Special Collections of the University Libraries of Notre Dame).

Meyerhoff's commitment to the AAGBBL and his ambition for its success and growth were demonstrated by his efforts to expand the Chicago-based league and his plans to establish AAGBBL–affiliated leagues in other sections of the country and continent. Table 4 illustrates that the greatest expansion in the league occurred during Management's Administration. It grew from a six-team league in 1944 to a ten-team league in 1948. Even though the league consisted of only six teams in 1945, Meyerhoff's Management Corporation created new league sites in Fort Wayne, Indiana, and Grand Rapids, Michigan, to replace Milwaukee and Minneapolis. Milwaukee and Minneapolis, it will be remembered, dropped out of the league during or after the 1944 season. In all, seven teams were added to the league under Management's Administration, and only two of these, Chicago and Springfield, Illinois, failed to prosper for more than one year.

Dr. Harold T. Dailey, President of the South Bend Blue Sox, thought the league's expansion to ten teams in 1948 was a mistake. In a caustic letter to Meyerhoff, he pointed out that a ten-team league was unwieldy and didn't even work in the major leagues. The main problem he foresaw for the AAGBBL was a dilution of player talent among too many teams. He feared a decrease in the quality of the "show," which in turn would reduce attendance and increase team deficits.[21]

Meyerhoff responded to Dailey's criticism by pointing out that the expansion to ten teams resulted "accidentally" when two established AAGBBL teams remained in the league after indicating they might withdraw. Meyerhoff further reminded Dailey that the League Board of Directors approved the ten team set-up and that the establishment of a team in Chicago did have some advantages. Primarily, it placed the AAGBBL in a better position to compete with the Chicago National Girls Baseball League for players, it opened up publicity possibilities in Chicago papers, and it put the AAGBBL in a position to control the development of girls' professional ball throughout the country. All of these attributes, Meyerhoff emphasized, were in the best interest of each member club.[22]

Table 4: AAGBBL Teams, 1943–1954
Dates of Entry and Duration of Play

Rockford Peaches, Ill.	1943–1954	Peoria, Redwings, Ill.	1946–1951
South Bend Blue Sox, Ind.	1943–1954	Muskegon Lassies, Mich.	1946–1950
Kenosha Comets, Wisc.	1943–1951	Chicago Colleens, Ill.	1948*
Racine Belles, Wisc.	1943–1950	Springfield Sallies, Ill.	1948*
Milwaukee Chicks, Wisc.	1944	Kalamazoo Lassies Mich.	1950–1954
Minneapolis Millerettes, Minn.	1944	Battle Creek Belles, Mich.	1951–1952
Fort Wayne Daisies, Ind.	1945–1954	Muskegon Belles, Mich.	1953
Grand Rapids Chicks, Mich.	1945–1954		

Source: *1944 Racine Belles Year Book*; *1945 Racine Belles Year Book*; *1946 Racine Belles Year Book*; *1947 Grand Rapids Chicks Year Book*; *1948 Racine Belles Year Book*; *1949 Peoria Redwings Year Book* (all Year Books obtained from the Meyerhoff Files or Dailey Records); Dailey Records, 1947–1954.

*The Colleens and Sallies were members of the AAGBBL's summer barnstorming teams in 1949 and 1950. They were used as rookie training teams, and games promoted publicity for new player tryouts throughout the populous South and Northeastern sections of the country.

As it turned out, Meyerhoff and the League Board of Directors should have heeded Dailey's warnings because the 1948 season did prove to be financially troublesome for the league. Failure of both the Springfield and Chicago teams to pay their way placed a financial burden on the remaining teams. Dailey also accurately predicted reduced attendance per team, but the decline was not as great as he had envisioned. Average team attendance dropped from 98,686 in 1947 to 91,074 in 1948, a decline of slightly less than 1 percent.[23] Diluting player talent among ten teams may have been a factor in this decline. However, it is suspected that postwar inflation, removal of travel restrictions, and rapidly developing and competitive commercial recreations accounted more directly for the decline in AAGBBL attendance in 1948.[24]

Expansion of the AAGBBL to ten teams was a risk Meyerhoff took based on projections for the long-range development of the league. He knew that if an AAGBBL team could attract significant attendance in metropolitan Chicago, sports enthusiasts in other urban centers might be persuaded to purchase franchises to develop a second AAGBBL-controlled league.[25] Meyerhoff did, in fact, explore the possibility of establishing other AAGBBL organizations in different parts of the country.

In September 1945, Meyerhoff discussed basing a "Southern Division" of the AAGBBL in Alabama with a Mr. James Price from Birmingham.[26] If the Southern Division had materialized, the Chicago-based league would have become the "Central Division." A "Western Division" was almost begun in California in 1946–1947. An estimated budget was drawn up in February 1946, for the "California Girls' Baseball League," and in March of the same year, Marty Fiedler of Los Angeles was granted permission by the League Board to use AAGBBL rules and the AAGBBL ball. The plan was to develop the AAG-

1946 Muskegon Lassies. *Left to right, front*: Gladys Davis, Jo Lenard, Sara Reeser, Dorothy Montgomery, Margaret Wenzell, Donna Cook, Irene Applegren, Evelyn Warwyshyn. *Back*: Dorothy "Mickey" Maguire, Erma Bergmann, Dorothy Stolze, Norma Metrolis, Arleene Johnson, Nancy Warren, Alva Jo Fischer, Charlene Pryer, Eileen O'Brien, Ralph Boyle (manager) (courtesy Jean Cione).

1946 Peoria Redwings. *Left to right, front*: Thelma "Tiby" Eisen, Mary Wood, Jane Jacobs, Terry Donahue, Mary Lawson, Annabelle Lee, Jane "Jeep" Stoll, Betty Tucker. *Back*: Betty Gerring (chaperone), Lillian Faralla, Jean Cione, Marion Bryson, Helen Machado, Rita Meyer, Kay Blumetta, Mary Reynolds, Mary Rountree, Johnny Gottselig (manager) (courtesy Jean Cione).

BBL game in California in 1946 and establish franchises there in 1947.[27] Although neither the Southern Division nor the Western Division materialized, the largesse of Meyerhoff's ambition for the AAGBBL was apparent.

Changes in the League's Organization and Financial Structure Under Meyerhoff

Had Meyerhoff possessed the financial resources of Wrigley, a Western Division of the AAGBBL might have become a reality. The time and the interest of key people seemed poised for it. However, Meyerhoff did not have an extra $100,000 to contribute to the development of a new league as Wrigley had in 1943. Differences in Meyerhoff's and Wrigley's financial situation had other impacts on the AAGBBL. These were manifested through changes in the league's organizational and financial structures.

It will be remembered that the entire league was operated as a non-profit organization under the Trustees. When Meyerhoff assumed control of the league in the fall of 1944, the respective teams were organized as an association of member clubs identified as the "All-American Girls Professional Ball League" ("The League"). "The League" then entered into an agreement with an organization established by Meyerhoff entitled "The Management Corporation of the All-American Girls Professional Ball League" ("Management"). "Management" was a profit-based organization.[28] In essence, the new organizational structure consisted of a non-profit organization administered by a profit-based organization (figure 3). This dichotomy is important because it later portended serious conflicts among league personnel.

It should be emphasized that the financial base of the Trustee structure was shared between team guarantors and Wrigley during the 1943 season. The franchise system insti-

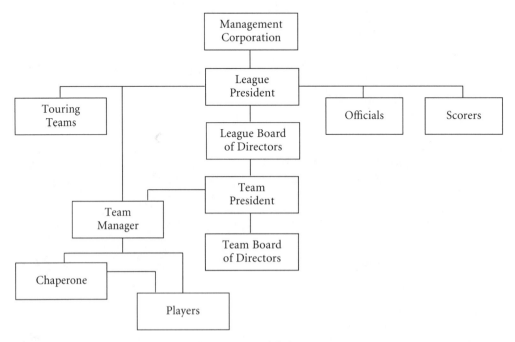

Figure 3: The Organizational Structure of the AAGPBL/AAGBBL, 1945–1950

1948 Chicago Colleens. *Left to right, front*: Doris Tetzlaff, Charlene Barnett, Betty Whiting, Marilyn Olinger, Beulah Georges. *Middle*: Doris Cook, Betty Tucker, Dave Bancroft (manager), Mirtha Marrero, Migdalia Perez. *Back*: Arleene Johnson, Jo Kabick, Eleanor Callow, Dolores Wilson, Doris Reid, Margaret Johnson (chaperone) (courtesy Northern Indiana Center for History).

tuted at the beginning of the 1944 season shifted the financial burden of league operations to team stockholders, but league deficits still appeared to be underwritten by Wrigley's financial resources.[29] The financial structure of the AAGBBL at the beginning of Meyerhoff's administration remained essentially what it had been during the 1944 season under the Trustee structure. The franchise system was retained as well as the three cent per admission charge paid for league office operations. The Management Corporation rendered the same services to the teams as the Trustee Administration had performed.[30] Under the Management structure, however, team franchise owners became responsible for the entire financial burden of local team operations, league operations, and any deficits.[31] Unlike Wrigley, Meyerhoff didn't have the financial backing to underwrite league deficits,[32] and there was considerable evidence to suggest that large deficits were incurred annually during Management's Administration, 1945–1950.

League Board Meeting Minutes made it clear that, as years passed, expenses and personnel salaries became greater (inflation), attendance dropped, and deficits increased. Table 5 provides a comparison of club operating statements for 1948 and demonstrates the nature of deficits incurred.

Table 5: AAGBBL Team Operating Expenses, 1948

Team	Total Yearly* Expenses	Profit (+) Loss (−)
Fort Wayne	$ 72,275.00	$−2,677.48
Grand Rapids	119,073.75	−7,852.47
Kenosha	62,828.68	−26,308.29
Muskegon	80,094.13	−17,336.33
Peoria	77,831.47	−183.31
Racine	79,761.48	−28,577.29
Rockford	70,396.68	−10,288.84
South Bend	79,547.60	+236.16

SOURCE: "All-American Girls Baseball League — Comparative Club Operating Statements — Year 1948," Meyerhoff Files, Drawer 75, All American Girls Budget Folder.
*Includes local as well as league expenses.

It must be acknowledged that the 1948 season was particularly costly for the league because the Springfield franchise folded in mid-season, and the other teams voted to carry expenses for it and maintain it as a traveling team. This turned out to be a costly operation. Yet the mid-season folding of one or more teams had not been an uncommon occurrence and it was something that continued to plague the league nearly every season.

The initial procedure employed for distributing league expenses during Management's administration was merely a division of the league budget by the number of teams, to determine each team's pro-rata share of the total budget. For instance, in 1946, the league budget totaled $79,450.57. Divided among the eight operating clubs, each team's share amounted to $9,931.32.[33] The problem with this procedure was that it did not take

1948 Springfield Sallies. *Left to right, front*: Luisa Gallegos, Janet Jameson, Margaret Murray, Doris Neal, Ruby Stephens. *Middle*: Shirley Stovroff, Jane "Jeep" Stoll, Pat Scott, Carson Bigbee (manager), Marge Wenzell, Evelyn Wawryshyn, Julia Gutz. *Back*: Mildred Meachem, June Schofield, Esther Hershey, Erma Bergmann, Doris Barr, Barbara Barbaze, Jean Marlowe, Mary Rudis (chaperone) (reproduced from the original held by the Department of Special Collections of the University Libraries of Notre Dame).

into account discrepancies in the population base of respective league cities. Thus, Kenosha, with a population of 48,765, was expected to obtain the same revenue through gate receipts as Grand Rapids, which had a population of 164,292.[34] This discrepancy led to the adoption of an expense-sharing plan formulated by Albert K. Orschel. In brief terms, the Orschel Plan stipulated "...that the expenses of the league should be shared by the various members in accordance with their ability to pay, their ability to pay being measured [by the previous year's] attendance."[35] In addition to an equitable payment of $5,000 per team, each club was assessed five cents for the first 50,000 admissions and ten cents for all admissions over 50,000. See Table 6 for a comparison of the high and low teams' contributions under this plan, which suggests how it worked in 1947.

Table 6: AAGBBL Expense-Sharing Plan, 1947

	Kenosha	*Grand Rapids*
1946 Attendance	53,098	134,900
Initial Payment	$5,000.00	$5,000.00
5 cents/first 50,000	2,500.00	2,500.00
10 cents/ea. Admission over 50,000	309.80	8,499.00
Total Payment for 1947	$7,809.80	$15,999.00

SOURCE: "All-American Girls Baseball League Suggested Plan for Sharing of Expenses," 24 March 1947, Meyerhoff Files, Drawer 75, Albert K. Orschel Correspondence and Plan Folder.

The Orschel Plan was revised in 1949 to attain greater equity of league expenses between the teams with the lowest and highest attendance. The revised plan was based on costs for an average league attendance of 730,000. The year 1949 was another economy year, so league costs were reduced as much as possible. This was reflected in the revised Orschel Plan. In the new plan, all teams paid Management $3,500 plus a straight three-cent admission charge. This alleviated the wide discrepancy between the league payments of teams with high and low attendance, exemplified again by Kenosha and Grand Rapids (Table 7). The final provision of the 1949 plan stipulated that any other shortages of league funds after these payments should be divided equally among the eight clubs.[36]

Table 7: AAGBBL Expense-Sharing Plan, 1949

	Kenosha	*Grand Rapids*
Initial Payment	$ 3,500	$ 3,500
1948 Attendance @ 3 cents for 1949 season	59,000	125,000
Total Payment to league	$ 5,270	$ 7,250

SOURCE: "Suggested Revision of Orschel Plan for 1949," AAGBBL Board Meeting Minutes, 4 February 1949, Dailey Records.

Management's Administration and Administrators

Another important way the Management structure differed from the Trustee structure was that it established a league governing board consisting of one representative from each team.[37] Team representatives to this board included team presidents or a designated proxy. This governing board was designated the League Board of Directors.

The establishment of the League Board of Directors solved the problem of team representation in league management noted as a major disadvantage of the Trustee structure. The agreement between "The League" and "Management" placed the responsibility for developing, supervising, and regulating play on Management, while the League Board retained control of league government by majority vote. Thus team directors obtained what amounted to control of league management without having to assume administrative responsibilities for it.[38]

The powers of the League Board of Directors included the following:

1. Approval or dismissal of member clubs
2. Appointment of special committees
3. Approval of annual and supplementary budgets prepared by Management
4. Approval of the league president selected by Management
5. Discipline of club members
6. Determination of admission charges
7. Determination of visiting teams' percentage of gate receipts
8. Determination of the per-admission charge to be paid Management for each game
9. Description of procedures for handling contracts, releases and waivers
10. Determination of the minimum and maximum player limits per team; approval of umpires selected by the league president
11. Establishment of league rules and procedures[39]

Under the Management structure, the league president served as a liaison between "The League" and "Management." He presided at all meetings of the League Board of Directors as an ex-officio member of the board. He was accorded the privilege of casting a deciding vote in case of a tie on all matters except election to membership and amendment of the constitution.[40] Other prescribed presidential duties stipulated that he serve as the final authority on rule interpretations, league personnel disputes, and game protests. He was further charged with securing and supervising umpires, processing waivers, and levying and collecting fines for violations.[41]

The first league president under the Management structure was Max Carey. Carey's first association with the AAGBBL was in the capacity of manager of the Milwaukee Chicks team during the 1944 season. His prior association with professional baseball included a distinguished major league playing career.

> One of the greatest major league outfielders of all time, Max scintillated with the Pittsburgh Pirates over a period of fifteen years and wore the livery of the Brooklyn Dodgers for four more, in addition to serving as manager of the latter club.[42]

At the time, Carey held the National League all-time record for the most stolen bases, and before becoming involved with the AAGBBL had been active as a minor league manager.[43] A measure of Max Carey's major league baseball prowess is exemplified by the fact that he was eventually inducted into the Baseball Hall of Fame.

One of Carey's major contributions to the AAGBBL was the development of a continental organization of commissioners who scouted outstanding female players in the United States and Canada (Table 8). Anna May Hutchison, who played in the league from 1944 to 1950, noted, "They had good scouts and they knew what they were looking for. They got top notch ball players."[44] Carey also developed a player-rating chart, used by scouts and managers to determine the caliber of a player's ability (see Appendix 5).[45]

Left: Arthur E. Myerhoff, AAGBBL Commissioner, 1945–1950 (ca. 1960s, courtesy Judy Meyerhoff Yale). *Middle:* Max Carey, AAGBBL President, 1945–1949 (reproduced from the original held by the Department of Special Collections of the University Libraries of Notre Dame). *Right:* Fred Leo, AAGBBL President, 1950–1951 (courtesy Northern Indiana Center for History).

Max Carey apparently performed yeoman service for the league during his term as president. The League Board of Directors extended him a vote of thanks for his fine work in each of the years 1946 through 1949. In 1946, the board voted him a bonus of $1,000.00, and in 1947 he received a $350.00 bonus. In 1949, the board voted to name the post-season play-offs the "Carey-Cup Play-offs" in his honor.[46]

Carey tendered his resignation as league president at the 1949 November board meeting. His professed reason for resigning was to consider other baseball administrative offers. Dr. Dailey, president of the South Bend team, suggested, however, that Carey was coerced into resigning. Dailey didn't explain the grounds for Carey's dismissal, but the fact that Carey remained in the AAGBBL as manager of the Fort Wayne Daisies in 1950 and 1951 indicated that other baseball offers were tenuous rather than actual.[47]

Table 8: AAGBBL Commissioners, 1946

United States		*Canada*	
William Alligood	N. C.	Hub Bishop	Regina
William Allington	Calif.	M. Blandford	Toronto
William Ballinger	Tenn.	M. L. Clouston	Saskatoon
Edward Dunk	Rochester/Syracuse	Myrtle Cook	Montreal
E. F. Englebert	Maryland	Gail Egan	Calgary
Harold Greiner	Indiana	C. M. Hollingsworth	Edmonton
Andrew Hale	Colorado	Joseph Mathewson	Winnipeg
Marion Huey	Florida	Dick Newell	Vancouver
Puss Irwin	Texas	William Westwick	Ottawa
Kenneth Jones	Illinois		
E. J. Lacerda	Mass.		
A. W. Milner	Ohio		
Al Nickolai	Missouri		
A. K. Rowswell	Pa.		
C. W. Rupp	Ohio		

Lad Slingerland	Michigan		
Edward Wenzell	Detroit		
M. Wilson	N.Y. District	Chief Scout	Bill Wamby
George Winter	Arizona		
Fred Zirkel	Wisconsin		

SOURCE: "Tops in Girls Sports," AAGBBL Brochure, 1946, Meyerhoff Files

The second and last president of the AAGBBL under the Management structure was Fred K. Leo. He served as president of the league during 1950, the last year of the Management structure. He was elevated to the position of league commissioner during the first year of Independent Team Ownership, 1951.[48]

Fred Leo's association with the AAGBBL began when he helped organize the Peoria Redwings team in 1946.[49] His background included experience in newspaper work, radio announcing, and sports officiating. Leo began working as a publicist for the league as early as 1947 and eventually became Max Carey's assistant and then his successor.[50] A measure of Fred Leo's contributions to the league was reflected in the tribute paid him by the league board upon his resignation toward the end of the 1951 season.

> RESOLVED: That the Board of Directors of the AGBL in regular meeting convened at South Bend, Indiana, on October 1, 1951, expresses its thanks and appreciation for the loyal, diligent and faithful services rendered by Fred K. Leo, as its commissioner; the League recognizes and extols Mr. Leo's loyalty and personal and financial integrity and ability and heartily recommends him for these qualities in any enterprise or activity in which he may hereafter become engaged.[51]

League Board Meeting Minutes suggested that both Max Carey and Fred Leo worked diligently on the league's behalf and supported progressive changes in the game. It was

1947 AAGBBL Board of Directors. *Left to right, front:* Judge Edward J. Ruetz, President, Kenosha Comets, Chairman of the League Board of Directors; Max Carey, League President; William Wadewitz, President, Racine Belles; Harry Hanson, President, Rockford Peaches; H.C. Hyslop, Vice President, Kenosha Comets; *Back:* Henry Herbst, President, Fort Wayne Daisies; Dan Clark, President and Secretary, South Bend Blue Sox; Dr. Harold T. Dailey, Vice President, South Bend Blue Sox; A. H. Sommer, President, Peoria Red Wings; Nate Harkness, President, Grand Rapids Chicks; C. L. Sundquist, Business Manager, Muskegon Lassies (courtesy Jnell Ruetz).

during Carey's administration (1945–1949) that frequent changes were made in league rules, which brought them into closer proximity with Major League Baseball. One of the most significant changes occurred in 1948, when overhand pitching was legislated.[52]

Advantages and Disadvantages of the Management Structure

In many respects, the Management structure was the ideal structure for the AAG-BBL. It enabled local franchise holders to assume or delegate responsibility for local operations; it allowed them to control the management of league affairs while freeing them from the administrative responsibilities of overall league concerns such as publicity, promotion, scouting, and screening personnel. At the same time, it gave them the services of one of the outstanding advertising agencies in the vicinity, an agency that had personnel who were interested, knowledgeable, and experienced in promoting organized baseball. The league's relationship with Meyerhoff's advertising agency reaped incalculable returns in national, international, and local publicity (see Chapter 5).

The major weakness of the Management structure was the dichotomy of Management's expense to team administrators and the fact that they perceived Management accruing profits at their expense. For instance, Management's gross share of gate receipts in 1948 amounted to more than $19,000.[53] Net profit from this amount totaled $6,607.80.[54] When team directors observed Management profits next to their deficits, they naturally began to question the efficacy of their agreement with Management.

The league's initial agreement with Management was established for a two-year period. Extensions of the initial agreement were considered regularly. At the end of the 1945 season, the League Board of Directors voted to extend the agreement through the 1949 season, and at the end of the 1947 season they voted to extend it through the 1951 season.[55] The agreement document provided that the League-Management relationship could be dissolved at any time if each member club paid a pro-rata share of $10,000 to Management. This was the amount Meyerhoff had paid Wrigley for the league's assets in 1944.

During the 1949 season some lobbying took place among team presidents to buy Meyerhoff out. Dr. Dailey noted that "All during the later part of the season of 1949 much discussion was batted around about the cost of Management and the thought was to get rid of it."[56] Team directors were finding it increasingly difficult to maintain teams on a subsidy basis and recognized the necessity of developing a self-supporting structure for all teams.[57] Expenditures for Management were a logical target for their discontent.

The financial status of teams in the league after the 1949 season was not much better than it had been after the 1948 season (Table 5). In 1948, only South Bend showed a profit of $236.16, and deficits of the other seven teams totaled $93,224.01. Although two teams showed profits totaling $15,327.86 in 1949, losses did not show a substantial decline. Total losses for six teams in 1949 amounted to $90,847.97.[58]

The 1950 season, rather than being a year of financial recovery, was nearly a financial disaster for the league. Two teams, Rockford and Peoria survived the season only by making public fund drives in mid-season.[59] Grand Rapids also held a public fund drive, but receipts of $4,000 from this campaign were insufficient to cover a $20,000 operating deficit. The Grand Rapids team was able to finish the season only because the players and manager agreed to continue playing without assurance that their full salaries would be paid. They were further saved by Jim Williams, owner of the Grand Rapids Jets, a men's semi-pro team, who agreed to assume team operations in his ball park so the team could finish the season.[60] In addition, it was necessary for the Muskegon franchise to move to Kalamazoo in June because the Muskegon Board of Directors ran out of operating funds.[61]

Emergency economies implemented by the League Board of Directors in 1950 included discontinuance of player meal money at the end of July and authorization of team management to revise player salaries.[62] In addition, Management, under duress, agreed to lower its share of gate receipts from three cents to one-and-a-half cents per admission.[63] The entire situation was summed up in the words of the chairman of the Rockford Peaches team in a letter to Management and associate members of the AAG-BBL.

> We believe that the interests of Girls Baseball as established and conducted by the AAGBL are immediately threatened by the financial condition of the League and its clubs. A crisis is at hand and all parties involved must recognize this fact.[64]

The letter went on to appeal to Management to modify its financial agreement with the league for the organization's financial survival.

The League Board of Directors were not unaware of the causes for the financial crisis that faced them during the 1950 season. Factors contributing to the league's financial woes, cited by directors at various times, included:

1. A shrinkage of the amusement dollar, inflation, and a concomitant decline of attendance at all types of sporting events[65]
2. Higher player salaries[66]
3. Fluctuation of league cities' economy such as the instability of labor and salaries which contributed to the dissolution of the Muskegon franchise in mid–1950[67]
4. Changes in the AAGBBL game from softball to baseball which required extended and expensive training of new talent[68]
5. League directors' inability to concur on player allocations to balance team competition, which was complicated by negative fan reaction to trades they didn't understand[69]
6. Team administrative mismanagement[70]
7. The influx of television[71]

The factor they didn't mention, but which obviously underlay everything else, was the limit of their personal wealth. They could not sustain significant losses year in and year out, nor did they have enough wealthy backers behind them to do so. This is the aspect in which directors of the AAGBBL differed most in relation to the majority of administrators of men's professional teams.

The combined effect of all of these forces impelled team directors to consider implementing rigorous financial economies for the 1951 season or curtailing operations completely. They adopted the former alternative because they wanted to continue operating this league. Their first major economic retrenchment was to sever League-Management relations.[72]

Denouement of the Management Corporation Administration

The AAGBBL's Management Corporation Administration, 1945–1950, was characterized by multiple changes, both within the league's structure and within the larger social structure. Within the league's structure, local franchise holders obtained representation in central league affairs through the League-Management agreement and the institution of the League Board of Directors. This agreement, however, proved more costly than the directors originally envisioned. Progressive changes in the AAGBBL game brought it into closer approximation to baseball to increase the game's spectator appeal, but they also reduced the league's talent pool. Fewer players could make an immediate transition from softball to AAGBBL baseball. Veteran players who, over the years, adapted to the league's game changes commanded increasingly higher salaries, exacerbating the league's unstable financial situation.

Important alterations were taking place in the postwar social milieu within which the AAGBBL operated. Most of these changes had negative effects on the league. The lifting of government price controls and postwar inflation tended to shrink the amusement dollar which had been relatively bountiful during the war years. The rise of commercial amusements during the postwar period placed the AAGBBL in a competitive position it had not faced during wartime. Industrial reconversion and postwar strikes affected team directors' ability to maintain their financial commitments to the league. In addition, Americans regained their mobility in the late 1940s as gasoline and rubber rations were lifted and automobiles, instead of tanks, once again began to roll off assembly lines. As a result, the AAGBBL began to lose the relatively captive audience it had catered to during the war. Finally, television's rising star boded ill for all of baseball, especially the minor league variety. Baseball fans no longer had to limit their spectating to the local nine — they could watch their favorite major league team from the comfort of their living rooms.

In retrospect it seems clear that the AAGBBL was doomed in 1950. Certainly league directors were fighting oppressive odds. Nonetheless they determined to continue the fight to preserve the league on their own, without assistance from a professional advertising agency. The conditions under which they operated after the 1950 season are the subject of Chapter 6.

5

Expansion of Public Exposure: Publicity and Promotion, 1945–1950

When Arthur Meyerhoff assumed control of the AAGBBL in the fall of 1944, he did so on the basis that he would carry forth the same principles of operation Wrigley inaugurated in 1943.[1] Since Meyerhoff had collaborated with Wrigley in creating the publicity themes and promotional campaigns of the Trusteeship Administration, his assumption of control of the league ensured a continuance of its publicity and promotion strategy. The Management Corporation Administration, under Meyerhoff's direction, was therefore characterized not by a change in publicity themes or promotional tactics, but by an expansion of publicity and promotion through the mass media, spring training camps and tours, summer barnstorming tours, and post-season exhibition tours.

AAGBBL Publicity in the Mass Media

At the beginning of Chapter 3, it was noted that the AAGBBL was featured in a number of popular periodicals as well as trade and sport magazines. Between 1943 and 1952, at least 34 articles featuring the AAGBBL appeared in thirteen periodical issues, ten trade magazines, eight sport magazines and two prominent newspaper weeklies.[2] Thirty-three of these features appeared between 1943 and 1950, the years of Wrigley and Meyerhoff's administration of the league. Twenty-six of the total 34 features (76 percent) appeared during Management's Administration, 1945–1950. It was during the Management Administration also that the first newsreel, radio, and television coverage of the AAGBBL occurred.[3]

In 1946, for instance, a Racine, Wisconsin, radio station, WRJN, "scheduled an elaborate program of play-by-play indirect wire broadcasts of many games [and covered] all the Racine Belle's games out of town in the Shaughnessy play-offs."[4] In 1947, Muskegon and Grand Rapids radio stations began broadcasting AAGBBL games, as did Chicago in 1948.[5] In 1948 also, a Chicago television station, WBKB, contracted to televise the home games of the Chicago Colleens. Patricia Stevens, Inc., a famous modeling school, sponsored these telecasts.[6] In 1947, Grantland Rice produced a Sportlight film entitled "Diamond Gals" which was purportedly still in popular demand three years later.[7] Finally, four major newsreel companies and two television producers were present at the 1950 spring training camp to film league activities.[8] Of no less importance, the league office originated a continuous stream of news releases of major importance for local newspaper publicity.[9]

It must be re-emphasized that these events didn't just happen; they were solicited by personnel employed by Meyerhoff to obtain public exposure for the league through the mass media. Meyerhoff, like Philip and William Wrigley before him, believed in "stoking" the advertising furnace. It was his profession. His dedication to promoting and obtaining public exposure for the AAGBBL was further evidenced by his organization of a Chicago-based AAGBBL minor league, and spring, summer, and post-season tours.

The Chicago Girls Baseball League: The AAGBBL's Minor League

Starting in 1946, AAGBBL cities began offering Junior League Girls Baseball through their park and recreation departments. The Junior Leagues incorporated the AAGBBL uniform and rules of play. At first glance they seemed to be impromptu, individual city based projects. However, the establishment of the Chicago Girls Baseball League (CGBL) in Chicago, beginning in 1946, lends a wider scope to the establishment of the Junior Leagues. Both they and the CGBL were conceived and implemented at the same time to train younger players in the unique AAGBBL game. The CGBL was a notch above the Junior Leagues because players in the CGBL were signed to contracts. Taken together, however, the Junior Leagues and the CGBL were conceived and implemented to begin training young girls to play the AAGBBL game.

Meyerhoff recognized the need for teaching young players the AAGBBL game because it was no longer softball but baseball. He needed new recruits every year to replace veterans retiring for various reasons. He observed early on that it took time to train softball players, even good softball players, to adjust to a game with longer basepaths, pitching distance, and different strategies. He also recognized that he could not rely on high schools and colleges to train young players in the finer points of skill, strategy, and competitiveness demanded by the AAGBBL game because the predominant philosophy in schools and colleges at the time was diametrically opposed to the AAGBBL. Accepting this, he recognized that the training of young players depended on park and recreation programs where most of the original players were found. Thus, he not only encouraged team directors to establish Junior Leagues in their cities, he also accessed the Chicago Park Department and some of its personnel to recruit and train young players from the populous metropolitan area to play AAGBBL baseball. These park and recreation leagues served as economic training grounds for future AAGBBL players. Madonna's song, "This Used to Be My Playground," from *A League of Their Own*, becomes much more poignant given this background.

In 1945, Mr. Leonard (Len) Zintak returned from the war and took a job as Athletic Director and Baseball Coach for both boys' and girls' teams at Chicago's Marquette Park. At the time, the girls were playing "softball" or "kittenball" with a 14-inch ball. Len held clinics for the youngsters on weekends which featured ex–major league players. One weekend, Rogers Hornsby attended a Marquette Park clinic and was impressed with the quality and efficiency of Len's program. He was impressed enough to mention Len as a good baseball man in a conversation with Max Carey sometime later. Through this contact, Max recruited Len to organize an AAGBBL minor league and operate it within the Chicago Park System.[10] Thus, Len became "Director of Schools and Try-outs and Affiliates of the League."[11] It should be remembered that this was not the first contact the AAGBBL's Chicago office had with the Chicago Park System. At the league's inception, Mr.

Wrigley consulted with Vern Hernlund, head park supervisor, to help draw up the first rules of play for the league.

Max Carey's contact with Len Zintak must have occurred sometime during the summer of 1946 because Mary Lou Studnicka Caden recalled that the four-team Chicago Girls Baseball League was preceded by two trial teams during the winter of 1946 and the summer and winter of 1947.

> Lenny Zintak ... had information put out in all the Chicago Parks announcing the formation of girls' teams. Lenny had some friends [who] helped him hold tryouts all over the city. We had enough girls for two teams on the south side of the city and were playing games in the parks. The team line-ups weren't set and the girls played different positions on both teams, trying to balance the teams. That winter we studied the game indoors at Marquette Park. Each player had a playbook and Lenny would diagram possible plays on a chalk board. We'd meet for two hours every Saturday. Some of the players were still in school and some players worked, so Saturday was best for meetings.
>
> We started out with the modified softball and went from fast pitch underhand to overhand at the same time they changed in the AAGBBL. We wore the same type of uniforms as the AAGBBL. Dimensions of the field were the same as the AAGBBL.[12]

Mary Lou was one of those girls who loved to play baseball and played with the boys at Marquette Park. She noted that she "could only play practice games as girls weren't allowed to play in league games," but she "managed to play in a lot of pick up games in the neighborhood."[13]

A 1948 press release from the AAGBBL's Chicago office on April 12, 1948, announced the formation of the *four team* Chicago Girls Baseball League. The press release is copied here in its entirety because of its historical significance.

> The birth of the Chicago Girls Baseball League was due to the fact that the interest has grown and the demand for franchises has increased to a point where a farm system became necessary to train girls for the All-American Girls Baseball League. The Chicago League will be composed of four teams, the Northtown Debs and the Northtown Co-eds sponsored by Mel Thillens, a north side business man, civic leader, sportsman and owner of the North Town Stadium, and the Blue Island Stars and the Blue Island Dianas to be fielded by the Blue Island Recreation Commission, headed by chairman Dr. Frank Tracy, and will be played at the Blue Island Stadium.
>
> All traces of softball have disappeared in the game with the inception of a 48 foot pitching distance, 72 foot base paths and an 11 inch ball. The pitchers are allowed to deliver the ball in any fashion they deem effective. All official baseball rules are used.
>
> Each team has a maximum roster of 15 players, a manager and a chaperon. The league is headed by Max Carey, President of the All-American Girls Baseball League, and is supervised by Leonard N. Zintak, former recreation leader and baseball man. All team personnel play a total of 50 games per season, 25 home games and 25 traveling games.
>
> The chaperon assigned to each team is responsible for administering first aid, uniforms and equipment, making living and traveling arrangements, and seeing to the general health and welfare of her charges. A high standard of conduct and behavior is maintained at all times.
>
> New prospects, from the Chicago area, are signed to agreements which protect their amateur standing before a definite contract is offered to play professional ball. All players are signed to these agreements with the league at the league headquarters in the Wrigley Building, Chicago. Players are rated and assigned on the basis of baseball ability by the use of a point system and rating charts. Players are allocated to the four clubs by the league to insure equitable balance and competition. All league players receive a complete course in the fundamentals of baseball at both indoor and outdoor schools and are

Hitting lesson from a pro: *Left to right:* Mary Lou Studnicka, Lenny Zintak, Rogers Hornsby (courtesy Mary Lou Studnicka Caden).

selected to play on the basis of athletic ability as well as their character and deportment. All girls are insured and receive expense money. Upon development girls are moved up to the All-American Girls Baseball League and will play in the major league of girls baseball that has attracted nearly a million spectators in 1947 in the 8 cities in which they played.

Tryouts will be held at Northtown Stadium on April 24th and at Blue Island Stadium on April 17th. Both tryout schools will begin at 2:00 P.M. All girls are asked to bring their own glove and heavy jacket. The Northtown Stadium is located at Devon and Kedzie and the Blue Island Stadium is at 125th and Western Avenue. [14]

The players in the Chicago Girls Baseball League were signed to contracts just as their "Big League" sisters were. This distinguished them as Minor League players rather than Junior League players.

OFFICIAL PLAYERS CONTRACT
OF
CHICAGO GIRLS BASEBALL LEAGUE

The Chicago Girls Baseball League is a League affiliated with the All-American Girls Baseball League, whose purpose it is to develop, supervise and regulate the playing of Girls' Baseball under such high standards of personal conduct, fair-play and good sportsmanship as will secure the approval of the American public.

The Chicago Girls Baseball League, hereinafter called the "League," desires to procure the services of _____ of _____ of _____ hereinafter called the "Player," to participate in the playing of ball as a part of any team operated by the League.

Term and Obligations
1. Subject to the provisions of Section 6 hereof, the League employs the Player for the 1948 baseball season conducted by it, on the terms and conditions herein set forth. The Player agrees to play ball as part of any team operated by the League and to faithfully serve the club to which she is allocated, and pledges herself to the League to conform to such high standards as may be set by the League and to abide by all rules and regulations adopted by the League.

Expense Allowance
2. The signing of this contract will authorize the club to which the player is assigned, to pay an expense allowance of not in excess of $_____ per week, to be paid at the end of each week so long as the Player is on the roster of said club.

Regulations
3. The Player and the League accept as part of this contract all rules and regulations set up and adopted by the All-American Girls Baseball League, which said rules and regulations by reference thereto are hereby made a part of this contract.

Rule Violations
4. The League or the Club to whom the Player is assigned may impose reasonable fines for violations of rules by the Players.

Options
5. The Player, by the execution of this contract, hereby grants to the All-American Girls Baseball League the first option on her services as a member of any club of said All-American Girls Baseball League; and the Player agrees, as promptly thereafter as this option may be exercised, to report for services to the club of the All-American Girls Baseball League to whom she has been assigned.

Termination
6. During the initial training period of the Player, the League shall have the right to terminate this contract without notice. At the end of the training period the League shall have the right to terminate this contract at any time on fourteen (14) days' prior notice. [15]

The 1948 CGBL rosters included the following players, managers and chaperones:

Airborne: Lorraine "Fitz" Fitzgerald, a CGBL Debs player who might have made it to the AAGBBL if it hadn't been for a broken leg (courtesy Lorraine Fitzgerald).

BLUE ISLAND STARS

Tillie Page	Helen Potaczyk
Arlene Kotil*	Frances Romane
Audrey Schenck	**Dolores Niemiec**
Frances Schiedel	**Betty Frances**
Jean Leback	Marie McCormack
Mary Lou Studnicka	Shirley Zarbock
Lorraine Kiekow	Betty Martiniak
Joan Holderness	*Florence Hay*
*Rosemary Turner***	

Player Pool: McKenna, Thayer, H. Schiedel

Manager: **Mitch Skupien**
Chaperone: Frances Romane

BLUE ISLAND DIANAS

Gladys Rick	Charlotte Janikowski
Lorraine Janikowski	Frances Sifrer
Hazel Smith	Dolores Dominiak
Angeline Metros	Frances Gonlag
Lorraine Klabacha	Lois Bochmann
Janet Cox	Josephine Topa
Anna Mae O'Dowd	Marge Murray
Lucille Gregorash	*Prudence Penny*

Player Pool: Roos, Fritsch

Manager: Ken Maier
Chaperone: Bernice Cunningham

NORTH TOWN CO-EDS

Shirley Sutherland	**Therese McKinley**
Peggy Fenton	Nyema Lindblade Heim
Dolores Mueller	Elaine Wyse
Dolores Pringle	Violet Palumbo Morrison
Elaine Hurt	Barbara Davis
Barbara Davis	Grace Frick
Betty Wilson	*Doris Calacurcio*
Barbara Heim	*Joyce Perce*

Player Pool: Schnieder

Manager: Floyd Jacobson
Chaperone: Dorothy Morgan

***Those who graduated to the AAGBBL**

NORTH TOWN DEBS

Ruth Berryman	Andy Anderson
Phyllis Carlson	Marilyn Boss
Kathleen Monihan	Lois Bellmen
Dutch Harms	**Eileen Gascon**
Lorraine Fitzgerald	Elizabeth Berberich
Nancy Marsh	Alice Sprayer
Dolores Koopman	**Joan Sindelar**
Gloria Schweigerdt	*Shirley Danz*
Sally Wolenberg	*Jean Disselhorst*
Marion Thornton	*Marlene Schaer*

Player Pool: Johnson

Manager: William Biebel
Chaperone: Nettie Rapp

***Players Listed on a different, (earlier/later) roster*

Others, not listed above, who played in the CGBL in 1948 and advanced to the AAGBBL, to the best of Lenny Zintak's memory: **Beatrice Allard, Ange Armato**.[16]

According to former CGBL player Betty Francis, most of the girls who played in the CGBL came out of the Chicago Park System and that "a lot tried out and never made our league or the AAGBBL."[17] Joan Holderness, one of several players who advanced from the CGBL to the AAGBBL recalled "playing many games at Northtown Stadium."[18] Delores Bajda, noted that games were also played at Shrewbridge Field, Cole Lenzi Field, and Thillens Stadium.[19]

Mary Lou Studnicka Caden, another graduate from the CGBL to the AAGBBL related her CGBL experience in fairly thorough detail:

> We had a chaperone for each team and they were usually playing chaperones. The players received $2.00 a game [expenses] and the chaperones got $7.00 a game. The chaperones drove a lot of the younger girls to and from the games. We usually played one week night and one Sunday afternoon game. Sometimes we played curtain opener games for the fastpitch kitten ball teams that played around Chicago—New Orleans Jax, Music Maids, Bluebirds, etc. They were a rough bunch. When the [AAGBBL] league started a team in Chicago, the Colleens, we also played before their games. Then we'd sit in the stands and watch the "pros" play.

> Many of the girls [who] started with Lenny eventually made it up to the AAGPBL. Among them were Dolly Niemiec, Gloria "Tippy" Schweigerdt, Ginger Gascon, Arlene Kotil, Mary Lou Studnicka, Dolores Mueller, Betty Francis and many more.

1948 North Town Debs: *Left to right, front*: Gloria "Tippy" Schweigerdt, "Boots" Berberich, Nancy Marsh, Kathleen "Toots" Monahan, Eileen "Ginger" Gascon. *Middle*: Joan "Jo" Sindelar, Shirley Danz, Lois "Punky" Belman, Lorraine "Fitz" Fitzgerald, Prudence Penny (Captain), "Jody." *Back*: Mary (?), Sally (?), Coach Bill Biebel, "Dutch" Harms, Lynn (?) (courtesy Lorraine Fitzgerald). *Below:* Blue Island Stars Uniform Patch (courtesy Betty Francis).

... Many of the Chicago farm team girls went on tour with two teams, the Colleens and the Springfield Sallies to promote the [AAGBBL].

... Mitch Skupien, one of the men [who] coached the farm teams was hired to manage the Grand Rapids Chicks in 1951. That was the year I finally went up to the "Pros." Mitch had been my manager in Chicago, and I had an offer from the Chicks, so I accepted.[20]

Mary Lou affirmed that the CGBL operated through 1950 as she played in the league from its infancy in 1946 through its last year, 1950.[21] Not surprisingly, the league ceased operating after team owners bought Meyerhoff out at the end of

Rayson's Sports CGBL Team: *Back*: Coach Bill, "Champ" Mueller, Mary Lou Studnicka, two unidentified players, Gloria Schweigert, unidentified, Coach Mitch Skupien. Front, All unidentified. (courtesy Mary Lou Studnicka Caden).

the 1950 season. The loss of the CGBL after the 1950 season would further constrict the AAGBBL's talent pool.

A number of the CGBL players earned spots on the 1949 and 1950 rookie touring teams. Among them were Arlene Kotil, Joan Holderness, Betty Francis, Joan Sindelar, (the CGBL's 1948 Player of the Year), Anna Mae O'Dowd, and Renae Youngberg.[22]

Some players, like Renae Youngberg, hopscotched from the CGBL to the AAGBBL. In 1949, Rayson's Sports took over sponsorship of the North Town Coeds, and the Rayson Manager, Mitch Skupien, recruited Renae to play for Rayson's.[23] She was a strong player, however, and only spent three weeks with Rayson's before being sent to join the touring teams.[24] Renae recalled that her mother was contacted by Max Carey's secretary asking her to bring Renae to the Wrigley Building to sign a contract and report to Ardmore, Oklahoma to play for the Springfield Sallies.

According to Joyce Smith, "Rayson's was a major sporting goods outlet in the Chicago area with several stores throughout the city."[25] Recruiting a major business to sponsor an AAGBBL team was consistent with Wrigley's and Meyerhoff's method of operation for establishing teams in league cities. It's not surprising, therefore, to find Thillens and Rayson's sponsoring CGBL teams in Chicago.

Spring Training and Exhibition Tours

Spring training in the AAGBBL was a unique affair during the Trustee Administration and most of Management's Administration. It differed considerably from the traditional practice of major league baseball in which each team made its own pre-season training arrangements. Spring training for AAGBBL teams between 1943 and 1948 was a collective affair where all league teams trained together at a central location. This was necessitated by the yearly reallocation of players to equalize team talent. The centralized spring training camp gave administrative personnel an opportunity to judge the relative talents of all players and enabled them to distribute that talent to respective teams as equitably as they could agree upon.

For the 1943 season, the first season of play, league administrators were working with previously unknown quantities; all players were rookies. Thereafter, each team retained a core of approximately ten regulars. The returning players and rookies were scrutinized during spring training for assignment to a team or dismissal. Spring training was also the only time administrative personnel, such as managers and team presidents, had to evaluate the ability of all rookies, and until 1949, spring training was the primary vehicle through which new talent was acquired. Therefore, it was deemed an essential feature of league operations.

The AAGBBL was subject to the same travel restrictions as major league baseball during World War II. During the war, baseball spring training camps had to be held in the north rather than in the south as was customary.[26] Consistent with the demands of the war, the AAGBBL's first spring training program was held in Chicago's Wrigley Field. The second year of play, spring training was held a bit further south in Peru, Illinois. World War II transportation restrictions were still in effect in the spring of 1945, the third year of league operations, and the first year of Meyerhoff's administra-

Two minor leaguers who made it to the pros: Arlene Kotil (left) and Joan Sindelar. Joan was the Chicago Girls Baseball League 1948 MVP (courtesy Leonard Zintak).

1949 Rayson's sports stars who became big leaguers: Renae Youngberg (left) and Gloria "Tippy" Schweigerdt (courtesy Renae Youngberg).

tion. The league's spring training camp for 1945 was again held in Chicago, at Waveland Park, and was followed by a pre-season exhibition tour to nearby military bases.[27]

By 1946, wartime transportation restrictions had been lifted and from 1946 to 1948 the AAGBBL was involved in ambitious spring training and exhibition programs. These were initiated, arranged and organized by Meyerhoff's Management Corporation with the approval of the League Board of Directors. Reminiscent of Major League Baseball's tradition of spring training in southern climes, all AAGBBL teams were assembled for spring training in Pascagoula, Mississippi, in 1946; in Havana, Cuba, in 1947; and Opalocka, Florida, in 1948. After ten days to two weeks in training camp, the teams paired off and played exhibition games en route to their return to open regular season play in northern league cities (see Figure 4). These spring training and exhibition programs had both positive and negative effects. On the positive side, they afforded "an excellent opportunity to introduce girls professional baseball" to southern communities.[28] In this respect, the spring training and exhibition tours also proved to be a valuable player recruiting medium.[29] The promotion and publicity attendant to the exhibition tours attracted sand lot players to the league from remote areas of the country.

Available league records didn't document how many players were attracted to the AAGBBL in this way, but in 1946, Doris Sams, born and raised in Knoxville, Tennessee, first heard of the league through a radio spot announcement.

> One day, a little boy in our neighborhood came running over to the house and told me that on the radio they had announced that there were two [girls'] professional baseball teams coming through our town. I couldn't believe it — girls playing baseball! He said all I had to do was go over and talk to the coach and try to get a try-out with him. It rained that day and they didn't get to play there, so I had to go up to the hotel.
> Leo Murphy was in the room and I introduced myself and told him I had been playing fast pitch for several years. He told me, "well, you can't try-out here, so you'll have to go to Chattanooga, that's where we're going." So I went to Chattanooga with him and he took me to another little city or two. Then he said, "go on back home and get your clothes and meet us up in Michigan." Well, I did that and I ended up on the Muskegon Lassies' ball club.[30]

Doris Sam became an outstanding pitcher and outfielder in the AAGBBL. She was the first player in the league to earn Player of the Year honors twice, which she accomplished in 1947 and 1949.

Delores "Dolly" Brumfield White was another prospect discovered during the 1946 spring training excursion. News of the training camp appeared in her local newspaper, *The Mobile Press Register.* Dolly had been pitching boys' baseball in her home town and she practiced with a local men's team at a nearby school yard. Members of the men's team saw the ad in the paper and encouraged her family to take her to the AAGBBL tryouts held in conjunction with spring training in Pascagoula. At the time, Dolly was only thirteen and her parents felt she was too young to join the league. However, her skills were impressive enough that Max Carey contacted her parents the following year and she was able to join the AAGBBL's spring training excursion to Cuba. She became a member of the league at that time and played from 1947 through 1953.[31]

Oklahoma native Earlene "Beans" Risinger, an outstanding overhand pitcher for the Grand Rapids Chicks, related that her first knowledge of the AAGBBL came from newspaper publicity promoting an exhibition game in Oklahoma City during the spring of 1947. Risinger, who lived in small, rural Hess, Oklahoma, which she claimed wasn't even on the map, and who "learned to throw a baseball very young," went to Oklahoma City for a tryout and subsequently became an AAGBBL player.[32] If the league hadn't conducted these spring training camps and tours or arranged for the newspaper ads and the radio announcements, these three and other exceptional ball players would never have had the opportunity to play professional baseball.

Figure 4: 1947 Pre-Season Tour Agenda
South Bend and Kenosha

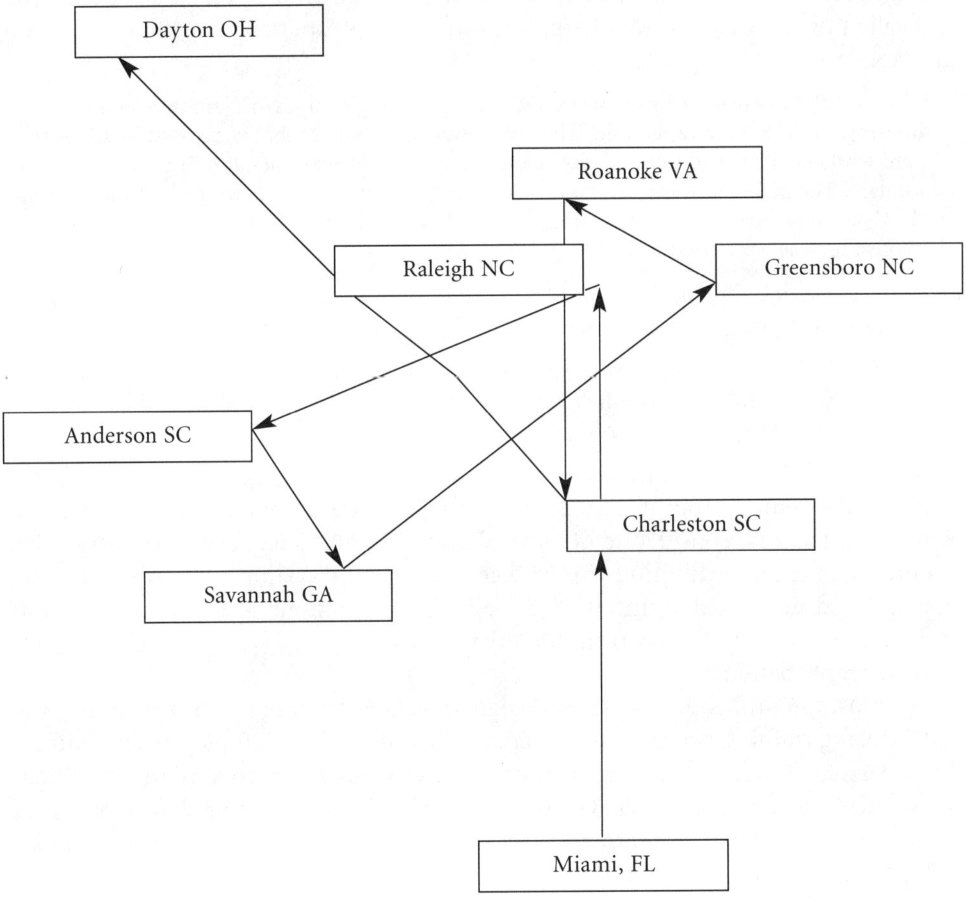

SOURCE: Chet Grant AAGBBL Records, University of Notre Dame Joyce Sports Research Collection, South Bend, Indiana.

Another positive aspect of the exhibition tours was the league's arrangement for exhibition games sponsored by local charities. The charities benefited from any proceeds after expenses were met. A local charity promoting a game drew more notice, spectators and larger gates. Officials from the Lexington, Kentucky, Colored Orphans and Industrial Home, for instance, received a $300.00 check from AAGBBL games played there in May 1947.[33] Noting Meyerhoff's soft spot for disadvantaged children, his hand is obvious in the organization of such events. In this way, he successfully satisfied several objectives: The AAGBBL was subsidized, local charities were enriched, and the league was exposed to the largest crowds possible.

For the players, these spring training and exhibition tours from south to north were among their most memorable experiences. The opportunity to travel and to learn about different sections of the country while playing ball was beyond the scope of their expectations.

Negative aspects of the first southern spring training excursion included poor accommodations and playing facilities, exhausting traveling tours, and considerable financial expense. The first league experience with a combined training camp in the South and an exhibition tour north was deemed the worst by some in regard to poor accommodations and training facilities. In 1946, Harold T. Dailey, then a director of the South Bend Blue Sox, recalled the Pascagoula, Mississippi, training camp experience in 1946 in not too kindly terms:

> That was the worst mess I ever saw for a spring training camp. No diamonds and the housing conditions were terrible. They were war built houses that were used by the shipyard workers. They had not been used and were alive with roaches and bugs of all kinds.... The ball field was a rutted infield and the other diamonds were all grass. We got the diamonds repaired and they tried to build ... extra diamonds that [were] finished about the time we were through.[34]

Jean Faut, a rookie who made good at that first 1946 southern spring training camp, remembered Pascagoula as "Cockroach Haven."

> You didn't even have to open your suitcase before they'd be inside. I think we bought out that place of DDT. You'd have the lights on at night and sprinkle it all around and across the doorway or they'd come through the door — it was really bad.[35]

Since 1946 was the league administration's first experience with a central southern training camp and exhibition tour, the schedule for the homeward bound exhibition trip was probably also the least considerate of players' physical endurance. Dailey observed that the South Bend team's exhibition trip in 1946 was "a bad traveling trip with long night jumps and bad mountain country."[36] If Dailey's observations were accurate, league administration learned a lesson from the mistakes of 1946, and spring training in 1947 was considerably better.

The most ambitious preseason campaign sponsored by league administration was the 1947 spring training program in Havana, Cuba. More than 200 players and administrative personnel were transported by train to Miami and by air from Miami to Havana for a two-week training session. They were housed in the Saville-Biltmore Hotel in Havana and practiced at the Gran Stadium del la Habana.[37] Marie "Blackie" Wegman, a rookie in 1947, detailed the trip to Cuba:

> I still remember we left in April [from Cincinnati] and took a train to Louisville. There was a train coming from the West and a train coming from the East and they met in Louisville. There was an iron railing there and all these girls came off of both trains and just met at this railing and were shaking hands [and saying] "How ya doing," and "How ya been," and all this. Dot [Mueller] and I looked at each other and said, "Hey this looks like it might be pretty much fun."
>
> Then we got on another train and went to Florida. Then we flew from Florida to Havana. It was evening [in Cuba] and when we got over the University of Havana, I can still remember the pilot circling the field. They had all the lights turned on so we could see it. He circled the plane around the field so we could see where we were going to play.[38]

Even though this was the most extensive spring training trip undertaken by the league, it turned out to be the most economical of the three. The 1946 excursion to

Pascagoula and back for eight teams cost $2,786.15 per team; the 1948 campaign to Opalocka, Florida cost $3,976.23 per team for ten teams; and the 1947 Cuban trip and tour for eight teams amounted to $2,775.32 each.[39] As Arthur Meyerhoff reflected 30 years later:

> The total expense charged each team for the Cuban enterprise was a fraction of its cost because of the exhibition games that helped finance the enterprise. It was an extremely elaborate setup and looked expensive, and I could never convince the directors that the cost was slightly over perhaps what it would have cost them to train in their own home town feeding and housing the girls.[40]

League personnel had better accommodations and practice facilities in Havana than in Pascagoula or Opalocka. The only drawback to Havana for the players was the food. According to Jean Faut, "some of the players couldn't find anything they could eat, but I loved the seafood, so I [did] great."[41] See Figure 4 for a representative example of the spring training exhibition tours the teams made on the way home from Havana.

Arthur Meyerhoff recalled that the AAGBBL's spring training appearance in Cuba in 1947 resulted from Max Carey's Cuban contacts.[42] Another baseball general manager who had contacts in Cuba was Branch Rickey. In 1947 the Brooklyn Dodgers also conducted spring training in Havana, Cuba. The Dodgers' reason for training in Havana rather than Florida, as was their custom, was the presence of Jackie Robinson on their roster. They didn't want to risk training in the South with him or exposing him to unnecessary humiliation.[43]

Between the Dodgers and the AAGBBL, Cuban fans were treated to a good deal of entertaining baseball in the spring of 1947. Possibly because of the novelty of seeing skirted female baseball players, Cuban spectators (almost exclusively male) attended the AAGBBL exhibition games in greater numbers than they did the Dodger exhibition games.[44] An account of the Cuban reaction to AAGBBL games, preserved by Dr. Dailey, newly elected president of the South Bend team, gives some indication of the popularity of the girls' teams among the Cubans.

> The Americanos became the rage of all baseball-mad Cuba. Hundreds turned out to see them practice. And no less than 50,000 wildly enthusiastic fans watched the round-robin tournament which concluded the training program. In the opening game of the final series between the Racine Belles and the Muskegon Lassies, the crowd numbered over 20,000 and gave convincing proof that Cuba had taken girls baseball to its heart.[45]

The AAGBBL spring training camp in Cuba acted as a stimulus for the development of a similar Cuban girls' baseball league. According to a league office news release, the Cuban girls league was organized "by a group of sports loving Cubans headed by Rafael Leon."

> Working in close co-operation with Max Carey and other AA League Officials, the Latin American loop was patterned after Carey's Organization. The All-American game, known as Girls Baseball, was adopted along with all of the AA rules and regulations.[46]

This Cuban girls' baseball league apparently had its genesis in late 1946 or the very first months of 1947 in preparation for the AAGBBL's spring arrival. Late 1946 to early 1947 was also the time when the All-American league office was making arrangements for the Cuban spring training campaign. According to Isabel Alvarez, she, along with other Cuban girls, were recruited and trained in the AAGBBL game before the All-Americans arrived in Cuba.[47] They were recruited from the streets of Havana by Raphael Leon, a

All eight AAGBBL teams descending la escalinata de la Universidad de la Habana, 1947 (courtesy Betsy Jochum).

wealthy beer merchant. On weekends he housed the girls at his ranch, fed them well, and taught them the AAGBBL baseball game. They were also provided with AAGBBL–style uniforms. Isabel especially remembered the exhibition game with the American rookies because, at only age 14, she pitched in that game.[48] Again, either through Max Carey or Wrigley Company contacts in Cuba, a well-to-do citizen was recruited to sponsor and develop girls' baseball teams. The objective had to be an exhibition game between the Cuban girls and the All-Americans during the AAGBBL's 1947 spring training excursion. Such a contest would be viewed as a means of heightening spectator interest and attendance.

Indeed, when the All-American Racine Belles and Muskegon Lassies prepared to play a best two-out-of-three game series to conclude round robin exhibition games in Cuba, an unusual event occurred. "On Saturday night, May 4, when the first game of the series was played, the program included an exhibition game between the American rookies and a team of Cuban girls. Upwards of 20,000 crowded the spacious stands and cheered every move...."[49]

As a result of the AAGBBL's Cuban campaign, players from the subsequently devel-

1947 — A visit to Sloppy Joe's in Havana: Standing, *Left to right:* Betty Whiting, Kay Blumetta, Amy Irene Applegren, Dottie Hunter, Alma Ziegler, Annabelle Lee, Doris Tetzlaff. Seated, Dorothy "Snookie" Harrell, Lil Faralla, Faye Dancer, Jane "Jeep" Stoll, Dottie Ferguson, Vivian Kellogg, Betty Luna, Thelma "Tiby" Eisen, Dorothy "Kammie" Kamenshek, Inez Voyce, Irene "Ike" Kotowicz (courtesy Dorothy "Snookie" Harrell Doyle).

oped "Latin American Feminine Basebol League" (LAFBL) and players from the AAG-BBL joined forces and played a post-season exhibition tour in Cuba in the fall of 1947.[50] Other post-season tours featuring Cuban and AAGBBL players occurred in the winters of 1948 and 1949. These will be discussed at greater length under the heading "Post-Season Exhibition Tours," later in this chapter.

A more immediate effect of AAGBBL play in Cuba featured the importation of the first Cuban girl to play with AAGBBL teams in the United States. Eulalia Gonzales, "Viyalla" (the smart one) to Cuban fans, was, according to her parents, 19 years old. Her visit to the United States as a member of the Racine Belles required intervention from Cuban President Grau. Viyalla came from a very poor family and had no birth certificate, a requirement for a visit to the United States. President Grau "issued a special certificate of permission for the girl to tour the States with the Belles."[51] Viyalla was the product of junior girls teams in Havana and "because of her exceptional ability [she] often played in exhibition games with and against men's teams."[52]

It was suggested that Viyalla's presence with the AAGBBL was basically a good will

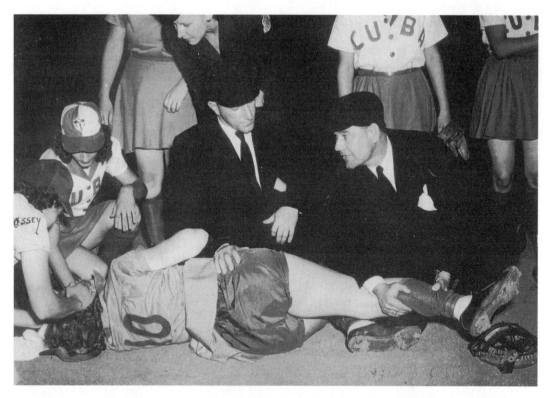

Rossey Weeks (left) consoling Marion Watson Stanton. Umpire on the right is Gadget Ward. Notice Cuban players' uniforms. This game may have been played during one of the AAGBBL's fall tours to Cuba (courtesy Grand Rapids History & Special Collections Center Archives, Grand Rapids Public Library, Grand Rapids, MI).

gesture and that her tenure with the AAGBBL would be short.[53] Arthur Meyerhoff noted that "Viyalla returned to Cuba because she was just plain lonesome. We even went so far as to provide another Cuban to come along as a companion when we found out she was unhappy. She was very young and missed her home environment."[54]

Other Cubans to join and continue to play in the AAGBBL in succeeding years included Gloria Ruiz, Georgiana Rios, Violet Zonia, Luisa Gallegos, Mirtha Marrero, Migdalia Perez, Ysora Castillo, and Isabel Alvarez. Isabel pointed out that "We had very well organized women's baseball in Cuba."[55] She also noted that she was only 14 when some of the older girls came to the United States in 1948 and that her Cuban manager told her she would go to the United States when she was 15. In 1949, she did come to play in the AAGBBL along with Migdalia "Mickie" Perez, Mirtha Marrero, and Ysora "Chico" Castillo.[56] Isabel credited her mother with planning and securing her career in baseball in the United States after the AAGBBL's spring training there.

> My mother told me she wanted me to be a baseball player. She planned my life in baseball.... She saw the opportunity when the Americans came to Cuba. She loved baseball. She used to listen to Cuban professional baseball on the radio. When the Americans came to Cuba, I pitched when we played with the Americans. They mixed up the teams for an exhibition game.
>
> [At 15] I could not be afraid. My mother trained me that way.... I could never say, "Mama, I am lonely or afraid." She'd probably think I was crazy if I said that. She knew

Above: Four Cubans who became Colleens in 1948: *Left to right:* Mirtha Marrero, Julia Gutz, Migdalia "Mickey" Perez, Luisa Gallegos (reproduced from the original held by the Department of Special Collections of the University Libraries of Notre Dame). *Left:* Isabel "Lefty" Alvarez (courtesy Northern Indiana Center for History).

the future, the opportunity to come to the United States. She knew besides baseball, it was a great opportunity to come to the United States.[57]

Isabel became a member of the 1949 Chicago Colleens touring team and remembered that the first English words she learned "since I had to eat were 'hamburger' and 'chocolate milkshake.' Whenever we went to a restaurant, that's all I ate, but I don't know for how long. I didn't know what else [to order]." She explained that between 1949 and 1952 she "went back and forth [to Cuba]. In 1953

I didn't have to go back because I applied for citizenship papers. One of the families I stayed with in Fort Wayne helped me to become a citizen."[58]

One can only imagine the culture shock and language barrier encountered by these brave young Cuban girls. They must have loved baseball very much to travel so far from home and family to play.

The 1948 centralized spring training camp and exhibition tour in Opalocka, Florida, was the last one of its kind approved by the League Board of Directors. Their primary reason for canceling these excursions was to curtail expenses. A motion to institute a cheaper spring training program had been made, but not acted upon, as early as September 1946.[59] A similar motion, calling for teams to train in league communities, was made after the 1947 season and defeated.[60] A reduction of the league from ten teams back to eight teams in 1949 created a temporary surplus of players. This, plus financial deficits resulting from the failure of the Springfield club in mid-season of 1948, led the board to agree that there was no necessity for an expensive spring training site in 1949.[61] Further discussion on this matter led to a consensus that spring training in hometowns was an excellent idea for the 1949 season.[62]

From 1949 forward, spring training and exhibition tours were arranged by each team rather than by Management. Some teams joined in cooperative training camps in nearby communities and played exhibition games in towns and cities adjacent to their own. Others trained in their local communities and then joined another team for an exhibition tour in neighboring states.[63]

The decentralization of spring training was a significant step toward the decentralization of league administration. In their quest to cut costs, team administrators also began cutting cooperative ties that had bound the league together from its inception. Furthermore, they began cutting ties with Meyerhoff's Management Corporation. The considerable professional publicity and promotion afforded by the annual spring training campaigns was continued by Meyerhoff through the rookie tours he organized and subsidized in 1949 and 1950. After the 1950 season, however, this type of promotion and publicity for the league became non-existent. Publicity and promotion throughout the country were assets the league could ill-afford to lose for player procurement purposes. In Arthur Meyerhoff's words, "I think that one lesson these gentlemen who took over the League didn't understand was that one must spend money to make it, and, as they eliminated the elements that made the League in the first place, the League deteriorated."[64]

With the discontinuance of centralized spring training and exhibition tours, the league lost a basic program for obtaining public exposure in the populous and remote southern and eastern sections of the nation. It also lost considerable ability to observe the talents of prospective players outside the Chicago vicinity. The spring exhibition tours had not only served as a league promotional program but also as a vehicle for player tryouts in far-flung communities. The League Board of Directors' conclusion that a surplus of players would exist for the 1949 season was valid, since a reduction from ten to eight teams did occur that year, leaving a balance of approximately 30 veterans from which to restock remaining teams. However, the player surplus of 1949 was a luxury the league was not to enjoy again, and player procurement became a major league concern thereafter.

Summer Barnstorming Tours

With the league's adoption of overhand pitching in 1948, the institution of longer base paths, and the use of a smaller ball (10⅜"), it became increasingly apparent that special training for rookies was necessary before they could adjust from softball to baseball as played by the AAGBBL. As time progressed, it also became obvious that few rookies could make an immediate adjustment to the caliber of ball played in the AAGBBL. Meyerhoff perceived the gap in public exposure and player training left by the discontinuance of the centralized spring training camps and exhibition tours. To fill the void, he sponsored a summer barnstorming tour during the 1949 and 1950 seasons. His purpose was to provide continued training of rookies not quite skilled enough for the AAGBBL, but too good to cast aside. He also wanted to continue publicizing and promoting the league on a broad scale to draw in still unknown talent. As he had with the exhibition tours after spring training in the previous years, he combined girls' baseball with support for charities. Barbara Liebrich, one of the tour chaperones emphasized:

> Most people don't understand that this was a very, very worthwhile thing. We played for charities: the milk fund, the shoe fund, the fireman's fund.... We'd go into a town, and in the 1940's, children needed help for shoes or "milk funds" they used to call them. We'd go in and play our game and take our expenses, and then the fund would get what we had left over and would help their fund give out shoes and that.[65]

There is no question that the summer barnstorming program was Meyerhoff's idea and project. The League Board of Directors' response to his proposal for the tour indicated that they wanted little to do with it.

> The directors stated they would have no objection [to the summer barnstorming tour], provided no game was held within 100 miles of any of our cities. No promotion, publicity or any other expenses [were] to be charged to the League. Management [would] purchase the necessary uniforms from the Springfield and Chicago Clubs, and ... reimburse the League for uniforms formerly used by the Springfield Club and now the property of the League.[66]

The summer barnstorming tour Meyerhoff organized for the 1949 season consisted of two teams, the now defunct Chicago Colleens and Springfield Sallies and a few of the outstanding CGBL players. The Colleens and Sallies played exhibition games in southern Illinois, Missouri, Oklahoma, Arkansas, Louisiana, Tennessee, Texas, Florida, Alabama, Mississippi, Georgia, South Carolina, North Carolina, Virginia, New Jersey, New York, Pennsylvania, Ohio, West Virginia, and Indiana. The tour began June 11 and ended September 5, 1949.[67] Altogether, 76 games were played before 112,661 spectators for an average attendance of 1,238 per game. The total cost of the tour was $50,957.05. Receipts from ticket sales totaled $47,440.12, leaving a deficit of $3,516.93, which Meyerhoff apparently underwrote.[68]

More than 600 prospects attended tryout sessions held in tour cities prior to games. "After a most critical classification" procedure, 11 (3.67 percent) were considered capable of playing with the league or the 1950 summer barnstorming tour.[69] Tour supervisor Leonard Zintak presented a favorable evaluation of the tour's training and scouting missions.

> Sixteen girls from the tour are ready to join regular league teams for the 1950 season. They have received careful instruction and have played in more than sixty games—which is a seasoning process without equal.

1949 Colleens and Sallies ready to board the bus. *Left to right, standing:* Shirley Danz, Gert Alderfer, Lillian Shadic, Fran Janssen, Helen Walulik, Mary "Wimp" Baumgartner, Isabel Alvarez, unidentified, Pat Barringer. *In Bus:* Unidentified, Joan Sindelar, Lois Bellman, Barbara Liebrich, Margaret Berger, Sue Kidd, Anna Mae O'Dowd, Betty Francis, Toni Palermo, Barbara Payne, Walter Fidler (bus driver) (courtesy Renae Youngberg).

    A further result of the tour was the indoctrination of a group of very young girls in the methods of baseball. The tour afforded these girls an opportunity to acquire skill through competition with more experienced players.

    The tour became an efficient scouting system — drawing in new talent from remote points, developing young players until they could meet the standards of the League, and seasoning others to become a nucleus for further training.

    Some of the players on the tour who are only fifteen and sixteen years old have been judged the best prospects for future League work. They came from sections of the country where they would never have been found but for the Barnstorming Tour.[70]

Gloria Cordes Elliott was one of the players recruited to the league through the 1949 barnstorming tour. Her ball playing experience came from having five sisters and five brothers. An older brother was an outstanding pitcher from Staten Island. Gloria recalled, "He used to ask me to play catch with him and while I was playing catch, he taught me how to throw a knuckleball and a curve ball, and I learned how to throw a pretty good fastball, so I became a baseball pitcher."[71] Gloria was another one of those players who played only baseball with the neighborhood boys.

Girls weren't allowed to play baseball at the time I was growing up, but having the brothers and playing ball with them, I was allowed to play on the pick-up teams and that was about all the baseball I could play, but it was a lot. I was always welcome to play with the boys' teams.

In 1949, when the touring teams from the girls league came to Staten Island to play a game, my friends and I went out to watch the game. While we were there, we were allowed to try out. Lenny Zintak was managing the girls on tour and he asked if anyone knew how to pitch, so I told him I did. He took me aside, and I just threw a few balls, and he said okay we'd hear from him. The next thing I was invited to a try-out in South Bend, Indiana. That was in the spring of 1950. From that try-out I was placed on the ... Kalamazoo Lassies team.

It was just a chance of a lifetime — I mean for someone who loved to play baseball as much as I did, to get involved with this league, was just phenomenal.[72]

Besides having a brother teach her how to pitch, Gloria was further prepared for her tryout in South Bend in the spring of 1950 by minor league pitcher George Bamburger, who eventually became a noted pitching coach for the Baltimore Orioles when they had five 20-game winners. He would go on to manage the New York Mets and the Milwaukee Brewers. When Gloria was preparing for tryouts in South Bend, he and some friends were getting ready to go to their teams. As she explained:

My brother taught me how to throw the ball, but I knew nothing about pitching. With the help of George Bamburger and two of the other players who were getting ready, they showed me how to hold runners on base, how to follow through, and taught me a lot about pitching that I would not have otherwise known. So I think that was a major factor in my going right into the league.[73]

Just as some players were discovered as a result of the spring training excursions that were organized between 1946 and 1948, others, like Gloria Cordes Elliott, were discovered as a result of the 1949 and 1950 rookie tours organized and administered by Meyerhoff.

By the end of the 1949 season it had begun to dawn on league board members that new players entering the league required special training to adapt to AAGBBL baseball. At a board meeting in August of 1949, " it was ... decided that there definitely would have to be schools during the winter to teach girls to play our game."[74] Apparently the winter training schools never materialized because at a June 1950 board meeting, "Mr. Allington suggested that we do whatever we can right now toward building up our tour teams as it is the only place we can get future players for our league."[75]

The summer tours were not only utilized as a player training and scouting program but also as a means of obtaining reactions to equipment and facility changes. Murray Howe, the tour advance man, made the following report to Meyerhoff regarding implementation of a new, smaller ball:

Its appearance, with the red seams and smaller size, satisfies the fans that we are playing *baseball* and the girls all think it is an improvement and are satisfied with it.[76]

... since the new ball came in, we haven't heard that old gripe about "They're using a softball." When we ran out of new [balls] for two games, and had to revert to the old ball temporarily, the old cry came back though. Just ⅜ of an inch and red seams, plus a real "crack" when the bat hits the ball, has made more friends for the game than you can imagine.[77]

During the 1950 tour, the teams experimented with 80-foot base paths and the league later adopted 85-foot base paths.[78]

Records for the 1950 summer barnstorming tour were not as complete as those for the 1949 tour, but there was evidence to suggest that it was as successful, if not more so, than the 1949 tour. The 1950 tour was concentrated in the New England states and a report submitted to Meyerhoff mid-way through the season was quite positive and optimistic.

> As you can see by the financial report following Hagerstown, the tour is doing fairly well.... With seven weeks remaining, there is a good chance of showing a profit by the end of the season.... The sponsors and crowds are well pleased with the shows ... which is what really counts.[79]

Two of the summer barnstorming tours' most prestigious exhibitions took place during the 1950 season. One was an exhibition game in Washington, D.C.'s, Griffith Stadium and the other was a three-inning exhibition game in New York's Yankee Stadium. A news release dated August 7, 1950, gave the following report of the Washington, D.C., games:

> The 2 barnstorming rookie teams of the AAGBBL made a terrific hit recently when they played two games in Griffith Stadium in Washington, D.C. ... More than 4,500 were on hand at Washington both nights and fans seeing the game for the first time were highly impressed.[80]

The AAGBBL games in Griffith Stadium were played when the Senators were out of town, and except for the thrill of playing in a beautiful, major league park, for the players, those games lacked the glamour of their exhibition in Yankee Stadium just prior to a Yankees-Phillies' (Philadelphia Athletics) game. As one might expect, playing in Yankee Stadium was a "thrill," and a "most memorable" experience for the players.

The Colleens played out of the Philadelphia dugout and the Sallies played out of the Yankee dugout. Rookie Mary Moore, from Lincoln Park, Michigan, and a member of the Sallies remembered the "*great* thrill" it was to play in Yankee Stadium:

> Walking onto that field was like in a movie. It was just so beautiful and manicured. It was—I mean words can't describe it actually.... We [met] Casey Stengel, Joe DiMaggio, Phil Rizzuto, [and] Yogi Berra. Billy Martin was there — of course there was a whole lot of them there. It was just awesome.[81]

Mary also experienced one of those "most embarrassing moments" in Yankee Stadium that day:

> We played very good ball ... and you could just hear the crowd "oooh" and "aaah." I can remember that it had been raining prior to the game. Of course they had the [infield] covered ... but the rest of the field was wet. We, of course, had our uniforms on, nice and clean for this big day. I was running to first trying to beat out a hit and peeled off of first into foul territory, not remembering that it had been raining. I slid into the mud — talk about embarrassed and all muddy, oh, my gosh! Here [I was] in a nice white, clean uniform —full of mud![82]

Chaperone Barbara Liebrich related that before the teams arrived at Yankee Stadium it was "promised that they'd move the bases to our regulation. When we got there, they said, 'No way. The bases are going to be where they are and the pitchers are going to have to pitch from 60 [feet]....' [Despite the larger diamond], we put on a good exhibition and they seemed to enjoy it, and they did broadcast the game.[83] Liebrich also shared insight into a couple of the Yankee players:

> ... I was in the New York Yankee dugout and Yogi Berra was there. He took our ball, and it was a little bit oversized compared to the regular [ball]. Yogi was hitting fungoes with

Colleens, Sallies All-American League Girl Baseballers

1950 Colleens and Sallies: Colleens *(top), left to right:* Ysora Castillo, Norma Berger, Lois Bellman, Barbara Berger, Toni Palermo, Shirley Danz, Betty Francis, Isabel Alvarez, Florence Hay, Arlene Kotil, Beverly Hatzell, Patricia Barringer (Manager/Chaperone), Joan Sindelar, Anna O'Dowd, Helen Walulik, Frances Janssen. Sallies *(bottom), left to right:* Anne Georges (Manager/Chaperone), Ginger Gascon, Doris Cook, Migdalia Perez, Lillian Shadic, Renae Youngberg, Mary Baumgartner, Sue Kidd, Kay Lionikis, Gertrude Alderfer, Barbara Payne, Barbara Liebrich, Betty Degner, Norene Arnold, Jane Moffet, Elma Steck (courtesy Northern Indiana Center for History).

our balls out to the outfielders. You ought to have seen the funny expression on their faces when the outfielders caught the ball!

Phil Rizzuto was there — he said we could use any bat that was in the bat rack of the Yankees. We had little Toni Palermo, and he told her if she wanted to, she could use his glove.[84]

Other players remembered their encounters with the major leaguers. Joan Sindelar, from Chicago, noted, "I sat next to Casey Stengel and talked to him, and we had a delightful conversation. I met all the Yankees. We were just so, so thrilled."[85] Pat Courtney, from Everett, Massachusetts, had been released from the Grand Rapids Chicks after a month of play earlier that season, but "received a letter asking if I'd like to play for the Chicago Colleens touring team. Would I ever! Boy I jumped at the chance. I joined the team in Orange, New Jersey.... We played at Yankee Stadium where I met Connie Mack which was the highlight of my brief career."[86]

Jane Moffet, an exceptional athlete from Pitman, New Jersey, had no prior organized playing experience before she joined the tour in 1949. She was in her second year of being groomed for the league through the rookie tour program. Her Yankee Stadium experience was quite unique compared to that of the other players with the touring teams, but she, too, could recall specific aspects of the event.

> Not being a Yankee fan and never having played on an organized baseball or softball team, I was not really excited or impressed that I was playing at "The Stadium." To me it was another game and another ball park.
>
> The Yankees had just completed their infield play and were returning to the dugout. I was preparing to warm up our pitcher and found myself in the dugout with several Yankee ball players. I was with Yogi, Joe D., Whitey Ford, Casey Stengel and others. Casey and Yogi were very friendly and stayed with us in the dugout talking baseball. Joe D. went directly to the locker room to receive treatment on his heel. I went out and warmed up the pitcher, and we played our three inning game. We remained for the Yankee/Phillies' contest.
>
> Little did I know then what I know now, that we both have become part of baseball history. I am now a devoted Yankee fan and very cognizant of their history and the role they have played in the game of baseball.
>
> All in the life of a rookie.[87]

Lenora Mandella, recruited from McKeesport, Pennsylvania, in 1949, and assigned to the tour in 1950 remarked:

> "We played two games at Griffith Stadium in D.C. ... [but] for me Yankee Stadium was the bigger thrill as we were only playing three innings prior to the Yankee's game. At that time we had the opportunity to meet some of the players, mainly Joe DiMaggio [and] the manager, Casey Stengel. The crowd was overwhelming, cheering ... on both the Sallies and Colleen players.[88]

Chaperones Barbara Liebrich and Pat Barringer enjoyed a special after-game experience while the players were changing and getting ready to board the bus. Barbara recalled that she and Pat had to stay in their chaperone uniforms for a post-game interview:

> Dizzy Dean was the broadcaster and they wanted to interview us on TV. When we got up there, his brother, Paul Dean was there. We were supposed to be on for ten minutes or whatever, and he said, "To heck with the Yankees," and we did the whole half hour! Dizzy Dean and Paul Dean wanted to take both Pat and I out to steak dinners, but we had these little cherubs waiting to get on the bus and go, so we had to refuse. But it was a fun time and something we'll never forget.[89]

Lenora Mandella captured the AAGBBL players' collective excitement over Yankee Stadium day as she recalled the post-game atmosphere on the bus.

> While we were on the field and bench, we had to keep it cool, as we were under the scrutiny of our managers and chaperones and had to be ladies. But that night on the bus ride to the next city, can you imagine 30 players going totally nuts! You couldn't hear yourself think! A day I will never forget as long as I live.[90]

A news release after the Yankee Stadium exhibition reported favorable fan reaction and media attention. It also illustrated how the exhibition game attracted new talent.

> The recent appearance of the AAGBL farm teams in Yankee Stadium at New York was very favorably received and the way has been paved for a second appearance of the game in the Yankee home park. In a letter to the league the Yanks said the fan reception was exceptional. "The game was carried in its entirety on television and there has been a great deal of interesting comment around the city since." There were a good many telephone

calls from young girls seeking information as to where they might contact the league and the Newsreel people asked the Yankee secretary about getting in touch with the tour for pictures. The newsreels will film the game on August 29th at Rochester, N.Y. as a result of their inquiry to the Chicago office.[91]

At the end of the 1950 season, tour supervisor Mitch Skupien reported that ten or twelve players out of 30 had developed enough skill to play in the league.[92] Skupien concluded his report of the 1950 summer tour by admonishing the League Board of Directors to develop some system of player recruitment. He informed them that he "definitely ran across some material that [was] good."

> Somebody should be working on these right away ... to keep them interested. Some of the girls I looked at I would have liked to have taken along instead of some that the league sent me but was afraid to release the girls given me for fear of making the league angry.[93]

Skupien's advice, however, went unheeded. Although the League Board of Directors talked of continuing the tour in 1951 after they had severed relationships with Meyerhoff's Management Corporation, a 1951 summer barnstorming tour did not materialize, and the problem of player procurement continued to plague the league.[94]

At the beginning of the 1952 season, league directors were again reminded "that the league must do something to ensure future talent in order to survive...."[95] Organization of a barnstorming tour patterned after Meyerhoff's 1949 and 1950 tours was initiated and implemented for the month of August 1952.[96] As far as can be determined this was the last summer barnstorming tour sponsored by the AAGBBL. The cessation of touring teams was one of the signs that signaled the beginning of the end of the league. Cessation of tours limited the league's public exposure to its immediate locales, constricted the league's player procurement potential and limited its player development program to the Rookie Rule (discussed in Chapter 7).

Post Season Exhibition Tours

In addition to spring training camps, spring exhibition tours, and summer barnstorming tours, Meyerhoff also sponsored some post-season exhibition tours. The purpose of these tours was two-fold. First, Meyerhoff wanted to promote the league internationally, and secondly, he wanted to realize a profit from it. The post-season tours, like the spring and summer tours, served as promotional programs for the league and further demonstrated the largesse of Meyerhoff's ambitions for the league. How much profit he realized is questionable. However, if he could have exchanged cash for players' love of playing, their growth and development, education through travel, deep camaraderie, and unforgettable memories, he would have been a very rich man. It is hoped that he and Philip Wrigley had some idea of the rich impact the AAGBBL had on the lives of more than 600 young women.

The first post-season exhibition tour sponsored by Meyerhoff was an outgrowth of the 1947 pre-season spring training camp in Cuba. Plans for this initial post-season tour featured an exhibition series of two AAGBBL All-Star teams and a "Latin American Feminine Basebol League" (LAFBBL) All-Star team. The Latin American countries on the agenda included Cuba, Santo Domingo, Puerto Rico, Venezuela, Panama, and Mexico, with concluding games in Texas. The question might be asked why Meyerhoff would organize tours in these countries and the answer is quite simple: As mentioned in Chapter

2, Wrigley had gum tappers in Central and South America. He also had business interests in Puerto Rico, for in Thomas Van Hyning's book about Puerto Rico's Santurce Crabbers, he noted that Pedrin Zorilla "spent his free time playing amateur baseball for the Buick and Wrigley teams."[97] If Wrigley had business offices in Puerto Rico, it is not a stretch to assume he had business offices and/or gum tappers in Cuba as well. The infrastructure of contacts and administrative personnel was already in place for Meyerhoff to utilize in the pursuit of his plan to establish an International League of Girls Baseball.

Latin American Feminine Basebol League patch (top background red, bottom blue) (courtesy Arthur Meyerhoff, 1974).

The two AAGBBL teams Meyerhoff organized to take to Cuba were named the "Atlantidas" and "Norteñas" for tour purposes, while the Cuban team was listed as the "Columbianas." Forty-four games were scheduled from September 24 through November 10, 1947.[98] The League Board of Directors authorized Meyerhoff to proceed with the tour and they agreed to loan him players to participate in it. They did not appropriate any funds to help Meyerhoff conduct the tour, but by the terms of the Management Agreement they were not bound to do so.[99] Meyerhoff's sponsorship of the summer barnstorming tours demonstrated his commitment to promoting the AAGBBL nationally; his sponsorship of the post-season tours signified his interest in promoting the AAGBBL on an international scale.

As it turned out, the three touring teams completed their nine-day exhibition series in Cuba but were unable to complete the remainder of the schedule.[100] Dorothy "Snookie" Doyle recalled that some of the AAGBBL players, besides herself, who embarked on this tour included Tiby Eisen, Kammie Kamenshek, Maddy English, Edie Perlick, Mary Reynolds, Erma Bergman, Ruby Hefner, Nancy "Hank" Warren, Dottie Schroeder, Betsy Jochum, Marge Stefani, Rita Meyer Moellering, Mary Rountree, Mildred "Mid" Earp, Betty Trezza, Connie Wisniewski, Ernestine "Teeny" Petras, and possibly Faye Dancer.[101]

Cancellation of the tour after the Cuban exhibitions may have occurred because of an attempt on the part of the Cuban promoters to swindle more funds than were in their contract. A letter from one of the players to league president Max Carey strongly suggested this possibility.

> Incidentally, Max, this might interest you. Manuel [Parra] told two of our kids that one of the reasons the October tour failed was because of a falsification on his part. It seems our boat stop after 9 days in Havana was to have been Puerto Rico. The guarantee wasn't too good from there. In order to be assured of more returns he added $8,000 to the transportation bill. The Puerto Ricans were not quite as dumb as he thought. They checked with the airlines and learned of the overcharge.[102]

At this point, the remainder of the 1947 Latin-American tour was cancelled. In a letter to players involved in the tour, and apologizing for the cancellation, Max Carey included these reflections:

> Personally, I feel that all of us have been enriched through our experiences in Cuba and it is my hope that future developments in South and Central American countries will again offer us opportunities for the building and extension of Girls Baseball.[103]

In a sense, this statement was prophetic because AAGBBL players and teams did become involved in Latin American tours in the winters of 1948 and 1949.

Just three months after the 1947 post-season Cuban tour, in mid–January 1948, a contingent of AAGBBL players joined two Latin American Feminine Basebol Teams for exhibition games in Maracaibo and Caracas, Venezuela. An average of 7,000 fans attended each of the nine games the two teams played in Venezuela. The game drawing a high attendance figure of 12,000 was a contest between one of the LAFBBL teams and a group of Venezuelan girls. The AAGBBL contingent that accompanied this tour included Mildred Earp, Dorothy Kamenshek, Senaida (Shoo Shoo) Wirth, Ruby Stephens and Mary Rountree.[104] Rountree attributed the success of the Venezuelan tour to the extensive publicity it received.

> We received the most extensive publicity I've ever seen for a baseball team. It was like the [Chicago] Herald sport page the day before the Orange Bowl. It wasn't just one day but a week before we got there and each day while we were there.[105]

Publicity, of course, was Meyerhoff's forte. Not more than a month after the 1948 January tour, several of the same AAGBBL players again joined the Cuban teams for an exhibition tour in Cuba and Puerto Rico. This time the AAGBBL contingent included Senaida Wirth, Ruby Stephens, Mildred Earp, Dorothy Kamenshek and Helen Filarski.[106] This was not to be the end of the AAGBBL's adventures in Latin America.

The apparent success of these combined AAGBBL/LAFBBL exhibitions prompted Meyerhoff to propose an "International League of Girls Baseball." It was designed as a winter league, playing in Florida in December, Venezuela in January, Puerto Rico in February and Cuba in March. Each of the teams was to bear the name of its respective country. Meyerhoff's plan was to pattern it after the All-American Girls League in the United States with the Management Corporation acting in a supervisory capacity. Each country or club was to have its own local president.[107] The financial structure of the proposed league, as outlined by Meyerhoff, was almost identical to that of the AAGBBL.

> A charge for Management of $2,500 per team, or 3 cents per admission, whichever amount is greater and which will act as both a franchise fee and the payment for Management services. All expenses of the league office and league operations to be borne prorata by each club. Management will contract for team managers, players, league administrators, such as the president and business manager at the lowest possible costs. All budgets will be approved by the presidents of the 4 clubs, and Management will be responsible for the proper disbursement of funds.[108]

This "International League of Girls' Baseball" didn't fully materialize, but there's evidence to indicate that definite steps were taken in that direction in Cuba and Puerto Rico. For instance, Isabel Alvarez remembered training at the Cuban ranch of Rafael Leon where she and other girls were well fed and taught the game of baseball as played by the All-Americans. Although only 14 at the time, she remembered the baseball training, wearing the AAGBBL–style uniforms, and pitching against AAGBBL teams during the spring of 1947.[109]

In addition, Judge Ruetz's personal AAGBBL memorabilia contains a picture from the 1947 Cuban trip that included the Judge with Max Carey, Rafael Leon, and two other gentlemen. The Cuban players' AAGBBL–style uniforms and the Judge's picture would indicate a strong connection between the Chicago office and Leon, the Cuban organizer.[110] It's quite possible that Leon was contacted and even subsidized to organize and train teams in preparation for the AAGBBL's arrival in 1947. Leon would later accompany the Cuban girls who joined the All-Americans for the Central and South American Tour in 1949. A Spanish scorecard collected from that tour listed him as "President of the Latin American Feminine Basebol League."[111] In effect, he was Max Carey's Cuban counterpart. His ties to Meyerhoff's Management Corporation can only be conjectured, but the data presented above seems to suggest that it's a reasonably valid conjecture.

Furthermore, during the 1949 Central and South American tour, to be discussed in detail in the next few pages, at least two AAGBBL–style teams existed in Puerto Rico in 1949. These teams may have been organized after the Cuban teams and, with a handful of All-Americans, may have toured Cuba and Puerto Rico in February of 1948. This theory is based on the fact that the Puerto Rican teams also wore the AAGBBL–style uniforms.

In a March 1949 Puerto Rican newspaper, discovered at the Northern Indiana Center for History as part of Annabelle Lee Harmon's memorabilia, there's a picture of a dispute at home plate. All players are wearing AAGBBL–style uniforms. The translated caption under the picture reads:

> ARGUING WITH THE UMPIRE — Lavone Paire, catcher of the North American Stars team, argues bitterly with umpire Brown while the catcher from Boricua (local nickname for Puerto Rico) joins the dispute. Paire made a great hit but didn't make it to first base because one of the Boricuas players had called time out before the play was completed. Paire asked for an explanation from the umpire who finally won the discussion.[112]

Another unidentified article, possibly from the same news magazine, shows a picture of a first basewoman in a white AAGBBL–style uniform stretching for the ball while a runner crosses the bag. Across the back of the first basewoman's uniform is the name "DENIA." The headline of the article, translated from the Spanish, reads, "Cubans and Americans Dominate the Boricuas; Play Today in Mayaguez." The last two paragraphs of the article recorded the scores: "Cubans: 9 runs, 8 hits, 1 error; *Denia* 1 run, 2 hits, 7 errors. Americans: 14 runs, 13 hits, 3 errors; *Nun* 1 run, 1 hit, 9 errors.[113] Again, the uniform is too much of an AAGBBL icon not to theorize collaboration between the AAGBBL's Chicago office and Puerto Rican girls' team organizers.

At the conclusion of the 1948 season, Meyerhoff organized another tour of Central and South America in cooperation with the Latin American Feminine Basebol League. This time, however, two AAGBBL teams were joined by some Cuban players.[114] This tour was possibly stimulated by a previous AAGBBL/Latin American tour player's observation that South America promised lucrative potential for such an experiment. Mary Rountree assessed Venezuela as a potential gold-mine for league exhibition games.

> The Venezuelan people have loads of money. The land overflows with oil instead of water. Since there are no manufacturing houses in Venezuela, and the government imposes the highest duties on imported goods of any country in the world, there is nothing for the people to do with their money. It flows like water. I would safely say that had two All American teams gone to Venezuela on a guarantee and percentage basis, they could have cleared the easiest $50,000 the League ever made.[115]

Mary's letter may have added to Meyerhoff's interest in establishing an international league. It may have at least added to his research of the possibilities. At any rate, a Central and South American tour was organized between January and March of 1949.

In a letter to players to secure recruits for the South American Tour, Max Carey wrote, "Briefly, this shapes up as the most pretentious tour undertaken by any baseball organization and has been designed to sell Girls Baseball to Latin-American countries."[116] It appears, therefore, that Meyerhoff used this tour to "show and tell" the AAGBBL to Central and South American countries in an effort to make the International League of Girls Baseball a reality.

Whatever the stimulus, two AAGBBL teams were accompanied by a contingent of Cuban girls, and they played exhibition games in Guatemala, Nicaragua, Costa Rica, Panama, Venezuela, and Puerto Rico from late January to mid–March of 1949.[117] For this tour, the two teams were labeled the "Americanas" and the "Cubanas." As the rosters in Table 9 indicate, the "Americanas" team consisted of AAGBBL players only, and the "Cubanas" team consisted of Cuban and American players. Dorothy "Kammie" Kamenshek recalled that she and Mary Rountree began as "Americanas" but were switched to the "Cubanas" to help equalize the competition.[118]

From pre-game publicity in *The Guatemala Bulletin* of Friday, January 28, 1949, it was learned that the "Cuban branch of the league has only been organized for a little over two years, but they have made surprising progress in this short time."[119] If accurate, this observation corroborates Isabel Alvarez's contention that the Cuban players began training in late 1946 or at least by January of 1947. It also indicates that the Cuban players were organized in preparation for the AAGBBL's spring training excursion to Cuba in 1947.

For the Central and South American tour in 1949, the players' transportation, hotel, and meals were guaranteed, and they were contracted for "fifty dollars a week minimum — more if guarantees and earnings warrant[ed]."[120] In addition, each series winner was promised an additional split. They were limited to 40 pounds of luggage and admonished to remember that they were representatives of America.

> Remember ... that you should appear your best in both dress and demeanor. You are good-will ambassadors for the U.S.A. in a foreign country which needs idealistic inspiration. If you accomplish that, it will make your trip to Central American lands worth while and repay the efforts of the All-American League.[121]

The AAGBBL and Cuban contingents (see Table 9) arrived in Guatemala City, Guatemala, January 26, 1949, where they spent four days. Their itinerary for other major cities included Managua, Nicaragua (9 days); San José, Costa Rica (3 days); Balboa, Panama (4 days); Caracas, Venezuela (9 days); Barquisimita, Venezuela (2 days); Maracaibo, Venezuela (4 days); and San Juan, Puerto Rico (10 days).[122] After arriving in Guatemala, their transportation between cities was mostly by two-engine prop planes. Annabelle Lee Harmon recalled the thrill of sitting in the cockpit of one of the planes.[123] Kammie Kamenshek related the concern she and others felt about the plane trips:

> [The] pilots seemed suspect to most of us. They never weighed the amount of luggage we had. [On] taking off from Caracas we had to climb fast to make the mountains, and on this occasion we had to return because of too much weight.[124]

Most games were played in major cities, like Caracas, where "the fields were in good shape and well kept," the crowds were large (three to one male), and "very enthusiastic and especially interested in the blonde players."[125] Occasionally, however, the teams ventured into the countryside. Ruth Richard, who kept a diary of the trip, was impressed by the contrast between Managua and Leon, Nicaragua. Leon was a little town some 68 miles from Managua via "The Bullet" train.

Top: Americanas y Cubanas ready for take-off: *Left, bottom to top:* Doris Tetzlaff, Irene Kotow-icz, Betty "Mo" Trezza, Dorothy "Kammie" Kamenshek. *Middle, bottom to top:* Annabelle Lee, Maggie Villa. *Right, left to right:* Mary "Windy" Reynolds, Thelma "Tiby" Eisen, Margaret "Mobile" Holgerson (courtesy Annabelle Lee Harmon). *Bottom:* South American Tour Contingent. Recognizable from far right: Rafael Leon, Mirtha Marrero, Mary Rountree, Kammie Kamenshek, Isabel Alvarez (courtesy Dorothy "Kammie" Kamenshek).

[We] rode thru [*sic*] dirt streets, saw one storied bldgs.—homes, farms, towns, and transportation [were] very crude. Farmers brought their produce in by ox-cart, women sold candies and fruits on street corners—carried everything on their heads in baskets and large pans.

There were two rooms upstairs [in the hotel] with cots in them—we used the larger one to undress in. No running water—only a pitcher, a basin, and a towel for 32 girls. Who wants to wash anyway!

Homes were very small and primitive—people slept in hammocks. Most women and children were bare-footed and poorly dressed.

Played ball in the dust bowl. Stands were small and made of hardened clay. Seats were folding chairs—roof was tin.[126]

Table 9: 1949 South American Tour Scorecard*

American Stars *(Uniforme Blanco)*			**Estrellas Cubanas** *(Uniforme Verde)*		
Nombre	*Pos.*	*Num.*	*Nombre*	*Pos.*	*Num.*
Ruby Stephens	P	18	Shirley Stownoff (Shirley Stovroff)	C	2
Irene Kotowicz	P	23	Marge Holgerson	P	16
Erline Resinger (Earlene Risinger)	P	88	Migdalia Misas	P	4
Mary Annabelle Lee	P	16	Adelina Garcia	P	12
Lavone Paire	C	7	Nancy Warren	P	21
Ruth Richard	C	66	Betty Golsmith (Betty Goldsmith)	P	20
Charlene Varnett (Charlene Barnett)	2b	12	Isabelita Alvarez (Isabel Alvarez)	P	6
Dottie Schroeder	SS	10	Mirta Marrero Mirtha Marrero	P	18
Marge Villa	Rf	6	Consuelito Forness (Consuelo Furnes) ?	C	15
Jane Stoll	Cf	13	Rita Briggs	C	19
Edith Perlicks (Edythe Perlick)	Lf	24	Zonia Vialat (Zonia Violet)	C	13
Iness Voyce (Inez Voyce)	1b	45	Betty Trezza	3b	3
Doris Fetzlaff (Doris Tetzlaff)	3b	15	Ma. E. Dominguez	SS	9
			Thelma Eisen	Cf	24
			Mary Reynolds	Lf	11
			Dottie Kamenshek	1b	22
			Isora del Castillo	3b	7
			Migdalia Perez	Rf	17
			M. Silverstein	P	(None given)
Dottie Hunter	Chaperona		Sra. Mercedes Hernandez de Leon	Chaperona	
John Rawlings	Dirigent (Mgr.) (ex–Segunda base del N.Y. Giants)		Dair Bancroft (Dave Bancroft)	Dirigent (Mgr.) (Ex–siore del equip de los Gigantes de N.Y.)	
Max Carey	Presidente del Circuito Americano de Base Ball Femenino		Sr. Rafael Leon	Presidente Liga Latinoamericana De Base Ball Femenino	

Annabelle Lee Harmon observed that some games were "played in old bull fight rings, and everything was made of adobe. [One] was just an old cattle field really, with adobe seats around it. Those adobe seats had been used for so many hundreds of years [hollows] were worn in them."[128] At one of these "cattle field" sites, Annabelle took a picture of Tiby Eisen showing off by leaning against a cow pulling a cart. The cow didn't see the humor and gave Tiby a good kick in the shin. Tiby was thankful the kick didn't break her leg.[129]

When games were played in more remote areas of the country, the food, too, was suspect. Kammie Kamenshek noted: "In one town away from the main cities I survived on catsup and bread. We felt we could trust this food. We were told to stay away from the water, so most of us drank Coca-Cola or beer."[130] Annabelle remembered drinking Orange Crush and that the food was an unending menu of "chicken and yellow rice," and sometimes the chicken was suspect:

> In one place they had the chickens on top of the hotel. We'd go up on the top of the hotel and count the chickens to see [how many they used]. This one night they gave us chicken and its [skin] was black. We thought, oh, no, was it a buzzard or a crow or what. We went up [on the roof] and counted the chickens, and yeah, they were all there.
>
> A few years ago, I went to a Chinese market, and the chickens were all black. Their skin was black.[131]

On this point, Annabelle agreed that the black-skinned chickens the players were fed in South America may have been a specialty, but at the time, all the players were afraid they were being served something else!

Tiby Eisen posing with a cart cow in a small Nicaraguan town (courtesy Annabelle Lee Harmon).

Even in the cities, the hotels "were below American standards for the time. Showers were central and sometimes the restrooms were for both male and female."[132] Annabelle Lee Harmon recounted the scene from a hotel window with a view of a lake and a river. "You could see the women out there washing their clothes, pounding them on rocks and laying them on bushes [to dry]."[133] The whole experience was an education in cultural differences for these young American women.

If ground level was sometimes oppressive, flying from city to city, aside from being nerve-wracking, offered sights of grandeur.

> We flew above mtns. ranging up to ... 11,000 feet that surround the city of San José....
> [We] also saw an active volcano.
> [We] flew over the Columbia River, then almost directly east over a solid blanket of clouds—saw a beautiful range of mountains jutting above the clouds topped with snow. The sun was very bright and made everything more beautiful.[134]

As would be expected of a Meyerhoff enterprise, promotion and publicity were prevalent wherever the teams played. The Panama *Star & Herald* reported the presence of Mr. Aurelio H. Zeledon, advance agent for the baseball girls.[135] He, of course, was responsible for submitting pictures and texts to newspapers for pre-game publicity, distributing large posters for prominent businesses to display, and arranging transportation to parade the players through town upon their arrival.[136] Ruth Richard noted that the players paraded through Guatemala City in jeeps, and in San José, Costa Rica, they rode through "the city with horns blaring and pamphlets flying." Radio broadcasts were also utilized to publicize games.[137]

Then, of course, there were those excursions that left indelible marks on impressionable young women. In Managua, Nicaragua, February 1, 1949, there was the unforgettable evening spent with General Somoza and the president of Nicaragua at the president's palace. Kammie and Tiby were impressed that the Nicaraguan general and president "were there to greet us before we played."[138] And, as Kammie Kamenshek explained and Tiby Eisen confirmed:

> We were invited to the president's castle for an evening of feast, dance, and entertainment. We all attended and the president was having such a good time that no one was allowed to leave. Our managers, Johnny Rawlings and Max Carey wanted us to leave but we were not allowed. This was one time we broke curfew and could not be fined. We all laugh about this. We danced all night—the rumba and other Latin American dances. [A] good time [was] had by all except our managers![139]

Tiby remembered that the president's son was "taken" with the very blonde Dottie Schroeder, that General Somoza—"the first Somoza" [Anastacio Somoza] ... introduced the president to us, but ... Somoza sat in the big chair and the president stood behind him."[140] She didn't fully understand the significance of the Nicaraguan dictator/puppet president relationship at the time, but she "loved that Latin music," and being a blonde who loved to dance, she had lots of young men approach her and invite her in Spanish and with hand signals to "twirl around."[141] Annabelle never forgot that upon leaving the banquet, Somoza's son was "standing in the doorway there, shaking my hand, and he took my hand and said, 'If there's anything I can do *to* you, let me know.'"[142]

Not only did General Somoza dine with and entertain the players, but the front page of *La Nueva Prensa* pictured him throwing the first ball to begin a game between "los equipos cubano y norteamericano." The translated picture caption read: "General Anastasio Somoza, Minister of Defense, threw the first ball in the game between the Cuban and North American teams day before yesterday afternoon."[143] Another picture caption on the same page noted: "Dori Schroeder connects for a tremendous hit for the North Americans during the game day before yesterday."

A news release from the AAGBBL office in Chicago on February 10, 1949, announced and perhaps embellished General Somoza's reaction to the exhibition games in his country:

> America's newest good-will ambassadors to the Latin Americas, the All-American Girls Baseball teams currently on tour with their president Max Carey, continue to spread the fame of girls' baseball and so well have they done their job that the Nicaraguan Minister of War, General Simosa [sic], has publicly stated that he intends to import a Yankee manager to teach the young women of his country how to play this new game.
>
> The Nicaraguan Dictator witnessed all the games the All-Americans played in his country and he openly admitted his pleasure. Newspaper accounts of his reaction put him on record as one of the game's newest and most enthusiastic fans.[144]

Another memorable excursion for the players during this tour was a visit to the Panama Canal. Ruth Richard documented that the teams arrived in Balboa, Panama, on February 10, that they were housed in an officers' barracks, and that they played ball at several G.I. camps on the 11th. By the 12th, they were pretty tired, but their schedule was full.

> Rode 50 miles today to Cristobal — played in Mt. Hope Stadium. Cubans vs. a [team] of Negroes for five innings then our two teams. After the game we were dead tired but were ushered off to see one of the locks in the Panama Canal. It all turned out to be very interesting but scientifically complicated. We saw a Swedish freighter go thru [sic] and a U.S. transport that was taking a group of G.I.'s to Japan. Back to the barracks, supper and another ball game. Mickey [Migdalia Perez] hurled for the Cubans and Beans [Earlene Risinger] for the Americans. Game was good and so was the crowd.[145]

The visit to the canal was especially memorable for Tiby Eisen who was "always interested in electronics."

> I remember [the Panama Canal trip] well because I was talking to a guy, ... watching him maneuver things to open the canal and so on. He said, "Come on, I'll let you press the button." "Really!" [I said.] I pressed that button and the locks started to work and I didn't wash my hands for a week! I never forgot that! I came home and bragged about that![146]

In Costa Rica, the All-Americans and Cubans were honored when the U.S. Ambassador and his wife attended their game played at the National Futbol (Soccer) Stadium on March 8, 1949. An article on the sports page of a San José, Costa Rica, newspaper reported the game in superlative terms (not uncommon for Latin American sports writers according to Guatemalan-born translator Monica Rivera):

> ... The game was formidable, and many teams here would wish to do the great plays, without poses or acting, that the Cubans and North Americans displayed. From the first turn at bat until the last second, the game was played with mastery and the calm dignity of the best players, and the public gave, play by play, deserved enthusiastic applause, and the teams responded with faster plays each time showing courage and passion in every play.
>
> Both teams were equally skilled, which increased the color of their play. They committed hardly any errors and the few that occurred took nothing away from the hard work these young players displayed throughout the entire spectacular performance.

> ... This great duel ended in the triumph of the Cubans by the score of 3 to 1. It was a just reflection of the excellent job of the fielders, particularly Cuban Marrero, right fielder, who was the best of the two teams.[147]

On March 9, both teams were invited by the International Base-Ball School in Costa Rica to a "sumptuous dance given in honor of the distinguished Cuban and American [girl] athletes that are visiting us." The rest of the invitation read, "This social event will occur Wednesday, February 9, 1949, at 9 P.M. in the spacious ballroom of the San José Golf Club. Casual Dress."

Price: Gentlemen 8.00   Ladies 2.00   Murrillo Orchestra

In Maracaibo, Venezuela, sportswriter Angel E. Machado, focused on interviewing Johnny Rawlings who "was sensational in the infield of the Big Leagues." Johnny's final comment, as recorded in this article, reflected Meyerhoff's objective for an international league: "I hope," he said in closing, "that next year we find one or two clubs here that we can play against and have good international competition."[148]

For those who played, the Central and South American tour was a unique opportunity they were thrilled to experience. As Kammie and Tiby pointed out, how many women from the United States had the opportunity to travel to Central and South America in the late 1940s?[149]

The 1949 Central and South American tour was to have included Santo Domingo in the Dominican Republic and Cuba, but it was unclear whether or not games were actually played in those countries.[150] It was painfully clear that Puerto Rico, the Dominican Republic, and Cuba did not provide the guarantees on which the tour was predicated.[151]

Although the "International League of Girls' Baseball" did not fully materialize, the games in Cuba in '47 and Central and South America in 1948 and 1949 certainly illustrated the scope of Meyerhoff's aspirations for the promotion of girls' baseball. It also demonstrated the extent to which he pursued the project he began in 1945 with just six teams. Who knows how many girls in North and South America today would love to see the emergence of a champion of girls baseball with the imagination, resources and commitment of Philip Wrigley and Arthur Meyerhoff combined!

Promotional Loss and League/Management Relations

According to AAGBBL President Max Carey, the financial failure of the 1949 Latin American Tour was caused by failure of the Latin Americans to carry out their contracts.[152] One result of the tour's failure was that the players involved in the tour received only half of the salary they had been guaranteed. Some of the players apparently thought they were being taken advantage of because they pressed the issue until the other half of their salaries were paid.[153] This incident strained already weakened ties between Meyerhoff's Management Corporation and the League Board of Directors.

It should be remembered that 1948 was a financially debilitating year for the AAGBBL. In addition, the league experienced a player raid conflict with the professional softball league in Chicago during the 1949 and 1950 seasons. The Latin American tour players, who for the most part were veteran star AAGBBL players, took advantage of the conflict between the two leagues and threatened to jump to the Chicago league in 1950 if not paid the balance of their salaries for the 1949 Latin American Tour.[154] When these players demanded the balance of their salaries, Meyerhoff, maintaining that the tour failure was not his fault, agreed to pay half of what was still owed them, a total of $2,362.48. The

Publicity poster used in Puerto Rico (courtesy Northern Indiana Center for History).

League Board of Directors were then pressured into paying the remaining $2,362.48 out of the league treasury.[155] This circumstance didn't please league directors, especially at a time when they were already badly in debt and money was tight.

Harold Dailey, president of the South Bend team, was very critical of this incident. He expressed a strong suspicion that "Meyerhoff welched on the whole deal and then slipped out of the money owed as wages."[156] Dailey reported further that "all during the latter part of the season of 1949 much discussion was batted around about the cost of Management and the thought was to get rid of it."[157] (It should be pointed out that Dailey's personal notes and letters throughout the Management Corporation Period implied a personal dislike for Meyerhoff and for the Management structure.) Some of the other team presidents, however, were not as committed to disassociating with Meyerhoff at that time as Dailey. He conceded that at "a Board Meeting the board was divided on the thing and the money to buy [Meyerhoff] out was not forthcoming."[158]

Judge Edward Ruetz, president of the Kenosha Comets, was one of those who didn't think the time was right to dissolve the league's contract with Meyerhoff. The reasons he set forth for continuing the League-Management relationship were compelling: (1) the member clubs were not financially able to buy out their contract with Management; (2) the member clubs didn't have the knowledge or resources to adequately procure and train new players; (3) the member clubs were not organized or financially able to procure new franchises for those that were failing — this had always been Management's responsibility; and (4) the member clubs should adhere to the contract they made with Management and this contract was not scheduled to expire until 1951. Ruetz rested his argument against dissolving the League-Management agreement largely on the important role Management played in procuring and training new players and promoting the AAGBBL.

> I think this last summer the Management Corporation did more to develop girls to our type of ball than ever before. Thirty girls in a [stationary training camp — proposed by the anti–Management faction —] for the season playing ball to an empty park would not produce the experience and the ability that those same 30 girls would receive under the exhibition tour that Meyerhoff sponsored this last season. In addition, the exhibition tour gave hundreds of girls the opportunity, for the time, to see the type of game we are playing in our league and its introduction in those many communities will probably start many girls playing our type of ball, which could not be accomplished under a program that places the girls in a stationary camp.
>
> [We must not overlook] the fact that we introduced a new type of game and that one cannot develop girls as fast as though we were playing a game that had been standard for years.[159]

In the end, however, Ruetz's rationale succumbed to Dailey's opinion among league board members.

Those league directors who began to be disgruntled with Meyerhoff's Management Corporation in 1948 and 1949 failed to appreciate that a considerable portion of any profits he realized from franchise fees and his percentage of gate receipts were pumped back into promotional and training programs such as the summer and post-season tours. Meyerhoff became the scapegoat for the league's financial troubles, but he could not have proceeded with these programs without the majority consent of the League Board of Directors.

Meyerhoff, like Wrigley before him, sought every opportunity to promote the

AAGBBL, not only through increased exposure in the mass media, but also through extensive spring training camps, spring exhibition tours, summer barnstorming tours and post-season tours. These promotional efforts were aimed at selling the AAGBBL game and logically contributed to the growth in popularity the league experienced in the immediate postwar years. Attendance at league games, for instance, rose steadily from 450,313 in 1945 to 910,747 in 1948. The decline began in 1949 when attendance dropped to 585,813 and it continued to decline thereafter.[160] The financial losses Meyerhoff incurred through his promotional programs were risks he took in the interest of the league's long-term future. He believed it was necessary to spend money to make money and he also believed the league would eventually become a profitable venture.[161] Unfortunately, he could not convince the league directors of the AAGBBL's long-term potential. They needed immediate returns. In the face of rising costs and diminished returns, to their own businesses as well as to the AAGBBL, they finally viewed the league's strong centralized government, including its strong centralized publicity and promotional programs, as an insupportable drain on their bank accounts.

It is suspected that Management's profit-based structure contrasted with the non-profit nature of local team organizations, exacerbated the conflict between Meyerhoff and the League Board of Directors. If this were the case, given human nature, it would not seem illogical to conclude that, as budget cutting became necessary, among the first items to be deleted were those that characterized Management — centralized league publicity and promotion. Whether these were the underlying motives or not, at the end of the 1948 season, the extensive spring training and exhibition tours were discontinued, and the post-season tours were cancelled after the 1949 South American tour. The summer barnstorming tour, which Meyerhoff organized and maintained at his own expense in 1949 and 1950, was the last vestige of a centralized league publicity and promotional campaign. This is not to say that publicity and promotion were solely responsible for the league's success, but that they contributed significantly to it. Where would today's major league baseball be without its regular publicity and promotional gimmicks?

League directors could not directly measure the effect Meyerhoff's promotional programs had on local attendance or on player procurement and training, so they considered them expendable items when it came to cutting the budget. The long-term value of advertising required individuals such as Wrigley and Meyerhoff to appreciate that anyone could sponsor a girls' baseball league, but that "the trick was to sell it."

6

Independent Team Owners, 1951–1954

Following the dissolution of the League-Management agreement, league directors immediately reorganized under the rubric of the American Girls Baseball League (AGBL).[1] Popularly, however, the league continued to be identified as the All-American Girls Baseball League (AAGBBL). The general framework of the American Girls Baseball League differed in two important respects from that of the Management Corporation. A commissioner was instituted to conduct league business instead of Management, and all team personnel were placed under team rather than league control (Figure 5). These changes affected other aspects of league structure.

League Administrative Personnel, 1951–1954

Under the administration of Independent Team Owners, the commissioner served as the only paid officer in league administration. Under the Trustee and Management Administrations, the league subsidized the president, a secretary, and a publicity agent. The commissioner basically fulfilled the responsibilities of a league business manager and voted during league board meetings only in the event of a tie. Essentially, he performed the same responsibilities as those of the president under the Trustee and Management structures.[2]

Fred Leo, league president during the 1950 season, was elected as the first commissioner under the new structure.[3] When Fred Leo became league commissioner in 1951, Kenosha Municipal Court Judge Edward J. Ruetz ascended to the position of league president.

Judge Ruetz was a natural choice for league president as his vibrant association with the AAGBBL had begun before day one of the league's existence. His son, Edward J. Ruetz, Jr., remembered:

> It would have been nigh on to impossible to find a bigger sports fan in Kenosha than my dad. In his college days, he played industrial league baseball for a Racine tire manufacturing company team. He counted sports figures among his friends and regularly attended gatherings of present and former sports stars in Chicago and Milwaukee. He was the pitcher for the Kenosha County Courthouse softball team, which performed weekly on the diamonds of Lincoln Park in one of the city leagues. "Packer Backer" is a term that had to be invented to describe such complete and unadulterated fans of the Green Bay Packers as dad. His long-standing, good-natured feud with Doc Pechous, the Chicago Bear's volunteer training camp physician and a neighbor, over which was the better team was a legend in its own time. Long after he had retired from the Municipal Court Bench,

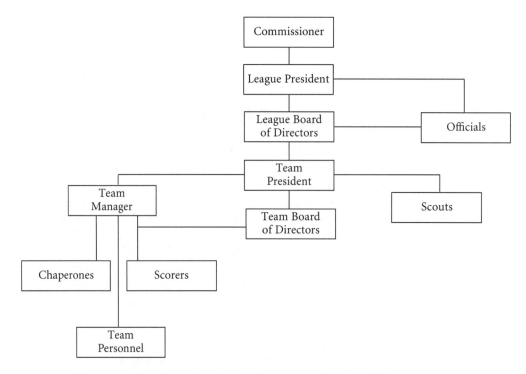

Figure 5: The Organizational Structure of the AGBL, 1951–1954

he told me of having a strange dream one night in which he was on his bench granting Sainthood to the Packer's offensive line. When he wasn't in the stands for games, he was listening on the radio — baseball, football, basketball, hockey — whatever contest could be found on the dial — day or night and sometimes well into the night.

It is not strange then, that when Phil Wrigley, owner of the Chicago Cubs baseball team was looking for someone in Kenosha to join him in a very unusual venture, he sent his advertising agency head, Art Meyerhoff, to see dad. Meyerhoff owned a gentlemen's farm in Kenosha County, escaping from the big city to this retreat on week-ends and he knew the territory. Calling at Dad's office in the court house, Meyerhoff explained that the war (1942) threatened to drain the major leagues of their players. If this should happen, Wrigley, and Branch Rickey, wanted to establish a league of women baseball players to move into the major league parks. Cities around Chicago would become the places where this league would be developed. Racine, Kenosha, Rockford, Illinois and South Bend, Indiana had been selected to initiate this venture. Would the Judge, Meyerhoff asked, be interested in heading up the Kenosha baseball club —finding the investors and establishing the organization? Is the Pope Catholic? Does the sun rise in the east and set in the west? You betcha he would, and with great relish![4]

From that first visit with Arthur Meyerhoff, Judge Ruetz remained an involved supporter and fan of the AAGBBL. He served as president of the Kenosha team from 1944 to 1951 and was elected chairman of the league's executive committee organized in 1947 to handle emergency situations. He served as chairman of the executive committee until he was elected league president in 1951, when Fred Leo was elevated to the position of league commissioner.[5] When Leo resigned at the end of the 1951 season, Ruetz naturally ascended to the position of league commissioner even though Kenosha did not field a team in 1952. However, Ruetz stipulated that he would act as commissioner under the condition that he would not have to assume any administrative duties, and Fort Wayne Daisies president Harold Van Orman became the last league president.[6] At this point, some reshuffling of titles and responsibilities was done by the league board to further economize. One of the board members, Earle E. McCammon, league representative from Kalamazoo, was hired by the board to assume league administrative duties at a savings of $4200.[7] McCammon enlisted his wife's clerical assistance at "substantial savings to the league."[8] After the 1952 season, Reutz bowed out of the commissioner's job and McCammon's title was changed at that time to commissioner and general manager.[9] He served in that capacity through 1954, the last season of league play.

Judge Ruetz: President, Kenosha Comets, 1944–1951; Chairman, League Executive Board, 1947–1950; AGBL President, 1951; AGBL Commissioner, 1952 (courtesy Jnell Ruetz).

Commissioner McCammon was distinguished as the originator and head of Kalamazoo's Economy Homes, Inc. He, like most other team presidents, was a sports enthusiast as well as a successful businessman. His enthusiasm for sports began in his youth, evidenced by his record for playing intercollegiate football, basketball, and baseball at Illinois State Normal School in Bloomington.[10] McCammon's first involvement with sports promotion began with his purchase of Kalamazoo's Lucky Strike Bowling Alley, "which he later sold to start Economy Homes, Inc...."[11] McCammon continued supporting sports participation through Economy Homes which sponsored softball, bowling, and basketball teams. When Kalamazoo was considered for an AAGBBL franchise in 1950, McCammon emerged as the primary supporter for the project.

> McCammon not only spent days and days in putting over the deal but he ... made trips to most other league cities and to league meetings at Chicago to see that Kalamazoo's interests were protected and ... given a sound squad that could hold its own in league play.[12]

Earle McCammon: President, Kalamazoo Lassies, 1950–1954; AGBL General Manager 1952; AGBL Commissioner, 1953, 1954 (reproduced from the original held by the Department of Special Collections of the University Libraries of Notre Dame).

1952 Kalamazoo Lassies: *Left to right, front:* Jean Lovell, Doris Sams, Carrie Hunt (Bat Girl), Kay Blumetta, Gloria Cordes, Jenny Romatowski. *Middle:* Fern Shollenberger, Dottie Naum, Betty Francis, Mary Carey, Bonnie Baker, Jean Marlowe. *Back:* Agnes Allen, Elaine Roth, Doris Cook, Ruth Williams, Dolly Pearson, June Peppas, Mitch Skupien (Manager) (reproduced from the original held by the Department of Special Collections of the University Libraries of Notre Dame).

The significance of McCammon's enthusiasm for the AAGBBL was reflected in his election to the position of business manager in 1951, after only one year's association with the league. His subsequent election to the commissioner and general manager position in 1952 was further testimony to his commitment to the league and to the quality of his services.

Changes and Characteristics of the Independent Team Owners' Administration

The basic difference between Independent Team Owners and the Trustee and Management Administrations rested in placing all playing and management personnel under the control of each individual team rather than under the control of a central league office.[13] Other major changes inaugurated under Independent Team Owners included:

1. Elimination of a centralized scouting program
2. Elimination of the player allocation procedure and institution of a draft procedure for placement of new players

3. Establishment of a monthly salary limit per team
4. Establishment of minimum and maximum player limits
5. A requirement that individual clubs assume responsibility for hiring and paying official scorers
6. A prohibition against hiring female managers (to be discussed in Chapter 9)

The Independent Team Owners' Administration was characterized by continual financial retrenchments, and a swinging of the administrative pendulum from centralized to decentralized and back to centralized government. Major items deleted from the league budget in 1951 included scouting expenses, tickets, and a league secretary's salary.[14] Each team assumed its own scouting and ticket expenses as well as responsibility for all personnel salaries, including those of the manager, chaperone(s), and players. These had all been provided by the central league office under the Trustees and Management.

Prior to 1952, the only salary limit set by the league was a player salary limit of $100 per week.[15] Not all players earned the $100 limit, but it was supposedly the top salary outstanding veterans could earn. However, teams occasionally fudged on the $100 limit to retain better players. Dorothy "Kammie" Kamenshek, for instance, remembered that her top salary was $125 per week.[16] A letter from Rockford business manager Carl Glans to inform Dorothy "Snookie" Doyle of her salary for 1948 explained that the league president had to be consulted before a player's salary could be raised above the salary limit. Snookie was informed: "There [were] not many who were raised above the salary limit, but we are happy to say that you were one of the two from our club whose salary was raised, over the salary limit." A "P.S." at the end of the letter advised, "Reference to the salary, keep that confidential."[17] The implication here was that team administrators didn't want the word spread that they could lobby for salaries above the published limit even though they were willing to do so to retain key players.

At the beginning of the 1952 season, the league board enacted a new team player limit of 16 or 17 as well as a new team salary limit. The salary limit for 16 players was set at $5400 per month and for 17 players it was set at $5700 per month.[18] Under this system, individual player salaries continued to differ, but a team was limited to expending not more than $5700 for all of its players' salaries. At the beginning of the 1954 season, the player salary limit was reduced to $4400 per month with an individual player salary limit of $400 per month, $115 of which was designated as expense money.[19] Effectively, substantial cuts in player salaries began in 1952, and by 1954 veteran players' salaries were cut from a potential $500 per month to $285 per month after expenses.

By 1952, some of the older players were aware that the league's financial stability was in jeopardy, and they opted to seek "real jobs," a college education, or play in the Chicago league rather than return to the AAGBBL. Joyce Hill Westerman, who began playing in the league in 1945, noted that by 1952 "things weren't looking too good in the league, and there were a few times when our salaries were held up for a week or two, and I thought, well, I think it's time to stay home."[20] Jo Lenard, who began playing in 1944, recalled that at the end of the 1953 season, the "league was sort of going down and I quit ... and went to college."[21] Jean "Buckets" Buckley, who joined Kenosha as a rookie in 1950, noted that when Kenosha folded at the end of the 1951 season, "you could feel the deterioration of the league ... it was going downhill."[22] She also observed that between the veterans and the rookies "there was some jealousy because we were the young crowd. We were displacing the veterans. They were cutting all the veterans and replacing them with rookies, and so they got us for half the salary of the veterans."[23] Whether team boards actually cut veterans to reduce budgets is open to conjecture. They may have offered them substantially lower salaries resulting in the players' decisions to play somewhere else, or to pursue a career, or to become a full-time wife and mother.

The primary aspect in which Independent Team Owners demonstrated a tendency to shift from decentralized back to centralized government occurred in the distribution of player talent. Player distribution during Trustee and Management administrations was based on an allocation system. Teams retained a core of eight to ten players each year and the remaining players were placed in a collective pool and assigned to teams by a player allocation committee composed of team presidents and managers. This procedure was determined to be the best method for maintaining a competitive balance within the league.[24] The player allocation procedure nonetheless became a thorn in the side of team boards of directors who felt their teams suffered discrimination through the allocation process.

When Independent Team Owners assumed control in 1951, the allocation system was replaced by a draft system. Teams retained as many players as they desired each year and any new acquisitions were obtained via a player draft.[25] At the beginning of 1954, however, dissatisfaction with the draft system led to the establishment of a combination pool-draft procedure for distributing player talent. Under this system, teams maintained a core of eight players and placed the rest in a pool, but the distribution of the pooled players took the form of a draft rather than an allocation. That is, the team in last place during the preceding season had the first choice of the pooled players; the team second to last, the next choice and so on.[26]

Neither the draft system nor the pool-draft experiment accomplished the desired end of equalizing team talent. On May 16, 1954, the league board voted to re-establish a balancing or allocation committee which would redistribute the pooled players in an attempt to equalize team talent once again. Thus, the Independent Team Owners reverted to the centralized procedure of player distribution utilized under the Trustee and Management administrations. All board members were admonished to abide by the decision of the new balancing committee (which had been a major bone of contention during Management's administration) because league survival depended on it. Board members were reminded that "...this year the league cannot afford to have any team so far behind in the standings by the middle of the season that it will no longer draw a crowd and consequently fail as Muskegon did last year [1953]."[27]

The Independent Team Owners' Administration was also characterized by a steady shrinkage in the number of league teams. The eight teams that started with Independent Team Owners in 1951 (South Bend, Rockford, Kenosha, Grand Rapids, Fort Wayne, Kalamazoo, Peoria and Battle Creek Belles) decreased to six teams in 1952 and 1953 (South Bend, Rockford, Grand Rapids, Fort Wayne, Kalamazoo, and Battle Creek '52/Muskegon Belles '53) and fell to five teams in 1954 (South Bend, Rockford, Grand Rapids, Fort Wayne, and Kalamazoo). About two-thirds through the 1953 season the Muskegon franchise failed and was carried as a traveling club by the rest of the league for the remainder of the season.[28] This action, as it had in the past, contributed to enlarged deficits for all remaining teams.

Losses incurred during the 1953 season resulted in the League Board of Directors decision to vote to suspend play as of March 1, 1954:

THE AMERICAN GIRLS BASEBALL LEAGUE SHALL SUSPEND OPERATION FOR 1954 AS OF MARCH 1, 1954, WITH EACH CLUB RETAINING FRANCHISES AND PLAYERS SHOWN BY CURRENT ROSTERS.[29]

Although losses incurred during the 1953 season were the immediate cause for this decision, it was clear that the 1953 season losses were only a part of a cumulative series of events that persuaded league directors to vote for suspension of play in January 1954.

> After a good deal of informal discussion with ideas brought out from each representative, a decision was finally made in the light of facts as appeared, that because of consistent losses by all clubs in the last few years, even with league overhead cut drastically, and a tapering off of attendance in general due to TV and other amusement competition, that league operations would be suspended for the year 1954, unless something would happen before March first to make it appear feasible for all clubs (6) to look forward to operation throughout the season without failure of any club before completion of the season.[30]

In addition, the recession of the mid–1950s had hit league cities, affecting employment, which in turn affected attendance at entertainment spectacles. The South Bend Directors' report to the League Board of Directors at the end of February 1954 drew attention to this situation.

> South Bend reported an all-out effort had been made to raise money in their town, but with the Studebaker plant entirely down, and South Bend employment situation as it is and [since it] had been recently declared a "distress area" along with Battle Creek, Michigan, it had proven impossible to raise enough money to make a start on plans for 1954.[31]

Despite this dismal picture, league directors were loathe to suspend operations, and at the February board meeting they voted to extend the deadline date for suspension from March 1 to March 20, 1954.[32] On April 10, 1954, league directors voted to adopt a five-team plan for league operations. The five cities to sponsor AAGBBL teams during 1954, the last season of play, included South Bend, Rockford, Grand Rapids, Fort Wayne, and Kalamazoo.[33]

There was no clear indication why league directors' decided to continue play during the 1954 season. One factor may have been avid lobbying on the part of fan clubs, which were active in all league cities. In Rockford, at least, the fan club was credited with ensuring that city's franchise in the league for the 1954 season.

> A lot of credit must be given to the Peaches Fans' Association for carrying the ball in reorganizing the club and in forming the new corporate board of directors. Praises are due many, many persons—including association prexy Dottie Kamenshek—in this civic effort, but special notice must be given to Joye Newton, the gal who spearheaded the drive which put over the deal.[34]

There seemed to be enough community support left for AAGBBL teams to make directors reluctant to give up on it just yet. In addition, players and ex-players residing in league cities were doing their own lobbying to keep the league active.

The most notable change inaugurated in the game during the administration of Independent Team Owner was the adoption of the regulation nine-inch baseball and extension of the base paths first from 72 feet, to 75 feet, and then to 85 feet, and the extension of the pitching distance from 55 feet to 56 feet, and finally to 60 feet. The final revision of equipment and facility changes took place on July 1, 1954, in an attempt to stimulate lagging attendance. Although not initiated until July, adoption of the nine-inch ball was first considered at a league board meeting held May 2, 1954.

Mr. Taylor [Grand Rapids] introduced a new baseball, which was made by Wilson Brothers in the same size and weight as the balls used in major league baseball. He asked the group to give some consideration to the idea of adopting this ball for our game, with the result of added interest to the game, elimination of some errors and adding to the year home-run total. Mr. Taylor thought, too, that a smaller ball should be easier for the girls to handle than the larger one now used in our league.[35]

No decision to change to the nine-inch ball was reached until the league directors' June 10, 1954, meeting. By that time, all teams had had the opportunity to experiment with the smaller ball and the reaction was unanimously favorable for its adoption:

> THE AMERICAN GIRLS LEAGUE HEREBY ADOPTS THE NINE-INCH REGULATION BASE BALL FOR LEAGUE PLAY, WITH BASES TO BE SET AT 85 FEET, THE PITCHER'S BOX AT 60 FEET (USING 59 FEET TO START).[36]

Adoption of the nine-inch ball for league play was delayed until July 1, so the surplus of ten inch balls on hand could be used up.[37]

Advantages and Disadvantages of the Independent Team Owners' Administration

The major advantages of the Independent Team Owners' Administration were minimization of intra-league personnel conflicts and reduction of league and team deficits. The major intra-league personnel conflicts during Management's administration of the league had primarily involved disagreements related to player allocation procedures. Suspicions were articulated that certain team presidents, to ensure their team would be the strongest, manipulated members of the allocation committee. Harold T. Dailey, a director for the South Bend team, complained that 1950 had been a bad year for his team,

Ad announcing implementation of the major league 9" ball featuring Betty Wagoner (reprinted with permission of the *South Bend Tribune*, South Bend, Indiana).

and noted that besides bad attendance, "We were taken for a ride after Ruetz and Black got Rockford lined up by not having to give up any players during the year."[38] This was one of frequent criticisms of the allocation system during Management's tenure, especially since the allocation committee was empowered to switch players from team to team throughout the season to keep competition balanced. Team directors and fans objected to this procedure.[39] Players undoubtedly resented the procedure also. After the institution of Independent Team Owners in 1951, and the adoption of the draft system, intraleague squabbles were not mentioned as frequently or as blatantly in League Board Meeting Minutes or in Dailey's personal notes as they had been during Management's administration.

Complete financial statements were not available for the Independent Team Owners' administration of league affairs, but a few figures indicate that substantial savings were realized during that time. For instance, in 1951, the first year under Independent Team Owners, the league budget was established at $28,668 as opposed to $43,595 in 1950, the last year of Management's reign.[40] Most of these reductions resulted from the deletion of league office personnel, scouting, and promotional functions.

Unfortunately, individual team deficits continued to total significant amounts. At the end of the 1953 season, losses for five teams in the league totaled approximately $44,500 or $8,900 per team.[41] Compared to the per team deficit of $9,300 in 1948 and $11,250 in 1949, the 1953 reduction of per team losses was not that substantial.

The major disadvantage of the Independent Team Owners' Administration was the decentralization of scouting and player procurement programs. Fred Leo anticipated this problem when the league reorganized at the end of the 1950 season. In a news interview he commented on the potential player-procurement problems likely to arise under the Independent Team Owners' Administration.

> My one concern is the ability of the individual clubs to come up with qualified player talent since there are bound to be inequalities in the abilities of individual clubs to cope with those most successful.... Discovery of capable replacements will always be our number one problem, just as it is in any sport. We're handicapped being the only [women's] league in the country playing real baseball, and the length of time necessary to make baseball players is costly and time consuming.[42]

Player procurement did constitute a major problem for teams operating under the guidance of Independent Team Owners. The only programs implemented to alleviate player shortages during this period consisted of a rookie tour in August of 1952[43] and retention of the Rookie Rule inaugurated in 1950.

The Rookie Rule, instituted in the spring of 1950, stipulated that each club had to have a rookie in the game at all times.[44] Before the season opened, this rule was modified to read that each team must have a rookie in each game at all times "on defense." This allowed teams to maintain a strong veteran batting line-up.[45] (The American League's Designated Pinch Hitter isn't as new a concept as some might think!) A rookie was defined as a player who had played fewer than five months or had participated in less than 50 games in the league. Pitchers were classed as rookies if they had pitched less than 50 innings.[46] Fourteen reasons were listed to justify adoption of the Rookie Rule and one-third of them pertained to player development.

1. Because we do not have sufficient players to complete and balance eight clubs.
2. For the development of new players.

...

7. The development of the new players will be equally distributed among all teams, and every club will share in the development of new players.

8. It places the responsibility of the development of the players on each club and manager.

...

13. It is the most direct and economical plan the league has for the development of new players.[47]

This rationale for the Rookie Rule was offered the last year of Management's Administration when Meyerhoff was sponsoring a barnstorming tour composed of two rookie teams that played throughout the east and south during the entire summer. These touring players were also on call to the league.

In pre-season board meetings in 1952, the Rookie Rule was re-examined because some team directors wanted to abolish it. The league had sponsored no summer tour in 1951, the first year of the Independent Team Owners, and no plans had yet been formulated for a 1952 summer tour. Bill Allington, veteran league manager, who had helped formulate the Rookie Rule, expressed the sentiments of those on the board who were in favor of retaining the rule. The Rookie Rule, he pointed out,

> ... was not a perfect solution to the problem of securing new talent for the league, still ... it was the only way to insure some source of obtaining new players with the present situation which did not allow for touring teams or other means of developing or discovering talent.[48]

Allington's observation appeared to be the strongest argument for retaining the rule.

An extension of the Rookie Rule was instituted in 1953 in an attempt to equalize team strength as well as to train new players. The new rule, which took effect June 1, 1953, stipulated that first division clubs must put two rookies in their line-up as opposed to one for second division teams.[49] This modification apparently didn't solve the problem either because those who opposed the rule were successful in having it abolished before the beginning of the 1954 season.[50] No alternative player procurement plan was proposed when the Rookie Rule was deleted, but none may have seemed necessary. The league decreased from six to five teams in 1954, resulting in a temporary player surplus.

Fort Wayne's Harold Van Orman, the AAGBBL's last president, 1952–1954 (courtesy Arthur Meyerhoff, 1974).

Comparison of the Three League Structures

An evaluation of the separate league administrations reveals that each had its strengths and weaknesses. The almost completely centralized governance of the league during the Trustee Administration (1943–1944) was essential for launching league operations in the relatively short period of time available between the fall of 1942 and the spring of 1943. The establishment of the league as a non-profit organization with high standards for the game and its personnel contributed to its public acceptance in the midst of the social upheaval occasioned by World War II. In addition, Wrigley's resources ensured the league's financial survival during its formative years. The main drawback of the Trustee Administration stemmed from its failure to provide local guarantors a voice in the conduct of league affairs.

The Management Corporation Administration (1945–1950) resolved the problem of representation for local franchise holders by establishing a League Board of Directors comprised of team presidents who governed league affairs. Management can also be credited with continuing extensive publicity, promotions, and player procurement campaigns. However, Management's costliness and profit-based super-structure led to increasingly large team deficits and resentment from team administrators who bore the financial deficits of the league. Progressive changes inaugurated in game play also worked to Management's disadvantage. As the game became more like baseball and less like softball, the available player pool from which the league could draw was diminished. Game changes, deemed essential for increasing spectator appeal, necessitated expensive and time-consuming training to turn softball players into baseball players. In addition, the player allocation system inaugurated under the Trustees and carried on by Management fostered intra-league personnel conflicts which, taken with increased financial deficits and player procurement difficulties, led to Management's dissolution.

The Independent Team Owners' Administration (1951–1954) effectively reduced league expenses, though team deficits continued to be a problem. Intra-league conflicts also appeared to be effectively diminished with the elimination of the player allocation system and the introduction of a draft system for player placement. However, the decentralization of league scouting and player procurement programs under this administration further inhibited the league's ability to attract and train new talent.

Each change in league administration sought to alleviate the disadvantages of the previous administration. It is impossible to say whether or not administrators of each new structure analyzed the problems their system might foster as well as the problems it might solve. Although league board members professed awareness of the social forces impinging on the league's success after the war, there was no evidence to suggest that they systematically sought solutions to the problems engendered by these forces. It appeared rather that they merely reacted to yearly deficits by initiating policy changes, which, though immediately economical, were sometimes detrimental to the league's long-term future. Unlike Major League Baseball owners, AAGBBL team administrators did not possess the necessary personal wealth to regularly sustain annual losses occasioned by rising prices and falling attendance figures characteristic of the post–World War II period. In this respect the AAGBBL suffered the same fate as many men's minor league baseball teams.[51]

7

Decentralization of Publicity and Promotion, 1951–1954

The decentralization of league publicity and promotion was a major fall-out of the decentralization of league administration between 1951 and 1954. However, the process of de-emphasizing centralized league publicity and promotion began at the end of the 1948 season. It was at this time that the League Board of Directors began systematically cutting the publicity budget. This process continued through the end of the 1952 season.

Reduction of Extensive Centralized Publicity and Promotion

Meyerhoff's proposal for the 1949 publicity budget, submitted in October 1948, totaled $7,365.00. As part of an overall economizing, the league board reduced this item to $4,000.[1] Table 10 indicates this cutback was consistent with league publicity expenditures before 1948. Nonetheless, the league publicity cutback in 1949 and all subsequent budget reductions for publicity had the effect of placing the AAGBBL in almost immediate jeopardy as a public entertainment enterprise.

During the war, travel restrictions and minimal competition from other recreational pursuits made the AAGBBL a primary sports spectacle in the Midwestern communities that sponsored it. When travel restrictions were lifted after the war, and as television began its rapid expansion in 1948 and 1949, the AAGBBL faced strong competition in a rapidly expanding leisure market.[2] Confronted with these circumstances, league directors should ideally have increased publicity and promotion budgets each year beginning in 1949 instead of decreasing them. Ironically, the League Board of Directors were all businessmen who expressed awareness of the social forces infringing upon the AAGBBL's popularity, i.e., television and other amusement competition.[3] Table 10 suggests, however, that their consciousness of these external problems was not accompanied by a recognition of the value of an extensive centralized publicity program to combat them.

Disadvantages of Decentralized Publicity and Promotion

Decentralization of the league at the end of the 1950 season placed the burden of responsibility for publicity and promotion on individual team managements. The disadvantage of independent team publicity efforts was the fact that local management did not always have the experience or expertise required for effective promotional and publicity campaigns. The South Bend organization typified this problem. The president of the team during the 1951 season wanted to curtail expenditures, and one item he reduced

Table 10: Comparison of League Publicity and Promotion Budget
with Seasonal Attendance, 1943–1954

Year	No. Teams	Publicity & Promotion Budget	Total Attendance Per Season
1943	4	?	176,612
1944	6	$5,067.00	259,658
1945	6	4,102.46	450,313
1946	8	4,066.80	754,919
1947	8	4,809.51	789,488
1948	10	8,445.40	910,747
1949	8	3,341.15	585,813
1950	8	468.00	481,981
1951	8	500.00	?
1952	6	200.00	?
1953	6	?	?
1954	5	?	270,000*

SOURCE: *Financial Records*: "All American Girls Baseball League Budget: League Expenses, 1945 Season, 1946 Season, 1947 Season," Meyerhoff Files, Drawer 75, Budget Folder; "Statement of 1944 and Estimated Cost of League Operation for 1945," Dailey Records, 1943–1946; "League Expenses—Total Year of 1948," Dailey Records, 1947–1949; "League Expenses of December & Total Expense for 1949," Dailey Records, 1947–1949; "All American Girls Baseball League Expenses to December 31, 1950," Dailey Records, 1950a; AAGBBL Board Meeting Minutes, 25 October 1950, including recommended budget for 1951, Dailey Records; "American Girls Baseball League Bulletin," 12 December 1951, including recommended budget for 1952, Dailey Records, 1952. *Attendance Records*: "League Attendance Figures for 1943–1949, Dailey Records, 1952; AAGBBL News Release, 21 November 1950, Dailey Records, 1950a.

*Estimated attendance needed for league to break even in 1954. Based on 45,000 attendance for each of six teams. AAGBBL Board Meeting Minutes, 29 February 1954, Dailey Records.

was publicity and promotion. In his 1951 records, Harold Dailey commented several times that the team president didn't want any special nights or promotions.[4] Toward the end of June 1951, Dailey lamented:

> Even with a great team we are not drawing the fans and that is because we are doing no promotion. We must get on the ball and get a lot of promotion from now on or we are in the hole.[5]

The South Bend team was not the only organization in the league to demonstrate reticence, or at best, lethargy, in regard to publicity and promotion. In mid–March 1951, league president Fred Leo issued a bulletin to all team presidents requesting publicity information on spring training sites, exhibition games and opening dates.[6] By mid–April only one team had complied with this request.[7] More than halfway through the 1951 season, team presidents began to wake up to the need for promotion. A league news release dated August 16, 1951, observed: "Many special nights have been planned the last month of the season by clubs throughout the circuit to bolster lagging gates."[8]

At an early 1952 pre-season board meeting, inadequate promotion during the 1951 season was discussed and the new league president, Harold Van Orman from Fort Wayne, Indiana, urged that more promotion be done during the 1952 season.[9] One method of facilitating publicity, discussed at a previous board meeting, involved the submission of a glossy print of each player to the league office, which in turn could disseminate mats to league city sports editors. Team managements demonstrated an apparent inability to appreciate the utility of this publicity material. A record of team managements' reluctance to submit glossy prints of players first appeared in the April 23, 1952, board meeting minutes.

President Van Orman again stressed the importance of publicity for the league, but said that it is impossible for the league office to do much about publicity when it has no material with which to work. He urged each and every club to get in all items possible which would be of interest to the public — and again asked that just as soon as girls arrive ... a picture of each one be made and sent to [the] League office.[10]

The appeal for player pictures was repeated at board meetings held immediately after the 1952 season and immediately before the 1954 season.[11] A discussion at a 1954 pre-season meeting suggested that the request had also been ignored during the 1953 season. It further indicated that team managements were finally becoming aware of the advantages of centralized league publicity.

> ... someone brought up the need for pictures of players to be available to the newspapers. Mr. McCammon reminded board members that each year he had requested action photos from clubs to be sent to the league office so mats could be made and available at all times to all newspapers in the league — so far [the] request has gone unheeded so Mr. O'Brien made the following motion:
>
> > EACH CLUB MUST FURNISH THE LEAGUE Office WITH ACTION PHOTOS OF EACH OF ITS PLAYERS ALONG WITH A BACKGROUND STORY OF EACH PLAYER, NOT LATER THAN MAY 25TH OR BE SUBJECT TO A FINE.
>
> This motion was supported by Mr. Smith and unanimously carried.[12]

Characteristics of Team Publicity and Promotion Programs, 1951–1954

The publicity and promotional efforts of team managements from 1951 to 1954 were almost exclusively directed at their local populaces. The most common events included special nights for players, managers, industries, lodges, civic groups, adjacent communities, ladies' and children's benefits and holiday fetes.[13] In addition to the well-established daily newspaper reports, special nights and radio broadcasts appeared to be the primary promotional tools utilized by team administrators between 1951 and 1954. All of these strategies were continued from practices begun during the Trustee and Management Administrations. As previously mentioned, some communities, such as Kalamazoo, made better use of available promotional tactics than others, namely South Bend and Rockford.[14] Whereas South Bend and Rockford pinched promotional pennies, Lee Elkins in Kalamazoo spent them with beneficial results. June Peppas, Kalamazoo pitcher and first basewoman reflected:

> I've always said the demise of the league was for lack of advertising and promotion. Lee Elkins took over the Kalamazoo Lassies in the spring of '52. He owned and operated McNamara Trucking, also McNamara Racing cars along with the Lassies. His sports operations were run businesses.
>
> He had people in advertising and baseball management. I remember Ann Chatham, our business manager and her assistant who went to baseball management school. We were in fourth place our last year and probably out-drew the other teams due to the advertising and promotional work done.
>
> I remember "The King and His Court," the Scottish Band, fourth of July fireworks, also giving bags of groceries away for some promotional works. We had Junior Lassies, [and] a fan club that followed us to some towns. When we won the playoffs from Fort Wayne in 1954, there were many Kalamazoo fans in the stands in Fort Wayne.
>
> We even had our own bus that he bought equipped with a radio, refrigerator, our own

Jean Faut Night: *Left to right:* Jean Faut, unidentified, Joe Boland, *South Bend Tribune* Sports Writer and South Bend Blue Sox Director. Special nights for players and managers were a common promotional tool for AAGBBL Teams (reproduced from the original held by the Department of Special Collections of the University Libraries of Notre Dame).

driver, and across the back a card table with card games going on most of the night. Sometimes before leaving the Kalamazoo Stadium (CAA Field) Jean Lovell would wheel it around the track. We thought we were in heaven.

I believe other directors got tired of getting out there to push their team or maybe tired of it all, or maybe thinking there wasn't much in it for them. Who knows now![15]

Two distinctive promotions developed by Independent Team Owners were actually conceptualized during the latter part of the 1950 season. This was the last year of Management's ownership of the league, and the first year of Fred Leo's presidency. The first of these promotions was a mid-season all-star game, and the second involved competitions with or against men's teams.[16]

The first All-Star game since the July 1,1943, night game in Wrigley Field was played July 7, 1952, at South Bend, Indiana. The game consisted of a contest between the team that was leading the league as of July 1 (the South Bend Blue Sox), and an All-Star team composed of players from the rest of the league who were elected as All-Stars by newspaper and radio representatives.[17] Thereafter, an annual All-Star game was held through 1954, the last year of league competition. The All-Star game proved to be a popular event with fans and a successful venture financially for the league, netting more than $1250 in 1952 and 1954.[18]

The first record of an AAGBBL team competing against a men's team was found in the board meeting minutes of August 21, 1950: "Permission was given for the Peoria Redwings to play against an Old-Timers ball team made up of men in the town."[19] This event was a novelty promotional gimmick to boost income because the Peoria team was in financial difficulty at the time.[20] The league board's permission for this event broke its traditional position against such exhibitions.[21] Ironically, the league office had just reiterated this stance during the first week of August 1950, when a Florida men's league offered to buy Dorothy Kamenshek's (Rockford first basewoman's) contract. Fred Leo reported that the board would not release Kamenshek from her contract, 1) because Rockford couldn't afford to lose her and 2) because "...we felt that women should play among themselves and that they could not but appear inferior in athletic competition with men."[22] Leo's and the league's position was more definitively elaborated in a 1950 McCall's feature story on the league.

> It is an iron rule of the league that the girls shall never play against teams of men or boys. Fred Leo said: "Every single member of our board agrees on one thing. This is a girls' game and our girls are not imitating men. It wouldn't prove a thing, it would simply be carnival stuff, if we played one of our teams against men. We think we are doing a little something to give girls confidence in themselves, the players and the women who come to watch the players. We are not interested in a meaningless competition with men. We are interested in showing a million people a year — and I hope it will turn into two million — that young women can put on a fine ball game all by themselves."[23]

The league board didn't have much difficulty compromising its standards on this issue when an exhibition game between an AAGBBL team and a local men's team was judged to be beneficial to the league's pecuniary interest, as in the Peoria case.

Most of the contests involving an AAGBBL team and a men's team were reported in the latter half of the 1954 season after the league's adoption of the nine-inch baseball. In these instances, teams exchanged batteries to equalize competition somewhat. Their primary purpose, of course, was to stimulate attendance.[24]

Aside from all-star games and women's versus men's competitions, the last major promotional effort by the league board between 1951 and 1954 was the adoption of the nine-inch baseball and extension of the diamond to 85-foot base paths with a 60-foot pitching distance. The reduction of the ball size and expansion of the diamond was agreed upon by the league board in view of the fact that it "might provide new interest and help gate receipts throughout the league."[25] This was the last step in the evolution of the AAGBBL game from softball to baseball, and it suggested that each equipment and facility change was ultimately viewed as a promotional tool.

National and International Publicity and Promotion, 1951–1954

Despite team managements' reluctance to subsidize and support centralized league publicity and promotion after 1949, the league did obtain some national and international publicity for the Independent Team Owner's Administration, 1951–1954. Nearly all of this publicity occurred during the 1951 and 1952 seasons, however, and was probably achieved through the efforts of Fred Leo, who served as a publicity agent for the league under Meyerhoff before he became league president in 1950.[26] Prior to his employment as a league publicity agent, Fred Leo was employed as a newspaper reporter, radio announcer, and sports official. He was also instrumental in organizing the Peoria Redwings AAGBBL team.[27] His background bespoke considerable experience with the methods and functions of promotion and publicity, and he was the last league president to have had intimate contact with Meyerhoff's advertising agency.

"Dottie Schroeder, Ball in Glove, Makes Great Play on Wide Throw for Brush Tag at Second Base." This picture was taken during a game between Kalamazoo's 1954 All-City Squad and the Grand Rapids Black Sox. Dottie Schroeder was the only female member of the Kalamazoo All-City Squad. The game was played as part of a late August benefit program. This picture illustrates that AAGBBL rules stipulating its players should not compete with or against men were relaxed at times (Kalamazoo *Gazette*, Aug. 29, 1954 — Used with permission of the Kalamazoo Gazette).

For the 1951 spring training camp, Fred Leo organized newsreel and television coverage of league activities.[28] It is highly possible that this promotional effort on Leo's part provided the league with its last national exposure, all of which was reaped in 1952 after his resignation. He was at least responsible for initiating a *Holiday* magazine feature, which appeared in June 1952.[29] In July 1952, Fox-Movietone produced a newsreel feature of the league entitled "Kalamazoo Klouters," narrated by Mel Allen.[30] August 1952 witnessed the last national exposures recorded for the AAGBBL: a feature in *The Woman* magazine and the appearance of Bonnie Baker, then a member of the Kalamazoo team, on the CBS television program *What's My Line*.[31] A couple of other non-local promotional efforts involving league players were a 1951 pre-season eastern tour by the Fort Wayne Daisies and the Battle Creek Belles and a 1951 post-season tour by the South Bend Blue Sox through Indiana, Missouri, and Texas. Since these tours involved individual teams, rather than the entire league, they appeared to be isolated team efforts rather than centralized league undertakings.[32] The last cooperative, far-reaching league promotional and player training effort was the rookie tour to eastern states in August of 1952.[33]

Toward the end of the 1952 season, league administrators investigated the possibility of a post-season Philippine or European U.S.O. tour and another Cuban tour. They were understandably wary of the Cuban proposal and concluded that the U.S.O. proposal was suggested too late for adequate planning and administrative action.[34] The U.S.O. proposal may have materialized as a result of a feature story of the league broadcast by the "Sports Answer Man" over sixty-odd Armed Forces stations around the world.[35] The league board pursued the possibility of a Far East tour during the 1953 season, but transportation and lodging couldn't be worked out with the army.[36]

AAGBBL Publicity and Promotion, 1943–1954

The AAGBBL's promotional history helps account for its success and failure. It could be said that the quantity and quality of publicity and promotional campaigns during the Trustee Administration, 1943–1944, contributed significantly to the league's success during the war years. Not only did league publicity reassure the public that it was attempting to reinforce the prevailing social concept of femininity, it also directed attention to the fact that the league was formulated to contribute to community welfare, to provide entertainment for families, and to provide recreation for war workers. Furthermore, every effort was made to keep the league in the public eye through daily newspaper coverage and feature articles in nationally popular periodicals. Publicity and promotion under the Trustees set the tone for "selling" the AAGBBL.

Under the direction of Arthur Meyerhoff's Management Corporation, 1945–1950, league publicity continued to emphasize the same themes established under the Trustees. With the dissolution of restrictive wartime legislation, Meyerhoff was able to expand national publicity and initiate both national and international promotional tours as well as maintain established local publicity and promotional efforts. Meyerhoff's promotional programs reinforced the league's player recruitment program and helped maintain interest in the league immediately after the war when competitive amusements began to flourish. Management continued to "sell" the league at home and also endeavored to sell it abroad.

When the League Board of Directors began cutting publicity and promotional expenditures in 1949, they began undercutting a cornerstone on which the league had been built. The league board's disassociation with Meyerhoff after the 1950 season resulted in the decentralization of league administration including the decentralization of league publicity and promotional efforts. Some teams were unable to devote adequate funds to promotion and publicity or did not have the professional personnel to direct such programs. Inadequate publicity and promotion during a time when competition with other leisure activities became intense boded ill for the league's future. Whatever the reasons, Independent Team Owners failed to successfully "sell" the league to the public. A side effect of their failure to "sell" the league, one that team owners didn't seem to fully comprehend, was their inability to attract new players to the league on a nationwide scale.

The AAGBBL may have folded even if the quality and quantity of publicity and promotion had not declined. However, the league's demise may also have been postponed a few years, if not indefinitely, with a continued and concentrated "stoking" of a centralized advertising program.

PART III

Team Administration

A good crowd (Collections of the Public Museum of Grand Rapids).

8

Team Administrative
Structure and Personnel

The description of "league" administrative personnel and structure conveyed in Part II is essential to an understanding of the AAGBBL. Of no less importance to a fuller understanding of the league is a knowledge of "team" administrative structure and personnel. Part III describes team administrative organization, examines team administrators' motives for supporting the AAGBBL, and examines the role team managers and chaperones played in league operations. Chapter 8 deals with team administrative structure and personnel, Chapters 9 and 10 focus on team managers and chaperones respectively.

Characteristics of Team Organizational Structure and Personnel

Local team administrative structures were established when the franchise system was instituted in 1944, and they remained essentially the same through the 1954 season. Team administrative structures consisted of team boards of directors composed of a president, vice president, secretary-treasurer, and various numbers of directors.[1] The South Bend Blue Sox Organizational Chart provides a model of team administrative structure (Figure 6).

During the Trustee and Management Corporation Administrations, the team boards of directors were composed of business and civic leaders in each participating city who contributed financial support for their teams.[2] They also tended to be individuals with considerable community influence and a strong interest in sport and youth.[3] Ken Sells, first league president, for instance, recalled that the first person he approached in Kenosha, Wisconsin, to organize an AAGBBL team was Municipal Court Judge Edward J. Ruetz. Sells reported that Judge Ruetz "became very interested in our proposition because of his sincere interest in juvenile delinquency."[4] As reported in Chapter 7, Judge Ruetz was also an avid sports fan, and he was immediately interested in heading up a team in Kenosha and finding investors to support it.[5]

As a result of his willingness to spearhead the organization of an AAGSBL team, Judge Ruetz was unanimously selected as president of the Comets by his fellow subscribers and served in that capacity throughout the team's tenure in the league. In early 1944 the Judge was described by *Kenosha News* Sports Editor Eddie McKenna as "an ardent participant as well as an avid spectator in sports, [who] will lend his wisdom, experience, and integrity in guiding the Kenosha Girls Professional Ball Team...."[6] In 1945, McKenna emphasized:

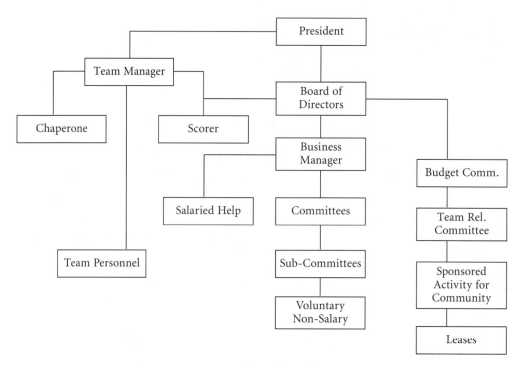

SOURCE: Chet Grant AAGBBL Records, University of Notre Dame Joyce Sports Research Collection, South Bend, Indiana.

Figure 6: Organizational Structure of the South Bend Blue Sox, ca. 1951–1954

> "Judge Ruetz is recognized as one of the best informed representatives in the league. His ability as a competitor in athletics, his sportsmanship attitude, and sense of fair play and integrity establishes him as a pillar of authority and respect in the eyes of team managers and league officials.[7]

During 1947, McKenna attributed Ruetz's selection as the league's Executive Committee Chairman "to his integrity, sound foresight, business acumen, and mastery of legal intricacies."[8] If Wrigley, Sells, and Meyerhoff were as fortunate in recruiting team leaders in other league towns who were as enthusiastic, as dedicated, and of such caliber and influence as Judge Ruetz in Kenosha, it's no wonder that league teams were so well accepted by their communities.

The *1947 Muskegon Yearbook* featured a photograph and brief biographical profile of all team presidents and affirmed:

> These men and their associates work for the mutual interests of players, fans, and the entire community to provide our cities with the finest and best in sports entertainment, community recreation, and youth development.[9]

A reiteration of the profiles of these team presidents acquaints the reader with the type of industrial, business, and civic leaders who gave their personal time, energy and resources to the promotion of AAGBBL teams in their respective communities. These men, as team presidents, also served on the League Board of Directors. The dates in brackets beside their names indicate the years each individual served on the League Board of Directors.[10]

The Kenosha Comets honored by a visit from Connie Mack and Al Simmons, June 4, 1947 (reproduced from the original held by the Department of Special Collections of the University Libraries of Notre Dame).

W. R. WADEWITZ, RACINE [1944–1949]: Vice President of Western Printing Litho. Company. A veteran of World War I and former all-around athlete, he [was] a Vice President of the Manufacturers Association of Racine, member of the Board of Trustees and Honorary Life Member of Racine Elks, Chairman of Racine Cemetery Commission and very active in American Legion and Civic Affairs.

N. J. HARKNESS, GRAND RAPIDS [1945–1950]: President, Michigan Distributors, Inc. A graduate of Northwestern University and a Captain in World War I, he [was] President of the Grand Rapids Chamber of Commerce and President of the Grand Rapids Veterans Counseling Center. He [served] on the Board of Directors of the Kent County Family Service and [was] a member of the Peninsular Club, University Club, Kent Country Club, American Legion, Elks, Torch Club, and White Lake Yacht Club.

DAN A. CLARK, SOUTH BEND [1945–1949]: Director of Clarke's Restaurants. An outstandingly popular and vigorous young business man in South Bend, he [was] well known for his civic work and his interest in the development of youth. A 32nd Degree Mason, he [was] a member of Notre Dame Alumni Association, an honorary life member of the Fraternal Order of Police Lodge No. 36, a life member of the International Association of Fire Fighters Local No. 362, and the Musicians Local No. 278.

HARRY HANSON, ROCKFORD [1944–1947]: President, Damascus Steel Products Corporation. A member of the Rockford Rotary Club, Past Commander of the Knights Templar and well known for his special interest in Boys' Club work, he [did] much to make Rockford an outstanding girls baseball center. He [served] on the Board of Directors of the Salvation Army.

W. R. Wadewitz
Racine Belles
(1944–1949)

J. L. Mueller
Fort Wayne Daisies
(1947–1949)

N. J. Harkness
Grand Rapids Chicks
(1945–1950)

L. A. Prescott
Muskegon Lassies
(1947)

Dan A. Clark
South Bend Blue Sox
(1945–1950)

Judge Edward J. Ruetz
Kenosha Comets
(1943–1951)

Harry Hanson
Rockford Peaches
(1944–1947)

A. H. Sommer
Peoria Redwings
(1945–1950)

1947 AAGBBL team presidents (from 1947 Muskegon Lassie's Yearbook) (courtesy Northern Indiana Center for History).

J. L. MUELLER, FORT WAYNE [1947–1949]: Lincoln National Life Insurance Company national sales leader for a quarter of a century, he [was] Past President of the Fort Wayne Basketball Association, an ardent golfer and senior champion at Fort Wayne Country Club. He [served] as General Chairman of the Community Chest and [was] active in American Red Cross, YMCA, War Bond, Civic Theatre and Philharmonic Orchestra activities. A member of the Chamber of Commerce and active in many other civic and fraternal organizations.

L. A. PRESCOTT, MUSKEGON [1947]: manager, Bennett Pumps Division of John Wood Manufacturing Company, he taught school in Muskegon for eleven and a half years before becoming a successful works manager in industry. He was manager of athletics at Muskegon High School and continued his interest in sports as a civic leader. He [was] a three-time President of the Greater Muskegon Chamber of Commerce and [was] Director of the Muskegon Manufacturers Association.

EDWARD J. RUETZ, KENOSHA [1943–1951]: municipal Judge of Kenosha, his list of civic achievements would fill a volume. He [was] former President and Board Member of the local and State Bar Associations, Chairman of Kenosha Post War Planning Committee, Chairman of Recreation Committee of Kenosha Chamber of Commerce, Executive Committee Red Cross, Executive Committee U.S.O., and meritorious certificate holder from the American Legion.

A. H. SOMMER, PEORIA [1945–1950]: director Keystone Steel & Wire Company, he [was] a graduate of Bradley University with a background of civil engineering and construction, Chairman of the Southwestern Section of the American Institute of Mining and Metallurgical Engineers and a Director of the National Open Hearth Steel Committee. He [was] a Director and member of the Budget Committee of the Peoria Community Chest and Council and a member of the Peoria Association of Commerce.[11]

Harold Dailey's records and league team yearbooks (1944–1949) suggested that these men served as team directors before and/or after their term as team president. Their continued presence at team board meetings and/or league board meetings was significant in that it contributed continuity and stability to the conduct of team and league affairs. The impact these men and others like them had on the acceptance of AAGBBL teams in their communities cannot be measured retrospectively, but their high public profiles could only add a positive impact to community support for teams.

The Independent Team Owners' Administration dawned with new leadership for most AAGBBL teams. There is some indication that the new leaders were less financially solvent than original team directors and therefore more profit-minded than their predecessors.[12] Whether the cause was lack of funds or desire to realize a profit, between 1951 and 1954, team directors sacrificed some of the quality that had characterized AAGBBL operations in the past. It was during this time that player salaries and expense allowances were drastically reduced; that teams began to travel in station-wagon caravans instead of on buses; that publicity and promotional budgets were cut; and that a full-time chaperone became an option instead of a requirement.

Team Directors' Motives for Supporting the AAGBBL

The question arises as to why leading businessmen from substantial Midwestern industrial cities contributed their support to the All-American Girls Baseball League. The war was certainly a persuasive factor in their initial willingness to undertake sponsorship of AAGBBL teams. They were quite likely promoting women's employment in their businesses, and their promotion of a women's spectator sport, while not what might be expected, was not inconsistent with wartime circumstances. The fact that the AAGBBL enterprise was presented to them by a businessman of Philip Wrigley's stature must have been persuasive in itself. In addition, the high standards on which the league was based, and its emphasis on femininity and skill undoubtedly appealed to these men.

The foregoing factors help explain leading businessmen's initial involvement in the AAGBBL but there is also the question of why they continued to sponsor AAGBBL teams up to five and six years after the war, in the face of regular annual deficits. There are several hypotheses in answer to this question, none of which are sufficient in themselves to fully explain the actions team sponsors chose after the war. Taken together, however, they help account for the continued time, energy, and financial contributions local businessmen gave their AAGBBL teams after the war.

There was, for instance, the non-profit, civic service image projected by the league, which presented a two-fold attraction for team sponsors. On one hand, it identified their businesses with an organization promulgating a contribution to community welfare. This was a beneficial public image to foster. On the other hand, because the AAGBBL was a non-profit organization, contributions to it were tax deductible. Then too, there were undoubtedly those who believed that if they could endure deficits long enough, their team would fulfill its potential, become a winner, and break even at the gate, if not realize a considerable profit to erase preceding deficits. The original team directors, for instance, were aware that league attendance demonstrated continual increases from 176,000 in 1943 to more than 910,000 in 1948.[13] Their expectations for continued increases in attendance figures must have been optimistic in the immediate postwar years.

Furthermore, there was the suggestion that once involved in the league, franchise holders' civic and personal pride prompted them to hold on to teams longer than was warranted by financial returns. Harold Dailey, South Bend Blue Sox director and president, in reflecting on the reasons businessmen continued to sponsor AAGBBL teams when deficits were mounting, made the following observation:

> To me, a dentist, it is funny that businessmen will not take the time to see where their money goes in this league when they are so tough in their own business. Perhaps it is as Ken Sells said, the short skirts and the girls do a lot of it.... I do not believe that is the case. It is the fact that it is a civic thing and town pride is the answer.[14]

Perhaps as time passed, franchise holders in the various cities considered sponsorship of AAGBBL teams a symbol of community or financial status they were loathe to relinquish. This state of affairs was alluded to when Wilbur Johnson, longtime official of the Rockford team, notified the League Board of Directors in the spring of 1950 that Rockford's days in the league were numbered if the financial decline continued, but parenthetically remarked, "...we are not going to lay down or quit."[15]

Finally, it comes down to a question of why anyone supports a professional ball team. William Wrigley, Jr., suggested in 1930 that he owned a professional baseball team for love of the game and not for financial returns.[16] Perhaps some of the men who subsidized AAGBBL teams acted out of a similar motive — it was their chance to "own" a ball team.

Fluctuating Franchises

Whatever forces may have motivated local businessmen to support AAGBBL franchises during and after the war, operational deficits began to dissuade them with increasing frequency after the 1948 season. This is illustrated by a listing of franchises reorganized and dropped during the league's history (Table 11). "Reorganized" here refers to the establishment of new team leadership.

The difference between the franchises dropped from 1944 to 1948 and those dropped after 1948 was that new franchise locations were easily established for the earlier dropouts. It became increasingly difficult for the league to find new franchise locations for later dropouts. Although businessmen from such cities as Chicago; Dubuque, Iowa; Benton Harbor, St. Joseph, Saginaw, and Flint, Michigan; Dayton and Toledo, Ohio; and Madison, Wisconsin, expressed interest in obtaining an AAGBBL franchise after 1950, none were actually able to collect sufficient funds to establish a team.[17]

Table 11: AAGBBL Franchises Dropped and Reorganized, 1944–1954

Franchises Reorganized	Date	Franchises Dropped	Date
Peoria	Dec. 1949	Minneapolis	July 1944
Muskegon	Dec. 1949	Milwaukee	Sept. 1944
Grand Rapids	Aug. 1950	Springfield	June 1948
South Bend	Nov. 1950	Chicago	Nov. 1948
Rockford	Nov. 1951	Muskegon	June 1950
Peoria	Nov. 1951	Racine	Feb. 1951
Kalamazoo	Mar. 1952	Kenosha	Aug. 1951
Rockford	Apr. 1954	Peoria	Jan. 1952
		Battle Creek	Aug. 1952
		Muskegon	July 1953

SOURCE: *Minneapolis Tribune*, 23 July 1944, p. S1; Dailey Records, 1943–1946; AAGBBL Board Meeting Minutes, 16 June & 11 November 1948; 21 December 1949; 11 June, 21 August & 8 November 1950; 6 February, 7 August & 14 November 1951; 9 January, 12 March & 15 August 1952; 12 September 1953, Dailey Records.

Another puzzle related to team organizations concerns the reason why team administrations in some cities (Peoria, Muskegon, Grand Rapids, South Bend, Rockford, and Kalamazoo) reorganized after they suffered major financial setbacks. The reorganization of league administration that took place at the end of the 1950 season may have been one factor encouraging local businessmen to renew or assume team franchises. The league budget under Independent Team Owners was significantly reduced, which possibly induced old and new administrators to be optimistic about the possibilities of breaking even or realizing a profit. Some of those who assumed control of old franchises may have been optimistic that their efforts would succeed where others had failed. Or, maybe they saw it as *their* chance to "own" a ball team.

The assumption of team ownership by one individual rather than by a group of businessmen marked a major change between Management's administration and that of Independent Team Owners. This was not a widespread practice, but it did occur in three instances. In mid–August of the 1950 season, the Grand Rapids directors were faced with an immediate cessation of operations and approached Jim Williams, owner of the Grand Rapids Jets (a semi-pro men's team) and Bigelow Field, and asked him if he would be interested in supporting the team in his field for the remainder of the season. He agreed, and his motive for doing so illustrated what may have been the reaction of other directors and other individuals for underwriting sagging AAGBBL teams: "I thought it was good politics to [let the Chicks use my park] since [they] ... definitely built themselves up a clientele."[18] Williams continued to operate the Grand Rapids Chicks through two-thirds of the 1952 season, until his park burned down.[19]

Lee Elkins in Kalamazoo performed another "eleventh hour" rescue of an AAGBBL team in the spring of 1952. He purchased the club "after the franchise rights had been lifted from the former owners when they failed to meet the extended deadline offered by the league."[20] Elkins, like Williams, was already involved in sports promotion. Although his specialty was race cars rather than baseball teams, Elkins invested considerable resources into training personnel and promoting the Lassies.[21]

In 1951, when the Kenosha team gave notice that it was curtailing operations in mid–July, Harold Van Orman, who later served as league president as well as president of the Fort Wayne Daisies, volunteered to subsidize the team through the second half of the season. His interest in supporting the Kenosha team appeared more immediately selfish than either Williams' or Elkins' team sponsorships. He agreed to handle the Kenosha team under the following conditions:

1. That when disposal of the franchise at the end of the season was undertaken, he be permitted to sell it for whatever loss might be sustained.
2. That should the league operate with 6 teams in another year, the players belonged to him and he would be permitted to sell them at his own price, again to recoup any possible loss.
3. That the league payments for the remainder of the year due from the Kenosha club be waived by the league.[22]

The majority of board members present accepted his proposal.

Community Support for Fading Franchises

Public reaction to announcements that franchises were to be terminated may also have fanned the optimism of prospective administrators in assuming AAGBBL franchises. In 1950, for example, the Peoria, Grand Rapids, and Rockford administrations made special public appeals for funds to see their teams through the season.[23] The amount netted by the Rockford fund drive was undetermined, but the team remained in the league, implying a positive response. The Grand Rapids fund drive netted approximately $4,000, and the Peoria campaign realized more than $8,000.[24] Neither of these totals was sufficient to cover each team's deficits, but they were substantial enough to persuade team administrators to maintain or assume team support for the remainder of the season.[25] Most importantly, these fund drives stimulated positive public reaction to the threatened loss of their respective AAGBBL teams. A portion of a fan's letter to the *Peoria Star* in response to the threatened loss of the Redwings reflected the positive fan sentiment in that community.

> Can't some kind of benefit be arranged to keep the Redwings ... there should be enough people in Peoria interested to help the cause for the sake of the town kids to keep them here. Why not put on an "auction" like they did at Exposition Gardens. I am sure every merchant would donate something and other people too, it wouldn't need to be big things, like refrigerators & etc., as at Exposition Gardens.... I think it is a shame if Peoria doesn't have enough civic pride to keep [the Redwings] here.[26]

Further involvement of the general community in team support was evidenced by the development of several fan clubs during the 1950s. Rockford and Fort Wayne reportedly held fan club organizational meetings of "amazing proportions." The Rockford Fans Association was supposed to have numbered more than 1,000 members and about "250 people attended a fan meeting at Peoria."[27] A South Bend Fan Club was organized in 1952 based on the "successful fan club operations in Fort Wayne and Rockford."[28] The purposes of these organizations were four-fold: (1) to publicize girl's baseball; (2) to sell tickets; (3) to promote park improvements; and (4) to build club membership.[29] The Rockford Fan Club demonstrated the effectiveness of fan club organizations by successfully raising funds to insure Rockford's representation in the league for the 1954 season.[30] As former Peach and 1952 Rockford Fan Club President, Dorothy "Kammie" Kamenshek, observed:

> We were very well accepted. When we developed a fan in the city, they were "died-in-the-wool" fans. You'd have the same corps of fans that showed up every game. Maybe when your team was doing real well, [or maybe during] a special series is when the others ... that didn't come all the time, would come.[31]

This kind of community involvement served as a type of peer pressure that encouraged local businessmen to continue supporting AAGBBL teams despite the deficits they incurred. Teams and their fan clubs became integral parts of the community. This broad-based support provided a persuasive voice to team owners to not "lie down or quit."

The local businessmen who volunteered to support teams in 1943 and those who followed were financially responsible for the league's continued existence through 1954. Whatever their motives for assuming and continuing to support and subsidize a non-profit organization that incurred annual deficits, they are to be commended for underwriting AAGBBL teams. They provided the players and the people in their communities an opportunity to be part of an historically unique women's professional baseball league for twelve memorable years.

9

Team Managers

From its inception, every effort was directed toward establishing the AAGBBL as a bona fide professional organization. Significant amounts of money were spent to recruit the best players from all over the United States and Canada. Once recruited, they were contracted to devote 100 percent of their time to playing professional baseball during the season, and they were paid a substantial weekly wage to do so. The personnel administering the league were professionals, and league publicity emphasized that it was a professional venture. The employment of ex–major league professional baseball players as team managers also contributed to the league's professional image. League president Ken Sells noted that he was "especially fortunate at the time we started this league in finding good baseball men available."[1] The availability of good baseball men occurred in 1943 because many men's minor league teams ceased operations due to war manpower demands and restrictions on travel and night baseball.[2]

Managers' Baseball Backgrounds

The first four AAGBBL managers included Bert Niehoff, Eddie Stumpf, Johnny Gottselig and Josh Billings. Of these individuals, only Johnny Gottselig lacked major league baseball experience or wide experience as a player, coach, or manager in minor league baseball.[3] Although Gottselig's professional sport career revolved around the Chicago Black Hawks Hockey Team, he was the only one of the four original managers known to have had experience coaching women's softball. Russian-born and raised in Canada, he was a prime professional baseball pitching candidate before hurting his arm while in college. Gottselig coached the Regina–Moose Jaw Royals Women's Softball Team in 1939 when they qualified for the International Tournament.[4]

The AAGBBL policy of hiring ex-professional male ball players for team managers continued throughout the league's history. As Table 12 (see pages 156 and 157) illustrates, 21 of the 34 male managers listed, or nearly two-thirds of the total, had major and/or minor league baseball experience. Not only were these men capable teachers of the game, but they were drawing cards in themselves. Chet Grant, destined to become an AAGBBL manager himself, recalled that at first he "wouldn't go around the corner to witness a hybrid travesty on the national pastime; that is, baseball professionally presented by short-skirted young women with oversize ball, undersize diamond, softball pitch and baseball lead-off base."[5] In his words, he was first lured to an AAGBBL game by a manager's baseball reputation.

In 1944, when the circuit was expanded to include ... the Milwaukee Chicks, I did go around the corner to greet the Chicks because their manager was Max Carey, the ex-basestealing champion of the National League.[6]

Max Carey, as has already been observed, became AAGBBL President in 1945, after a term as manager for the Milwaukee Chicks in 1944. He rounded out his career with the AAGBBL as manager of the Fort Wayne Daisies from 1950 to 1951, and he was beloved by his players. Thelma "Tiby" Eisen, from California, judged herself to be a "B" player and wasn't sure she'd make it when she tried out for the AAGBBL. She credited Max Carey with her success as a lead-off hitter, base-stealer, and fielder because he was such "a wonderful teacher and coach."[7] Viola "Tommie" Thompson Griffin echoed Tiby's observation that he was "a wonderful teacher."[8]

Other famous major leaguers, besides Max Carey, who managed in the AAGBBL were Dave Bancroft, Leo Murphy, Johnny Rawlings, Bill Wambsganss, and Jimmie Foxx. Bancroft had more than 40 years of baseball experience behind him when he joined the AAGBBL. The highlights of his career consisted of four World Series appearances, the first with the Phillies in 1915, and the other three with the New York Giants in the early 1920s. He also acted as a player-manager for the Boston Braves in 1924.[9]

Leo Murphy spent 25 years in organized baseball as a catcher, and he played and managed in several Midwest minor leagues, with the Cincinnati Reds, and the Pittsburgh Pirates.[10] He was well known to Midwestern baseball enthusiasts. At the time Murphy became manager of the Racine Belles, he was a local resident of the city, a member of the team's field commission, and a member of the team's special Board of Strategy.[11]

Johnny Rawlings played for several major league teams including the Cincinnati Reds, the Boston Braves, the New York Giants, and the Pittsburgh Pirates. Rawlings and Bancroft were well acquainted, having played shortstop and second base for the Giants in the 1921 and 1922 World Series.[12]

Bill Wambsganss' baseball career spanned 19 years, but his claim to fame came from performing the only unassisted triple play in World Series history. He executed this feat as a second baseman for the Cleveland Indians in the 1921 series against the Brooklyn Dodgers.[13] In the fifth inning of the fifth game he caught a line drive, forced a runner on his way to third, and tagged the runner approaching from first.

The manager with the most successful win-loss record in AAGBBL history was not one of the aforementioned stellar professional performers, as might be expected, but a man of wide baseball experience nonetheless. William Baird "Bill" Allington played 20-odd years of minor league ball in the West Coast League, the Southern League, and the Western League. He lived in the Los Angeles area, and his career included minor parts in the baseball films *It Happens Every Spring* and *The Stratton Story*. He was characterized as a "dedicated ballplayer" and "a no-nonsense executive on the field."[14] His involvement with women's softball began about 1939 when he started coaching women's teams in the Los Angeles area. He was credited with recruiting several players from Los Angeles who later became AAGBBL stars.[15] They included Dorothy "Snookie" Harrell Doyle, Lavone "Pepper" Paire Davis, Dottie Wiltse Collins, Faye Dancer, and Annabelle Lee Harmon.[16] Through his association with women's softball in the Los Angeles area, Allington was employed as the AAGBBL's West Coast Scout before joining the league as manager of the Rockford Peaches in 1944.[17]

Allington's eight years with the Rockford Peaches was a record of longevity with one

Table 12: AAGBBL Managers, 1943–1948

City	1943	1944	1945	1946	1947	1948
Battle Creek						
Chicago						Dave Bancroft†*
Fort Wayne			Bill Wambsganss*†	Bill Wambsganss*†	George Johnson Daddy Rohrer†	Dick Bass/ Harold Greiner§ Thelma Eisen Vivian Kellogg Mary Rountree
Grand Rapids			Benny Meyers	John Rawlings*	John Rawlings*	John Rawlings*
Kalamazoo						
Kenosha	Josh Billings*	Marty McManus*	Pres Cruthers* Eddie Stumpf*	Pres Cruthers*	Ralph Shiners*	Chet Grant
Milwaukee		Max Carey*†				
Minneapolis		Bubber Jonnard*†				
Muskegon				Ralph "Buzz" Boyle*†	Bill Wambsganss	Bill Wambsganss
Peoria				Bill Rogers Johnny Gottselig§	Johnny Gottselig§ Leo Schrall	Leo Schrall
Racine	Johnny Gottselig§	Johnny Gottselig§	Chas. Stist† Leo Murphy§†*	Leo Murphy§†*	Leo Murphy§†*	Leo Murphy§†*
Rockford	Eddie Stumpf*	Jack Kloza Bill Allington§†	Eddie Ainsmith* Bill Allington§†	Bill Allington§†	Bill Edwards Eddie Ainsmith*	Bill Allington§†
South Bend	Bert Niehoff*†	Bert Niehoff*†	Marty McManus*	Chet Grant	Chet Grant	Marty McManus*
Springfield						Carson Bigbee*

*Major League Experience; †Minor League Experience; §Women's Softball Managerial Experience

**According to Mary "Wimp" Baumgartner, Bonnie Baker was the first and only woman to actually sign a contract to manage an AAGBBL team (Kalamazoo) during the 1950 season. Other women were appointed as interim managers, but did not sign a contract to manage. Two other women, Pat Barringer and Barbara Liebrich, were employed to manage and chaperone the Rookie Touring Teams in 1949 and 1950.

SOURCE: *Dailey Records*, 1943–1954; *1944 Racine Belles Year Book*, pp. 5, 7, 27; *1945 Racine Belles Year Book*, p. 4; *1946 Racine Belles Year Book*, pp. 11–12; *1948 Racine Belles Year Book*, p. 9; *1947 Grand Rapids Chicks Year Book*, p. 11; *1947 Muskegon Lassies Year Book*, pp. 21, 67; *1949 Peoria Redwings Year Book*, pp. 19, 31; *1949 Muskegon Lassies Year Book*, p. 4. Additional information obtained from Mary "Wimp" Baumgartner September 27, 2004, at the AAGPBL Reunion in Kalamazoo Michigan. Empty spaces designate the absence of a team for that year. Some managers who assumed duties in mid-season may not be represented.

team unrivaled by any other manager in the league. His nearest competitors were Leo Murphy and Johnny Rawlings who served five consecutive years at Racine and Grand Rapids, respectively (see Table 12). Allington's record of success was also unrivaled. In ten years in the league, eight at Rockford and two at Fort Wayne, his teams topped the season's standings five times and were finalists in the post-season play-offs eight times. His Rockford Peaches won the post-season championship four times: 1945, 1948, 1949, and 1950.[18] Allington's nearest rival in this category was Johnny Rawlings, who in five years at Grand Rapids earned all-league honors three different seasons. Rawlings' Chicks won the post-season play-off in 1947; in 1948, they led in team standings at the end of regular season play; and in 1949, they were finalists in the post-season play-offs.[19]

Allington's success was attributed to "his patience and teaching techniques with rookies."[20] Helen Filarski Steffes agreed:

> Bill Allington was one heck of a coach. If you didn't learn from Bill, you had it. He taught me everything I know about professional ball. [The transition to the AAGBBL] was like night and day — bigger diamond, smaller ball, hard ball rules.... If I didn't have Bill, I wouldn't have made it.[21]

Table 12: AAGBBL Managers, 1949–1954

City	1949	1950	1951	1952	1953	1954
Battle Creek			D. Bancroft*† Guy Bush*	Guy Bush* Joe Cooper		
Chicago	Pat Barringer** (Rookie Tour)	Pat Barringer** (Rookie Tour)				
Fort Wayne	Harold Greiner§	Max Carey*†	Max Carey*†	Jimmie Foxx*†	Bill Allington*§	Bill Allington*§
Grand Rapids	John Rawlings*	John Rawlings*	Mitch Skupien§	J. Gottselig§ Woody English*	Woody English*	Woody English*
Kalamazoo		Lenny Zintak§ Bonnie Baker**	Norm Derringer	Mitch Skupien§	Mitch Skupien§	Mitch Skupien§
Kenosha	Johnny Gottselig§	Johnny Gottselig§	Johnny Gottselig§ Teeny Petras			
Milwaukee						
Minneapolis						
Muskegon	Carson Bigbee*	Leonard Zintak§			Joe Cooper	
Peoria	Leo Schrall	Leo Murphy*†§ Mary Reynolds	John Rawlings*			
Racine	Leo Murphy*†§	Norm Derringer				
Rockford	Bill Allington†§	Bill Allington†§	Bill Allington†§	Bill Allington†§	John Rawlings*	John Rawlings*
South Bend	Dave Bancroft*†	Dave Bancroft*† Karl Winsch*†	Karl Winsch*†	Karl Winsch*†	Karl Winsch*†	Karl Winsch*†
Springfield	Barbara Liebrich** (Rookie Tour)	Barbara Liebrich** (Rookie Tour)				

Jean Cione, former member of the Rockford Peaches, testified that Allington always had the players thinking about baseball. She recalled, for instance, that he utilized bus rides as skull sessions and that players had great respect for his baseball knowledge.[22] Another Allington hallmark was his insistence that players have a rule book and know the rules. Katie Horstman recalled that he "was very stern. He made us have a rule book and we had to study it. He got us up at 7:00 A.M. on road trips and gave us strategy questions."[23] Helen Filarski Steffes remembered:

> (He quizzed) us all the time on the bus, even in the middle of the night. One time it was pitch dark and Bill turned on the lights and asked me the infield fly rule.... He made us aware of the importance of rules and regulations.[24]

On the down side, some players considered Allington's approach too sarcastic and observed that he ruined some rookies by putting too much pressure on them.[25] Some of the players who competed against Allington's teams viewed him as a man obsessed with winning.[26] All-in-all, however, Allington's baseball knowledge, discipline, and attention to detail made him an outstanding manager in the AAGBBL.

After the AAGBBL's demise in 1954, Allington did not abandon his interest in women's baseball or softball. In concert with booking agent Mat Pascale from Omaha, Nebraska, Bill organized and managed an All-Star Squad of former AAGBBL players from 1955 to at least mid–1958.[27] Allington's "All-American World Champions" barnstormed the United States from late April to early September playing 75 to 85 games a season. They played exclusively against men's teams on regulation baseball fields with the only deviation from baseball rules being an exchange of pitchers and catchers. In 1955 and 1956, Bill's All-Americans "performed in more than 150 cities and towns covering 23 states and Canada ... and travel(ed) over 20,000 miles annually by automobile."[28]

Top left: Bill Allington. *Top right:* Dave Bancroft. *Bottom left:* Johnny Rawlings. *Bottom right:* Marty McManus (all photographs reproduced from the original held by the Department of Special Collections of the University Libraries of Notre Dame).

According to team member Katie Horstman, ten or eleven players and Bill piled into his Studebaker station wagon and Joanie Berger's sedan with a few bats and balls, their gloves and a duffel bag apiece. Bill, Joanie Berger, Dottie Shroeder, and Pickles Lee shared driving time and, as Katie explained:

> "We'd play in one city and then drive maybe 300 or 400 miles, [sometimes] sleep in the car until we hit the next town and played again. It wasn't easy, but we all enjoyed it. We just loved to play baseball.[29]

Allington's "All-American World Champions": *Left to right:* **Manager Bill Allington, Joanne Weaver, Dottie Schroeder, Katie Horstman, Joan Berger, Gertie Dunn, Ruth Richard, Dolores Lee, Jean Smith, Jean Geissinger, Maxine Kline (courtesy Katie Horstman).**

Booking agent Mat Pascale preceded the team, arranged games and supplied posters for publicity. When the team arrived to play in mostly small cities of between 4,000 to 15,000 they'd do a little advertising of their own:

> Right before a game we would get on a fire truck, have our signs with us, and go through town about 4:00 P.M. [The driver] would blow the sirens and we advertised that way ... and that's how we would get people to the games.[30]

They played in a dust storm in Kansas and dodged a tornado in Minnesota, but possibly their most eventful experience occurred in a small, south Texas town. It was a vivid memory for team member Katie Horstman:

> The bookie scheduled the games, so we never knew who we were playing. We just played ball against the men and that was it. Well [in this town] it happened to be a black team. In Texas [mid–1950s] whites did not play against blacks.
>
> We couldn't find the ball park, so we asked the sheriff where the ball park was. He asked, "Why do you want to know that?" We said we were playing, and Bill's attitude was "we're going to play, that's it, no matter if we have a war or whatever." The sheriff said, "You can't play that team."
>
> I was sitting in the back seat so I piped up and said, "Oh, well, why not?" He said, "Well, they're black." I said, "Well, who cares?" I'm from Ohio, you know — who cares?

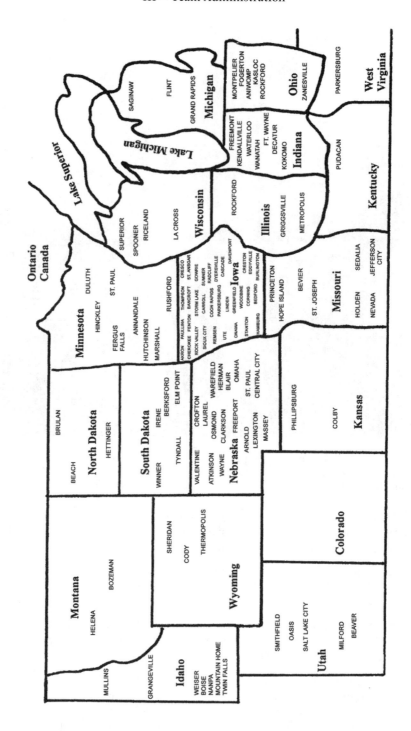

Figure 7: All-American World Champions' Tour Stops, 1955–1956 (adapted from a map contributed by Katie Horstman).

He said, "Well, we don't do that around here." Bill said, "Okay, fine." So we went on down the street and asked somebody else who told us where [to go]. It was way back someplace, in a valley, a beautiful ball park. There was music and everything else, and we were in seventh heaven.

We didn't know the sheriff was following us. I mean to tell you, he had about five cop cars ... and he wasn't going to let it happen, and he didn't let it happen. He went to a black man and I hate to tell you all the things he called him, and he said, "If you have this game, I'm going to send you right across the border." It was right on the border of Texas and Mexico.... They drew their guns and everything. That was scarey.... Unbelievable! I had no idea about segregation or anything — I was from Ohio.[31]

Katie recalled that by season's end they hadn't made much money, but they'd made expenses playing for between fifty cents and fifty dollars a night per player. Their motivation for these grueling summers: love of the game. The last three stanzas of Jean DesCombes Lesko's poem about "The Barnstorming Babes" pretty well sums it up.

> We stick together not for money alone
> For we can all get jobs if we return home.
> But, we love the game and deep down inside
> There's a glowing warmth and a heartfelt pride.
>
> There may be no trophy for winning the game
> But the pressure's there just the same.
> We must make the catch or hit the long drive
> For these are the things on which we thrive.
>
> So we'll travel around from pillar to post,
> Go without sleep, and live on toast.
> For our love of the game we'll give it our best,
> After the season, then we'll rest.[32]
> — Courtesy of Jeneane DesCombes Lesko

Dolores "Pickles" Lee: Throwing two balls to two different catchers as part of the pre-game entertainment for Allington's World Champions (courtesy Northern Indiana Center for History).

In August of 1957, Allington's All-Stars returned to South Bend and staged an exhibition game with a collection of ex–Blue Sox players. This was the first game in three years his touring squad had played against other women.[33] Allington's last involvement with women's softball was his term as coach of California's championship Orange Lionettes in the late 1960s.[34]

Women Managers

Table 12 indicates that some teams employed players as managers. It should be noted that in each case where a woman manager was employed, their managing terms began in the middle or toward the end of a season. In some situations, only two or three weeks of the season remained when women managers took over. This was the case when three players, Thelma "Tibby" Eisen, Vivian Kellog, and Mary Rountree, together assumed management of the

Fort Wayne Daisies in 1948, and when Ernestine Petras assumed management of the Kenosha Comets in 1951.[35] These women were retained as managers as a matter of convenience and economy, though they must also have demonstrated the capability to handle the position of field manager. Thelma "Tiby" Eisen acknowledged that, as captain of the team, stepping into the role of manager was not difficult for her "because I analyzed everything constantly and let the manager know if he made a mistake."[36]

Bonnie Baker, Mary Reynolds and Ernestine Petras managed for half a season or more. Baker became player-manager for the Kalamazoo Lassies when they were transferred from Muskegon in mid–June 1950. According to Mary "Wimp" Baumgartner, Bonnie was the only female manager signed to a manager's contract.[37] Earle McCammon, president of the Kalamazoo team, stated at a league board meeting that retention of Baker as team manager was an economy measure.[38] Mary Reynolds was given management responsibilities of the Peoria Redwings after the resignation of Leo Murphy, who ostensibly resigned "to give the faltering Redwings a chance to resolve their financial problems and stay in the league the balance of the season." In a personal memo, Harold Dailey suggested that Murphy was forced to resign.[39] Ernestine Petras also assumed management responsibilities of a team in financial troubles. When she became manager of the Kenosha Comets during the last half of the 1951 season, they had become an orphan team and were being subsidized by league president Harold Van Orman, Jr.[40] In each of the foregoing cases, it was more convenient and more economical for team directors to delegate team management to veteran female players or player-chaperones than to engage qualified male managers.

All of the women who assumed team manager positions had four or more years of experience in the AAGBBL. Bonnie Baker, for instance, had played in the league since it began in 1943. She was specifically traded to the Kalamazoo team from South Bend in 1950 so she could act as manager at Kalamazoo.[41] Mary Reynolds, who joined the Peoria team when it first organized in 1946, was named player-chaperone at the beginning of the 1950 season and subsequently became team manager in mid-season.[42] Ernestine Petras first joined the league in 1944 as a member of the Milwaukee Chicks team. She was captain of the Kenosha Comets when elected to serve as manager in 1951.[43] Thelma Eisen also joined the league in 1944 as a member of the Milwaukee Chicks, and Vivian Kellog started with the 1944 Minneapolis Orphans.[44] Mary Rountree's association with the league began when she joined the Peoria Redwings in 1946.[45] The longevity of these players' association with the league suggests they were strong performers who demonstrated leadership qualities on and off the field.

Of all the players who served as team managers, special permission had to be obtained from the League Board of Directors for Ernestine Petras to manage the Kenosha team the last few weeks of the 1951 season.[46] This resulted from the league board's decision to prohibit the employment of feminine managers after the 1950 season.[47] The apparent reason for this legislation stemmed from negative fan reaction and player disrespect for female managers. Harold Dailey offered this rationale in a memo dated August 29, 1950:

> Talked with several of the fans [at Kalamazoo–South Bend game] and Baker's day is over as manager with Kalamazoo if the fans have a thing to say about it. They feel that it would be a better team if they had a man manager. Also that the Peoria team was not good with Reynolds at the head. [Ruth] Williams told me that there was no team work there and that the girls would not follow the signals with Reynolds on the coaching line.[48]

Above: Bonnie Baker (courtesy Northern Indiana Center for History). *Above, right:* Mary Rountree. Ernestine "Teeny" Petras (both photographs reproduced from the original held by the Department of Special Collections of the University Libraries of Notre Dame).

It can't be ignored that Peoria and Kalamazoo were at the bottom of league standings when the female managers were installed and their positions didn't change any by the end of the season.[49] Had either team been able to improve its standings, then player and fan reaction to female managers may have been positive instead of negative and the league board's action prohibiting them may not have occurred. This is hypothetical

of course, but it is often demonstrated in professional sport that male managers become scapegoats for losing teams. The fact that a similar reaction to female managers was intensified to excluding them from further managerial positions was not inconsistent with male/female roles during the 1950s. They obviously had an uphill battle to fight and a very slippery slope on which to fight it.

On the other hand, it is not illogical to postulate that fan and player reaction would have been supportive if the particular teams in question had been able to improve their standings under the guidance of female managers.

Mary "Windy" Reynolds with Peoria Redwings Manager Leo Schrall (courtesy Terry Donahue).

AAGBBL Policies and Regulations for Team Managers

Salaries for regular AAGBBL managers varied, but a new manager could earn $2500 for five months' work and was eligible for a 20 percent annual raise from 1943 to 1947.[50] If a manager coached a championship team he was likely to receive a bonus from team administrators. Bill Allington, for instance, was awarded a $500 bonus under such circumstances at the end of the 1945 season.[51] In January of 1947, league administrators voted to extend a $250 allowance to managers during the two-week spring training camp. This was in addition to their regular salary.[52] The following year (1948), the league board attempted to set a ceiling on managers' salaries by imposing a $3600 maximum salary limit, including bonuses.[53] Apparently some managers' salaries were getting out of hand. As nearly as could be determined, this legislation was dropped during the administration of Independent Team Owners (1951–1954).

An examination of Table 12 indicates a fairly constant turnover among AAGBBL managers. Only four of the 34 male managers maintained an association with the league for six years or more, whereas 13 served one-year terms. The reasons for AAGBBL manager dismissals or retirements were similar to manager dismissals in most other sport enterprises. Some were dismissed because they didn't produce winning teams or because they disagreed with team directors.[54] Some had or developed drinking problems or attacked officials.[55] Others retired to assume better positions elsewhere. Leo Schrall, for instance, resigned as coach of the Peoria Redwings after the 1949 season to assume a full-time coaching position at Bradley University.[56]

Under the Trustee and Management Corporation administrations, employment and release of managers was a league and not a team responsibility, though team administrations were allowed to approve or disapprove the acceptability of a specific manager.[57] There didn't appear to be any problems with the assignment and release of managers under this procedure until the 1947 season. Nor was the problem clearly defined, but the following action by the league board indicated that a snag was encountered either in the signing or release of managers.

> It was moved, seconded and unanimously adopted that the League Office shall have the choice of a new manager for any team. If the Office deems the choice unwise, and the club still wishes to hire said prospect, then the matter will be brought up before the Executive Committee who will present a full report to the Board at the following meeting.
> In case of releasing a Manager, then the Executive Committee shall sit in as a Trial Board. At this meeting, the Manager shall be present, together with the Club President. If a member of the Executive Committee is the President of the Club in dispute, another Board member shall be appointed to act on the Trial Board to determine all facts on the situation.[58]

When the league switched to Independent Team Owners in 1951, this policy became obsolete as the hiring of all personnel reverted to individual team administrations.

When AAGBBL administration changed in 1951 from the Management Corporation to Independent Team Owners, one thing that did not change was the practice of employing, whenever possible, ex-professional male baseball players as team managers. Team administrators adhered to the philosophy that these men were best qualified to manage women's professional baseball, that they contributed to the league's professional image, and perhaps that the ex-pros, in themselves, acted as spectator drawing cards.

10

Chaperones

Young women who played for amateur softball teams in the 1940s and 1950s generally lived and played in their home environs; and except for those who played in some metropolitan centers, amateur players played in only one or two games per week. AAGBBL players, on the other hand, hailed from all sections of the United States and Canada, including a few from Cuba. They were full-time ball players three and a half to four months during the summer, playing an average of a game a day and a double-header or two on the weekends. These conditions made the institution of a chaperone desirable for the sake of propriety. American social mores of the time did not sanction women traveling about supervised only by a male manager. In this respect, the institution of chaperones, at the beginning of the Trustee Administration, paralleled practices employed by women's AAU and college athletic teams.[1]

League administrators not only had to contend with general public approval, but also with parental approval, as most players were between 18 to 25 years of age and single. Some were recruited as young as 14 or 15. As mentioned in Chapter 3, it was natural for parents of single young women to be reluctant to allow their daughters to move to strange, and often far-away towns to travel about the Midwest supervised only by a male manager. The league's employment of chaperones, therefore, not only enhanced its public image but also placated protective parents.[2]

When Canadian Terry Donahue was asked whether her parents had reservations about her joining the AAGBBL in 1943, she responded that her dad was for it but her mother was especially hesitant about the idea. She acknowledged that staying in private homes and the existence of "the chaperone turned the tide for my Mom."[3] Joyce Hill Westerman also testified that "the chaperone was a factor in my parents letting me go as well as how much I wanted to go."[4] Recruited from Alabama, Delores "Dolly" Brumfield White emphasized that because of the chaperone and Margie (Holgerson — another player from Alabama), her folks let her go to tryouts in Havana, Cuba, in 1947 when she was only 14.[5] Audrey Haine Daniels also noted that her mother was persuaded to allow her to join the league because of the chaperones' presence.[6] Except for chaperones, a number of worthy players may never have enjoyed the opportunity to play in the league in the first place. Thus, Wrigley's institution of the chaperone as an integral part of team operations involved considerable wisdom and foresight.

In retrospect, other players acknowledged the important role chaperones played in their well being. As Dorothy "Kammie" Kamenshek observed, "They were not just a chaperone. They took care of our injuries, our meal money, assigned us rooms, and were our confidants if we needed someone because we were all very young."[7] Thelma "Tiby" Eisen emphasized, "It was important for the girls to be able to talk to a woman about physical things, instead of a man. I remember Max Carey ... was like a father figure to us, but you wouldn't go to him for certain things."[8] Dolly Brumfield White, recruited to the league at age 14, testified how chaperones took special care of younger players:

> I remember with South Bend, it was my first year. I was in a hotel room with several of the girls. They were playing poker. In walks the chaperone. She breaks up that game to get me out of there. I'm not supposed to be in there [while] those girls [are] playing poker. At home my Daddy played poker and it was all right, but she was looking after me. She was in charge of protecting me.
>
> I saw a lot of movies, but I didn't know until recently that the chaperone had assigned players to take me to the movies. I just thought we were going to the movies.[9]

Shirley Burkovich, 16 when she left Pittsburgh, Pennsylvania, to join the league as a Muskegon Lassie, recalled Helen Hannah Campbell's dealings with a prospective date:

> Even if you wanted to go out with someone, you had to get permission. [The chaperone] had to approve it, especially with teenagers.... After a game, this young boy asked me to go to the movies and I said, "We'll have to get permission." He said, "Well, okay." So I went to Helen [Hannah Campbell] and she said, "Well, I'll have to see him." So I told him, "You'll have to meet the chaperone." He kind of smiled and said, "Okay." He went in and came out, and this time he wasn't smiling, he was laughing, and he said to me, "I didn't want to marry you, I just wanted to take you to the movies."
>
> I didn't ask what she asked him, but I'm sure he had to go through the paces. That's the way it was. They didn't let us go just wandering off. The chaperones were very important to the team, especially the younger girls.[10]

For younger players especially, chaperones served more than an administrative role; they served as surrogate mothers.

The chaperone had an especially important role when it came to player injuries. Besides treating minor injuries, the chaperone, rather than the managers, assumed the role of team physician in deciding when a player with a major injury should return to the field. As Helen Hannah Campbell explained, the chaperone was the one who talked to the doctor and the player and decided on a player's fitness to play. This was important because players didn't want to lose their positions and would not be totally forthright with their managers regarding the seriousness of their injuries. Thus, the manager deferred to the chaperone's judgment on injury matters.[11]

Chaperones' Backgrounds

Table 13 provides a listing of most, if not all, of the individuals who served as chaperones during the AAGBBL's twelve-year history. The first chaperones were selected on the basis of their experience "directing girls in schools and other fields of athletics" and on their own experience in organized sport.[12] As might be expected, several chaperones employed by the AAGBBL were physical education instructors. One of the first chaperones who exemplified all of these qualities was Marie "Teddy" Anderson.

Marie Teichman Anderson was an outstanding athlete in her day, having traveled through 38 states, five provinces of Canada, and seven Mexican states with sport teams. She held world records for the 220-yard dash and the indoor high jump, and she equaled world records in the 50- and 100-yard dashes, the 60-yard low hurdles, and the hop, skip, and jump. She was a graduate of Lake View High School in Chicago and the American College of Physical Education. When she was employed by the AAGBBL, she was a phys-

Table 13: AAGBBL Chaperones, 1943–1948

City	1943	1944	1945	1946	1947	1948
Battle Creek						
Chicago						Margaret Johnson
Fort Wayne			Helen Rauner Harrington	Helen Rauner Harrington	Marian Stancevic	Gerry Reiber
Grand Rapids			Dorothy Hunter*	Dorothy Hunter*	Dorothy Hunter*	Dorothy Hunter*
Kalamazoo						
Kenosha	Ada Ryan	Lex McCutchen	Lex McCutchan Catherine Behrens	Jo Hageman*	Jo Hageman*	Jo Hageman*
Milwaukee		Dorothy Hunter				
Minneapolis		Ada Ryan				
Muskegon				Eunice Kessler Frances Grube Eileen O'Brien*	Helen Hannah	Helen Hannah
Peoria				Betty Gerring Irene Ives	Mildred Baker	Ruth Waco
Racine	Marie Anderson	M. Anderson Virginia Carrig	Ruth Peterson Jo Winter Mildred Wilson	Mildred Wilson	Mildred Wilson	Mildred Wilson
Rockford	Marie Timm	Marie Timm	Marie Timm	Mildred Lundahl Millie Deegan	Mildred Lundahl	Dorothy Green* Mary Moore
South Bend	Rose Way	Helen Moore	Lucille Moore	Lucille Moore	Lucille Moore	Lucille Moore
Springfield						Mary Rudis*

*Former AAGBBL Player; +Player-Chaperone. Note: Empty spaces indicate team was not active in the AAGBBL.

SOURCE: *1944 Racine Belles Year Book*, pp. 6–7; *1945 Racine Belles Year Book*, pp. 8–10; *1946 Racine Belles Year Book*, pp. 8–10; *1947 Grand Rapids Chicks Year Book*, pp. 6–9; *1947 Muskegon Lassies Year Book*, p. 21; *1948 Racine Belles Year Book*, pp. 10–13; *1949 Peoria Redwings Year Book*, pp. 10–16; 1950 Kenosha Comets Scorecard, Northern Indiana Center for History (NICH), Dailey Records, 1943–1954; *Kalamazoo Gazette* (Mich.), 18 May 1954, p. 33, 27 April 1953, p. 16; *Grand Rapids Press* (Mich.), 21 May 1953, p. 41; "Fort Wayne Daisies 1953 Official Program and Scorebook," p. 3, contributed to the author by Marilyn Jenkins, Grand Rapids, Michigan; 1953 South Bend Scorecard, NICH. Additional information obtained from Mary "Wimp" Baumgartner, August 27, 2004, at the AAGPBL Reunion in Kalamazoo, Michigan.

ical education instructor who had coached championship teams in swimming, basketball, track, softball, volleyball, and ice-skating.[13]

Ruth Peterson, one of Marie's successors for the Racine Belles, had been an active athlete, had supervised women's athletic teams, and was a physical education instructor at Racine's Washington Junior High School when she became the Belles' chaperone. Her athletic career included experience as a pitcher for Racine's Davis Shoe Softball Team, many times city champions. She also pitched for the girls' baseball team at the University of Wisconsin and participated on field hockey and track squads. Peterson earned her degree from Kendall College of Physical Education in Chicago.[14]

Mildred Wilson, Racine Belles' chaperone from 1946 to 1949, had a background similar to that of her predecessors. A native of Brooklyn and a physical education graduate from Long Island University, Wilson was a sports star in her own right. She managed and played catcher for the New York Celtics Softball Team, the Metropolitan Champions. She was also an outstanding basketball star, and her New York team ran up a string of 32 consecutive wins during the winters of 1945 and 1946.[15]

Table 13: AAGBBL Chaperones, 1949–1954

City	1949	1950	1951	1952	1953	1954
Battle Creek			Pat Barringer	Pat Barringer	Kay Kimball Pat Barringer	
Chicago	Barb Liebrich* (Tour Team)	Barb Liebrich* (Tour Team)				
Fort Wayne	Gerry Reiber	Doris Tetzlaff*	Doris Tetzlaff*	Doris Tetzlaff*	Doris Tetzlaff*	Margaret Ryan
Grand Rapids	Dorothy Hunter*	Dorothy Hunter*	Dorothy Hunter*	D. Hunter* (Last half)	Dorothy Hunter*	Dorothy Hunter*
Kalamazoo		Helen Hannah Alice Hohlmayer*	Helen Hannah	Barbara Liebrich*	Barbara Liebrich*	Barbara Liebrich*
Kenosha	Jo Hageman*	Teeny Petras+ Beth Goldsmith*	Jo Hageman*			
Milwaukee						
Minneapolis						
Muskegon	Helen Hannah	Helen Hannah Alice Hohlmayer*			Kay Kimball Pat Barringer*	
Peoria	Elizabeth Dailey	Mary Reynolds+	Alice Hohlmayer*			
Racine	Mildred Wilson	Irene Hickson+				
Rockford	Mary Moore Dorothy Green*	Dorothy Green*	Dorothy Green*	Dorothy Green*	Dorothy Green*	Marion Holloway
South Bend	Marge Stefani*	Marge Stefani*	Jean Faut+	Jean Faut+ Shirley Stovroff+	Irene Wagoner	Mildred Roark
Springfield	Pat Barringer* (Tour Team)	Pat Barringer* (Tour Team)				

In addition to those chaperones with physical education training backgrounds, others came to the league with a variety of experiences and as a result of former contact with league personnel. Alexandra "Lex" McCutchan hailed from Regina, Saskatchewan, and had done some teaching, but her introduction to the league came through her acquaintance with Racine manager, Johnny Gottselig.

> "Johnny Gottselig, manager of Racine in 1943, came to visit [in Kansas City, Missouri] and said they needed a chaperone because they were going to have two more teams in 1944. I knew him when I was young in Regina, Saskatchewan.
> My husband's health wasn't the best. He thought that because Wrigley was behind it, that that would be a good company to get in with. Johnny ... recommended me to Wrigley.[16]

Elizabeth Dailey, the 1949 Peoria chaperone, was a registered nurse. She served in the Army Nurse Corps from 1940 to 1945 and earned two battle stars and a bronze star while overseas.[17]

Dorothy Hunter was perhaps the first AAGBBL player to become a chaperone. A member of the Racine Belles in 1943, Hunter became chaperone of the Milwaukee Chicks in 1944. When the Chicks were relocated to Grand Rapids in 1945, she moved with them.[18] With the exception of the first half of the 1952 season, when team management didn't hire her for economic reasons, Hunter served as the Chicks' chaperone through 1954. In so doing, she established the longest tenure of a chaperone in the AAGBBL (see Table 13).

A native of Canada, Hunter gained her ball playing experience with championship teams in Winnipeg, Manitoba. During the winter months, she generally returned to Winnipeg, where she worked as a cashier in a large office. Eventually, however, she settled in Grand Rapids.[19] Hunter's length of service as chaperone for the Grand Rapids Chicks indicated her enthusiasm for the position and her expertise in carrying out her responsibilities.

Marilyn Jenkins, former Grand Rapids Chicks catcher, testified that Dorothy Hunter commanded considerable respect throughout the community and throughout the league. Her players especially respected her because, according to Jenkins,

> ... she took care of all our problems: our jewelry, our money, our chewing gum, our sewing, our [personal] problems, our strawberries [sliding bruises], and our dislocated fingers. She taped us together — she had a heck of a fishing tackle box — and she went to the hospital with all injured players. She had spunk, spark, and fight, and we all respected her.[20]

Dorothy Hunter may have been the exceptional chaperone, but Jenkins' remarks convey a sense of the value a good chaperone had for her players.

Helen Hannah Campbell, one of Muskegon's chaperones, was perhaps the most qualified woman to don the uniform of an AAGBBL chaperone. Born in 1915, Helen was the only child of James Harrison "Truck" Hannah, who played, coached, and managed in the Pacific Coast League. He also played in the majors for the Yankees and the Tigers, and he concluded his 30-year baseball career back in the minor leagues as a manager. In his career in the Pacific Coast League, "Truck" played for and later coached and managed the Los Angeles Angels. At that time, the Angels were the triple–A farm team for the Chicago Cubs. Helen remembered attending spring training at Catalina Island every year with the Angels and Cubs.[21] The intertwining of her life with Wrigley's baseball organizations began in childhood as a result of her father's baseball career.

A

Left: Dorothy "Dottie" Hunter. Milwaukee and Grand Rapids Chicks chaperone 1944–1954 (courtesy Marilyn Jenkins). *Right:* Helen Hannah Campbell. Muskegon and Kalamazoo Lassies' chaperone, 1947–1951 (courtesy Helen Hannah Campbell).

beloved daughter who adored her father, Helen grew up immersed in the golden age of baseball. She frequently shared the company of baseball notables such as Joe DiMaggio and his brothers, Ted Williams, Lefty O'Doul, the Lillard brothers, Buck Newsome, Jigger Statz, Miller Huggins, Babe Ruth, Ty Cobb, and Lou Gehrig.[22]

> To me, these baseball greats "were either in [our] league, on our team, or in our home, and they were just like neighbors. They were compatriots of my father in his profession, and I didn't know I was supposed to be honored by knowing who they were, or what they were, or what they said to me."[23]

Later on, when people would ask if she'd ever shaken Babe Ruth's hand, she'd think, "I'd like to have a nickel for every time I probably did."[24]

With a father whose life's vocation and avocation focused on playing, coaching, and managing baseball, Helen absorbed the game from the inside out long before she joined the Muskegon Lassies in 1947. In addition, by 1947, she'd acquired considerable organizational and leadership skills. A graduate of Woodbury College, Helen's first major employment experience came as administrative assistant to Mr. Jim Crowell, Director of Purchases for the Wrigley Company's west coast holdings. These included The Santa Catalina Island Company; The Wilmington Transportation Co.; Catalina Airlines; the Los Angeles Angels (AAA) Baseball Club; and Fleming and Weber, a real estate company. Most of these holdings supported the Catalina Island Company.

Helen explained that she didn't believe her father pulled any strings to help her acquire the job. However, because of her father's long association with the Angels, Mr. Crowell knew she had just graduated and had "a pee-wee-dink job with an insurance company." When he approached her about working for him, she was very pleased because the job "was with baseball — it was with the company my Dad was with."[25] In addition, her office location was at the ball field.

> For the first several months, my offices were in the tower that was the landmark of the baseball diamond (42nd and Avalon Blvd.) in Los Angeles. At the top of the tower was a clock (on all 4 sides of the tower) but ... it spelled out "Wrigley Field" in a circular formation instead of the numbers 1 to 12.
>
> But when the Wrigley contingent from Chicago rented a complete floor in an office building (across the street from the Biltmore Hotel), they assigned two offices to the Director of Purchases ... and they transferred us from the ball tower to downtown.[26]

After five years of working with Wrigley Company purchasing, Japan bombed Pearl Harbor, Wrigley loaned Catalina Island to the government for military training, and Helen's position became obsolete. Before long, however, she found employment as personnel director of 500 men in a ship-fitting factory. This lasted until she felt the constraints of being in a dead-end job. Before she could seek another position, however, she had to obtain an availability certificate. Acquiring such a certificate was necessitated by the war-related nature of her work place, but her boss stubbornly refused to grant her continued requests for one. Not to be held back unjustly, she circumvented her recalcitrant supervisor by joining the Marine Corps in the fall of 1943.[27]

After basic training at Camp Le Jeune, North Carolina, and a little KP duty at Cherry Point, Helen was transferred to El Toro Air Base in Santa Ana, California. There she assumed command of a $100,000 clothing warehouse for the 2,000 female Marines on base. She remained at El Toro until World War II ended. In the fall of 1946, she was discharged as an inactive organized reserve.[28] Thus, between 1936 and 1947, before she joined the AAGBBL, Helen's employment and military experience honed her organizational and leadership qualities. She especially acknowledged the impact of Marine life in this regard.

> My four years in the Marine Corps put me in good stead for regimentation and discipline and expecting orders to be carried out. I was firm but fair. They [the players] were buddies to me. I wanted to instill confidence in me for them.[29]

After being discharged in the fall of 1946, Helen attended winter baseball league meetings in Los Angeles with her father. It was there she first met Max Carey, a prior acquaintance of her father's. Max, now President of the AAGBBL, recognized her potential as a first class chaperone candidate because he offered her the Muskegon chaperone job at that time. Helen didn't accept immediately since she was involved in a business venture with some fellow service personnel. However, Max contacted her again in the early spring of 1947 and offered her the job a second time. With the lure of Cuba as a spring training site, Helen decided it sounded like "an interesting project" and agreed to try it for a year.[30] Once again, her life was impacted by Wrigley baseball, but this time it was Wrigley *women's* baseball that captivated her.

That "interesting project" began with a bang just after the AAGBBL contingent landed in Havana, Cuba. The chaperones were faced with trying to corral 200 wired, hungry young female ball players inside the Biltmore Hotel while Cinco de Mayo madness was happening outside. On top of that, the hotel failed to have adequate food on hand for the group. Helen described the scene:

> Of course, those [girls] who were on the third and fourth floors were tying bed sheets together and dropping them out the window and talking to the vendors who were going along, and having them [tie] stuff in baskets. [We] were trying to get those baskets away from them because there was no place they could properly prepare whatever they might have brought up — or even get them to wash that food and fruit, or whatever, because of the bad stories we'd heard about the Cubans' gardens. So that was a chore to begin with.[31]

The frantic was juxtaposed with the humorous when Alva Jo "Tex" Fischer convinced a young Cuban Don Juan leering at Helen in the dugout that the "AAGBBL" initials on the shield adorning Helen's navy blue uniform represented her name. The young man questioned, "Su nombre?" Tex, poker-faced, and in all seriousness, nodded and pronounced it: "AGABUBBLE." The young man, bewildered, turned and walked away, never to return. Tex sat down by Helen and remained poker-faced, so Helen just laughed to herself, and the humor of the incident remained vivid in her memory the rest of her life.[32]

Other aspects of chaperoning that Helen recalled included the 24/7 nature of the job from spring training to the end of play-offs; how "the managers depended upon the chaperone probably more so than the girls did"; how the "chaperone became like a surrogate mother of the team"; how her duties were many and varied, including making hotel reservations, arranging for buses for away games, checking the girls' housing, disbursing checks and meal money, doing banking for some players, laundering and packing uniforms, making trips to the hospital, waging a continual battle about the thing that bothered her most — "those damned strawberries that they used to get."

> They wouldn't allow me to put a dressing on that would stay on and then have to put any kind of shorts on top of it. Then the next thing, they were in the ball game, and they'd slide into second base again and pull all of that stuff off. Oh, it was an icky job. I felt sorry for them because some of those sores would last a whole season.[33]

Helen also emphasized the strong relationship that existed between the players and the community by the time she joined the league in 1947. This made her job of finding housing for them less of a chore.

> Families clamored to house the girls if they were baseball fans. They adored the Lassies. If they weren't baseball fans and they housed girls, they became baseball fans. Those who housed girls often had a son or daughter gone because of marriage or the war.[34]

Then there were the players' unforgettable practical jokes. Helen noted that she experienced short-sheeting and housekeeping carts propped in front of her hotel room doors. On her first road trip with the Lassies, the California girls put an artificial garter snake in her hotel room.... She picked it up and started to pet it and said, "What should we name it?" Their expectations for a good laugh at her expense were quickly quelled! The California girls, nicknamed "the prune pickers," concocted another humorous prank Helen recalled fondly:

> During my second year, I bought some mirrored dark glasses. When we went into Peoria [to play], they all bought mirrored sun glasses in a drug store. All 16 lined up on the sidewalk to get on the bus, and they all had on mirrored sun glasses![35]

Besides a willingness to tackle the physical tasks of the job, the qualities of a good chaperone as displayed by Helen included firmness, caring, patience, understanding, dedication, and a sense of humor!

During the Lassies' last two years in Muskegon, 1948–1949, Helen assumed the added responsibilities of General Manager for the team along with her chaperoning duties.[36] When asked if she had problems with men taking her seriously in this administrative capacity, she responded:

> No. I don't know whether they were surprised or scared. I had 12 officers and 125 enlisted [all men] under me in the Marine Corps, so I had a background in leadership and the vocabulary of a leader. When I assumed the role as G.M., the future of the league was shaky, so I said, "What have I got to lose?[37]

She tackled the G.M. job as a challenge and with the fervor that prompted the 1999 L.A. Angels' Booster Club president to characterize the then 84-year-old Helen as "a Real Dynamo."[38] After all, he noted:

> When Helen isn't tangled up with baseball, her retirement time is filled with volunteering at the Nixon Library, the Fountain Valley Police Department, the Women Marines, the Gene Autry Museum, the pharmacy at her HMO, and last but not least, her international traveling.[39]

At the end of her fifth year as chaperone for the Lassies, Helen determined to quit because "five

Helen Hannah Campbell. Retired U.S. Marine Corps Master Gunnery Sgt. E-9 (courtesy Ruth Davis).

years was enough and the league was deteriorating and going down hill."[40] That decision was enforced when she returned home to Southern California. There she found a government letter surprising her with the news that she was drafted back into active duty due to the onset of the Korean War. Striving always to gain the highest rank possible during her military career, Helen remained a Marine for a total of 32 years. She retired at the top of her classification in 1975 as Master Gunnery Sergeant E-9. Semper Fi, Helen!

AAGBBL Chaperone Policies

Chaperones were paid between $250 and $300 per month plus expenses during the first years of league operation.[41] Lex McCutchan noted that her "salary was $75 a week. In 1944 that was a good salary compared to what I was earning on a good job."[42] South Bend chaperone Lucille Moore also testified that this was a considerable sum at the time.[43] Chaperones' salaries, like players' salaries, were reduced as the league's financial situation declined. In 1954, for example, chaperones were paid $300 a month but $115 of this amount was designated for expenses.

A paraphrased list of chaperones' duties suggests that if they were conscientious, they earned every penny of their wages. Chaperones were required to:

1. Be responsible for the appearance, conduct, and behavior of the players over whom they were appointed and be accessible to players at all times.
2. Attend all team meetings and practices and be on the field one hour before game time to minister to any player needs.
3. Visit and approve players' living quarters and eating places.
4. Approve all players' social engagements.
5. Maintain general contact with players at all times.
6. Acquire a general knowledge of league regulations and supervise their execution.
7. Enforce the league rules prohibiting players from wearing slacks, shorts, or dungarees in public, from spring training through the final date of any play-off series.
8. Enforce the league rule prohibiting players from wearing boyish bobs or short hair cuts at any time.
9. Post a list of all eating places and taverns placed out of bounds by the club board of directors in the clubhouse.
10. Acquire a general knowledge of first aid and be responsible for filling the first aid kit.
11. Be responsible for making room assignments and distributing towels and soap.
12. Check players in thirty minutes before traveling time.
13. Be responsible for handling meal and taxi money on road trips.
14. See that curfew hours are regularly followed.
15. Make all hotel room assignments and supply hotels with room lists.
16. Report any player to the manager who habitually ignores league standards.
17. Hold regular meetings with the manager regarding any problems.
18. See that players do not fraternize with other teams' personnel.
19. Decide on the permissibility of card playing in rooms.
20. Approve all players' change of residence.[44]

In essence, a chaperone acted as an overseer of team personnel, a road secretary, an equipment manager, a trainer, a first aid dispenser, and an assistant manager. Some also assisted in the coaching boxes during games.[45] If chaperones failed to perform their duties as outlined, they were subject to a fine. Any violations of rules and regulations by players not reported by a chaperone to the manager or league office made her subject to the same fine as the player.[46]

Some chaperones had trouble fulfilling the responsibilities the league office outlined for them or else grew negligent in their supervision. At a league board meeting in November 1945, it was agreed that "managers and chaperones shall co-operate more fully than they have or did last year regarding the conduct of players."[47] It was emphasized that "chaperones shall be fined along with players for any infringement of a rule."[48] This same item was re-emphasized at league board meetings in June 1947, in April 1950, and in February 1952.[49] The fact that players lived in a dozen or more different locations while "at home" suggests chaperones' duties were difficult to perform and that infractions occurred. One chaperone pointed out to league administrators that "supervision of the girls at home is almost impossible."[50] She suggested that league administrators try to rent a large home or dormitory space on local school campuses to house the players under one roof while they were "at home." No records were encountered to indicate that any action was taken on this suggestion.

Chaperones' dress, like players' uniforms, came under the jurisdiction of the League Board of Directors. In 1946, chaperones' uniforms consisted of a shirtwaist dress with an AAGBBL emblem on the left breast.[51] A jacket of contrasting shade complimented the dress. At a league board meeting in June 1946, league directors endorsed legislation which stipulated, "On very hot nights, the chaperones will be allowed to take off their coats while sitting on the bench, but must wear them if they must go on the field."[52] This legislation apparently aroused a protest from chaperones because at a September 1946 board meeting the chaperone jacket policy was revised to state, "In the future, chaperones may wear

Eight chaperones in Cuba. *Left to right:* Mildred Baker (Peoria), Mildred Wilson (Racine), Jo Hageman (Kenosha), Helen Hannah (Muskegon), Mildred Lundahl (Rockford), Marian Stancevic (Fort Wayne), Dottie Hunter (Grand Rapids), Lucille Moore (South Bend) (courtesy Northern Indiana Center for History).

what they please on the field."[53] League directors conceded that donning a jacket on a hot, muggy, Midwestern summer night to coach at one of the bases or attend to an injury was not that critical.

The league stopped supplying chaperones with uniforms in 1950 or 1951 as an economy measure. The uniform, however, gave chaperones public visibility and by the February 1952 Board Meeting, it was deemed a desirable practice to re-instate.

> President Van Orman instructed each club to obtain a chaperone uniform and to insist that the chaperone wear the uniform at all places where she appears. In case of a player-chaperone, she should assume the chaperone attire after games, at hotels, on the bus, etc., — or at all times when appearing publicly, except when on the field when she would necessarily wear her uniform.[54]

The specific style of uniform adopted in 1952 was left to the discretion of each club, though it was stipulated that chaperone uniforms "should be patterned after that of an air-line stewardess, with cap."[55] This type of uniform had previously been adopted in 1947 under the Management Administration.[56]

In October 1949, a change was instituted in the league's chaperone system. A motion was made at a league board meeting that "each club employ player-coach-chaperones for the 1950 season."[57] Prior to this time, chaperones had been employed strictly as chaperones and had not simultaneously participated as players. Jo Hageman may have been an exception to this practice as the suggestion was made at a league board meeting that she be utilized as a player-chaperone in 1946. However, no confirmation of her actually having participated as a player and a chaperone in 1946 was discovered.[58] With this possible exception, the chaperone's position was considered a full-time responsibility, and the duties assigned to her suggested, until 1950, it was just that.

According to ex-manager Chet Grant, the league board's decision to utilize active players in the dual capacity of chaperone was, indeed, justified as an economy measure.[59] This seems consistent since it will be remembered that 1949 and 1950 were financially debilitating years for the league. Players who served as player-chaperones were paid more than other players, but less than the full combined salary of a player and a chaperone. Shirley Stovroff, 1952 South Bend player-chaperone, for example, earned $318 per month as a player and an additional $159 per month for doubling as the team's chaperone.[60] Thus, South Bend saved $100–150 per month that would have been required for a full-time chaperone.

The move to switch from full-time to part-time chaperones did not take place without considerable dispute, despite the financial savings. One league board member urged his colleagues to retain full-time chaperones at a January 1950 board meeting.

> Mr. Johnson made an urgent appeal that we retain the present chaperone set-up or program and not utilize a player as a chaperone. Considerable discussion took place, but Mr. Johnson's motion to continue the present chaperone system was dropped for want of a second. Therefore, the resolution regarding the player-coach-chaperone adopted at the October 2, 1949 meeting will still prevail.[61]

The overriding concern at this time was how to curtail expenses, and the majority of the board members obviously believed dropping the full-time chaperone policy was a viable step in this direction.

The chaperone controversy, however, was not settled with this legislation. In 1950, four teams, South Bend, Rockford, Grand Rapids, and Muskegon, elected to retain full-time chaperones.[62] At the end of the 1950 season, an agenda item for a league board meeting concerned returning to the full-time chaperone system:

> This suggestion will be met with mixed emotion but in the interest of maintaining our game at a high level, qualified people in this position can be of tremendous value. Naturally a poor chaperone will do a poor job and it is for this reason that many clubs are still unsold on the value of having a chaperone.[63]

The issue of returning to the full-time chaperone system was still controversial at the board meeting of September 20, 1950. Some team presidents were for it, and some were against it.[64] Although no action on the matter was taken at this particular board meeting, a compromise was reached later, allowing those who desired to employ a full-time chaperone to do so while at the same time allowing those who wanted to employ part-time chaperones to do so. New league rules, adopted in February 1951, stated: "A chaperone may also participate in the team's activities as a player-coach, but such duties shall in no way lessen her responsibilities in enforcing rules of conduct."[65]

Some observers have suggested that the League Board of Directors' decision to compromise on a full-time chaperone adversely affected the league's social image. Former manager Chet Grant remarked, for example, that the

> ... decline and fall of the AAGBL coincided with the regression of emphasis on the feminine factor by club directors who succeeded the pioneers. By 1950, for instance, the full-time chaperone, the AAGBL's figure of feminine gentility, had been made optional to the extent that a player might double as duenna.[66]

Given the social expectations for women during that time, Grant's observation may have been credible.

Utilizing players as player-chaperones made sense to the League Board of Directors after the first few years of play. Board members became acquainted with individual players, recognized their leadership abilities, and trusted their integrity. It's obvious that some board members believed veteran players who, by experience, knew team and league procedures, understood proper medical treatments; and those who knew which players and what places to watch could do a better job of chaperoning than someone unconnected with the game or the league. The fact that utilizing player-chaperones would benefit the financial situation at hand didn't hurt either. The main downside to this theory was the human tendency of player-chaperones to be too lenient with their teammates, which in some instance, may have resulted in adverse fan reaction and support.

Whatever the case, the long-term concern with chaperone issues by the League Board of Directors indicates something of their concept of the importance of the position to the players, to the managers, and to the league's image.

PART IV

The Players

The Peg to First. *Left to right:* Dottie Ferguson Key, Ruth "Tex" Lessing (reproduced from the original held by the Department of Special Collections of the University Libraries of Notre Dame).

11

Player Recruitment and
Player Backgrounds

A history of the AAGBBL is incomplete without a discussion of the players, for it goes without saying that their personalities and performances largely contributed to the league's success. The scope of this book, which deals primarily with the organization and operation of the league, limits the focus on players to the league's player recruitment policies and some sociological aspects of their backgrounds (Chapter 11); to a discussion of AAGBBL player policies and regulations (Chapter 12); and to an examination of the accomplishments of a few league All-Stars (Chapter 13). In the bibliography, refer to authors Lois Browne, Patricia Brown, Barbara Gregorich, Diane Helmer, Susan Johnson, Sue Macy, W.C. Madden, and Carolyn Trombe for works that give greater scope to the players.

Player Recruitment

During the Trustee Administration (1943–1944), the league office professed that players were selected on the basis of "the recognized professional sports principle of getting the very best obtainable players throughout the country...."[1] This statement indicates league administrators attempted to recruit the most highly skilled players available in the nation. A 1943 *Time* magazine article, however, hinted that the first players recruited were selected as much on the basis of their physical appearance as on the basis of their softball skill. The author of the article claimed that league scout Jim Hamilton "turned down several outstanding players because they were either too uncouth, too hard-boiled, or too masculine."[2] Given the publicity campaigns emphasizing "femininity" (Chapter 3), it's quite likely physical appearance was an important consideration in player selection for administrators who attempted to maintain a public image of the league that reflected the highest contemporary standards of femininity as well as the highest standards of skill.[3] It was not improbable, therefore, that given two players with similar skill, the more "feminine" appearing of the two would be selected to play. Arthur Meyerhoff maintained, however, that skill was not generally sacrificed for appearance in player selection. He observed that it was easier to educate a skilled player in the elements of feminine charm, for show purposes, than to make an excellent ball player out of an unskilled but attractive woman.[4]

Available evidence seems to corroborate Meyerhoff's claim that exceptional skill was a major consideration in player selection. Among the first AAGBBL players were those publicized for their "feminine" appearance or accomplishments, but they also enjoyed successful softball careers with amateur teams contending for city, state, regional, national, and world championships.

Among the more publicized of the star amateurs who participated the first year of league play were Chicagoans Ann Harnett (2nd base), Irene Ruhnke (short stop), Clara Schillace (outfield), and Edythe Perlick (outfield). These players competed with and against each other in Chicago's intra-city competitions. Harnett, Ruhnke, and Schillace were also veterans of national and world softball tournaments.[5] It's quite likely these four were hand-picked for their looks as well as their skill, for publicity purposes. Clara Schillace reported that she was approached by league president, Ken Sells, himself.

> Ken Sells approached me — I played in a Chicago league. My older brother, my mentor, thought it was fake and had a lawyer friend check it out. I signed and decided to go with the yellow team [Racine] with Shirley Jameson and Joanne Winter — we all came from the Chicago league. I was one of the first four to sign.[6]

Sells also personally recruited Shirley Jameson who mentioned that he "called Dundee High School [where I taught] in the early spring and left a message for me to call him at the Wrigley Building to talk about playing in a professional league."[7]

Among the outstanding Canadian players to participate during the first season of play were Helen Nicol (later Fox) from Calgary, Mary "Bonnie" Baker from Regina, and Terrie Davis from Toronto. As a teenager, Nicol pitched for the Edmonton team that won the Western Canadian Championship. Bonnie Baker made Canadian softball history as a catcher for the Army and Navy Bombers, and Terrie Davis participated in three world championship tournaments with the Toronto Sunday Morning Class team.[8]

Other premiere players recruited for the first year of play who were publicized for their "femininity," but who also played on city, state, or national championship softball teams before joining the AAGBBL included outfielder Shirley Jameson from Dundee, Illinois; pitcher Sonny Berger from Homestead, Florida; catcher Marion Wohlwender from Cincinnati, Ohio; second sacker Mary Lou Lester from Nashville, Tennessee; and first base standout Janice O'Hara from Beardstown, Maryland.[9] Each of these women was featured as an outstanding player in 1943 pre-season and early season publicity, and many of them lived up to their reputations throughout the season. The league city sportswriters' unofficial All-Star Team for 1943 included eight of the thirteen previously mentioned players, namely Ann Harnett, Clara Schillace, Edythe Perlick, Shirley Jameson, Helen Nicol, Sunny Berger, Bonnie Baker, and Terry Davis.[10] These players may have embodied the league's "femininity" standard, but they also demonstrated ball playing skills of a high professional caliber, indicating that skill was a prime requisite, if not *the* prime requisite for player selection.

It is not surprising that these players and others like them found their way to the AAGBBL. Municipal, state, regional, and national American Softball Association tournaments were the starting place for early scouts since women's softball competition in high schools and colleges was predominantly confined to dispersed leagues. Battery mates Elizabeth "Lib" Mahon and Viola "Tommie" Thompson Griffin, played organized softball for a textile mill in Greenville, South Carolina, before joining the AAGBBL. Among the players recruited for the 1944 season, "Lib" reported, "The president of the Greenville Spinners [men's] Class 'A' team told me about it."[11] Vivian Kellogg recalled that she "played in a state championship tournament in 1943 [and] was scouted there and signed for a try-out in 1944."[12] Annabelle Lee and Marge Callaghan Maxwell both played in a

World Softball Tournament in Detroit in 1943. As Marge, from Vancouver, British Columbia reported:

> I was playing in a World Softball Tournament in Detroit in 1943. A scout approached my manager, but I didn't know until after the tournament was over. I had to get special permission from the government to go because I worked as a squad leader at Boeing, an "essential" war job. I didn't go until half way through the 1944 season.[13]

Betty Trezza, also recruited for the 1944 season, noted that she "was playing in a softball tournament in Central Park, New York. After the game was over, a scout came up to me and asked if I'd like to play out west."[14]

Similarly, a considerable number of players who entered the league between 1943 and 1949 had a history of high-level competition behind them. Table 14 depicts the highest level of softball competition 83 individual players experienced before they joined the AAGBBL. Nearly half (44.5 percent) of those individuals for whom this information was available had participated on city, state, regional, national, or world championship teams prior to joining the AAGBBL.

Table 14: Previous Softball Experience of 83 AAGBBL Players*

Level of Competition	No.	Percent	Championship Teams No.	Percent
City Teams	33	39.7		
City Champions	17	20.5	17	20.5
State Tournaments	6	7.2		
State Champions	10	12.0	10	12.0
National Tournaments	4	4.8		
National Champions	2	2.4	2	2.4
World Tournaments	1	1.2		
World Champions	4	4.8	4	4.8
Province Team	1	1.2		
Regional Champions	4	4.8	4	4.8
High School	1	1.2		
Totals	83	99.8	37	44.5

SOURCE: *1944 Racine Belles Year Book*, pp. 9–14; *1945 Racine Belles Year Book*, pp. 11–16; *1946 Racine Belles Year Book*, pp. 14–19; *1947 Grand Rapids Chicks Year Book*, pp. 13–17; *1947 Muskegon Lassies Year Book*, pp. 21–31; *1948 Racine Belles Year Book*, pp. 14–19; *1949 Peoria Redwings Year Book*, pp. 21–29; Player Profiles, Meyerhoff Files, Drawer 19, Biographies of Players Folder; *Kenosha Evening News*, May-June 1943; *Rockford Register-Republic*, 1 September 1943, p. 13; *Kalamazoo Gazette*, July 1950.

*Some players naturally had experience in more than one category of competition listed. For the purposes of this table, only the highest level of competition recorded for each player was utilized.

Although some reference was usually made about players' appearance or feminine accomplishments in league publicity, their playing skill or potential was also emphasized.

During Management and Independent Team Owner administrations, league administrators continued to emphasize skill and femininity for players in league publicity, but more emphasis seemed to be placed on skill than on femininity as time progressed. If nothing else, the emphasis on skill was necessitated by league administrations' efforts to continuously substitute baseball equipment, facilities, and regulations for the more common women's softball. Only the most skilled softball players were able to adjust to overhand pitching and longer base paths, which created problems for player procurement. This was acknowledged in a league news release in 1950. It observed that since this was the "only league in the country playing this game, it [was] difficult to secure adequate player talent of a caliber qualified to replace many of the stars...."[15]

During the later part of Meyerhoff's Management Administration, 1947–1950, when the league converted to overhand pitching, some players were discovered who had grown up with baseball backgrounds. Wilma Briggs, recruited from East Greenwich, Rhode Island, in 1948, credited her baseball background to her father.

> My father let me play on his baseball team. I played [with] the high school team one summer. I played outfield and first base. During my senior year I tried out for the team and played some outfield. The All-American League was my first experience playing with women. I was glad the league pitched overhand because I'd never played softball.[16]

Some of those with baseball experience were located as a result of Meyerhoff's extensive national publicity as well as both pre-season and rookie tours. Choctaw, Arkansas, native Sue Kidd ascribed her entry into the AAGBBL in 1949 to these factors:

> I played baseball with my father and the boys all the time. I was allowed to play on the boys' baseball team in high school. The Superintendent of Schools taught me the drop I had—a real good curve ball. I had a guidance counselor in school who tried to get me interested in college. I always told her I was going to play professional baseball and she'd tell me, "Sue, there's no such critter as professional ball [for girls]."
>
> Then one day during my junior year she got me out of class, all excited, and showed me this *Life* magazine and there it was, pictures and a story of this baseball league. Of course, I was excited about that! [Then] in June it came out in the paper that these two traveling All-American [rookie] teams were playing in Little Rock.
>
> So I went down and tried out one day and they told me to go home and pack my bags. My mother had to wash and iron all night—said she cried all night because I was only 15—but some of the girls who were a few years older told her they'd take care of me and they did: Fran Janssen and [Mary] "Wimp" Baumgartner, and of course they've been faithful friends all these years.[17]

Delores "Dolly" Brumfield White, a 1947 Alabama recruit, indicated that organized sports for girls didn't exist in Alabama at the time. She credited the development of her baseball skills to playing catch "for hours" with a member of the men's church softball team who lived next door. In addition, she played with boys and men on the school playground. Management Corporation publicity highlighting the 1947 spring training camp in Pascagoula, Mississippi, constituted her introduction to the league.

> [I played] with the men who built the ships in the shipyards when they would come to the school yard to play. They let me play with them if there was somebody missing from the infield. I got to fill in. They're the ones who went to my parents when they saw something in the paper about Pascagoula having try-outs. That's how I got to go.[18]

Shirley Burkovich, who "came from a baseball family," also confirmed that she "never played softball." She noted that her playing experience in Pennsylvania was limited to playing baseball "with the boys ... on playgrounds, and on vacant lots, and in the streets, [and] under the street lights.... When we played, we just played for fun."[19] Her introduction to the league was also the result of publicity announcing tryouts in Pittsburgh.

> [My brother] saw an ad in the paper [in 1949] that they were having a try-out for the All-American Girls Baseball League. So he said to me, "Why don't you go down there and try out?" ... I was just 16 years old, and I was scared. I said, "I'm not going down there [with] all those people." ... So he took the day off of work and took me. He said, "We'll just sit in the stands and watch. You don't have to go down [to the field]. We'll just watch."

Well, we sat there, I don't know for how long, and he said to me, "I think you're as good as any of those girls down there." I said, "You think so?" I was getting antsy up [in the stands] anyway, seeing everybody playing and I was sitting up there, and I thought, well maybe I will give it a try. So that's what I did. I went down and Lenny Zintak was there and Dolly Pearson and Shirley Jameson. Shirley was helping him with try-outs.[20]

Although a considerable number of the league's most skilled players came from the Chicago area, outstanding players were recruited from all sections of the United States and several Canadian Provinces. The 60 players chosen to play for the league in 1943, for instance, hailed from 17 States and five Provinces of Canada.[21] With the addition of two more teams in 1944, players in the league represented 26 different States plus the same five Provinces of Canada.[22] Table 15 suggests that almost half (41 percent, 1943–1949; 45 percent, 1951) of the league's players were recruited from nine Midwestern states (Illinois, Indiana, Kentucky, Michigan, Minnesota, Missouri, Ohio, Wisconsin, and Iowa) and a solid majority (61.5 percent, 1943–1949; 77 percent, 1951) were recruited from 17 Midwestern and Northeastern States—the nine Midwest states just mentioned plus Maryland, Massachusetts, New Jersey, New York, Pennsylvania, Rhode Island, Virginia, and West Virginia.

Table 15 also confirms that the AAGBBL recruited players on a nationwide scale. The area the league tapped for talent appeared to be somewhat more limited beginning in 1951 than in previous years. This resulted from economic cutbacks including the discontinuance of pre- and post-season tours. The change in league administration to Independent Team Owners at this time altered the league's player procurement procedure from a centralized operation to an individual team responsibility. Team managements generally didn't have the contacts or the resource personnel in place for securing players on the nationwide scale that was characteristic of the Trustee and Management administrations. Dorothy Hunter, a league chaperone from 1944–1954, suggested that the general caliber of players recruited to the AAGBBL between 1951 and 1954 was somewhat below that of players recruited during the Trustee and Management administrations. She attributed this to restricted recruitment practices.[23]

Some General, Sociological Player Characteristics

Generally, players' motives for joining the AAGBBL stemmed from love of the game and a strong desire to play.[24] For most, playing with the AAGBBL was a dream come true. Winnipeg, Manitoba, native Dorothy Hunter captured this sentiment in June 1943 when she first joined the league as a player for the Kenosha Comets. She noted, in a newspaper interview: "...if anyone had told me two months ago that I would be in the United States, playing softball on a Major League team and getting paid for it, I would have thought that I had a pipe dream."[25] Dorothy "Kammie" Kamenshek described her thoughts about joining the league: "I was elated. I thought I was going to be able to do what I really wanted to do and maybe get paid for it."[26] Gloria Cordes Elliott stressed, "It was just a chance of a lifetime for someone who loved to play baseball as much as I did to get involved with this league. It was just phenomenal."[27]

Available biographical data for 92 AAGBBL players who joined the league between 1943 and 1949 indicated they ranged in age from 15 to 28 years old, though the majority joined the league between the ages of 18–22 (see Table 16). Height and weight figures were not available for all of these individuals, but statistics for those whose personal data

Table 15: Number of Players from
Respective States/Provinces, 1943–1949 & 1951

States/	1943–1949		1951– All 8 Teams		Midwest States '43–'49		Midwest States 1951		Midwest & NE States '43–'49		Midwest & NE States 1951	
Provin.	No.	%	No.	%	No.	%	No.	%	No.	%	No.	%
Alberta	2	1.7										
Manit.	5	4.3	6	3.6								
Ontar.	4	3.4										
Sask.	8	6.8	2	1.2								
Cuba	1	.9	4	2.4								
Ala.				.6								
Ariz.	2	1.7	2	1.2								
Ark.	1	.9	1	.6								
Calif.	9	7.7	9	5.4								
Fla.	4	3.4	3	1.8								
Ga.				.6								
Ill.	24	20.5	25	15.1	24	20.5	25	15.1	24	20.5	25	15.1
Ind.	1	.9	11	6.6	1	.9	11	6.6	1	.9	11	6.6
Iowa			1	.6			1	.6			1	.6
Ky.	1	.9			1	.9			1	.9		
La.	1	.9	1	.6								
Md.	1	.9	2	1.2					1	.9	2	1.2
Mass.	4	3.4	11	6.6					4	3.4	11	6.6
Mich.	8	6.8	19	11.4	8	6.8	19	11.4	8	6.8	19	11.4
Minn.	1	.9			1	.9			1	.9		
Mo.	2	1.7	2	1.2	2	1.7	2	1.2	2	1.7	2	1.2
N.J.	1	.9	7	4.2					1	.9	7	4.2
N.Y.	3	2.5	9	5.4					3	2.5	9	5.4
N. Car.			4	2.4								
Ohio	12	10.2	10	6.0	12	10.2	10	6.0	12	10.2	10	6.0
Okla.			1	.6								
Ore.	1	.9										
Pa.	3	2.5	17	10.2					3	2.5	17	10.2
R.I.			2	1.2								
S. Car.			1	.6								
S. Dak.			1	.6								
Tenn.	5	4.2	1	.6								
Tex.	2	1.7										
Va.			2	1.2							2	1.2
W. Va.			3	1.8							3	1.8
Wisc.	11	9.4	7	4.2	11	9.4	7	4.2	11	9.4	7	4.2
Totals	117	100	166	99.7	60	51.3	75	45.1	72	61.5	128	77.0

SOURCE: The 1943–1949 figures represent individual player profiles compiled from the yearbooks and newspapers cited in Table 14 and player profiles in Meyerhoff Files, Drawer 19, Biographies of Players Folder. The 1951 figures were compiled from eligible player lists for all eight 1951 teams in Dailey Records, 1951a.

was available suggested the *majority* ranged between 5'2" and 5'6" in height and 121–145 pounds in weight. *Individuals* ranged in height between 4'11" and 5'11" and from 95 to 160 pounds in weight (see Table 17). For the most part, they were average sized young women.

Table 16: Age of Selected AAGBBL Players Upon First Joining the League

Age	No.	Percent
15	1	1.1
16	1	1.1
17	6	6.5
18	17	18.5
19	14	15.2
20	11	11.9
21	11	11.9
22	11	11.9
23	7	7.6
24	7	7.6
25	4	4.3
26	0	0.0
27	1	1.1
28	1	1.1
Totals	92	99.8

SOURCE: Same as Table 14.

Table 17: Height and Weight for Selected AAGBBL Players

Height	No.	Percent	Weight	No.	Percent
4'11"	2	2.2	Under 100	1	1.4
5'	0	0.0	100–105	1	1.4
5'1"	3	3.4	106–110	0	0.0
5'2"	12	13.5	111–115	2	2.9
5'3"	12	13.5	116–120	5	7.2
5'4"	16	17.8	121–125	9	13.0
5'5"	15	16.8	126–130	16	23.2
5'6"	13	14.6	131–135	6	8.7
5'7"	6	6.7	136–140	10	14.5
5'8"	4	4.5	141–145	8	11.6
5'9"	3	3.4	146–150	7	10.1
5'10"	2	2.2	151–155	2	2.9
5'11"	1	1.1	156–160	2	2.9
Totals	89	99.7		69	99.8

SOURCE: Same as Table 14.

The majority of those for whom information was available were cited as being employed in another occupation during the off-season. Among these, 21 different occupations were identified with 35 percent being employed in some type of office work, either as clerks or secretaries. Factory workers totaled 18.2 percent of those sampled, though in most cases the individual's specific task was not identified. Some of these unspecified factory jobs might actually have been office-type work rather than assembly-line work. Of those sampled, a little more than 12 percent were teachers and half of the teachers were physical education teachers, exclusively or in part. Table 18 presents a listing of some of the other occupations in which AAGBBL players were involved during the off-season.

Another marked characteristic of AAGBBL players for whom personal data was available was their other sport interests. Although it was not specifically stated in some cases, it was presumed that the sports interests cited for players were sports in which they participated. As can be seen from Table 19, AAGBBL players' sport interests other than softball/baseball included 35 other activities ranging from archery to volleyball. The ten sports commanding the greatest number of participants were those, perhaps with the exceptions of horseback riding, ice skating, and bowling, which were available within the school curriculum. These included basketball, swimming, tennis, track and field, volleyball, golf, and field hockey. Slightly over 59 percent of the 93 individuals for whom this information was available participated in from one to three other sports, and 83 percent participated in from one to five other sports (see Table 20).

When the AAGBBL folded, many players remained active in sports. Some, like Dorothy "Snookie" Doyle, Thelma "Tiby" Eisen, and Arleene Johnson Noga returned to championship caliber amateur softball.[28] Some enjoyed outstanding success in other sports. Sue Kidd, Fran Janssen, and Betty Wagoner, for instance, played national championship caliber basketball with the South Bend Rockettes.[29] Jean Faut and Jean Havlish became successful professional bowlers.[30] Joanne Winter played three years on the LPGA tour and was sponsored by Racine's Western Printing Company — one of her AAGBBL team sponsors. She noted that Mickey Wright and Betsy Rawlins were very good to her, and that after three years on the tour, she became a golf teaching pro.[31] Jennie Romatowski represented the U.S. as a member of the National Field Hockey and Lacrosse teams.[32] AAGBBL players were talented athletes. Many followed their love of competitive play to the AAGBBL and beyond.

Table 18: Occupations of Selected AAGBBL Players

Occupation	No.	Percent
Bank Work	2	3.0
Bowling Alley Attendant	1	1.5
Cab Driver	1	1.5
Commercial Artist	1	1.5
Department Store Manager	2	3.0
Factory Work	12	18.2
Fashion Model	1	1.5
Interior Decorator	1	1.5
Monogramist	1	1.5
Newspaper Writer	1	1.5
Nurse	1	1.5
Office/Clerical	23	35.0
Photography	2	3.0
Recreation Director	1	1.5
Sales Clerk	2	3.0
Science Research	1	1.5
Student	3	4.5
Teacher	4	6.1
Physical Education Teacher	4	6.1
Telephone Operator	1	1.5
Totals	65	98.4

SOURCE: Same as Table 14.

Table 19: Sport Interests of Selected AAGBBL Players

Activity	No.	Percent
Basketball	50	53.8
Bowling	49	52.7
Swimming	28	30.1
Tennis	28	30.1
Horseback Riding	21	22.6
Track and Field	20	21.5
Ice Skating	19	20.4
Golf	16	17.2
Volleyball	13	14.0
Badminton	10	10.7
Field Hockey	10	10.7
Fishing	6	6.4
Speed Skating (Ice)	6	6.4
Bicycling	5	5.4
Hunting	5	5.4
Ice Hockey	3	3.2
Skiing	3	3.2
Soccer	2	2.1
Archery	2	2.1
Camping	2	2.1
Dance	2	2.1
Hiking	2	2.1
Horseshoes	2	2.1
Roller Skating	2	2.1
Rowing	2	2.1
Bobsledding	1	1.1
Boxing	1	1.1
Curling	1	1.1
Figure Skating	1	1.1
Flying	1	1.1
Football	1	1.1
Handball	1	1.1
Motorcycling	1	1.1
Target Shooting (Rifle)	1	1.1

SOURCE: Same as Table 14.

NOTE: This table was compiled from the published sport interests of 92 AAGBBL players. It includes all the sport interests for each player.

Table 20: Number of Sport Interests of Selected AAGBBL Players

No. of Sports	No. of Players	Percent
1	21	22.6
2	14	15.1
3	20	21.5
4	12	12.9
5	11	11.8
6	4	4.3
7	5	5.4
8	3	3.2
9	2	2.1
10	1	1.1
Totals	93	100.0

SOURCE: Same as Table 14.

Only a few AAGBBL players were married when they joined the league. In 1946, for example, only 12 of 144 players were married, and only three of those had children.[33] Interviews with ex-players suggested these 1946 figures were fairly representative for the average number of players who were married during any given year of the league's history.[34] Some retired from the league when they married, and some, of course, were married after the league folded.[35]

As nearly as can be determined, black players didn't fit the AAGBBL's "All-American" concept. There were a few who tried out for at least one AAGBBL team. A pre-season news story from a May 10, 1951, South Bend, Indiana, newspaper noted:

> Two Negro girls, the first in the American Girls Baseball League, worked out with the Sox at Playland Park yesterday. The two [were] Elizabeth Jackson, an infielder, and Marie Mazier, an outfielder, both from South Bend.[36]

At a post-season league board meeting in November 1951, "The question of hiring colored players was discussed at length, with various views from different cities."

> The consensus of the group seemed to be against the idea of colored players, unless they would show promise of exceptional ability, that in the event a club did hire one of them, that none of the clubs would make her feel unwelcome.[37]

The South Bend team had another black player try out in June of 1952, but she apparently did not make the team, for no further mention of her appeared in the city's newspaper coverage.[38] Jean Faut recalled that black players had tried out with the team, but her impression was that they did not appear to take the trials seriously. If the board meeting minutes can be taken as the prevailing attitude toward blacks at the time, perhaps the black players perceived a futility in taking the tryouts seriously. To Jean Faut's knowledge, none of the other AAGBBL teams ever employed a black player.[39]

Apparently the segregation of black and white leagues, common within organized men's major and minor league baseball through the mid–1950s, also existed among women's softball teams in the Midwest. The *Fort Wayne Journal Gazette* (Ind.) printed a picture of the Babb's Angels, "Female Negro Softball Team," holders of the "state Negro title" in July 1954.[40] The black players who tried out for the South Bend AAGBBL team may have participated on this team or in this league.

Reasons for player retirement from the AAGBBL included injuries, mother-hood, marriage, lack of childcare, sick

Jean Faut as a Member of the Professional Women's Bowling Association (courtesy Jean Faut Fantry).

family members, education, job conflicts, inter-league competition and advancing age. The most common reasons for player retirement appeared to be injuries and family related circumstances. In 1950, for example, the league lost at least 25 players. Among these, three quit because of approaching motherhood; four retired or planned to retire as a result of marriage; three opted to attend to ill family members; one was forced to quit because she couldn't find adequate child care; two switched to another league; two took another job; two retired due to advanced age; and seven were sidelined with injuries. The injuries that ended players' careers were as diverse as one might expect. Broken ankles and legs, fractured fingers, concussions, and back injuries were among those itemized for players lost during the 1950 season.[41] Annabelle Lee Harmon acknowledged that her AAGBBL career was shortened when she suffered partial paralysis from hitting the back of her head while sliding into home plate. She recovered after a year of doctoring with a chiropractor, but returned to softball in Southern California instead of returning to the AAG-BBL.[42]

The reaction of league administrators toward the loss of players due to family responsibilities included being understanding, tolerant, and even expectant. Manager Leo Murphy pretty well summed up the sentiments of managers and league administrators on this point when he observed:

> ... after seven years of operation we couldn't expect anything else ... and actually we're proud and happy that these kids go on to the fulfillment of a worth while life reaping the benefits that we know our game provides. It does make it tough to replace them, however, since most of them have become well established and replacements are not only difficult, but costly to come by.[43]

William Chafe, author of a book dealing with the changing roles of women between 1920 and 1970, suggested that there was a re-emphasis on women's place in the home in the postwar years.[44] If the loss of AAGBBL players during 1950 can be taken as an example, the re-emphasis on women's place in the home affected some AAGBBL players as well as those in society at large.

League publicity largely failed to relate players' individual backgrounds after the Trustee Administration. If there was such publicity, it recorded only the bare outlines of family relationships and playing careers. Very little printed data relayed players' thoughts, or feelings, or perceptions about their AAGBBL experiences. In broad terms, ex-players interviewed prior to 1976 and from 1993 to 2004 conveyed that the AAGBBL offered them the opportunity to play professionally a game they loved.[45] In addition, it offered them, in one observer's eyes, the opportunity to display their skill in a game requiring "a very great deal of skill..."; to show that they were good at something, and to have people yell their approval at them.[46]

The AAGBBL also offered players the opportunity to travel, meet a wide variety of individuals, and broaden and enrich their lives. This was true for those recruited from metropolitan areas, like Madeline "Maddy" English, from the Boston area, who acknowledged that the league exposed her to different people and different cultures and created a special sisterly bond among teammates.[47] Dorothy "Snookie" Harrell Doyle and Thelma "Tiby" Eisen, Los Angeles natives, testified that they had the opportunity to meet people from all over and travel to all parts of the U.S., Cuba and, in Tiby's case, Central and South America — an education in itself.[48] Cincinnati native Dorothy "Kammie" Kamenshek lived the American Dream through the AAGBBL. Kammie, a first generation American whose father passed away when she was a child, affirmed that without the money she earned playing for the AAGBBL, she would never have had the opportunity to go to college and become a physical therapist. Nor would she have become head of physical therapy in Los Angeles County.[49] Her quest for excellence on the ball field obviously carried over into a quest for excellence in her chosen life's work. This trait undoubtedly applied to other AAGPBL players who pursued college and/or further careers at the end of their ball playing days.

Those from small towns and rural areas were especially affected by the opportunity to play in the AAGBBL. Rosemary "Stevie" Stevenson, a Stalwart, Michigan, native avowed: "It gave me an opportunity to get out and see the world, meet some wonderful people, and have an opportunity of a lifetime that 500 some women had. It was super neat."[50] Sue Kidd, from Choctaw, Arkansas, acknowledged, "It made a big impact on my life. I got to travel and meet people from all over the country and from other countries even. It helped me grow up. It taught me to be independent."[51] Dolly Brumfield White, who hailed from Prichard, Alabama, noted that traveling from the deep South to the far North as well as to Cuba exposed her to many different cultures and greatly enriched her adolescent years. Dolly, like Kammie, attended college with her AAGBBL earnings. She, like a number of her league-mates became a teacher. When she speaks to groups about her AAGBBL experiences, she illustrates the cultural diversity she experienced during her first year with the league, as a 14 year old, by talking about her teammates.

> The catcher was from [eastern] Canada, Bonnie Baker. The first baseman was from Colorado, Theda Marshall, better known as "Teke." Second baseman — Marge Stefani. She was the old war horse that got on my case and stayed on me, from Detroit, Michigan. You know, she [was always yelling at me]: "You gotta have pepper over there. Let me hear you over there. I can't hear you over there, Dolly! Come on!" She sounded like a circus barker.
> Then the third baseman was Pauline "Pinky" Pirok from Chicago, Illinois. The shortstop was [Senaida] "Shoo Shoo Wirth, my roommate from Tampa, Florida. Left field — Daisy Junor, western Canadian.... Center field — Betsy Jochum from Ohio. Right field — Lib Mahon, South Carolina. Marie "Red" Mahoney [from Houston, Texas] was a utility [player]. Jaynne Bittner [from Lebanon, Pennsylvania] was the rookie pitcher that year. Ruth Williams [was from Nescopeck, Pennsylvania].... The point is, these were the better players from all over the country that were now on one team.[52]

Thus, AAGBBL teams became mini-melting pots of society and afforded players an opportunity to rub shoulders with diverse opinions and viewpoints from all over the country that couldn't help but broaden their perspective of the world.

Earlene "Beans" Risinger's story represents another outstanding example of the opportunity and personal advancement a player could gain through participation in the AAGBBL. Risinger grew up in tiny, rural Hess, Oklahoma, where girls' basketball and softball were popularly supported. Her father, a sandlot first baseman, taught her to throw overhand when she was very young. There was a great deal of poverty in Risinger's home town during and after the Depression, and she worked in the cotton fields for fifty cents an hour so she could have shoes on her feet and clothes to wear. Her family was so poor they couldn't afford a newspaper, so she'd go to the local grocery store to read it. One day, in 1947, she read that the AAGBBL was scheduling tryouts and an exhibition game in Oklahoma City. Excited about possibly playing for such a league, she contacted the sportswriter who in turn contacted the AAGBBL's Chicago office. She received a letter back inviting her to Oklahoma City for a tryout. To Risinger, "That's when life began."

1953 Fort Wayne Daisies Infield. *Left to right:* Shirley Crites (3B), Jean Havlish (SS), Jean Geissinger (2B), Delores "Dolly" Brumfield (1B) (courtesy Jean Havlish).

After graduation, [there] I was with really no future. Going to college never was even thought about, as there was no money for college. So after being frustrated and working in the cotton fields for fifty cents an hour, I thought [the AAGBBL] might be my future as there were no factories or anything like that anywhere nearby.

[After a favorable try-out in Oklahoma City] I borrowed money from a bank and started for Rockford, Illinois on a train.... By the time I got to Chicago, and had to change trains, I was so homesick that I took the first train back to Hess, Oklahoma. I then went back to the cotton fields to repay the bank.

Then, in 1948, a second chance came. They had a team in Springfield, Illinois, which wasn't so far away, so I made that on the bus. The manager of the team, Carson Bigbee and the chaperone, Mary Rudis took me under their wings, and I made the team as a pitcher. The greatest year of my life was 1948. I [went] home at the end of every season as I still wasn't weaned away from home.

The [reduction] of the league [from ten to eight] teams brought about my allocation to Grand Rapids, Michigan in 1949, the home of the

Pitcher Earlene "Beans" Risinger (courtesy Northern Indiana Center for History).

Grand Rapids Chicks, whose manager was Johnny Rawlings. In January of 1949, I was asked to go on the South American tour, and I jumped at the chance. During this tour, Johnny Rawlings taught me the fine points of pitching.

I played for the Chicks through 1954, and then when the league disbanded, I had the opportunity to go to x-ray school at Butterworth Hospital in Grand Rapids. Following that training, I began working in an orthopedic surgeon's office, and I have been there ever since [as of 1975].

When I say baseball did everything for me, it's true. Possibly I would still be in Hess, Oklahoma, which isn't a bad place to live if you have a profession and can drive some place to work. At that time, I had nothing, and now I feel satisfied with my life, and I am a very happy person.[53]

Summary

This brief account of league player recruitment policies and players' sociological characteristics only provides a silhouette of players' AAGBBL experiences. It is enough to suggest that girls and women all over North America learned and loved softball/baseball from their youth. They were highly skilled, if also "feminine" appearing individuals who gained their pre-professional playing experience largely through community amateur softball teams or by playing baseball with the neighborhood boys. AAGBBL players tended to be sport-oriented individuals who came from nearly every section of the North American continent, but, except for a few Cubans, only those of Caucasian lineage had the opportunity to compete with the league. AAGBBL players discontinued their ball playing careers for various reasons, and a re-emphasis on women's place in the home during the postwar years may have contributed to this process for some.

What this account does not do is relate, on a broad scale, the players' human side: their character traits; the obstacles they encountered and overcame, or succumbed to. Nor does it relate the humor and pathos they experienced. League publicity largely failed to explore the personal aspects of players' lives, and in the mid–1970s, when the core of this work was composed, too few players were accessible to explore this avenue of inquiry. In the current revision, an effort has been made to incorporate as much as possible from player interviews conducted by Dr. Janis Taylor in 1993 and Ms. Mary Moore from 1996 to 2004 and beyond. However, this task is better dealt with in other works.[54]

12

AAGBBL Player Policies
and Regulations

Chapter 11 provided some insight into league player recruitment procedures and players' general sociological characteristics and individual accomplishments, important dimensions of their AAGBBL careers. League policies and regulations governing player conduct, salaries, and inter-team transactions provide another dimension of their AAGBBL experience. The changes which occurred in these regulations over the years also provide insight into the interaction between league administrators and players. This chapter examines these facets of league operations.

Player Conduct Rules

The rules established by league administrators for player conduct, were, like the institution of chaperones, an effort to maintain a public image of high standards for feminine conduct. These rules remained essentially the same throughout the league's history, though some became more explicit and others were added or deleted as time progressed. Table 21 presents a comparison of conduct rules published about 1945, 1947, and 1951. It illustrates the evolution in administrations' formulation of conduct rules and suggests that some players tested the letter and spirit of these rules, not uncommon for spirited, competitive young women.

Most notable in this regard were rules 1, 2, 10, 11, and 13 (see Table 21). Rule 1, concerning the league's dress code, became more specific as time progressed, implying that players took advantage of any loophole they could exploit. Rule 2, which prohibited smoking and drinking in public places, became more explicitly restrictive in regard to drinking regulations as time progressed, but more liberal in regard to smoking regulations. The 1951 rules outlined acceptable drinking practices in detail but offered no legislation against smoking as in previous years. The league's liberalized smoking regulations reflected a growing acceptance of female smokers in society at large.

Rule 10, which legislated the length of player uniforms, was also liberalized in the 1951 rules. That is, no regulations on the length of players' skirts were mentioned in the 1951 conduct rules. Previous regulations stipulated that uniform skirts could be no shorter than six inches above the knee. Player complaints that the length and fullness of the skirts inhibited fielding and pitching efficiency ultimately had their effect. At least that was the recollection of Dorothy "Kammie" Kamenshek and Nancy Mudge Cato as to why the skirts became sleeker and shorter.[1]

Inter-team player fraternization, or socializing with opponents, seemed to be a per-

Table 21: Evolution of Player Conduct Rules

ca. 1945	*1947*	*1951*
1. Always appear in feminine attire when not actively engaged in practice or playing ball. This regulation continues through the Shaughnessy Playoffs. At no time may a player appear in the stands in her uniform.	Always appear in feminine attire when not actively engaged in practice or playing ball. This regulation continues through the Shaughnessy Playoffs. AT NO TIME MAY A PLAYER APPEAR IN THE STANDS IN HER UNIFORM, OR WEAR SLACKS OR SHORTS IN PUBLIC.	Always appear in feminine attire. This precludes the use of any wearing apparel of masculine nature. MASCULINE HAIR STYLING, SHOES, COATS, SHIRTS, SOCKS, T-SHIRTS, ARE BARRED AT ALL TIMES. Dress for the occasion. Feminine attire acceptable by the general public at picnics, on the bus, and at the beach are permissible. No one will be allowed to appear off the bus in slacks, shorts, or dungarees.
2. Smoking or drinking are not permitted in public places.	Smoking or drinking are not permitted in public places. Liquor drinking will not be permitted under any circumstances. Other intoxicating drinks in limited portions with after-game meal only, will be allowed.	CONSUMPTION OF ANY LIQUOR OTHER THAN BEER OR WINE IS PRO-HIBITED AT ALL TIMES. Beer and wine may be consumed in moderation with the after-game meal only. Your appearance in public bars is prohibited.
3. All social engagements must be approved by the chaperones.	All social engagements must be approved by the chaperones. Legitimate requests for dates can be allowed by chaperones.	[Same as 1947.]
4. All living quarters and eating places must be approved by the chaperones.	All living quarters and eating places must be approved by the chaperones. No player shall change her residence without the permission of the chaperone.	[Same as 1947.]
5. For emergency purposes it is necessary that [players] leave notice of [their] whereabouts at [their] home phone.	[Same as 1945.]	[Same as 1945.]
6. Each club will establish a satisfactory place to eat and a time when all members must be in their individual rooms. In general the lapse of time will be two hours after the finish of the last game.	[Same as 1945.]	CURFEW WILL BE ENFORCED ON THIS BASIS: 12:30 OR TWO AND HALF HOURS AFTER THE CONCLUSION OF THE BALL GAME.
7. Always carry your employee's pass as a means of	[Same as 1945.]	Always carry your employee's pass as a means of identifica-

ca. 1945	*1947*	*1951*
identification for entering the various parks. This pass is NOT transferable.		tion at various parks. This pass is NOT transferable and violators of this rule will be subject to pass cancellation.
8. Relatives, friends, and visitors are not allowed on the bench at any time.	[Same as 1945.]	[Same as 1945.]
9. Due to shortage of equipment, baseballs must not be given as souvenirs without permission from the management.	[Same as 1945.]	[Not delineated in 1951 rules.]
10. Baseball uniform skirts shall not be shorter than six inches above the knee cap.	[Same as 1945.]	[Not delineated in 1951 rules. Pictures of players between 1951 and 1954 indicate this rule was not in effect.]
11. In order to sustain the complete spirit of rivalry between clubs, the members of the different clubs must not fraternize at any time during the season.	In order to sustain the complete spirit of rivalry between clubs, the members of different clubs must not fraternize at any time during the season. After the opening day of the season, fraternizing will be subject to heavy penalties. However, this means in particular, room parties, auto trips to out of the way eating places, etc. However, friendly discussions in lobbies are permissible with opposing players.	FRATERNIZATION ON AND OFF THE FIELD IS PROHIBITED EXCEPT BY SPECIAL PERMISSION FROM THE CHAPERONE.
12. When traveling, the members of the clubs must be at the station thirty minutes before departure time. Anyone missing her arranged transportation will have to pay her own fare.	[Same as 1945.]	[Not delineated in 1951 rules.]
13. [Not delineated in 1945.]	Players will not be allowed to drive their cars beyond their city's limits without the special permission of their manager. Each team will travel as a unit via method of travel provided for by the league.	Players will not be allowed to drive cars out of town except by express permission of the chaperone.
14. [Not delineated in 1945.]	[Not delineated in 1947.]	When in uniform, no jewelry, regardless of type, will be permitted.

ca. 1945	*1947*	*1951*
15. Not delineated in 1945.	[Not delineated in 1947.]	Association by any player with persons of questionable or undesirable character shall be grounds for expulsion from the league.

SOURCE: 1945 Rules: Meyerhoff Files, Drawer 19, Rules and Regulations Folder; 1947 Rules: Meyerhoff Files, Drawer 19, 1947 Rules and Regulations Folder; 1951 Rules: "American Girls Baseball League Rules," (Adopted for Playing Season 1951), Dailey Records, 1951a.

petual problem for league administrators, as shown in Rule 11. In 1945, fraternization was categorically prohibited, but in 1947 and 1951 it was allowed under certain conditions. The league's policy of allocating players every year must have undermined the intent of this rule. Players could become good friends on a team one year, be allocated to different teams the next year, and be expected to act as if they were unacquainted. Not a rule social young women would be likely to uphold. League administrators conceded that they couldn't eliminate fraternization so they attempted to govern it. The success of their efforts to regulate fraternization could not be measured, but given human nature and especially the unqualified loyalty young women tend to have for their friends, it can only be conjectured that this particular rule was often disregarded.

Rule 13, governing players' use of their cars, was not invoked until 1947 because it was not a problem until then. Wartime travel restrictions and domestic shortages of raw materials would have rendered automobiles beyond the means of most AAGBBL players. Postwar affluence and the elimination of travel and fuel restrictions changed this situation. These changes in the larger social milieu resulted in enough problems for league officials that they felt it necessary to regulate players' use of private cars.

Players interviewed about their experiences in the AAGBBL generally agreed, in retrospect, that the conduct rules were "quite reasonable and appropriate," "necessary to the public image," and "consistent with the times."[2] Jean Cione, who played for Rockford and several other league teams, pointed out that a number of the league conduct rules were similar to those employed at Eastern Michigan University, where she attended college during the school year.[3]

Players interviewed between 1993 and 2004 noted that they thought league conduct rules were reasonable. Elizabeth Mahon, however, did note that the older she became, the more onerous some of the conduct rules became.[4] Complaining and grumbling over some of the rules was also acknowledged, but general player compliance with league conduct rules was the prevalent recollection.

Player Salaries and Salary Problems

Table 22 provides a picture of the evolution of player salaries from 1943 to 1954. Ken Sells, the league's first president, noted that it would have been difficult to obtain players for less than the $40–85 per week salaries established during the war.[5] The necessity for high salaries (by the standard of the day) was motivated by competition with Chicago's Metropolitan Girls Major Softball League. This was explained in a Chicago newspaper report just after the AAGBBL announced it would begin operations in the summer of 1943.

Changes. *Left to right:* Amy Applegren, 1940s Rockford Pitcher, and Gloria Cordes, 1950s Kalamazoo Pitcher, illustrate changes in pitching style and changes in the fullness and length of the AAGBBL uniform skirts (both photographs courtesy Northern Indiana Center for History).

Table 22: AAGBBL Player Salaries, 1943–1954

Year	Low	High
1943–1947	$40/week	$85/week, expenses paid
1948–1949	$50/week	$100/week, expenses paid
1950	No minimum	$100/week, expenses paid
1951	$5400 salary limitation per team per month. No minimum or maximum player limits. Traveling expenses paid.	
1952–1953	$5400/month team limit for 16 players; $5700/month team limit for 17 players; traveling expenses paid.	
1954	$4400/month team limit; $400/month maximum; player salary of which $115 was designated for traveling expenses. No minimum player salary limit.	

SOURCE: AAGBBL Board Meeting Minutes, 14 November 1944; 19 February 1945; 16 November 1945; 21–22 February 1947; 1 May 1947; 30 January 1948; 17 March 1948; 18 January 1950; 25 October 1950; 28 May 1952; 10 April 1954; Dailey Records.

Rudy Sanders, president of the Metropolitan Girls Major Softball League, received the news of the imminent raid upon the amateur players with calm. "Wrigley is going to have trouble persuading most of the players to sign," he said. "Most of them have war defense jobs or other work by which they earn an average of $50 a week the year 'round now. They can hold these jobs and play nights with us, and live at home, untroubled by scheduled trips to other cities."[6]

In Chicago, the AAGBBL not only had to compete with high war industry salaries but with a combination of high war industry salaries and established, convenient, and highly organized amateur softball competition. It is suspected, however, that the lure of travel and playing ball full time outweighed the disadvantages Mr. Sanders noted, at least for such star Chicago players as Ann Harnett, Irene Ruhnke, Clara Schillace, and Edythe Perlick.

The establishment of a rival *professional* softball league in Chicago in 1944 contributed to the necessity for the AAGBBL to maintain wartime salaries during the postwar period. The National Girls Baseball League (NGBL) consisted of the major teams formerly identified with Chicago's amateur Metropolitan Girls Major Softball League. Although "Baseball" was used in this league's title, field sizes were that of softball, and the NGBL never adopted baseball rules or the overhand pitch as did the AAGBBL. The amateur Metropolitan League's reorganization into the National (Professional) League came about so players could be signed to contracts. This enabled team sponsors to prevent the AAGBBL from draining the best players from Chicago teams as occurred in 1943.[7] At the end of the 1946 season, the AAGBBL and the National League entered into a non-raiding agreement. This was revoked by the National League at the beginning of the 1948 season and re-established at the beginning of the 1950 season.[8]

In 1950, the Chicago League consisted of six teams: the Queens, the Music Maids, the Bloomer Girls, Rock-Ola, the Bluebirds, and the Cardinals. Former AAGBBLers on Chicago NGBL team rosters as of June 15, 1950, included Jo Kabick (1944–1947*), Marge Lang (1943), Eileen Gascon (1949 & 1951); Toni Palermo (1949–1950), Pauline Pirok (1944–1947), Audrey Wagner (1944–1948), Margaret Wigiser (1944–1945), Velma Abbott (1946–1948), Marge Smith (1948), Dorothy Whalen (1943), Lucella MacLean (1943–1944), Betty Tucker (1946–1949), Connie Wisniewski (1944–1949, 1952), Irene Kerwin (1949–1950), and Dorothy Wind, (1943–1944). Those on 1950 NGBL rosters who would later play in the AAGBBL included Betty Wanless (1953–1954) and Dolores Moore (1952–1954).[9]

It's obvious that both leagues vied for common talent and that a non-raiding agreement was beneficial to both. Some of the NGBL's 1950 players who played in the AAGBBL before 1947–48 may have gravitated to the Chicago league when the AAGBBL's base paths and pitching distances increased and when the change was made to overhand style pitching.

Although a rise in the maximum limit of AAGBBL player salaries coincided with the 1948 rift between the two leagues (see Table 22), AAGBBL salary raises pre-dated the inter-league feud. Max Carey, then league president, began working on a player classification system as a base for determining player salaries in the spring of 1947.[10] It wasn't until March 17, 1948, that the League Board of Directors approved Carey's plan, which took into account players' years of service as well as their individual contributions.[11] Although the rift between the AAGBBL and Chicago's National League may have been pending at the time this salary schedule was approved, the inter-league feud wasn't formally announced until nearly two months later on May 11, 1948.[12]

Players were not unaware of the salary bargaining powers the disagreement between the AAGBBL and the National Girls Baseball League provided. Several players on the Racine team held out for larger salaries prior to the beginning of the 1949 season. At a league board meeting held May 20, 1949, the vice president of the Racine team requested permission "to raise the salaries of Eleanor Dapkus, Edythe Perlick and several others ...

*Year(s) in the AAGBBL

if it was necessary to get them to sign."[13] He was granted permission to exercise his own judgment for these raises.

In the fall of 1949, Connie Wisniewski, star outfielder for the Grand Rapids Chicks, reportedly jumped to the Chicago League for $250 per week.[14] Connie's value to the Chicago league was her strong underhand pitching, which no longer served her in the AAGBBL. By mid–February 1950, star players from every team except South Bend were cited for being slow to sign their 1950 contracts.[15] The re-establishment of a non-raiding agreement between the AAGBBL and the NGBL during the first week of February 1950 saved both leagues considerable sums in salary expenses.

Later changes in the league's player salary policy reflected league administrators' efforts to maintain operation by reducing player salaries. This trend accompanied general economizing that began in 1950 and continued through the Independent Team Owners Administration. In consequence, better players were assured substantial salaries while newer and less skilled players were retained for considerably less.

The 1950 season was critical financially for the AAGBBL. Grand Rapids and Peoria almost dropped out of the league in mid-season due to insufficient attendance. The Muskegon team was relocated to Kalamazoo at league expense for the same reason. The League Board of Directors voted to rescind meal money expenses for traveling teams as an emergency economy measure in mid–July 1950 to counterbalance loss of revenue occasioned by the instability of the Muskegon, Peoria, and Grand Rapids franchises.[16] Player reactions to these financial crises were both positive and negative. The Peoria players voluntarily waived their salaries for a week to stave off financial disaster,[17] and Grand Rapids players chose to play through the whole month of August without assurance they would receive their salaries.[18] On the other hand, the South Bend players almost revolted when

1952 Grand Rapids Chicks. *Left to right, front*: Connie Wisniewski, Doris Satterfield, Jayne "Red" Krick, Mary Lou Studnicka, Margaret "Mobile" Holgerson, Eleanor Moore, Earlene "Beans" Risinger. *Back*: Woody English (Manager), Jean Geissinger, Marilyn Jenkins, Jean Smith, Renae Youngberg, Inez Voyce, Mary Rountree, Magdalen "Mamie" Redman, Dorothy Stolze (courtesy Northern Indiana Center for History).

they were notified meal money for travel had been cancelled. They threatened not to take the next road trip, but were eventually persuaded by team and league administrators to accept the retrenchment as a means of helping to support the Peoria and Grand Rapids personnel.[19]

Theoretically, teams were bound by league regulations to adhere to salary limits (see Table 22), but some evidence suggested that certain players received under-the-table payments for their play. In 1952, for instance, one of the South Bend players received a salary of $110 per week. Her contract, however, showed her weekly salary to be $80 per week. The remaining $30 per week was paid by one of the team directors who was reimbursed by the club for service expenses. The player in question benefited by receiving an extra $30 a month tax-free.[20] This particular player stipulated the terms of the arrangement, and it seems likely other star players negotiated similar arrangements beneficial to themselves.

Waiver, Trade, and Loan Policies

Intra-league player transactions included waivers, trades, loans, and allocations. Waiver and trade procedures were fairly straight-forward and consistent throughout the league's history. A club desiring to release a player placed her name on a waiver list in the league office and other teams had 48 hours to claim her. The team placing her name on the waiver list could also reclaim her within the 48-hour period. If a team did not claim the player, she was released. Trade regulations stipulated that 1) trades could not be consummated before June 15 or after August 15 of each season; 2) the receiving club was responsible for transportation expenses; 3) a trade was finalized only when all players involved had reported to their respective teams; and 4) the assignor club had to notify the assignee club if any assigned player had sustained a serious injury.[21]

During the Trustee and Management Administrations (1943–1950), all waivers and trades were subject to approval of the league president and involved no financial transactions between teams. During the Independent Team Owners Administration, however, teams were free to act independently on these matters. The procedure for placing a player on waivers was the same after 1950 as before, but the league president had no power to approve or disapprove the action. Trades under Independent Team Owners had to be reported to the league president after the fact, and a minimum sale price of $100 per player was established. Ten percent of this amount was paid to the league office to cover communication and administrative expenses.[22]

AAGBBL player loans and allocations were unique and were more characteristic of the Trustee and Management Administrations than of the Independent Team Owners. The league loan policy stipulated:

> It shall be a condition of the loaning of a player by one club to another that the loaning club (which is the club with whom the player is officially affiliated) shall have the right to recall her. A player shall not be loaned for more than two weeks to another club, and during that two weeks shall be considered on the roster of the loaning club. If at the end of the two weeks the loaning club wishes to retain her, upon request the loaning club may reclaim her. After two weeks, the loaning club will be deemed to have waived the services of said player. There can be no loans made after August 15th of each season.[23]

Player loans were a means of helping a team maintain its competitive standing in the event a key player was injured, suspended, ill, or otherwise unable to play for a short period of time. Provisions were made for loans during the Independent Team Owners Administration, but "only in emergencies and only with the approval of the Board of Directors."[24]

Although the theory behind player loans was good in principle — to help a team maintain competitive equity — there must have been bizarre consequences at times. Imagine the New York Yankees loaning their back-up shortstop to the Boston Red Sox for two weeks! First of all, the player wouldn't want to go, and secondly, he probably wouldn't play his best if he did go. Besides, the Red Sox wouldn't be happy with just any substitute; they'd want the best one. Then what would the Yankees do if their primary shortstop was hurt during a game with another team? An AAGBBL player involved in a loan situation must have been in a state of turmoil wondering if she would be able to return to the manager, teammates, and friends she started the season with or if she would have to make adjustments to new teammates, manager, chaperone, and housing arrangements for the rest of the season.

On the other hand, loan situations held the potential for positive results, as in the case of South Bend pitcher, Sue Kidd.

> ... [In]1951, we had a full roster and plenty of pitchers. Battle Creek was hard hit with injuries, and I was [asked to go to or was sent] to Battle Creek with the intent [that] I would return to South Bend. I was sad at the time; however, [when I got] to Battle Creek with Guy Bush as manager, he quickly had confidence in my ability and played me in the outfield and/or even second base, when I was not pitching. I pitched two very good games while there, I think, even winning both, but I'm not sure.... South Bend sent Jan Rumsey to Battle Creek and had me returned to South Bend. With Guy Bush giving me plenty of confidence and playing every game, I had mixed emotion about leaving Battle Creek. However, South Bend was in contention and we did go on to win the championship that year and again in 1952.
>
> As to the experience, it was great, and I did get to play some other positions in the future, usually at first base or outfield — not every game, but I did have more playing time.[25]

South Bend's Sue Kidd (reproduced from the original held by the Department of Special Collections of the University Libraries of Notre Dame).

It would seem, therefore, that the positive or negative effects of the loan policy depended on how the receiving team handled the loaned player. If a player was assured of playing time, as opposed to sitting the bench, being loaned could be an attractive alternative.

Allocation Procedures and Problems

The player allocation system, established during the Trustee Administration, was the primary means through which league administrators attempted to develop and maintain competitive equity among teams. The purpose of this maneuver, of course, was to develop close, season-long competition to maintain high spectator interest in all league cities, and thereby ensure maximum attendance and financial success for all league teams instead of one or two.

The allocation body for the first year of play (1943) consisted of the league president, team managers, and possibly other league officials. This group assigned players to teams after assessing their relative talents in spring training. The second year of the Trustee Administration, league officials had a year of competitive statistics to help them reshuffle player personnel.[26] Each team was allowed to retain a core of eight to nine veterans and the remaining players were either re-assigned to one of the league teams or released. Again, the effect on individuals who weren't among the core of retained players had to be unsettling — not knowing what team they'd be playing with at the beginning of spring training every year.

When the league reorganized under the Management Corporation in 1945, representatives from Rockford, Kenosha, and South Bend "expressed a desire to have some voice in the selection of players assigned to their teams."[27] Yet they also agreed that the principle of maintaining evenly matched teams was a good one. The resolution of the problem resulted in the establishment of an Allocation Board consisting of "the President of the member clubs, or a duly appointed representative, and the President of the League as Ex-Officio."[28] The Allocation Board approved "all player transactions by a majority vote, with the president of the League [casting] a vote in case of a tie."[29] Procedures outlined for the Allocation Board included the following:

1. Meetings of the Allocation Board are to be attended only by the Presidents of the Member clubs or their duly appointed representatives, and the President of the League, and by Managers of the ball clubs, who will have the privilege of conferring with their respective Club Presidents, and shall have the right to recommend selection of players for their individual ball clubs.
2. Allocation Day shall be set during spring training, after the League President and the Managers have had the opportunity to rate the ability of players.
3. Clubs with open positions have first choice on available players at all times during the season.
4. The selection of players shall be made in such a manner as to be fair and equitable to all member clubs having as a primary objective that all teams be as evenly matched as possible. If disputes occur in the selection of players, then the selection shall be based according to the standings of the clubs, with priority given to the last place club, and succeeding clubs in reverse order of their standings. New clubs shall make selections after old clubs have completed their roster of players.[30]

The player allocation system developed by AAGBBL administrators was theoretically sound, and the administration's adherence to it from 1943 to 1949 suggested that it held a measure of practical merit. Had its object of application been more mechanical and less human, it would have been an ideal system. What it couldn't account for were the unpredictable contingencies of human nature, such as players' refusal to be moved to another team, "luck, managerial ability, injuries, and play of rookies...."[31] The allocation system may have received less criticism from fans, players, and team directors if it had been limited to a pre-season operation. The fact that the Allocation Board had the power to redistribute players any time during the season finally created enough dissention that it was abandoned. In the meantime, league administrators attempted to deal with flaws inherent in the allocation procedure.

Structural changes in the allocation system occurred almost annually to alleviate imbalances experienced the preceding season. Many of these changes occurred in response to an effort to equalize each team's pitching strength. The allocation regulations adopted in 1945, the first year of the Management Administration, stipulated that a team could keep any ten players from the previous season's roster. In 1946, this rule was modified to read that a club could retain only two experienced pitchers among its ten returnees.[32] In 1947, teams were allowed to retain one player per position plus two pitchers.[33] In 1948, an expansion year, teams were allowed to retain only nine players, including two pitchers. Players who pitched and played another position could not be used as pitchers if they had been reserved for another position.[34]

After the 1949 season, enough dissatisfaction existed for the allocation procedure among league administrators that a special committee was established to examine its problems. This committee recommended that the "Allocation Board" be replaced by a "Balancing Committee" and that the make-up of the Balancing Committee consist of five elected individuals rather than a representative from each team. It was stipulated that the membership of the Balancing Committee would consist of the league president, two managers, and two team presidents (presumably none of whom would represent the same team). Other changes adopted by the Balancing Committee included 1) no mid-season switches involving playing regulars except in emergency situations; 2) all teams were required to declare all veterans who would be used as pitchers for pre-season balancing purposes; and 3) non-intervention with team personnel was to prevail during the season.[35] These changes reflected the major items of dissention fostered by the allocation procedure.

The good intentions of the new balancing procedure were short-lived. In a telegram to league president Fred Leo, dated June 30, 1950, Harold Van Orman, president of the Fort Wayne Daisies, protested the Balancing Committee's action of assigning two Fort Wayne regulars to bolster the Muskegon team just relocated to Kalamazoo.

> Ft. Wayne feels league beset with enough serious problems not to rock ship with dissatisfactions from personnel changes. We do not recognize board's right to take two regulars from our team in direct contradiction to our voted policy of no more tearing down. In addition, after season's start, regulars were not to be moved without club's express permission. We will not order our players to move as directed and request a meeting of board proper, with notice to take legitimate action. Ft. Wayne now one of league's most solid towns after many years of second division and profitless operation. Resent initiative and success being punished by arbitrary action.[36]

The last sentence of Van Orman's telegram reflected the conflict local directors experienced under the allocation system. On one hand, they wanted the league to be a success, but on the other hand, it was difficult for them to promote league welfare above their individual team's welfare. League interests tended to be subordinated to local interests, especially when it became a question of economics. This reaction became more marked as time progressed and deficit expenditures increased.

1952 Fort Wayne Daisies — Regular Season Champions. *Left to right, front:* Thelma "Tiby" Eisen, Dolly Vanderlip, Lois Youngen, Lavone "Pepper" Paire, Wilma Briggs. *Middle:* Doris Tetzlaff, Delores "Dolly Brumfield, Maxine Kline, Katie Horstman. *Back:* Katie Vonderau, Nancy Warren, Dottie Schroeder, Jeanne Weaver, Joanne Weaver, Betty Weaver Foss, Jaynne Bittner, Sally Meier, Pat Scott, Jimmie Foxx (manager) (courtesy Jean Havlish).

When the league reorganized under Independent Team Owners in 1951, provisions for player allocation were eliminated from league rules and regulations.[37] All playing personnel became the sole property of their respective clubs and league administrators no longer had jurisdiction over inter-team player transactions.

Abandonment of the allocation system eventually convinced team and league administrators that with all of its flaws, the allocation system was preferable to no allocation system. After three seasons without a player allocation system, equalizing team strength once again became a primary concern of the League Board of Directors. In notifying team presidents of a league meeting in February of 1954, Commissioner Earle McCammon reminded them:

> The desire of winning a pennant will have to be subordinated to the preservation of the league. In the past there have always been "wealthy" clubs that make this impossible, but by now I think all clubs realize the fact that the league is no stronger than the weakest club and that attendance depends on competition regardless of the level.[38]

The spring of 1954 witnessed a re-institution of the former Balancing Committee and a presidential admonition to team administrators "to abide by the decisions of the committee in this matter as a means of league survival — with the reminder that this year the league cannot afford to have any team so far behind in the standings by the middle of the season that it will no longer draw a crowd and consequently fail as Muskegon did last year."[39] The player allocation system, established in 1943 and maintained through 1949, was not a perfect solution to equalizing competition, but it proved more viable for the AAGBBL than the open competitive structure allowed during the first three years of Independent Team Ownership.

Harold Dailey's records indicated that some players resisted re-allocation and trades, just as some resisted compliance with league conduct rules and salary limitations.[40] Those who refused to be traded or re-allocated were suspended from the league.[41] Yet the Allocation Board, and Balancing Committee after it, were not inconsiderate of veteran players' individual circumstances and preferences. The allocation committee advised, at the end of the 1949 season, "that the board be especially careful in changing the 6 and 7 year players without determining whether they would move or quit the league."[42]

> ... some wish to end their playing days in the town in which they started. Some are married and have homes in the cities in which they have played so long. Better to retain them than lose them to another league or [have them] stop playing altogether.[43]

Based on a few player interviews as an indication of general player attitude, love of the game and the desire to play tended to counterbalance most players' disappointments at being traded or relocated to another team.[44] As Dolly Pearson Tesseine observed, "You got to know [other players] as you played against them. It was just a matter of getting used to different towns and different living arrangements."[45] Nonetheless, after a player had played with one team for several years and had become established in a particular league town, some quit playing in preference to moving to another city during the baseball season. Betsy Jochum, star outfielder for the South Bend team during the early 1940s, acknowledged this was the reason she quit playing with the AAGBBL.[46]

Summary

For the most part, AAGBBL player regulations were designed to insure the league's success. The conduct rules were established to insure a favorable public image. Changes in these rules occurred with changes in public opinion, and were exemplified by alterations in the league's smoking policy along with regulations governing the length of players' uniforms. League policies regulating salaries, loans, trades and allocations were aimed at obtaining highly skilled players and apportioning them to create the best possible competitive spectacle. League administrators' failure to adhere to this principle during Independent Team Ownership was later perceived by the league commissioner as contributing to the league's decline. Generally, players complied with regulations out of love for the game and a desire to play. Nonetheless, they were not altogether passively compliant as demonstrated by the evolution of conduct rules, salary dealings, and players' willingness to retire rather than be traded to another team.

13

AAGBBL All-Stars

Inflated views of player performances can be obtained by considering only league All-Stars' accomplishments. They, of course, were exceptionally good players, and, therefore, more was written about their feats than their less renowned compatriots. Nonetheless, a variety of observers have suggested that performances of the selected All-Stars were characteristic of the average AAGBBL player.[1] Still, the All-Stars tended to be somewhat more consistent in demonstrating outstanding performances. Before discussing All-Star performances, a brief introduction of league All-Star selection procedures is in order.

AAGBBL All-Star Selection Procedures

The AAGBBL didn't begin recognizing official All-Star teams, voted by team managers and sportswriters, until the end of the 1946 season. League city newspaper sports writers selected an unofficial All-Star Team at the end of the 1943 season,[2] but no evidence of a similar action was discovered for the 1944 and 1945 seasons.

Selection of All-Star Teams and Most Valuable Player Awards were traditional practices in men's Major League Baseball, and it was not clear why this tradition was not implemented in the AAGBBL until the end of the 1946 season. A basic difference did exist between the men and women's leagues, which may account for the AAGBBL's tardiness in recognizing an All-Star Team and selecting a Player of the Year. There were two men's leagues, the National League and the American League, and only one women's professional baseball league, the AAGBBL. The male All-Stars were selected within their respective leagues to compete against each other. The female All-Stars, until 1952, were elected to All-Star status, but never competed since there was no other league to compete against. This factor may have precluded the official naming of an AAGBBL All-Star Team between 1943 and 1946. Once the practice of selecting an All-Star team was officially assigned to league managers and sportswriters in 1946, it continued as a tradition for the remainder of the league's history.

In 1952, the League Board of Directors decided to create an All-Star Game to be held during the first two weeks of July, similar to the men's Major League Baseball All-Star Game.[3] The board adopted the following procedures for the conduct of this game.

> The team in top place as of the morning of July 1 will be the host team. Which [sic] team will play on July 7th, an All-Star team composed of players selected by the working press and radio. In case of a tie for first place as of this date, then the team with the highest standing at the end of the 1951 season will be considered the top team.
>
> The manager of the All-Star team shall be the manager of last year's play-off winner, and the expenses of the players and participants shall be taken from the proceeds of the

gate receipts, appropriate tokens or gifts for all participants to be purchased, with the remaining profits to be added to the league treasury.

In the event of a rain-out of the All-Star game, it was decided that the game would be cancelled with the league to bear all expenses involved.[4]

The 1952 All-Star Game proved to be a successful financial venture. More than $1250 was netted from the game which insured its repetition during the 1953 and 1954 seasons.[5]

Table 23 provides a listing of AAGBBL players elected to All-Star status. It also identifies those individuals chosen to receive the annual Player of the Year Award. Table 23 further reveals that several players selected for All-Star status earned the honor more than once. Among the prominent All-Star repeaters were those individuals who were named Player of the Year. These individuals' backgrounds and performances are discussed in the following pages.

Connie Wisniewski
Pitcher, Outfielder

The first AAGBBL player to be honored as Player of the Year was Connie Wisniewski. She earned the award on the basis of her stellar 1945 pitching performance for the Grand Rapids Chicks. Wisniewski joined the league at the age of 22 as a member of the Milwaukee Chicks. The Chicks were relocated to Grand Rapids at the beginning of the 1945 season. At 5'10" and 147 pounds, Wisniewski was one of the taller, stronger players in the league. When she joined the AAGBBL, she had been pitching for only two years, though she had played first base since she was eleven years old.[6] It didn't take her long to develop into a premiere softball pitcher in the AAGBBL. In 1944 she pitched in 36 games, held a 23–10 win-loss record and compiled an Earned Run Average (ERA) of 2.23. Her best pitching years, however, were 1945 and 1946. In 1945, Wisniewski earned the epithet "Iron-Woman Wisniewski" for facing more batters (1,367), pitching more innings (391), and working more games (46) than any other pitcher in the league. In addition to all of this, her 1945 ERA was a fantastic 0.81.[7] She even held the distinction of pitching and winning a double header in Racine during the 1945 season.[8] Wisniewski's 1946 statistics were equally impressive. She appeared in 48 games (nearly half the season's total), compiled a 33–9 win-loss record, and established an ERA of 0.96.[9]

Wisniewski's pitching fortunes began to change in 1947 when sidearm pitching became the predominant style. She appeared in 32 games in

Connie "Iron Woman" Wisniewski, 1945 Player of the Year. The 1944 Milwaukee Chicks rode the right arm of Connie Wisniewski to the 1944 World Series Championship versus Kenosha. Connie pitched 5 of the 7 game series and won four (reproduced from the original held by the Department of Special Collections of the University Libraries of Notre Dame).

Table 23: AAGBBL All-Star Teams, 1943, 1946–1954
(It is unknown if All-Star Teams were selected for 1944 and 1945)

Team Names are designated as follows:

BC	Battle Creek	FW	Fort Wayne	GR	Grand Rapids		
Ke	Kenosha	Ka	Kalamazoo	Mil	Milwaukee		
Min	Minneapolis	Mu	Muskegon	P	Peoria		
Ra	Racine	Ro	Rockford	SB	South Bend		

1943 (Unofficial)

Irene Hickson	C-Ra
Bonnie Baker	C-SB
Mary Nesbitt	P-Ra
Helen Nicol	P-Ke
Olive Little	P-Ro
Marge Berger	P-SB
Dorothy Kamenshek	1B-Ro
Marge Stefani	2B-SB
Ann Harnett	3B-Ke
Terrie Davis	SS-Ro
Shirley Jameson	OF-Ke
Clara Schillace	OF-Ra
Edythe Perlick	OF-Ra
Pauline Pirok	UI-Ke
Eleanor Dapkus	UO-Ra
MVP Unknown	

1946

Bonnie Baker	C-SB
Ruth Lessing	C-GR
Connie Wisniewski	P-GR
Joanne Winter	P-Ra
Carolyn Morris	P-Ro
Anna May Hutchison	P-Ra
Dorothy Kamenshek	1B-Ro
Sophie Kurys	2B-Ra
Madeline English	3B-Ra
Senaida Wirth	SS-SB
Merle Keagle	OF-GR
Elizabeth Mahon	OF-SB
Thelma Eisen	OF-P
Sophie Kurys	MVP-Ra

1947

Ruth Lessing	C-GR
Mildred Earp	P-GR
Anna May Hutchinson	P-Ra
Dorothy Mueller	P-P
Dorothy Kamenshek	1B-Ro
Sophie Kurys	2B-Ra
Mary Reynolds	3B-P
Dorothy Harrell	SS-Ro
Audrey Wagner	OF-Ke
Edythe Perlick	OF-Ra
Jo Lenard	OF-Min
Doris Sams	UI-Mil
Doris Sams	MVP-Mil

1948

Ruth Lessing	C-GR
Alice Haylett	P-GR
Joanne Winter	P-Ra
Lois Florreich	P-Ro
Dorothy Kamenshek	1B-Ro
Sophie Kurys	2B-Ra
Madeline English	3B-Ra
Dorothy Harrell Doyle	SS-Ro
Audrey Wagner	OF-Ke
Connie Wisniewski	OF-GR
Edythe Perlick	OF-Ra
Audrey Wagner	MVP-Ke

1949

Ruth Richard	C-Ro
Lois Florreich	P-Ro
Jean Faut	P-SB
Louise Erickson	P-Ro
Dorothy Kamenshek	1B-Ro
Sophie Kurys	2B-Ra
Madeline English	3B-Ra
Dorothy Harrell Doyle	SS-Ro
Elizabeth Mahon	OF-SB
Doris Sams	OF-Mu
Connie Wisniewski	OF-GR
Marge Villa	UI-Ke
Doris Sams	MVP-Mu

1950

Ruth Richard	C-Ro
Lois Florreich	P-Ro
Jean Faut	P-SB
Maxine Kline	P-FW
Dorothy Kamenshek	1B-Ro
Evelyn Wawryshyn	2B-FW
Fern Shollenberger	3B-Ke
Dorothy Harrell Doyle	SS-Ro
Betty Wagoner	OF-SB
Doris Satterfield	OF-GR
Doris Sams	OF-Ka
Jacqueline Kelley	UO-Ro
Alma Ziegler	MVP-GR

1951

Ruth Richard	C-Ro
Jean Faut	P-SB
Maxine Kline	P-FW
Rose Gacioch	P-Ro
Dorothy Kamenshek	1B-Ro
Charlene Pryer	2B-SB
Fern Shollenberger	3B-Ke
Alice Pollitt	SS-Ra
Eleanor Callow	OF-Ro
Doris Sams	OF-Ka

1952

Ruth Richard	C-Ro
Rita Briggs	C-BC
Maxine Kline	P-FW
Rose Gacioch	P-Ro
Gloria Cordes	P-Ra
Jean Cione	P-BC
Betty Foss	1B-FW
Joan Berger	2B-Ro
Fern Shollenberger	3B-Ke
Dorothy Schroeder	SS-FW

1953

Ruth Richard	C-Ro
Jean Faut	P-SB
Eleanor Moore	P-GR
Earlene Risinger	P-GR
June Peppas	1B-Ka
Alma Ziegler	2B-GR
Fern Shollenberger	3B-Ka
Dorothy Schroeder	SS-Ka
Doris Satterfield	OF-GR
Nancy Jane Stoll	OF-Ka

1951		1952		1953	
Connie Wisniewski	OF-GR	Eleanor Callow	OF-Ro	Joyce Ricketts	OF-GR
Jean Faut	MVP-SB	Doris Sams	OF-Ka	Rose Gacioch	UI-Ro
		Joanne Weaver	OF-FW	Jenny Romatowski	UO-SB
		Dorothy Harrell Doyle	UI-Ro	Jean Faut	MVP-SB
		Alice Deschaine	UI-Ro		
		Doris Satterfield	UO-GR		
		Connie Wisniewski	UO-GR		
		Betty Foss	MVP-FW		

1954	
Ruth Richard	C-Ro
Jean Lovell	C-Ka
Gloria Cordes	P-Ka
Nancy Warren	P-Ka
Janet Rumsey	P-SB
Rose Gacioch	P-Ro
June Peppas	1B-Ka
Nancy Mudge	2B-Ka
Fern Shollenberger	3B-Ka
Dorothy Schroeder	SS-Ka
Eleanor Callow	OF-Ro
Jean Smith	OF-GR
Joyce Ricketts	OF-GR
Betty Wanless	UI-SB
Wilma Briggs	UO-SB
Joanne Weaver	MVP-FW

1952 Hosts *South Bend Blue Sox*		1953 Hosts *Fort Wayne Daisies*		1954 Hosts *Fort Wayne Daisies*	
Shirley Stovroff	C	Rita Briggs	C	Rita Briggs	C
Mary Baumgartner	C	Lavone Paire	C	Lavone Paire	C
Jean Faut	P	Maxine Kline	P	Maxine Kline	P
Jette Vincent	P	Jaynne Bittner	P	Katie Horstman	P
Dorothy Mueller	P	Pat Scott	P	Neola La Duc	P
Sue Kidd	P	Marilyn Jones	P		
Joyce Hill Westerman	1B	Betty Foss	1B	Betty Foss	1B
Charlene Pryer	2B	Jean Geissinger	2B	Jean Geissinger	2B
Delores Brumfield	2B				
Barbara Hoffman	3B	Katie Horstman	3B	Jean Havlish	3B
Gertrude Dunn	SS	Jean Havlish	SS	Mary Weddle	SS
Jo Lenard	OF	Wilma Briggs	OF	Joanne Weaver	OF
Elizabeth Mahon	OF	Joanne Weaver	OF	Lois Youngen	OF
Nancy Jane Stoll	OF	Jean Weaver	OF	Virginia Carver	OF
Lou Arnold	UI	Alice Blaski	UI	Alice Blaski	UI
Betty Wagoner	UO	Shirley Crites	UO		
		Donna Lee Norris	UO		

SOURCE: *1944 Racine Belles Year Book*, p. 24; *1947 Grand Rapids Chicks Year Book*, p. 19; *1948 Racine Belles Year Book*, pp. 33–35; *1949 Peoria Redwings Year Book*, pp. 33–35; "Managers All-Star Teams," Dailey Records, 1947–1949; "1950 All-Star Teams," Dailey Records, 1950a; "Daisy Fan Club Newsletter," December 1951, Dailey Records, 1951; "Bulletin," Dailey Records, 1952; *Fort Wayne Journal-Gazette* (Ind.), 12 July 1953; "Third All Star Game," Dailey Records, 1954.

1947 and her win-loss record dropped to 16–14 with a 2.15 ERA. These statistics placed her 19th among league pitchers, suggesting that side arm pitching negatively affected her pitching effectiveness.[10] In 1948, the pitching distance was extended to 50 feet, and overhand pitching was inaugurated. For all practical purposes, this change marked the end of Wisniewski's pitching career in the AAGBBL. In 1948 she pitched only eight games and her win-loss record was a poor 3–4 with an ERA of 2.47.[11] But Wisniewski's versatility was reflected in her ability to become an All-Star outfielder when her pitching days were over. In 1948 she appeared in 118 games as an outfielder and batted .289, third among all league players.[12] Wisniewski's performance in the outfield earned her election to the AAGBBL All-Star Team in 1948. Every year she played in the league thereafter, including 1949, 1951, and 1952, she was one of the league's All-Star outfielders.[13]

At the end of the 1949 season, Wisniewski jumped to the Chicago National Girls Baseball League where she reportedly commanded a salary of $250 per week ($150 more than the AAGBBL paid).[14] The Chicago league, which still employed softball rules, including underhand pitching, hoped to employ her as a pitcher.[15] Despite the financial rewards of the Chicago league, Connie Wisniewski found the social atmosphere of the AAGBBL more to her liking and she returned to the Grand Rapids Chicks in 1951.[16] She either retired at the end of the 1952 season or returned to the Chicago League because her name did not appear in league statistics for 1953 and 1954.[17]

Sophie Kurys, Second Base

Sophie Mary Kurys, native of Flint, Michigan, was the AAGBBL's base stealer extraordinaire. As opposing Peoria catcher Terry Donahue noted, "Sophie was great at stealing. The key to her success was that she got a great jump on the pitcher. She was a hard one to throw out."[18] Sophie joined the league in 1943 and played with the Racine Belles from 1943 through the 1950 season. In 1951, Kurys jumped to the Chicago league but returned to the AAGBBL at the beginning of the 1952 season. Her return to the AAGBBL in 1952 was short-lived as she returned to the Chicago league in early June 1952.[19]

Sophie Kurys, 1946 Player of the Year, and base stealer extraordinaire (courtesy Northern Indiana Center for History).

Kurys, at 5'5" and 125 pounds, was only 18 years old when she joined the Racine Belles at second base in 1943, but she already had the credentials of an outstanding ball player. Her previous softball career included positions on several teams in her home city including the 1939 Michigan State Championship team. She had "won the Most Valuable Player Award in the State Tournament at Lansing at the age of 14 and in the same year won the Matt Pentathlon with a score of 4,693 out of a possible 5,000..."—a mark unequaled by 1944.[20] In other words, she was an outstanding athlete with "speed to burn."

Sophie Kurys stole only 44 bases in 1943, but every year thereafter she led the league in stolen bases by significant margins. The following figures tell their own story:[21]

Table 24: Sophie Kurys' Base Stealing Statistics

Year	Base Path Length	Kurys' Stolen Bases	Nearest Competitor
1944	68'	166	127
1945	"	115	92
1946	72'	201	128
1947	"	142	83
1948	"	172	102
1949	"	137	78
1950	"	120	75

These figures suggest that Sophie Kurys was a better-than-average batter who acquired a fair number of walks. Her statistics support this observation. Her lifetime AAGBBL batting average, 1943–1950, was a respectable .257, and she averaged 72 walks per year.[22] Kurys' batting average ranked in the league's top 20 every year but 1947 when she ranked 22nd.

Sophie's best all-around year in the AAGBBL was 1946, the year she was selected as the AAGBBL's Player of the Year. The league news release describing her accomplishments during the 1946 season observed: "Kurys was a spectacular performer in every department of play in the past season."

> She batted second in the league for the full season and she established no less than five new all-time league records—for stolen bases (201), for runs scored in one season (117), for bases on balls in one season (93), for runs scored in one game (5), and for fielding percentage at second base in one season (.973). She played a very important part in the championship effort of her team and continued as a standout star in the post-season playoff series, leading all players in hitting, scoring runs, and stealing bases.[23]

There was little question that Sophie Kurys deserved the Player of the Year Award in 1946.

Kurys' appearance at second base on four of the five All-Star Teams selected between 1946 and 1950 was further tribute to her consistent, outstanding play during her AAGBBL career (see Table 23). At the end of 1950, her last full season of play in the AAGBBL, she was still a league standout. Although she was not selected as the league's All-Star at second base in 1950, she led "the league in four departments of specialized play, namely in runs scored with 95; hits, 185; and stolen bases, ... 120; and was tied with Eleanor Callow of Rockford for first in home runs with 7."[24] A player profile in the *1946 Racine Belles Year Book* summed up Sophie Kurys' attributes in these terms: "Sophie is without question one of the top performers of the league in all departments of play, a scrappy team player, a great competitor, a great infielder, a good hitter, and a stand-out base runner...."[25]

Doris Sams
Pitcher, Outfielder

Doris "Sammy" Sams, a native of Knoxville, Tennessee, was 20 when she began playing with the Muskegon Lassies in 1946. She played eight years of organized amateur

1946 All-Stars (courtesy Northern Indiana Center for History).

Doris Sams, Player of the Year — 1947 and 1949 (courtesy Northern Indiana Center for History).

softball prior to joining the AAGBBL. During her pre–AAGBBL experience, Sams played in eight State Tournaments and in 1941 she played on the team representing Tennessee in the National Amateur Softball Tournament. At 5'9" and 145 pounds, she, like Connie Wisniewski, was one of the taller, stronger players in the league. She was characterized as "a girl that is always calm, cool, and collected, even when the going is rough."[26] Nancy Mudge Cato, a Kalamazoo player who occasionally pitched against Sams, observed that as a batter she never appeared to be ready to hit the ball. Cato attributed Sams' consistently high batting average to her quick wrists.[27] In 1952 Sams hit twelve home runs to set a new record in that category. The previous all-time league record for most homers in a season was 10, set by Eleanor Dapkus of Racine in 1943.[28] Sams hit the tie-breaking homer in late July 1952, at Fort Wayne.[29]

1947 All-Stars (courtesy Northern Indiana Center for History).

Doris Sams was the first AAGBBL player to earn the Player of the Year Award twice, which she accomplished in 1947 and 1949. In 1947, she was honored with the award for winning 11 of 15 games as a pitcher and compiling a .280 batting average (third among league regulars) and playing the outfield with distinction when not pitching.[30] Her continued improvement as a double-duty player led to her selection for the Player of the Year Award again in 1949:

> All the bespectacled Knoxville girl did to gain the recognition was to lead the League in hitting with a mark of .279; lead the League in total number of hits with 114; win 15 games and lose 10 as a pitcher and play the outfield 85 nights to compile a fielding average of .976.[31]

Sams appeared on five All-Star Teams during her eight-year tenure with the AAG-BBL, including the years 1947, 1949, 1950, 1951, and 1952 (see Table 23). If an illness hadn't kept her out of the first half of the 1953 season, she may well have been named to the 1953 All-Star Team.[32] After appearing in 45 games during the last half of the 1953 season, Sams led all outfielders in fielding percentage with a perfect 1.000 mark, and her .312 batting average was good enough to rank her sixth among all league batters.[33]

Audrey Wagner
Outfielder

Audrey Wagner, the fourth AAGBBL player to earn the Player of the Year Award, was one of the youngest players to join the league. She was only 15 years old when she began playing as an outfielder for the Kenosha Comets in 1943. Wagner, a native of Bensonville, Illinois, showed steady improvement from 1943, when she batted .230 and fielded at a .926 percentage, through 1948, when she was named the league's Player of the Year. Wagner fielded 1.000 in 1948, and league publicity asserted that she won the Player of the Year Award "because of her exceptional hitting and all-around play."

> She won the League batting crown with a mark of .312, the second successive year in which she had topped the .300 mark, a great accomplishment in girls baseball. Wagner holds the all-time league record for most hits in one season, 130, most long hits in one season, 41, and most doubles in one season, 25.[34]
> Miss Wagner missed ten games in the early part of the season but was well up in all departments. She had four home runs, three less than Connie Wisniewski, who lead the department, had fourteen triples, one less than the leader Eleanor Callow of Rockford, and checked in with sixteen doubles. She batted in 56 runs, swiped 53 bases, and led in total number of base hits with 130.[35]

Audrey Wagner's absence during the first part of the 1948 season was due to her attendance at Elmhurst College as a pre-med student. Lex McCutchan, one of Audrey's chaperones, recalled that Audrey took the "L" train from Chicago to play weekends until school was over and that she loved animals. "When she was 16 she smuggled a puppy into camp one time in her duffel bag. She petted every horse or dog we'd see. I thought she might become a vet."[36] In 1950, Audrey, like Connie Wisniewski, jumped to the Chicago league, her motive being to attend medical school while she played ball.[37] By 1963, Audrey

Audrey Wagner, 1948 Player of the Year (reproduced from the original held by the Department of Special Collections of the University Libraries of Notre Dame).

Wagner had become a physician and surgeon in Inglewood, California.[38] According to some of her AAGBBL acquaintants, she utilized the funds she earned playing professional ball to defray her medical school expenses.[39]

Audrey loved the game and continued to play when the opportunity arose at least through her 50th year. This author had the privilege of competing against her in a slow-pitch tournament in Eureka, California, during the summer of 1978. By this time, Audrey had moved her medical practice to Crescent City, California. She was playing right field for the Crescent City team when I encountered her. When "Doc" came up to bat, everyone's attention focused on her because she could still "clobber the stuffing" out of the ball! Though her hair had grayed and she'd gained a few pounds, her playing skills appeared undiminished. Recognizing her from my thesis research, I introduced myself, and enjoyed a memorable visit. It was sad to learn, just a few years later, that she'd been killed in an airplane crash.

1948 All-Stars (courtesy Northern Indiana Center for History).

Alma Ziegler
Pitcher, Second Base

The sports writers' unofficial choice for the 1950 Player of the Year was Alma Ziegler, Grand Rapids' pitcher-second basewoman. Why this selection was *unofficial* was not clear. Perhaps it was because the managers could not concur on a player of the year for 1950, so the sports writers were left to their own choice. No evidence was available to suggest that the managers did not concur with the sports writers' selection of Alma Ziegler as the league's 1950 Player of the Year, but absence of the managers' input may have resulted in the *unofficial* status of the selection. The rationale given by the sports writers for their selection of Alma for this award is as follows:

> ... for the honor, Ziegler had 19 mound victories against 7 defeats to lead the pitchers in the won and lost records and performed at second base with brilliance when not on the mound. She played in all but one of her team's games and played an important role in the battle staged by the Chicks to come from deep in the second division to a play off berth at the end of the season.[40]

Ziegler played second base for the Chicks' team beginning in 1944, when it was first organized in Milwaukee. In 1948 she began pitching and played second base when not on the mound.[41] She continued to perform as a Chicks' pitcher-second basewoman through the 1954 season.[42]

Alma Ziegler was not a player who compiled overpowering statistics. As far as can be determined, she led the league in fielding percentage only once, in 1953, with a .954 mark.[43] Her highest league batting average was .198, and her lifetime average through

1953 was only .173.[44] What she lacked in statistics she apparently made up for in hustle, intelligence, and inspiration. A player profile in the *1947 Grand Rapids Chicks Year Book*

described Ziegler as "the spark plug of the team ... in there yelling directions on every play that comes up."[45] An indication of her value to the team was the fact that she was elected captain of the Chicks in 1944 and remained captain of the team through the 1954 season. In addition, she worked for the team as a publicist and office clerk in the off-season. Her teammates characterized her as a person possessed with boundless energy and enthusiasm.[46]

Ziegler's overall statistics for 1950 were average for her, a .174 batting average and a .940 fielding average at second base. She ranked third in ERA among pitchers with a 1.38 mark.[47] The sports writers' selection of Alma Ziegler as Player of the Year in 1950 may have been as much in recognition of her consistent and invaluable inspiration to her teammates as for her baseball skills. The same may be said for her selection as a member of the 1953 All-Star team.[48]

Alma "Ziggy" Ziegler, 1950 Player of the Year (courtesy Dorothy "Snookie" Doyle).

Jean Faut
Pitcher, Third Base

Jean Faut was considered *the* outstanding overhand pitcher in the AAGBBL by a number of her peers.[49] Her baseball experience in Allentown, Pennsylvania, her home town, certainly prepared her for the role of an outstanding pitcher when the AAGBBL switched to overhand pitching in 1948. While in high school, Jean Faut, "a baseball bug," spent her leisure time playing with a local men's semi-pro team when they practiced at a field located about two blocks from her home. She gained her experience pitching batting practice for the men. Her pitching skills became good enough for the team manager to invite her to pitch in one of the team's exhibition games. As she recalled, she traveled on a couple of exhibition tours with the semi-pro team.[50]

Jean Faut joined the AAGBBL as a rookie in 1946 when she was selected to play third base for the South Bend Blue Sox.[51] From 1947, when the league permitted side arm pitching, through 1953, she was a regular pitcher for the Blue Sox. In 1951, she began serving double duty for the Blue Sox, playing third base when not pitching. A hitter of above average ability, she was an asset to the team's offense. In the three years she played regularly, 1951–1953, she batted .258, .296, and .275 respectively.[52]

Faut was one of the AAGBBL's most outstanding overhand pitchers. Over seven seasons, 1947–1953, she compiled a pitching record of 132 wins and 61 losses.[53] Her ERA for six of these seven years averaged out to a tidy 1.24, and she led the league in this department in 1950 (1.12), 1952 (0.93), and 1953 (1.51).[54] The years she did not lead the league in ERA she ranked fifth or better, except in 1948 when she ranked seventh.[55] The only pitchers to earn a lower seasonal ERA than Faut were Mildred Earp, who compiled a 0.68 record in 1947, and Alice Haylett, who registered a 0.77 record in 1948. From 1947 to 1954, there was no other AAGBBL pitcher who approached Faut in lifetime ERA or in lifetime wins and losses.[56]

Faut pitched two perfect games in her career with the Blue Sox. The first occurred July 21, 1951, against Rockford, and it was the first perfect game to be pitched during the league's overhand era. The following description of that event was reported in a South Bend paper the following day:

> Faut fanned 11 during her nine-inning stint and only two balls were hit to the outfield, one foul which was caught by Betty Wagoner in right. There wasn't a really hard chance for the Sox defenders during the entire game.
>
> Jean, who was never sharper, was behind only two batters. She threw three balls to Eleanor Callow in the fifth and then fanned her. One other time she threw three balls, then two strikes, and the batter grounded out.[57]

Jean Faut, Player of the Year — 1951 and 1953 (reprinted from the original held by the Department of Special Collections of the University Libraries of Notre Dame).

Faut's second perfect game occurred September 3, 1953, at Kalamazoo. It was the second perfect game for Jean as well as just the second perfect game of the league's overhand era.

> The third-place Lassies hit only three balls out of the infield against the blazing fastball and darting curve of the Blue Sox ace, who won her 17th game of the season for the South Bend team. Kalamazoo didn't get anything that even looked like it might have been a base hit.[58]

Faut's best overall year was 1952 when she compiled a .296 batting average and a .908 pitching percentage with 20 wins and 2 losses in 23 appearances. She also compiled her best ERA of 0.93 in 1952.[59] Jean Faut also made a significant contribution to the Blue Sox's 1952 post-season championship with three victories in the play-offs. In the final game, she pitched and helped her own cause by hitting two triples which aided the Blue Sox's 6–3 win.[60] Faut lost the voting for Player of the Year to Betty Foss of Fort Wayne by one point in 1952, but her 1951 and 1953 superior performances enabled her to earn the award for those years.[61] Besides Doris Sams, Jean Faut was the only other AAGBBL player to be selected as Player of the Year twice.

Forty years later, Betty Wagoner, one of Jean's teammates asserted, "Jean was the best player in the league. I was glad I was on her team."[62]

Faut received considerable support in her baseball career from her husband, Karl Winsch, who had a brief major league pitching career with the Philadelphia Phillies before hurting his arm.[63] Although they were married in 1947, Jean retained the use of her maiden name as a player. Karl became manager of the Blue Sox in 1951,[64] and served as manager through the 1954 season.[65] He was perceived as a tough but good manager and this evaluation was upheld by the fact that the Blue Sox won the AAGBBL post-season play-off during two years of his management, 1951 and 1952.[66] In the early 1990s, Karl didn't hesitate to share his opinion that "Jean was the greatest pitcher in the league. She was a terrific ball player. She pitched two perfect games ... one against Rockford, the best hitting team in the league."[67]

Betty Weaver Foss
First Base, Third Base

Another married player who won the Player of the Year Award was Betty Weaver Foss. A native of Metropolis, Illinois, Foss gained her playing experience competing with and against boys in her hometown.[68] She began playing at third base for the Fort Wayne Daisies in 1950 after "persuading her husband and parents that she might have a future in the game."[69] Her judgment was borne out by the end of July 1950. By that time she had earned recognition as the "most sensational rookie in the game's history."[70] League publicity described her skill and accomplishments in superlative terms:

1951 All-Stars (courtesy Northern Indiana Center for History).

There isn't any question about her being the fastest and strongest performer in the league. [She was 6' tall, 175 pounds.] On many occasions she has hit infield rollers of average speed that are easy outs when other runners are involved, but she is across first base before the fielders can grab the ball. That's when she doesn't hit solidly. When that happens the ball travels tremendous distances and on line drives she has spun several infielders around with the power she exerts with the bat. Able to hit to all fields, she finds opposing pitchers walking her in circumstances that would make the old baseball strategists shudder.[71]

Foss performed well in the field, but "at the plate and on the bases is where she ... made a tremendous impression with fans throughout the 8 team league."[72]

Betty Foss won the league batting championship in 1950 with a .346 average and led the league in doubles with 24.[73] In 1951, she again led league batters with a .368 average, was high in doubles (34), total bases (176), and tied with three others in homers with 4.[74] Although she came in second to her younger sister, Joanne Weaver, in the 1952 league batting race with a .334 average, she led the league with 79 runs, 135 hits, 207 total bases, 26 doubles, 17 triples, and 74 RBIs.[75] Her 1952 offensive performance was instrumental in her selection as the league's Player of the Year, which she won by a 25–24 vote over Jean Faut.[76] She also led the league in four categories in 1953. She posted the most runs, 99; the most hits, 144; the most total bases, 144; and the most stolen bases, 80.[77] She also posted her fourth consecutive .300 plus batting average in 1953. Her .321 season mark earned third place among all league batters that year.[78]

Joanne Weaver
Outfielder

When Betty Foss joined the Fort Wayne Daisies in 1950 as a rookie, her 14-year-old sister, Joanne Weaver, accompanied her and became a utility player for the Daisies.[79] A third Weaver sister, Jean, joined the Daisies in 1951.[80] It was Jo Weaver, however, who was destined to outshine her older sister Betty Foss' batting feats in the course of the next four years. She had an ideal athletic frame for a woman at 5'11" and 130 lbs., and she "roamed the outfield with the grace of a doe."[81]

In 1952, Jo held the league batting lead for fourteen straight weeks and edged sister Betty out of the league batting crown with a .346 average.[82] She performed the same feat in 1953 with an identical .346 batting average.[83] In 1954, Jo Weaver was elected the league's Player of the Year with good cause. By mid–August 1954, she led the league in five categories: She had a .430 batting average, scored 98 runs, had 125 base hits, acquired 214 total bases, and stole 76 bases.[84] Her end-of-the-season batting average of .429 remains the highest professional baseball batting average into the twenty-first century. Her nearest rival was Nap Lajoi, who hit .4265 in 1901. Ted Williams, the last major leaguer to hit over 400, attained an average of .4057 in 1941.[85]

The sisters Jo, Betty, and Jean began playing ball when they were in grade school. According to a newspaper interview in the late 1970s, Jo explained, "We used to play out in the cow fields back home. My dad was a baseball nut, but my mother didn't know what first base even meant. My sisters and I were always playing ball. I just simply had natural ability to play."[86]

One of Jo's fond memories of her AAGBBL days was meeting Babe Zaharias. "She was in town playing in a [golf] tournament and she came out that night to watch us. I

Betty Weaver Foss (left)—1952 Player of the Year; Joanne Weaver—1954 Player of the Year (reproduced from the original held by the Department of Special Collections of the University Libraries of Notre Dame).

hit a grand slam homer that night."[87] Looking back on her AAGBBL playing days, she echoed many players' sentiments when she said, "It was a thrill for me ... because here I was doing the thing I loved best and being paid for it."[88] Jo loved playing, and the Daisies loved her. Fort Wayne's regular appearance in post-season play-offs from 1950 to 1954 attests to the contributions of Jo Weaver and Betty Weaver Foss.[89]

Dorothy Kamenshek
First Base

Dorothy Kamenshek, first basewoman for the Rockford Peaches, was never recognized as Player of the Year, but if there had been an award for "Player of the League" Dorothy Kamenshek most certainly would have won it. Always in the top ten in batting average, and usually the top five, she was considered the best fielding first basewoman in the league. She wasn't known as a power hitter, but as a place hitter. Opposing first basewoman June Peppas acknowledged that "Kammie could bunt anywhere she wanted."[90] Kamenshek noted that hitting came naturally to her but credited her ability to bunt to manager Bill Allington. In her words, "He taught me bunting. He'd have me out there for hours bunting and dropping the ball down on a handkerchief at third base and at first base."[91]

The 1952 All-Star Team — The First League-Wide All-Star Team to Play Together. *Left to right, front*: Ruth Richard (C), Rita Briggs (C), Joan Berger (2B), Fern Shollenberger (3B), Alice Deschaine (Ut. Inf.), Dorothy "Snookie" Doyle (Ut.Inf.), Alma Ziegler (P), Gloria Cordes (P). *Back*: Dottie Green (Chaperone), Eleanor Callow (LF), Betty Weaver Foss (1B), Maxine Kline (P), Dottie Schroeder (SS), Rose Gacioch (P), Sadie Satterfield (Ut.OF), Doris Sams (CF), Connie Wisniewski (Ut. OF), Joanne Weaver (RF), Bill Allington (Manager) (reproduced from the original held by the Department of Special Collections of the University Libraries of Notre Dame).

Although she didn't produce the flashy outstanding year that would have given her recognition for Player of the Year, her consistent fielding and hitting earned six straight awards as the league's All-Star first basewoman — seven if 1943 is counted (see Table 22). During her ten seasons in the league, 1943–1951 and 1953, Kamenshek compiled a fielding average of .982 and a lifetime batting average of .293.[92] She led the league in fielding at first base in 1949 with a record of .995, and she led the league in batting in 1946 and 1947 with averages of .316 and .306 respectively.[93] Some other categories in which Kamenshek led the league included most hits, 129 (1946); most singles, 102 (1945), 120 (1946), 113 (1948); fewest strikeouts, 6 (1944), 10 (1946), 6 (1947) 14 (1948); and most times at bat, 447 (1944), 419 (1945).[94]

Wally Pipp, a former New York Yankees' star, voiced a tribute to Kammie's consistent, outstanding play in 1950. He described Kamenshek as the "fanciest fielding first baseman I've ever seen, man or woman."[95] Shortly thereafter officials of the Fort Laud-

Dorothy "Kammie" Kamenshek, "One of the Greatest Players in the League" (reproduced from the original held by the Department of Special Collections of the University Libraries of Notre Dame).

1952 South Bend Blue Sox, First All-Star Opponents and 1952 World Champions. *Left to right, front:* Jo Lenard (LF), Jette Vincent Mooney (P, 2B), Betty Wagoner (CF), Sue Kidd (P, RF), Jean Faut (P, 3B), Earle McCammon (League Business Manager), Gertie Dunn (SS), Marge Wenzell, (RF, 3B, 2B). *Back:* Karl Winsch (Manager), Lou Arnold (P), Joyce Westerman (1B), Mary "Wimp" Baumgartner (C), Mary Lou Graham (Bat Girl), Janet Rumsey (P), Mary Froning (OF) (courtesy Jean Faut Fantry).

erdale club in the Florida International Baseball League attempted to buy her contract from the AAGBBL. Board officials turned down the offer on the basis that Rockford couldn't afford to lose her and on the principle that women should play among themselves because they "could not help but appear inferior in athletic competition with men."[96] This was Kamenshek's own reaction to the Florida League offer. She told one sports writer:

> I'd never play in a men's league.... To begin with, no woman could cover the extra distance on a men's diamond and play day in and day out. It would be too much. Then, too, a woman would be at a physical disadvantage competing with men standing over 6 feet tall and outweighing her by 60 or 70 pounds.[97]

Many years later "Kammie" observed, "in that era I thought it would just be a publicity stunt." More importantly, she also pointed out that "they offered me less money than I was making. The [men's] minor leagues were very poorly paid at that time."[98]

The same sports writer observed that it was "probably no exaggeration to say that Kamenshek today is one of the really great woman athletes in the country."

> She's not so versatile as Babe Didrickson, of course, and hasn't the flair for publicity that marks such feminine competitors as Gorgeous Gussie Moran, but her accomplishments in baseball are certainly far above the average.[99]

Kamenshek's consistent high caliber performance in the field and at bat made her one of the AAGBBL's best all-around players. Not only did she possess excellent mechanical skills, she also displayed intensity and level-headedness. A Peaches' and Kamenshek fan wrote of his/her admiration of Kammie in 1945:

> In reviewing the games and hearing the pitchers given lots of credit, which they surely deserve, and giving the other players their due, I still start and finish with your excellent ability to *play ball* not only literally, but in your attitude of a real good sport. Whether you're winning or losing, whether decisions are questionable, you always play ball with the same fine spirit. I'm not the only one who has noticed this and when the going is tough — just remember it pays — for people *do* notice and admire this kind of spirit and control.[100]

Besides being a dedicated ball player, Dorothy Kamenshek was devoted to the AAG-BBL. Her devotion to the league was manifested by her involvement in the Rockford Peaches Fan Club after she retired as a full-time player. She retired as an active player at the end of the 1951 season with a back injury, but resumed her playing career on a part-time basis in 1953, playing only in the Peaches' home games. Kamenshek became involved in the Peaches' Fan Club organization in 1952, and assumed the presidency of that organ-

1953 All-Stars. *Left to right, front:* Fern Shollenberger, Betty Wagoner, Jane "Jeep" Stoll, Alma "Ziggy" Ziegler, Ruth Richard, Jean Faut, Marge Russo, Mary "Wimp" Baumgartner. *Middle:* Rose Gacioch, Dolly Pearson, June Peppas, Jenny Romatowski, Katie Vonderau, Jean Lovell, Joyce Ricketts. *Back:* Eleanor Callow, Sadie Satterfield, Eleanor Moore, Earlene "Beans" Risinger, Dottie Schroeder, Dottie Hunter (Chaperone), Karl Winsch (manager) (courtesy Jean Havlish).

ization in 1953. She continued to hold this position and was instrumental in guarantee-ing the Rockford team's continued participation in the league during the 1954 season.[101]

Summary

AAGBBL All-Star performances were comparable to what one might expect of All-Star performers in any baseball league. In addition, their skill attracted and entranced audiences. Former spectators, twenty to twenty-five years after the AAGBBL's demise, vividly recalled feats of AAGBBL All-Stars such as Wisniewski, Kurys,' Sams, Wagner, Faut, Ziegler, Foss, Weaver and Kamenshek.[102] Their skillful performances made indelible impressions, the kind of impressions spectators cannot get enough of seeing, so they go back again and again. In this way the All-Stars and their teammates contributed to the AAGBBL's success. As one league sportswriter aptly observed when league administrators voted to discontinue play in 1955:

> Those who missed seeing a girls' baseball league game, perhaps forever, really missed something.
>
> — Jerry Hagan
> *Kalamazoo Gazette*
> 2 February 1955

PART V

Beyond the Playing Field

"We're all for one, we're one for all, we're All-Americans...." All-Americans preparing for an old-timer's game at the 1986 National Reunion in Fort Wayne, Indiana. *Left to right, back:* Helen Rauner, Betsy Jochum, Jaynne Bittner, Joyce Westerman, Sue Kidd behind Mary Froning, Tiby Eisen, Dottie Collins, Wilma Briggs, Fran Janssen, Lou Arnold, Jean Faut Eastman. *Front:* Helen Callaghan St. Aubins, Lib Mahon, Isabel Alvarez, Jean Geissinger Harding, Mary "Wimp" Baumgartner (seated), Arlene Avery, Beaty Kemmerer, Jackie Kelley, Marge Callaghan Maxwell (courtesy Ruth Davis and photographer Mary Dierstein).

14

The Newsletter and
the First National Reunion

After the League — Before the Newsletter

After the league folded in 1954, each player's life followed its own path. Some returned to their home towns; some stayed in league cities where they played; and some followed jobs or husbands to new locations. Players tended to leave their playing days behind them. Their new positions and responsibilities weren't conducive to discussing their playing days, and most of them didn't think of their playing days as anything out of the ordinary at the time. Some who tried to discuss their experiences in the AAGBBL tired of hassling the "was it softball or baseball" question. Nonetheless, they had competed at the highest level possible, and when the league was gone, there was an inner void that demanded another avenue of involvement.[1] Although their baseball days had come to an end, many continued to be sports participants.

In 1962–63, previous South Bend usher, statistician, and #1 fan, Arnold Bauer and ex–business manager Ed Des Lauriers embarked on the project of locating and surveying ex-players. Arnold and his wife had housed many of South Bend's players over the years. As he noted in a summer 1983 newsletter, "we had 4 girls each year and sometimes [many of the other girls] were probably over to our home on a Saturday night for a feed after the ball game."[2] Why Arnold and Ed undertook this survey is not known, though it may have been that Arnold and his wife simply wondered what "their girls" were doing. The survey these two gentlemen sent out in 1962–63 sought to discover if the players were married or working, or both, at what jobs, what their opinions were about their league experience, and whether or not they were still participating in sports. They sent out "over 400 letters" and received 148 responses.[3]

From this survey, ex-players reported participation in softball, basketball, volleyball, field hockey, lacrosse, bowling, golf, badminton, swimming, skating, water skiing, tennis, hunting, fishing, skiing, and curling. The most often mentioned activities were bowling, golf, basketball, volleyball, and softball. Some reported coaching rather than participating. Those who coached mentioned softball and basketball most frequently. Twenty-nine (19 percent) either did not respond to this question or reported they were not participating in any sports.[4]

By the early 1960s each ex-player was busily involved in adult life — working or raising a family or both, competing in or coaching sports, or spending their leisure time in other pursuits. Those who responded to Bauer and Des Laurier's survey, "without exception stated the years spent [in the league] were a rewarding experience.... And almost all stated they had formed many lasting friendships. Many also asked if a reunion couldn't be arranged."[5] This mention of "a reunion" may have planted a seed in the players' hearts and minds to reunite. If so, it remained dormant until after children were raised and lives settled. It would be nearly 20 years later before "a reunion" would be seriously considered by former players.

Between 1962–63 and 1980, some widespread social movements occurred in the United States. Among them were desegregation and the feminist movement. Desegregation focused on equal rights and opportunities for blacks and minorities, and the feminist movement focused on equal rights and opportunities for women. Some dismissed the feminist movement as left-wing radicalism, but it found fertile soil and mushroomed throughout the country. By the early 1970s women's studies courses were blossoming on college and university campuses. Young female students, especially master and doctoral candidates, were researching every aspect of women's history. This book's roots and bulk as a master's thesis, for instance, grew out of Dr. Ellen W. Gerber's Women's Sport History Course at the University of Massachusetts, Amherst during the early 1970s.

In addition, a vast assortment of women's organizations popped up in local communities during the 1970s. Fort Wayne, Indiana's Women's Bureau (FWWB), for example, was established in 1975. The FWWB, like many of its clones, identified itself to women in the community as "a support group, a network, a sanctuary, a solution and a refuge. The FWWB [was/is] composed of dedicated women extending support, encouragement, and individual assistance to all women searching for solutions."[6]

Women and their importance in society as well as in the home became the focus of intense study and examination. The historical studies in colleges and universities were fueled by the discovery of women who had accomplished much in their day despite social taboos that hedged their lives. Each historical figure, discovered and revealed, increased the growing consciousness of girls and women everywhere that they were capable of doing or being what they desired. They gained courage to fight the taboos that hedged their lives. Within this milieu, the AAGBBL was rediscovered, researched and revealed.

The completion of this author's master's thesis in the mid–1970s was possibly the first in-depth primarily historical study of the league. Marjorie Pieper and Maria Sexton both provided excellent historical overviews of the AAGBBL in 1953, but their objectives were to compare AAGBBL standards with the existing standards for girls and women's sports in schools and colleges. Their purpose was to present a scientific-based comparative study rather than an in-depth historical study.

The Development and Decline of the All-American Girls Baseball League was completed in September of 1976 for the University of Massachusetts, Amherst. A few months before this, Michigan resident and graduate student Sharon Roepke began investigating the league. Roepke, too, was touched by the feminist movement. Her interest in the AAGBBL was piqued during a baseball discussion with an older friend who commented that he had seen AAGBBL games. Being a baseball fan and softball player, and never having heard of the AAGBBL, Roepke set about investigating it. She was a Kalamazoo resident and began her search with microfilm copies of the *Kalamazoo Gazette*. From there she embarked on finding ex-players and interviewing them. By the summer of 1977 Roepke had discovered *The Development and Decline* and requested a copy of it. Her request was gladly granted and interview tapes and a microfilm copy of Dr. Dailey's records were also shared with her. It was rewarding to know that another researcher was interested in using *The Development and Decline* as a basis for continued research of the AAGBBL.[7]

Sharon Roepke was a Michigan resident, which provided her the opportunity to search out ex–AAGBBL players still located in league states around the Chicago Circle. Being a clinical psychologist, Sharon was keenly interested in individual's league experiences rather than the organizational and operational structure of the league as presented in *The Development and Decline*. She searched out, contacted, interviewed players, and gathered information. Each ex-player she contacted and interviewed motivated her to search for others. Ultimately, she traveled more than 40,000 miles from New York to Manitoba in search of All-Americans. One of the players she interviewed in Allegan, Michigan, was June Peppas, who owned and operated a printing company. Through Sharon, a loose community of players began to reconnect, and she developed an address list which she later shared with June Peppas.[8]

Sharon Roepke (courtesy Sharon Roepke).

A 1976 visit to the Baseball Hall of Fame in Cooperstown led Roepke to comment that she "found virtually nothing on women or the AAGBL. Women were considerably more invisible than the Negro Leagues."[9] As a result of this visit, Sharon began asking why the league was not recognized by the Hall of Fame. Eventually, this became an important question for the players.

Sharon's obsession with the AAGBBL led her to write and present academic studies of the league's history, as this author had done in the earlier 1970s. She presented her findings at annual meetings of the North American Society for Sport History, the Popular Culture Association, the Society for American Baseball Research (SABR), and possibly others.[10] Later, she embarked on creating the first AAGBBL baseball cards. Most importantly, through her contact with a growing number of ex-players, and because of her belief that the league and players should be recognized for their place in baseball history, she began stirring the players' thoughts about the historical importance of their experience. Soon they themselves picked up the ball and began throwing it around with the skill, tenacity, persistence, and teamwork that highlighted their playing days.

The Newsletter and the First National Reunion

In 1977 or 1978, two ex–AAGBBL players, Dorothy "Kammie" Kamenshek and Marge Wenzell, visited ex–Fort Wayne Daisy and Kalamazoo Lassie, June Peppas in her Allegan, Michigan, home. In the process of discussing where other ex-players were, and how they were doing, and do you know where who is, "reunion" entered the conversation.[11] The key here was that they didn't just talk about it; they began collecting names and addresses and writing letters.

In October of 1980, June Peppas, who co-owned a printing company in Allegan, Michigan, sent a letter to previous players whose addresses she had collected over a period of time. Her purpose was to round up as many AAGBBL player addresses as possible and "reacquaint [everyone] with the past and the present." In this way she hoped to stimulate interest in a nation-wide reunion.[12] June sent out a bona-fide newsletter in January of 1981. It's heading read: "All-American Girls Professional Baseball League — *TODAY'S NEWS.*" It was a type-written, double-spaced, five paragraph, one-page letter. The date and June's return address completed the letterhead. The first paragraph noted that it had been "38 years since the All American League first started." The second paragraph stated:

> We originally sent out six letters to those that we were sure of having correct addresses. That was in October 1980. So far our biggest and only response has been from Dottie Kamenshek, but we are hoping after this letter to you, we will be getting many many more addresses, etc. Let us make it work. Send us all the current info that you can so that all might enjoy receiving from the "Newsletter" and from each other.

The third paragraph informed:

> As we receive new addresses and info, it will be passed on to you in updated material. Such as: Kammie suggests that in the near future we can get together in some centrally located place for a reunion. Sounds great and it would take a lot of planning. We are now encountering those that have reached the point of wanting [to] or [are] already retiring. The above get together could be worked among those persons.

The fourth paragraph explained the letterhead as an old printer's attempt "to give some identity to our original meaning."[13] The fifth paragraph served as a closing.

June's third letter, dated February 1, 1981, was a one-side of one-page, double-columned, typewritten newsletter. Mailings for this issue totaled 130+. The opening sentence of the February '81 issue stated, "Our response last month was fantastic ... so decided that another issue was in order. If this keeps up, I'll have to start typesetting instead of [using] the typewriter."[14] In response to players who requested back issues of the Newsletter, June explained, "The first two (Oct. '80 & Jan. '81) were only starters to get going. The Feb. [1981] [issue] was our first biggie."[15]

Headings from the February 1981 newsletter included *News, Point of Interest, Info Needed, East Coasters, 1981 Summer Reunion, Mailing Envelopes, Who Knows,* and *Letters.* The *News* paragraph announced:

We are trying to get some publicity from the old league city newspapers. To date Kalamazoo has put out three articles, since Oct., and will very soon see if they will put out one from us. Maybe in this way we can locate more people.[16]

June Peppas, creator of *Today's News,* the first AAGPBL Newsletter Editor from 1980 to 1982 (courtesy Ruth Davis).

Info Needed solicited "information on wrong addresses, names, illnesses and those no longer with us. Sharing is Caring." *Who Knows* asked, "where can we find: Dottie

Schroeder, Kay Blumetta, Wilma Briggs, Bonnie Baker ... and many many more." *1981 Summer Reunion* read:

> J.B. [Jaynne Bittner] mentioned a get-together of those that might want or have the time. Let's hear from those who might want to get the ball rolling. Of course we think MI would be a great place. Enough interest has been shown — so let us do something about it.[17]

Letters reported the contents of responses to the previous newsletter(s): RENAE YOUNG-BERG'S, trip to Florida; VIVIAN KELLOG'S recollection of the league song and desire to sing it "if we would let her"; MILLIE DEEGAN retired and very busy playing golf and officiating, but not so busy that she wouldn't have time to attend a reunion; JAYNNE BITTNER sharing ideas for a reunion and finding people; RITA BRIGGS offering to be involved with planning a reunion and adding names to the list; SARAH LONETTO encouraging continuance of the newsletter and the addresses provided; and JENNY ROMATOWSKI sharing how busy she'd been with field hockey and teaching over the years but that she planned to retire two years hence.[18]

The next edition of the newsletter, March 1981, was type-set and consisted of at least two pages back to back. (There were some address pages that may have been sent with the March newsletter, but it was not clear if this was the case.) The *Letters* section was longer, an *In Memory Of...* section was added, more addresses were listed, and a picture of an AAGBBL exhibit in the Grand Rapids Museum was included. The call for a reunion continued. Almost every month, thereafter, a newsletter was printed and illustrated with old and new pictures and newspaper clippings and a reunion was promoted. The newsletter became a sounding board and a platform from which players could communicate with everyone at once. It stimulated and reconnected them. It was informative, caring, sharing, and professionally presented. It's content tugged at players' heart strings. Philomena Francisco Zale captured the impact of receiving a newsletter for the first time:

> For about a minute or two my first thought when I looked at my mail and I saw the envelope, "AAGPBL," [was] Geeze is it time for spring training already! Then I remembered that thirty years had passed since my playing days. [I] just couldn't wait to open my mail and read its contents. The memories that came rushing to me were great....[19]

The newsletter was launched, and through the spring and summer months of 1981, it continued to expand and to solicit unknown addresses. It continued to keep the concept of a "reunion" fresh in its recipients' minds. By the September 1981 newsletter, for example, "reunion" was a constant theme in the *Letters* columns. Sarah Jane "Salty" Sands Ferguson wrote, "My thoughts on the reunion — I feel that since the league was started in Chicago that is where it should be held." Marie "Blackie" Wegman offered that "As to the reunion question: I think it would be appropriate to hold the reunion in one of the cities that had a team in the league.... I just think a league city would be nicer. It seems a business in one of these cities would be more likely to help back a reunion than some city who never heard of us." Dolly "Vanderlip" Ozburn volunteered:

> I would love a reunion. I would be happy to serve on a planning committee. If 4 or 5 people could be selected or volunteer to meet one weekend, I would be willing to come. From looking at the addresses, Chicago would be a good place to get a planning group together. I am sure the group, whomever it might be can't use everyone's ideas but it would be a start....[20]

In the same issue, Sugar Koehn penned the remark that she "was very pleased about Merrie's thesis and [copies] have been passed around." June added, "If ever a reunion, Merrie is invited." Without question, this author was and is forever grateful for being included with that group in that and other events. It is gratifying to theorize that *Development and Decline* contributed something to the players' sense of the historical importance of their AAGBBL experience and that it may have been one of the reunion's building blocks.

"The Newsletter" and "The Reunion" were entwined from the beginning, and it was no wonder that mini-reunions began sprouting up. On July 25, 1981, June Peppas held an "AAGBL" picnic at her home in Allegan, Michigan, "for some fun, eats & drinks, and lots of chatter." From this event she informed her readers: "We plan on lots more gatherings in the very near future to discuss the many possibilities that have come forth from **your** many letters." This gathering was reported in the September 1981 issue of *TODAY'S NEWS*, complete with a picture of bathing beauties Marilyn Jenkins, Joyce Ricketts, [Earlene] Beans Risinger, and June beside the pool. Below the picture was a checklist survey. The items were brief and to the point: "I would like to attend a reunion," "I would attend if it were in — July, August," I would like to help organize —call me, write me," "name."

In the meantime, the July '81 Newsletter reported that "Mary 'Bonnie' Baker was reached (via Ruth Williams) and had an exciting time catching up on what everyone [had] been doing through the years." At the end of August '81, some former Blue Sox organized a mini-reunion. As Lib Mahon stated for *South Bend Tribune* sports writer Bob Towner:

> Bonnie had as much to do with us getting together as anyone. She called me to say she and her husband would be attending a convention in Madison, Wis., and that if she were this close (to South Bend) we might as well get together. We called some of the others who live here and I got in touch with June Peppas who played for the Kalamazoo team and edits a little newsletter most of us receive.[21]

Others present at the South Bend mini-reunion included Ruth Williams Heverly, Connie Wisniewski, Jenny Romatowski, Marie Kruckel, Twila Shively, Barbara Hoffmann, Janet "Pee Wee" Wiley Sears, Betty Wagoner, Lou Arnold, chaperone Lucille Moore, Mary Jane Clark (widow of one-time team director Dan Clark), former manager D.C. "Chet" Grant, league umpire Barney Zoss, and Arnold Bauer, "our No. 1 fan and statistician."[22] Can't you just hear them all throwing in their two cents worth on the "Reunion" topic.

About a month later, the Fort Wayne Women's Bureau and radio station WMEE sponsored the first "Run, Jane, Run — Women in Sports" weekend September 26 & 27, 1981 at Tah-Cum-Wah Recreation Center. The function included a "weekend of volleyball and softball tournaments and a 5 kilometer run" in a celebration of women athletes and as a "grass roots fund raiser for the Fort Wayne Women's Bureau."[23]

The final featured event of the "Run, Jane, Run" weekend was a reunion of ex–Fort Wayne Daisies and an exhibition game between former Daisies and former Junior Daisies with a few other league personnel thrown in. The pro-old timers defeated the juniors 21–8 "in a laugh-filled, three-inning game. To be accurate, each run the Daisies scored counted as three."[24] Former league personnel participating in the game included Maxine Kline Randall, Vivian Kellogg, Betty and Jo Weaver, Isabel Alvarez, June Peppas, Dottie Collins, Elizabeth Mahon, Jaynne Bittner, Jean Geissinger Harding, Rita Briggs, Marilyn Jones Doxey, Mary "Wimp" Baumgartner, Norma Taylor, Sally Meier, Beverly Hatzell, Twila "Twi" Shively, and former Jr. league players Edie Moody, Arlene Avery, and Ruth Davis. Ruth had also been a bat girl for the South Bend Blue Sox. Manager

Lined up for the 1981 "Run, Jane, Run" Exhibition Game. *Left to right:* Mary "Wimp" Baumgartner, Bev Hatzell, Barb Hoffman, Twi Shively, Ruth Davis, Arlene Avery (courtesy Ruth Davis and photographer Mary Dierstein).

Harold Griener and chaperones Jerry Rieber and Helen Harrington rounded out team personnel. Umpires Barney Zoss and Vern Krauss adjudicated play.[25] June Peppas and Lib Mahon, remember, had also attended the gathering in South Bend just a month before. Reporting on the "Run, Jane, Run" event in the October '81 Newsletter, June noted:

> Sharon Taylor-Roepke [showed] a slide presentation of the league." ... Saturday and Sunday were spent reminiscing and being happy with old friends again. Dottie Collins provided two scrapbooks for everyone's viewing that started in the '30s and went through '54 — and were approximately 2 feet square in size.... [The] game drew about 1,000 old and young Daisy fans who thor-

Ready for a "Run, Jane, Run" Game in Fort Wayne. *Left to right:* Bev Hatzell, Maxine Kline, and Jean Geissinger Harding (courtesy Ruth Davis).

oughly enjoyed the [underhand] game and wanted more. There also were many autographs seekers to be had.... I wonder if anyone else got up stiff Monday morning?[26]

To the best of Ruth Davis' recollection, she was sitting at a picnic table with "Lib Mahon, Twi Shively, Wimp Baumgartner, Arlene Avery, Betsy Jochum, and Barbara Hoffman when the "Reunion" topic surfaced. Lib Mahon, at some point in the conversation, expressed the opinion that a national reunion would be too difficult to organize. Ruth, one of Lib's former students who had remained a good friend, recalled her response as something like, "How difficult can it be?"[27] With such an utterance, in that group, chances are she was instantly elected to the post of reunion organizer. At any rate, she embraced the challenge "hatched at a picnic table after the 'old timers' game in Fort Wayne" and ran with it. She soon wondered what she had committed herself to, but as she observed many years later, she grew up with the league in a time and place where she never learned things could not be done. As she concisely explained, "I did what I did because I didn't know that I couldn't."

Ruth Davis as a South Bend Blue Sox bat girl (courtesy Ruth Davis).

> I think ... perhaps that is the greatest legacy of the League, that it presented a model for all of us growing up at that time that we *could* do what ever we set our minds to— because we didn't know that we couldn't. We saw women who were participating in a sport where women had never played before (professionally). We saw those same women go on to become pioneers in physical therapy, medicine, aviation, education, law. We saw some of them become rich, some become famous in other fields, and some dedicate their lives to the poor, to the church, and to humanity. The women who played in the League were not just great athletes; they were the best that this country had to offer in so many ways.... I know that not everyone fell into that mold, but if I were a statistician, I'll bet that the greats outweighed the not so greats at a statistically higher rate than in the general population.[28]

Ruth had the resolve, and June had the addresses and the newsletter. This dynamic duo was able to announce in the headline of the December '81 newsletter: "Reunion has been set." Between October and December, plans had been made and finalized. Ruth had arranged "THE REUNION" at the Chicago City Center Holiday Inn for July 8, 9, 10, and 11, 1982. As Ruth later explained:

> Chicago was chosen as the site for a number of reasons: easy access for members to fly in from across the country; P.K. Wrigley's idea for the league was born in Chicago, and I

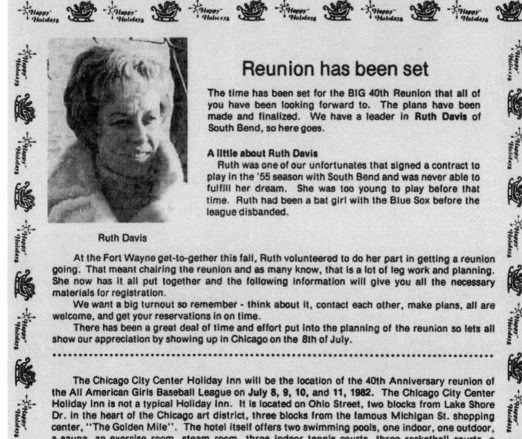

ALL AMERICAN GIRLS PROFESSIONAL BASEBALL LEAGUE

c/o June Peppas
228 Trowbridge St.
Allegan, MI 49010
616/673-3372 or 673-3594

TODAY'S NEWS

DECEMBER 1981 - Issue no. 9

MERRY CHRISTMAS

Reunion has been set

The time has been set for the BIG 40th Reunion that all of you have been looking forward to. The plans have been made and finalized. We have a leader in **Ruth Davis** of South Bend, so here goes.

A little about Ruth Davis
   Ruth was one of our unfortunates that signed a contract to play in the '55 season with South Bend and was never able to fulfill her dream. She was too young to play before that time. Ruth had been a bat girl with the Blue Sox before the league disbanded.

Ruth Davis

   At the Fort Wayne get-to-gether this fall, Ruth volunteered to do her part in getting a reunion going. That meant chairing the reunion and as many know, that is a lot of leg work and planning. She now has it all put together and the following information will give you all the necessary materials for registration.
   We want a big turnout so remember - think about it, contact each other, make plans, all are welcome, and get your reservations in on time.
   There has been a great deal of time and effort put into the planning of the reunion so lets all show our appreciation by showing up in Chicago on the 8th of July.

....

   The Chicago City Center Holiday Inn will be the location of the 40th Anniversary reunion of the All American Girls Baseball League on July 8, 9, 10, and 11, 1982. The Chicago City Center Holiday Inn is not a typical Holiday Inn. It is located on Ohio Street, two blocks from Lake Shore Dr. in the heart of the Chicago art district, three blocks from the famous Michigan St. shopping center, "The Golden Mile". The hotel itself offers two swimming pools, one indoor, one outdoor, a sauna, an exercise room, steam room, three indoor tennis courts, three racketball courts, a French style restaurant, a cocktail lounge, a piano bar and free parking. (A word of caution: Blazers will fit, but vans will not fit in the garage. It has a clearance of 6' 6''.) Pets are permitted

(continued on page 2)

REUNION◾ *July* 1982 ◾CHICAGO

Announcing the reunion (courtesy Jean Geissinger Harding).

wanted to get the Cubs involved and there were a great many attractions available for various interests and physical abilities.[29]

Activities planned for the four-day event included a Cubs game, a boat tour, a golf outing, a jazz tour, a banquet, and "in-hotel activities in a huge room that the hotel set aside for the duration of the reunion. I'm not sure that room was ever empty!" All that was left was for everyone to sign up and make reservations. By the end of February 1982, 200 reservations were on hand and more were coming.[30]

Between December and July, Ruth enlisted the hotel "planner" to assist with arranging events and finding Patty Berg to speak at the banquet. Ruth was a busy lady during those months:

> There were numerous trips to Chicago, to the hotel, to the ballpark, to the cruise line. Telephone contacts were almost daily both with Chicago and with June. Twi Shively was my right hand in South Bend. She did everything from stuff envelopes to keeping me from going off the deep end when things weren't going smoothly. June Peppas had her own printing company and was instrumental in getting information out to the women in a timely fashion.
>
> As the time for the reunion drew closer and the attendees were set, I hand-lettered the name tags (no computer back then!). Then we decided to make favors for the banquet by hand, little baseball spikes painted on river stones. For several nights all the ball players living in South Bend sat in my recreation room painting stones, and the tables, and each other.[31]

Who knew river rocks could become so precious. Get a bunch of goal-oriented women together in one place with an objective before them, and, in time, anything can and did happen.

The Women's Sports Foundation was approached to sponsor the event, which they agreed to do. For publicity, June solicited local newspapers and other media to cover the event. The hotel planner and the Women's Sports Foundation arranged national publicity. The major TV networks were notified, and *That's Incredible* and *Good Morning America* responded. *Good Morning America* followed through by inviting Lavone "Pepper" Paire Davis and Dorothy "Kammie" Kamenshek for an interview.[32] As Pepper recapped in the fall '82 newsletter:

> The voice on the phone was muffled, I heard a name mumbled and something else I couldn't understand — then I heard, "This is *Good Morning America*." Being of unsound mind and a suspicious nature, I almost replied, "Oh yea, well this is *Goodnight Irene* and I'm hanging up." But I didn't, ... and I still can't believe it yet, and we've been there and back. Anyhow, amidst the confusion of phone calls from New York writers and talent coordinators, calls from the airport, Kammie and I yakking back and forth — somehow, next thing I know I'm parking my wide body alongside Kammie on a 747's likewise. It's 2 P.M. L.A. time and a five hour flight and we're on our way.

Pepper continued with a detailed, entertaining account of the remainder of the trip and the experience of being a part of *Good Morning America*.

On July 8, 1982, "The lobby of the Holiday Inn's Chicago Center resounded with shrieks, giggles, and gasps ... as one after another, members of the old All-American Girls Professional Baseball League checked in for their first-ever reunion, and recognized each other — after first checking name tags!"[33] It truly was a heart-bursting, eye-filling scene to behold — the hotel lobby's atmosphere soaked one's soul with love and joy.[34] In the words of Ruth and June in the August '82 newsletter:

It [was] a beautiful experience to be a part of the reunion of so many wonderful people. As we sat in the lobby, watching you enter the front door, many tentatively, (wondering if anyone would remember?) we could see the apprehension turn to absolute joy as names rang out and people enfolded each other in love that years and distance had not been able to diminish.

... The lobby became the scene of the world's biggest love-in! Looking around as we sat there, it was evident that even the hotel staff was caught up in the spirit of happiness that seemed to burst the confines of cement and steel.

... If it never happens again, it happened this once — a reunion never to be duplicated and always to be remembered in everyone's hearts— Forever.[35]

Such an event, experienced so deeply by so many, would have sequels—first, in Fort Wayne in 1986, in Scottsdale, Arizona, in October of 1988, then at Cooperstown's National Baseball Hall of Fame in November 1988. By Cooperstown, the mantle of love had broadened and deepened, and the awe of that historical event at least equaled if it did not eclipse the first national gathering. Thereafter, national reunions were scheduled every two or three years until 2000, when they were organized on a yearly basis.

June Peppas published the newsletter from October 1980 through August of 1982. After the first reunion, an anonymous, undated letter went out which announced, "DURING OUR CHICAGO REUNION, JUNE STATED THE NEWSLETTER MAY END. NOW, WE CAN NOT ALLOW THIS TO HAPPEN, CAN WE!"[36] The letter noted that June thought she wasn't getting enough information from the players and that the newsletter was becoming an expensive project. It closed with this appeal: "COME ON PEOPLE, LET'S NOT LET THE SOURCE OF OUR CONTACT FADE, LET US DO OUR SHARE, AND KEEP THE NEWSLETTER GOING. DO IT NOW, TODAY, AND THRU OUT THE COMING YEARS, TILL WE MEET AGAIN."[37] Insufficient written and financial contributions became recurring themes in the newsletter's continuing existence between 1981 and 1986. When materials to publish and funds to mail became slim, at least some of the players responded with letters and funds, because the newsletter continued to arrive in the mail. Thankfully, when June Peppas felt her purposes with the newsletter had been fulfilled, others took it over to keep the bond of caring and sharing alive.

In an undated newsletter, published sometime between September and December of 1982, June advised her compatriots that she was passing the newsletter baton on to another:

> The newsletter has been a wonderful "Labor of Love" over the last two years. And it DID what I wanted to accomplish — locate and continue locating as many AA's as possible, and (through the work of Ruth Davis) have that BIG reunion.
>
> Now it is time for my part to come to an end. BUT — the newsletter will continue under the leadership of Shirley Stovroff. Shirley also has a print shop — located in CA — and as many of you may not have realized, the printing of the last newsletter

Shirley Stovroff, second newsletter editor, 11/82–1/84 (reproduced from the original held by the Department of Special Collections of the University Libraries of Notre Dame).

was done by Shirley. The two of us have spent time discussing and evaluating the newsletter and Shirley wants—with my many blessings—to take over. For this Shirley a BIG THANKS!

Under Shirley, the newsletter's title, "TODAY'S NEWS," was dropped and the letterhead was adorned with the "AAGBBL" shield and "All-American Girls Professional Baseball League." Shirley published the newsletter from November 1982 through January 1984. Accompanying the January '84 issue was a notice which read.

> DEAR AAGBBLers,
>   Due to business and personal activities, I am no longer able to publish the newsletter.... Your new publisher will be ... the one and only PEPPER PAIRE. Yep, she has all the qualifications, bats and throws right and is very cute. Give her all the help that you can. I know everything will be much better in Pepper's capable hands. Hope you enjoy my last newsletter and good health to you all.[38]

The letterhead of Pepper's first issue of the newsletter featured the title "EXTRA INNINGS" and a logo composed of crossed bats with a ball in the center of the X, AAGPBL arched above the ball and the year arched below it. The league dates, 1943, 1954 appeared on the crossed bats. This was encompassed by a baseball diamond with the figure of an AAGBBL player at home plate. Pepper wrote and forwarded the following hand-written letter sometime between January 12, 1984, and the publication of her first issue, dated February 18, 1984:

> ... I'm going to get out a volunteer letter — don't know exactly *how* I'm going to do it. Don't know exactly *what* it's going to be like. But—I do know the *why*! It's because I don't want to lose that "Loving Feeling" I've had since "June and Ruth" got us together again. I can still feel the "glow" of Chicago and remember the wonderful warm pages we turned out of the past! We can keep that feeling alive if we care![39]

Pepper performed yeoman service, publishing the newsletter by hand, without the assistance of a printer, until after the 1986 reunion in Fort Wayne. She and Dottie Collins decided to collaborate on the publication of the newsletter at that time. Following the reunion, the October 1986 newsletter notified the membership:

> Pepper and I [Dottie Collins— see reference below] have been working on a new system for the News Letter. We are open for suggestions to improve our plan.
>   We have set dates so that you can count on your News Letter 3 times a year, to be in the mail by April 15th, August 15th, and December 15th. There may be times when we will put out a special edition depending on the amount of News we have and how important that you receive it in a hurry. You might call this News Letter a Special Edition.
>   Pepper (Paire) Davis will be writing your News Letter. In order for her to achieve this, she must hear from you — stories, jokes, vacation plans, memories of the league, your health, poems, etc. Dottie Collins will have it printed and mailed....
>   Bo Shaffer will be our printer and has offered to help us in any way to obtain our goal.[40]

The new newsletter title was simplified and featured "All-American Girls Professional Baseball League," each word printed directly under the word above with the figure of the AAGPBL player to the right of the title with league dates under the player. This logo was used from October 1986 through August 1987. After the organization of the Players' Association in September 1987, the logo was changed to include the AAGPBL Shield with league dates under it. To the right the shield appeared "All-American Girls

Professional Baseball League Players Assoc., Inc." This logo remained in use from September 1987 through August 1993.

Pepper continued to contribute a section about west coast events for several years after October of 1986, but Dottie assumed the duties of compiling and publishing the remainder of the newsletters at this juncture.

At the 50th reunion in South Bend in 1993, there was a contest for the players to submit and vote on a title for the newsletter. The October 1993 newsletter arrived with the new letterhead logo, *TOUCHING BASES*. To the title's left was the AAGPBL shield, and to its right the figure of an AAGBBL runner touching a base. In the

Lavone "Pepper" Paire Davis, third newsletter editor, *Extra Innings*, 1984–1986 (courtesy Ruth Davis).

President's Message under the letterhead, Mary "Wimp" Baumgartner mentioned the new title. "Note," she said, "the graphics and new name of our newsletter. I'm very pleased with the selection made by our members. Boy do we have excellent taste."[41]

Dottie Collins would continue to compile the newsletter until Jeneane "Jeanie" Des-Combes Lesko assumed the duty of its publication January 1, 2001. Jeneane converted the newsletter to magazine status to decrease mailing costs. Her efforts were aided by advanced computer technology, and volunteers Linda Lundin and Kathy Bertrand, "The Gals in Sports." Others who later joined the newsletter staff under Jeneane Lesko were Suzy Lewis and Shelley McCann.[42] Jeneane maintained the *TOUCHING BASES* letterhead, but changed the style of print and added "All American Girls Professional Baseball League Players' Association, Inc.," across the face of the magazine. The background of the bottom half of the shield to the left of the title changed from black to light gray to white. On the September 2004 issue, the figure of a base runner touching a base was changed to that of an infielder touching a base before throwing a ball.

As the newsletter continued, so too did mini-reunions, especially in Fort Wayne. "Run, Jane, Run" became an annual event, and all were invited to attend. Most AAGBBL members who attended these annual gatherings lived in nearby states. They couldn't resist those three-inning games. "Run, Jane, Run" eventually expanded from a weekend to a week-long activity, and Dottie Wiltse Collins became involved in its organization and

Jeneane DesCombes Lesko, fifth newsletter editor as of 2001 (courtesy Jeneane DesCombes Lesko).

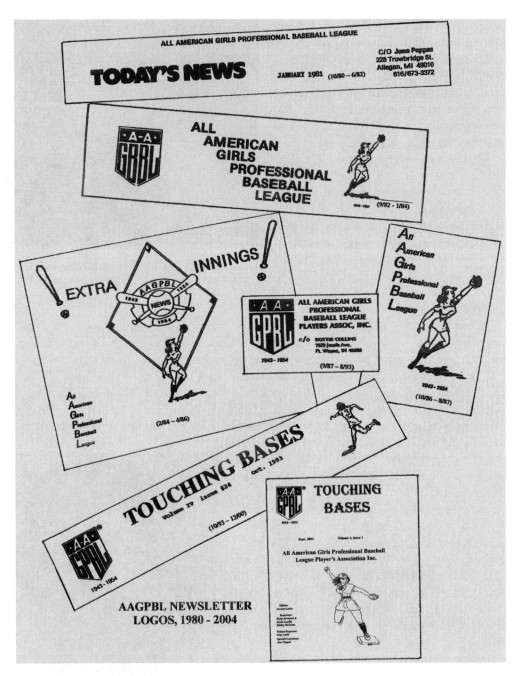

AAGPBL Newsletter Logos, 1980–2004 (courtesy Jean Geissinger Harding and Jeneane Des-Combes Lesko).

administration. (Anyone who has seen Dottie Collin's scrapbooks understands the impact of her involvement — thorough and meticulous.) During the "Run, Jane, Run" events between 1982 and 1985, the players lobbied for another national reunion. This time, Dottie Collins took up the challenge.

The August 1985 newsletter informed players that the response of those interested in another national reunion was "great," and was all that was needed to start work. The players were advised that their reunion would "be a part of "Run, Jane, Run — Women in Sports" during the week of September 16–21, 1986. Dottie organized a reunion committee consisting of herself, Dona Schaefer from the Fort Wayne Women's Bureau, former league players Mary "Wimp" Baumgartner, and Isabel Alvarez, former chaperone Helen Harrington, and former manager Harold Greiner. The objectives of the reunion were twofold: "To allow more time for *all* to be together and [to] make it a fun time with as little expense ... as possible."[43]

Included in the September 1985 newsletter was a copy of an official invitation from the Fort Wayne Convention and Visitors Bureau to Dottie Collins, formally inviting the AAGBBL to celebrate its Second National Reunion in Fort Wayne in 1986:

> On behalf of His Honor, Mayor Moses, the Greater Fort Wayne Chamber of Commerce, and the Hotel/Motel Association, the Convention and Visitors Bureau would like to take this opportunity to officially invite the All American Girls Professional Baseball League to hold their 1986 reunion in Fort Wayne ... Indiana's Choice City.[44]

As the article above noted, the newsletter had become the "lifeline" that linked the players together. Combined, the newsletter and large and small reunions which materialized all over the country between 1980 and 1986 cemented a wide, deep, solid bond among the players. The 1986 reunion would become the springboard from which the players' desire for recognition by the Baseball Hall of Fame would take flight. This goal concomitantly resulted in the establishment of the All-American Girls Professional Baseball League Players' Association (AAGPBL-PA) and the establishment of a central archives for AAGPBL memorabilia. The 1986 reunion was also the breeding ground for *A League of Their Own*.

15

The Archives and the
Baseball Hall of Fame

Prelude

As early as May 1981, the AAGPBL newsletter contained proposals for an archives and a display at the National Baseball Hall of Fame in Cooperstown. A letter from this author, who was delighted to have received one of the first copies of the newsletter, urged:

> There are a lot of people with a lot of scrapbooks and other memorabilia of the league that will be thrown away if they don't do something positive with it. I would like to suggest that ex-players either send now, or make provisions in their wills to send all their AAGBBL memorabilia to the University of Notre Dame's Sports and Games Collection. If everyone deposited their memorabilia in a central location, it would sure make future study of the league richer and easier. I suggest Notre Dame because I know there is already a nucleus of material there.[1]

The same newsletter contained a letter from an active Sharon Roepke who had recently communicated with the Hall of Fame:

> I had to drop you [June Peppas] another quick note to share my excitement about some new developments with the National Baseball Hall of Fame. I called the historian a few days ago and had a long conversation with him about the appropriateness of having a display on the AAGBL in the Hall of Fame. We shared pleasant disagreements but I think I succeeded in giving him new information that impressed him.... Do you suppose you could mention this in the next newsletter. I'd like to know what people might be willing to loan the Hall of Fame for this purpose or perhaps give to them for a permanent collection. This may be a dream come true for me and I'm sure some others will feel similarly. I was very disappointed with the Hall of Fame when I was there in 1976 and found virtually nothing on women or the AAGBL. Women were considerably more invisible than the Negro Leagues.
>
> Please have people direct their suggestions to me and I'll pass them on to Mr. Kachline. I think later on we may want to start a letter writing campaign — but I'd hate to swamp them right away. I'm certain we could get hundreds of fans and players to support this project.
> I would think that the sort of items they would be interested in would include: the various size balls, bats, gloves, action photos, scrapbooks, uniforms, jackets, hats, posters, etc.—all those items I've found fascinating....[2]

Through their letters, Merrie and Sharon voiced their passions for an archives and recognition by the Hall of Fame. They were inspired by the feminist movement, by their love of baseball/softball, and by their love of the All-American Girls' Baseball League.

They were inspired most of all by the women they had read about and met, by the women they had come to admire, respect, and treasure, and with whom they could identify, albeit vicariously. How they, like countless other girls and women, would have loved to experience the opportunity to play professional baseball like their fathers, brothers, male cousins and acquaintances.

Sharon, who had searched out and interviewed many individual players and league personnel between 1976 and 1981,[3] had obviously made the Hall of Fame an objective. In addition, she also lobbied ex-players she talked with to make it their objective.

However, those who read and responded to the newsletter in 1981 weren't, as yet, overly concerned about an archive or recognition by the Hall of Fame. Of all the letters posted in the newsletters between May 1981 and July 1982, there was only one reference to an archives, and only three reference to the Hall of Fame. Irene Hickson was "concerned, like many of us as to what will happen to our memorabilia."[4] Regarding the Hall of Fame, Ruth Williams Heverly was quoted in the July 1981 newsletter as saying that she "would also like to see something develop from the 'Baseball Hall of Fame' article." June Peppas, the newsletter editor, replied to her, "We'll all have to let them know our feelings Ruth. We are waiting for the word from Sharon Roepke."[5]

The second newsletter reference to the Hall of Fame came from a Mr. Cecil Johnson, a collector of baseballs. Johnson contacted June Peppas, and from this encounter contacted Mr. Clifford Kachline, Baseball Hall of Fame Historian. He sent a copy of Mr. Kachline's response to June who printed it in the October 1981 newsletter. In that letter, Mr. Kachline responded to Mr. Johnson that he knew about the league but wasn't aware "that the league switched from a 12-inch ball to smaller balls and eventually to a regulation baseball." He also confessed:

> At one point a few years ago when we were developing plans for the expanded, modernized Museum there were thoughts of a section devoted to "Women in Baseball." We might have included brief reference in that section to this league. However, the idea went by the boards when we began running out of space, time and money. Maybe sometime in the future we'll be able to pursue this again.
>
> ... We would be interested in obtaining more information and material on this league for our files here at the Hall of Fame, and I feel certain a good story on the league would make an acceptable piece for a future SABR [Society for American Baseball Research] Research Journal. If you have any more thoughts on this subject, please let me know.[6]

Eight months later, in June 1982, a month before the first national reunion, Sharon Roepke reported the following:

> Clifford Kachline says they're changing directors so that would delay a display (AAGPBL), but says he'll keep in touch. He says they're interested in **donations** not **loans** of mementoes—particularly uniforms, photos, etc. I'll be talking to baseball writers at N.A.S.S.H. [North American Society for Sport History] this year about the need for their support with Cooperstown—many are friends with Mr. Kachline....[7]

Outside of the previous four references, there seemed to be an overall lack of information to report in the newsletter concerning an archives or the Hall of Fame. This is understandable if one remembers that those who received and read the newsletter at this time were engrossed in reconnecting with each other through the newsletter and mini-reunions. For most, even a national reunion was off in the distant future until December 1981.

Though not reported in the newsletter, group discussions about an archives and recognition by the Hall of Fame must have transpired during the mini-reunions which occurred between May of 1981 and the First National Reunion in July of 1982. Sharon Roepke attended the first "Run, Jane, Run" mini-reunion in Fort Wayne in September 1981. Her contact with the players and the Hall of Fame resulted in discussions of recognition by the Hall of Fame at that gathering. Quite possibly, it also cropped up in other mini-reunions around the country.

In addition, "archives" and "Hall of Fame" became central topics for discussion at the First National Reunion in Chicago in July of 1982. This author, for one, addressed those present at the closing banquet and urged them again to establish a central location for their memorabilia to enable future researchers a wider, deeper, and more available picture of their history. That was my dream for them at the time. Boy did I dream small compared to what they accomplished in the next twenty years.

The September/October 1982 newsletter confirmed that the Hall of Fame, at least, was an important subject of discussion among the players during that First National Reunion. This issue of the newsletter was primarily a pictorial record of the reunion with a scattering of articles. One of the articles informed everyone, "The 'Goodmorning [sic] America' people called and invited Dottie Kamenshek, and Pepper Paire to be their guests on Tuesday, July 20th [1982]." The article pointed out that "David Hartman, after the interview, went back on the air and stated one of the prime interests of our people was to be recognized as a League in the Hall of Fame."[8] Hartman's announcement confirms that the Hall of Fame question had become a focus for at least a nucleus of players at the 1982 reunion. Otherwise, he would not have had the information from which to make such an announcement. It's interesting to note, too, that even at this early date the concept of recognition for the "League" superseded recognition for individual members of the league. This idea didn't just materialize on *Good Morning America*— it had been hashed out beforehand.

Another indication that the Hall of Fame as well as an archives were hot topics at the first national reunion was a September 1982 article in the *Fort Wayne News Sentinel* about the league. Dottie Collins was interviewed and the reporter noted: "What Collins and other former AAGPBL players would like is a Hall of Fame." "At least a place where we can put our memorabilia," Dottie said. She also made a pitch for an archives in this article. "I'd like it [archives] here in Fort Wayne but haven't had much luck with the project. There is a chance we might be in the Smithsonian Institution. But that's not definite."[9]

The September/October 1982 issue of the newsletter confirmed that interest was out there for preserving and displaying AAGBBL memorabilia at the Smithsonian Institution. Ex-player Joan Kaufman, somewhere along the line, had met and discussed the AAGBBL with Mr. Donn Rogosin[10] who either worked for or had connections with the National Museum of American History. This museum was an affiliate of the Smithsonian Institution in Washington, D.C. Mr. Rogosin, in turn, contacted Ellen Roney Hughes, the organization's Museum Specialist, Division of Community Life. Her letter to Joan Kaufman conveys extreme interest in AAGBBL memorabilia:

> Dear Ms. Kaufman:
>   [Donn Rogosin] just phoned and told me of meeting you. I'm so excited about the possibility of collecting materials from the AAGBL, I couldn't wait to contact you!
>   For several years we have been researching and collecting in the field of American women's sports history. The subject is so fascinating and yet so few people know much about it. I hope to help correct that with an exhibition sometime in 1985. While we have been able to collect some very fine artifacts, we have a long way to go to obtain enough

Betsy Jochum standing beside the Smithsonian Institution's display of her AAGBBL experience and uniform for a Traveling Exhibition entitled *Sports: Breaking Records, Breaking Barriers.* The exhibition opened October 6, 2004, in Washington, D.C., and was scheduled to tour the United States for two years beginning in January 2005 (courtesy Betsy Jochum).

material to support a major exhibition. To collect a uniform and other artifacts from the AAGBL would be a dream come true! Don told about the wonderful poster which you are donating and I can't thank you enough. He mentioned that you have a copy of the rules of behavior which would be outstanding, if you could part with it or if we could copy the original. He also said that you know someone who has a uniform. I would like very much to get in touch with that person so I can try to obtain one for the National Collections. Any help you can give us would be appreciated.[11]

Within a year, Ms. Hughes had acquired a complete uniform for the Smithsonian. It was donated by South Bend Blue Sox outfielder Betsy Jochum and is still displayed there.

The following letter reflects the fact that this writer's reunion speech urging players to find a place to preserve their AAGBBL memorabilia had found a champion in the person of Dottie Wiltse Collins. Dottie took it upon herself to begin pursuing the establishment of an archives almost immediately after the First National Reunion. She wrote this letter September 17, 1982:

First [I] want to tell you [Merrie Fidler] that you really added that extra touch to our reunion in Chicago. Your speech touched a lot of hearts and for one inspired me.

Since returning home it has been so great getting phone calls and letters from so many of the gals and at this point I can't help but think what a shame that so many years passed by that we had no contact. Now that the contact has been made, I for one am going to hang on to it.

Your dream of a place for everyone's AAGPBL memorabilia has become my dream and in talking to others they all want it so very bad.

In talking to the media here in Ft. Wayne (who all knew the AAGPBL) they agree there is a heritage that should be preserved.

... I have been doing a lot of talking here in Ft. Wayne, mostly trying to get ideas. I might add I'm getting a lot of input. I think I could interest Ft. Wayne in this project, but need to know from you what direction you are going in. The Ft. Wayne Historical Society is very interested but I'm not sure this is the right direction. Every time I mention it, someone gives me a different idea.

I did a spot on local sports tonight asking former fans to check attics and basements for anything they may have saved from the Daisie [sic] era. Thought that was a start no matter where we have it.

... I would really love to hear from you on this—any input or whatever. Your dream has become an obsession with me 'cause I really feel that the history of our league and the girls who played it—it should be preserved.[12]

June Peppas and Ruth Davis's organization of the First National Reunion in 1982 provided a forum where a number of ex-players were exposed to the ideas of an archives and recognition by the Hall of Fame. These two objectives would not be realized for six more years, but the seed was planted in the players' hearts and minds at that first reunion. Others could shout "archives" and "Hall of Fame" into infinity, but only when the drive came from within the family of ex-players did these objectives have a chance to materialize.

Not only did Dottie Collins take up the challenge of establishing an archives, she also became involved in helping to organize annual mini-reunions that kept the twin flames of "archives" and "Hall of Fame" burning in the players' consciousness. In the same letter of September 1982, she explained:

I do have a reason for all this which you may not be aware of. The Ft. Wayne Women's Bureau is having their 2nd annual "Run, Jane, Run" Women in Sports weekend. For the second year they have included a mini reunion and an exhibition game between former Ft. Wayne Daisies and other members of the AAGPBL. Last year we had about 12 girls. This year in spite of just being in Chicago, we have 25+ coming.

I'm sure the Chicago reunion was a one shot deal. But have been assured by the Ft. Wayne Women's Bureau that this will be a yearly event and will give the girls a chance to have a place to meet every year. Maybe they can't make it every year but at least the girls will know that if not 1982, maybe 1983 or '84.

On Sat. 25th Sept., we are playing a game. No doubt about 4 innings. Last year we packed the stands and there was very little coverage on it. This year it's being covered almost daily. In fact, I have another T.V. 30 min. spot tomorrow on it. I'll get some of the coverage to you when it's over. UPI has expressed interest in it, as well as *Sports Illustrated* and several others.

So my point is with a yearly reunion here in Ft. Wayne and if nothing really big develops for the AAGPBL memorabilia, what better place than Ft. Wayne if something can be worked out?[13]

Dottie Collins' early resolve to establish a site for yearly reunions and her obsession for establishing an archives began in Chicago. Like June Peppas with the newsletter and the reunion, Dottie didn't just talk about her commitment for preserving and advancing the history of the AAGBBL, she lived it. Her "obsession" to preserve and promote the league's history became a personal commitment of time, energy, and resources that would stretch, unwaveringly, two decades into the future.

In the fall of 1982, the newsletter recorded a letter from Mr. Kachline to Sharon Roepke in which he notified her that discussions for "updating and adding to the Museum exhibits" included a "'Women in Baseball' display which has been on our list for the past several years." He cautioned that collection of memorabilia and pictures necessary for a display would delay such an exhibit at least until the spring of 1984, and that such a display would "encompass not just the AAGBL, but also other women who have been involved in professional baseball as players (Jackie Mitchell, for instance), scouts and executives."[14]

The next mention of the Hall of Fame in the newsletter didn't occur until July 1983, when Sharon Roepke submitted a letter in which she complained, "Cooperstown is proving a damned disappointment at the moment. I feel like I'm back at square one since the historian [Kachline] left." In this same letter, she advanced the need for a central archives site even to the point of receiving "memorabilia directly if anyone wants to do that — with the understanding that eventually I will make arrangement to donate it to a larger collection.... Regardless, I would like to see us at least keep track of what memorabilia is out there and who has it. It's important if scholars are to re-write history, that they have access to the information."[15]

From July 1983 to April 1986, no further reference was found in the newsletter to either an archives or the Hall of Fame. However, propitious things were happening in the background. Mini-reunions continued to flourish around the country, including the annual "Run, Jane, Run" in Fort Wayne. Many letters and mini-reunion pictures festooned newsletters during these years, keeping players connected.

According to Jean Geissinger Harding, the Hall of Fame topic was occasionally discussed at the annual "Run, Jane, Run events." She recalled that Sharon Roepke attended "Run, Jane, Run" events and spoke to those gathered about the Hall of Fame a "couple of times."[16] Dottie Collins must also have expressed her concern for the establishment of an archives when ex-players were gathered for "Run, Jane, Run." As a result, between 1982 and 1986, thoughts about these two topics were percolating in a nucleus of players' minds.

Sharon Roepke unveiled the first ever All-American Girls Baseball League Star Series Baseball Cards at "The New Agenda" Conference convened early in 1984 by the U.S. Olympic Committee and the Women's Sports Foundation. The purpose of this conference was to establish a new direction for women's participation in sports in the next decade. Among those attending this conference was an as yet "unfound" All-American, Karen Violetta Kunkel. Karen recognized the baseball card reproduction on Sharon's T-shirt and introduced herself. At this time, Karen was the moving force behind and director of the Great Lakes Sports Training Center and U.S. Olympic Training/Education center at Northern Michigan University. The February 1984 newsletter reported that she "might make the R.J.R. this year."[17] Her addition to the newsletter mailing list and to the list of participants at "Run, Jane, Run" proved invaluable to the organization and operation of the AAGPBL Players' Association in years to come.

Also in 1984, Sharon Roepke visited the Hall of Fame with her AAGBBL Baseball Cards and ex-player Rita Meyer Moellering. There she and Rita met Ted Spencer, the Hall's new curator. In the course of conversation, Sharon asked him if he would consider doing an exhibit on women's baseball, the AAGBBL specifically. He acknowledged that he didn't know much about the league, so she gave him a copy of a pamphlet she had written on the league's history ("Diamond Gals") as well as a packet of about 18 AAGBBL Baseball Cards she had created.[18] When he read the information Roepke gave him and examined the baseball cards, it connected in his mind that his grammar school physical education teacher in Quincy, Massachusetts, may have played for the League He was correct. That teacher was Mary Pratt, who pitched for the Rockford Peaches and Kenosha

Left to right: Bill Guilfoile, Mary Pratt, Ted Spencer, and first AAGBBL President Ken Sells at the Opening of the Baseball Hall of Fame's "Women in Baseball" exhibit, Nov. 5, 1988 (courtesy Mary Pratt).

Comets between 1943 and 1947. In fact, Mary pitched a no-hitter against Dottie Collin's Minneapolis Millerettes in 1944. The baseball cards, the historical summary, and the student-teacher connection ruminated in his mind from 1984 onward.[19] Thus, Roepke's research, writing, and baseball cards generated a receptive attitude in Spencer for establishing a women's baseball exhibit at the Hall of Fame. When others made inquiries of him about a women's exhibit two years hence, Roepke's ground work had been laid.

In the August 1985 newsletter, Dottie Collins included a flyer announcing that the Second National AAGBBL Reunion would be held in Fort Wayne in conjunction with "Run, Jane, Run" in mid–September 1986. Dottie followed this up with a Christmas brochure detailing reunion events. One item of interest in this brochure was that players could expect themselves to be filmed at the reunion for a proposed AAGBBL documentary by Kelly Candaele and Kim Wilson from Los Angeles. Kelly, a son of former AAGBBLer Helen Callaghan Candaele Staubins, was a labor organizer and was dating Kim who worked for ABC *Movies of the Week*.[20]

The next reunion letter from Dottie Collins, in January or February 1986, noted that Dr. Janis Taylor from Northwestern University would also be filming to produce a documentary of the AAGBBL at the fall '86 reunion. Taylor had just completed doctoral study at Northwestern University in broadcasting and film. She heard about the players reconnecting from Katie Horstman, former Fort Wayne Daisy. Katie had been one of Janis's high school teachers and, later, a softball teammate. Her first thought when Katie mentioned that a reunion was coming up was, "Let's do a documentary."[21] Katie referred her to Dottie Collins and the 1986 national reunion was destined to be the focal point of two documentary productions. At the end of her newsletter notice that Janis Taylor would be filming also, Dottie admonished her readers: "Make sure you gals all have your hair done before you arrive 'cause there will be a lot of filming going on."[22]

In April of 1986 the Hall of Fame once again came to the fore in the newsletter with the announcement that Kelly Candaele and Kim Wilson had begun video-taping some of the California players, including Faye Dancer, Tiby Eisen, Pepper Paire Davis, and Kelly's mother, Helen. By this time, Kelly and Kim already had plans to "obtain funding from various foundations for promoting women in sports; they had a director lined up; they were searching for film on the league; and they had established that the documentary was a nonprofit venture. In relation to the Candaele/ Wilson documentary, current newsletter editor Pepper Paire Davis wrote: (Misspellings are purposefully hers.)

A duplicate of Ted Spencer's baseball card of Dottie Collins (courtesy Sharon Roepke).

> Pretty fantastic, huh, gals?? We will be immortalized on celluloid for the future!!!!! About time we got some recognization for our part in Woman's Sports History!!! Perhaps a film on the AAGPBBL might be the trumpet to topple the "Walls of the Great Hall of Fames of Baseball"!!!! Incidently, Where does it say "Mens" Baseball Hall of Fame...???????"[23]

Events simmering on the back burner began to boil to the surface. At the second national reunion in Fort Wayne in September 1986 they gained a full head of steam.

Recognition by the Baseball Hall of Fame

Two interrelated, catalyzing events occurred in the fall of 1986 that led directly to the establishment of an archives and recognition of the AAGBBL by the Hall of Fame. One event involved Janice Mall, a reporter for the *Los Angeles Times,* who contacted Bill Guilfoile, the Hall of Fame's publicity director. She called regarding the Hall's intentions about recognizing the AAGBBL. Mall's timing was on target because for some time prior to her call, Bill Guilfoile and Ted Spencer had frequently discussed the subject, and Spencer continued to thumb through Roepke's baseball cards now and then. When Guilfoile and Spencer discussed Mall's call, "both men sensed the inherent draw of such a display and ... realized the time for such recognition was now." [24] Bill Guilfoile placed Spencer in charge of talking with the reporter and encouraged him to express a positive response. As a result, when Janet Mall of the *Los Angeles Times* connected with Spencer for a telephone interview, he responded that "Cooperstown would love to do an exhibit," but space and lack of memorabilia were substantial hurdles.[25]

The second catalyzing event of the fall of 1986 was the formation of an AAGPBL committee to "look further into opening the door for us at the Hall of Fame. The committee [was] composed of Lynn Haber, a writer [from] Boston, Mass., Karen Violetta Kunkel, Sharon Taylor-Roepke, Danielle Barber, and yours truly — Dottie Collins." The October 1986 newsletter announced the formation of the committee and solicited assistance in obtaining the names of people who might be able to help. The committee urged each member to report what she would be "willing to give to the Baseball Hall of Fame if we are able to achieve our goal." They explained: "We need to have a list to show them. None of the memorabilia will be collected until we have ... signed an agreement with the Baseball Hall of Fame that it will be a permanent display. Send info to Dottie Collins."[26]

The December '86 newsletter recorded the Hall of Fame Committee's first report: "Lynn Haber has made contact with Cooperstown and Karen Kunkel has been writing letters. I'm sure you all realize that it is going to take time but the committee is enthused. For our first report we will put it this way: AAGPBL AT BAT — IT'S THE FIRST INNING — FIRST HITTER WALKED AND IS ON FIRST BASE."[27]

Publication of the *Los Angeles Times* article occurred January 4, 1987. It's concluding paragraphs must have set off fireworks in actively involved AAGPBL hearts and minds.

> The Women's Sports Foundation included a history of the league in its current newsletter and suggested that people who think it should be in the Hall of Fame should write.
> The Cooperstown people don't need to be persuaded. Asked if the Hall of Fame had plans for an exhibit about the All-American Girls League, curator Spencer said, "The answer is absolutely. We're not just showing the major leagues. We should be showing *baseball.* There's no opposition within the staff here [to an exhibit on women in the sport]. It's going to happen." But Spencer had two problems: "I don't have the space and I don't have the materials. Right now all I've got is a set of [Girl's League] baseball cards."
> Spencer said the museum has plans for expansion within the next couple of years, which will provide space for the women's exhibit as well as some other new ones. The display will include other information about women in baseball — some have been minor league administrators and umpires for example — but the focus of the exhibit will be the All-American Girls Baseball League, Spencer said.
> The problem of materials is less easily solved. "If someone would deluge us with old uniforms, it'd be spectacular," Spencer said. Other possibilities for display would be special bats and balls, such as autographed ones. When people offer materials like scrapbooks and old photographs, the museum makes copies and returns the originals, he said. Anyone who would like to offer information or material on women's baseball and particularly on the All-American Girls Baseball League [should write] to the Hall of Fame. [Write to] Spencer at Box 590, Cooperstown, N.Y. 13326.[28]

Dottie Collins swept aside the memorabilia problem in the opening paragraph of her January 12, 1987 response to Ted Spencer's *Times* comments:

> In regards to the article in the *Los Angeles Times*, January 4, 1987, in which you stated that you were interested in Memorabilia from the All American Girls Professional Baseball League, we would like you to know that there is a variety of memorabilia available.[29]

When Spencer received Dottie's letter he knew exactly what it was because she was the subject of one of those baseball cards he had in his desk drawer. When he opened the letter, Spencer acknowledged, "...I got really excited and I opened the letter — I didn't even read it. I just saw her phone number and I called."[30] Then, according to Carolyn Trombe's biography of Dottie Collins:

> Spencer told Dottie how thrilled he was to hear from her because she was one of the women on the cards and with her he felt a special rapport. That bond grew with time, as Ted worked alongside Dottie to make the dream of the exhibit come true. Dottie served as Ted's number one contact person for the All-American League and its history. "She was the guiding light, the heart and soul of the whole operation from here on," Spencer said. "Because I really felt it was her drive that it all came about in the time that it did. She wasn't pushy; she was never adversarial. She was always total cooperation, excitement, and positive thinking. She was the glue that held the whole thing together." The respect went both ways. "Without Ted Spencer we would never have made the Hall of Fame," Dottie stated matter of factly.[31]

The only sticking point for the All-Americans, through at least October of 1987, was that they didn't want to share a display with other women in baseball at Cooperstown. They wanted their own, separate exhibit. In a president's letter to league members published in the October 1987 newsletter, June Peppas spoke for the Board and presumably most of the membership:

> It is our belief that one of our prime responsibilities is our place in Cooperstown Hall of Fame. Now that we have organized along with our Media Center, we hope to have more clout. Cooperstown has offered us only a part of a permanent display to be shared with other women in baseball such as officials, owners, bus. managers etc. This is not what we want. We want our own permanent display with the opportunity for the league to be inducted into the Hall of Fame. But this is going to be a great undertaking which will involve time, effort and skills on the part of many of our people. All Americans, we plan on going forward.[32]

The AAGPBL Board and the majority of the membership looked upon a "display" as a showcase only. They wanted induction, which included full recognition with a ceremony. They wanted the Hall of Fame to INDUCT THE WHOLE LEAGUE as an honorary member.[33] Such a proposition, of course, was contrary to the scope of the Hall of Fame. Administrators at the Hall of Fame would have had to induct all of Major League Baseball first.

At this juncture, approximately 200 ex-players were members of the Players' Association (see Chapter 16). Among this many individuals, disagreements were bound to exist on any issue. The Hall of Fame project was no exception in this regard. In addition to those who lobbied for induction of the whole league, there were those who petitioned the Hall of Fame to induct selected individuals rather than the whole league. However, this was a small faction, as most players ascribed to the "All for one, and one for all" creed.[34]

Ted Spencer also recalled that there was a hard-line faction of ex-players from whom he received "a very terse letter saying we will stand for nothing but full induction." His personal reaction to this attitude was quite negative, but through a conciliatory letter he tried to point out to the individual representing this group that the Hall of Fame was looking at a bigger picture than just the AAGPBL. The Hall's administrators were looking at the larger historical landscape of *all* American women who played baseball from the mid–1800s forward. They had to consider not just the AAGBBL, but all those pioneer women who played baseball before the AAGBBL entered P.K. Wrigley's thoughts. In Spencer's words:

[The AAGPBL] wouldn't have had a league if it wasn't for all the [women] who said "we love the game" and suffered to play 100 years before [the AAGBBL]. And they played individually, and they played as men, or they played with men, and they were really known more as oddities than anything else. They were more like "Alligator Face Boy" or something. I mean they really ... had to play against great social opposition, but they loved the game. And that is part of our mission, to show just how strong the pull of the game is.[35]

Spencer also observed, however, that the AAGBBL was "obviously head and shoulders the high water mark ... the apex of the [women in baseball] story."[36]

The Hall of Fame would not budge from its position of a "Women in Baseball" display, and, from an overall historical perspective, rightly so. Conflict between the AAGPBL and the Hall of Fame over this fundamental principle could have derailed the whole project, but by April 1988, a compromise of sorts had been worked out. The AAGPBL Board acquiesced to being a part of a "Women In Baseball" permanent display rather than standing on a principle that would exclude them altogether. Administrators at the Hall of Fame acquiesced to "unveiling" the display — a concept never before entertained. Dottie Collins reported that "Ted Spencer stated they had never had to deal with an unveiling of a *display* before, but he would do it."[37] Thus, the staff at the Hall of Fame maintained their historical perspective and the AAGPBL was honored with a formal "unveiling" recognition ceremony. Whatever the bartering process had been, Ted Spencer commended Dottie Collins as the "glue" that held everything together.[38]

In Dottie Collins, both Merrie Fidler and Sharon Roepke found the same AAGPBL champion for their dreams of an archives and recognition by the Hall of Fame. Dottie had pitched for the Fort Wayne Daisies while a member of the AAGBBL. In the game of the AAGPBL vs. the Hall of Fame, she also pitched masterfully, keeping her team in the game for almost two years until the dream of recognition by the Hall of Fame became a reality.

Dottie Collins pitching in a "Run, Jane, Run" old-timers' game, mid–1980s (courtesy Mary Dierstein).

Establishing an Archive

From the September 1986 Fort Wayne Reunion until the opening of the Hall of Fame display in 1988, Dottie Collins had an excellent supporting team. In addition to the immediate members of that first Hall of Fame

Committee (Lynn Haber, Karen Violetta Kunkel, Sharon Roepke, Danielle Barber), Dottie solicited support from the rest of her AAGPBL colleagues. In an April 1987 AAGPBL Newsletter article entitled "COOPERSTOWN 1989" she wrote:

> The exact date I do not recall, but one day in January [1987] my telephone rang and upon answering it the gentleman on the other end identified himself as Mr. Ted Spencer from the Baseball Hall of Fame in Cooperstown, New York. He said he had been swamped with mail in regards to our league and instead of writing us a letter he felt that we deserved a telephone call to let us know that we had been accepted into the Baseball Hall of Fame. Our conversation was long giving details on how we should go about preparing the items for display. Mr. Spencer described the display as being 8' by 8.' Along with preparing the items, space also has to be made available so that is why we are saying — 1989.
>
> It will be a large project. Our first objective will be to set up an archives. A place for this has not yet been determined but several locations are in mind. From the archives items will be selected for Cooperstown, the rest will remain in the archives and under our control. Part of the archives will be a traveling archives which can be sent to member cities or anyone who requests it.
>
> Here is what we need from you — suggestions and ideas as to what should go to Cooperstown.... How we can include everyone who wants to be a part of it.... Items that you might have that would be important to us that you would be willing to donate to either Cooperstown and/or the archives ... *VOLUNTEERS who would be willing to work with us and meet with us* ... We need Legal advice — Any attorneys out there — Please give us a call. This is not a small job, it will take a lot of time and work. It is also going to take money to set up the archives — So when the time comes, we hope you will be there to help.[39]

An extra edition of the newsletter, the printing of which was now also in Dottie's hands, appeared in June 1987. It announced the results of the May 23rd meeting with those who responded to the April appeal. Those who attended the meeting included Fran Janssen, who hosted the meeting, Earlene (Beans) Risinger, Jean Geissinger Harding, Karen Violetta Kunkel, Dottie Wiltse Collins, June Peppas (via the telephone), and Sharon Roepke. The first order of business was deciding to organize to achieve their goal and deciding on a name for the organization. Thus, in response to the call of the Hall of Fame and the concomitant need for an archives, "The All-American Girls Professional Baseball League Players Association, Inc." (AAGPBL-PA) was created. It was established as a non-profit organization committed to preserving the AAGPBL's history and its place in baseball's history.[40]

With recognition by the Hall of Fame forthcoming, and with the Players' Association established, the need for an archives was pressing. More than that, finding a place where memorabilia could be collected, catalogued, and stored for the Hall of Fame display was an immediate necessity. And, it was immediately dealt with. Between that first organizational meeting for the Players' Association on May 23, 1987, and publication of the June 1987 extra edition of the newsletter, Karen Violetta Kunkel had assumed the position of Executive Director and Director of Archives. The temporary site for the archives would be Northern Michigan University in Marquette, Michigan, where Karen was also the director of the Great Lakes Sports Training Center and the U.S. Olympic Training and Education Center. In Karen's words, the administration at Northern Michigan University played a significant supporting role in establishing the first AAGPBL archives:

> My background had nothing in it about an archives. I did have Northern Michigan University, and they had an archives, so I went for advice. Blessed again! There were students available to intern with me on the project but no money in the History Department

budget to pay them. I needed help. I went to the University President, Dr. James Appleberry. I explained the project, its importance, and the need for financial help. Dr. Appleberry ... provided budget support along with student labor for developing the AAGBBL
archives.[41]

Once this temporary site for the archives was determined, the next step was to notify
the players on the mailing list. Dottie extended an appeal to them in the June 1987 extra
edition:

> HERE IS YOUR FIRST JOB: — Go over your items carefully that you wish to donate to
> the archives and/or the National Baseball Hall of Fame. Write each item down and
> describe it in detail. Example: Kenosha Comets Year Book — 1945 — Picture (Team)
> Racine Belles — 1950. — Individual Picture — Name — Year. — Balls — Year, size, signed by
> what team. — Bats Belonging to whom. Uniform, team, condition — complete or incom-
> plete.
>   This information is to be sent to Karen Kunkel (address below), her grad students will
> catalog everything so that we will know exactly what we have. After everything has been
> catalogued and we have gone over it we will contact each of you when we are ready to
> receive the material. There will be papers for you to sign and clippings & pictures you
> send will be copied and photographed and then returned to you unless you specify other-
> wise. We are interested in anything that you might have pertaining to the league. We are
> in hopes that you will make this your number 1 priority now and get this information
> into us right away.[42]

A form was developed so players could designate whether they were contributing "a
straight gift with no return," a "loan for a specified period of time, or on loan but would
be in their will for someone upon their death."
According to Karen, "volumes of things" were
received at the University and she and her student
assistants "started receiving and cataloging items
and storing them according to the History Department recommendations."[43]

Karen Violetta Kunkel ca. 1986 (courtesy Karen Violetta Kunkel).

In August 1987, Betsy Jochum wrote that John
Kovach, head of displays and sports materials at
the Northern Indiana Historical Society (NIHS)
had set up an AAGBBL display for opening day at
South Bend's new Coveleski AAA Baseball Park
the previous April. The event was feted by a parade
including the Budweiser Clydesdales pulling a
Studebaker wagon, Studebaker antique cars, and
a group of South Bend Blues Sox carrying signs
identifying them as members of the AAGPBL from
1943 to 1954. This group consisted of Janet "Pee
Wee" Wiley Sears, Lou Arnold, Frank Yuhasz
(Loyal Fan), Twila Shively, and Betsy Jochum.
According to Betsy, "The streets were lined with
crowds of people all the way to the ball park."[44]

The South Bend players' contact with John
Kovach in April of 1987 would lead to a formal
offer to the AAGPBL–PA Executive Board to per-

manently house their archives at the NIHS Museum. Lib Mahon, acting as a liaison between the two groups in September 1987, advised the board that the museum had plenty of room, and a display would be seen all year round by those touring the museum or holding meetings there. She also reported "enthusiasm in the Mayor's Office, and throughout the business community" for this project. Lib, Lou Arnold, and Sharon Roepke were assigned to look into this offer and report back.[45]

By April 1988, the AAGPBL Board was discussing matters of safeguarding donor rights, storage, insurance, and cataloging in relation to establishing a permanent archives at NIHS. At this time, the newsletter noted that Lib Mahon and Betsy Jochum were obtaining additional information for establishing a permanent archives in South Bend. However, it was decided "that the memorabilia should remain at Northern Michigan University until Cooperstown has made their selection, then the proper legal papers [could be] drawn up for the complete transfer to a permanent archives."[46]

By early August 1988, newsletter recipients were notified that the date for the Cooperstown display had been set for November 5, 1988; that Ruth Williams Heverly was coordinating events with Cooperstown; that the Hall of Fame people "agreed that the 'Life Time Roster' listing everyone's name who played in the league will be included in the display case"; and that "they are submitting a list of memorabilia ... they wish to place in the display."[47]

Newsletter readers were also advised in August '88 that plans for transferring the archives from Northern Michigan University to NIHS would be completed August 22, 1988. On that date, according to Karen Violetta Kunkel, her secretary, Dawn Wilder, "along with student help loaded a box truck with all the records and items and drove it from the University to South Bend. Fran Janssen, representing the board at the time, was there to receive the items on behalf of the Players' Association."[48]

Those still wishing to contribute items were directed to contact a board member for proper donation procedures. In addition, it was noted that "all memorabilia, even though housed at the Indiana Historical Society will remain the property of the Players' Association."[49] A letter to the Board from John Kovach at NIHS on September 14, 1988, extended thanks to the AAGPBL for selecting NIHS to house their archival collection. Kovach observed:

> The All-American Girls Professional Baseball League played an important role in our history, both socially and athletically. The new exhibit at Cooperstown and interest in the league is proof of that.
>
> Over 80 items were selected from the archives to be sent to Cooperstown for possible inclusion in their exhibit. As some of you may know, an exhibit was done at the Stanley Coveleski Regional Stadium in South Bend this past summer. The response to that was so strong, that we intend to do a larger one there next season.
>
> Some of the other plans for the archives will include: a future exhibit at the Historical Society (perhaps during Women's History month — February or during the summer months); exhibits at other museums (the Royal Ontario Museum has inquired about the collection holdings) and perhaps some sort of traveling exhibit. Of course the collection will also be open to researchers to help them with their projects.[50]

Once memorabilia was collected and housed, and items for Cooperstown shipped off, the AAGPBL Board's attention refocused on Cooperstown.

AAGPBL Players' Association's first board of directors during the Baseball Hall of Fame recognition activities, November 3–6, 1988. *Left to right, front:* Jean Geissinger Harding, Earlene "Beans" Risinger, Arleene Johnson Noga, Faye Dancer. *Back:* Karen Violetta Kunkel, Fran Janssen, Dottie Wiltse Collins, Vivian Kellogg, Joanne Winter, June Peppas, and Wilma Briggs (courtesy Jean Geissinger Harding).

The Cooperstown Unveiling

The reunion/recognition at Cooperstown transpired during November 3, 4, and 5, 1988. One hundred and fifty ex–AAGBBL players, their families, and many more well-wishers attended the event. Those who arrived on November 3 experienced ever-increasing, shared anticipation for the opening of the AAGBBL exhibit. When Dottie Collins and Hall of Fame president Howard C. Talbot pulled the drapes to unveil the "Women in Baseball" exhibit on November 5, 1988, at 1:00 P.M., deep emotions surfaced. Pride and joy bubbled from the toes to the nose, overran the eyes, and had to be shared with hugs all around the rest of the day and night. The league song erupted spontaneously

Merrie Fidler in front of the "Women in Baseball" exhibit at the National Baseball Hall of Fame, November 5, 1988.

in the Hall and all over Cooperstown from 1:00 P.M. to whenever. It was the first curtain rising ever for a Hall of Fame display. It was the first ever exhibition "event" in the Hall of Fame's history.[51] As Ted Spencer would recall sixteen years later:

> [We] looked out and there [were] 1200 people. Here's a day where we have 400 people. That's what we'd have on a Saturday in November, 400 people. The place was [packed], and they sang that [AAGBBL] song all day long.... And this museum [had] never had that much noise! It was great.
> ... To me it changed the whole direction of the museum because it brought home how important the game is culturally.[52]

For everyone who experienced that Cooperstown weekend, it was a "once-in-a-lifetime" event, but especially for the players. Their letters in the December 1988 newsletter effervesced with gratitude to the AAGPBL Board and the wonder of it all.

Lois "Tommie" Barker wrote, "Well, our big week at the Hall of Fame has come and gone but I assure you the honor of being just a small part of it and the memories will always be held close to my heart forever.... You'll never know the joy you brought by doin' what ya done."

Ruth Richard noted, "Now my family knows why I enjoyed playing for the All Americans. They couldn't get over how friendly all the players were. That's one week-end they will never forget. It was the greatest!!!"

Irene "Choo-Choo" Hickson remarked, "You made us so happy and proud to be a member of our league and best of all the Hall of Fame. One other time I was that happy and proud, was when I made one of our teams...."

Tiby Eisen and Charter Member Peggy Mack exclaimed, "This past weekend in the quaint little town of Cooperstown, New York, was the experience of a lifetime and now it is the memory of a lifetime."

Beverly Stuhr Thompson wrote, "I wish I could put into words how I really feel, about last weekend. I'm trying to tell my Mother and friends what it was like when the display opened."

Lou Arnold shared, "The only way I could honestly tell you my true feeling is— if my heart could hold this pen. My heart is about to explode, I'm so thrilled about being in Cooperstown."

Jean Marlowe noted, "'Twas better medication than my Doctors could prescribe for me!"

Doris Sams relayed that "she just can't come down off her high. Was quite a thrill for her to see her picture in the display, along with her trophy and bat."

Ros Scarborough related for Teeny Petras, "Teeny's been on cloud nine since Cooperstown and hasn't come down. When she went to get the paper in the candy store, she was signing autographs for hours, [and] the owner begged her to stay longer because he never sold so many papers. Cooperstown and seeing the players after so many years is a memory she will treasure forever."

Jean Lovell Dowler stated, "We had a really great time in Cooperstown, which was a once in a lifetime event!"

Kay "Swish" Blumetta wrote, "Back in Jersey once more and finally coming down out of the clouds! It was a beautiful and unforgettable time we all had for sure."

Maddy English penned, "My family, friends and I had a marvelous time. Enjoyed seeing everyone and seeing the display; it was really a thrill."

Katie Horstman confirmed, "Coooperstown was a real DREAM."

Sara Sands Ferguson informed, "Was talking with one of the employees at the Hall and he told us that they did not have the crowd or excitement of our magnitude even at the induction of WILLIE STARGELL this summer. Quite a tribute to the AAGPBL I think."

In like manner, Canadian Marge Callaghan Maxwell relayed, "My ex-boss says I bumped GRETSKY & LEMNIUS off the front page of the sports section. I have sure had a lot of phone calls from people to congratulate me. They think it is fantastic. I really enjoyed myself down there...."

Anna May Hutchison wrote, "What a let down after such an exciting week-end in Cooperstown. That was truly an emotional time in my life and it is hard to realize that it has come and gone so quickly, as it seems like it was just yesterday that the plans were in the making. I've talked to or received messages from some of the girls and the feelings are of the 'Biggest Thrill of a Lifetime.'"

Vivian Kellogg called just before press time to share that she was "really riding a high — received a letter of congratulations from none other than former PRESIDENT GERALD R. FORD. He wrote: 'I vividly recall the league when it played its games at the Old South High School Field in Grand Rapids. I was an avid fan. It was excellent baseball.'"[53]

Wilma Briggs called to tell "about the welcome when she returned home. There was a huge sign at school reading —'WELCOME BACK MISS BRIGGS — OUR HALL OF FAMER.' But her 3rd grade class did not think that was enough and seemed to be very upset that the PRESIDENT had not contacted any of us. They felt he should be told — without any help from 'Briggsie' in the spelling or grammar department (21) letters were sent to the President."

At the same time, in South Bend, former Blue Sox pitcher Lou Arnold was also writing letters to solicit recognition from the President. Two were sent with no response. In the third, she wrote that if this were a men's league gaining recognition by the Hall of Fame, he would not only have written, he would have called.[54] Whether it was a combination of "Briggsie's" third grade class's letters and Lou's appeals, or whether it was Lou's threat of labeling him sexist, a letter signed by President Ronald Reagan acknowledging the honor accorded the AAGPBL was posted to Dottie Collins on January 10, 1989:

> I am happy to add my congratulations to those received by the All American Girls Professional Baseball League after the opening of the "Women in Baseball" exhibit at the National Baseball Hall of Fame.
>
> As professionals in our national pastime of baseball, you were pioneers among women in the world of professional sports. Your achievements on the diamond came through exceptional dedication and discipline, and I know you agree it was surely worth the effort. Baseball is always a memorable and enriching experience, and you can reflect and rejoice that the example you and others set is now depicted at Cooperstown to inspire and inform your fellow Americans and visitors from abroad for years to come.
>
> Again, congratulations to you and your coaches, umpires, owners, and many fans. Nancy joins me in sending warm best wishes always. God bless you.[55]
> — Ronald Reagan

How wonderful the Hall of Fame event transpired during these ladies' lifetime. How wonderful they could drink from the cup of honor they never in their wildest dreams imagined possible for them. When they played baseball in the AAGBBL, they felt blessed just to be able to play the game they loved at its highest level. They never dreamed of Cooperstown because they were girls (women). Now, however, they could revel in the honor of being recognized as a part of baseball's history in the National Baseball Hall of Fame in Cooperstown, New York. Beyond that, the All-Americans were assured that future generations of girls browsing through the Hall of Fame could envision their history, their love of the game, and their accomplishments, and understand that, as girls, they, too, had the ability to play baseball, if not yet the opportunity to do so.

From November 5, 1988 onward, an undying glimmer of possibilities for future generations of girls to play baseball will forever emanate from baseball's shrine, the Hall of Fame. As first AAGPBL president Ken Sells reflected, "I still have to believe the display in Cooperstown will inspire some individual or group to again start a Girls Professional Baseball League."[56] AAGPBL president June Peppas expressed a similar thought when she wrote to her colleagues in the post–Cooperstown newsletter:

> Cooperstown has come and gone All Americans. If we never do anymore we have gotten our display there for all America to see. Every man, woman, boy and especially the girls that travel through their hallowed halls will now see the All American Girls Professional Baseball League. They will see action shots, individuals, lots of league memorabilia, and above all they will see the names, hometowns and years played by our players. For this we should all be very very proud.[57]

Thus it transpired that a permanent AAGPBL Archives and a permanent "Women in Baseball" exhibit at the National Baseball Hall of Fame both occurred in the latter part of 1988. Like the Newsletter and the First National Reunion, the Cooperstown "Women in Baseball" display and the AAGPBL Archives at the Northern Indiana Historical Society Museum evolved hand-in-hand.

Epilogue

Both NIHS and the Hall of Fame would soon discover that their permanent All-American displays would become one of their most popular exhibits. Both institutions would also frequently solicit additional memorabilia from the players in order to be able to rotate their displays as well as to loan out materials for temporary exhibits to other institutions.

By the spring of 1989, for instance, AAGPBL board president June Peppas wrote for the May newsletter: "Since Cooperstown we have been deluged with museum requests. Among those contacting us: The Royal Canadian Museum, The Canadian Baseball Hall of Fame, and The Smithsonian Institute." June continued her update with an appeal for additional memorabilia.

> To be able to meet their requests, we must have ... memorabilia such as complete uniforms and/or parts of, balls, gloves, posters, B/W or color action/non-action shots, patches, trophies or other things you may feel important. The above are items we feel are of greatest importance. At this time _WE DO NOT NEED SCRAPBOOKS_.
>
> Dig hard All Americans, we need your help. Check those closets, get into the attic or the basement and dig out. It does no one any good buried away for eventual throwing out and look how much good it can bring to so many people and future young women athletes. So _LET'S ALL PUT FORTH AN ALL AMERICAN EFFORT_.[58]

Also in the spring of 1989, Ted Spencer related that he was receiving "two to four inquiries about [the AAGPBL] weekly." He also encouraged AAGPBLers to attend the Hall of Fame's 50th year reunion that June.[59] These observations and appeals were just the first few leaks in the dike of demands for AAGPBL information and artifacts that would emanate from and flood these two institutions in years to come.

Northern Indiana History Center

By the fall of '89, AAGPBL Board Meeting Minutes recorded that "The memorabilia is now the property of the Northern Indiana Historical Society, at South Bend, Indiana," so the "memorabilia will be properly cared for under their control." During the same meeting, Diane Barts, museum registrar, presented future plans for a new "historical complex to be built on the grounds at the Oliver family mansion."[60] Completion of the new complex would move the AAGPBL collection from the old and crowded Court House to a new, expanded facility in late 1994.

It was not until March 29, 1990, however, that the AAGPBL archives were formally presented to the Northern Indiana Historical Society by Dottie Collins. Other AAGBBLers present at this event included Betsy Jochum, Lib Mahon, Twi Shively, Nancy DeShone Rockwell, Fran Janssen, "Pee Wee" Wiley Sears, and umpire Barney Zoss. Lou Arnold, it was reported, "was there in spirit." During the months from August 1988 to March 1990 and beyond, the South Bend players were kept busy helping to catalogue artifacts and photographs. Lib Mahon, Betsy Jochum, Twi Shively and Fran Janssen performed the bulk of the work in completing this time-consuming, tedious project. Once artifacts were catalogued, photographs required identifications and cataloging.[61] Fran Janssen reported that the museum staff enjoyed listening to the photo identification ses-

Formal presentation of the AAGPBL Archives to the Northern Indiana Historical Society (now Northern Indiana Center for History), March 19, 1990. Standing, *left to right:* Janet "Pee Wee" Wiley Sears, Twi Shively, Betsy Jochum, Dottie Collins, Fran Janssen, Nancy DeShone Rockwell Dinehart, Lib Mahon. Seated: League Umpire Barney Zoss (courtesy Fran Janssen).

sions in the balcony above the main floor of the old South Bend Court House. There was much banter and laughter as the pictures were viewed, identified, and catalogued.[62]

Fran noted that she and volunteer Merle Blue, a former local high school history teacher, aided the move to the new museum in late 1994. They moved all of the museum's paper records and files, including those of the AAGPBL, from temporary storage in the offices above the Carriage House of the Oliver Mansion downstairs to the archives in the new building. Part of the new building was actually attached to the Carriage House. This task involved numbering shelves, listing the location of items on the shelves, physically moving items, and submitting the lists to be computerized. These two performed yeoman service for the museum and the league.[63]

One benefit of the new facility was that it could house a permanent AAGPBL display inside in an eight-foot by ten-foot display case. Outside, in a six-foot by six-foot area, the AAGPBL logo on a bronze plaque was set in the brick walkway leading to the museum's front door. Surrounding the plaque, in a diamond formation, each AAGPBL team name was inscribed on individual bricks. On the home plate end of the diamond, a bronze baseball was implanted in a brick and "1943–1954" was inscribed on either side of the ball.[64]

By December of 1990, more than 1,000 photos had been catalogued. NIHS registrar, Diane Barts, was soliciting written and taped accounts of life in the AAGPBL from former players, managers, chaperones, umpires, or anyone else reading the newsletter.[65] Also in 1990, the committee working on cataloguing pictures and other memorabilia suggested that anyone sending anything to the archives should submit a personal history with it and identify names and locations of pictures.[66]

The AAGPBL Board contributed funds annually to the archives for preservation of their materials, and in January 1993, they established the beginnings of an endowment fund to help perpetuate the collection. The board also established an agreement with NIHS for using the AAGPBL logo for saleable items with the profit from such sales to be used to protect AAGPBL memorabilia.[67]

As of 1997, NIHS and Cooperstown were trading materials, NIHS's title was changed to Northern Indiana Center for History (NICH), and a new executive director was on board. Although NICH was the avowed location for the league's memorabilia, some players, such as Vivian Kellogg, preferred to deposit their photos and artifacts at Cooperstown. The Board "stressed the need of cooperation between the two" institutions.[68]

Possibly in the face of an unintended but emerging competition for memorabilia with the Hall of Fame by 2000, Cheryl Taylor, NICH Executive Director, advised the AAGPBL Board that "the All American Collection [was] the most important collection" the museum had and the "most requested collection" by researchers. Thus, she began lobbying the AAGPBL Board and the players to continue contributing to the collection. She also indicated that she wanted to "expand the exhibit and include some audio and video" materials.[69] By 2004, NICH had as many as 25 calls each month pertaining to the AAGPBL during the busiest spring months. The museum applied for and received a $15,000 grant from SBC Communications which they used to "scan all the photos in the collection as well as many of the scrapbooks and other media."[70] The scanned photos were to be viewable over the internet by the fall of 2004. Plans were also under way to enlarge the AAGPBL permanent display and compliment it with a computerized kiosk for viewing the scanned pictures.[71] The AAGPBL collection's continued popularity at NICH through the years has insured its maintenance, growth, and advancement into the future.

The Baseball Hall of Fame

While NICH's AAGPBL collection was established and growing, Ted Spencer admitted that the Hall of Fame was experiencing "the most popular exhibit" they'd ever done by "a thousand percent." "I mean," Spencer continued, "I've been here 22 years now [2004], and I never get more than a handful of letters for any one exhibit for one reason or another. The first year [of the "Women in Baseball" exhibit] alone, I stopped counting at two hundred. And that's a significant statement."[72] Public response to the display confirmed Bill Guilfoile and Ted Spencer's vision of the value of a "Women in Baseball" exhibit. Ted Spencer also affirmed that the public's response to the AAGBBL display was instrumental in expanding the Hall of Fame's role in preserving and promoting the history of baseball.[73]

As a result, a continuing and growing relationship was generated between the Hall of Fame and the AAGPBL. This was not something the administrators at the Hall of Fame had envisioned when they opened the "Women in Baseball" display in November 1988. Ted Spencer observed that the "Women in Baseball" exhibit received so much attention, especially after the movie, *A League of Their Own*, that the Hall of Fame administrators couldn't ignore it. Here again, the AAGPBL's popularity with the public promoted itself on its own merits.

The affable relationship between the Hall of Fame and the AAGPBL would blossom in the fall of 1995 when an article in the September newsletter announced: "HALL LIBRARY TO START WOMEN IN BASEBALL COLLECTION." This was the Hall's effort "to honor and document the lives and careers of women who have played baseball" by establishing a separate file for each player in the AAGPBL. In addition, it was a response to continued requests by school children for information about the AAGPBL. As Tim Wiles, Hall of Fame Public Services Librarian at the time, explained, "...a significant portion of these requests were for information on particular players, usually from the same towns as the students making the requests. Without individual files, we didn't have much to send these kids."[74]

Wiles encouraged all players to contribute whatever they could so the Hall of Fame would have an individual file for each AAGBBL player, just as it had for each man who played Major League Baseball.[75] Stimulated by calls and letters full of questions, a follow-up letter by Wiles in the January 1996 newsletter itemized the kinds of things the files could contain.

> We are interested in newspaper clippings from both your AAGPBL days and thereafter. If you want your file to reflect your career as a softball player, coach, teacher, or whatever, and you have clippings, send them along. If you receive an award or if a youth baseball field is named after you, send us a clipping.
>
> We'd love to have COPIES of your rule books, contracts, charm school books, letters from the league or the team, fan mail from the 40's and 50's or from today, diaries or letters which are relevant to baseball, programs, scorecards, scrapbooks, etc. It's your file in the Hall of Fame. Put whatever you want in it. The files will be used in the future by two kinds of researchers. The first will be interested in the league, or in women's sports in general. The second kind of researchers will be your descendants several generations from now. They will be interested not just in your playing career but also in the other events of your life. If you are a champion bowler, they'll probably find that interesting. I'm just speaking from our experiences with the files of nineteenth century male baseball players. When their great-grandchildren come in, they are fascinated by every detail.
>
> We are interested in photographs as well. If you send a photograph, make sure that you tell us two things about it: 1.) Do you want us to copy it and give it back, or are you giving it to us? Second, please try to identify as many of the people in the photograph as possible. In this way, you are doing a service to other players who might not have so much in their files.[76]

Not only did the Hall of Fame Library want to establish files for each individual, they also intended to create "files on each team in the AAGPBL as well as files on lawsuits filed by girls who just wanted to play little league." Because they were developing files on "Women in Baseball," they would also have files for "players on the Colorado Silver Bullets, & files on other important women in baseball," including umpires, and individuals who had played for barnstorming teams and the Old Negro Leagues.[77]

A little more than a year later, Wiles reported to newsletter readers, "We currently have 37 'great' files, which are chock full of clippings, etc., and another 35 'good' files which generally contain one slim article about a player. 35 and 37 make 72. I know the league had almost ten times that number of players."[78] By 2004, Wiles would state that the actual number of AAGPBL biographical folders was difficult to determine because they were integrated alphabetically with all the other biographical files. He did estimate,

however, "that most living players have a file, [as well as] most of the well-known players who are already deceased." In addition, he stated, "We ... sent questionnaires to all
living players in 1997, and our return rate was eventually about 80 percent I think —
which of course [was] fabulous. Those questionnaires are available to anyone, and are
frequently consulted by students."[79]

In addition to the above, the Hall of Fame currently holds about a dozen scrapbooks
and approximately 150 individual photo files donated by players and league personnel
since 1995. All AAGPBL teams have clipping and photo files, and there are around "40
subject files in the library with headings like AAGPBL — schedules, stats, batboy/girls,
night games, playoffs, jewelry, stadiums, etc."[80] Obviously, the lure of having one's files
and memorabilia in The National Baseball Hall of Fame could not be ignored by players
who had not already committed their clippings and artifacts to NICH before Tim Wiles'
solicitation of mementos in 1995.

In the spring of 1997, Ted Spencer, curator at the Hall of Fame, requested AAGPBL
players to send in additional memorabilia because the Hall was "planning to expand [the]
"Women in Baseball" exhibit over the next several years. As you know," he told them,
"the current exhibit is very popular, and we receive many requests to make it bigger and
richer in historical detail."[81] As Spencer indicated to Carolyn Trombe, Dottie Collins'
biographer, the new display would be impressive. It's intended to be a three-dimensional
exhibit and will include a space to walk through. He also indicated that the new display
would include more historical memorabilia related to pre- and post–AAGBBL women
involved in baseball, but that the AAGBBL would still be, as they presently are, the "apex"
of the display.[82]

About 1997, the Hall of Fame also instituted a Mother's Day event in cooperation
with the AAGPBL. This event became "somewhat of a tribute to the women who played
the great game of baseball."[83] The 2002 Mother's Day weekend in Cooperstown, for
instance, was also feted as the "10th anniversary salute to the film *A League of Their
Own.*" Those in attendance from the movie included "Garry Marshall, Tracy Reiner
(Betty Spaghetti), Lori Petty (Kit), and Megan Cavanaugh (Marla Hooch). Penny Mar-
shall, who directed the film, returned to Cooperstown along with members of the All-
American Girls Professional Baseball League. The weekend's events were capped by an
"evening roundtable discussion in the Hall of Fame Gallery hosted by film critic Jeffrey
Lyons." Round table participants from the AAGPBL included "Mary Moore, Jane Moffet,
Dolly White, Madeline English, Gloria Cordes, and Helen Steffes."[84] Also in 2002, Delores
"Dolly" Brumfield White, AAGPBL board president, became a member of the Hall of
Fame's Educational Advisory Council.

In 2003, plans were announced for the production of the Hall of Fame's second Electronic Field Trip. The topic was "Women's Baseball." The "Women in Baseball" Electronic Field Trip (EFT) occurred on March 18, 2003, and was entitled "Dirt on Their
Skirts: 150 Years of Pioneers in Women's Baseball." It delivered "a timeless [history] lesson of [baseball] to the largest classroom in the world, with the broadcast of a live electronic field trip for nearly 20 million students across the country directly from Wrigley
Field in Chicago." The program took place during Women's History Month; it celebrated
the 60th anniversary of the AAGPBL; and it was designed for grades 7 through 12. Participants included "students from Chicago's Lake View High School, as well as Draper
Middle School in the Mohonasen (N.Y.) School District, and students from the Dolgeville (N.Y.) School District."[85]

EFT co-hosts included the Hall of Fame's research librarian, Tim Wiles, Silver Bullets player Julie Croteau and coach Phil Niekro. Participants from the AAGPBL included "Helen Hannah Campbell, Shirley Burkovich, Jane Moffet, Isabel "Lefty" Alvarez, Audrey Haine Daniels and her husband Bud, Earlene "Beans" Risinger, Terry Donahue, Jean Cione, and Delores "Dolly" Brumfield White. All of these ladies were interviewed from Wrigley Field. Mary Pratt joined the telecast live from Cooperstown, and Alice "Lefty" Hohlmayer joined in from San Diego, California."[86] Other Hall of Fame participants included Jane Forbes Clark, chairperson, and president Dale Petroskey.[87]

During the two 90-minute segments that included a combination of live T.V. broadcasts and internet curriculum, students had the opportunity to call in and e-mail questions to the participants. According to Jeff Arnett from the Hall of Fame:

> "Women in Baseball" aired live in 33 states, with additional broadcasts showing in Toronto, Ontario, and Glasgow, Scotland. Initial numbers estimate a live audience ... in excess of 15 million students with another six to eight million expected to view the program via tape delay, the Internet and video.[88]

A Hall of Fame press release credited the following organizations for supporting the program.

> The program [was] broadcast to schools through a partnership among Ball State University, Best Buy's Children Foundation, Project View, a federally funded interactive technology program based in Schenectady, Apple Computer and the National Baseball Hall of Fame and Museum. Additional sponsors [included] the Chicago Cubs and the AAGPBL."[89]

In the fall of 2003, the Hall of Fame continued with its exploration of long-range lessons which included the AAGPBL. An article in the September 2003 newsletter from the Hall of Fame announced:

> Our video conference efforts are poised for a move to the next level as we prepare to deliver distance learning from the Museum's Bullpen Theater. The 56-seat mini-auditorium/classroom has been retrofitted with nearly $90,000 in new technology to combine education and public programs in a unique setting. Finally, we are nearing an agreement with the *New York Times* to exclusively publish a 16-page *Newspapers In Education* [NIE] tabloid on standards-based, historical lessons in baseball. The tab will be available to all syndicate papers of the *Times*, as well as to individual classroom subscribers. The NIE feature will be released in September 2003.... Conservative estimates show the insert will initially reach 50,000 students in 2,000 classrooms in at least 18 cities.[90]

The lessons to be broadcast included one for Women's History: "Dirt on Their Skirts."

Cooperstown hosted a 60th AAGPBL Anniversary Reunion Ceremony in September of 2003. During a brief ceremony for the players on the east side of the Library, the Hall's president, Dale Petroskey, announced that a statue of an AAGBBL player would be placed on the lawn nearby. This project was conceived, researched, and presented to Mr. Petrosky during the 2003 Mother's Day weekend by Jane Moffet, AAGPBL treasurer. Her objective was to add to the league's history and legacy at the Hall of Fame. The plan she presented to the Hall of Fame was for a life-sized bronze statue of a player in an AAG-BBL uniform swinging a bat. To Jane, the statue had to be a batter because all players batted, but they didn't all pitch or catch or play first base. Her purpose, of course, was that the statue would represent each player and exemplify the motto of "All for one and one for all."[91]

When Hall of Fame president Dale Petroskey announced that the Hall of Fame would undertake the statue project, he also announced that it would finance the statue — a very big item. In addition, he explained that the Hall would employ the same sculptor to do the AAGBBL statue who had done the statues of Roy Campanella and Johnny Padres that currently stand on the lawn outside of the Hall of Fame Library. The target date for the unveiling of the AAGBBL statue was tentatively set for the spring of 2006.

Concluding Note

In 1972, when this volume began as a master's degree project, researching the AAGPBL was a "pulling teeth" experience. One had first to discover the existence of the AAGBBL and then to dig to uncover primary source material accurately reflecting its history. One had to dig harder to find more than a handful of ex-players, and most of the time they were stumbled upon.

Between 1976 and November of 1988, when Sharon Roepke visited and revisited the Hall of Fame, all the Hall ever contained relating to the AAGBBL were a few Dell Annual Booklets entitled "Major League Facts and Figures." These booklets included general information and statistics on the AAGBBL. This was a happenstance too, because Marie Keenan, who compiled the "Facts and Figures" for Major League Baseball, was also AAGBBL president Max Carey's secretary.[92] The "Facts and Figures" booklets were in the Hall of Fame because they were a source for men's Major League Baseball statistics—certainly not because they happened to include AAGBBL information. In essence, the existence and history of the AAGBBL was rather well buried after the end of the 1954 season until recognition by the Hall of Fame in 1988.

Today, however, thanks to many contributing factors and individuals, there are two major resource centers that preserve and promote the existence and history of the AAGBBL. At the Northern Indiana Center for History and the Hall of Fame alike, casual observers and serious researchers can visit to obtain visual and auditory impressions of, and factual information about, the AAGBBL. Both the NICH in South Bend, Indiana, and the National Baseball Hall of Fame in Cooperstown, New York, welcome the casual observer and the intent scholar to visit and be surrounded by primary and secondary source materials related to the AAGBBL.* All are welcomed to examine inspiring written records, authentic memorabilia, and auditory and photographic documentation of the fun-loving, dedicated, skilled, and intense "girls" who loved and played the game of baseball at its highest level.

---

*The Special Collections Department at the University of Notre Dame's Library also contains valuable AAGBBL documents, and the staff there is as accommodating as the staff at the two institutions that were the focus of this discussion.

16

The Organization of the
Players' Association and
A League of Their Own

The Player's Association: 1987–1992

At the AAGPBL National Reunion in Fort Wayne, Indiana, in September 1986, Dottie Collins, Karen Violetta Kunkel, Sharon Roepke, Lynn Haber, and Danielle Barber formed a committee to obtain recognition by the Baseball Hall of Fame. In a video interview with documentarian Dr. Janis Taylor at the '86 reunion, Dottie stressed:

> Of course, you know we are wanting recognition by the Baseball Hall of Fame. Not recognition as an individual person or an individual team, but just recognition *that we did exist*. That to all of us would be the greatest thing that could happen.[1]

Why it took from the end of the reunion in early September 1986 until late January 1987 for Dottie to write to Ted Spencer at the Hall of Fame is conjecture. The fact that she did and that he was eagerly receptive to her appeal was a matter of the right people being in the right place at the right time under the right circumstances (see Chapter 15). When Dottie received Ted Spencer's phone call in January 1987 indicating that the Baseball Hall of Fame was interested in creating a "Women in Baseball" display, the wheels were set in motion for the 22-month journey to the "hallowed halls."

One of the first things Dottie did for the committee was to send out a general appeal for help from the players through the April 1987 newsletter. After explaining that Ted Spencer had called; that this would be a large project requiring the establishment of an archives; and that everyone's input and memorabilia were needed; Dottie appealed for "*VOLUNTEERS who would be willing to work with us and meet with us....* Let us hear from you," she wrote, "so we can set the process in motion when we meet in May."[2] In response to Dottie's appeal, Fran Janssen offered her South Bend, Indiana, home as a meeting site since it was centrally located for Dottie in Fort Wayne and others who were interested in attending from Chicago and a few Michigan cities.[3]

That first organizational meeting took place Saturday, May 23, 1987. Those who arrived at Fran Janssen's home in response to the April newsletter's appeal included "Earlene 'Beans' Risinger, Jean Geissinger Harding, Karen Violetta Kunkel, Dottie Wiltse Collins and Sharon Roepke."[4] June Peppas was unable to attend the meeting but the group consulted with her by telephone.[5] The agenda this group dealt with between May 23 and the first week in June 1987 was varied and impressive. Besides agreeing to establish a formal organization to better coordinate matters with the Hall of Fame, they accomplished the following:

1. They selected a name for the organization: The All American Girls Professional Base-ball League Players' Association, Inc. .
2. They elected an Executive Board from among those present plus June Peppas who had initiated the newsletters and assisted with the reunions:

Chairperson	June Peppas
Vice Chairperson	Fran Janssen
Secretary	Jean Geissinger Harding
Treasurer	Dottie Collins
Parliamentarian	Earlene "Beans" Risinger
Development Officer & Archives Director	Karen Violetta Kunkel

3. They recruited a Board of Directors from various geographic areas to represent the membership:

Wilma Briggs (East)	Arleene Johnson Noga (Canada)
Faye Dancer (West)	Lillian Jackson (Chicago)
Joanne Winter (South)	

4. They set up a Board of Ex-Officio Advisors — Individuals who were not players, but who were instrumental in advancing the purposes of the association:

Sharon Roepke — Researcher, Writer, Speaker, Hall of Fame Promoter
Sue Macy — Researcher, Writer
Lynn Haber — Researcher, Writer
Dona Schaefer — Coordinator for baseball games at "Run, Jane, Run" in Fort Wayne.

5. They hired an attorney: Gary Walker (Karen Violetta Kunkel's tennis partner's hus-band.)
6. They assigned Jean Geissinger Harding, her daughters, and Joanne Winter the job of designing a permanent logo to be voted on at the September '87 meeting in Fort Wayne.
7. They enlisted Dottie Kamenshek, Marge Wenzell, Tiby Eisen, Faye Dancer, and Pep-per Paire Davis to begin composing a league history.
8. They gathered (from 1980 to 1987) a list of 500 names of ex–AAGPBL players to cre-ate a Lifetime Roster and made it a goal to discover the hometown and years of play for each player.
9. They undertook the establishment of a temporary archives at Northern Michigan Uni-versity in Marquette, Michigan, under the direction of Karen Violetta Kunkel.[6]

All of this information was published in the extra edition of the newsletter mailed June 15, 1987. Beyond itemizing the less-than-month-old state of the association, the committee, through Dottie, appealed for additional help in the areas of (1) identifying personal items to be loaned to the temporary archives at Northern Michigan University, (2) adding to the list of known managers and chaperones, and (3) contributing funds to help "get these projects off the ground." Along with each individual identifying what per-sonal mementos to loan, they were instructed to write each item down and describe it in detail, and mail the written lists to Karen Violetta Kunkel. Once Karen received the lists, they were catalogued by her grad students. This way, the AAGPBL Board knew what was available to loan to the Hall of Fame. Once specific items were designated for loan to the Hall of Fame, players who had the items were notified as to what specifically to send to the archives. In addition, ex-players were invited to attend Fort Wayne's "Run, Jane, Run" scheduled for September 16–19, 1987. They were notified that the interim board intended to meet at this time and all were invited to attend.[7]

By July 20, 1987, the association's articles of incorporation as a non-profit organization was deposited with the Michigan Department of Commerce. The same was officially filed by the State of Michigan in Lansing, Michigan, September 9, 1987. The expressed purposes for which the corporation was organized were as follows:

1. Research, collect, document, and preserve the history of the All American Girls Professional Baseball League.
2. Encourage and provide opportunities for social interaction of the membership.
3. Establish an "official" voice and disseminate historical, educational, and factual information regarding the All American Girls Baseball League.[8]

Much, if not all, of the business acumen for the swift realization of the organizational aspects of the association came from Karen Violetta Kunkel's professional background and experience. As Karen explained, "My background, education, and career had given me experiences in much of what I thought we should do at the onset to preserve the history of the league and to give its players and league personnel the recognition that was due."[9] Karen further noted that she'd had "little playing time as a rookie and left midway through her first season with appendicitis that required surgery." Nonetheless, her brief tenure with the league instilled a respect for and identification with the AAG-BBL:

> I was proud to have a contract with the league and to be with such wonderful athletes. I believed in the "one for all and all for one" motto and felt that after all those years I could give something back for a wonderful opportunity and experience. After a conversation with Dottie Collins, I suggested we consider making a Players' Assoc., invite some interested people, form a committee, and proceed. Everyone was asked to come to our first meeting with ideas. I drew up an organizational plan, some sample by-laws, and other ideas for discussion at the first meeting of our committee in early spring of 1987 at Fran Janssen's house in South Bend, Indiana.... At this meeting the first official by-laws and a procedure manual were developed. We also drew up some objectives for the Association:
>
> 1. Try to locate all of the players of the League, which included anyone who had a contract with the league regardless of how many years played. This was a difficult task which required locating records and married names, (some with more than one). Forty-four years had passed [since the league was inaugurated in 1943].
> 2. Provide another opportunity for those located to get together again.
> 3. Preserve our memorabilia and history.
> 4. To become recognized as a legitimate part of baseball history and be included in the displays at the National Baseball Hall of Fame in Cooperstown, NY.[10]

Karen reflected that Jean Harding became the association's secretary and held that position forever [through 2000], "giving us the finest set of records anyone could ask for."

> Dottie Collins worked on a news letter and [locating] players along with Fran who networked with everyone to get us going [and spent] hours of writing and rewriting suggestions for everything. Lil [Jackson] worked on a watch with our logo and networked. Beans [Earlene Risinger] networked and called volunteers for various jobs. Dottie and her committee worked on the Hall of Fame and I worked on registering marks and logos and

establishing an archive. June kept us sane and organized that first year. I think without her people, business, and organizational skills we would have failed.[11]

AAGPBL Board members recognized the value of Karen's contributions. Dottie Collins expressed the board's gratitude to Karen in the October 1987 newsletter: "For all the work, energy, and help — we want to give our sincerest thanks and deepest appreciation to Karen Kunkel. Karen, without your help and expertise, it would have been a long, unbelievable task."[12]

In the June and August 1987 newsletters, Dottie Collins continued to solicit ideas, suggestions and criticisms from the readership. Outside of the Hall of Fame and the archives, discussed in Chapter 15, the board and interested ex-players focused on some additional projects. Those that claimed their attention in 1987 and 1988 included (1) establishing a Media Center for educational information and press releases; (2) creating, registering, and protecting marks and logos; (3) licensing businesses to produce saleable items, especially jewelry to symbolize identification with the league; (4) compiling an accurate league history; (5) compiling a life-time roster of all players who signed a contract to play in the league; and (6) pursuing a commemorative stamp to be issued in the league's honor. Early on, these were recurrent topics in Board Meeting Minutes and the newsletter. A more complete discussion of these foundation projects follows.

The Media Center

By August of 1987, Karen Violetta Kunkel assumed the additional responsibility of administering the new association's "Media Center." This became a necessity when writers and reporters from the news media in general learned that the Hall of Fame would be recognizing the league. At this point, the news media began calling Dottie, who yelled "Help!" and Karen came to the rescue. Along with the archives, the Media Center was located at Northern Michigan University, where media packets were made up. When writers or researchers called anyone anywhere in the country, they were directed to the association's Media Center at Northern Michigan to obtain official information. The prepared media packets included a history of the league and other data required for story writing. In this way, the association provided consistent, professional information for inquiring minds.[13] More than that, media packets were eventually distributed to more than 850 radio, TV, and newspapers across the country. This effort also helped the board spearhead the effort to unearth and enfold "lost" All-Americans.

A committee of media representatives was established and covered all geographic areas of the country. Those selected had volunteered their services and resided in different areas of the country. This group included Ruth Williams Heverly (East), Dorothy Schroeder (Mid-West), Evelyn Wawryshyn Moroz (Canada), Jean Faut Eastman (South), Rita Meyer "Slats" Moellering (Mid-South), and Marge "Poncho" Villa Cryan (West). These six served uninterrupted terms as media reps from 1987 through 1993 when organizational down-sizing became a consideration, and the association's need for widespread news releases was more than satisfied by the advent of the movie, *A League of Their Own*. In 1990, Terry Donahue, from the Chicago area, joined the media rep ranks and served through 1993.[14]

Marks and Logos

At the First Annual Meeting of the new Players' Association in September 1987, a logo was chosen. According to the October '87 newsletter, "There were many to choose from, but all present thought [the] shield having been used by all the teams in the league should be the official logo."[15] The only difference between the Players' Association shield and the shield that decorated team uniforms from 1946 through 1954 was the substitution of a "P" standing for "Professional" in the place of one of the "Bs" in the original "Base Ball"* or AAGPBL instead of AAGBBL.[16] The newsletter had used the AAGPBL designation from the January 1981 issue forward. The "P" for "professional" left no doubt in anyone's mind that this was a "professional" baseball organization, not an amateur or semi-professional group.[17] Once selected, the board recognized the importance of trademarking its logo to protect it so others could not use it without permission. They also understood the possibilities of drawing royalties from the logo.[18] An article entitled "Logo" in the December 1988 newsletter informed association members of the following:

> This is our registered trademark, we own it, it is the only thing that belongs to us. No one can reproduce our logo, and what this means is that anyone who uses our logo without our permission can be sued. It is a marketable item for us, so anyone who wishes to use the logo only need to ask our permission to do so. We have a system for allowing our logo to be used. Any manufacturer can write to us for a form to fill out. In return they will pay a nominal fee of $25.00 for a licensing fee. This is standard practice with any marketable item, but what it means to us, we can control the use of it and get a percentage of the profits. We can get a guarantee uniformity of its use, as it will never change, it must be used as it is. If you have any questions on using the Logo in any form please contact the board before doing so.[19]

Unfortunately, in future years it became necessary for the board to demand "cease and desist" orders for misuse of the marks and logos by some former players. In response to membership abuse of the association's marks and logos, the December 1992 newsletter devoted three quarters of a page to showing and discussing the association's current marks and logos. These included the association name: "All American Girls Professional Baseball League"; the letters "AAGPBL"; the team logo as worn on team uniforms; the uniform itself, including anything depicting a skirt as a baseball uniform; and the league logos ("AAGSBL, AAGPBL, AAGBBL, and AGBL"). The membership was also advised that "Any merchandise ordered by you bearing our marks or logo, must have board approval. Merchandise sold in stores or at our reunions must have prior board approval.... Any abuse of the marks and logos will be dealt with by the Association's Attorney."[20]

Player misuse of the association's marks and logos cropped up again later in the 1990s. Not that it was a huge problem, but one that required constant vigilance since failure by the organization to police the use of its marks and logos could result in their loss.[21] Misuse of the marks and logos also indicated that the board occasionally had unpleasant matters to deal with. All was not always smooth sailing, nor could one expect 250 individuals, plus or minus, to see eye to eye on everything all the time.

Charms, Rings, and Watches

One area where board-approved league marks and logo licenses were readily dispensed was with jewelry manufacturers. In the spring of 1982, long before the Players' Association was formed, league members began creating jewelry to symbolize their special experience. The first to be mentioned in the newsletter was a charm commemorat-

---

*Throughout the remaining chapters, AAGBBL is used to refer to the league as it existed from 1943 until 1954. AAGPBL is used to refer to the Players' Association.

ing the first national reunion in 1982. It was designed by Dorothy Kamenshek, Marge Wenzell, and Shirley Stovroff. The charm was designed to be worn as either a bracelet or a necklace. It was one inch in diameter and made of gold-plated bronze. Its design included the AAGBBL logo and 40th year, 1982.[22]

In the fall of 1987, when plans for Cooperstown were well under way, Jaynne Bittner, working with the AAGPBL Board and Balfour Company, created an AAGPBL players' ring. It was something the players had been requesting for years. In June of 1988, Arleene Johnson Noga wrote Jean Geissinger Harding that she had received her ring and thought it was "just beautiful" and that she "had many favorable comments on it."[23]

A watch with the AAGPBL logo on its face was another jewelry item that became very popular for players and associates alike. Watches were licensed as early as 1992 and continued to be popular saleable items through 1998 and beyond.[24]

Another one-inch diameter pendant was licensed in October 1998. It included an AAGPBL skirted batter with "All American Girls Professional Baseball League, 1943–1954" inscribed around its perimeter.[25]

League History

Along with several other projects, the compilation of an official, documented history of the league was viewed as a vital need by the league board in 1987. Among other things, it was essential to have accurate information for the Media Center. Committees were set up for different years the league existed. Joanne Winter headed the committee dealing with the years 1943–1946. Her completed section of the project acknowledged content contributions from first league president Ken Sells, Merrie Fidler, Marge Pieper, and league members Dorothy Kamenshek, Dottie Collins, June Peppas and Sophie Kurys. A copy of this document is retained at the Baseball Hall of Fame. Ex-chaperone Dottie Green chaired the committee for 1947–1950 and ex–Grand Rapids catcher Marilyn Jenkins took over for the years 1951–1954. In 1990, the last year the committee was active, June Peppas substituted for Marilyn Jenkins, and June Emerson stepped in when Dottie Green passed away. June Emerson also assumed the task of integrating the three sections of the history project, but she passed away suddenly before completing it. It is not known if the integrated history of the league undertaken by the players was ever completed.[26]

Lifetime Roster

The lifetime roster project actually began back in October of 1980 when June Peppas decided to find as many of her ex–league mates as possible. With impending recognition by the Hall of Fame in 1987, finding ex-players took on immediacy. One of the association's goals was to have a lifetime roster completed and in the display at Cooperstown. The roster was designed to include not only each player's maiden name, but her hometown, and the years she played in the AAGBBL. Information was solicited from the players in the October 1987 newsletter. Dottie Collins emphasized, "It would be a shame to send your name into Cooperstown with either no information by it or the wrong information."[27] At this point a committee was formed to help find the "lost" All-Americans and to solicit maiden name, home town, and years spent in the league for those whose information was not known. The "Lost All-American" committee members for 1987–88 included Dottie Collins, Nancy "Hank" Warren, June Emerson, Dottie Schroeder, Fran Janssen, and Maxine Kline. Others who would serve on this committee in future years were Ellen Tronnier, Marjorie Peters, Sheri Kadlec, Betty Moczynski, and Therese McKinley Uselmann.[28]

Dottie Collins notified the board at the September '87 meeting that the lifetime roster project aimed to locate all ex-players. At that time, 244 were known and 37 of those were deceased. The task ahead involved finding 257 members. By September 1988, the list of known members had grown to 329. In November 1995, the board's search for lost All Americans improved when Dr. Leslie Heaphy from the Society for American Baseball Research (SABR) "offered the resources of SABR to help locate 'Lost' All Americans. They provided the same service for the Negro League in helping to find former players."[29] At this time there were still 138 individuals unaccounted for. A little less than two years later, Board Meeting Minutes recorded that the lifetime roster project could be laid to rest with the announcement that "This project is finally completed after years of review of records and stat sheets." Copies were printed and given to each player, the Northern Indiana Center for History, and Cooperstown.[30]

Commemorative Stamp

One project the AAGPBL attempted to accomplish before the Cooperstown unveiling was the issuing of a commemorative stamp. The board began work on this project in September of 1987. They quickly learned that this was an uphill battle. The postal service Philatelic and Postal Services Department notified them that ideas for stamps did come from everyday postal customers like themselves. They were also informed, however, that more than 2,000 letters suggesting stamp issues arrived every month. While they were assured their letter would be placed in the committee's file for review, they weren't given any encouragement for a stamp being issued in their honor. Fran Janssen submitted a letter to the newsletter in December 1988 encouraging members to write to the Citizen's Stamp Advisory Committee and include recent AAGPBL clippings from local newspapers, *Sports Illustrated*, and *USA Today* regarding the Hall of Fame display.[31]

Renewed attempts to acquire a commemorative stamp occurred in 1989,1990, 1995, 1997, 1998, and 2002. All with no result to date. The 2002 effort holds the most promise of realization at this writing. It was begun with a letter writing effort by Jon Richards, son of Lou Stone Richards, former Belle and Blue Sox player. Jon sent a copy of his appeal to the postal service to President George W. Bush's White House Chief of Staff, Andy Card. Card's response led Jon to state that Mr. Card was "rendering some valuable assistance towards this worthy goal."[32] The January 2004 newsletter reported that "both Richards and Card ... are working hard to make the stamp a reality." Why would Andy Card, President Bush's Chief of Staff, take an interest in a stamp to commemorate the AAGPBL? His Little League coach was— Lou Stone Richards![33] We may see a "Women in Baseball" stamp series yet.

The formal organization of the Players' Association met with some resistance among the ranks of ex-players. There were those who felt occasional reunions were sufficient and did not necessitate the creation of a formal organization.[34] Again, the attainment of a unanimous agreement on such a project among 200+ individuals cannot be considered realistic. However, as can be seen from examining the names of players who helped on project committees in the foregoing paragraphs, an impressive number of All-Americans joined "the team" to help the Players' Association take flight and soar. See Appendix 1 for a listing of AAGPBL committee members from 1987 to 2004.

Lou Stone Richards with President George W. Bush and Andy Card, September 7, 2003 (White House photograph by Tina Hager, courtesy the White House).

The Documentaries

It may not seem logical, but the breadth of articles mandates that a discussion of the documentaries that preceded and prompted the major motion picture *A League of Their Own* must begin with the AAGPBL Newsletter undertaken by June Peppas in October 1980. It was through the newsletter that players began to reconnect. It was here that players were exposed to newspaper articles, museum displays, and every kind of publicity imaginable about themselves. It was here they learned that their colleagues were accorded various honors. It was from this source that they absorbed an idea of their worthiness and their newsworthiness.

In the March 1981 issue, for instance, half of an 8½ × 11-inch page was devoted to a picture of a Grand Rapids Museum exhibit for the Chicks. A June 1979 *Post-Dispatch* (city unidentified) newspaper article about "Girls of Summer" covered the inside foldout of the June 1981 newsletter. The July '81 newsletter included three 3 × 5-inch pictures of "Alva Jo Fischer Memorial Softball Complex" located in "Lady Bird Johnson Community Park" in San Antonio, Texas. The same issue was adorned with a newspaper article from the *Knoxville News-Sentinel*, July 5, 1981, entitled "Mrs. Ump." It featured Cartha Doyle Childress who played for the Rockford Peaches in 1947. Millie Deegan sent in a copy of a 1974 Western Electric Company article picturing her giving batting instructions and describing why she was inducted into New Jersey's Softball Hall of Fame. It was reprinted in the October 1981 newsletter. The back page of the December '81 issue featured Dottie Kamenshek's election to *Who's Who* in Orange County, California. The list goes on. Unfortunately, the newsletter didn't always identify the source of the news articles it reprinted, but here's a further listing from newsletters published between 1982 and 1992. The dates given are dates the articles were reprinted in the AAGPBL Newsletter.

Title of Article & Player(s) Featured	*Location*	*Newsletter Date*
"A's Crash Dolly's 49th" (Dolly Pearson Tesseine)	Mt. Pleasant, MI	Feb. 1982
"Chicks Baseball to Revive Memories"	Grand Rapids, MI	Mar. 1982
"Reunion spurs memories of Rockford Peaches"	Rockford, IL	Mar. 1982
"Alice McNaughton feels at home on the diamond"	Fairfield, CA	May 1982
"Girls' pro baseball league made impact"	Kalamazoo, MI	May 1982
"Ft. Wayne Daisies 2nd Mini-Reunion"	Ft. Wayne, IN	Nov. 1982
"Katie Horstman Chosen Citizen of the Year"	Minster, OH	Feb. 1983
"Memories of Redwings"	Unidentified	Feb. 1983
"Manitoba's girls of summer"	Winnipeg, Manit., Can.	June 1983
"Her Best Friends Were Diamonds" (Pepper Paire Davis)	Los Angeles	June 1983
"This Ump's A Lady" (Dolly Konwinski)	Unidentified	Jan. 1984
"Mt. Everest" (Karen Violetta Kunkel)	Kalamazoo, MI	Jan. 1984
"Olive Little inducted in Softball Hall of Fame"	Portage la Prairie, Can.	Feb. 1984
"Diamonds & Lace"	Los Angeles, CA	Feb. 1984
"Olive's Success traced to father" (Olive Little)	Winnipeg, Can.	Feb. 1984
" 'Maddy' English honored at gala retirement party"	Everett, MA	July 1984
"Thelma Eisen was a pioneer ballplayer"	West Los Angeles	Mar. 1985
No title — Mary Baker inducted to Sask. BB Hall of Fame	Saskatchewan, Can.	Aug. 1985
"Golf teacher for 22 years..." (Joanne Winter)	Phoenix, AR	April 1986
"It's a special delivery..." (Helen Hannah Campbell)	Orange County, CA	April 1986
"Girls ballclub reunites"	USA Today	Oct. 1986
"Katie Horstman Inducted into Hall of Fame"	Minster, OH	Dec. 1986
"Alice DeCambra to enter baseball Hall of Fame"	Somerset, MA	Dec. 1987
"Diamonds were the best friend of many..."	Arizona	Dec. 1987
"Baseball Belles can still put a sparkle on those diamonds"	Unidentified	April 1988
"Women on the Diamond"	South Bend, IN	April 1988
"Lucella Ross to Journey to Cooperstown"	Lloydminster, (?)	April 1988
"She played hardball for Ft. Wayne Daisies" (Kay Blumetta)	North Plainfield, NJ	April 1988
"Baseball Hall of Fame to honor Brooklynite" (V. Kellogg)	Brooklyn, MI	Aug. 1988
"Miz Mo Hits the Big Time" (Betty "Mo" Trezza)	Brooklyn, NY	Aug. 1988
"Girls on the Diamond" (Betty Cornett & Wanita Dokish)	Unidentified	Oct. 1988
"Jean Smith One of the 'Girls of Summer'"	Harbor Springs, MI	Oct. 1988
"Pratt Goes to Bat" (Mary Pratt)	Quincy, MA	Oct. 1988
"The Lady is a Champ" (Betty Trezza)	Brooklyn, NY	Oct. 1988
"Baseball Hall to induct Noga" (Arleene Noga)	Regina, Sask., Can.	Dec. 1988
"They were the girls of summer" (Jean Havlish, Nancy Cato)	Minneapolis, MN	Dec. 1988
"Women Won't Strike Out in SB HOF" (Evelyn Adams)	Unidentified	Dec. 1989
"Stevenson among inductees" (Rosemary Stevenson)	Marquette, MI	Dec. 1989
"Alumni Assn. Honors Hancock Hall-of-Famer" (A. Lafser)	Unidentified	April 1990
"This Dolly played pro shortstop" (Dolly Pearson Tesseine)	Michigan	Aug. 1990
"Former Baseball Standouts..." (Margaret Russo Jones)	Dolgeville, NY	Aug. 1990
" 'Curly Top'— The Girl Who Waved" (Violet Schmidt)	Indiana	Aug. 1990
"U.P. Sports Hall banquet Saturday" (Rosemary Stevenson)	Marquette, MI	Aug. 1990
"Local Baseball Greats Named..."(Mildred Deegan)	New Jersey	Aug. 1990
"Baseball dreams came true for Mary Baker"	Regina, Sask., Can.	Aug. 1990
"Former Blue Sox Honored Tonight"	South Bend, Ind.	Dec. 1990
"Winthrop's Pat Brown tosses out first ball at Red Sox game"	Boston, MA	Dec. 1990
"Veteran leaguers play ball ... at movie tryouts"	Skokie, IL	Aug. 1991
"Dorothy Hunter"	Grand Rapids, MI	Aug. 1991
"Young aces CWGA" (Barbara Parks Young)	Clinton, CT	Dec. 1991

The point of this list is that these are just the newspaper articles reprinted in the newsletters between 1982 and the end of 1991. How many more were published in how many other cities in the U.S. and Canada may never be known. In addition, a list of magazine articles would be just as impressive. How many people read these articles throughout North America? How many movie goers were already primed by the printed word to see the All-Americans on the big screen by 1992?

It is this author's contention that each newspaper or magazine article served as a current of heat that built the thermal pattern for a thundercloud that was to become *A League of Their Own*. Each new article seen by the All-Americans or those close to them generated more and more articles until they all formed an ephemeral swirl over the nation that finally captured the attention of filmmakers in Southern California and Michigan. The breakthrough occurred in 1986 at the Second AAGBBL National Reunion in Fort Wayne, Indiana.

In a December 1985 Christmas brochure — almost a year before the Second National Reunion — Dottie Collins announced that Kelly Candaele and Kim Wilson in Los Angeles were in the process of filming a documentary of the league. This was followed in the January/February 1986 issue of the newsletter by the announcement that Dr. Janis Taylor of Northwestern University was also planning a documentary of the league. Newsletter readers were informed that Candaele/Wilson and Taylor planned to do some of their filming at the 1986 national reunion in Fort Wayne.

Jan Taylor explained that the impetus for her documentary came from the fact that she had just earned a doctorate in film and broadcasting from Northwestern University. Added to this was the fact that she'd been a former student and one time softball teammate of Katie Horstman, an ex–Fort Wayne Daisy.[35] When she heard from Katie about the 1986 reunion, filming a documentary was a natural step for her to take. Her efforts culminated in "When Diamonds Were a Girl's Best Friend."

Dottie Collins, Lil Jackson, Irene Kotowicz, Phyllis Koehn, Philomena Francisco Zale, her husband Tony, Lou Arnold, and Wimp Baumgartner were invited to attend the premiere of "When Diamonds Were a Girl's Best Friend" at Northwestern University at the end of May 1987. Dottie Collins wrote in the June 1987 newsletter:

> There were two showings with a reception and buffet after the presentation. Everyone there was interested, gracious, and curious about the All American Girls Professional Baseball League, asking us millions of questions and we even signed autographs and baseballs.
>
> ... The Producer and Director, Janis Taylor, caught the emotions and feelings of all the players as they reminisced about the past.
>
> The Documentary was humorous and heart warming.... [36]

Janis Taylor's film contained historical scenes of the All-Americans obtained from the National Archives, as well as home movies. It also contained interviews with players and chaperones as well as scenes from an Old-Timer's Game in Fort Wayne, Indiana.[37] The film placed first in the documentary category in the Chicago CAN Illinois Community Television Competition and Festival. It also won an award in the Oswego Herland Film and Video Festival in Oswego at the Oswego Art Guild in New York.[38] Those who viewed it became part of the thermal build-up for bigger things to come.

Kelly Candaele, a son of former All-American Helen Candaele Staubins, was dating Kim Wilson in Los Angeles, California. She just happened to work for ABC *Movies of the Week* in that city and contributed knowledge of the movie industry. Kelly recounted that he had studied history in college and knew there were "many aspects of women's history that were hidden — repressed or never remembered."[39] He also noted that he had been "a fan of the documentary format from [his] college years — mostly political and cultural films."[40] As Kelly and Kim interacted, and Kim saw pictures of Kelly's mother as an All-American player, one conversation led to another and they decided to undertake a film project dealing with the AAGBBL. Kelly's goal "was to share a part of my Mom's life that I had heard about growing up and to honor her experience and achievements."[41] He noted:

> ... we got involved into looking closer at the documentary world — how funding was done — what were people shooting on — and [realized] that people who really wanted to make a film could do so much easier by starting with documentaries rather than banging [their] head against the wall with Hollywood feature film producers.[42]

Kelly's account of how the documentary of *A League of Their Own* materialized is intriguing. Once he and Kim decided to do a documentary, they knew they had to find some footage of the league. They knew this would anchor the film and make it interesting to distributors. The rest reads like a story book.

> We found a lot of the footage at the National Archives in D.C. and other stuff from the women themselves. I had lunch with a local LA reporter about another issue and mentioned the baseball league. She said she wanted to do a three part segment for nightly news on the women and the league which [she did].
>
> We took that series and used it as a trailer. We ended up at the local PBS station KCET and met with a producer there. He told us he took the trailer home and showed it to his daughter and she loved it.
>
> The station agreed to pay for a director and allow us to fly to Ft. Wayne to film a reunion and also to allow us full use of their editing facilities. When we finished the film it was sold to National PBS for a nation wide airing. It received a great deal of publicity and myself and my mom were on the *Today Show* the morning that it aired.
>
> Penny Marshall's assistant saw the film and showed it to her. She called myself and Kim to her house to meet one evening shortly after that and things went from there.[43]

Of course, there were numerous hurdles along the way: negotiating contracts, dealing with attorneys, obtaining rights—"it's what can drive most film makers crazy."[44] The documentary of *A League of Their Own* aired nationwide September 30, 1987, and the thunderstorm began fulminating.

A League of Their Own

After the documentaries aired, producers came knocking on the AAGPBL Players' Association's door. An offer from the Orion Film Company was recorded in the April 1988 Board Meeting Minutes. An independent film company, Sundance Producers, met with the board on May 7, 1988, at president Peppas' residence in Allegan, Michigan. A follow-up meeting was held with this group on May 28. In September of 1988, Karen Violetta Kunkel reported receiving "a few contacts by film companies." Between September and November 1988, the board decided to sign a contract with Longbow Productions of California.[45]

According to Ted Spencer, Penny Marshall, a rabid baseball fan, saw the Hall of Fame's news release about the "Women in Baseball" display and decided to attend. She spent the whole weekend "hiding in plain sight" behind sunglasses and a pulled-down

Annabelle Lee Harmon with Penny Marshall (courtesy Annabelle Lee Harmon and Penny Marshall).

baseball cap. Spencer related that she seemed most comfortable attending different events with the players, and that she left with the idea that she wanted to do a movie about this group.[46] Penny described it this way:

> ... One day I saw a documentary [*A League of Their Own*] on the All-American Girls Baseball League of the 1940s. It was about a group of courageous women who were recruited to play baseball when the young men who played ball had gone off to fight World War II.
>
> I chose to direct *A League of Their Own* because I thought it was a story that needed to be told, and told with accuracy, inspiration and humor....[47]

A newspaper article was reprinted in the August 1989 newsletter entitled "Yours Truly" by Tim Kiska. The newspaper, city, and date, were not identified, but presumably it came from a Hollywood publication. It announced:

> **Works in progress**: Longbow Productions, the brainchild of former Detroit TV producer Bill Pace..., personality Ronnie Clemmer and Detroit businessman Richard Kughn appears finally to have caught the Hollywood brass ring.
>
> The company now has a deal to do a feature-length movie with 20th Century Fox. "It's about a women's baseball team," says Pace.... **Lowell Ganz** and **Babaloo Mandell** ... will work the typewriter while **Penny Marshall** ... will direct. No title yet, though working titles are *The Girls of Summer* and *In a League of Their Own*.[48]

By the September 21, 1989, board meeting, Karen Violetta Kunkel notified those in attendance that there was a first draft of the movie and "in the opinion of those who read it, it will do honor to the league."[49] At this meeting, Karen Violetta Kunkel, now AAGPBL–PA Executive Director, was appointed the Players' Association's Public Relations Director for all matters relating to the movie. According to Marie "Blackie" Wegman, Karen served the board with distinction as liaison with the producers. On the set one day, Marie observed:

> They worked until seven thirty [P.M.] and Karen had been there since five thirty in the morning. She puts in long days. I can appreciate how rough the job had to be at times for Karen. She had the task of trying to convince Penny Marshall that maybe she knew a little bit more about what the league was all about.[50]

During the Players' Association's general membership meeting, September 23, 1989, Mr. Ron Clemmer from Longbow Productions and Mr. Elliott Abbot from Penny Marshall Productions were introduced. They indicated that 20th Century–Fox would be doing the filming. They cautioned the membership to refrain from publicizing the film until the release date was near. Clemmer and Elliott further explained that selecting filming locations, hiring actors, actresses, doubles, and preparing costumes would take considerable time. They also indicated that it was their hope to have the movie premiere in the Midwest. Harriett Miller from the Fort Wayne Women's Bureau addressed the group and responded that she would "vie for the film's premiere in Fort Wayne."[51]

Ultimately, four primary locations were selected for filming: Huntingburg, Indiana, became the home of the Rockford Peaches; Evansville, Indiana, doubled as the home of the Racine Belles; Chicago's Wrigley Field was used for the tryout scenes; and only Cooperstown would do for the Baseball Hall of Fame scenes.[52] Auditions were held in Los Angeles and New York, and some AAGPBL members were invited to observe. In the L.A. area, Pepper Paire Davis related that she expected to see "baseball players trying out for acting parts." Instead, she observed "actresses trying out for baseball parts."[53] Karen Violetta Kunkel affirmed, however, that the baseball auditions were bona fide undertakings. Penny, herself, confirmed that "All of the actresses I cast had to pass a baseball fielding and hitting test before they were hired — even Madonna."[54] Not that they were expected to be professionals, but that they could demonstrate basic baseball skills.[55]

Karen also noted that USC Assistant Baseball Coach Bill Hughes traveled to all of the filming sites and had a skills rating chart, which Karen and coaches from each local area were required to use to rate each prospective cast member's baseball ability. Karen noted that once the cast was selected, they met at a Holiday Inn in Skokie, Illinois, with AAGPBL ex-players from the surrounding area. She was in charge of inviting the ex-players to play catch and mingle with the cast for a day. This enabled the cast to "get a feel for" the players they would be depicting in the film.[56]

West Coast tryouts were held at the University of Southern California, where head coach Rod Dedeaux and his staff "put the gals through their paces—warm-up drills—calisthenics—laps around the field — ground balls—hitting practice — all that great spring training stuff—remember gals?" Pepper noted that she "would have liked to own the 'Sloan's Linament' concession the next day!"[57]

Later on, Penny Marshall invited the L.A. "girls," Pepper, Tiby Eisen, Faye Dancer, Alice "Lefty" Hohlmayer, Inez Voyce, Anita Foss, Kammie Kamenshek, Marge Wenzell, and loyal league-ite Peggy Mack to her home to interact with the ladies in the cast. Peggy Mack wrote to the newsletter that the "evening was so very much fun."

> The evening was fun — with the chatting and the League members giving the cast girls a
> bit of Know-how — of how to throw, how to slide and just a lot of "how to's. We ended
> the evening sitting around a big coffee table and singing the [league] song....[58]

Filming of *A League of Their Own* endured some problematic incidents. Some were
not uncommon for Hollywood. Others were unique to the nature of the film's subject.
Of the more common variety, there were constant script changes, changes in location,
changes in the lead actress — Geena Davis for Debra Winger, and even changes in the
filming company — Columbia Pictures for 20th Century–Fox.[59] From July to October
1990, filming was on hold, but by October things were looking up. By this time, however, filming had to wait for the return of summer weather.

Once filming began, the not-so-common problems faced by the production crew
included the use of period gloves and shoes and an uncommonly hot summer. Most cast
members had difficulty catching the ball with the period gloves, so tennis balls and nerf
balls were disguised as baseballs. Each baseball cover sewn over a tennis or nerf ball
required an hour and a half's work. The shoes were inexpensive period look-a-likes with
period-correct spikes. The spikes frequently caused the cheap soles to break in the middle which necessitated the continual purchase of more shoes. The hottest Midwest summer on record for a hundred years was another unexpected problem. Temperatures of
105–110 degrees every day caused frequent delays for wardrobe changes and hairdo and
make-up redos so sweaty brows and sweaty clothes wouldn't appear on the screen.[60]

By the fall of 1990, the self-appointed interim Executive Board of the Players' Association had fulfilled its role of establishing the organization. It had provided a framework
for the organization to build on, established an archives to preserve league memorabilia
and history, gained recognition by the Baseball Hall of Fame, promoted and publicized
the league, and arranged for additional reunions to offer continued social opportunities
for its members. The movie project, contracted in the fall of 1988, was well under way,
and it was time for a member-elected board to assume further responsibilities. The new
Executive Board elected by association members in the fall of 1990 included Joan Holderness, president; Barbara Liebrich, vice president; Mary "Wimp" Baumgartner, assistant vice president; Jean Geissinger Harding, secretary; Dottie Wiltse Collins, treasurer;
and Wilma Briggs, sgt. at arms.[61] Karen Violetta Kunkel was retained as executive director and continued as the association's liaison with the movie production crew.

During July of '91, the AAGPBL Board was advised that casting and training were
progressing well and filming would begin soon in Chicago.[62] The cast and crew worked
long and diligently between July and November and completed filming at Cooperstown
on October 31, 1991.

Marie "Blackie" Wegman attended filming at Evansville with her brother Bill and
her sister-in-law Carol. Her reconstruction of the experience for the newsletter was priceless:

> When we hit Evansville I started to get excited. When we found the ball field we
> couldn't believe our eyes. People were lined up at least five or six across in a line that
> wound all around the paths in the park almost to the street. We found out later that
> between nine and ten thousand people had shown up to sit in the grandstands. We were
> fortunate to find a parking place off behind the park and we walked to the first barricade.
> I told the attendant I was an old ball player and I would like to see KAREN KUNKEL. She
> took us to the next barricade and my words were repeated. Then they took us across the
> lot to the gate and the grandstand. The security fellow heard the story and he took us to

the ramp to another fellow and he told us to go into the grandstand. All this time we were walking past all these people. I didn't even look at them, I was afraid of what they were thinking. I turned a corner in the grandstand and the first person I saw was BETSY JOCHUM. Down the row was LOU ARNOLD AND HER GODCHILD, CAROL, & PEE WEE (Wiley) SEARS & LEX MCCUTCHAN. I was truly dumb founded. Lou luckily had a seat next to her for me and Bill and Carol found a seat behind us. We sat through a lot of shooting and we had to take off our glasses and watches, but I think we had such a great time that it's immaterial whether we made the movie or not. It is impossible to imagine the food that was given out — Peanut Butter and Jelly sandwiches, hot dogs, hamburgers, egg salad or chicken salad, cases of apples, bananas, an assortment of candy, and when we were sitting along the left field fence one of the crew brought us ice cream. I could not get enough of the "Outfits" the people were wearing, soldiers, sailors, marines, waacs, waves, all the women in dresses and hats of all shapes and sizes and men in suits and hats. It was near 80 degrees and Lou said the women had to wear panty hose and I was happy to be sitting there.

Then Karen Kunkel came and got us and took us to the tent where the cast ate their meals. It was her lunch break because she spends every minute out on the field where they are shooting. There was a buffet table waiting for us, spaghetti dinner, salad, fruit, dessert.

When I caught my first glimpse of a [AAGBBL] uniform I could feel my pulse beating faster. They look so authentic. When they were shooting the scene at home plate and celebrating the victory, I could feel the chills and goose bumps.... After eating we went back to the ball field and there were a few benches along the field fence. We were permitted to sit there and watch some more of the filming. The whole infield was filled with boom cameras, lights, lenses, etc. & production people. They really go over every play to try to make it perfect. They worked a long time at second base and home plate. Then Karen took us out on the infield amid all the equipment to watch the play at home plate. Unbelievable. Penny was sitting there in her chair and all the stars of the film were in the vicinity. I watched one play on the two screens that Penny watches instead of the live action. The screens show what will be seen in the movie. Geena Davis is the catcher but her stunt double went through the scene over and over until they checked everything. Then Geena came out and on the second try they had what they wanted. The players were just as Dusty and Dirty as we used to get. They certainly weren't afraid of old Mother Earth.

I was interested in the kind of baseballs they were using. They were a little smaller than the one we used and were of varying hardnesses. I felt three of them — one like a hardball — another was a baseball covered tennis ball — and the third was like a nerf ball. A technician told us it took an hour and a half to sew the seams by hand.

Then Karen introduced us to the cast — Geena Davis, Lori Petty — Tom Hanks and Madonna actually stopped and talked to us. They said that was rare because of the problems people could cause her. Rosie O'Donnell played third base and had a bandage around her knee. I asked her if it was a baseball

Marie "Blackie" Wegman as a player (courtesy Northern Indiana Center for History).

injury, but she said it was a prop. She asked if I saw the error she made at third and I said "No, but I saw the neat pick-up you made on the bad throw from the outfield." She just laughed. She is funny. She led the crowd in singing between shootings. We were going to meet Penny Marshall, but she was called away to handle some business.[63]

There was much promotion of the movie before it was released and the players contributed their time and efforts toward this end. Gloria Cordes Elliott, Betty "Mo" Trezza, and Dottie Collins were interviewed on *Good Morning America*; Audrey Kissel Lafser and Erma Bergmann were interviewed on radio and T.V.; and Marie Wegman and Pat Scott had newspaper, radio, and T.V. interviews.[64] These were just the few who wrote into the newsletter to apprise AAGPBL readers of their efforts.

In Florida, Columbia Pictures requested Karen Kunkel to organize ex-players from that state and those nearby to attend Major League Baseball Spring Training Camps where they could be easily interviewed by newspaper, radio, and television personnel covering the men's teams. The "Grapefruit League" became a publicity stage for *A League of Their Own* as ex–AAGBBL players turned out at every Florida spring training site to promote "their" movie.[65]

Premieres of the movie were scheduled in the South, East, Midwest, Southwest and West for the last week of June. Columbia wrote to the Players' Association requesting player appearances for autograph sessions to promote the movie. Some premieres were employed as fund raisers. Whether it was for fund raisers or just to promote the movie, the players joined forces as they had so many times on the field in years past. The tentacles of teamwork stretched from shore to shore.

> **Dottie Collins**: Lompoc, California, where Helen (Callaghan) Staubin lives raised money for their softball leagues and Helen was in attendance there. The girls in the LA area attended one at Columbia Studio, with a party afterwards. New York gals were able to attend one and we hear that Dottie Green was in attendance there. Fort Wayne held a fund raiser for the All Americans and Fort Wayne Women's Bureau. About 150 former players, family and friends attended along with local Fort Wayne people. From all reports, everything has been a success and everyone is having lots of fun.

> **Earlene "Beans" Risinger** (Grand Rapids, Mich.): Well, Grand Rapids finally woke up to the *League of Their Own* and they, (media) had us running. On Wed., July 1, off we went at 7:30 A.M. to a radio talk show on WOOD — then 8:30 WLAV, then at 10:30 out to golf course to throw balls around and an interview to have on 11:00 news. Then had to be at the movie theater at 6:00 to greet and sign the small poster for fans, etc. Surprising how many old fans showed up, new ones also, many of our friends. It was wild. The publicity person for the New Star Theater was on the ball. Renae Youngberg came in, as did Doris Cook and June Peppas, even though they were Lassies. Also the WOOD TV did a line thing on 6:00 news. Another TV, 13, interviewed us and had it on 11:00 news.

> **Gene Travis Visich** (New York): What a wonderful time (again) for the AAGPBL! Apparently, everyone loved the movie and now we will be known world-wide. The phone and the mail hasn't stopped for over a month, and it has been great fun to be a part of all the hoopla. I saw Dottie Collins and Moe Trezza on TV and I can't believe that Sports channel came to my house to film me and some of my memorabilia and incorporated it into a really great segment about the league. Friends and relatives from all over have sent me articles about other gals, so I have much to put together into a huge scrapbook! I and my 84-year-old Mother and my Daughter Andrea, attended the premiere at the Ziegfeld Theater in NY and then went to the Tavern On the Green for the reception afterward. What an exciting evening. Got to see Penny Marshall, Madonna, Tom Hanks and the thrill of the nite was being introduced to and having my picture taken with Rosie O'Donnell. At

the premiere in NY I was asked for my autograph by a number of people and it brought back memories of kids outside of the Rockford stadium so many years ago. The movie incorporated a little of everything, humor, pathos, action and was sweet and sassy with a little bit of Hollywood thrown in! I can't wait for South Bend next year. Seeing the girls again is so touching. It is a special feeling we have for each other and I do believe we are truly an All American Classic.[66]

When screenings opened to the general public on July 4, 1992, the thunderstorm turned into a lightning show that spotlighted All-Americans throughout the country. They performed exceedingly well.

Charlene "Shorty" Pryer Mayer (Portland): This has been some 3 weeks—starting with an interview, then on a local TV sports news, then our local Minor League Class A (Oakland A's Farm Team) had me throw out the first ball, then the Portland paper, then a Portland TV station sent a reporter and photographer down, we spent 3 hours together, the last 2 hours out on a ball diamond playing catch and my hitting his over-hand pitches. My arm was sooooooo sore from playing catch, almost renewed my tennis game—HA. Then I got a phone call from a lady in another town, who's mother kept two Rockford Peaches at her home when this lady was a teenager, and another lady who was visiting her daughter up here from Calif., was recruited and given a contract to try out, but the league fired the scout and didn't honor the contract. Lots of acquaintances and friends and working buddies called, it got to where Jack would say "you get the phone, it's probably Hollywood." You see, it's not like I was in a town that ever heard of this league or Shorty Pryer, and the whole thing was a big surprise to everyone. They even had me stand up in church and take a bow!

Betty "Mo" Trezza (Brooklyn): The movie certainly gave our league exposure and all us gals. I can't believe how popular we have become. I've been on TV shows, talked on the radio and in three local papers. This all happened in the last month.

Ann Meyer Petrovic (Tucson): Things are happening in Tucson. Betty Tucker, Lil Jackson and myself have been on radio and TV. We really enjoyed that. We always go the three of us together. I'm enjoying it while I can. The movie was great.

Rossey Weeks (Jacksonville, Fla.): Seems Penny Marshall has made the women of the league immortal. Since the movie there has been a flurry of attention in Jacksonville about my playing in the league. Besides TV I've been asked to be on radio.... I'm taking ... five plus some more kids in the neighborhood to see "A League of Their Own." You may never hear from me again. Months from now the movie house will find me under popcorn, candy wrappers and drink cups.

Helen Waddell Wyatt: We have been having a ball over this film. We have had interviews on TV, Radio, Newspapers and magazines, people calling us from all over the country. We had the premiere then a party after. Really whooping it up here. We were even in a parade.

Lucella MacLean (Canada): They have really kept me busy for the past two weeks. I had phone calls from Toronto, Ontario, North Battleford, Sask., Calgary and Edmonton, Alberta and Vancouver. On July 3rd, CFRN TV out of Edmonton sent a couple of people here to our home to do some filming. I was at the Premiere in North Battleford on July 2nd, as well as the one here on June 29th.

Pat Scott (Kentucky & Ohio): Well we had a great time over the movie here in Kentucky and Ohio. Marie Wegman and myself were joined by three other all Americans, Anna May Hutchison, Joyce (Hill) Westerman and Audrey (Haine) Daniels. We were all on TV a number of times. Marie and I were on a radio talk show. We were at the premiere of the movie in Cincinnati July 1st. A pretty good movie.

Rosemary Stevenson (Grand Rapids, Mich.): Well — what did you think of the movie? I thought they did a good job on it! Eight of us were at the New Star Theatre in Grand Rapids to sign autographs on July 1st. They also did a coverage on Channel 8 & 13, then on July 2nd, Earlene Risinger, Dolly (Niemiec) Konwinski, Marilyn Jenkins and myself were on WCUZ radio station. Now the Muskegon Cinema 12 Theatre wants to give us a night on August 1st at 6 P.M. to sign autographs.

Lou Calacito: Boy what a merry go round I have been on since the Movie — *League of Their Own* has been out. I was interviewed by KUSA Channel 9 and was on the 5 & 10:30 sports programs to talk about the league. They also sent me a tape of it.

Gloria "Tippy" Schweigerdt (Chicago): So many wonderful events have happened in the last three weeks for us ladies from Chicago. Last week we were guests at Sox Park and treated like royalty. Last Saturday on Fox 32 they showed the events from the ball park plus interviews from the field and from my home. The night before Sox Park, Burt Constable, who writes for the *Daily Herald*, took me to the premiere of the Movie. Terry Donahue and myself are scheduled Wed., July 8th to be on *Good Morning America*.

Katie Horstman (Ohio): I've been answering the phone every morning since the movie commenced. Lima, Dayton, St. Marys, Sidney, Celina, Minster, Radio, TV, and Hard Copy have been calling me.

Mava Thomas: I have been having a great time with so many telephone calls, individuals sending me copies of the papers with nice notes attached and talking to me in person. Have signed so many of the pictures and also the copy of the *League of Their Own*. TV 20 took a video when I was out playing with the boys All Star Baseball Team, so made the evening news on the 30th of June. The writer with the *Buffalo Gram* wrote a two-page coverage of my Dad and had a picture of me and write-up in which he mentioned that I had played for the AAGPBL. I went to the special screening in Clearwater as I said and then to the paid screening and also the opening so have enjoyed it three times. I helped them set-up a display in the glass case at the Theater where it is showing.[67]

Retiring AAGPBL Players' Association president Joan Holderness addressed the membership through the November/December 1992 newsletter to express her gratitude to them for their part in promoting the movie. She perceptively observed that she didn't "think any of us realized at [the] time what an impact this movie would have on the general public, or on our own lives."[68] It's doubtful if Joan realized, at that time, that the effects of *A League of Their Own* would not diminish, but would stretch a decade and more into the future.

First of all, the movie, in one fell swoop, exploded the historical existence of the league into every little dot on the North American map and wherever it debuted in the rest of the world. As Terry Donahue pointed out, "If it hadn't been for that movie, we all would've been dead and gone and no one would have ever known about us."[69] After the film's debut, *everyone* old enough and able to go to the movies knew about "this feminine phenomenon of sports Americana!"[70]

Secondly, the movie enriched the individual lives of the All-Americans still living and many family and friends of the deceased. Much of this will be covered in the next chapter in detail, but briefly, as Shirley Burkovich stated, "When the movie came out, that's what brought us to the attention of the public." Reflecting on the film a dozen years later, Wilma Briggs, echoed Shirley's sentiments:

> *A League of Their Own* did wonders for spreading the word about our league. I've signed more autographs since the movie than I did while I was playing. And I've been inducted into 5 Halls of Fame. Also, I was named 15 out of 50 of Rhode Island's Greatest Sports Figures from 1900–2000 by *Sports Illustrated*. WOW! God has surely been good to me![71]

The public attention and the players' gracious response to it resulted in inductions into local baseball halls of fame; invitations to throw out the first pitch at major league games; invitations to teach youngsters the fundamentals of the game; recognition by sports foundations; recognition for being outstanding athletes, and more. Because of *A League of Their Own,* AAGBBL players received individual as well as collective honors and accolades in their golden years that heretofore were reserved for men's Major League players in their youth and middle years. The film revealed a concept that is still just beginning to emerge in this country. It revealed that there is meaning and importance to girls' and women's participation in sport.

Beyond these effects and expectations, *A League of Their Own* became a cultural phenomenon. As documentarian Kelly Candaele reflected a dozen years later:

> It's interesting how the term "A League of Their Own," took on a cultural presence far larger than we intended. President Clinton used the phrase "There's no crying in politics" on the campaign trail. And Hillary points to the movie as being an inspiration to her when she was deciding to run for the Senate (it's in her book).[72]

Current AAGPBL Players' Association president Delores "Dolly" Brumfield White recognized this element when she wrote her President's Message to the membership in September 2001:

> The popularity of the movie continues to be a major method to tell the story of our league. Lines used in the movie are often used in advertisements, interviews, in the media, and general conversations. How often do you hear [or see] the title "A League of Their Own" used?

The movie congealed the gathering thunderstorm of public awareness of the AAG-BBL. It flooded the players with public accolades and honors, but it did not dissipate in a short period of time as is common of thunderstorms. The effects of the film linger yet and patter gently through our collective thoughts and emotions because the film plays common chords in our lives that unite us. In America, sport, and especially baseball, does that.

17

The Players' Association, 1990–2004

The Executive Boards

The All-American Girls Professional Baseball League Players' Association operated under four executive boards from its inception in May of 1987 through and beyond the printing of this book in the spring/summer of 2006. As was stated in previous chapters, the first board was a self-appointed board and was initially established to represent the players in dealings with the Baseball Hall of Fame, the archives, and the film industry. From 1987 to 1998 the Executive Board was complimented by a six-member Board of Directors (five from 1987 to 1990) who acted as area representatives. Thus, a full board consisted of 11–12 members. However, the full 12 members of the board rarely met due to distance and travel expenses. When they met as a body, it was generally at national reunions, which for the most part were held biannually from 1991 to 2000. Beginning in 2000, reunions were scheduled annually. Other meetings, throughout any given period, were generally attended primarily by the Executive Board. The original Executive Board members, who established the Players' Association in 1987 (June Peppas, Fran Janssen, Dottie Collins, Jean Geissinger Harding, Earlene Risinger, and executive director Karen Violetta Kunkel), saw themselves as an interim board organized quickly to deal with expedient matters. They served from September 1987 through September of 1990. Their vision, courage, and commitment laid a substantial foundation upon which their successors could build.

1990–1992[1]

The Players' Association's first *elected* Executive Board took office in late September 1990, and experienced several personnel changes before a new board took office in September of 1992. Board president Joan Holderness, secretary Jean Geissinger Harding, and treasurer Dottie Collins served for this administration's two years. Executive vice president Barbara Liebrich was replaced by Kate Vonderau in 1991 and assistant vice president Mary "Wimp" Baumgartner was replaced by Barbara Sowers, also in 1991. Barbara Liebrich, however, continued to serve in 1992 as a replacement at sgt. at arms for Wilma Briggs. Besides serving as assistant vice president, in 1990, Wimp Baumgartner chaired the Policy and Procedure Manual Committee. She and associate Joyce Smith manned this committee through 1993, with Joyce assuming sole responsibility for Policies and Procedures during 1994.

Although the 1990–92 board's term of service was short, its plate was full. The issues the first elected board faced included (1) whether or not to establish a corporate headquarters; (2) obtaining a legal advisor; (3) improving coordination with media and area representatives; (4) establishing new committees to deal with the budget, Cooperstown, the lifetime roster, and recognition and awards; (5) reviewing the Policy and Procedure Manual; (6) coordinating with the affiliate and ex-officio members; (7) updating the players' directory, the computer list, release forms, and non-profit status; (8) reviewing history materials, AAGPBL player cards, and voting procedures.[2]

In the span of its two-year existence, the first elected board accomplished most of the tasks on its initial list. Its members opted not to establish a corporate headquarters because no further mention of this item was encountered in the board minutes. Legal counsel, of course, was obtained, new committees were established, and the need for ex-officio officers abandoned. Reorganization of the media and area representatives was achieved, a new players' directory was printed, and the organization's non-profit status was updated. The association's voting procedures were modified, and the Policy and Procedure Manual was revised by Mary "Wimp" Baumgartner and Joyce Smith and duly accepted by the board. The computer database for players, and player stats, originated in late 1988 by Joan Holderness, was updated and expanded to include not only players, and player records, but chaperones, managers, bat girls/boys, umpires, honorary members, affiliate members, and associate members. Joan continued work with the database after her presidency, and she maintained a close working relationship with Cooperstown to update the AAGPBL's lifetime roster there.[3] As Wimp Baumgartner noted upon Joan's resignation in 1994, she "volunteered immense amounts of her time, talent and money" as creator and chair of the database committee.[4] The first elected board also addressed league history materials and player cards, but these projects were passed on to the next administration for completion.

Other major challenges to confront the first elected board were how this non-profit organization should deal with movie royalties and what the future of the organization should be after the movie was released. By the time the movie was released, the main objectives for which the organization was established were accomplished, namely, recognition by the Hall of Fame, the establishment of a national archives, and completion of movie licensing and filming. Realization of these major accomplishments prompted discussions of the continuing need for the Players' Association and whether to continue it as it was or dissolve and restructure it. Ultimately, these larger conflicts were resolved by membership votes at the 1991 and 1992 annual meetings. The membership stipulated that the association should continue to operate as originally structured, and the problem of movie royalties would be passed on to the next administration.[5]

1993–1998[6]

The second Executive Board, elected to office in September 1992, included Mary "Wimp" Baumgartner, President; Kate Vonderau, Executive Vice President; Barbara Sowers, Assistant Vice President; Jean Geissinger Harding, Secretary; Dottie Wiltse Collins, Treasurer; and Wilma Briggs, Sgt. at Arms. The only new officer to the previous 1991 slate was President Baumgartner. This board, as the one that preceded it, would experience turnovers in the positions of executive and assistant vice presidents. Those to serve as executive vice presidents during this period included Jean Faut Eastman (1994–95), Sue Zipay (1996), and Joyce Smith (1997–1998). Those to serve as assistant vice presidents included Nancy DeShone Rockwell (1994–1995), Jean Faut Eastman (1996) and Sue Zipay (1997–1998).

President Baumgartner advised the membership in the November/December 1992 newsletter that her initial goals were (1) to work with the reunion committee to have the best 50th reunion ever; (2) to continue addressing the baseball card problem; (3) to deal with problems related to licensing, logos, marks, and merchandising; (4) to explore the viability of employing an executive director; (5) to keep the association informed and united; and (6) to keep the association before the public. Wimp's message in the October 1993 newsletter, newly titled *TOUCHING BASES*, suggested that her first objective was successfully achieved. She wrote to the membership:

> Greetings: To the tough, tenacious survivors of the Greatest Show on Earth, and to all other members. It seems from the letters we are receiving everyone enjoyed the memorable 50th.
>
> Each display at the Northern Indiana Historical Society was a joy to behold. They were very well done and much of our memorabilia was shown.... I wish everyone could have felt the emotion one gets in seeing all our memorabilia in one place.[7]

By the end of 1994, the desire to employ an executive director had been abandoned; problems with logos, marks, and merchandising had been laid to rest; and an agreement with the Fritsch Baseball Card Company assured players they could acquire their own baseball cards. Association members continued to be informed of the Executive Board's actions through the newsletter and reunions, and a system was established for keeping the AAGPBL-PA before the public: A Grant of Permission Form was distributed to players to ascertain those willing to represent the association at benefits, ball games, autograph signing programs, and other personal appearance requests received by the board.[8] When an organization or individual contacted the board for players to attend festivities or autograph signing sessions, the board then had a list of participants in all areas of the country who were willing to comply.

The efficient handling of President Baumgartner's original goals led to the establishment of others. The most important of these were to provide and maintain operational expenses for the Players' Association; to revise the by-laws into a manageable, flexible document; and to investigate ways to streamline the organization to reduce expenditures and optimize effectiveness. By the end of 1998, movie royalties were invested and merchandising contracts signed which gave the association an annual income. The by-laws were revised, a Policy and Procedure Manual was composed, and restructuring of the association became a reality.[9]

Under Mary "Wimp" Baumgartner's administration, some other notable accomplishments were recorded by the association. At Dorothy "Kammie" Kamenshek's suggestion and through her committee's efforts, the board was able to notify the membership in 1994 that they were all eligible to apply to BAT (Baseball Assistance Team). BAT is a program that provides one-time assistance to former professional baseball players in dire need.[10] At least one former AAGBBL player found assistance through this organization.

In the September 1996 newsletter, President Baumgartner announced the existence of several other noteworthy items. The first of these was an internet website created by Canadian Reg Langeman, who was "interested in the historical and educational background of our league."[11] Reg, looking to develop an historical website, happened to see *A League of Their Own* at an overnight hotel stop on the way to a softball tournament in Alberta, Canada. After seeing the movie and researching the league, he discovered that Canadian women from his local area played in the AAGBBL, and that he had worked with the niece of two former Canadian AAGBBL players. He started the website out of his own interest and was later contacted by the Players Association regarding his unintended illegal use of copyright materials. An agreement was worked out between them and he maintained the website until his children grew older, required more of his time, and the website became increasingly demanding. After a time he found he was "getting 20–30 e-mails each day as well as many requests from students to 'hook them up' with one of the players." He could tell "when and where the movie *League of Their Own* was being televised as [he] would get flooded with requests from certain parts of the country."[12]

Mary "Wimp" Baumgartner (courtesy Ruth Davis).

The second notable item to which President Baumgartner alerted the membership was the establishment of a Reunion Support Fund. This fund was initiated and supervised by Jean Faut Eastman to provide financial assistance for All-Americans who would not otherwise be able to attend reunions. The third notable item identified in the September 1996 newsletter was Mary Moore's consent to take up the project of videotaping players' oral histories begun by Janis Taylor at the 1993 Reunion in South Bend. Wimp Baumgartner notified the membership to be ready for oral history tapings at the reunion in Myrtle Beach, South Carolina, in her inimitable manner:

> ... we will continue to tape oral histories as these tapes will preserve our individual characteristics. If you plan to attend the next reunion and haven't been taped, have your hair curled, wear a big grin, get your facts straight, and be ready for candid camera.[13]

The oral history project was important to President Baumgartner and she viewed the reunion support as a means of enabling those not financially able to attend reunions so everyone's oral histories could be preserved. In her words:

> Everyone's story is unique in that some players played a limited time and others for years; some played with lots of ability and others played to the best of their ability. Everyone contributed in their own way and all have a story to tell and preserve for all time. We will have your voice, your physique, personality and humor on tape. This factual information on individuals and how they perceived their experiences during their playing days will be recorded in your own way, verbally and visually.
>
> ... In obtaining oral histories from as many members as possible, we are able to collect, document and preserve our history.[14]

This researcher blesses Mary "Wimp" Baumgartner for her vision and Mary Moore for her dedication and persistence in pursuing this project. The oral histories accomplish exactly what Wimp projected they would accomplish. It is a treat to watch and listen to them.

1999–2004[15]

At the Palm Springs, California, reunion in late 1998, a new Executive Board was elected. The previous board's restructuring of the Executive Board term lengths resulted in the election of Delores "Dolly" Brumfield White to a two-year term as president and Jean Cione was elected to a two-year term as vice president. Dottie Collins continued as treasurer, and Jean Geissinger Harding continued as secretary. Under the restructuring process achieved by the Baumgartner administration, the assistant vice president, sgt. at arms, and six director positions were deleted. However, the four-member Executive Board was rounded up to six with the addition of two representative positions. One representative post was held by Jean Faut Eastman (1999–2002). The other representative post was held by Mary Pratt (1999–2000).

In late 2000, the Executive Board make-up changed with the resignation of Dottie Collins from the board. Her position as treasurer was assumed by Jane Moffet (2000–?) who was elected to the representative post previously held by Mary Pratt. The board then assigned Shirley Burkovich to fill the vacated position. Jean Geissinger Harding also resigned her secretarial post in late 2000, but continued to serve on the board in an advisory capacity through 2001. Sue Macy was assigned by the board to fill Jean's vacated position and secretarial duties (2000). Jean Faut Eastman retired at the end of 2002 and Jeneane DesCombes Lesko was elected to replace her (2003). Jeneane took over compilation and publication of the newsletter for Dottie Collins at the beginning of 2001.

At the time this book was published, and after additional elections, the Executive Board consisted of Delores "Dolly" White, President (2005–2008); Jean Cione, Vice President (2005–2008); Jane Moffet, Treasurer (2005–2008); Sue Macy, Secretary (2005); Shirley Burkovich, Representative (2005); and Jeneane Lesko, Representative (2005).

As Joyce Smith succinctly stated, previous boards "paved the way and got over most of the high hurdles" and "unraveled most of the ... knotty problems" the association faced prior to 1998.[16] Thus, newly elected president, Dolly White, could focus her attention on continuing the association's original purposes. In her message to the membership in the January 1999 newsletter, she encouraged all members to harken back and join in to promote social activities and opportunities for the members; to help research, collect, document, and preserve the history of the AAGPBL; and to continue to disseminate educational information regarding the history of the league and its personnel.[17]

One step toward the ongoing realization of these goals was to schedule annual instead of bi-annual reunions as of 2000. This afforded members the opportunity to gather and interact every year if they so desired. In addition, President White and others began to act as hubs for the expanding, instant communication network provided by e-mail. Those without computers were encouraged to enlist the assistance of children, grandchildren, friends, or neighbors to be their internet contact. Illnesses, injuries, accidents, deaths, special honors, and immediate association business could be shared among the ranks of players and associates in a matter of hours or days instead of months or years. This helped establish and maintain close personal relationships among players and associates.

Some significant steps toward preserving the league's history by the administration elected at the end of 1998 included the production of an historically accurate documentary and the erection of an AAGBBL statue at the Baseball Hall of Fame. If all followed the blueprint, these projects were scheduled to be completed by the end of 2006. As far as disseminating educational information regarding the history of the league, the 1999–2003 board members and some of their colleagues were active participants in the Hall of Fame and Ball State University's production of an electronic field trip featuring "Women in Baseball," which reached an estimated 20 million students worldwide.[18]

Members of the board and their teammates also attended annual Fan Fest festivities held in conjunction with Major League Baseball's All-Star Game each year since 1999. As one observer noted when she attended Fan Fest in Milwaukee in 2002, "Where would you find 3 floors of wall-to-wall baseball with information and displays for MLB, the AAGPBL and the Negro League and it's not Cooperstown? IT'S FAN FEST."[19]

Although the Player's Association as a whole didn't become involved with Fan Fest until 2000, ex-players Alice "Lefty" Hohlmayer and Lavone "Pepper" Paire Davis actually pioneered the AAGPBL's presence at Fan Fest celebrations. They were invited to attend the Fan Fest in San Diego, July 10–14, 1992, where they "signed autographs ... every day until 10 P.M."[20] In 1999, another AAGPBL player, Mary Pratt, was invited to a Fan Fest when it was held in Boston. At this time Mary was on the Executive Board of the Players' Association and realized what an opportunity it was for promoting and perpetuating the league's history. From this point forward, President Dolly White and other association members attended the annual Fan Fests from 2000 through spring 2005, and a Fan Fest Committee was established to organize AAGPBL representation at this annual event on a continuing basis. Ex-players who attended Fan Fest, set up an AAGBBL display table, signed autographs, and answered fan questions for four or five days each year.

Members of this board, namely newsletter editor Jeneane DesCombes Lesko, and vice president Jean Cione, inherited the website from volunteer creator Reg Langeman and board liaison Joyce Smith in 2002. They, along with Jeneane's son, Matthew, continue to update and expand the newsletter to preserve and disseminate the league's history. It is also used as a vehicle through which researchers can connect with players in their area. In 2000, it was estimated that the AAGPBL website would receive 50,000 hits for the year. In 2003, the website received an average of 18,698 hits per month with a high during the month of April of 27,850. Website searchers for 2003 clicked in from Canada, South America, Australia, Africa, and all 50 states.[21] As website liaison Jean Cione, noted:

> ... we get requests from anybody from a 6th grader to a doctoral thesis researcher, and they all want to know more about you [AAGBBL players]. I'm probably the person who knows most what the world thinks of you, and I wish you could get some of the requests that I get. You would feel very special. You're revered by young people and people your own age.
> ... The website has opened the world up to you.[22]

In 2004 the Executive Board added a Women's Baseball Committee to maintain contact with, and support for, the emerging women's baseball programs in the country. Another innovation the board instituted in the spring of 2004 was the stipulation that each association committee would henceforth include an associate (non-player) member. Prior to this time, with only one or two exceptions, only former players were eligible for Executive Board or other committee positions. Now, however, the board realized that preservation of the association rested with associate members because as each year passed, fewer and fewer ex-players remained. They reasoned that if associates became caretakers of the association and kept it viable, the league's existence and history would continue to be preserved and perpetuated.

In Tribute

That first handful of players who met in Fran Janssen's South Bend, Indiana, home to incorporate had no way of knowing the far-reaching legacy they were creating. The players present at that occasion consisted of June Peppas (via telephone), Fran Janssen,

Jean Harding, Dottie Collins, Earlene Risinger, and Karen Violetta Kunkel. All maintained, and will continue to maintain, a close relationship with the association until their dying day. They are to be lauded for their commitment to the organization they created. Of this group, a Meritorious Service Tribute Above and Beyond the Exceptional must be accorded Dottie Wiltse Collins and Jean Geissinger Harding who served as executive board treasurer and secretary, respectively, from 1987 to 2000. It's impossible to assess the number of headaches, hours, and personal expense these two devoted to the Players' Association during the first 14 years of its existence. It is not impossible to deduce that their continued presence on the Executive Board helped stabilize and steer the association through transitional years. They are to be commended for their commitment to, and passion for, the AAGPBL Players' Association.

Individual Awards and Honors

In a letter to this author describing her role in the First National AAGBBL Reunion in 1982, former bat girl Ruth Davis observed:

> The women who played in the League were not just great athletes; they were the best that this country had to offer in so many ways…. I know that not everyone fell into that mold, but if I were a statistician, I'll bet that the greats outweighed the not so greats at a statistically higher rate than in the general population.[23]

As one peruses the pages of the AAGPBL Newsletters from 1981 to the present, the reality of Ruth's observation becomes apparent. Some became doctors, lawyers, professors, and teachers. Some worked in factories or as office clerks. Some became mothers and devoted their lives to their families. Many coached their own and others' youngsters to play the game they loved. Most demonstrated a caring, giving nature that bespoke specialness. This is richly illustrated in the awards and honors attributed to them individually.

The following litany is in tribute to the players. As outstanding, skilled athletes and, just as importantly, as outstanding people, they were the AAGBBL. Their performances and personalities sealed its success. They did not contribute to its demise. Unfortunately, the paragraphs below are not all-inclusive. They reflect only those awards and honors reported in the newsletters or accidentally encountered by the author from other sources. It is certain that not everyone reported their awards and honors to the newsletter. In addition, although the author attempted to examine the newsletters carefully for individual awards and honors, some may have been missed. Sincerest apologies are extended if this occurred. For the most part, awards and honors are listed by the date awarded. In some cases the date of the award was not given, so the date of the newsletter in which it was reported is cited. If a single player received several awards through the years, an attempt was made to report them collectively.

Prior to the Newsletter[24]

As early as 1960, honors and awards for AAGBBL players started trickling in. Gertrude, "Gertie" Dunn was inducted into the West Chester [PA] Athletic Hall of Fame in 1960 for baseball, field hockey and lacrosse. "In the 1970s she joined the Pennsylvania Sports Hall of Fame."[25] Joanne Winter received the award for LPGA teacher of the year in '69, and in 1979 she was elected to the Arizona Softball Hall of Fame. In 1974, Millie

Deegan was honored as only the fourth woman to be inducted into the New Jersey Softball Hall of Fame. Among her qualifications were 20 years in organized softball in the state, first as a player and then as a coach. Winning 20 straight state titles in a row didn't hurt. In 1977, Earlene "Beans" Risinger was inducted into the Jackson County, Altus, Oklahoma Baseball Hall of Fame along with Yankee great Mickey Mantle. Beans also relayed that Jaynne Bittner was inducted into the Pennsylvania Hall of Fame.

The 1980s[26]

The 1980s witnessed more awards and honors for previous AAGBBLers. Dorothy "Kammie" Kamenshek was listed in *Who's Who* in Orange County, California, where she served as head of Physical Therapy for Los Angeles County. In 1981, she was highlighted in *Sports Illustrated* as the league's "Best All-Around Player," and *Sports Illustrated for Women* recognized Kammie as the 100th member of the "100 Greatest Female Athletes of the 20th Century" in its November 29, 1999, issue. Less than eleven months later, on October 24, 2000, Kammie's athletic and professional achievements were honored when she was inducted into the Ohio Women's Hall of Fame by Governor Bob Taft.[27]

The July 1981 newsletter reported that a Memorial Softball Complex had been named after Alva Jo Fischer in Lady Bird Johnson Community Park in San Antonio, Texas. According to Millie Deegan, Alva Jo was "Always working with the youth."

The February 1983 newsletter noted that Katie Horstman, former student and longtime educator at Minster, Ohio, High School, was selected as "Citizen of the Year." In 1986 Katie was the first woman inducted into the Minster Hall of Fame. The September 2003 newsletter reported that by that date Katie was inducted into the Ohio Track Hall of Fame and the National Track Hall of Fame. Her 2003 honors included inductions into the Ohio Women's Hall of Fame and into the Northeast Indiana Baseball Hall of Fame.

Others who received awards in the mid–1980s included Margaret Wigiser, first supervisor of girls' programs in PSAL in New York, who had an outstanding female student-athlete award named after her. In 1986 Sophie Kurys was inducted into the Greater Flint, Michigan, Area Sports Hall of Fame, and Jean Cione was inducted into the Eastern Michigan University Athletic Hall of Fame.[28] In 1987, Mary "Wimp" Baumgartner received the Nancy Rehm Memorial Award in Fort Wayne, Indiana. The award recognized an "outstanding woman who has contributed her time and energy to better the sports programs for all girls and women in all walks of life."[29] Wimp would also be the first woman inducted into the Hall of Fame at the University of Indianapolis in 1989. Also in 1987, Terry Donahue was inducted into the Saskatchewan Baseball Hall of Fame along with 19 men. Arleene Noga followed Terry Donahue into the Saskatchewan Hall of Fame in 1988, and during the summer of 2004, the Ogema Heritage Grandstand in Ogema, Saskatchewan, Canada, was renamed the Arleene Johnson Noga Grandstand for her contributions to sports in the area.

Terry Donahue (courtesy Ruth Davis).

About this time, Mary Pratt was recognized for becoming a member of the Boston University Sports Hall of Fame as one of New England's all-time great female athletes. Mary was inducted into the Boston Garden's Hall of Fame in 1995, and into the National High School Hall of Fame in 1998. Her induction into the National High School Hall of Fame recognized her as a "trailblazer in the field of women's sports for more than 60 years [and] as someone who contributed toward the advancement of the role of women in sports." Mary was also the 2003 recipient of the Sports Museum of New England's Legacy Award for her contribution to New England Sports.[30]

Four All-Americans were honored by the St. Louis Cardinals during the summer of 1989. They included Audrey Kissel Lafser, Rita Meyer Moellering, Edna Franks Dummerth, and Erma Bergmann. Audrey Kissel Lafser was also honored as the Hancock Alumnus of the Year in December of 1989. In the same month, an article appeared recognizing Jean Havlish as one of only two women from Minnesota to be inducted into the WIBC Hall of Fame and the only bowler inducted into the Minneapolis Sports Hall of Fame. It was noted that she was on the Bowlers Journal All American team in 1969–1970 and listed in the *World Book Encyclopedia*. In 2000, Jean was also honored as No. 78 in the top 100 sports figures in Minneapolis/St. Paul Minnesota.

Jean Havlish's induction into the WIBC Hall of Fame, St. Louis, Missouri, 1987 (courtesy Jean Havlish).

The 1990s[31]

Recognitions in the 1990s continued, especially after the appearance of *A League of Their Own*, when the country as a whole became aware of its All-Americans. Prior to *League*, however, Rosemary Stevenson became one of ten new inductees in the Upper Peninsula (Michigan) Sports Hall of Fame in April of 1990. The year 1990 also featured Ellen Tronnier's induction into the Wisconsin Softball Hall of Fame. Locally, the South Bend White Sox honored ten AAGPBL Blue Sox in a pre-game event in August of 1990. The ten so honored included Barbara Hoffman, Marie Kruckel, Frances Janssen, Lou Arnold, Janet Wiley Sears, Nancy Rockwell, Lillian Luckey, Dottie Christ, Betsy Jochum and Elizabeth Mahon. In Boston, the Red Sox, in like manner, honored Pat Brown, Maddy English, Pat Courtney and Mary Pratt. Pat Brown was granted the honor of throwing the first ball to Red Sox catcher Tony Peña.

In the Philadelphia area, Jane Moffet was inducted into East Stroudsburg University Sports Hall of Fame for field hockey and basketball in 1990. The Philadelphia Sports Hall of Fame inducted her in 1998 for baseball; and in 1999 she was doubly honored when she was inducted into the Pitman High School Hall of Fame for field hockey and basketball and into the Gloucester County Hall of Fame for field hockey, basketball, and baseball. Jane also held the distinction of being listed in *Who's Who in American Education* and *Who's Who in American Women*.[32]

In 1991, besides previous inductees Terry Donahue, Arleene Johnson Noga, Bonnie Baker and Christine Jewitt Beckett, the Saskatchewan Baseball Hall of Fame inducted the rest of Saskatchewan's 25 AAGBBLers into its hallowed halls:

Janet Anderson Perkin	Betty Berthiaume Wicken	Julie Dusanko
Gene George McFaul	Thelma Grambo Hundeby	Lucella MacLean Ross
Ann Surkowski Deyotte	Lena Surkowski Delmonico	Elsie Wingrove Earl
Daisy Junor	Agnes Zurowski Holmes	Marguerite Jones Davis
Ruby Knezovich Martz	Mildred Warwick McAuley	Catherine Bennett
Virginia Carigy	Betty Petryna Allen	Muriel Coben
June Emerson	Hazel Measner Wildfong	Velma Abbot[33]

The induction was held at North Battleford, Saskatchewan, on April 6, 1991, and was "very successful. The overall Master of Ceremonies was Patricia Dewar of Saskatoon while Brenda Zeman did the installation ceremonies, the Right Honourable Lieutenant Governor Sylvia Fedoruk was the guest speaker while Gene McFaul of North Battleford said grace and Arleene Noga gave the toast to the queen."[34]

After the release of *A League of Their Own*, the Women's Sports Foundation honored the AAGPBL at its Women's Sports Awards Banquet in 1992. This was the first WSF awards banquet attended by AAGPBL representatives. Those who represented the AAGPBL at this event were Jean Faut Eastman, Betty Trezza, and Marilyn Jenkins.

Honors and awards for AAGBBL players snowballed during the decade of the 1990s. In May of '92 Vivian Kellogg was inducted into the Jackson Bowling Hall of Fame. Later (1994), Vivian would be honored when the village of Brooklyn named one of its new

Vivian Kellogg Field (courtesy Fran Janssen).

four-diamond softball fields after her. Vivian, along with Earlene "Beans" Risinger and Dolly Niemiec Konwinski, were invited to participate in a Michigan High School Athletic Association Leadership Conference for Women in Sports in 1993.

Sue Kidd, Tiby Eisen, Arleene Noga, and Wimp Baumgartner represented the league at the induction of the AAGPBL as a league into the Slippery Rock Hall of Fame in 1993. Eleanor Dapkus Wolf and Elizabeth "Lib" Mahon joined Dolores Mueller Bajda and Terry McKinley Uselmann, Phyllis Koehn, and Terry Donahue as honorees of the Chicago Old Timers Baseball Association. Later, Lib would be inducted into the South Bend, Indiana, Sports Hall of Fame.

In February of 1994, Amy Applegren was inducted into the Greater Peoria Sports Hall of Fame, and Mary Wisham was honored when West Putnam dedicated a softball field in her name. The news article announcing the event noted, "No name in Putnam County is more readily associated with women's softball than Mary Wisham," and that "she had been a role model to youth on and off the playing field ... to be the best they can."[35] The Greater Akron Baseball Hall of Fame inducted Jane Jacobs Badini in 1994 — its first woman ever. About the same time Rossey Weeks was added to the Jacksonville, Florida, Sports Hall of Fame Honor Roll, and Lou Erickson Sauer's AAGPBL exploits were recorded on a bronze plaque by ex-classmates and mounted on a building at the town's new sports complex. In '95, Dolores "Pickles" Lee was inducted into the Hudson County Athletic Hall of Fame.

The year 1996 was honor-filled for All-Americans. Early on, Betsy Jochum and Twila Shively were honored by the Chicago Old Timers' Baseball Association. Then professional golf teacher Joanne Winter was awarded the LPGA Ellen Griffin Rolex Award "designed to recognize an individual, male or female, who has demonstrated in their teaching the spirit, love and dedication, as Griffin did to golf students, teaching skills, and the game of golf."[36] The Alberta, Canada, Sports Hall of Fame inducted Helen Nicol Fox in "recognition of her prolonged and meritorious record as a multi-sport Athlete involved in softball, ice hockey, speed skating, baseball and golf."[37] Then there was the day that Alta Little had the honor of throwing the first pitch at a Texas Rangers game, being the dinner guest of, and sitting in a box seat with the Rangers' general partner, George W. Bush. In September 1996, the Fort Wayne Daisies were honored when Diamond No. 2 at the Tah-Cum-Wah Community Center was "dedicated and renamed Daisies Field" in honor of the 1945–1954 Daisies."[38] Some of those in attendance included Dottie Collins, Isabel "Lefty" Alvarez, Mary "Wimp" Baumgartner, and Tiby Eisen. Also, Janet Rumsey received the Jack Cramer Award for "sportsmanship, dedication, and people who are good athletes, who are really nice people,"[39] and Connie Wisniewski was inducted into the Grand Rapids Hall of Fame in October of that year. Connie was also inducted into the Polish Sports Hall of Fame.

In 1996, Jean Peterson Fox was inducted into the Bureau County Sports Hall of Fame; Erma Bergmann was inducted into the St. Louis Softball Hall of Fame; and, in Michigan, Dolly Pearson Tesseine became a member of the Michigan Amateur Softball Hall of Fame. Maggie Brooks, Lynd Legislator 17th District, proclaimed May 26, 1996 "All-American Girls Professional Baseball League Day" in Irondequoit and Monroe Counties and saluted Gloria Cordes Elliott "for her contribution to the sport of baseball as a member of the Racine Belles and Kalamazoo Lassies in 1950–1954, and [to] honor her efforts to preserve the dignity and legacy of that game by working with young people."[40] From Susan Molinari, U.S. Congress, Gloria also received the Sports History Award as a

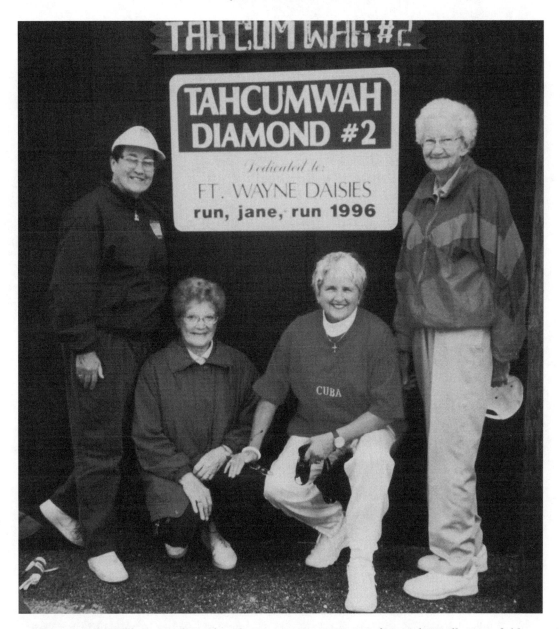

Tah-cum-wah Field #2 — Dedicated to the Fort Wayne Daisies. *Left to right:* Dolly Brumfield White, Arleene Johnson Noga, Isabel Alvarez, Fran Janssen (courtesy Fran Janssen).

symbol of the significant contributions she made to the role of women in sports and to the role of women throughout society. Ms. Molinari noted that Gloria's accomplishments truly put her in a league of her own. Gloria was also inducted into the Staten Island Sports Hall of Fame in 1997.

In 1997 Jean Faut Eastman became a charter inductee into the South Bend, Indiana Hall of Fame at Coveleski Stadium. She was recognized for her exceptional pitching including four no-hit and two perfect games. In Wisconsin, Annastasia "Stash" Batikis was inducted into the Southeastern Wisconsin Educators' Hall of Fame in April of 1997.

Annastasia taught for 35 years in Manitowoc and Racine "where she was a leading force in developing interscholastic track, basketball and gymnastics programs for girls."[41]

"On June 28, 1997, history was made in Miami, Florida. On that day the first Cuban female professional baseball player, Ysora 'Chico' Kinney del Castillo, was inducted into the Cuban Baseball Hall of Fame."[42] Up to that date, only Cuban-born males who had played amateur or professional baseball could be nominated for this honor by the Federation of Cuban Players in Exile. In September '97, the Colorado Rockies honored Earlene "Beans" Risinger in a tribute to Women in Baseball. Meanwhile, in Columbia, South Carolina, Viola Thompson Griffin was inducted into the South Carolina Athletic Hall of Fame.

In 1998, Midland Park posthumously honored "a great lady," Carol Habben, with *A Field of Her Own* near the high school. The Board of Education president challenged the young girls in the audience to "use Carol as an example to set ... lofty goals and aspirations in all that you do."[43] Also, the Chicago Old Timers honored Irene Kotowicz and Ginger Gascon in the spring of '98, and during that summer the Texas Rangers honored 10 "Girls of Summer" with an exhibit and pre-game festivities. Those in attendance included Barbara "Bobby" Payne, Mary Lou Caden Studnicka, Charlotte "Skipper" Armstrong, Marie "Red" Mahoney, Sue Kidd, Catherine "Katie" Horstman, Alta Little, Ruth "Tex" Lessing, Jaynie Krick (who threw out the first ball), and Delores "Dolly" Brumfield White. In late 1998, Dolly White was inducted into the Henderson State University Hall of Fame, and in 2004, she was selected as the Distinguished Alumna of the Year by her undergraduate school, the University of Montevallo in Alabama — known as Alabama College in Dolly's day.[44]

Ysora Castillo, entertaining an audience during the 1949 Rookie Tour (courtesy Leonard Zintak).

Like the Rangers, the Detroit Tigers also presented a salute to women in baseball in July '98. Among those slated to attend were Mary Moore, Helen Filarski Steffes, and Rose Gacioch who lived in a retirement community. Rose and her retirement residence friends needed $400 to attend the event. A story in the local paper brought sufficient donations from the community to get the group to the ball game. Rose, Mary, Helen, and approximately 22 other unnamed, former AAGPBLers signed autographs before the game.[45]

The National Baseball Hall of Fame at Cooperstown displayed an exhibit during the summer and fall of 1998 entitled "Short Stop From Sadorus." The exhibit honored Dorothy Schroeder (1928–1996), her rural farm roots, and baseball in the heartland. Dorothy was the only player to play all 12 years of the AAGBBL's existence.

Capping off 1998's honors, the Canadian Baseball Hall of Fame inducted all 64 Canadians who played in the AAGBBL:

Marge Callaghan Maxwell
Colleen McCulloch
Mildred Warwick McAuley
Lee Surkowski Delmonico
Elsie Wingrove Earl
Ruth Middleton Gentry
Helen Nicol Fox
Anne J. Thompson
June Emerson
Betty Petryna Allen
Christine Jewitt Beckett
Marion Watson Stanton
Doris Barr
Mary "Bonnie" Baker
Dorothy Ferguson Key
Olga Grant
Ruth Mason
Evelyn Wawryshyn Moroz
Thelma Grambo Hundeby
Hazel Measner Wildfong
Helen Nelson Sandiford
Jeanne Gilchrist

Penny O'Brian Cooke
Kay Heim McDaniel
Terry Donahue
Lucella MacLean Ross
Audrey Haine Daniels
Alice Janowski
Julie Sabo Dusanko
June Schofield
Lillian Hickey
Mae Stark
Daisy Junor
Marjorie Hanna
Dorothy Cook
Muriel Coben
Eleanor Callow
Ethel Boyce
Ethel McCreary
Thelma Golden
Gladys Davis
Velma Abbott
Vicki Panos
Martha Rommelaere Manning

Betty Carveth Dunn
Arleene Johnson Noga
Janet Anderson Perkin
Anne Surkowski Deyotte
Agnes Zurowski Holmes
Joan Schatz
Barbara Barbaze
Betty Berthiaume Wicken
Catherine Bennett
Marguerite Jones Davis
Doris Shero Witiuk
Mary Justra Shastal
Dorothy Hunter
Olive Bend Little
Ruby Knezovich Martz
Shirley Smith
Gene George McFaul
Thelma Walmsley
Helen Callaghan St. Aubin
Yolande Teillet Schick[46]

Induction ceremonies for these players took place on June 4, 1998, in St. Marys, Ontario, Canada. The date marked the "160th anniversary of the first recorded baseball game in Canada, played in Beachville, near Woodstock."[47] It also marked the first ever on-site induction at the new multimillion-dollar Hall of Fame and Museum. Mr. William J. "Bill" Rayner, Ontario native and confirmed baseball fan, spent ten months preparing an 80-page induction nomination proposal to submit to the Canadian Baseball Hall of Fame. He was assisted by Arleene Johnson Noga, the Canadian director of the AAGPBL Players' Association. "The Canadian women were elected to the hall on the first ballot ... (29 out of 34 induction committee members voted for the women)." "'It was an opportunity to make a statement about honoring all excellence and not being gender-exclusive,' Hall of Fame board member Ashleigh Barney of London said."[48] It was a memorable day for the Canadian All-Americans— as memorable as Cooperstown for American players.

The year 1999 dawned with an honorable event for the AAGBBL and especially for Annabelle Lee Harmon in Southern California. She was featured on Edison International's float "The Great American Pastime" in the Pasadena Tournament of Roses Parade on New Year's Day. The float celebrated 100 years of American baseball, featuring four, 17-foot tall, flower-covered baseball players who represented four different eras of the game. One represented a player from the turn of the century, one represented the National Negro Baseball League, one represented the All-American Girls Baseball League, and one represented a modern team.[49]

The Elgin Sports Hall of Fame inducted Charlene Barnett into its ranks in 1999, and Dottie Wiltse Collins and Joanne Weaver were inducted into the Fort Wayne, Indiana,

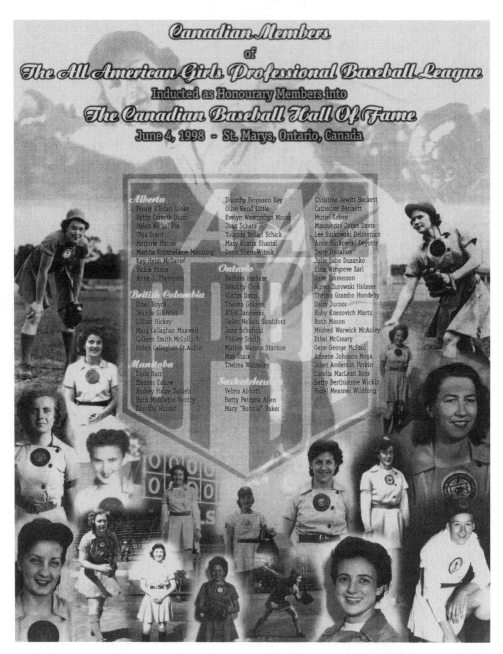

Canadian Members of The All American Girls Professional Baseball League Inducted as Honourary Members into The Canadian Baseball Hall Of Fame June 4, 1998 - St. Marys, Ontario, Canada

Alberta
Penny O'Brian Cooke
Betty Carveth Dunn
Helen Nichol Fox
Olga Grant
Marjorie Hanna
Martha Rommelaere Manning
Kay Heim McDaniel
Vickie Panos
Anne J. Thompson

British Columbia
Ethel Boyce
Jeannie Gilchrist
Lillian Hickey
Marg Callaghan Maxwell
Colleen Smith McCulloch
Helen Callaghan St. Aubin

Manitoba
Doris Barr
Eleanor Callow
Audrey Haine Daniels
Ruth Middleton Gentry
Dorothy Hunter

Dorothy Ferguson Key
Olive Bend Little
Evelyn Wawryshyn Moroz
Joan Schatz
Yolande Teillet Schick
Mary Kustra Shastal
Doris Shero Witiuk

Ontario
Barbara Barbaze
Dorothy Cook
Gladys Davis
Thelma Golden
Alice Janowski
Helen Nelson Sandiford
June Schofield
Shirley Smith
Marion Watson Stanton
Mae Stark
Thelma Walmsley

Saskatchew
Velma Abbott
Betty Petryna Allen
Mary "Bonnie" Baker

Christine Jewitt Beckett
Catherine Bennett
Muriel Coben
Marguerite Jones Davis
Lee Surkowski Delmonico
Anne Surkowski Deyotte
Terry Donahue
Julie Sabo Dusanko
Elsie Wingrove Earl
June Emmerson
Agnes Zurowski Holmes
Thelma Grambo Hundeby
Daisy Junior
Ruby Knezovich Martz
Ruth Mason
Mildred Warwick McAuley
Ethel McCreary
Gene George McFaul
Arleene Johnson Noga
Janet Anderson Perkin
Lucella MacLean Ross
Betty Berthiaume Wicklin
Hazel Measner Wildfong

Canadian Hall of Fame honors Canadian All-Americans (courtesy Arleene Johnson Noga).

Baseball Hall of Fame that same year. They would also be recognized as two of northeast Indiana's top 50 athletes by the *Fort Wayne News Sentinel* in late 1999. Collins was selected as number 16 on the top 50 list and Weaver as number 28.

In its 1999 induction ceremonies, the Ohio Baseball Hall of Fame honored South Bend's Betsy Jochum. Charlene "Shorty" Pryer Mayer was honored posthumously the same year when the Wilson Elementary School ball field in Medford, Oregon, was named in her honor. Shorty spent 25 years working with Medford students.

Annabelle Lee Harmon and "The Great American Pastime." Edison International's Tribute to Baseball at the 1999 Tournament of Roses Parade (courtesy Annabelle Lee Harmon).

Charlene "Shorty" Pryer (courtesy Ruth Davis).

[She coaxed] speedy runs, strong swings and artful catches from hundreds of students.... The School Board decided to "do something nicer" than a wooden sign on the backstop, so [they planned] for a concrete pedestal with a plaque recalling Mayer's life.... [An older] youngster wrote, "I was in kindergarten when you were here, I remember you being short, with short hair and an angel. But, now you are an angel in heaven's hands, and we all know that you will be in the big playground in the sky, watching all us kids from up above."[50]

Washington State resident Jeneane DesCombes Lesko was inducted into Ohio Northern University's Athletic Hall of Fame in 1999. In the summer of 1999 she was invited to participate in the opening ceremonies at the Grand

Opening of Safeco Field in Seattle. On the field with former Seattle Baseball Greats to celebrate the History of Baseball in that city, she received a huge ovation from the fans as the AAGPBL representative. Annually, she and Rose Powell are invited to the Girls' Little League Softball World Series for 14–15 year olds where they participate in the pre-game events and throw out a first pitch. In 2001 Jeneane was inducted into the Grand Rapids Sports Hall of Fame as a former Chick's player.[51]

The 2000s[52]

In 2000, the AAGPBL held a reunion in Milwaukee. There they were honored with a permanent display at Miller Park. The ceremony was the first held in a Major League Baseball park to honor the whole league. Also in 2000, Wilma "Willie" Briggs was inducted into the Rhode Island Scholar-Athlete Hall of Fame. The article announcing this event included the information that Wilma had previously been inducted into the East Greenwich Athletic Hall of Fame (first woman inducted), and that she was "recognized by *Sports Illustrated* as one of the 50 Greatest Sports Figures of Rhode Island, 1900–2000 (15th)."[53] Wilma was also inducted into the Northeast Indiana Baseball Hall of Fame in 2004.

The 2000 Seattle Mariners held a "Tribute to Women in Baseball" and displayed an honorary banner of Dorothy "Snookie" Doyle at their stadium. Ten AAGPBLers were invited to this event, including Dorothy Kamenshek, Snookie Doyle, Pauline Crawley, Lois Youngen, Doris Shero Witiuk, Rose Folder Powell, Jean Faut Eastman, Marge Wenzell, and Jeneane DesCombes Lesko.

Madeline "Maddy" English (courtesy Ruth Davis).

In Everett, Massachusetts, Madeline "Maddy" English received the distinctive honor of having a new school named after her. She was the first female after whom a municipal building was named in Everett. The naming of the school was opened up to the students, who had to write an essay to justify their choice. The winner was Tiffani Macarelli, who summarized her essay by writing, "Maddy English is not only a role model to sports fans and players, but to people of all ages and interests. Maddy English shows many great qualities and shows that being a team player is the best kind of person to be in life."[54]

In 2001, The Chicago Old Timers Hall of Fame honored Dottie Collins, Joyce Hill Westerman, and Annastasia "Stash" Batikis; Jenny Romatowski was inducted into Eastern Michigan University's Hall of Fame; the Grand Rapids Chicks team was the first team inducted into the Grand Rapids Sports Hall of Fame; and Pat Scott was inducted into the St. Henry High School Hall of Fame. Pat was honored by her hometown of Walton when the city dedicated the baseball field at the Walton Community Park in her name.

Dolly Konwinski was selected as an honoree by the Chicago Old Timers Baseball Association in 2001, and she experienced an unannounced honor at Major League Baseball spring training in Orlando, Florida, the same year. In line a little late to get tickets to a Yankees and Cardinals game to see Big Mac (Mark McGwire), she and her husband began chatting with the young man who announced tickets were sold out. Dolly relayed the outcome of the conversation to newsletter readers:

... We talked about the movie [*A League of Their Own*], and how much he [the young man] enjoyed it. Before we knew it, he asked how many tickets we wanted for each of the games. Six I said. Our tickets were waiting at the window. "Now, how about throwing out the First Pitch?" [he asked] Yankees and Braves. "Sure," I said!

Bring on the "Cardinals." Joan Holderness and Dee White came to the game, and Joan and I went into the dugout with McGwire. Yep, autographs and all.[55]

The year 2002 witnessed the induction of Vivian Kellogg, Maxine Kline and Dottie Schroeder (posthumously) into the Fort Wayne Old Timer's Baseball Association. It was also the year Annastasia Batikis and Ellen Tronnier were honored with plaques on the Milwaukee Brewers Walls of Honor at Miller Park in a pre-game ceremony. Jenny Romatowski was named Distinguished Graduate — Class of 1946 by the State of Michigan and the article noted that she had previously been inducted into the Wyandotte Sports Hall of Fame, Michigan Amateur Sports Hall of Fame, National Polish-American Sports Hall of Fame, and Eastern Michigan University Hall of Fame.

In July of 2002, the Society for American Baseball Research featured a panel discussion by AAGPBL players Vivian Sheriffs Anderson, Jackie Mattson Baumgart, Betty Moczynski, Joyce Hill Westerman, Annastasia Batikis, and Mary Froning O'Meara. In November, Jackie Baumgart was honored by the Wisconsin Old Timers Baseball Organization. Also in 2002, Terry McKinley Uselmann was selected as Woman of the Year for her parish. Her contributions to her school and the parish she was associated with were many and varied. Among them:

> [She] taught CCD, worked Fun-Fest, started a girl's softball program and ran it for 10 years; co-chaired "Target Sound-proof" which soundproofed the parish hall; received for the parish the first Marian Award for girl scouts; was Medical Missions Chairperson.
> [Her] current activities include being a Lector/Commentator, Minister of Care, member of the Bereavement Committee, and [she] heads the St. Matthew Circle.
> ... She currently has two part time jobs: one as a starter at the Glenview Park District Golf Course; and one as an Usher for Event Venue Services at the Rosemont Theater and All State Arena.
> Her greatest contribution to our club and the entire parish as a whole is the generosity of time and talents.[56]

During the 2002 season, the Toronto Blue Jays Organization erected banners at the Skydome depicting hometown heroes. One of the sixty-foot outdoor banners gave tribute to the AAGPBL and featured Arleene Johnson Noga. In August 2002, "the state of New Jersey commemorated Women's Equality Day by honoring Jane Moffet and Teeny Petras and all the women ballplayers of the AAGPBL."

> They were honored for their pioneering efforts in playing professional baseball during and after World War II and thereby contributing to the status of women in sports and in effect enhancing the equality and status of women.[57]

The April 2003 newsletter revealed that Jean Marlowe had been inducted into the Northeastern Pennsylvania Sports Hall of Fame and was about to be inducted into the Pennsylvania Sports Hall of Fame. In Rockford, Illinois, the YWCA honored Dottie Ferguson Key with the Janet Lynn Award for Sports for her contributions and leadership in the community. The Milwaukee Brewers selected Betty Moczynski and Mary Froning O'Meara to join those on their Walls of Honor. The St. Louis Cardinals honored Erma Bergmann, Audrey Kissel Lafser, and Edna Frank Dummerth in a pre-game ceremony in June of 2003.

The AAGPBL was extended an historic invitation to the White House for a special ceremony recognizing the league's contributions to the game of baseball during the September 2003 Tee Ball game. Those representing the league included Helen "Gig" Smith, Lou Stone Richards, Dolly Brumfield White, Gloria Cordes Elliott, Ruth Richard, Jean Faut Fantry, and Karen Violetta Kunkel.[58]

As of this writing in the fall of 2004, the "new" AAGPBL honorees depicted in the newsletter included Dolores Bajda, Ginger Gascon, Terry Donahue and Terry Uselmann who were featured on the July 4th Northbrook, Illinois, Park District's float honoring the AAGPBL. Thelma "Tiby" Eisen was inducted into the Jewish Sports

Left: Arleene Johnson Noga, representing 64 Canadian women who played in the AAGBBL, Toronto Blue Jays' Skydome main entrance, 2002 baseball season (courtesy of Arleene Johnson Noga). *Below:* The Milwaukee Brewers honor the AAGPBL (courtesy Fran Janssen).

All-Americans honored at a White House T-ball game, September 7, 2003. *Left to right:* Karen Violetta Kunkel, Gloria Cordes Elliott, Helen "Gig" Smith, Jean Faut Fantry, President George W. Bush, Ruth Richard, Lou Stone Richards, Dolly Brumfield White (White House photograph by Tina Hager, courtesy the White House).

Left: Thelma "Tiby" Eisen honored by Jewish Sports Hall of Fame (courtesy of Sue Macy). *Above:* Chicago Old-Timers honor Lou Arnold, September 2004 (courtesy of Lou Arnold).

Hall of Fame. At ceremony's end, Tiby was "mobbed by fans of all ages who were clamoring for her autograph."[59] The September 2004 newsletter noted that Lou Arnold was honored by the Chicago Old Timers Association and Joyce Hill Westerman and Grace Piskula were added to the Milwaukee Brewers Walls of Honor. In Canada, Millie Warwick McAuley was granted the honor of throwing out the ceremonial first pitch for the Women's World Cup of Baseball.

Via e-mail, Player Association secretary Sue Macy notified the membership that 2004's Women's Sports Foundation's AAGPBL honorees included Marilyn "Jonesy" Doxey and Terry Donahue. Sue also noted that on the west coast Snookie Doyle, Tiby Eisen, Maybelle Blair, Shirley Burkovich, and Lee Delmonico were introduced on the Jumbotron at Dodger Stadium in the early part of September. Afterward "they could barely get to the parking lot without signing autographs for everyone from little kids to the women who worked in food services." A few weeks later this group "minus Snookie but plus Helen Hannah Campbell were guests at *Fortune Magazine*'s Most Powerful Women Summit ... and met former Texas Governor Ann Richards, Billie Jean King, Arianna Huffington and lots of other powerful women." Sue also announced that co-sponsors MassMutual and Office Depot were awarding their Sports Visionary Award to the AAGPBL at the Success Strategies for Businesswomen Conference scheduled for February 27 to March 1, 2005, in Boca Raton, Florida.[60]

Another e-mail message from Player Association president Dolly White informed the membership that Rose Gacioch would be honored posthumously with induction into

the Wheeling, West Virginia, Hall of Fame on November 27, 2004. Rose had the distinction, as a teenager, of playing with the All Star Ranger Girls, one of the last "Bloomer Girl" barnstorming baseball teams. In the words of Barbara Gregorich, she was "a worthy link between the great tradition of bloomer girl baseball and the well-paid and well-played AAGBL."[61] When Rose was interviewed about her career and the AAGBBL's recognition by the Baseball Hall of Fame, she was recorded as saying: "Now I got something on Pete Rose. I got there before he did."[62]

One might suggest that the foregoing honors and awards garnered by the All-Americans were bestowed on them merely because they were baseball players or "because of the movie." When one becomes acquainted with them, however, it is realized that their honors were richly deserved because most are gracious, generous, gregarious, and magnanimous. As a result, not only are they more than deserving of their awards and honors, they have become their own best ambassadors.

Rose Gacioch (courtesy Ruth Davis).

AAGPBL Ambassadors

Here again, the data presented is in tribute to the players; it was collected from the AAGPBL Newsletters and reflects only what was reported there. It does not pretend to be inclusive or to have garnered every single item in which players were involved in representing, promoting, and preserving the legacy of their association. Again, the author apologizes if someone's efforts were overlooked. The intent is to illustrate how much the players continued to give to the public after their playing days were over. Their largesse continues to return to them, since what they gave served to keep the AAGPBL in the public's eye and to perpetuate their association.

Benefits[63]

Former AAGBBL players frequently gave of their time to raise funds for others. In the Los Angeles area, for example, Katie Horstman, Maybelle Blair, Shirley Burkovich, Snookie Doyle, Tiby Eisen, Annabelle Lee Harmon, Lee Delmonico and ex-chaperone Helen Hannah Campbell frequently attended fund raisers all over the Los Angeles area. In 2003, for instance, Katie, Maybelle, and Shirley helped publicize the annual Golf Classic fund-raiser for the Sunset Haven Senior Citizen facilities in Upland, Apple Valley, and Hemet. These facilities are long-term care service providers for low-income seniors. In 2004, four or five of the seven attended one or more fund raisers for the Jr. Seau Kids Organization in February; the Celebrity Golf Tournament Fund Raiser for inner city youth of Yorba Linda in April; and a Heart Association Fund Raiser event in Ontario, also in April.[64]

Dolly Niemiec Konwinski in Michigan was a tireless fund raiser for cancer research. At reunions, she recruited her ex-teammates to sign balls and posters to be auctioned off for breast cancer research because she knew "that someday, with all the research, we can 'wipeout' this kind of cancer."[65]

Delores "Dolly" Brumfield White, retired professor at Henderson State University in Arkadelphia, Arkansas, was another active 1998 fund raiser. Her efforts were directed toward raising funds to benefit Henderson State's softball facility.

Baseball/Softball Events[66]

AAGPBL players were loyal supporters of baseball/softball events where they tirelessly signed autographs. In Rochester, New York, in 1995, for instance, Gloria Cordes Elliott, Sarah "Salty" Sands Ferguson, Norma Dearfield, Wilma Briggs, Lenora Mandella,

A few Southern California AAGPBL ambassadors, ca. 2002. *Left to right:* Shirley Burkovich, Marge Wenzell, Dorothy "Kammie" Kamenshek, Lee Surkowski, Thelma "Tiby" Eisen, Pauline Crawley, Dorothy "Snookie" Doyle (courtesy Kammie Kamenshek and Marge Wenzell).

Joanne McComb, Mary Moore, Helen Filarski Steffes, and Dolly Pearson Tesseine attended a baseball camp for girls ages 8 to 18. The article didn't mention how many autographs they signed, but the picture showed them prepared to sign as many as desired.

Anna May Hutchison, Joyce Hill Westerman, and Annastasia Batikis represented the Players' Association at the 1995 Field of Dreams Celebrity Ball Game. A newspaper reporter noted that "The Belles signed hundreds of autographs and were introduced and loudly applauded in a ceremony preceding a celebrity game.... One family "commented that in comparison to some of the male ball players for whom autograph signing was merely a business, the Belles were gracious, wonderful and caring. In other words," the reporter commented, "when it comes to dealing with young fans, the former Belles are in a league of their own."[67]

Sarah Jane "Salty" Sands Ferguson regularly attended opening ceremonies for her local area's little league programs in the 1990s. She was often featured throwing the first pitch of the first game of the season. Young fans continued to clamor for her autograph at these events.

Tiby Eisen, Maybelle Blair, and Shirley Burkovich attended a game between the "Silver Bullets" and a San Diego Military Baseball Team in 1996 and signed autographs for fans as they left the game. At a Rockford Peaches mini-reunion in '96, 32 former players shared the honor of signing autographs during four different sessions of the day — about four-and-a-half hours total.

In 2004, the newsletter reported that The Pitch & Hit Club of Chicago invited Terry Donahue, Lou Arnold, Janet "Pee Wee" Wiley Sears, and Toni Palermo to their annual awards evening. The foursome obliged by participating in a pre-dinner autographing session attended by more than 1,000 guests. On the west coast, Maybelle Blair, Snookie Doyle, Annabelle Lee, and Shirley Burkovich attended a Cucamonga Quakes (Class A team) autograph signing event for middle school kids. In Houston, Mary Lou Studnicka Caden, Dolly Brumfield White, Marie "Red" Mahoney, Shirley Burkovich, and Katie Horstman talked with fans and signed autographs at the annual Major League Baseball Fan Fest activities.

When they weren't signing autographs, AAGBBL players were lending their presence in support of baseball or softball. One such event was the 23rd Annual Baseball Awards Dinner in Los Angeles in 1989 attended by Anita Foss, Inez Voyce, Tiby Eisen, Hedy Crawley, Snookie Doyle, Faye Dancer, Annabelle Lee Harmon and Helen Hannah Campbell. In Canada, Evie Wawryshyn Moroz, Arleene Johnson Noga, Audrey Haine Daniels, Marge Callaghan Maxwell, and Jeanne Gilchrist shared attendance at four baseball clinics for girls 8 to 18 sponsored by Major League Baseball, Canada. These clinics were held during the summer of 1999. Teeny Petras was present at the Waretown Opening Day for the Athletic Association 1998 baseball and softball programs to throw out the first pitch. In 2003, Wilma Briggs attended a baseball-for-girls opening day celebration in Rhode Island to lend her inspiration to the program.

In 2002, Jeneane DesCombes Lesko organized and coached her own women's baseball team. They played in a 24-hour marathon game at Electric Park in Tucson, Arizona. Each player collected $1000 in donations for the benefit of U.S. doctors for Africa, "specifically for the relief of pregnant African mothers with AIDS to prevent new-borns from being born with AIDS."[68] Sixty-two players attended the event and were divided into three large teams with plenty of subs, and they rotated every two hours. Jean was up all night coaching, and even pitched for one team for four innings because they were

All-Americans at the 2004 Fan Fest in Houston, Texas. *Left to right:* Shirley Burkovich and Katie Horstman (courtesy Shirley Burkovich).

short on pitchers. According to Jean, "It was great fun." The event netted about $40,000 and a commendation from the U.S. Doctors from Africa.[69]

The Southern California players' 2004 calendar, from February through August, included attendance at five Sports Educators of America Free Baseball Clinics. Their schedule also included attendance at The Olympic Softball Team Tour in Cathedral City, Opening Day Event for Rancho Cucamonga Quakes (Class A Anaheim Angels Farm Team), a Softball Clinic at Dodger Stadium, a Softball Clinic at Angels Stadium, a Kids in Sports Softball Clinic in Hawthorne, and an International Softball Tournament in Irvine. In addition, they spoke to a sixth grade class in Anaheim, to a Women's Club Luncheon in Redlands, and to an Anaheim School District Workshop attended by 800 student athletes.[70] These ladies were truly busy ambassadors for their association.

Mr. Charlie Coleman, president of the Ontario, California, Fast-pitch Softball Association (OFSA), eloquently praised the contributions of Southern California AAGBBLers in a letter of appreciation to Shirley Burkovich and her volunteers. Many event sponsors throughout the country could undoubtedly echo his sentiments:

> Please accept our sincere thanks for all you did during our Memorial Day Tournament. I have come to know that a big part of our success in these events is due to the tireless contributions of your time, the joy you show to the children and your endless desire to autograph whatever it may be until there is nothing left to sign. All this you've done for

mere tokens of a greater appreciation that can never be defined by material items. Your presence made our event so memorable for all those who attended.

It was such a great joy for me to watch how people of all ages flocked to you and the Ladies. As I watched people follow you any place you went, walked towards you just so they might catch that one chance at an autograph from a Baseball Hall of Famer, I was impressed by the genuine desire, of you all; to hear the stories, share the moment, encourage the youth to growth and show us older ones how to give back.

I know that all the people of OFSA will never forget how great it was when the Ladies came to be with us. You have to know you've been "adopted" by the OFSA family. Whenever I talk to anyone about a ceremony we need to prepare for, everyone asks if we can get **our** Ladies from the "League of Their Own" to be there. We're hoping that you all will consider us, OFSA, as part of your family.[71]

The September 2004 newsletter recorded that Dolly Konwinski provided her granddaughter with a replica of a Chicks' uniform, and they, with Marilyn Jenkins, Rosemary Stevenson, and Beans Risinger, appeared at a "baseball game to help Catholic Social Services at 'Go to Bat for Kids' night."

Meetings[72]

From the beginning of the association, AAGPBL players attended and/or spoke at a variety of organizational meetings. Dottie Collins recorded being invited, in 1987, to attend a luncheon in Indiana put on by the Girls Clubs of America, The Women's Sports Foundation, and the National Association of Sports for Girls and Women. In 1988 Jean Havlish and Nancy Mudge Cato were among the first AAGPBL representatives to participate on a panel at a Society for American Baseball Research Conference. In 1997, former South Bend and Fort Wayne players attended a round table discussion about the AAG-BBL at DePauw University. Those attending included Lou Arnold, Pee Wee Wiley Sears, Dottie Wiltse Collins, Amy Applegren, Twila Shively, Betsy Jochum, Fran Janssen, and Wimp Baumgartner. Also in '97 an AAGPBL contingent was invited to attend a fast pitch softball tournament and festivities at the University of Wisconsin–Eau Clair. Participants included Jackie Mattson Baumgart, Mary Froning O'Meara, Shirley Palesh, Dolly Vanderlip Ozburn, Lou Erickson Sauer, and Ellen Tronnier.

In 1999, Helen "Gig" Smith was deployed by the league to go to Hawaii to "BRAG about" the AAGPBL at four different army institutions. She was uniquely qualified for the task having been a World War II WAAC. According to Gig, "The response was wonderful.... I was proud to say I'd been in the Army as well as in the AAGPBL, and it made them happy, too."[73]

The year 2001 witnessed the busy Californians' attendance at a Women in Sports Celebration at the Anaheim Convention Center for high schools in the Anaheim area. Those feted were Marge Wenzell, Dorothy Kamenshek, Dorothy Doyle, Annabelle Lee, Tiby Eisen, Lee Delmonico, Pauline Crawley, Maybelle Blair, Shirley Burkovich and Helen Hannah Campbell. In the Northwest, Jeneane DesCombes Lesko spent time signing autographs and answering questions at Fan Fest in Seattle along with five other former players.

Jean Faut Fantry attended scheduled appearances at the Varsity Club in Rock Hill, South Carolina, the University of Pittsburgh, and the College of Art & Design in Savannah, Georgia, in 2003. Also in 2003, the California contingent of Maybelle Blair, Pauline Crawley, Marge Cryan, Lee Delmonico, Pepper Paire Davis, Snookie Doyle, Tiby Eisen,

Anita Foss, Annabelle Lee, Inez Voyce, and Shirley Burkovich participated in a panel discussion at a baseball exhibit featured by the Los Angeles County Natural History Museum. In the Chicago area, in 2003, Terry Donahue, Dolores Bajda, Terry Uselmann, and Ginger Gascon attended a Chicago Historical Society affair which honored the AAGPBL.

Grand Rapids, Michigan, and South Bend, Indiana, players did their part in 2003 as members of a panel discussion and autograph session at Grand Rapids' Van Andel Museum Center in conjunction with its AAGBBL exhibit. Those participating included Marilyn Jenkins, Beans Risinger, Jaynne Bittner, Mary Moore, Helen Steffes, Doris Cook, Rosemary Stevenson, Lou Arnold, and Pee Wee Wiley Sears. In California, Tiby Eisen was interviewed on the popular T.V. show, *Dinner and a Movie*, prior to the showing of *A League of Their Own*. In Atlanta, Jean Cione represented the AAGPBL at the "Women of Experience" Brunch prior to attending the Women's Final Four Basketball Championships.

In 2004, Joyce Hill Westerman participated on a panel at the University of Wisconsin–Parkside in celebration of Women's History Month. Joyce and Ann Batikis appeared at the Racine Heritage Museum in May of 2004 to share their AAGBBL experiences with third- to fifth-grade students. Fran Janssen, Betsy Jochum, and Lou Arnold gave a talk to seniors 55 and older at the Northern Indiana Center for History in South Bend in March of 2004. Vivian Kellogg spoke to a group who came to the Brooklyn branch of the Jackson District Library to hear of her AAGBBL experiences. Helen "Gig" Smith addressed a diversity conference at McLean School in Potomac, Maryland in 2004. In response to her presentation, Mr. Christopher Fusco wrote that she was outstanding, that it was a pleasure to meet her, and that they were "thrilled with both her presentation and overall message."[74]

Student Research[75]

As they were in other realms, so too were the All-Americans generous, gracious, and caring when students involved with history projects approached them for information about themselves and their experiences in the AAGBBL. Whether for book writers, like this author, or for graduate study students such as Debbie Shattuck in 1981, or college, junior high, and high school students later on, players gave of their time, energy, and materials to be of assistance. In this manner they also contributed to the promotion and preservation of their legacy.

A League of Their Own spawned young students' interest in investigating the league. The August 1992 newsletter, for instance, featured pictures, an article, and a letter from Roman Arellano's teacher. Roman, a student at Amundsen High School on the north side of Chicago, constructed a history display project on the AAGBBL with the help of Lou Arnold, Terry Donahue, Dolores Mueller Bajda, and Janet Wiley Sears. He won at two levels of the Chicago Metro Fair, and was invited to the State History Fair but was unable to attend. In the Ravenswood-Lake View History Fair, however, he won first place and $250.[76]

As other students wrote to her for help, Dottie Collins appealed to the membership to contact her if they wouldn't mind helping young people who were writing for information. Besides assisting students herself, she began acting as a match-maker to connect young students with ex-players living near them who could assist with their research. After Reg Langeman developed the AAGPBL website and coordinated with the Players' Association, most of the match-making was done through the internet. Jean Cione assumed website match-making duties in 2001. Sometimes the newsletters didn't report who helped whom, but they did report the results of the contact.

In 1994, for instance Mikell Brough-Stevenson wrote, possibly to Dottie Collins, "Thank you for your letter and all the wonderful information, it helped me win FIRST place in the History Day Fair.... Thanks a million!"—Mikell[77]

A grateful parent's letter published in the January 1999 newsletter captures the positive sentiment parents and student experienced while working with AAGPBL players:

> Just a quick note to let you know about little Jennifer whom so many of you helped when she was a mere 5th grader trying to do a research paper on the All-American Girls Professional Baseball League. On October 21st [1998] she turns 21. She is a junior at the University of Iowa where she will complete a major in Sociology this January and one in Journalism next January. Since the end of her freshman year she has been working for the Women's Sport's PR Dept. of the Univ. and this past summer her Women's Tennis Media Guide won an award for the "Best of the Big Ten Schools." She recently was asked to submit articles to a new women's sports publication which will be featured online and have separate issues pertaining to high school sports, college sports, and professional sports.
>
> Her father and I know that all of her success as a writer, and her interest in sport's media in particular, stems back to the wonderful experience of her fifth grade project. Had the 22 women whom she located and interviewed not been so encouraging and helpful she might not have discovered her talent for research and interview. Had she been able to simply go to the library and look up information in a book she would not have learned how to keep researching a subject until she found answers. It was both a trying and exciting time for her. To all the women who have crossed our lives, we, the Dudas send out gratitude and thanks.—Diana Duda[78]

Students, like Amber Jenkins and Marcie Flanagan, and Colleen, Stefanie and Amanda frequently conveyed their own gratitude.

> Dear Dottie:
>
> I pestered you last year for addresses and information for a social studies project and unfortunately, my partner and I came in second. We became determined to improve this year. With kindness and generosity of yourself and six other players, last month we were awarded First Place, Best of Division, and Grand Champions. In May we will be advancing to the state social studies fair.
>
> I wanted to thank you for being so instrumental in helping me understand, and learn about the league. Thank you so much and wish me luck.
>
> Amber Jenkins and Marcie Flanagan
> Richwood High School; Class of 2000[79]

> Thank you so much for answering our letter. We were thrilled to get all the information. It was exciting to learn that Gloria Cordes Elliott lived here too. She came over, talked to us, and gave us much information and articles and pictures to use for our project. It was so nice of her. We received a "200" on the report, and will be in our school fair. Thank you so much.
>
> Colleen — Stefanie — Amanda[80]

In 2002, AAGPBL Players' Association president Dolly White wrote to her teammates through the newsletter that the "AAGPBL continues to be a popular topic for student history reports. Our Web site puts us in contact with today's students as well as researchers seeking information about our League."[81]

In the spring of 2004, a History Day Competition was held that involved 700,000 students from all 50 states and American Samoa. Some students who focused their research on the AAGPBL fared very well. Alex Tyson's AAGPBL display won first place in the Tulare County, Wisconsin History Day. A group from Akron-Westfied Community School in Akron, Iowa, placed 11th in the nation with their project entitled, "The Girls of Summer: Paving the Way for Women in All Seasons." They performed their project at the national competition at the University of Maryland where they were awarded the opportunity to perform again at the Smithsonian Museum of American History in Washington, D.C.[82]

Erin Schmidt, a thirteen-year-old from Haven, Kansas, won second place in her History Day Regional Competition and second place in the Kansas State Competition with her project, "The Women of the AAGPBL: Exploring a New Game of Baseball." Her second place at the state competition earned Erin the opportunity to display her project at the National History Day Competition at the University of Maryland where she was awarded a bronze medal. Erin's project was also selected for display at the Smithsonian. She was surprised when a reporter and photographer from the *Wichita Eagle* interviewed her at the Smithsonian and an article about her AAGBBL project appeared on the paper's front page the next day. In addition, the day at the Smithsonian garnered its own personal rewards for her:

> I had many people, both young and old stop by to look at [my display] and ask questions. I even heard one gentleman say to his wife that it was the most interesting display at the museum even though it wasn't a permanent display.[83]

Ex-AAGPBL player Joyce McCoy, who lived close by, personally worked with Erin to help organize all the information players shared with her. In the May 2004 AAGPBL Newsletter, Erin expressed her gratitude to all those who helped her win her awards "by giving their time to respond to her questions and sending pictures and items for her to display:"

> Gert Alderfer, Bea Arbour, Lou Arnold, Helen Austin, Annastasia Batikis, Wilma Briggs, Wimp Baumgartner, Delores Brumfield White, Shirley Burkovich, Erma M. Bergmann, Dottie Collins, Alice Deschaine, Cartha Doyle, Marilyn Doxey, Edna Dummerth, Thelma Eisen, Gloria Elliott, Lou Erickson, Jean Havlish, Alice Hohlmayer, Joan Holderness, Katie Horstman, Betsy Jochum, Vivian Kellogg, Maxine Kline, Dolly Konwinski, Marie Kruckel, Sophie Kurys, Marie Mansfield, Joyce McCoy, Jane Moffet, Anna O'Dowd, June Peppas, Grace Piskula, Mamie Redman, Violet Schmidt, Janet Sears, Ellen Tronnier, and Mary Wisham.[84]

Erin noted that she mailed out 65 questionnaires and received 47 back "along with signed baseball cards." Forty of the players also sent signed baseballs or softballs to use in her exhibit. In addition, Erin noted that they sent newspaper clippings, copies of team pictures, and a program. Joyce McCoy, her mentor, provided Erin with a copy of her Hall of Fame certificate, a letter written home to her mother, and a copy of her first check stub. As part of her project, Erin interviewed several players by phone, including Lou Arnold, Wimp Baumgartner, Betsy Jochum, Dolly Konwinski, Sophie Kurys (who gave her advice on improving her own play), Jane Moffet, and Dolly White.

Besides the student history competitions, Erin's research led to additional opportunities. She was interviewed by the curator of the Reno County Museum for a quarterly magazine article, she was asked to display her work and give a presentation at a local business women's meeting, and she graciously shared her experiences with this writer.

Erin, as previously noted, was extremely thankful for the widespread assistance she

Erin Schmidt with her AAGPBL History Project (courtesy of Erin Schmidt).

received from the All-Americans and explained that she felt she was "very fortunate to have made friends with these pioneers of women's sports and honored that they would help me tell their story and take an active interest in my project."[85] Erin maintained contact with some of the All-Americans who helped her at the end of her history competitions. She was especially thrilled when Joyce McCoy attended one of her softball games at the Twelve and Under World Tournament in Hutchinson, Kansas. She also enjoyed an extra special experience when Alice "Lefty" Hohlmayer McNaughton "called and asked me to meet her at a 14 and 16 and under tournament that she was invited to attend in Blue Springs, Mo. It was very thrilling to meet her and her son Shawn and hear her stories about her years in the league."[86] At this writing, Erin planned to keep in touch with the AAGPBL friends she made and to continue to share her work with others.

Erin's experience with the All-Americans is just one example of their willingness to go the extra mile for students on a yearly basis. For more than a decade, All-Americans, like those who helped Erin, enriched students' lives and provided relationships that had far reaching effects. They are to be commended for their magnanimous natures.

On the other hand, the All-Americans confirmed that they, too, were rewarded by their interaction with students. Their personal rewards extended to their association. Students who researched the league will never forget the players who helped them or the All-American Girls' Baseball League. Like Erin, they will pass their knowledge and love of the league on to others and to the next generation. They may even become the next generation of associate members to carry the Players' Association into the future.

Summary

The Executive Boards of the AAGPBL's Players' Association carried through with the purposes the organization's founders visualized in 1987. They committed themselves to preserving and perpetuating the AAGPBL's history; to publishing a regular newsletter to maintain contact with each other; to scheduling and promoting regular reunions for the social benefit of the membership; and to presenting a unified, historically accurate picture of the league and of themselves to the media and to the public.

The Executive Boards and the Directors of the Players' Association diligently pursued and accomplished objectives they set for themselves. They supervised the completion of the lifetime roster, established an archives, gained recognition by the Baseball Hall of Fame, and successfully negotiated a major motion picture depicting their playing days.

The realization of these objectives lead to the formulation and realization of others. Among them were the establishment of flexible policies and procedures for the association's governance, contracting for baseball cards, protecting their marks and logos, and establishing an oral history record of their individual and collective experiences.

They determined to keep their history alive through the establishment and maintenance of a web page; coordination of educational programs with the Baseball Hall of Fame; and setting up a viable, nationwide network of ex-players who generously donated their time, energy, and expertise to benefit others and ultimately to benefit their association. They perceived the historical value in promoting the erection of a life-sized statue commemorating the AAGBBL at the Baseball Hall of Fame, of planning for the production of an historically thorough and accurate documentary, and of providing for the association's future by involving non-playing members in its governance. They planned to

AAGPBL 2005 Office Depot Visionary Sports Awards Presentation Attendees. *Standing, left to right:* Joan Holderness, Sue Zipay, Helen "Gig" Smith, Katie Horstman, Dolly Konwinski, Jean Faut Fantry. *Seated, left to right:* Sue Macy (AAGPBL Associate Member and Board Secretary), Jane Moffet (AAGPBL Board Treasurer), and Marilyn "Jonesy" Jones Doxey.

maintain contact with, and support emerging women's baseball programs in the United States. Their hope has always been that future generations of girls and women would have the opportunity to play baseball as they did in the 1940s and 1950s.

To the credit of the individual members of the Players' Association, they cooperated in publicizing, promoting and perpetuating their legacy by unselfishly giving of themselves to benefit others. They graced many occasions with their presence and signed innumerable autographs at benefits, meetings, and softball and baseball events. Many actively encouraged young students to discover and display the league's unique place in history. To their credit as outstanding people, they were widely honored for what they contributed to their communities when their playing years ended. Collectively, the members of the AAGPBL Players' Association truly functioned in "A League of Their Own" as athletes and as the best humanity has to offer.

How fitting, then, that the AAGPBL Players' Association was honored on February 28, 2005, as recipient of Office Depot's "Sports Visionary Award." This award was established to "recognize women whose extraordinary dedication, vision, leadership and commitment have helped to change the lives of so many women."[87] It was presented at the Gala Visionary Award Dinner of Office Depot's "Success Strategies for Businesswomen Conference." Notable keynote presenters at the conference included author and poet Maya Angelou, ABC's Barbara Walters, Chief designer Kathy Ireland, and Xerox's Chairman and CEO, Anne Mulcahy.

The award was presented by Cheryl Crocker, Office Depot's Regional Vice President of Stores, to player spokesperson Katie Horstman. Other AAGPBL players in attendance included Marilyn "Jonesy" Jones Doxey, Helen "Gig" Smith, Jean Faut Fantry, Jane Moffet, Dolly Konwinski, Joan Holderness, and Sue Zipay. They were accompanied by associate member and AAGPBL Board secretary Sue Macy.

True to form, the AAGPBL's player representatives met people at the regular conference events and were scheduled to sign autographs for a half hour on the last day of the conference. Once again, they demonstrated their willingness to go above and beyond what was required. AAGPBL Board secretary Sue Macy observed:

> At the beginning of the [autograph] session, Office Depot started playing *A League of Their Own* on a TV monitor. When [the players] finally stopped signing autographs, the closing credits of the film were playing. They'd signed for almost two hours, and people had skipped the last session to stand in line waiting for autographs. The line went halfway around a huge ballroom![88]

These players and their league mates were great athletes, and they are great people. Office Depot's presentation of the "Sports Visionary Award" to the AAGPBL Players' Association was a wonderful tribute to their extraordinary qualities.

PART VI

Summation

Dorothy "Snookie" Harrell Doyle. Autograph signing had just begun (courtesy Snookie Doyle).

18

Summary and Conclusions

The All-American Girls Baseball League, 1943–1954

The All-American Girls Softball League (AAGSBL) emerged from the onset of World War II and the development of softball as a sport for American women between 1900 and 1940. It is unlikely the AAGSBL would have been created if organized softball had not become a popular sport for American women by the early 1940s. League administrators needed a player talent pool to draw from, and they found it in the many amateur and semi-professional women's softball leagues that materialized in the U.S. and Canada by the late 1930s. These leagues found their genesis primarily through the efforts of national softball organizations and playground and industrial recreation programs.

With the talent pool in place, the creation of the AAGSBL was stimulated by the manpower demands of World War II which threatened the existence of men's Major League Baseball. The potential wartime demise of Major League Baseball presented a possible void in major league parks. For baseball team owner Philip K. Wrigley, a logical alternative was to replace men's baseball with a similar, already popular sport employing women participants. That sport was softball.

Philip K. Wrigley, entrepreneur and owner of the Chicago Cubs, established the AAGSBL as a professional organization. However, he based its administrative structure on a non-profit rather than a profit-based foundation. Given the wartime social climate, he felt this was the most honorable tack to follow. Wrigley employed professional personnel to administer the league; he utilized a professional advertising agency to promote it; he hired ex–professional baseball players as managers; and he paid players a professional wage to devote themselves exclusively to playing baseball during the season.

The AAGSBL was a league of teams established in specific Midwestern cities to play on a regularly scheduled basis almost every day for three to four months of the year. This is what distinguished the AAGSBL from the barnstorming Bloomer Girl Baseball Teams which entertained crowds beginning in the 1890s, or basektball's Red Heads, who became a popular touring attraction in the 1940s.[1] The AAGSBL was unique. It was America's first, non-barnstorming, professional *team* sport for women. Shortly after its creation, it was renamed the All-American Girls Professional Ball League (AAGPBL) to distinguish it from softball.

The AAGSBL/AAGPBL utilized Major League Baseball rules for spectator appeal, except for underhand pitching and shorter pitching and base path distances. The league employed softball's underhand pitching exclusively until 1946, when sidearm pitching was introduced. In 1946 the league's name was changed to reflect the rules it played by, and it was thereafter identified as the All-American Girls Base Ball League (AAGBBL).

In 1948, full overhand pitching was instituted and this change finalized the league's identity as a women's professional *baseball* league. The only differences between the AAG-BBL game and men's Major League Baseball at this point were shorter base paths (72 feet) and pitching distance (50 feet) and a slightly larger ball (10⅜ inches). Since the AAGBBL employed Major League Baseball rules to govern its games, the game it played after 1947 can be considered to have been as truly "baseball" as either Little League or high school or college "baseball." In 1954, the differences in ball size and pitching distance were eradicated and only a five-foot difference in the base path distance remained. Thus, although the league started as a softball league, after 1947 it truly became a baseball league. Not all women softball players could play AAGBBL baseball, but those who could played it well.

Initially, the AAGSBL was administered by a Board of Trustees comprised of Philip K. Wrigley, Branch Rickey, and Paul V. Harper. Branch Rickey served mostly as a figurehead, so for all practical purposes, the league operated under the aegis of Wrigley and Harper. Ken Sells, former assistant to the Cubs' general manager, was appointed by the Trustees as the league's first president. He was largely responsible for the day-to-day administrative duties associated with the league from its inception in early 1943 until the end of the 1944 season. Sells played a key role in persuading Wrigley to place the operation of the league under his command for the 1944 season when Wrigley contemplated disbanding the girls' league with the survival of men's baseball. The governance of the league during the Trustee Administration was largely autocratic, although team sponsors were consulted on some matters.

The Trustee Administration (1943–1944) was largely characterized by what Wrigley considered high standards of professionalism and intensive and extensive publicity and promotion. The league's non-profit, trustee structure also gave it an aura of benevolence. These characteristics, coupled with the employment of team chaperones and publicity themes of "Recreation for War Workers," "Community Welfare," "Family Entertainment," and "Femininity," were designed to give the league a favorable public image and broaden its spectator appeal. The Trustees' enlistment of leading citizens in league cities as team guarantors can only have aided this effort.

At the end of the 1944 season, Wrigley sold the AAGPBL to his advertising agent, Arthur E. Meyerhoff. Meyerhoff established a "Management" superstructure to administer league affairs. Whereas "The League" remained a non-profit organization, "Management" was established as a profit-based organization. Meyerhoff organized a League Board of Directors, comprised of team presidents, to govern league affairs. In this way he democratized the league's governance system. With the assistance of league presidents Max Carey and Fred Leo and the League Board of Directors, Meyerhoff administered the league from 1945–1950.

The Management Corporation Administration (1945–1950) largely reflected the philosophy and practices of the Trustees, but was further characterized by experimentation with game changes, extensive and varied publicity programs, and extensive player procurement programs. These programs were accompanied by extensive expenditures, which team management became less and less able or willing to afford as wartime business affluence decreased.

At the end of the 1950 season, team presidents chose to sever relationships with Meyerhoff's Management Corporation and to administer their teams on an independent basis in the interest of economizing. In so doing, they severed many of the cooperative ties that had bound the league together from its inception, including a centralized promotional program and centralized player procurement and allocation programs. They did, however, retain the League Board of Directors, the centralized league governing body established by Meyerhoff.

The Independent Team Owners Administration (1951–1954) was characterized by economic retrenchment through decentralization of league affairs. Scouting, publicity, and personnel were the three main areas in which league control was relegated to team control after 1950. Player salaries decreased and pre-season training excursions were restricted to local areas. Post-season tours were also discontinued between 1951 and 1954. Despite these efforts to economize, AAGBBL team administrators could not make ends meet, and the league folded at the end of the 1954 season. During its twelve years of operation, however, it became a recognized part of community life in its Midwestern cities.

The Success and Decline of the AAGBBL

The All-American Girls Baseball League was more than a novelty. To be sure, it first appeared as a novelty, and in those cities in which it survived a season or less, it can be considered to have remained a novelty. However, in communities such as Racine, Kenosha, South Bend, Rockford, Peoria, Fort Wayne, Grand Rapids, and Kalamazoo, it was more than that. As one Grand Rapids historian pointed out, the "All-American Girls Baseball League received tremendous community support for several years," and "names such as Gabby Ziegler and Connie Wisniewski became household words."[2]

Based on high moral and professional standards of the day, and supported and promoted by leading businessmen to fill a spectator entertainment need for the benefit of their communities, the AAGBBL attracted a diverse audience. It appealed to all ages and both sexes, and it became family entertainment. More importantly, the very durability of its existence in more than a half dozen Midwestern cities attested to the fact that it attracted a clientele of considerable proportions. One cannot escape asking why it achieved this measure of success, and why the success declined.

To answer a question with a question, why does any spectator sport flourish and endure, then disintegrate? Is a spectator sport's success based on its ability to maintain a balance between its internal policies and changing external social conditions? This at least seems to help account for the fate of the All-American Girls Baseball League. The interaction between the league's internal policies and external conditions affords a basis for analyzing the AAGBBL's success and decline.

First of all, the AAGBBL's existence was based on the availability of a large talent base in the form of thousands of amateur and semi-professional women's softball teams. When the league began operations in 1943 as the All-American Girls Softball League, the rules established by league administrators to govern play did not appreciably restrict this talent pool. It was in 1948, when league administrators implemented overhand pitching for purposes of spectator appeal, that the league lost its broad base of player talent. Most women of the time had obtained their early playing experience in softball and had difficulty adjusting to the longer distances and different pitching style employed by the AAGBBL game.

When the league first began, considerable funds and effort were expended to obtain the best available talent throughout the United States and Canada. This practice was expanded during Management's tenure, not only through the establishment of a nationwide system of scouts, but also through spring training tours, summer barnstorming tours, and post-season exhibition tours. Just three years after the league adopted overhand pitching, the AAGBBL's centralized player procurement program was abolished. This event severely limited teams' abilities to obtain the best available players throughout the continent. The logical outcome of this eventuality was a decline in the caliber of player skills, which in turn affected the game's spectator appeal. Thus, AAGBBL administrators committed two fundamental tactical errors in their player procurement program as time progressed: (1) They inaugurated a game beyond the experience of their talent pool, and (2) they progressively restricted, rather than expanded, their scouting programs. In essence, internal policies became inconsistent with external realities.

From 1943 to 1946, the AAGBBL was an innovative, entrepreneurial leisure-time enterprise that took advantage of peculiar wartime conditions. Arthur Cole observed that such enterprises are based on two fundamental conditions, a populace's available leisure time and its available discretionary income.[3] The amount of leisure time the inhabitants of AAGBBL cities had during the war isn't known, though one observer noted that 48-hour work weeks were the rule.[4] If this was the case, the amount of leisure time available in AAGBBL cities wouldn't have been great, but the number of leisure activities available to people during the war weren't great either. In addition, gasoline and rubber rationing meant that inhabitants' pleasure-seeking was largely restricted to local areas. At the same time, because of restrictions on consumer goods, the populace of AAGBBL cities had considerable discretionary income since they were, for the most part, employed in war industries. Under these conditions of significant discretionary income and circumscribed leisure time, the AAGBBL commanded a captive audience.

It must be recalled that early AAGBBL administrators exerted every publicity and promotional effort to attract available audiences. Toward this end they utilized daily press coverage and compelling social themes such as "Femininity," "Recreation for War Workers," "Community Welfare," and "Family Entertainment." However, in 1949, when travel restrictions were lifted, when strikes and unemployment hit league cities,[5] and when other commercial leisure-time activities began to proliferate, league administrators began cutting their publicity and promotional budgets. What was needed at this time were more expenditures for promotion and publicity to keep the AAGBBL in a competitive position with other growing leisure-time attractions. The league's internal policies on this matter were based on the need to economize, not on the need to meet the demands of changing external social conditions.

Then came television. Television brought ever popular Major League Baseball and other professional sports into the everyday grasp of ever-increasing segments of the population by 1950. Television is considered to have contributed directly to the decline of minor league baseball in the 1950s, but even though some minor leagues disintegrated with the advent of television, others had major league teams to subsidize them — possibly from television income.[6] In 1954, the AAGBBL, sometimes equated with AA minor league ball, had neither a parent organization nor a multimillion-dollar owner to subsidize it.

Had Wrigley remained committed to the league, and better still, had he been able to persuade other baseball magnates to become involved in and remain committed to the AAGBBL, the league could have weathered the financial storms it met between 1949 and 1954. As it was, the AAGBBL's backers were businessmen in mid-sized cities with considerably less discretionary income than Philip Wrigley. With the loss of war industry contracts, they became increasingly dependent on short-term returns. Financially they could not remain committed to the AAGBBL's long-term survival despite any reluctance they may have felt in relinquishing their interests in the league. Unfortunately, changes among the league's administrative personnel did not prove conducive to its ability to cope with changing external financial conditions.

Less obvious, but contributing something to the league's success and decline was its position on equalized competition. Under Wrigley and Meyerhoff, players were owned by the league and allocated to teams with the forethought of giving every team as equal a share as possible of the available talent to insure every team's success rather than one team's success. This was important for a "one-of-its-kind" league. There was evidence to support the position that team presidents chafed at this principle of enforced cooperation. After the 1950 season, when team sponsors bought out Meyerhoff's interests in the league, they dispensed with the allocation system in favor of an "each-team-for-itself" policy of player procurement. It wasn't until 1954 and the loss of several franchises too low in league standings that Independent Team Owners realized unregulated competition seldom produces the best results. They also failed to see that the vulnerability of the AAGBBL to changing economic conditions required more, rather than less, equalization of competition and intra-league cooperation.

Finally, there is the vague realm of the AAGBBL's social image to consider. Given the fact that the AAGBBL was created in the middle of World War II, when women were involved in nearly every occupation imaginable except fighting at the front, it was important for administrators to emphasize femininity in league publicity, conduct rules, uniforms, and the institution of chaperones. Perhaps all of this early emphasis on femininity was just an obsession of its upper class administrators and had no real impact on league communities. Perhaps. However, when one considers that the league existed in cities believed by some to be the "Bible Belt" of the Midwest,[7] then the femininity image that league administrators attempted to establish contains considerably greater importance.

It is difficult to say whether league administrators emphasized femininity less as time progressed. It wasn't emphasized less in publicity materials published in national, trade, and sport magazines, but it wasn't strongly emphasized in league city newspapers after 1943. Some observers saw league administrators' willingness to exchange full-time chaperones for part-time chaperones in the 1950s as a de-emphasis on femininity.[8] Whether the public was even aware of, or cared about, this change is debatable. A few ex-players suggested that, internally, administrative emphasis on femininity did decrease with time,[9] which may or may not have been sensed by the public. These things can only be conjectured now. However, if the emphasis on femininity was a vital factor in the league's public acceptance during wartime, when rigid social expectations for women were relaxed, then an equally strong emphasis on the league's feminine image would have been more important in the postwar period when an emphasis on the narrow social role for women resurfaced. Relaxing of the league policy of emphasizing femininity, if in fact it did occur, would have been one more incident contributing to the observation that internal league policies were out of sync with external social conditions.

If one were limited to citing just one of these several factors that contributed to the league's decline, then changes in administrators' financial resources, coupled with changes in the external economy, would have to be selected as that one factor. As discussed previously, however, there were other discrepancies between internal league policy and external social conditions that contributed to the league's decline. It seems the best explanation of the league's extinction considers all of these factors together, rather than one alone.

Future Considerations

It is tempting to apply lessons of the past to present and future conditions, but this inclination must be resisted since the present never completely replicates the past, nor the future the present. However, general guidelines can be elicited from past events for present and future instruction. Such guidelines can be extracted from the AAGBBL experience for present and future attempts to establish women's professional team sports. The most important of these would seem to be:

1. Establish a strong internal structure including:
    a. dependable and long-range financial backing;
    b. employment of professional administrative personnel;
    c. establishment of the broadest possible player procurement program to obtain the best possible talent;
    d. establishment of and maintenance of an extensive publicity and promotional program;
    e. development of some means of equalizing competition among teams, and make sure the participants are aware of the rationale for equalization.
2. Conduct an evaluation of the social context into which the activity is to be injected, including research to affirm:
    a. the extent of the talent base;
    b. the potential audiences' discretionary time, income, attitudes, and alternative leisure-time options.
3. Constantly evaluate the social milieu and implement procedures to adjust to major social changes. Communicate these adjustments to the players.
4. Immediately institute and support programs to maintain and enlarge the existing talent pool.

The history of the AAGBBL provides a model of a women's professional team sport that enjoyed social approbation and considerable success. It asserts that similar present and future endeavors have potential for success. Given proper research, committed and financially secure administrators, and intelligent organization, women's professional team sports can become viable spectator attractions.

Those of us who never viewed an AAGBBL game first-hand need only discuss the league briefly with a participant or eyewitness to conclude that we "really missed something."

> When I knew that the AAGBBL had played its last game, it was the saddest day of my life because I knew nobody was going to see that game again, or those uniforms again, or those girls again, playing so well. It was a once in a lifetime thing, that's the way I felt.
> — Dorothy Hunter
> Grand Rapids Chicks Chaperone
> 3 January 1976

Beyond the Playing Field, 1980–2004

When Dorothy Hunter, ex-player and chaperone, lamented the demise of the All-American Girls Baseball League during an interview with this author in 1976, neither of us, nor any of Dorothy's AAGBBL colleagues, had any idea the whole country — indeed, the whole world — would have the opportunity to see that game and those uniforms again. *A League of Their Own* could not portray the real-life expertise the All-Americans displayed. However, the silver screen trumpeted their existence and conveyed a credible account of their history across continents as no other medium could have done.

The advent of the feminist movement in the 1970s inspired a renewed interest in women's history in colleges and universities throughout the U.S. It helped motivate this author and Sharon Roepke to follow their love of baseball/softball by traveling into the past to rediscover and reveal the AAGBBL to themselves and their acquaintances. In so doing, they stirred the hearts and minds of action-oriented All-Americans to contemplate the joys of reassociating with former teammates.

Dorothy "Kammie" Kamenshek, Marge Wenzell, and June Peppas visualized a reunion. June Peppas created the newsletter in 1980 as a vehicle through which she could reconnect with her teammates and reconnect them with each other after 25 to 35 years. Ruth Davis, a former AAGBBL bat girl, accepted the challenge of organizing that First National Reunion. When June decided to relinquish the newsletter after the Chicago reunion, it was kept alive by Shirley Stovroff and Lavone "Pepper" Paire Davis. Dottie Collins assumed publication of the newsletter at the end of 1986 and passed it on to Jeneane DesCombes Lesko at the end of 2000. This lifeline kept players connected and helped rebuild their common identity.

After the 1982 Chicago reunion, other players began setting objectives. Dottie Collins, especially, determined that the All-Americans should hold more reunions, establish an archive, and pursue recognition by the Hall of Fame. The Fort Wayne Women's Bureau's "Run, Jane, Run" events made annual mini-reunions in Fort Wayne a natural. Then Dottie and her Fort Wayne colleagues organized the Second National Reunion, where documentarians Kelly Candaele, Kim Wilson, and Janis Taylor filmed the first historical league documentaries.

Pursuit of recognition by the Hall of Fame increased and a positive response from Ted Spencer scrambled All-Americans into action. Enter Karen Violetta Kunkel, whose personal history provided the acumen for organizing, and for determining purposes and objectives — whose educational resources provided an environment for cataloguing and collecting memorabilia for a Hall of Fame Exhibit. Add Fran Janssen, Earlene "Beans" Risinger, Jean Harding, and June Peppas, and many others (see Appendix 1) who were all willing to devote time, energy, expertise, and personal resources to achieve desired goals. Mix in John Kovach from the Northern Indiana Historical Society and South Bend Blue Sox players Lib Mahon, Betsy Jochum, Fran Janssen again, Lou Arnold, and Pee Wee Wiley Sears who helped establish the AAGBBL archives.

Now the snowball effect took over. Penny Marshall and other producers saw the Candaele/Wilson documentary, *A League of Their Own*. Longbow Productions won the Player Association Board's agreement to produce a feature film. The Baseball Hall of Fame recognized the AAGBBL on November 5, 1988. Penny Marshall was there to observe and mingle with the players. She decided she wanted to co-produce the movie.

When completed, *A League of Their Own* was a huge success and the players began reaping the recognition, honors, and awards they so richly deserved. They took pride in and ownership of their association and did everything they could to publicize, promote, and perpetuate the legacy that mushroomed into a living, breathing entity.

The All-Americans didn't fold up shop, go home and pull down the shades after *A League of Their Own* played out its run. As of this writing, they kept attending reunions and supporting and promoting their association by donating their time, energy, and resources to attend all manner of events and meetings. They supported their association leaders' goals and objectives. Their Executive Boards established a strong, yet flexible organization that registered and protected their marks and logos. They assumed responsibility for a web site initiated voluntarily by Reg Langeman, a "new" Canadian fan. They joined with the Baseball Hall of Fame and Ball State University to produce an educational history program that reached approximately 20 million students worldwide. They persuaded the Baseball Hall of Fame to erect a statue in their honor. They were honored by the White House. They pursued the production of an historically accurate documentary film to be used for educational purposes. They supported and promoted emerging women's baseball programs. They perceived the need to train those who respect and admire their heritage to take over when they are gone. They did everything within their power to perpetuate their legacy so that Dorothy Hunter's lament over the near-extinction of their experience would never again be voiced.

They were, they are, they will always be P.K. Wrigley's All-American Girls. Their hearts join in singing "We're all for one, We're one for all, We're All-Americans." Philip Wrigley, Ken Sells, Arthur Meyerhoff, Max Carey, Fred Leo, Judge Ruetz, Earle McCammon, Harold Van Orman, and all their team sponsors, managers, chaperones, and fans must be very proud.

PART VII

Appendices

Rhubarb at home plate — *Left to right:* Umpire Gadget Ward, Dottie Naum, Merle Keagle (reproduced from the original held by the Department of Special Collections of the University Libraries of Notre Dame).

Appendix 1: AAGPBL Players' Association Offices and Committee Positions Held, 1980–2004

Newsletter Editors

1980–1982	June Peppas
1983	Shirley Stovroff
1984–1986	Lavone "Pepper" Paire Davis
1987	Dottie Wiltse Collins, Lavone "Pepper" Paire Davis
1988–1989	Dottie Collins
1990	Dottie Collins, Sandy Oberpheltzer
1991–1923	Dottie Collins, Mary "Wimp" Baumgartner
1994–2000	Dottie Collins
2001–2004	Jeneane DesCombes Lesko

National Reunion Committees

(Some committee members may not be listed due to lack of information.)

1982 **Chicago, IL:** Ruth Davis

1986 **Fort Wayne, IN:** Dottie Collins, Mary "Wimp" Baumgartner, Isabel "Lefty" Alvarez, Helen Harrington, Harold Greiner, Dona Schaefer

1988 **Scottsdale, AZ:** Sophie Kurys, Nickie Fox, and Connie Wisniewski

1988 **Cooperstown, NY:** Ruth Heverly Williams

1991 **Clearwater, FL:** Barbara Sowers

1993 **South Bend, IN:** Nancy Rockwell, Fran Janssen, Lou Arnold, Elizabeth "Lib" Mahon, Betsy Jochum, Twila Shively

1995 **Indian Wells, CA:** Thelma "Tiby" Eisen, Maybelle Blair, Lillian Faralla, Jean Faut Eastman

1997 **Myrtle Beach, SC:** Jean Faut Eastman, Helen "Gig" Smith, Ruby Heafner, Mildred Meacham, Delores "Dolly" Brumfield White, Barbara Parks Young

1998 **Palm Springs, CA:** Maybelle Blair, Donna McLain, Shirley Burkovich, Pauline "Hedy" Crawley, Dorothy "Snookie" Doyle, Maymie DePrima, Phyllis Gallagher, Thelma "Tiby" Eisen, Peggy Mack, Mary Lou Swangan

2000 **Milwaukee, WI:** Jackie Baumgart, Ellen Tronnier, Annastasia Batikis, Mike Corona, Mardi Timm, Joyce Hill, Jean Kowalkowski

2001 **Grand Rapids, MI:** Dolly Konwinski, Marilyn Jenkins, Earlene "Beans" Risinger, Doris Cook

2002 **South Bend, IN:** Fran Janssen, Betsy Jochum, Lou Arnold, Janet "Pee Wee" Wiley Sears, Lucy Sears, Nancy DeShone Dinehart

2003 **Syracuse, NY:** Shelley McCann, Vita Lobdell, Tim Wiles, Lisa Tamilia, Jenny Brown, Kristine Fernandez, Gail Dean, Karen Kockenbery

2004 **Kalamazoo, MI:** Ede Moody, Susan Beechler, Mark DiMeglio, Liz Lake, Karen Christensen, Sandy Kristen, Janet Pfau, Izzy Forester

AAGPBL Executive Boards: 1987–2004

1987–1990

President	June Peppas
Vice. Pres.	Fran Janssen

Secretary   Jean GeissingerHarding
Treasurer   Dottie Wiltse Collins
Parliament.   Earlene Risinger
                 Karen Violetta Kunkel: Devel-
                 opment Officer ('87); Public
                 Relations Ch. ('88); Archives
                 Director ('88); Executive
                 Director and Movie Advisor
                 ('90–92)

1991–1992

President   Joan Holderness
Exec. V.P.   Barbara Liebrich ('91);
                 Kate Voderau ('92)
Assist. V.P.   Mary "Wimp" Baumgartner
                 ('91); Barbara Sowers ('92)
Secretary   Jean Geissinger Harding
Treasurer   Dottie Wiltse Collins
Sgt. at Arms   Wilma Briggs ('91); Barbara
                 Liebrich ('92)

1993–1998

President   Mary "Wimp" Baumgartner
Exec. V.P.   Kate Vonderau ('93); Jean Faut
                 Eastman ('94–'95); Sue Zipay
                 ('96); Joyce Smith ('97–'98)
Assist. V.P.   Barbara Sowers ('93); Nancy
                 Rockwell ('94–'95); Jean Faut
                 Eastman ('96); Sue Zipay
                 ('97–'98)
Secretary   Jean Geissinger Harding
Treasurer   Dottie Wiltse Collins
Sgt. at Arms   Wilma Briggs

1999–2004

President   Delores "Dolly" Brumfield
                 White
Vice Pres.   Jean Cione
Secretary   Jean Geissinger Harding
                 ('99–'00); Sue Macy ('01–'04)
Treasurer   Dottie Wiltse Collins
                 ('99–'00); Jane Moffet
                 ('01–'04)
Representative   Jean Faut Eastman Fantry
                 ('99–'02); Jeanie DesCombes
                 Lesko ('03'); Representative
                 Mary Pratt ('99–'00); Jean
                 Geissinger Harding ('01);
                 Shirley Burkovich ('02–03)

AAGPBL Directors

1987–1990
Wilma Briggs

Faye Dancer
Lillian Jackson
Arleene Johnson Noga
Joanne Winter

1991

Dolores Moore
Faye Dancer
Lillian Jackson
Arleene Johnson Noga
Blanche Schachter
Terry McKinley Uselmann

1992

Wilma Briggs
Faye Dancer
Lillian Jackson
Arleene Johnson Noga
Blanche Schachter
Mary "Wimp" Baumgartner

1993

Barbara Liebrich
Faye Dancer
Lillian Jackson
Arleene Johnson Noga
Dottie Green/Gloria Cordes Elliott
Jean Faut Eastman

1994

Joan Holderness
Thelma "Tiby" Eisen
Lillian Jackson
Arleene Johnson Noga
Gloria Cordes Elliott
Joyce Smith

1995

Sue Zipay
Thelma "Tiby" Eisen
Lillian Jackson
Arleene Johnson Noga
Gloria Cordes Elliott
Joyce Smith

1996

Nancy Rockwell
Thelma "Tiby" Eisen
Dolores Lee Dries
Arleene Johnson Noga
Gloria Cordes Elliott
Joyce Smith

1997

Nancy Rockwell
Thelma "Tiby" Eisen
Dolores Lee Dries
Arleene Johnson Noga
Gloria Cordes Elliott
Jean Faut Eastman

1998

Nancy Rockwell
Thelma "Tiby" Eisen
Dolores Lee Dries
Arleene Johnson Noga
Gloria Cordes Elliott
Jean Faut Eastman

Ex Officio / Advisors

1987–1991

Lynn Haber
Sue Macy
Sharon Taylor-Roepke
Dona Schaefer

Media / Area Representatives

1987–1993

East	Ruth Williams Heverly
Midwest	Dorothy Schroeder
Canada	Evelyn Wawryshyn Moroz
South	Jean Faut Eastman
Midsouth	Rita Meyer "Slats" Moellering
West	Marge Villa Cryan
Chicago	Terry Donahue (1990–1993)

1994–1995

East	Maddy English, Joan Knebl, Mary Pratt
Midwest	Dorothy Niemiec Konwinski, Ede Moody
Canada	Mary Baker
South	Adelline Kerrar
Southwest	Joanne Winter, Betty Tucker
West	Dorothy Kamenshek, Annabelle Lee Harmon

Archives Committees

1987	Elizabeth "Lib" Mahon
1988	Karen Violetta Kunkel
1989	Karen Violetta Kunkel

1990–1998	Fran Janssen, Ch., Lib Mahon, Betsy Jochum, Twila Shively, Lou Arnold
1999–2004	Fran Janssen, Ch.

History Committees

1987–1989	Joanne Winter, Marilyn Jenkins, Dottie Green
1989	Joanne Winter, June Peppas, June Emerson

Lost All-Americans Committees

1987	Dottie Collins, Nancy "Hank" Warren, June Emerson, Dottie Schroeder, Fran Janssen, Maxine Kline
1990	Ellen Tronnier, Marjorie Peters, Sheri Kadlec
1991–1994	Ellen Tronnier, Marjorie Peters, Betty Moczynski, Therese McKinley Uselmann

Hall of Fame Reunion Liaison

1988	Ruth Williams Heverly, Chairman

Nominating Committees

1989	Doris Cook, Marilyn Jenkins, Renae Youngberg
1991–1992	Vivian Kellogg, Jaynne Bittner, Jean Cione
1993	Gloria Cordes Elliott, Betty Trezza, Ruth Williams Heverly
1994	Renae Youngberg, Sue Zippay, Delores "Dolly" Brumfield White
1995	Renae Youngberg, Ch.
1996	Marie "Blackie" Wegman, Ch.
1997–1998	Gloria Cordes Elliott, Ch.
1999	On Hold
2001–2004	Nancy DeShone Dinehart

Statistician / Computer Records

1989–1993	Joan Holderness
1994	Joan Holderness, Dottie Wiltse Collins
1995	Dottie Collins, Nancy Rockwell
1996–1998	Dottie Collins, Nancy Rockwell,

Marie "Blackie" Wegman,
Jackie Cox

1999–2000	Mardi Timm
2001	Jean Cione
2002	Jean Cione, Cyn Hales
2003	Jean Cione
2004	Jane Moffet

Accountant

1989–1993	Pat Barringer
1994–2004	Professional Accountants

Policy and Procedure Manual

1990–1993	Mary "Wimp" Baumgartner, Joyce Smith
1994	Joyce Smith

Budget Committees

1990	Executive Board
1991–1993	Dottie Wiltse Collins, Pat Barringer, Joan Holland, Fran Janssen
1994–1998	Dottie Collins, Joan Holland, Fran Janssen
1999–2000	Dottie Collins, Ch.
2001–2004	Jane Moffet, Ch.

By-Laws Committees

1990	Fran Janssen, Rick Chapman, Joyce Smith

Saleable Items

1990–1992	Nancy "Hank" Warren
1993	Elizabeth "Lib" Mahon
1994–1996	Dottie Wiltse Collins
1997–1998	Dottie Collins, Marie "Blackie" Wegman, Lib Mahon
1999–2001	Shirley Burkovich

Humanitarian Committee

1990–1993	Helen Filarski Steffes, Connie Wisniewski, Carol Habben, Dolores Lee Dries, Marge Callaghan Maxwell, Helene Machado Van Sant
1996–2000	Helen Filarski Steffes, Ch.
2002–2004	Shirley Burkovich

5-Year Plan Committee

1991	Jean Geissinger Harding, Joan Holderness, Joyce Smith

Legislative Committees

1991–1992	Barbara Liebrich, Rick Chapman
1994	Joyce Smith, Nancy Rockwell
1995	Joyce Smith
1996–1998	Joyce Smith, Fran Janssen, Jean Geissinger Harding, Mary "Wimp" Baumgartner
1999	Jean Cione, Delores "Dolly" Brumfield White
2000–2002	Jean Cione

Area Representatives

1991	Lois Florreich, Marilyn Mack, Ede Moody, Jean Harding, Joan Knebl, Adeline Kerrar, Shirley Jameson, Alice McNaughton, Dolly Niemiec Konwinski, Dolores Moore, Roz Scarbrough
1994–1995	West: Dorothy Kamenshek, Annabelle Lee Harmon Southwest: Joanne Winter, Betty Tucker Midwest: Dolly Niemiec Konwinski, Ede Moody Canada: Mary Baker East: Maddy English, Joan Knebl, Mary Pratt South: Adeline Kerrar

Advisory Committee and Major Issues

1993	Dorothy Kamenshek, Mary Baker, Terry Donahue, Dorothy Green, Joanne Winter, Connie Wisniewski

Oral Histories

1993	Dr. Janis Taylor, Northwestern University
1996–2004	Mary Moore

Reunion Support Fund

1999–2004	Jean Faut Eastman Fantry

Web Site

1999–2001	Joyce Smith and Reg Langman
2002–2004	Jeanie DesCombes Lesko and son Matthew Lesko

Public Relations

1999–2004	Mary Pratt

Contracts and Royalties

1999–2001	Jean Faut Eastman Fantry
2001	Jean Faut Eastman Fantry, Jeneane DesCombes Lesko
2001–2005	Donna McLin

Special Documentary Committee

2002–2004	Jane Moffet, Jackie Baumgart, Karen Violetta Kunkel, Carmen Velez

Hall of Fame AAGPBL Statue

2003–2004	Jane Moffet, Wilma Briggs, Shelley McCann

Baseball Committee

2004	Delores "Dolly" Brumfield White, Mary "Wimp" Baumgartner, Donna McLin

Fan Fest Committee

2004	Delores "Dolly" Brumfield White, Shirley Burkovich, Carmen Velez

Vision Committee

2004	Jane Moffet, Jean Cione, Karen Violetta Kunkel, Merrie Fidler

Appendix 2: AAGBBL and AAGPBL Players' Association Highlights

1943   P.K. Wrigley issued a press release February 17, announcing plans to start the All-American Girls Softball League (AAGSBL)

The first game was played May 30, 1943: South Bend defeated Rockford 4–3 in 13 innings at Bendix Field in South Bend. It was the first game of a Sunday double header. South Bend also won the night-cap 12–9 in 9 innings. Racine and Kenosha's first game on the same date was rained out (*South Bend Tribune,* 31 May 1943).

The first night game in Wrigley Field featured two AAGSBL All-Star teams on July 1.

The league name was changed to the All-American Girls Base Ball League (AAGBBL) July 15, 1943.

The league name was changed to the All-American Girls Professional Ball League (AAGPBL) at the conclusion of the season.

1944   The league grew from four to six teams with the addition of Milwaukee and Minneapolis.

The second night games in Wrigley Field featuring four AAGPBL teams occurred July 18.

1945   Arthur Meyerhoff purchased the AAGPBL from P.K. Wrigley.

The Milwaukee and Minneapolis teams moved to Grand Rapids and Fort Wayne.

1946   The league was again renamed the All-American Girls Baseball League (AAGBBL) and became an eight team league with the addition of Peoria and Muskegon.

All eight teams attended spring training in Pascagoula, Mississippi, and played exhibition games on their return to their home cities.

Limited side-arm pitching was introduced.

1947   All eight teams attended spring training in Cuba and played exhibition games from Florida to their home cities.

Full side-arm pitching delivery was allowed.

The first post-season competition was organized in Cuba.

1948   The league grew to a maximum of ten teams with the addition of Chicago and Springfield.

The Chicago Girls Baseball League (CGBL), the AAGBBL's Minor League, was organized in Chicago.

All ten teams attended spring training in Opalocka, Florida.

Overhand pitching was instituted with a 10⅜ inch ball.

A second post-season tour was organized in Cuba.

1949   A winter tour through parts of Central and South America was organized during February and March.

The league was reduced to eight teams when Chicago and Springfield became rookie touring teams that played through the South and East from June to September for training and recruiting purposes.

1950   The league continued with eight teams and two rookie touring teams.

1951   Individual Team Owners purchased

the league from Meyerhoff and the league was officially renamed the American Girls Baseball League (AGBL), but continued to be popularly referred to as the AAGBBL.

The rookie touring teams were discontinued.

1952   The league was reduced to six teams. The first league-wide All-Star Game was played July 7.

1953   The league continued to operate with six teams.

1954   The league was reduced to five teams.

Use of the regulation baseball was instituted July 1.

The last game was played September 5, 1954. Kalamazoo defeated Fort Wayne in Fort Wayne to win the post-season championship.

1955–   Team owners voted to suspend play
1958   for the 1955 season January 31, at Kalamazoo, Michigan.

Allington's "World Champion" All-American Touring Team played in the Midwest, South, and Northeast

1963   Arnold Bauer sent out survey and compiled an address directory

1976   Merrie Fidler completed "Development and Decline of the AAGBBL, 1943–1954"

Sharon Roepke began finding and interviewing All-Americans

1978   June Peppas, Dorothy "Kammie" Kamenshek and Marge WEnzell propose a reunion

1980   First newsletter issued by June Peppas in October

1981   First Old-Timers Game at "Run, Jane, Run" in Fort Wayne, Indiana

Daisy Mini-Reunion 9/27, plus others in South Bend and Kalamazoo

1982   First National Reunion, Chicago, Illinois: Hosted by Ruth Davis, 7/8–10

Arnold Bauer published second address directory

Shirley Stovroff became newsletter editor, 11/82

"Run, Jane, Run" included Old-Timer's baseball game and golf

1983   Pepper Paire became newsletter editor 2/83

"Run, Jane, Run" held baseball game and golf, 9/24

1984   First Baseball Cards by Sharon Roepke

"Run, Jane, Run" with baseball game and golf

1985   "Run, Jane, Run" with baseball game and golf, 9/21

1986   Second National Reunion, Fort Wayne, Indiana, 9/18–21

Kelly Candaele/Kim Wilson and Dr. Janis Taylor filmed for documentaries

CBS's Ann Curry covered the event

Dottie Collins became newsletter editor

1987   Ted Spencer from the Baseball Hall of Fame called Dottie Collins 1/87

Players' Association organized in South Bend, May 23

First Players' Association Membership Meeting held in Fort Wayne, Indiana with "Run, Jane, Run" activities, 9/87

Members voted on Logo, approved Board as presented

Search begun for archives; Lifetime Roster begun

Explored creation of a league ring

Planned for Arizona and Cooperstown Reunions

1988   National Reunion in Scottsdale, Arizona

"Run, Jane, Run" baseball game and golf, Lifetime Roster created

"Women in Baseball" display opened in Cooperstown 11/5

Membership meeting held in Cooperstown, full 11 member Board present for the first time

1989   Movie contract signed with Longbow Productions

Annual Meeting with "Run, Jane, Run" baseball game and golf

1990   Annual Meeting in Fort Wayne, elections for new board held

Archives presented to Northern Indiana Historical Society — Lib Mahon

Longbow Productions joined with Columbia Studios

Joan Holderness computerized database

1991   Annual Meeting and National Reunion in Clearwater, Florida

Movie production began with Penny Marshall directing

1992   Movie Premiere of *A League of Their Own* during the last part of June

Annual Meeting with "Run, Jane, Run" in Fort Wayne, Indiana

1993 50th Reunion in South Bend, Indiana, with Museum Display
T.V. Series Premiered based on *A League of Their Own*
Oral histories taped by Dr. Janis Taylor
Address Directory printed
Women's Sports Foundation honored three AAGBBL Representatives in NYC
AAGBBL honored at Slippery Rock University's Symposium

1994 Annual Meeting in Fort Wayne with "Run, Jane, Run"
Baseball Card Contract signed with Ted Williams
Licensing Agreement signed with Global Marketing
Baseball Card Contract signed with Fritsch Card Company
First group of stats presented to Cooperstown and the Northern Indiana Historical Society
Opening of permanent display at Northern Indiana Historical Society
The Players' Association recognized by "BAT" (Baseball Assistance Team)

1995 Annual Meeting and National Reunion in Indian Wells, California
Official Baseball Cards on the market
Opening of "War Years" display in Cooperstown
Cooperstown established individual player files
Address Directory Printed

1996 Annual Meeting in Fort Wayne with "Run, Jane, Run"
Mary Moore began video taping oral histories
Trademarks registered
Second set of Baseball Cards printed

1997 Annual Meeting and National Reunion held in Myrtle Beach, North Carolina
Final set of stats to Northern Indiana Historical Society and the Baseball Hall of Fame
Official notification received from the Trade Mark Commission
The Logo and Name registered to the Players' Association, Inc.
Official Players' Roster printed
Address Directory printed
Medallion designed for members

1998 Annual Meeting and National Reunion in Palm Springs, California
Membership approved Bylaw changes and reduced Board from twelve to six, with elections every two years
Policy and Procedure Manual established
Certificate of Recognition given by Cooperstown to every player
Marketing now controlled by the Board
Public Relations Committee established and chaired by Mary Pratt to record former players' speaking engagements and special events
"Run, Jane, Run" in Fort Wayne with golf
Canadian Baseball Hall of Fame inducted 64 Canadian AAGPBL players, 6/4

1999 Annual Meeting in Fort Wayne
Last public appearance with "Run, Jane, Run"

2000 Annual Meeting and National Reunion in Milwaukee, Wisconsin
Dottie Collins retired from the Board, 12/31/00
Documentary agreement with V1
Reproduction of original uniforms
Cooperstown's first Mother's Day Program
First official representation at Major League Baseball's Fan Fest in Atlanta, Georgia

2001 Annual Meeting and National Reunion in Grand Rapids, Michigan
Chicks inducted into Grand Rapids Sports Hall of Fame
Cooperstown's Mother's Day Program
Major League Baseball Fan Fest in Seattle, Washington
Jean Geissinger Harding, last member of original Board, resigns 9/11

2002 Annual Meeting and National Reunion in South Bend, Indiana
Cooperstown's Mother's Day Program
Major League Baseball Fan Fest in Milwaukee, Wisconsin
Special Documentary Committee established

2003 Annual Meeting and 60th National Reunion in Syracuse, New York
Ceremony at Cooperstown: Hall of Fame announced an AAGBBL

Statue would be cast and placed in the sculpture garden area

Major League Baseball Fan Fest in Chicago, Illinois

Women's Sports Foundation invited three representatives to its banquet

Cooperstown's Mother's Day Program

Hall of Fame Statue Committee established

2004 Annual Meeting and National Reunion in Kalamazoo, Michigan

Major League Baseball Fan Fest in Houston, Texas

Cooperstown's Mother's Day Program

Women's Baseball, Fan Fest, and Vision Committees established*

This list of AAGPBL Highlights contributed by Jean Geissinger Harding and edited by Merrie Fidler.

Appendix 3: The League Song

Batter up!
Hear that call.
The time has come for one and all
To play ball.

For we're the members of the All-American League
We come from cities near and far
We've got Canadians, Irishmen, and Swedes

We're all for one
We're one for all
We're All-Americans!

Each girl stands her head so proudly high
Her motto do or die
She's not the one to need or use an alibi

Our chaperones are not too soft
They're not too tough
Our manager is on the ball
We've got a president who really knows his stuff

We're all for one
We're one for all
We're All-Americans!

Lyrics reprinted by permission of Lavone "Pepper" Paire Davis

Appendix 4: AAGBBL Champions

Play-Off Champions

1943	Racine Belles
1944	Milwaukee Chicks
1945	Rockford Peaches
1946	Racine Belles
1947	Grand Rapids Chicks
1948	Rockford Peaches
1949	Rockford Peaches
1950	Rockford Peaches
1951	South Bend Blue Sox
1952	South Bend Blue Sox
1953	Grand Rapids Chicks
1954	Kalamazoo Lassies

Batting Champions

1943	Gladys "Terrie" Davis, Rockford Peaches	.332
1944	Betsy Jochum, South Bend Blue Sox	.296
1945	Mary Nesbit Wisham, Racine Belles	.319
1946	Dorothy Kamenshek, Rockford Peaches	.316
1947	Dorothy Kamenshek, Rockford Peaches	.306
1948	Audrey Wagner, Kenosha Comets	.312
1949	Doris Sams, Muskegon Lassies	.279
1950	Betty Weaver Foss, Fort Wayne Daisies	.346
1951	Betty Weaver Foss, Fort Wayne Daisies	.368
1952	Joanne Weaver, Fort Wayne Daisies	.344
1953	Joanne Weaver, Fort Wayne Daisies	.346
1954	Joanne Weaver, Fort Wayne Daisies	.429

Pitching Champions

		W L	ERA
1943	Helen Nicol, Kenosha Comets	31–8	1.81
1944	Helen Nicol, Kenosha Comets	17–11	0.93
1945	Connie Wisniewski, Grand Rapids Chicks	32–11	0.81
1946	Connie Wisniewski, Grand Rapids Chicks	33–9	0.96
1947	Mildred Earp, Grand Rapids Chicks	20–8	0.68
1948	Alice Haylett, Grand Rapids Chicks	25–5	0.77
1949	Lois Florreich, Rockford Peaches	22–7	0.67
1950	Jean Faut, South Bend Blue Sox	21–9	1.12
1951	Alma Ziegler, Grand Rapids Chicks	14–8	1.26
1952	Jean Faut, South Bend Blue Sox	20–2	0.93
1953	Jean Faut, South Bend Blue Sox	17–11	1.51
1954	Janet Rumsey, South Bend Blue Sox	15–6	2.18

SOURCE: Bailey, John W., *Kenosha Comets, 1943–1951*. Badger Press, Kenosha, Wisconsin, 1997.

Appendix 5: AAGBBL
Point Rating Chart

POINT RATING CHART

Copyright 1945—All American Girls Baseball League

[This chart was created by AAGBBL President Max Carey]
(Copied from an original found at the Northern Indiana Center for History, South Bend, Indiana)

_____ Commissioner

_____ State or District

Extra Good	100
Good	80
Fair	60
Not Good	40
Bad	20
Very Bad	0

N.B.—Use this chart for individual player ratings or

NAME	Position	BATTING				RUNNING				FIELDING			THROWING		Team Spirit	Behavior	Cooperation	TOTAL	Height	Weight	Age
		Power	Swing	Bunting	Eye	Speed	Start	Stealing	Sliding	Judging Fly Balls	Ground Balls & Hands	Ground Covering	Arm	Distance							
1																					
2																					
3																					
4																					
5																					
6																					
7																					
8																					
9																					
10																					
11																					
12																					

PITCHERS

NAME	R	L	Speed	Slow Ball	Control	Stuff	Holding Runners On	Fielding	Batting	Poise	Stamina	Team Spirit	Behavior	Cooperation	TOTAL	Height	Weight	Age
1																		
2																		
3																		
4																		
5																		

Chapter Notes

Preface

1. See www.dunsmuir.com/babe.htm
2. Chet Grant, "I Managed Girls Baseball," *South Bend Tribune Michiana Magazine*, 9 July 1972.
3. Ted Spencer to Merrie Fidler, September 2004. Mr. Sells related this story to Mr. Spencer at the opening of the Baseball Hall of Fame's "Women in Baseball" exhibit, 5 November 1988.

Chapter 1

1. A starting point for those interested in the history of softball in Canada: Jenni Mortin, *Safe At Home: A History of Softball in Saskatchewan*, Published by Softball Saskatchewan and Saskatchewan Sports Hall of Fame and Museum, 1997.
2. Robert M. Yoder, "Miss Casey at the Bat," *Saturday Evening Post*, 22 August 1942, p. 48.
3. Norris A. Bealle, *The Softball Story*, Washington, D.C.: Columbia, 1957, p. 47.
4. *Ibid.*
5. *Ibid.*, p. 3.
6. Sam B. Warner, Jr., *Streetcar Suburbs: The Process of Growth in Boston, 1870–1900*, New York: Atheneum, 1973, pp. 117–152.
7. Jacob A. Riis, *The Battle With the Slum*, New York: Macmillan, 1902, p. 288.
8. Jane Addams, *Twenty Years at Hull-House*, New York: Macmillan, 1910; A Signet Classic, n.d., p. 29.
9. Riis, *The Battle With the Slum*, pp. 274, 309.
10. Henry S. Curtis, "New Games for the People," *Review of Reviews*, May 1912, p. 584.
11. Joseph Lee, "Preventive Work," *Charities* 6, 6 April 1901: 305.
12. Addams, *Twenty Years at Hull-House*, pp. 103, 243–244, 304–305.
13. Graham Romeyn Taylor, "Recreation Developments in Chicago Parks," *American Academy of Political and Social Science* 25, March 1910: 90; Bealle, *The Softball Story*, p. 164.
14. Gertrude Dudley and Frances A. Kellor, *Athletic Games in the Education of Women*, New York: Henry Holt, 1909, p. 212.
15. Dale A. Somers, *The Rise of Sports in New Orleans, 1850–1900*, Baton Rouge: Louisiana State University Press, 1972, pp. 118–119; *New Orleans Daily Picayune*, 5 May 1886; 25 December 1884; 27 December 1884.
16. David Q. Voigt, *American Baseball, vol. 2: From the Commissioners to Continental Expansion*, Norman: University of Oklahoma Press, 1970, p. 211.
17. Marjorie Sloan Loggiea, "On the Playing Fields of History, "*Ms.*, July 1973, p. 63.

18. Dudley and Kellor, *Athletic Games in the Education of Women*, pp. 213–214; Curtis, "New Games for the People," p. 584.
19. Elizabeth Burchenal, "A Constructive Program of Athletics for School Girls: Policy, Method and Activities," *American Physical Education Review* 24, (May 1919: 275.
20. Edwin E. Jacobs, "A Study of the Physical Vigor of American Women, Ph.D. dissertation, Clark University, ca. 1920, p. 91.
21. Helen Frost and Charles Digby Wardlaw, *Basketball and Indoor Baseball for Women*, New York: Scribner's, 1920, p. 91.
22. Everett B. Mero, *American Playgrounds: Their Construction, Equipment, Maintenance and Utility*, Boston, Mass.: American Gymnasia Company, 1908, p. 153; Curtis, "New Games for the People," p. 584; Dudley and Kellor, *Athletic Games in the Education of Women*, p. 212.
23. Mabel Lee, "The Case For and Against Intercollegiate Athletics for Women and the Situation Since 1923," *Research Quarterly* 2, May 1931: 119; Norma Leavitt and Margaret M. Duncan, "The Status of Intramural Programs for Women," *Research Quarterly* 8, March 1937: 70; M. Gladys Scott, "Competition for Women in American Colleges and Universities," *Research Quarterly* 16, March 1945a: 55 (The statistics used from this survey were compiled from "District" figures); Christine White, "Extramural Competition and Physical Education Activities for College Women," *Research Quarterly* 25, October 1954: 350.
24. Alice Allene Sefton, *The Women's Division National Amateur Athletic Federation: Sixteen Years of Progress in Athletics for Girls and Women, 1923–1939*, California: Stanford University Press, 1941, pp. 77–79.
25. Interview with Delores "Dolly" Brumfield White. Palm Springs, Ca: 9 January 2004.
26. Interview with Annabelle Lee Harmon, Costa Mesa, California, 26 April, 2004.
27. "Female baseball players plan Fort Wayne game," *Fort Wayne News-Sentinel*, 22 September 1982, p. 6.
28. Joseph Lee, *Constructive and Preventive Philanthropy*, New York: Macmillan , 1910; Jane Addams, *The Spirit of Youth and the City Streets*, New York: Macmillan, 1910; Jacob Riis, *The Battle With the Slum*.
29. Most of the promotion of organized sport programs focused on boys' needs. See: Joseph Lee, *Constructive and Preventive Philanthropy*, pp. 170–184; Henry S. Curtis, *Education Through Play*, New York: Macmillan, 191, pp. 220–237. These works include representative accounts of the value of games in developing boys' social and ethical characters.
30. Lee, *Constructive and Preventive Philanthropy*, p. 183.

31. William Henry Chafe, *The American Woman: Her Changing Social, Economic and Political Roles, 1920–1970,* New York: Oxford University Press, 1972, pp. 3–22.

32. Dudley and Kellor, *Athletic Games in the Education of Women,* pp. 3–44.

33. Mero, *American Playgrounds,* p. 153.

34. Henry S. Curtis, *The Play Movement and Its Significance,* New York: Macmillan, 1917, p. 38.

35. Riis, *The Battle With the Slum,* p. 267.

36. Arthur T. Noren, *Softball,* New York: Ronald Press, 1966, p. 11.

37. *Ibid.,* p. 12.

38. Howard S. Patterson, *Social Aspects of Industry,* New York: McGraw Hill, 1935, p. 214.

39. U.S. Bureau of Labor Statistics, *Health and Recreation Activities in Industrial Establishments, 1926,* Bulletin No. 458, Washington, D.C.: Government Printing Office, April 1928, pp. 59–93.

40. U.S. Bureau of Labor Statistics, *Welfare Work for Employees in Industrial Establishments in the United States,* Bulletin No. 250, Washington, D.C.: Government Printing Office, February 1919, p. 87.

41. U.S. Bureau of Labor Statistics, *Health and Recreation Activities in Industrial Establishments, 1926,* pp. 31–57.

42. *Ibid.,* pp. 55–58, 88–94.

43. *Ibid.,* p. 47.

44. *Ibid.*

45. Frank J. Taylor, "Fast and Pretty," *Collier's,* 20 August 1938, p. 38.

46. Clarke A. Chambers, *Seedtime of Reform: American Social Service and Social Action, 1918–1933,* Minneapolis: University of Minnesota, 1963; Ann Arbor: The University of Michigan Press, Ann Arbor Paperbacks, 1967, p. 240.

47. Frederick Lewis Allen, *Since Yesterday,* New York: Harper, 1939; New York: Bantam, 1965, p. 142.

48. *Ibid.*

49. Samuel E. Morison, Henry Steele Commager, and William E. Leuchtenburg, *The Growth of the American Republic,* Vol. II, New York: Oxford University Press, 1969, p. 504.

50. John R. Betts, "Organized Sport in Industrial America," Ph.D. Dissertation, Columbia University, 1951, p. 482.

51. Roy Smith Wallace, "Recreation," *Social Work Yearbook,* New York: Russell Sage Foundation, 1933, p. 429; Gilbert C. Wrenn, *Time on Their Hands: A Report on Leisure, Recreation and Young People,* Washington, D.C.: American Council on Education, 1941, pp. xix-xx.

52. Jean Faut to Mary Moore, oral history interview, AAGPBL Mini-Reunion, Fort Wayne, Indiana, 1996.

53. *Ibid.*

54. See Jan Taylor's oral history video tapes, AAGPBL Reunion, South Bend, Indiana, 1993. See also Mary Moore's oral history video tapes, AAGPBL Reunions, 1996–2004.

55. Wilma Briggs and Sue Kidd to Jan Taylor, oral history interviews, AAGPBL Reunion, South Bend, Indiana, 1993. Interviews with Dolly Brumfield White and Shirley Burkovich, Palm Springs, California, 9 January 2004.

56. "Softball," *Time,* 16 September 1935, p. 48.

57. Taylor, "Fast and Pretty," p. 23.

58. John Brown, Jr., "Softball Problems — Hearings on the Present Situation," *Recreation* 28, December 1934: 445–446.

59. Bealle, *The Softball Story,* p. 43.

60. Sefton, *Women's National Amateur Athletic Federation,* p. 38.

Chapter 2

1. John Rickards Betts, *America's Sporting Heritage, 1850–1950,* Reading, Mass.: Addison-Wesley, 1974, pp. 288–289.

2. Ken Beirn, Office of War Information, to Philip K. Wrigley, 18 December 1942, Arthur E. Meyerhoff Company All-American Girls' Baseball League Files, Drawer 19, 1943 Correspondence Folder, Wrigley Building, Chicago, Illinois, 1974. Unfortunately, the fate of these records is not now (2004) known. In late 1942, government plans were underway for the establishment of a second front in the European war. These plans demanded increased military and industrial manpower mobilization. For an intergovernmental account of European war strategy, see Herbert Feis, *Churchill, Roosevelt and Stalin: The War They Waged and the Peace They Sought,* Princeton, N.J.: Princeton University Press, 1957.

3. Ken Beirn to Philip Wrigley, 18 December 1942.

4. David Quentin Voigt, *American Baseball,* vol. 2: *From the Commissioners to Continental Expansion,* Norman, Okla.: University of Oklahoma Press, 1970, pp. 256–257.

5. Philip K. Wrigley to Merrie Fidler, 12 August 1975.

6. *Who's Who in the Midwest,* 14th ed., Chicago, Ill.: Marquis Who's Who, 1974–1975.

7. "Chewing Gum Is War Material," *Fortune,* January 1943, p. 100

8. *Ibid.,* p. 98.

9. *Ibid.,* p. 99.

10. Paul M. Angle, *Philip K. Wrigley: A Memoir of a Modest Man,* Chicago: Rand McNally, 1975, p. 34.

11. *Who's Who in the Midwest,* 1974–1975.

12. Angle, *Philip K. Wrigley,* p. 63.

13. *Ibid.,* pp. 63–64.

14. "Ladies of Little Diamond," *Time,* 14 June 1943, p. 73.

15. William Wrigley, Jr. with Forrest Crissey, "Owning a Big League Ball Team," *The Saturday Evening Post,* 13 September 1930, p. 25.

16. Angle, *Philip K. Wrigley,* p. 63.

17. Dorothy Kamenshek to Dr. Janis Taylor, oral history interview, 50th AAGPBL Reunion, South Bend, Indiana, 1993

18. Eileen "Ginger" Gascon to Mary Moore, oral history interview, 53rd AAGPBL Reunion, Fort Wayne, Indiana, 1996.

19. "*Chewing Gum Is War Material,*" p. 124.

20. *Ibid.*

21. Interview with Helen Hannah Campbell (who worked as an administrative assistant for Wrigley's purchasing department for three businesses related to tourism on Catalina Island), Costa Mesa, California, 26 April 2004.

22. " Chewing Gum Is War Material," p. 126.

23. *Ibid.*

24. Frank J. Taylor, "Fast and Pretty," *Collier's,* 20 August 1938, p. 38.

25. *Chicago Daily News,* 9 February 1943, Sports Section, p. 15.

26. Richard R. Lindeman, *Don't You Know There's a War On?* New York: Putnam's, 1970, p. 148.

27. *Ibid.,* p. 152.

28. Paul Gardner, "Now Lady Umpires!" *This Week,* 17 July 1943; Lindeman, *Don't You Know There's a War On?,* p. 152.

29. "Mr. Wrigley's Statement for the Press on the Girls' All-American Softball League," 17 February 1943, Meyerhoff Files, Drawer 19, 1943 News Release Folder.

30. Untitled AAGSBL Contract Agreement Between Board of Trustees and Local Guarantors, 1943, Meyerhoff Files, Drawer 19, 1945 Management Corporation Softball Enterprise Folder.

31. *Ibid.*

32. "All-American Girls Softball League," ca. February 1943, Meyerhoff Files, Drawer 19, 1945 Management Corporation Softball Enterprise Folder.

33. Maria Sexton, *Implications of the All-American Girls Baseball League for Physical Educators in the Guidance of Highly-Skilled Girls*, Type C Project, Advanced School of Education Teachers College, Columbia University, 1953.

34. Telephone interview with Maria Sexton, July 2004.

35. Interview with Arthur E. Meyerhoff, Rancho Santa Fe, California, 28 December 1972.

36. Arthur Meyerhoff to Philip Wrigley, 5 December 1942, Meyerhoff Files, Drawer 19, 1944 Miscellaneous Folder.

37. Jess Krueger to Arthur Meyerhoff, 9 January 1943, Meyerhoff Files, Drawer 19, 1944 Miscellaneous Folder.

38. "Notes on Meeting Regarding Softball Project," 22 December 1942, Meyerhoff Files, Drawer 19, 1944 Miscellaneous Folder.

39. *Ibid.*

40. *Ibid.*

41. Philip K. Wrigley to Merrie Fidler, 12 August 1975.

42. Voigt, *American Baseball*, 2:164–165.

43. "Mr. Wrigley's Statement for the Press on the Girls' All-American Softball League," 17 February 1943, Meyerhoff Files, Drawer 19, 1943 News Release Folder.

44. Philip K. Wrigley to Merrie Fidler, 12 August 1975.

45. "Evolution of the Ball Size Used in All-American Girls Base Ball League From 1943–1949, And Diamond Changes, 1943–46," Dailey Records, 1947–1949.

46. Ken Sells to Harold T. Dailey, n.d., Dailey Records, 1943–1946.

47. "For the Personal Information of Sports Editors," 15 July 1943, Meyerhoff Files, Drawer 19, 1943 News Release Folder.

48. *1944 Racine Belles Year Book*, p. 3. (Most yearbooks can currently be accessed at the Northern Indiana Center for History or the Baseball Hall of Fame.) AAGBBL Board Meeting Minutes, 3 April 1945 and 19 September 1945, Dailey Records.

49. "Ladies of Little Diamond," *Time*, 14 June 1943, pp. 73–74.

50. *Racine Journal Times* (Wis.), *Rockford Register-Republic* (Ill.), *South Bend Tribune* (Ind.), *Kenosha Evening News* (Wis.), Sports Pages, May–June, 1943. (Female softball players' emulation of male baseball stars may have been one effect of Ladies' Days at major league ball parks.)

51. "All-American Girls Softball League," ca. 1943, Meyerhoff Files, Drawer 19, 1945 Management Corporation Softball Enterprise Folder.

52. Joyce Smith to Merrie Fidler, 1 July 2004. Joyce's father was the bartender at this establishment.

53. Interview with Annabelle Lee Harmon, Costa Mesa, California, 26 April 2004.

54. "Notes on Meeting Regarding Softball Project," 22 December 1942, Meyerhoff Files, Drawer 19, 1944 Miscellaneous Folder.

55. "Early History of the League — Notes from [Frank] Avery," Dailey Records, 1943–1946; Bernard Friedman, *The Financial Role of Indiana in World War II*, Bloomington, Ind.: University Press, 1965, pp. 24–25; Mary Watters, *Illinois in the Second World War*, vol. II: *The Production Front*, Springfield, Ill.: Illinois State Historical Library, 1952, pp. 251–252; *Kenosha Evening News* (Wis.), 27 May 1943, p. 16.

56. Kyle Crichton, "Not So Soft," *Collier's*, 10 August 1935, pp. 24, 38; *Kenosha Evening News* (Wis.), 19 May 1943, p. 10; Carl Biemiller, "World's Prettiest Ballplayers," *Holiday*, June 1952, p. 50; Morris A Bealle, *The Softball Story*, Washington: Columbia, 1957, pp. 97–104, 116, 158–160, 113–115.

57. *Chicago Daily News*, 11 May 1943, Sports Section News clipping, Meyerhoff Files.

58. *Ibid.*, 14 July 1951, Dailey Records.

59. Bill Veeck with Ed Linn, *The Hustler's Handbook* New York: Putnam's, 1965, p. 323.

60. Interview with Maybelle Blair, Katie Horstman, Shirley Burkovich and Delores "Dolly" White, Palm Springs, California, 9 January 1993.

61. Telephone interview with Sophie Kurys, July 2004.

62. *Chicago Daily News*, 9 February 1943, Sports Section, p. 15.

63. Interview with Arthur E. Meyerhoff, Rancho Santa Fe, California, 28 December 1972.

64. Ken Beirn, Office of War Information, to Philip K. Wrigley, 18 December 1942, Meyerhoff Files, Drawer19, 1943 Correspondence Folder; Interview with Arthur E. Meyerhoff, Rancho Santa Fe, California, 28 December 1972.

65. Philip K. Wrigley to Merrie Fidler, 12 August 1975.

66. "Names Suggested for President of All-American Girls Softball League," Meyerhoff Files, Drawer 19, 1944 Miscellaneous Folder.

67. *Ibid.*

68. Voigt, *American Baseball*, 2:121.

69. Arthur Mann, "The Truth About the Jackie Robinson Case," *The Saturday Evening Post*, 20 May 1950, p. 20.

70. *Ibid.*

71. "Comeback at 77," *Time*, 31 August 1952, p. 39; "Branch Rickey Rides Again: The Return of the Mahatma," *The Saturday Evening Post*, 9 March 1963, p. 66; "The innovator," *Newsweek*, 20 December 1965, p. 58.

72. Philip K. Wrigley to Merrie Fidler, 12 August 1975; Angle, *Philip K. Wrigley*, p. 106.

73. Arthur E. Meyerhoff to Philip K. Wrigley, 25 May 1943, Meyerhoff Files, Drawer 19, 1943 Correspondence Folder.

74. Angle, *Philip K. Wrigley*, pp. 16–18; *Racine Journal Times* (Wis.), 3 May 1943, p. 8.

75. *1944 Racine Belles Year Book*, p. 27.

76. *Ibid.*

77. *Ibid.*

78. Ken Sells to Dr. Harold T. Dailey, n.d., Dailey Records, 1943–1946. Arthur Meyerhoff observed that Sells overstated his case in this sentence. He suggested that Sells should more properly have related that the Wrigley Company, the advertising agency, and the Cubs organization all cooperated with him rather than stating that they had been put at his disposal. Arthur Meyerhoff to Merrie Fidler, 13 May 1976.

79. Untitled document explaining "The Responsibilities and Benefits of the Guarantors and the League as Operator of the Club," Meyerhoff Files, 1945 Organization Folder; *Kenosha Evening News* (Wis.), 1 May 1943, p. 3.

80. "Early History of the League," n.d., Dailey Records, 1943–1946.

81. Marie Keenan, "All-American Girls Professional Ball League," *Major League Baseball: Facts, Figures and Official Rules* Racine, Wis.: Whitman, 1945, p. 131; Angle, *Philip K. Wrigley*, p. 183.

82. *1944 Racine Belles Year Book*, p. 3.

83. "Franchise Plan for Teams in the All-American Girls Softball League," 5 October 1943, pp. 1–2, Meyerhoff Files, Drawer 19, Franchise Material Folder.

84. *Ibid.*, p. 5.

85. *Ibid.*, pp. 5–6.

86. *1944 Racine Belles Year Book*, p. 3.

87. Keenan, *Major League Baseball*, p. 131.

88. *Milwaukee Journal*, 23 July 1944, Sports Section, p. 46.

89. "Report on All-American Girls Survey in Milwaukee," Meyerhoff Files, Drawer 19, 1944 Miscellaneous Folder.

90. *Minneapolis Tribune*, 23 July 1944, Sports Section, p. 1.

91. *Ibid.*; *1945 Racine Belles Year Book*, p. 10.

92. Keenan, *Major League Baseball*, p. 131; Ellen Gibson, "The Pay-Off," *Once A Year* (Milwaukee Press Club Publication), vol. 49, 1945, p. 18.

93. A comparison of the *Minneapolis Tribune* and *Milwaukee Journal* with the *Racine Journal-Times*, the *Rockford Register-Republic*, the *Kenosha Evening News*, and the *South Bend Tribune*, May–July 1944.

94. E.W. Moss, "Comparative Figures for Three Competing Classes of Baseball," *Baseball Bluebook*, Supplement No. 9-B, November 1945, p. 2.

95. *Ibid.*, pp. 3–4.

96. *Ibid.*

97. *Ibid.*, pp. 2–4.

Chapter 3

1. For instance, "Ladies of Little Diamond," *Time*, 14 June 1943; Herb Graffis, "Belles of the Ball Game," *Liberty*, 16 October 1943; Herb Graffis, "Queens of Swat," *Click*, September 1944; "Girls' Baseball," *Life*, 4 June 1945; J. Gordon, "Beauty at the Bat," *American Magazine*, June 1945; "Baseball Men Envy Her," *Seventeen*, September 1945; Jack Stenbuck, "Glamour Girls of Big-League Ball," *Magazine Digest*, July 1946; "Babette Ruths," *Newsweek*, 29 July 1946; Ben Gould, "Slide Nellie Slide," *Deb*, September 1946; Bill Fay, "Belles of the Ball Game," *Collier's*, 13 August 1949; Morris Markey, "Hey Ma, You're Out!" *McCall's*, September 1950; C.L. Biemiller, "Women's Prettiest Ballplayers," *Holiday*, June 1952.

2. *Kenosha Evening News* (Wis.), 6 May 1943, p. 3; Biemiller, "Women's Prettiest Ballplayers," p. 75; Angle, *Philip K. Wrigley*, p. 24.

3. William B. Furlong, "P.K. Wrigley: Baseball Magnate," *The Saturday Evening Post*, Summer 1972, p. 114.

4. Thomas Suhband, "A Man Who Made $32 grow to $13,000,000," *System*, February 1916, p. 181; Merle Crowell, "The Wonder Story of Wrigley," *The American Magazine*, March 1920, p. 16.

5. Furlong, "P.K. Wrigley," p. 86.

6. *Ibid.*, p. 110

7. Angle, *Philip K. Wrigley*, p. 31.

8. Interview with Arthur E. Meyerhoff, Rancho Santa Fe, California, 28 December 1972.

9. *Ibid.*

10. "Girls Baseball In Chicago for Hospital," *News of the Nation*, vol. IX, No. 2, n.d.; "All American Girls ... Professional Ball at Brewers' Park," *The Hotel Greeters Guide of Wisconsin*, 1944; Gertrude E. Hendriks, "Play Ball! Girls' Baseball Team Boosts Milwaukee in Sport Circles," *The Torch*, June 1944; "Beauty Invades the Ball Park," *Dodge News*, vol. 10, No. 2, 1945; Ellen Gibson,

"The Pay-Off," *Once A Year*, vol. 49, 1945; Norman Klein, "Baseball-Business Booster," *Forbes Magazine of Business*, 1 April 1947; Don M. Black, "Belles of Baseball," *The Ashlar*, April 1948; Fred Leo and Ray Seymour, "These Girls Play for Keeps!" *Moose Magazine*, July–August 1949; "Daring Damsels of the Diamond," *Allsports*, July–August 1949.

11. Marie Keenan, "All-American Girls Professional Ball League," *Major League Baseball: Facts Figures and Official Rules*, Racine, Wis.: Whitman, 1945; William C. Fay, "Bonnie's the Belle of the Ball Game," *Sport*, May 1946; Bill Kofender, "Gals Play Ball Too," *Sports Graphic*, June 1947; Robert Larimer, "Diamond Damsels," *Sportfolio*, October 1947; "Diamond Daisies," *Sport Life*, October 1949.

12. Michael Strauss, "Queen of Diamonds," *New York Times Magazine*, 4 August 1946; Adie Suesdorf, "Sluggers in Skirts," *This Week Magazine*, 31 July 1949.

13. *Kenosha Evening News*, 27 May 1943, p. 16.

14. *Kenosha Evening News*, 4 August 1943, p. 8; Bernard Friedman, *The Financial Role of Indiana in World War II*, Bloomington: Indiana University Press, 1965, pp. 24–25; Richard Kraus, *Recreation and Leisure in Modern Society*, New York: Appleton-Century Crofts, 1971, p. 207.

15. *Kenosha Evening News*, 1 June 1943, p. 9.

16. *Ibid.*, 20 August 1943, p. 8.

17. *Ibid.*

18. *Ibid.*, 1 May 1943, p. 3; 18 June 1943, p. 8; 29 June 1943, p. 8; *Racine Journal-Times* (Wis.), 9 May 1945, p. 16; 16 May 1945, p. 12.

19. *Chicago Tribune*, (Ill.) 1 July 1943, Sec. 2, p. 23; *Kenosha Evening News* (Wis.), 24 June 1943, p. 8; 2 July 1943, p. 8; *Chicago Tribune*, 2 July 1943, Sec. 2, p. 21.

20. *Chicago Tribune* (Ill.), 2 July 1943, Section 2, p. 21.

21. Jay Feldman, "The *Real* History of Night Ball at Wrigley Field," *The Baseball Research Journal*, Society for American Baseball Research, No. 21, 1992.

22. *Ibid.*

23. *Ibid.*

24. *Ibid.*

25. *Chicago Herald-American*, 12 July 1944, news clipping in Meyerhoff Files.

26. Memo, 12 July 1944, Meyerhoff Files, Drawer 19, Red Cross Game at Wrigley Field Folder.

27. *The Chicago Sun*, 18 July 1944, news clipping in Meyerhoff Files.

28. Interview with Dorothy Hunter, Grand Rapids, Michigan, 3 January 1976.

29. Meyerhoff Files, Drawer 19, Red Cross "Thank You" Night News Release Folder.

30. *Racine Journal Times*, 19 July 1944, p. 10.

31. *Ibid.*

32. Edward J. Ruetz, Jr., "Play Ball!" A bat boy's memories of the AAGBBL contributed by his wife, Jnell Ruetz, Littleton, Colorado, July 2004.

33. *Racine Journal Times*, 19 July 1944, p. 10.

34. "Notes on Meeting Regarding Softball Project," 22 December 1942, Meyerhoff Files, Drawer 19, 1944 Miscellaneous Folder.

35. "Ladies of Little Diamond," *Time*, 14 June 1943, pp. 73–74.

36. *Kenosha Evening News* (Wis.), 13 May 1943, p. 8.

37. Frank J. Taylor, "Fast and Pretty," *Collier's*, 20 August 1938, pp. 22–23; Robert M. Yoder, "Miss Casey at the Bat," *The Saturday Evening Post*, 22 August 1943, pp. 16–17, 48–49; Aaron Davidson, "The Batter Half," *Collier's*, 12 August 1944, pp. 18–19, 41.

38. Frederick W. Cozens and Florence Scovil Stumpf,

Sports in American Life, Chicago: The University of Chicago Press, 1953, p. 123.

39. Philip K. Wrigley to Merrie Fidler, 12 August 1975. Ken Sells' essay on the beginnings of the AAGSBL, Northern Indiana Center for History. No date is recorded on the hand-written document. This author suspects it was after the unveiling of the Baseball Hall of Fame's Display in Cooperstown or after *A League of Their Own* premiered.

40. Interview with Arthur E. Meyerhoff, Rancho Santa Fe, California, 28 December 1972; "Ladies of Little Diamond," p. 74.

41. *Kenosha Evening News* (Wis.), 13 May 1943, p. 8.

42. Madeline "Maddy" English to Dr. Janis Taylor, oral history interview, AAGPBL Reunion, 5 August 1993.

43. Joyce Hill Westerman to Dr. Janis Taylor, oral history interview, AAGPBL Reunion, South Bend, Indiana, 5 August 1993.

44. Interview with Dorothy "Kammie" Kamenshek, Thelma "Tiby" Eisen, Dorothy "Snookie" Doyle, and Marge Wenzell, Palm Desert, California, 9 January 2004.

45. Madeline English to Dr. Janis Taylor, oral history interview, AAGPBL Reunion, South Bend, Indiana, 5 August 1993.

46. Interview with Delores "Dolly" Brumfield White, Shirley Burkovich, Katie Horstman, and Maybelle Blair, Palm Springs, California, 9 January 2004. Audrey Haine Daniels to Dr. Janis Taylor, AAGPBL Reunion, South Bend, Indiana, 1993.

47. Terry Donahue to Dr. Janis Taylor, oral history interview, AAGPBL Reunion, South Bend, Indiana, 1993.

48. *Kenosha Evening News* (Wis.), 13 May 1943. p. 8

49. "Rules of Conduct for All American Baseball Girls," ca. 1945–1946, Meyerhoff Files, Drawer 19, Rules and Regulations Folder.

50. *Ibid.*

51. Judy Meyerhoff Yale to Merrie Fidler, 23 March 2004

52. Arthur E. Meyerhoff to Helena Rubinstein, 16 March 1944, Meyerhoff Files, Drawer 19, Beauty Salon Correspondence Folder; "Ladies of Little Diamond," p. 74.

53. *Kenosha Evening News* (Wis.), 20 May 1943, p. 14; 28 May 1943, p. 8.

54. Interview with Thelma "Tiby" Eisen, Dorothy "Kammie" Kamenshek, Marge Wenzell, and Dorothy "Snookie" Doyle, Palm Desert, California, 10 January 2004.

55. *Kenosha Evening News* (Wis.), 19 May 1943, p. 10; 20 May 1943, p. 14; 22 May 1943, p. 3; 5 June 1943, p. 3.

56. *Ibid.*, 25 May 1943, p. 8.

57. *Ibid.*, 18 June 1943, p. 8.

58. *Ibid.*

59. William Fay, "Bonnie's the Belle of the Ball Game," *Sport*, May 1946, pp. 26–28, 97–98, was the most outstanding example of "Bonnie Baker" publicity, but she was often pictured in other articles.

60. *Kenosha Evening News* (Wis.), 13 May 1943, p. 8.

61. *Ibid.*, 28 May 1943, p. 8.

62. *Ibid.*

63. Interview with Arthur E. Meyerhoff, Rancho Santa Fe, California, 28 December 1972.

64. Interview with Jean Faut, South Bend, Indiana, 6 January 1973.

65. William L. Chafe, *The American Woman: Her Changing Social, Economic and Political Roles, 1920–1970*, New York: Oxford University Press, 1972, p. 188; see also Katherine Archibald, *Wartime Shipyards: A Study in Social Disunity*, Berkeley: University of California Press, 1947, pp. 15–39.

66. Quoted in Betty Friedan, *The Feminine Mystique*, New York: Dell, 1963, p. 37.

67. Interview with Arthur E. Meyerhoff, Rancho Santa Fe, California, 28 December 1972.

68. *Racine Belles Year Book*, p. 3.

69. *Ibid.*, p. 4.

70. *Muskegon Lassies Year Book*, p. 2.

71. *Kenosha Evening News* (Wis.), 27 July 1943, p. 8; 6 August 1943, p. 8.

72. *Ibid.*, 27 July 1943, p. 8; 1943 Season Attendance Figures, Dailey Records, 1943–1946.

73. "A 96,000 Gate is an Even Break: A Special Report to the Peaches Fans, Sponsors and the General Public," Rockford Peaches, Inc., 1950, Dailey Records, 1950a.

74. *Ibid.*

75. Dailey Records, 1951a.

76. *Kenosha Evening News* (Wis.), 21 August 1943, p. 3.

77. *Rockford Register-Republic* (Ill.), 21 August 1943, p. 9.

78. AAGBBL Board Meeting Minutes, 7 June 1945, Dailey Records.

79. *Racine Journal-Times* (Wis.), 6 June 1945, p. 12.

80. *The Racine Belle*, vol. 1, no. 2, May 1948, p. 4, Meyerhoff Files, Drawer 25, 1947–1949 Folder; *Ft. Wayne Journal-Gazette*, 6 August 1952, p. 17; *1949 Muskegon Lassies Year Book*, pp. 6–9; "All-American Girls Baseball League —1948" and "General Forward 1947" Dailey Records, 1947–1949.

81. "Fort Wayne Junior Girls Baseball League 1963 Schedule and Score Card," pp. 6, 13. This schedule and scorecard was donated to the author by former AAG-BBL player Marilyn Jenkins, Grand Rapids, Michigan.

82. *Fort Wayne Journal-Gazette* (Ind.), 6 August 1952, p. 17.

83. Sally Reed, "Girls League Packs 'Em In," *Fort Wayne Journal-Gazette*, 8 April 1973. Contributed by Jean Geissinger Harding, July 2004.

84. *Ibid.*

85. Interview with Delores "Dolly" Brumfield White, Shirley Burkovich, Katie Horstman and Maybelle Blair, Palm Springs, California, 9 January 2004.

86. Interview with Ed Des Laurier, South Bend, Indiana, 6 January 1973.

87. *Kenosha Evening News* (Wis.), 1 June 1943, p. 9.

88. "Further History of Years Thru (sic) 1945–1946," Dailey Records, 1943–1946.

89. Voigt, *American Baseball*, 2:292.

90. Chafe, *American Woman*, p. 206.

91. "Radio Spot Announcement," Meyerhoff Files, Drawer 19, 1944 Announcement Folder.

92. *Milwaukee Journal* (Wis.), 26 July 1944, p. L2.

93. *Ibid.*, 23 July 1944, Sports Section, p. 6.

94. *Ibid.*, 11 August 1944, p. L10; "Notes on Meeting With Mr. Wrigley RE: Concerts in Milwaukee," 27 July 1944, Meyerhoff Files, Drawer 19, 1944 Milwaukee Pop. Concert Folder.

95. *Milwaukee Journal* (Wis.), 11 August 1944, p. L10.

96. AAGBBL News Release on Milwaukee Concert, 15 August 1944, Meyerhoff Files, Drawer 19, News Release Folder.

97. Alice Irwin (Meyerhoff Co.) to respective newsreel companies, 3 August 1944, Meyerhoff Files, Drawer 19, 1944 Correspondence Folder.

98. *Ibid.*, to respective magazine publishers.

99. Announcement, 4 August 1944, Meyerhoff Files, Drawer 19, 1944 Announcements Folder.

100. "Baseball, Maestro, Please," *Time*, 31 July 1944, p. 40.

101. Thomas A. Morgan and James R. Nitz, "Our Forgotten World Champions: The 1944 Milwaukee Chicks," *Milwaukee History: The Magazine of the Milwaukee County Historical Society*, Summer 1995 p. 43.

102. *Milwaukee Journal* (Wis.), 11 August 1944, p. L10.

103. Thomas J. Morgan and James R. Nitz, "Our Forgotten World Champions," pp. 34–36.

104. Crowell, "The Wonder Story of Wrigley," p. 16.

105. AAGBBL Board Meeting Minutes, 14 November 1944, Dailey Records.

106. and 1944 Attendance and Win-Loss Records, Dailey Records, 1943–1946.

Chapter 4

1. John H. Black to Mr. A.E. Meyerhoff, 10 October 1944, Meyerhoff Files, Drawer 19, 1944 Correspondence Folder.

2. "For the Personal Information of the Directors of the All-American Girls Professional Ball League," 15 March 1947, Meyerhoff Files, Drawer 25.

3. Keenan, *Major League Baseball*, 1945, p. 131; "Attendance Figures for 1943 and 1944," Dailey Records, 1943–1946.

4. "Management Agreement," 14 December 1944, p. 2, Meyerhoff Files, Drawer 75, 1950–53 Management Corporation Folder.

5. "Memorandum Regarding the Future Activities of the All-American Girls Professional Ball League," 3 November 1944, Meyerhoff Files, Drawer 19, 1945 Organization Folder.

6. John H. Black to Mr. A.E. Meyerhoff, 10 October 1944, Meyerhoff Files, Drawer 19, 1944 Correspondence Folder; Interview with Arthur E. Meyerhoff, Rancho Santa Fe, California, 28 December 1972.

7. Judy Meyerhoff Yale, "Arthur E. Meyerhoff Memorial Fund," Pamphlet. Biographical sketch of Arthur Meyerhoff and rationale for establishing a Memorial Fund in his memory for Chicago Youth Centers, Chicago, Illinois, April, 1998.

8. *Ibid.*

9. *Ibid.*

10. Telephone interview with Tiby Eisen, 30 June 2004.

11. Interview with Dorothy "Snookie" Doyle, Cathedral City, 27 April 2004.

12. Judy Meyerhoff Yale, "Arthur E. Meyerhoff Memorial Fund," Pamphlet. Biographical sketch of Arthur Meyerhoff and rationale for establishing a Memorial Fund in his memory for Chicago Youth Centers, Chicago, Illinois, April, 1998.

13. Ken Sells, Essay on the Organization of the AAGBBL, Northern Indiana Center for History, South Bend, Indiana.

14. Keenan, *Major League Baseball*, 1945, p. 130.

15. "History During 1946–47," Dailey Records, 1943–1946.

16. Interview with Jean Cione, Ypsilanti, Michigan, 17 June 1974.

17. Betty Carveth Dunn to Mary Moore, oral history interview, AAGPBL Reunion, Myrtle Beach, South Carolina, 1997.

18. Viola "Tommie" Thompson Griffin to Dr. Janis Taylor, oral history interview, AAGPBL Reunion, South Bend, Indiana, 1993.

19. *Ibid.*; Interview with Jean Faut, South Bend, Indiana, 6 January 1973.

20. Karen Violetta Kunkel to Dr. Janis Taylor, oral history interview, AAGPBL Reunion, South Bend, Indiana, 7 August 1993.

21. Dr. Harold T. Dailey to Arthur Meyerhoff, 18 November 1947, Dailey Records, 1947–1949.

22. Arthur Meyerhoff to Harold T. Dailey, ca. November 1947, Dailey Records, 1947–1949.

23. "League Attendance Records for 1943–1949," Dailey Records, 1952.

24. Richard Kraus, *Recreation and Leisure in Modern Society*, New York: Appleton-Century-Crofts, 1971, pp. 208–209.

25. Arthur Meyerhoff to Harold T. Dailey, ca. November 1947, Dailey Records, 1947–1949.

26. Arthur E. Meyerhoff to James E. Price, 14 September 1945, Meyerhoff Files, Drawer 19, 1945 Correspondence Folder.

27. Estimated Budget, California Girls Baseball League," Meyerhoff Files, Drawer 19, California Girls Baseball League Folder, 22 February 1946; A.E. Meyerhoff to Marty Fiedler, 25 March 1946, Meyerhoff Files, Drawer 19, Marty Fiedler Folder; AAGBBL Board Meeting Minutes, 10 April 1946, Dailey Records.

28. "Management Agreement," 14 December 1944, Meyerhoff Files, Drawer 75, 1950–53 Management Corporation Folder.

29. Angle, *Philip K. Wrigley*, pp. 110–111.

30. "Management Agreement," 14 December 1944, Meyerhoff Files, Drawer 75, 1950–53 Management Corporation Folder.

31. Constitution of the All-American Girls Professional Ball League, Article XIV, Meyerhoff Files, Drawer 19, 1945 Management Corporation Softball Enterprise Folder.

32. Interview with Arthur Meyerhoff, Rancho Santa Fe, California 28 December 1972.

33. "Audit to League Directors," 14 July 1947, Alfred C. Hales, CPA, Dailey Records, 1943–1946.

34. "All-American Girls Baseball League: League Expenses to 31 December 1946," Meyerhoff Files, Drawer 75, Budget Folder.

35. "All-American Girls Baseball League Suggested Plan for Sharing Expenses," 24 March 1947, Meyerhoff Files, Drawer 75, Albert K. Orschel Correspondence and Plan Folder.

36. "Suggested Revision for Orschel Plan for 1949," AAGBBL Board Meeting Minutes, 4 February 1949, Dailey Records.

37. "Management Agreement," 14 December 1944, Meyerhoff Files, Drawer 75, 1950–53 Management Corporation Folder.

38. John H. Black to Mr. A.E. Meyerhoff, 10 October 1944, Meyerhoff Files, Drawer 19, 1944 Correspondence Folder.

39. "Constitution of the All-American Girls Profession Ball League," Meyerhoff Files, Drawer 19, 1945 Organization Folder.

40. *Ibid.*

41. *Ibid.*

42. *1944 Racine Belles Year Book*, p. 27.

43. *Ibid.*

44. Anna May Hutchison to Dr. Janis Taylor, oral history interview, 50 AAGPBL Reunion, South Bend, Indiana, 7 August 1993.

45. Max Carey to A.E. Meyerhoff, 28 December 1944, Meyerhoff Files, Drawer 19, All-American Girls Professional Ball League Management Corporation Folder; "Further History of Years 1945, 1946," Dailey Records, 1943–1946.

46. AAGBBL Board Meeting Minutes, 29 July 1946, 10 November 1947, 13 October 1948, and 11 July 1949, Dailey Records.

47. *Ibid.*, 16 November 1949 and 15 March 1950; AAGBBL News Release, 21 March 1951, Dailey Records, 1951a.

48. News clipping, (source unnamed) 19 December 1950, Dailey Records, 1951a.

49. AAGBBL Board Meeting Minutes, 16 November 1949, Dailey Records.

50. Arthur E. Meyerhoff to Harold T. Dailey, ca. November 1947, Dailey Records, 1947–1949; AAGBBL Board Meeting Minutes, 16 November 1949, Dailey Records.

51. AAGBBL Board Meeting Minutes, 1 October 1951, Dailey Records.

52. *1948 Racine Belles Year Book*, p. 8; *1949 Peoria Redwings Year Book*, p. 59.

53. "AAGBBL Comparative Club Operating Statements—Year 1948," Meyerhoff Files, Drawer 75, All American Girls Budget Folder.

54. "AAGPBL Management Corporation Balance Sheet," 31 December 1948, Meyerhoff Files, Drawer 75, All American Girls Budget Folder.

55. "Management Agreement," 14 December 1944, Meyerhoff Files, Drawer 75, 1950–53 Management Corporation Folder; *Ibid.*, "Exhibit 'B,'" 20 August 1945; "Exhibit 'C,'" 10 November 1947.

56. Harold T. Dailey memo (preceding a letter to Judge Ruetz, 27 September 1949), Dailey Records, 1947–1949.

57. "Recommendations of the Peoria Club to Executive Committee of the AAGBBL," Dailey Records, 1947–1949.

58. "Comparative Operating Statements—Year 1948," Meyerhoff Files, Drawer 75, All American Girls Budget Folder; "Comparative Club Operating Statement — Year 1949," Dailey Record, 1947–1949.

59. "A Special Report to the Peaches Fans, Sponsors, and the General Public," Dailey Records, 1950a; AAGBBL News Release, 25 July 1950, Dailey Records, 1950a; *Peoria Star* (Ill.), 18 July 1950, p. B-2; AAGBBL News Release, 1 August 1950, Dailey Records, 1950b.

60. AAGBBL Board Meeting Minutes, 21 August 1950, Dailey Records.

61. *Ibid.*, 11, 16, and 30 June 1950.

62. *Ibid.*, 19 July 1950.

63. *Ibid.*, 16 June 1950.

64. Wilbur E. Johnson to "All-American Girls Baseball League Management Corporation and to the Members of the AAGBL," 14 June 1950, Dailey Records, 1950a.

65. *Ibid.*; Fred Leo to Team Presidents, 31 May 1950, Dailey Records, 1950a.

66. AAGBBL Board Meeting Minutes, 19 July 1950, Dailey Records.

67. *Ibid.*, 11 June 1950 and 29 February 1954.

68. AAGBBL News Release, 8 February 1950, Dailey Records, 1950a.

69. "League Meeting Called," 23 September 1949, Dailey Records, 1947–1949; Telegram from South Bend Directors to Management and Team Presidents, 3 October 1949, Dailey Records, 1950a; Harold Van Orman Telegram to Fred Leo, 30 June 1950, Dailey Records, 1950a.

70. AAGBBL News Release, 21 November 1950, Dailey Records, 1950a.

71. *Ibid.*; Earle McCammon Bulletin to Team Presidents, 12 June 1952, Dailey Records, 1952; AAGBBL Board Meeting Minutes, 24 January 1954, Dailey Records.

72. AAGBBL Board Meeting Minutes, 18 December 1950, Dailey Records.

Chapter 5

1. Interview with Arthur E. Meyerhoff, Rancho Santa Fe, California, 28 December 1972.

2. See "Published Materials" section of Bibliography.

3. Meyerhoff Files, 1948 Spring Training Release Folder; "History During 1946–7," Dailey Records 1943–1946; "History of the League During 1947 & 1948," Dailey Records, 1943–1946.

4. "History During 1946–7," Dailey Records, 1943–1946.

5. "History of the League During 1947 & 1948," Dailey Records, 1943–1946; *Fort Wayne Journal-Gazette* (Ind.), 24 June 1948, p. 19.

6. *Fort Wayne Journal-Gazette* (Ind.), 24 June 1948, p. 19.

7. *Kenosha Evening News* (Wis.), 29 April 1947, p. 8; AAGBBL News Release, 6 April 1950, Dailey Records, 1950a.

8. AAGBBL News Release, 24 April 1950, Dailey Records, 1950a.

9. Evident throughout Dailey Records, 1943–1954.

10. Telephone interview with Lennie Zintak, 20 July 2004.

11. "Operation of the League," contained in Marjorie L. Pieper's 1953 unaccepted Master's Thesis proposal to the University of Michigan entitled "The Origin and the Development of the All-American Girls Baseball League from 1943–1948 and Comparing Its Standards with Those of the National Section on Women's Athletics." Contributed by Jean Cione, former AAGBBL player and one of Marjorie's teachers. This document is also part of Joanne Winter's history of the AAGBBL, National Baseball Hall of Fame Library, Cooperstown, New York.

12. Mary Lou Studnicka Caden e-mail to Merrie Fidler, 20 June 2004.

13. Mary Lou Studnicka Caden to Merrie Fidler, 15 August 2004.

14. "Chicago Girls Baseball League News Article," Press Release, courtesy of Leonard Zintak, Huntley, IL, August 2004.

15. CGBL Player's Contract, courtesy of Leonard Zintak, Huntley, IL, August 2004.

16. Player Rosters and Winter "Group" List, courtesy of Leonard Zintak, Huntley, IL, August 2004.

17. Betty Francis to Merrie Fidler, 19 July 2004.

18. Joan Holderness to Dolly White, e-mail, 28 June 2004. Joan Holderness to Merrie Fidler, e-mail, 30 June 2004.

19. Dolores Bajda to Merrie Fidler, 3 September, 2004.

20. Mary Lou Studnicka-Caden e-mail to Merrie Fidler, 20 June 2004.

21. Telephone interview with Mary Lou Studnicka Caden, 2 August 2004.

22. Unidentified news clipping from Joan Sindelar's scrapbook, contributed by Yvonne Jacques, Phoenix Arizona, September 2004. Names noted by Lenny Zintak, August 2004.

23. Telephone interview with Mary Lou Studnicka Caden, 2 August 2004.

24. Joyce Smith for Renae Youngberg, e-mail to Dolly White and forwarded to Merrie Fidler, 28 June 2004.

25. *Ibid.*

26. Voigt, *American Baseball*, 2:299.

27. *1945 Racine Belles Year Book*, p. 7; "1945 Season Remarks," Dailey Records, 1943–1946.

28. *1946 Racine Belles Year Book*, p. 28.

29. Interview with Arthur E. Meyerhoff, Rancho Santa Fe, California, 28 December 1972.

30. Doris Sams to Mary Moore, oral history interview, AAGPBL Reunion, Myrtle Beach, South Carolina, 1997.

31. Interview with Delores "Dolly" Brumfield White, Palm Springs, California, 9 January2004.

32. Earlene "Beans" Risinger to Merrie Fidler, December 1975.

33. *Lexington Leader* (Kentucky), 1 June 1947, news clipping in Dailey Records, 1947–1949.

34. "Season of 1946," Dailey Records, 1943–1946.

35. Interview with Jean Faut, South Bend, Indiana, 6 January 1973. Reflecting on this comment, Meyerhoff suggested that the bugs were pinch bugs instead of cockroaches. He also affirmed that league administration was "constantly aware of [its] responsibilities from a health standpoint for the girls, and I believe that when the complaint came up it was investigated very thoroughly to be certain that the best possible conditions prevailed." A.E. Meyerhoff to Merrie Fidler, 8 June 1976. Mr. Meyerhoff may have confused Pascagoula (1946) with Opalocka (1948).

36. "Season of 1946, Dailey records, 1943–1946.

37. "History of the League During 1947 & 1948," Dailey Records, 1943–1946.

38. Marie "Blackie" Wegman to Mary Moore, oral history interview, AAGPBL Reunion, Fort Wayne Indiana, 1996.

39. Arthur E. Meyerhoff to Merrie Fidler, 8 June 1976.

40. "Training Camp Expenses," Dailey Records, 1950a; A.E. Meyerhoff to Merrie Fidler, 8 June 1976.

41. Interview with Jean Faut, South Bend, Indiana, 6 January 1973.

42. Arthur E. Meyerhoff to Merrie Fidler, 8 June 1976.

43. Voigt, *American Baseball*, 2:299.

44. *Kenosha Evening News* (Wis.), 14 May 1947, p. 10; Interview with Jean Faut, South Bend, Indiana, 6 January 1973; "History of the League During 1947 & 1948," Dailey Records, 1943–1946; Interview with Arthur E. Meyerhoff, Rancho Santa Fe, California, 28 December 1972.

45. "History of the League During 1947 & 1948," Dailey Records, 1943–1946.

46. AAGBBL News Release, 12 September 1947, Meyerhoff Files, Drawer 75, 1947 News Release Folder.

47. Interview with Isabel Alvarez, 22 May 2004, Fort Wayne, Indiana.

48. *Ibid.*

49. *1947 Racine Belles Yearbook*, p. 14. Contributed by Jean Cione, Bozeman, Montana, May 2004.

50. AAGBBL News Release, 12 September 1947, Meyerhoff Files, Drawer 75, 1947 News Release Folder.

51. *Racine Journal-Times* (Wis.), 6 May 1947, p. 10.

52. *Ibid.*, 7 May 1947, p. 16.

53. *Ibid.*, 6 May 1947, p. 10.

54. Arthur E. Meyerhoff to Merrie Fidler, 8 June 1976.

55. Isabel Alvarez to Dr. Janis Taylor, oral history interview, AAGPBL Reunion, South Bend, Indiana, 7 August 1993.

56. *Ibid.*

57. *Ibid.*

58. *Ibid.*

59. AAGBBL Board Meeting Minutes, 24 September 1946, Dailey Records.

60. *Ibid.*, 17 October 1947.

61. *Ibid.*, 26 September 1948. See footnote #20.

62. *Ibid.*, 6 October 1948.

63. Dailey Records, 1949–1954.

64. Arthur E. Meyerhoff to Merrie Fidler, 8 June 1976.

65. Barbara Liebrich to Mary Moore, oral history interview, AAGPBL Reunion, Palm Springs, California, 1–5 November 1998.

66. AAGBBL Board Meeting Minutes, 13 April 1949, Dailey Records.

67. Meyerhoff Files, Drawer 75, Barnstorming Tour Folder.

68. Meyerhoff Files, 1949 Exhibition Tour Attendance Folder.

69. Meyerhoff Files, Drawer 25, Report on the 1949 Summer Barnstorming Tour Folder.

70. *Ibid.*

71. Gloria Cordes Ellliott to Mary Moore, oral history interview, AAGPBL Reunion, Fort Wayne, Indiana, 19–22 September 1996.

72. *Ibid.*

73. *Ibid.*

74. AAGBBL Board Meeting Minutes, 10 August 1949, Dailey Records.

75. *Ibid.*, 30 June 1950.

76. Murray Howe to Arthur E. Meyerhoff, 28 July 1949, Meyerhoff Files, 1949 Correspondence Folder.

77. Murray Howe to Arthur E. Meyerhoff, 7 August 1950, Dailey Records, 1950b.

78. AAGBBL News Release, 7 August 1950, Dailey Records, 1950b.

79. Murray Howe to Arthur E. Meyerhoff, 16 July 1950, Meyerhoff Files, Drawer 74, 1950 Barnstorming Tour Folder.

80. AAGBBL News Release, 7 August 1950, Dailey Records, 1950b.

81. Mary Moore to Merrie Fidler, tape recorded memoir, March 2004.

82. *Ibid.*

83. Barbara Liebrich to Mary Moore, oral history interview, AAGPBL Reunion, Palm Springs, California, 1–5 November 1998.

84. *Ibid.*

85. Joan Sindelar to Mary Moore, oral history interview, AAGPBL Reunion, Myrtle Beach, South Carolina, 22–26 October 1997.

86. Pat Courtney to Mary Moore, oral history interview, AAGPBL Reunion, Palm Springs, California, 1–5 November 1998.

87. Jane Moffet to Merrie Fidler, 9 March 2004.

88. Lenora Mandella to Merrie Fidler, 2 February 2004.

89. Barbara Liebrich to Mary Moore, oral history interview, AAGPBL Reunion, Palm Springs, California, 1–5 November 1998.

90. Lenora Mandella to Merrie Fidler, 2 February 2004.

91. AAGBBL News Release, 22 August 1950, Dailey Records, 1950b.

92. AAGBBL Board Meeting Minutes, 20 September 1950, Dailey Records.

93. *Ibid.*

94. "AAGBBL Notes," 21 November 1950, Dailey Records, 1950a; AAGBBL Board Meeting Minutes, 25 June 1951, Dailey Records.

95. AAGBBL Board Meeting Minutes, 13 June 1952, Dailey Records.

96. *Ibid.*, 13 June 1952; 7 July 1952.

97. Thomas VanHyning. *The Santurce Crabbers: Sixty Seasons of Puerto Rican Winter League Baseball*, Jefferson, N.C.: McFarland, 1999, p. 7.

98. Copy of South American Tour Schedule, 15 August 1947, Meyerhoff Files, Drawer 74, S.A. Tour Folder.

99. "Management Agreement," 14 December 1944, Meyerhoff Files, Drawer 19, AAGSBL-Structure Folder.

100. Max Carey to Tour Players, 23 October 1947, Meyerhoff Files, Drawer 74, S.A. Tour Folder.

101. Dorothy "Snookie" Doyle telephone response to Merrie Fidler, 13 October 2004.

102. Mary Rountree to Max Carey, 31 January 1948, Meyerhoff Files, Drawer 74, S.A. Tour Folder.

103. Max Carey to Tour Players, 23 October 1947, Meyerhoff Files, Drawer 74, S.A. Tour Folder.

104. Mary Rountree to Max Carey, 31 January 1948, Meyerhoff Files, Drawer 74, S.A. Tour Folder.

105. *Ibid.*

106. AAGBBL News Release, ca. 16 February 1948, Meyerhoff Files, 1948 News Release Folder.

107. "Memorandum of All American Cooperative Organization Plans for Latin America," 18 April 1948, Meyerhoff Files, Drawer 74, S.A. Tour Folder.

108. *Ibid.*

109. Interview with Isabel Alvarez, Fort Wayne, Indiana, 29 May 2004.

110. This picture was contributed by Jnell Ruetz, Littleton, Colorado, July 2004. It could not be printed here because permission to print releases could not be obtained from the unidentified gentlemen.

111. See Spanish scorecard in Annabelle Lee Harmons memorabilia, Box 3, Northern Indiana Center for History, South Bend, Ind. Leon and his title are listed at the bottom of the Cuban roster.

112. *EL IMPARCIAL, El Diario Ilustrado,* San Juan, Puerto Rico, 11 Marzo de 1949. Annabelle Lee Harmon memorabilia, Box 3, Northern Indiana Center for History, South Bend, Ind. There were three large pictures of the game on what looks to be the front page of this illustrated news magazine.

113. Unidentified Puerto Rican newspaper clipping, but probably from *EL DIA,* Ponce, Puerto Rico, sometime during the week of 7–13 March 1949. Another identified article dated 10 March, from *EL DIA* mentioned the same park as the location for games and the same nickname for the local people. Annabelle Lee Harmons memorabilia, Box 3, Northern Indiana Center for History, South Bend, Ind.

114. Max Carey to Tour Players, 15 April 1949, Meyerhoff Files, Drawer 74, Latin American Tour Folder.

115. Mary Rountree to Max Carey, 31 January 1948, Meyerhoff Files, Drawer 74, S.A. Tour Folder.

116. Max Carey to Dorothy, "Snookie" Doyle, 22 October 1948. Contributed by "Snookie" Doyle, May 2004.

117. AAGBBL News Release, 10 February 1949, Meyerhoff Files, Drawer 74, 1949 Tour Publicity Folder. Ruth Richards Diary of tour agenda and events 4 December 1948 to 11 March 1949. Contributed to Merrie Fidler, 6 January 2004.

118. Dorothy "Kammie" Kamenshek to Merrie Fidler, 31 December 2003.

119. *The Guatemala Bulletin,* 28 January 1949. Copy of newspaper found in the Northern Indiana Center for History, South Bend, Indiana, Annabelle Lee Harmon Memorabilia, Box 3.

120. Max Carey to players, 4 December 1948, contributed by Ruth Richard, 6 January 2004.

121. *Ibid.*

122. Ruth Richard Diary, late January to early March, 1949, contributed to Merrie Fidler 6 January 2004.

123. Interview with Annabelle Lee Harmon, Costa Mesa, California, 26 April 2004.

124. Dorothy "Kammie" Kamenshek to Merrie Fidler, 31 December 2003.

125. *Ibid.*

126. Ruth Richard Diary, 4 February 1949, contributed to Merrie Fidler 6 January 2004.

127. Scorecard Roster of Americanas and Cubanas,

Northern Indiana Center for History, South Bend Indiana, Annabelle Lee Harmon Memorabilia, Box 3.

128. Interview with Annabelle Lee Harmon, Costa Mesa, California, 26 April 2004.

129. Interview with Dorothy "Kammie" Kamenshek, Marge Wenzell, Thelma "Tiby" Eisen, and Dorothy "Snookie" Doyle, Palm Desert, California, 9 January 2004.

130. Dorothy "Kammie" Kamenshek to Merrie Fidler, 31 December 2003.

131. Interview with Annabelle Lee Harmon, Costa Mesa California, 26 April 2004.

132. Dorothy "Kammie" Kamenshek to Merrie Fidler, 31 December 2003.

133. Interview with Annabelle Lee Harmon, Costa Mesa, California, 26 April 2004.

134. Ruth Richard Diary, 7 February and 14 February 1949, contributed to Merrie Fidler, 6 January 2004.

135. *Star & Herald,* Panama, R.P., 9 February 1949, p. 6. Annabelle Lee Harmons memorabilia, Box 3, Northern Indiana Center for History, South Bend, Ind.

136. See Annabelle Lee Harmon memorabilia, Box 3, Northern Indiana Center for History, South Bend, Indiana. This is not an extensive collection of newspaper clippings, but enough to get a sense of the publicity and promotion that attended the games: "All American League Girls Baseball Teams Staging Three Exhibition Games," *The Guatemala Bulletin,* 28 January 1949; "Empatada ayer la Serie de Base-ball Femenino," *La Nueva Prensa,* Managua, Nicaragua, 4 de Febrero de 1949; "Girl Baseball Players Due to Arrive in Canal Zone Tomorrow," *Star & Herald,* Panama, R.P., 9 February 1949;"All Star Girl Teams to Play at Mt. Hope This Evening at 7:30," *Star & Herald,* Panama, R.P., 11 February 1949; "'En Maracaibo No Hace Calor' Afirma Johni Rawlings" *Panorama,* Maracaibo, 4 de Marzo de 1949; A full page picture spread showing game action shots in *El Imparcial, El Diario Ilustrado,* San Juan, Puerto Rico, 11 de Marzo de 1949; "Equipos Femeninos de Beisbol Debutan Esta Tarde Parque Arecibo," *Diario de Puerto Rico,* 12 de Marzo de 1949, p. 17. There is one large poster in the collection which measures about 20" × 30."

137. *Star & Herald,* Panama, R.P., 29 January and 7 February 1949. Annabelle Lee Harmons memorabilia, Box 3, Northern Indiana Center for History, South Bend, Ind.

138. Interview with Thelma "Tiby" Eisen, Dorothy "Kammie" Kamenshek, Marge Wenzell, and Dorothy "Snookie" Doyle, Palm Desert, California, 9 January 2004.

139. Dorothy "Kammie" Kamenshek to Merrie Fidler, 31 December 2003.

140. Interview with Thelma "Tiby" Eisen, Dorothy "Kammie" Kamenshek, Marge Wenzell, and Dorothy "Snookie" Doyle, Palm Desert, California, 9 January 2004.

141. *Ibid.*

142. Interview With Annabelle Lee Harmon, Costa Mesa, California, 26 April 2004.

143. "Empatada ayer la Serie de Base-ball Femenino," *La Nueva Prensa,* Managua, Nicaragua, 4 de Febrero de 1949. There were four pictures on what looks to be the front page of this paper, and three of them dealt with the girls' game.

144. AAGBBL News Release, 10 February 1949, contributed by Annabelle Lee Harmon.

145. Ruth Richard Diary, 10–12 February 1949, contributed to Merrie Fidler, 6 January 2004.

146. Interview with Thelma "Tiby" Eisen, Dorothy Kamenshek, Marge Wenzell, and Dorothy "Snookie" Doyle, Palm Desert, California, 10 January 2004.

147. Sports page article from San José, Costa Rica,

probably 8 March 1949, located in Annabelle Lee Harmon's AAGBBL memorabilia, Box 3, Northern Indiana Center for History, South Bend, Indiana.

148. Angel E. Machado, "EN MARACAIBO NO HACE CALOR," AFIRMA JOHNI RAWLINGS," *PANORAMA*, Maracaibo, Venezuela, 4 Marzo de 1949.

149. Interview with Thelma "Tiby" Eisen, Dorothy Kamenshek, Marge Wenzell, and Dorothy "Snookie" Doyle, Palm Desert, California, 10 January 2004.

150. Max Carey to Tour Players, 15 April 1949, Meyerhoff Files, Drawer 74, Latin American Tour Folder.

151. *Ibid.*

152. *Ibid.*

153. Wilbur Johnson to Arthur Meyerhoff, ca. 24 August 1949, Dailey Records, 1947–1949.

154. Dailey's personal memo on South American Tour incident, Dailey Records, 1947–1949.

155. "Salaries of Players on Management's South American Tour," Dailey Records, 1947–1949.

156. Dailey's personal memo on South American Tour incident, Dailey Records, 1947–1949.

157. Dailey's personal memo preceding Ruetz letter, 27 September 1949, Dailey Records, 1947–1949.

158. *Ibid.*

159. Edward J. Ruetz to Harold T. Dailey, 27 September 1949, Dailey Records, 1947–1949.

160. "League Attendance Figures for 1943–1949, Dailey Records, 1952; AAGBBL News Release, 21 November 1950, Dailey Records, 1950a.

161. Arthur E. Meyerhoff to Merrie Fidler, 8 June 1976.

Chapter 6

1. AGBL Constitution, Article IV, Sec. 2, Dailey Records, 1951a.

2. "Constitution," Article IV, Sec. 2, Dailey Records, 1951a.

3. AAGBBL Board Meeting Minutes, 18 December 1950, Dailey Records.

4. Edward J. Ruetz, Jr., "Play Ball" [Memoirs of an AAGBBL Bat Boy], 2001. Contributed by Jnell Ruetz, July 2004.

5. AAGBBL Board Meeting Minutes, 18 December 1950. *Kenosha News*, spring 1947, spring 1951: These undated newspaper clippings were part of Judge Ruetz's scrapbook contributed by his daughter-in-law, Jnell Ruetz, July 2004. The spring dates were deduced from the content of the articles.

6. *Ibid.*, 20 February 1952.

7. *Ibid.*, 1 October 1951.

8. *Ibid.*

9. *Ibid.*, 15 October 1952.

10. *Kalamazoo Gazette* (Mich.), 13 July 1950, p. 30.

11. *Ibid.*

12. *Ibid.*

13. "Rules and By-Laws," 30 January 1951, Dailey Records, 1951a.

14. AAGBBL Board Meeting Minutes, 25 October 1950, Dailey Records.

15. See TABLE 21, Chapter 12.

16. Interview with Dorothy "Kammie" Kamenshek, Dorothy "Snookie" Doyle, Thelma "Tiby" Eisen, and Marge Wenzell, Palm Desert, California, 9 January 2004.

17. Carl Glans to Dorothy "Snookie" Doyle, 19 March 1948, contributed by Dorothy "Snookie" Doyle.

18. AAGBBL Board Meeting Minutes, 25 October 1950, Dailey Records.

19. *Ibid.*, 10 April 1954.

20. Joyce Hill Westerman to Mary Moore, oral history interview, AAGPBL Mini-Reunion, Chicago, Illinois, July 1999.

21. Jo Lenard to Mary Moore, oral history interview, AAGPBL Mini-Reunion, Chicago, Illinois, July 1999.

22. Jean "Buckets" Buckley to Mary Moore, oral history interview, AAGPBL Reunion, Grand Rapids, Illinois, 5–10 September 2001.

23. *Ibid.*

24. "Rules and Regulations of All-American Girls Baseball League," Article A, Sec. 4, Dailey Records, 1943–1946.

25. "Rules and By-Laws," 30 January 1951, Dailey Records, 1951a.

26. AAGBBL Board Meeting Minutes, 10 April, 2 May 1954, Dailey Records.

27. *Ibid.*, 16 May 1954.

28. *Ibid.*, 24 January 1954

29. *Ibid.*

30. *Ibid.*

31. AAGBBL Board Meeting Minutes, 29 February 1954, Dailey Records.

32. *Ibid.*

33. *Ibid.*, 10 April 1954.

34. *Rockford Register-Republic* (Ill.), 3 May 1954, p. B-3.

35. AAGBBL Board Meeting Minutes, 2 May 1954, Dailey Records.

36. *Ibid.*

37. *Ibid.*

38. Harold T. Dailey Memo, 22 August 1950, Dailey Records, 1950b.

39. Dailey Records, 1950a and 1950b.

40. AAGBBL Board Meeting Minutes, 25 October, 18 December 1950, Dailey Records.

41. *Ibid.*, 12 September 1953.

42. AAGBBL News Release, 21 November 1950, Dailey Records, 1950a.

43. AAGBBL Board Meeting Minutes, 7 July 1952, Dailey Records.

44. "Report of Balancing Committee," 15 March 1950, Dailey Records, 1950a.

45. AAGBBL Board Meeting Minutes, 20 April 1950, Dailey Records.

46. "Report of Balancing Committee," 15 March 1950, Dailey Records, 1950a.

47. *Ibid.*

48. AAGBBL Board Meeting Minutes, 28 May 1952, Dailey Records.

49. Kalamazoo Gazette (Mich.), 2 June 1953, p. 19.

50. AAGBBL Board Meeting Minutes, 10 April 1954, Dailey Records.

51. Voigt, *American Baseball*, 2:296–297.

Chapter 7

1. AAGBBL Board Meeting Minutes, 6 October 1948, Dailey Records.

2. Richard Kraus, *Recreation and Leisure in Modern Society*, New York: Appleton-Century Crofts, 1971, pp. 208–209.

3. AAGBBL Board Meeting Minutes, 24 January 1954, Dailey Records.

4. Harold Dailey personal memo, 2 June, 19 June, 25 June 1951, Dailey Records, 1951a.

5. *Ibid.*, 25 June 1951.

6. "Bulletin to Presidents," 21 March 1951, Dailey Records, 1951a.

7. "Bulletin to Presidents and Business Managers," 12 April 1951, Dailey Records, 1951a.

8. News Release, 16 August 1951, Dailey Records, 1951a.

9. AAGBBL Board Meeting Minutes, 20 February 1952, Dailey Records.

10. *Ibid.*, 23 April 1952.

11. *Ibid.*, 15 October 1952, 2 May 1954.

12. *Ibid.*, 2 May 1954.

13. For examples see news clippings in Dailey Records, 1951a for 11, 14, 16 July, 17 August 1951; Dailey personal memo, 3 July 1952, Dailey Records, 1952.

14. A perusal of newspaper coverage for league teams during May–September, 1953 and 1954, conveys the relative utilization and effectiveness of publicity and promotion by local team administrations.

15. June Peppas to Merrie Fidler 15 November 2003.

16. AAGBBL Board Meeting Minutes, 30 June, 13 July, and 21 August 1950, 24 January 1951, 9 January 1952, Dailey Records.

17. *Ibid.*, 13 June 1952; Souvenir Score Card: "First ... All Star Game, 1952," Dailey Records, 1952.

18. AAGBBL Board Meeting Minutes, 15 August 1952, 1 August 1954, Dailey Records.

19. *Ibid.*, 21 August 1950.

20. *Peoria Star* (Ill.), July and August 1950.

21. Interview with Arthur E. Meyerhoff, Rancho Santa Fe, California, 28 December 1972; "Notes on Meeting Regarding Softball Project," 22 December 1942, Meyerhoff Files, Drawer 19, 1944 Miscellaneous Folder.

22. *Peoria Star* (Ill.), 4 August 1950, p. B-2.

23. Morris Markey, "Hey Ma, You're Out!" *McCall's*, September 1950, p. 80.

24. *Grand Rapids Press* (Mich.), 10 July 1954, p. 23; *Kalamazoo Gazette* (Mich.), 9 August 1954, p. 13; *Fort Wayne Journal-Gazette* (Ind.), 24 August 1954, p. 15; News clipping, 20 July 1954, Dailey Records, 1954.

25. AAGBBL Board Meeting Minutes, 10 June 1954, Dailey Records.

26. *Ibid.*, 6 October 1948, 21 November 1949; "Special Bulletin to Presidents, 7 August 1951: A Letter of Resignation of Fred K. Leo," Dailey Records, 1951a.

27. *Ibid.*, 16 November 1949.

28. "Column Material," ca. 12 April 1951, Dailey Records, 1951a.

29. AAGBBL Board Meeting Minutes, 1 October 1951, Dailey Records.

30. *Ibid.*, 7 July 1952, Dailey Records; "Bulletin From McCammon," 20 October 1952, Dailey Records, 1952.

31. The article in *The Woman* was mentioned in "Bulletin From McCammon," 12 June 1952, Dailey Records, 1952; Bonnie Baker's appearance on "What's My Line," was mentioned in the AAGBBL Board Meeting Minutes, 15 August 1952, Dailey Records.

32. News clippings, Dailey Records, 1951a. "Girl Baseball Teams Play Here Tonight," *The Washington Post*, 14 May 1951, page 11.

33. AAGBBL Board Meeting Minutes 13 June 1952 and 7 July 1952, Dailey Records

34. AAGBBL Board Meeting Minutes, 7 July 1952, 15 August 1952, Dailey Records.

35. News Bulletin, 7 August 1952, Dailey Records, 1952; Chet Riggins, Producer of "Sports Answer Man" of the Armed Forces Information and Education Division, to Earl McCammon, ca. August 1952, Dailey Records, 1952.

36. AAGBBL Board Meeting Minutes, 17 June 1953, Orwant Records, McCammon Folder.

Chapter 8

1. *1944 Racine Belles Year Book*, p. 2

2. *Ibid.*; *1947 Muskegon Lassies Year Book*, pp. 4, 65.

3. *1949 Peoria Redwings Year Book*, p. 3.

4. Ken W. Sells to Harold T. Dailey, n.d., Dailey Records, 1943–1946.

5. Edward J. Ruetz, Jr., "Play Ball!" [Memories of an AAGBBL Bat Boy], donated by his wife, Jnell Ruetz, July 2004.

6. Eddie McKenna, subtitle: "Judge Ruetz Elected as President," *Kenosha News*, 14 March 1944.

7. Eddie McKenna, "Six New Players," undated 1945 article from *Kenosha News* in Judge Ruetz's scrapbook contributed by daughter-in-law Jnell Ruetz, July 2004.

8. Eddie McKenna, "Girls League Directors Elect Judge Ruetz Chairman," undated 1947 *Kenosha News* article in Judge Ruetz's scrapbook, contributed by daughter-in-law Jnell Ruetz, July 2004.

9. *1947 Muskegon Lassies Year Book*, p. 65

10. Dates of respective team presidents' tenure on the League Board of Directors was acquired from AAGBBL Board Meeting Minutes, 14 November 1944 to 1 August 1954, Dailey Records.

11. *Muskegon Lassies Year Book*, p. 65.

12. Interviews with former Grand Rapids business manager, Carl Orwant; chaperone, Dorothy Hunter; and players, Marilyn Jenkins and Joyce Ricketts; Grand Rapids, Michigan, 3 January 1976.

13. AAGBBL attendance figures, 1943–1949, Dailey Records, 1947–1949.

14. Dailey's Personal Memo, 15 September 1950, Dailey Records, 1950a.

15. AAGBBL Board Meeting Minutes, 31 May 1950, Dailey Records.

16. William Wrigley, Jr., With Forrest Crissey, "Owning a Big League Ball Team," *Saturday Evening Post*, 13 September 1930, p. 24.

17. AAGBBL Board Meeting Minutes, 18 December 1950, 25 June 1951, 10 July 1951, 9 January 1952, 28 May 1952, 15 October 1952, Dailey Records.

18. *Ibid.*, 6 February 1951.

19. *Ibid.*, 15 August 1952.

20. *Ibid.*

21. June Peppas to Merrie Fidler, 15 November 2003.

22. AAGBBL Board Meeting Minutes, 7 August 1951.

23. *Peoria Star* (Ill.), 18 July 1950, Sports page; "Special Report to the Peaches Fans, Sponsors, and the General Public," brochure in Dailey Records 1950a.

24. AAGBBL Board Meeting Minutes, 21 August 1950, Dailey Records; AAGBBL News Release, 24 July 1950, Dailey Records, 1950a.

25. *Ibid.*

26. *Peoria Star* (Ill.), 28 July 1950, p. B-2.

27. AAGBBL News Release, 7 March, 6 April, and 12 May 1950, Dailey Records.

28. AAGBBL News clipping, 9 January 1952, Dailey Records, 1952.

29. *Ibid.*, 25 January 1952.

30. AAGBBL Board Meeting Minutes, 29 February 1954, Dailey Records.

31. Interview with Dorothy "Kammie" Kamenshek, Marge Wenzell, Dorothy "Snookie" Doyle, and Thelma "Tiby" Eisen; Palm Desert, California, 10 January 2004.

Chapter 9

1. Ken W. Sells to Harold T. Dailey, n.d., Dailey Records, 1943–1946.

2. Frederick W. Cozens and Florence S. Stumpf, *Sports In American Life*, Chicago: The University of Chicago Press, 1953, p. 213.

3. *Kenosha Evening News* (Wis.), 21 May 1943, p. 10; 28 May 1943, p. 8; *1944 Racine Belles Year Book*, p. 27.

4. *1944 Racine Belles Year Book*, p. 5.

5. *South Bend Tribune Michiana Magazine* (Ind.), 9 July 1972, p. 3.

6. *Ibid.* Chet Grant was mistaken about the teams which joined the league in 1944. It was Milwaukee and Minneapolis rather than Milwaukee and Fort Wayne which joined the league in 1944. Fort Wayne replaced Minneapolis in 1945: *1944 Racine Belles Year Book*; *1945 Racine Belles Year Book*.

7. Thelma "Tiby" Eisen to Merrie Fidler, interview in Palm Desert, California, 10 January 2004.

8. Viola "Tommie" Thompson Griffin to Jan Taylor, oral history interview, AAGPBL Reunion, 6 August 1993.

9. South Bend Tribune (Ind.), 8 August 1949, sports page.

10. *1946 Racine Belles Year Book*, pp. 11–12.

11. *Ibid.*

12. *1947 Grand Rapids Chicks Year Book*, p. 11.

13. *1947 Muskegon Lassies Year Book*, p. 67.

14. Carl L. Biemiller, "Women's Prettiest Ballplayers," *Holiday*, June 1952, p. 77.

15. *1949 Peoria Redwings Year Book*, p. 31.

16. Annabelle Lee Harmon to Dr. Janis Taylor, oral history interview, AAGPBL Reunion, South Bend, Indiana, 6 August 1993.

17. *1944 Racine Belles Year Book*, p. 27.

18. *1944 Racine Belles Year Book*, pp. 15, 20–21; *1945 Racine Belles Year Book*, p. 21; *1946 Racine Belles Year Book*, p. 30; *1947 Grand Rapids Chicks Year Book*, p. 24; *1948 Racine Belles year Book*, p. 29; *1949 Peoria Redwings Year Book*, pp. 54–55; "Season 1949," Dailey Records, 1947–1949; "Season 1950," Dailey Records, 1950a; "All Star Team, 19 September 1950," Dailey Records, 1950a; News clipping, 14 September 1951, Dailey Records, 1951a; News clippings, 2, 11 September 1952, Dailey Records, 1952; "Financial Report, 1953 Play-Offs," Dailey Records, 1954; News clipping, 27 August 1954, Dailey Records, 1954; *Rockford Register-Republic* (Ill.), 6 September 1954, p. B4; *Kalamazoo Gazette* (Mich.), 6 September 1954, p. 17.

19. *Ibid.*

20. Biemiller, "World's Prettiest Ballplayers," p. 77.

21. Helen Filarski Steffes to Jan Taylor, oral history interview, AAGPBL Reunion, South Bend, Indiana, 6 August 1993.

22. Interview with Jean Cione, Ypsilanti, Michigan, 17 June 1974.

23. Katie Horstman to Jan Taylor, oral history interview, AAGPBL Reunion, South Bend, Indiana, 5 August 1993.

24. Helen Filarski Steffes to Jan Taylor, oral history interview, AAGPBL Reunion, South Bend, Indiana, 6 August 1993.

25. Interview with Dorothy "Snookie" Doyle and Dorothy "Kammie" Kamenshek, Palm Desert, California, 10 January 2004.

26. Interview with former Grand Rapids Chicks personnel, Carl Orwant, Marilyn Jenkins, Joyce Ricketts, and Dorothy Hunter, Grand Rapids, Michigan, 3 January 1976.

27. Evidence that Allington's All-Americans played into 1958 is confirmed by "All-Americans Put on Good Show, but Indians Win, 8–6," *Sleepy Eye Herald Dispatch*, Sleepy Eye, Minnesota, 22 July 1958. Contributed by Armand Peterson.

28. "World Champions Official Program," 1957, p. 1 and 6, courtesy of Katie Horstman. Interview with Katie Horstman, Palm Springs, California, 9 January 2004.

29. Interview with Katie Horstman, Palm Springs, California, 9 January 2004.

30. *Ibid.*

31. *Ibid.*

32. Contributed by Jeneane DesCombes Lesko, 31 March 2004.

33. *South Bend Tribune* (Ind.), 18 August 1957, p. 40; 28 August 1957, Sec. 3, p. 1.

34. Carole Ogelsby to Merrie Fidler, Amherst, Massachusetts, April 1973. Carole played for Bill Allington when he coached the Orange Lionettes in the Los Angeles area during the 1960s.

35. Bill Fay, "Belles of the Ball Game," *Colliers*, 13 August 1949, p. 44; AAGBBL News Release, 16 August 1951, Dailey Records, 1951a.

36. Thelma "Tiby" Eisen to Dr. Janis Taylor, AAGPBL Reunion, South Bend, Indiana, 6 August 1993.

37. *Kalamazoo Gazette* (Mich.), 16 June 1950, p. 24. Mary "Wimp" Baumgartner to Merrie Fidler, 23 August 2004.

38. AAGBBL Board Meeting Minutes, 5 July 1950, Dailey Records.

39. *Peoria Star* (Ill.), 31 July 1950, p. B-2; AAGBBL News Release, 1 August 1950, Dailey Records, 1950b; Dailey suggested that manager Murphy had been forced to resign, Dailey personal memo, 31 July 1950, Dailey Records, 1950a.

40. AAGBBL News Release, 16 August 1951, Dailey Records, 1951a.

41. "Season 1950," Dailey Records, 1950a.

42. AAGBBL News Release, 1 August 1950, Dailey Records, 1950b.

43. *1947 Grand Rapids Chicks Year Book*, p. 14; AAGBBL News Release, 16 August 1951, Dailey Records, 1951a.

44. *1945 Racine Belles Year Book*, pp. 8–9.

45. *1947 Muskegon Lassies Year Book*, p. 17.

46. AAGBBL News Release, 16 August 1951, Dailey Records, 1951a.

47. Dailey Notes, 21 November 1950, Dailey Records, 1950a.

48. Dailey personal memo, 29 August 1950, Dailey Records, 1950b.

49. "Season 1950," Dailey Records, 1950a; *Peoria Star* (Ill.), July 1950; *Kalamazoo Gazette* (Mich.), June 1950.

50. Manager's Contract, Chet Grant AAGBBL Collection, Joyce Sports Research Collection, University of Notre Dame Library, South Bend, Indiana; AAGBBL Board Meeting Minutes, 22 February 1946, Dailey Records.

51. AAGBBL Board Meeting Minutes, 19 September 1945, Dailey Records.

52. *Ibid.*, 22 January 1947.

53. *Ibid.*, 22 December 1947.

54. *Fort Wayne Journal-Gazette* (Ind.), 4 August 1949, p. 10.

55. "Brief Historical Summary of the South Bend Blue Sox, 1950," Dailey Records, 1950b; *Racine Journal-Times* (Wis.), 4 June 1945, p. 12.

56. *1949 Peoria Redwings Year Book*, p. 64.

57. "By-Laws," Article IV, 2:b, Meyerhoff Files, Drawer 19, AAGSBL Structure Folder; "The AAGPBL Articles of Association," p. 8, Meyerhoff Files, Drawer 19, 1945 Management Corporation Softball Enterprise Folder.

58. AAGBBL Board Meeting Minutes, 10 November 1947, Dailey Records.

Chapter 10

1. *Kenosha Evening News* (Wis.), 13 May 1943, p. 8.
2. *Ibid.*
3. Terry Donahue to Jan Taylor, oral history interview, AAGPBL Reunion, South Bend, Indiana, 5 August 1993.
4. Joyce Hill Westerman to Jan Taylor, oral history interview, AAGPBL Reunion, South Bend, Indiana 5 August 1993.
5. Interview with Delores "Dolly" Brumfield White, Palm Springs, California, 9 January 2004.
6. Audrey Haine Daniels to Dr Janis Taylor, oral history interview, AAGPBL Reunion, South Bend, Indiana, 5 August 1993.
7. Interview with Dorothy Kamenshek, Palm Desert, California, 10 January 2004.
8. Interview with Thelma "Tiby" Eisen, Palm Desert, California, 10 January 2004.
9. Interview with Delores "Dolly" Brumfield White to Merrie Fidler, Palm Springs, California, 9 January 1993.
10. Interview with Shirley Burkovich, Palm Springs, California, 9 January 2004.
11. Interview with Helen Hannah Campbell, Fountain Valley, California, 11 January 2004; Vivian Kellogg to Dr. Janis Taylor, oral history interview, AAGPBL Reunion, South Bend, Indiana, 5 August 1993.
12. *Kenosha Evening News* (Wis.), 13 May 1943, p. 8.
13. *1944 Racine Belles Year Book*, p. 9.
14. *1945 Racine Belles Year Book*, p. 5.
15. *1946 Racine Belles Year Book*, p. 13.
16. Alexandra "Lex" McCutchen to Jan Taylor, oral history interview, AAGPBL Reunion, South Bend, Indiana, 6 August 1993.
17. *Peoria Redwings Year Book*, p. 19.
18. *Grand Rapids Chicks Year Book*, p. 12.
19. *Ibid.*; Interview with Dorothy Hunter, Grand Rapids, Michigan, 3 January 1976.
20. Interview with Marilyn Jenkins, Grand Rapids, Michigan, 3 January 1976.
21. Interview with Helen Hannah Campbell, Costa Mesa, California, 25 April 2004.
22. *Ibid.* Chamberlain, Ryan, "SABR Nine Questions," *Society for American Baseball Research Bulletin*, May–June, 2004.
23. Interview with Helen Hannah Campbell, Costa Mesa, California, 25 April 2004.
24. *Ibid.*
25. Helen Hannah Campbell to Merrie Fidler, 14 July 2004.
26. *Ibid.*
27. Interview with Helen Hannah Campbell, Costa Mesa, California, 25 April 2004. .
28. *Ibid.*
29. *Ibid.*
30. *Ibid.*
31. *Ibid.*
32. *Ibid.*
33. *Ibid.*
34. Helen Hannah Campbell to Dr. Janis Taylor, oral history interview, AAGPBL Reunion, South Bend, Indiana, 7 August 1993.
35. Helen Hannah Campbell to Dr. Janis Taylor, oral history interview, AAGPBL Reunion, South Bend, Indiana, 7 August 1993.
36. Phone interview with Helen Hannah Campbell, 29 June 2004.
37. Chamberlain, Ryan, "SABR Nine Questions," *Society for American Baseball Research Bulletin*, May–June 2004.
38. Frazier, Russ, "Helen Hannah Campbell: May '99

Booster of the Month," *BOOSTER CHATTER: The Official Angels Booster Club Newsletter*, July 1999.
39. *Ibid.*
40. Interview with Helen Hannah Campbell, Costa Mesa, California, 25 April 2004.
41. AAGBBL Board Meeting Minutes, 14 November 1944, Dailey Records.
42. Alexandra "Lex" McCutchen to Dr. Janis Taylor, oral history interview, AAGPBL Reunion, South Bend, Indiana, 6 August 1993.
43. Interview with Lucille Moore, South Bend, Indiana, 6 January 1973.
44. "All-American Girls Baseball League Chaperone Contract," Meyerhoff Files, Drawer 75, 1948–1949 Springfield Sallies Folder.
45. "Fort Wayne Daisies Official Program and Scorebook," 1952, p. 5, contributed to the author by Marilyn Jenkins, Grand Rapids, Michigan.
46. "All-American Girls Baseball League Chaperone Contract," Meyerhoff Files, Drawer 75, 1948–1949 Springfield Sallies Folder.
47. AAGBBL Board Meeting Minutes, 16 November 1945, Dailey Records.
48. *Ibid.*
49. *Ibid.*, 25 June 1947; 20 April 1950, and 20 February 1952.
50. *Ibid.*, 24 September 1946.
51. *1947 Muskegon Lassies Year Book*, pp. 10–19.
52. AAGBBL Board Meeting Minutes, 15 June 1946, Dailey Records.
53. *Ibid.*, 24 September 1946.
54. *Ibid.*, 20 February 1952.
55. *Ibid.*, 23 April 1952.
56. *1947 Muskegon Lassies Year Book*, p. 19.
57. AAGBBL Board Meeting Minutes, 2 October 1949, Dailey Records.
58. *Ibid.*, 22 February 1946.
59. Interview with Chet Grant, South Bend, Indiana, 6 January 1973.
60. "Monthly Payroll of South Bend Blue Sox, Inc.," 9 June 1952, Dailey Records, 1952.
61. AAGBBL Board Meeting Minutes, 18 January 1950, Dailey Records.
62. "Season 1950," Team Roster Lists, Dailey Records, 1950a.
63. "Agenda for September Meeting," 13 September 1950, Dailey Records, 1950a.
64. AAGBBL Board Meeting Minutes, 20 September 1950, Dailey Records.
65. "AAGBBL Rules," 21 February 1951, Dailey Records, 1951a.
66. D.C.P. Grant, "I Managed Girl Baseball Teams," *South Bend Tribune Michiana Magazine* (Ind.), 9 July 1972, p. 6.

Chapter 11

1. "Mr. Wrigley's Statement for the Press on the Girls' All-American Softball League," 17 February 1943, Meyerhoff Files, Drawer 19, News Release Folder.
2. "Ladies of Little Diamond," *Time*, 14 June 1943, p. 74.
3. Management Corporation Softball Enterprise Folder, Meyerhoff Files, Drawer 19.
4. Interview with Arthur E. Meyerhoff, Rancho Santa Fe, California, 28 December 1972.
5. *Kenosha Evening News* (Wis.), 19 May 1943, p. 10; 20 May 1943, p. 14; 22 May 1943, p. 3; 24 May 1943, p. 8.

6. Clara Schillace to Jan Taylor, oral history interview, AAGPBL Reunion, South Bend, Indiana, 6 August 1993.

7. Shirley Jameson to Jan Taylor, oral history interview, AAGPBL Reunion, South Bend, Indiana, 7 August 1993.

8. *Ibid.*, 17 June 1943, p. 8; 18 June 1943, p. 8; 19 June 1943, p. 3.

9. *Ibid.*, 5 May 1943, p. 8; 17 June 1943, p. 8; 18 June 1943, p. 8; 19 June 1943, p. 3; 21 June 1943, p. 8; 22 June 1943, p. 8.

10. *1944 Racine Belles Year Book*, p. 24.

11. Elizabeth "Lib" Mahon and Viola "Tommie" Thompson Griffin to Jan Taylor, oral history interviews, AAGPBL Reunion, South Bend, Indiana, 5 August, 1993 and 6 August 1993 respectively.

12. Vivian Kellogg to Jan Taylor, oral history interview, AAGPBL Reunion, South Bend, Indiana, 5 August 1993.

13. Marge Callahan Maxwell to Jan Taylor, oral history interview, AAGPBL Reunion, South Bend, Indiana, 6 August 1993.

14. Betty Trezza to Jan Taylor, oral history interview, AAGPBL Reunion, South Bend, Indiana, 6 August 1993.

15. AAGBBL News Release, 24 July 1950, Dailey Records, 1950a.

16. Wilma Briggs to Jan Taylor, oral history interview, AAGPBL Reunion, South Bend, Indiana, 7 August 1993.

17. Sue Kidd to Jan Taylor, oral history interview, AAGPBL Reunion, South Bend, Indiana, 7 August 1993.

18. Interview with Delores "Dolly" Brumfield White, Palm Springs, California, 9 January 2004.

19. Interview with Shirley Burkovich, Palm Springs, California, 9 January 2004.

20. *Ibid.*

21. *1944 Racine Belles Year Book*, p. 8

22. *Ibid.*, p. 27.

23. Interview with Dorothy Hunter, Grand Rapids, Michigan, 3 January 1976.

24. Interview with Jean Faut, Elizabeth Mahon, and Betsy Jochum, South Bend, Indiana, 6 January 1973; Interview with Jean Cione, Ypsilanti, Michigan, 17 June 1974; interview with Nancy Mudge Cato, Elk River, Minnesota, 26 October 1974; Interview with Dorothy Hunter, Marilyn Jenkins, and Joyce Ricketts, Grand Rapids, Michigan, 3 January 1976.

25. *Kenosha Evening News* (Wis.), 5 June 1943, p. 3.

26. Dorothy "Kammie" Kamenshek to Dr. Janis Taylor, oral history interview, AAGPBL Reunion, South Bend, Indiana, 7 August 1993.

27. Gloria Cordes Elliott to Mary Moore, oral history interview, AAGPBL Reunion, Fort Wayne, Indiana 19–22 September 1996.

28. Interview with Dorothy "Snookie" Doyle, Thelma "Tiby" Eisen, Palm Desert, California, 10 January 2004. Arleene Johnson Noga to Mary Moore, oral history interview, AAGPBL Reunion, Myrtle Beach, South Carolina, 22–26 October 1997.

29. Sue Kidd to Dr. Janis Taylor, oral history interview, AAGPBL Reunion, South Bend, Indiana, 7 August 1993.

30. Jean Faut to Mary Moore, oral history interview, AAGPBL Reunion, Fort Wayne, Indiana, 19–22 September 1996.

31. Joanne Winter to Dr. Janis Taylor, oral history interview, AAGPBL Reunion, South Bend, Indiana, 7 August 1993.

32. Jennie Romatowski to Dr. Janis Taylor, oral history interview, AAGPBL Reunion, South Bend, Indiana, 5 August 1993.

33. "Babette Ruths," *Newsweek*, 29 July 1946, p. 68.

34. Interviews with Jean Faut Winsch, Elizabeth Mahon, and Betsy Jochum, South Bend, Indiana, 6 January 1973; Jean Cione, Ypsilanti, Michigan, 17 June 1974; Nancy Mudge Cato, Elk River, Minnesota, 26 October 1974.

35. See Dr. Janis Taylor's oral history interviews, 5–7 August 1993, and Mary Moore's oral history interviews from annual AAGPBL Reunions, 1996–2004.

36. AAGBBL News clipping, 10 May 1951, Dailey Records, 1951a.

37. AAGBBL Board Meeting Minutes, 14 November 1951, Dailey Records.

38. Memo, 4 June 1952, Dailey Records, 1952; *South Bend Tribune* (Ind.), June–August 1952.

39. Interview with Jean Faut Winsch, South Bend, Indiana, 6 January 1973.

40. *Fort Wayne Journal-Gazette* (Ind.), 18 July 1954, sports page.

41. AAGBBL News Release, 23 February, 15 March, 21 March, 6 April, 16 June, 1 July, 13 July, 1 August, 7 August 1950, Dailey Records, 1950a.

42. Annabelle Lee Harmon to Dr. Janis Taylor, oral history interview, AAGPBL Reunion, South Bend, Indiana, 6 August 1993.

43. AAGBBL News Release, 6 April 1950, Dailey Records, 1950a.

44. William Henry Chafe, *The American Woman: Her Changing Social, Economic, and Political Roles, 1920–1970*, New York: Oxford University Press, 1972, pp. 217–218.

45. Interviews with Jean Faut, Jean Cione, Nancy Mudge Cato, Marilyn Jenkins, Joyce Rickets, Betsy Jochum, Elizabeth "Lib" Mahon, 1973–1976; Dr. Janis Taylor oral history interviews, August 1993, and Mary Moore oral history interviews, 1996–2004.

46. Morris Markey, "Hey Ma, You're Out!" *McCall's*, September 1950, p. 80.

47. Madeline "Maddy" English to Dr. Janis Taylor, oral history interview, AAGPBL Reunion, South Bend, Indiana, 5 August 1993.

48. Interview with Dorothy "Snookie" Harrell Doyle, Thelma "Tiby" Eisen, Marge Wenzell, and Dorothy "Kammie" Kamenshek, Palm Desert, California, 10 January 2004.

49. *Ibid.*

50. Rosemary Stevenson to Dr. Janis Taylor, oral history interview, AAGPBL Reunion, South Bend, Indiana, 7 August 1993.

51. Sue Kidd to Dr. Janis Taylor, oral history interview, AAGPBL Reunion, South Bend, Indiana, 7 August 1993.

52. Interview with Delores "Dolly" Brumfield White, Shirley Burkovich, Katie Horstman, and Maybelle Blair, Palm Springs, California, 9 January 2004.

53. Earlene Risinger to Merrie Fidler, December 1975.

54. Thankfully, other authors have begun the task of exploring the players' lives to a greater extent than it was possible for this author to do. For the most prominent, see: Lois Browne, *Girls of Summer: In Their Own League*, Toronto, Canada: Harper Collins, 1992; Patricia I. Brown, *A League of My Own: Memoir of a Pitcher for the All-American Girls Professional Baseball League*, Jefferson, N.C.: McFarland, 2003; Barbara Gregorich, *Women at Play: The Story of Women in Baseball*, New York: A Harvest Original, Harcourt, Brace, 1993; Diana Star Helmer, *Belles of the Ballpark*, Brookfield, Conn.: Millbrook, 1993, Susan E. Johnson, *When Women Played Hardball*, Canada: Seal Press, 1994; Sue Macy, *A Whole New Ball Game: The Story of the All-American Girls Professional Baseball League* , New York: Henry Holt, 1993;

W.C. Madden, The *Women of the All-American Girls Professional Baseball League: A Biographical Dictionary*, Jefferson, N.C.: McFarland, 1997; Carolyn Trombe, *Dottie Wiltse Collins: Strikeout Queen of the All-American Girls Professional Baseball League*, Jefferson, N.C.: McFarland, 2005.

Chapter 12

1. Interview with Nancy Mudge Cato, Elk River, Minnesota, 26 October 1974. Interview with Dorothy "Kammie" Kamenshek, Palm Desert, California, 10 January 2004.

2. Interview with Elizabeth Mahon and Jean Faut Winsch, South Bend, Indiana, 6 January 1973; Interview with Jean Cione, Ypsilanti, Michigan, 17 June 1974; interview with Nancy Mudge Cato, Elk River, Minnesota, 26 October 1974.

3. *Ibid.*

4. *Ibid.*

5. AAGBBL Board Meeting Minutes, 14 November 1944, Dailey Records.

6. *Chicago Daily News*, 10 February 1943, Sports Section, p. 15.

7. *Ibid.*, 11 May 1943, Sport Editorial; 14 July 1951, Photo Section, "Hurray for Mama!"; "TV Glamazons Scramble for Baseball Crown," *TV Forecaster*, ca. June 1951, pp. 44–45, Dailey Records, 1951a.

8. AAGBBL Board Meeting Minutes, 24 September 1946; Letter from National Girls Baseball League President to Max Carey, 11 May 1948, Dailey Records, 1947–1949; AAGBBL News Release, 6 February 1950, Dailey Records, 1950a.

9. *Girls Baseball*, Publisher's Press, Chicago, Illinois, 15 June 1950. According to the editor's note, this publication in previous years had been the voice of the National Girls' Baseball League (NGBL). As of 1950, it claimed to be independent of the NGBL, though still committed to publicizing important facts and figures about the NGBL as well as other girls' baseball. The 15 June 1950 edition included an article about the AAGBBL and listed rosters for all 8 AAGBBL teams. This publication was contributed to the author by Dorothy "Snookie" Doyle, May 2004.

10. AAGBBL Board Meeting Minutes, 1 May 1947, Dailey Records.

11. *Ibid.*, 17 March 1948.

12. Letter from National Girls Baseball League President to Max Carey, 11 May 1948, Dailey Records, 1947–1949.

13. AAGBBL Board Meeting Minutes, 20 May 1949, Dailey Records.

14. "Bulletin to All Presidents," 1 December 1949, Dailey Records, 1950a.

15. AAGBBL News Release, 10 February 1950, Dailey Records, 1950a.

16. AAGBBL Board Meeting Minutes, 19 July 1950, Dailey Records.

17. *Peoria Star* (Ill.), 18 July 1950, p. B-2; Memo, 17 July 1950, Dailey Records, 1950a.

18. AAGBBL Board Meeting Minutes, 21 August 1950, Dailey Records.

19. Memo, 24 July 1950, Dailey Records, 1950a; Telegram from Fred Leo to Harold Dailey, 29 July 1950, Dailey Records, 1950a.

20. Memo, 24 May 1952, Dailey Records, 1952.

21. "Rules and Regulations of the All-American Girls Baseball League," ca. 1946, Dailey Records, 1943–1946.

22. "American Girls Baseball League Rules, Adopted for 1951," Dailey Records, 1951a.

23. "Rules and Regulations of the All-American Girls Baseball League," ca. 1946, Dailey Records, 1943–1946.

24. "American Girls Baseball League Rules Adopted for 1951," Dailey Records, 1951a.

25. AAGBBL Board Meeting Minutes, 14 November 1944, Dailey Records.

26. *1944 Racine Belles Year Book*, pp. 6–8; *1945 Racine Belles Year Book*, pp. 8–10.

27. AAGBBL Board Meeting Minutes, 14 November 1944, Dailey Records.

28. "Rules and Regulations of the All-American Girls Baseball League," ca. 1946, Dailey Records, 1943–1946.

29. *Ibid.*

30. *Ibid.*

31. AAGBBL News Release, 7 March 1950, Dailey Records, 1950a.

32. AAGBBL Board Meeting Minutes, 4 May 1946, Dailey Records.

33. *Ibid.*, 13 November 1946; 30 April–1 May 1947.

34. *Ibid.*, 20 January 1948; 21 April 1948.

35. "Report of Allocation Committee," 2 October 1949, Dailey Records, 1950a; AAGBBL News Release, 7 March 1950, Dailey Records, 1950a; Fred Leo to Team Presidents, 5 January 1950, Dailey Records, 1950a.

36. Harold Van Orman to Fred Leo, 30 June 1950, Dailey Records, 1950a.

37. "American Girls Baseball League Rules and Regulations, Adopted for Playing Season 1951," Dailey Records, 1951a.

38. Notice of League Meeting from Earle McCammon, 22 February 1954, Dailey Records, 1954.

39. AAGBBL Board Meeting Minutes, 16 May 1954, Dailey Records.

40. For examples see Memo, 8 August 1950, Dailey Records, 1950b; Memo 23 June 1951, Dailey Records, 1951; AAGBBL News Release, 21 June 1951, Dailey Records, 1951a.

41. AAGBBL Board Meeting Minutes, 25 June 1947, Dailey Records.

42. *Ibid.*, 2 October 1949, "Report of the Allocation Committee," Dailey Records, 1950a.

43. *Ibid.*

44. Interview with Jean Faut Winsch, Elizabeth Mahon, and Betsy Jochum, South Bend, Indian, 6 January 1973; interview with Jean Cione, Ypsilanti, Michigan, 17 June 1974; interview with Nancy Mudge Cato, Elk River, Minnesota, 26 October 1974.

45. Dolly Pearson Tesseine to Jan Taylor, oral history interview, AAGPBL Reunion, South Bend, Indiana, 7 August 1993.

46. Interview with Betsy Jochum, South Bend, Indiana, 6 January 1973.

Chapter 13

1. Interviews with Arthur E. Meyerhoff, Rancho Santa Fe, California, 28 December 1972; Chet Grant, Gadget Ward, Ed Des Lauriers and Lucille Moore, South Bend, Indiana, 6 January 1973; John Schultz, Minneapolis, Minnesota, 19 June 1975; Carl Orwant and Dorothy Hunter, Grand Rapids, Michigan, 3 January 1976.

2. *Fort Wayne Journal-Gazette* (Ind.), 18 July 1954, sports page.

3. AAGBBL Board Meeting Minutes, 9 January 1952, Dailey Records.

4. *Ibid.*, 23 April 1952.

5. *Ibid.*, 15 August 1952; 1 August 1954.

6. *1947 Grand Rapids Chicks Year Book*, p. 13.

7. "Babette Ruths," *Newsweek*, 29 July 1946, p. 69.

8. *1947 Grand Rapids Chicks Year Book*, p. 13.

9. *Ibid.*, p. 27.

10. *1948 Racine Belles Year Book*, pp. 21–22.

11. *1949 Peoria Redwings Year Book*, p. 45.

12. *Ibid.*

13. *Ibid.*, pp. 33–35; All Star List, Dailey Records, 1947–1949; "Daisy Fan Club Newsletter," December 1951, Dailey Records, 1952; "Bulletin," Dailey Records, 1952.

14. AAGBBL News Release, 10 February 1950, Dailey Records, 1950a.

15. *Ibid.*, 8 February 1950.

16. Marilyn Jenkins to Merrie Fidler, 4 January 1976.

17. Howe News Bureau Official AAGBBL Records, Dailey Records, 1953, 1954.

18. Terry Donahue to Jan Taylor, oral history interview, South Bend, Indiana, 5 August 1993.

19. *Fort Wayne Journal-Gazette* (Ind.), 14 June 1952, p. 11.

20. *1944 Racine Belles Year Book*, p. 11.

21. Figures compiled from *1945 Racine Belles Year Book*, pp. 17–18; *1946 Racine Belles Year Book*, pp. 24–25; *1947 Grand Rapids Chicks Year Book*, pp. 25–26; *1948 Racine Belles Year Book*, pp. 20–21; *1949 Peoria Redwings Year Book*, pp. 41–42; Howe News Bureau Official AAGBBL Records, 1949, 1950, Dailey Records, 1947–1949, 1950a.

22. *Ibid.*

23. *1947 Grand Rapids Chicks Year Book*, pp. 27–29.

24. Howe News Bureau Official AAGBBL Records, 1950, Dailey Records, 1950a.

25. *1946 Racine Belles Year Book*, p. 16.

26. *1947 Muskegon Lassies Year Book*, p. 27.

27. Interview with Nancy Mudge Cato, Elk River, Minnesota, 26 October 1974.

28. Howe News Bureau Official AAGBBL Records, 1 September 1952, Dailey Records, 1952; "Bulletin Announcing 1952 All-Star Selections," 1 July 1952, Dailey Records, 1952.

29. Bulletin, 7 August 1952, Dailey Records, 1952.

30. *1948 Racine Belles Year Book*, p. 33.

31. "Managers' Choice of Player of the Year — 1949," Dailey Records, 1947–1949.

32. *Kalamazoo Gazette* (Mich.), 19 July 1953, p. 29.

33. Howe News Bureau Official AAGBBL Records, 1953, Dailey Records, 1954.

34. *1949 Peoria Redwings Year Book*, p. 33.

35. "Managers' Choice of Player-of-the-Year and The All-Star Team of 1948," 18 November 1948, Dailey Records, 1947–1949.

36. Lex McCutchen to Jan Taylor, oral history interview, South Bend, Indiana, 6 August 1993.

37. AAGBBL News Release, 8 February 1950, Dailey Records, 1950a.

38. Survey of AAGBBL Players by Ed Des Lauriers and Arnold C. Bauer, South Bend, Indiana, June 1963. Contributed to the author by Elizabeth Mahon, South Bend, Indiana.

39. Interview with Elizabeth Mahon, South Bend, Indiana, 6 January 1973.

40. "The All-Star Team," 19 September 1950, Dailey Records, 1950a.

41. *1949 Muskegon Lassies Year Book*, p. 35.

42. Dailey Records, 1947–1949.

43. Howe News Bureau Official AAGBBL Records, 1953, Dailey Records, 1954.

44. *1945 Racine Belles Year Book*, pp. 18, 20; *1946 Racine Belles Year Book*, pp. 25, 27; *1947 Grand Rapids Chicks Year Book*, pp. 26–27; *1948 Racine Belles Year Book*, pp. 20, 22; *1949 Muskegon Lassies Year Book*, pp. 33, 37; Howe News Bureau Official AAGBBL Records, 1949–1953, Dailey Records, 1947–1954.

45. *Grand Rapids Chicks Year Book*, p. 13.

46. Interview with Marilyn Jenkins, Joyce Ricketts, and Dorothy Hunter, Grand Rapids, Michigan, 3 January 1976.

47. Howe News Bureau Official AAGBBL Records, 1950, Dailey Records, 1950a.

48. *Ibid.*, 1953, Dailey Records, 1954.

49. Interview with Jean Cione, Ypsilanti, Michigan, 17 June 1974.

50. Interview with Jean Faut Winsch, South Bend, Indiana, 6 January 1973.

51. *Ibid.*; *1947 Muskegon Lassies Year Book*, p. 37.

52. Howe News Bureau Official AAGBBL Records, 1951–1953, Dailey Records, 1951b, 1952, and 1954.

53. *1948 Racine Belles Year Book*, p. 21; *1949 Peoria Redwings Year Book*, p. 45; Howe News Bureau Official AAGBBL Records, 1949–1953, Dailey Records, 1947–1954.

54. *Ibid.*; Faut's ERA for 1949 was not available.

55. *Ibid.*

56. *Ibid.*

57. News clipping, 22 July 1951, Dailey Records, 1951a.

58. *South Bend Tribune* (Ind.), 4 September 1953, Sec. 3, p. 1.

59. *1948 Racine Belles Year Book*, p. 21; *1949 Peoria Redwings Year Book*, p. 45; Howe News Bureau Official AAGBBL Records, 1949–1953, Dailey Records, 1947–1953.

60. Howe News Bureau Official AAGBBL Records, 1 September 1952, Dailey Records, 1952; News clipping, 12 September 1952, Dailey Records, 1952.

61. "Daisy Fan Club Newsletter," December 1951, Dailey Records, 1952; "Bulletin Announcing All Star Team," 1952, Dailey Records, 1952; *Fort Wayne Journal-Gazette* (Ind.), 12 July 1953.

62. Betty Wagoner to Jan Taylor, oral history interview, South Bend, Indiana, 6 August 1993.

63. News clipping, 5 January 1951, Dailey Records, 1951a.

64. *Ibid.*

65. Dailey Records, 1951–1954.

66. News clipping, 14 September 1951, Dailey Records, 1951a; News clipping, 11 September 1952, Dailey Records, 1952.

67. Karl Winsch to Jan Taylor, oral history interview, South Bend, Indiana, 5 August 1993.

68. AAGBBL News Release, 7 August 1950, Dailey Records, 1950b.

69. *Ibid.* After 1950 she was switched to first base.

70. *Ibid.*

71. *Ibid.*

72. *Ibid.*

73. Howe News Bureau Official AAGBBL Records, 1950, Dailey Records, 1950a.

74. *Ibid.*, 1951, Dailey Records, 1951b.

75. *Ibid.*, 1952, Dailey Records, 1952.

76. "Bulletin," 1 July 1952, Dailey Records, 1952.

77. Howe News Bureau Official AAGBBL Records, 1953, Dailey Records, 1954.

78. *Ibid.*

79. AAGBBL News Release, 7 August 1950, Dailey Records, 1950b.

80. News clipping, 19 May 1951, Dailey Records, 1951a.

81. George Honold, "A 'shining star' in the Daisies' lineup," *Fort Wayne Journal-Gazette*, 8 May 1977. Contributed by Jean Geissinger Harding, July 2004.

82. Howe News Bureau Official AAGBBL Records, 1952, Dailey Records, 1952.

83. *Ibid.*, 1953, Dailey Records, 1954.

84. "Results of Poll for All-Star Game, By Representatives of Press and Radio, July 2, 1954," Dailey Records, 1954; Howe News Bureau Official AAGBBL Records, 15 August 1954, Dailey Records, 1954: These were the last official records available for 1954.

85. "Single Season Leaders for Batting Average," Baseball-Reference.com, Leaders.

86. George Honold, "A 'shining star' in the Daisies' lineup," *Fort Wayne Journal-Gazette*, 8 May 1977. Contributed by Jean Geissinger Harding, July 2004.

87. *Ibid.*

88. *Ibid.*

89. Dailey records, 1950–1954.

90. June Peppas to Jan Taylor, oral history interview, South Bend, Indiana, 5 August 1993.

91. Interview with Dorothy Kamensheck, Palm Desert, California, 10 January 2004.

92. *1944 Racine Belles Year Book*, pp. 16, 19; *1945 Racine Belles Year Book*, pp. 17, 20; *1946 Racine Belles Year Book*, pp. 24, 27; *1947 Muskegon Lassies Year Book*, pp. 35, 39; *1948 Racine Belles Year Book*, pp. 20, 22; Howe News Bureau Official AAGBBL Records, 1949–1953, Dailey Records, 1947–1949, 1950a, 1951b, 1952, and 1954.

93. Howe News Bureau Official AAGBBL Records, 1949, Dailey Records, 1947–1949; *1947 Grand Rapids Chicks Year Book*, p. 25; *1948 Racine Belles Year Book*, p. 20.

94. *1949 Peoria Redwings Year Book*, pp. 48, 50.

95. *Peoria Star* (Ill.), 4 August 1950, p. B-2.

96. *Ibid.*

97. *Rockford Register-Republic* (Ill.), 21 August 1950, p. 22.

98. Dorothy Kamensheck to Jan Taylor, oral history interview, South Bend, Indiana, 7 August 1993.

99. *Ibid.*

100. "A Peaches & Kamenshek fan," to Dottie Kamenshek, Rockford, Illinois, 11 September 1945. Contributed to the author by Dorothy "Kammie" Kamenshek, May 2004.

101. *Rockford Register Republic*, 6 May 1953, p. B5; 3 May 1954, p. B3.

102. Interviews with Chet Grant, South Bend, Indiana, 6 January 1973; John Schultz, Minneapolis, Minnesota, 19 June 1975, and Harold J. VanderZwaag, Amherst, Massachusetts, 26 January 1976.

Chapter 14

1. Telephone conversation with Jean Faut, March 2004.

2. *TODAY'S NEWS, AAGPBL Newsletter*, summer 1983. All newsletters cited hereafter were contributed by Jean Geissinger Harding, May 2004. Newsletters are also available at the Northern Indiana Center for History, South Bend, Indiana.

3. Player survey result booklet printed and distributed to respondents by Arnold C. Bauer and Ed Des Laurier. Contributed by Jean Geissinger Harding, May 2004.

4. *Ibid.*

5. *Ibid.*

6. Fort Wayne Women's Bureau Brochure, contributed by Jean Geissinger Harding, May 2004.

7. Susan Johnson interview of Sharon Taylor-Roepke, 29 September 1992; Sharon Taylor-Roepke to Merrie Fidler, 22 August 1977. Interview with Sharon Taylor-Roepke, 27 August 2004.

8. Interview with Sharon Taylor-Roepke, 27 August 2004.

9. *TODAY'S NEWS, AAGPBL Newsletter*, May 1981.

10. Sharon Taylor-Roepke to Merrie Fidler, 22 August 1977, 3 December 1977, 28 February 1978, 3 March 1982, 6 June 1982, and 16 July 1982.

11. Interview with Dorothy "Kammie" Kamenshek and Marge Wenzell, Palm Desert, California, 4 April 2004. Telephone conversation with Kammie and Marge, 14 July 2004.

12. *TODAY'S NEWS, AAGPBL Newsletter*, July 1981.

13. *TODAY'S NEWS, AAGPBL Newsletter*, January 1981.

14. *TODAY'S NEWS, AAGPBL Newsletter*, February 1981.

15. *TODAY'S NEWS, AAGPBL Newsletter*, March 1981, cited from Fran Janssen's letter.

16. *TODAY'S NEWS, AAGPBL Newsletter*, February 1981.

17. *Ibid.*

18. *Ibid.*

19. *TODAY'S NEWS, AAGPBL Newsletter*, March 1981.

20. *TODAY'S NEWS, AAGPBL Newsletter*, September 1981.

21. Bob Towner, "Blue Sox reunion draws players and memories," *South Bend Tribune*, 23 August 1981. Contributed by Jean Geissinger Harding, May 2004.

22. *Ibid.*

23. *1981 Run, Jane, Run Women In Sports*, Brochure, sponsored by the Fort Wayne Women's Bureau and WMEE Radio, 26 and 27 September 1981; and George Honold, "Daisies remember the good old days," *Fort Wayne Journal Gazette*, 28 September 1981.

24. George Honold, "Daisies remember the good old days," *Fort Wayne Journal-Gazette*, 28 September 1981.

25. *Ibid.*, and *TODAY'S NEWS, AAGBBL Newsletter*, October 1981.

26. *TODAY'S NEWS, AAGPBL Newsletter*, October 1981.

27. Telephone interview with Ruth Davis, 15 July 2004.

28. Ruth Davis to Merrie Fidler, 21 June 2004.

29. *Ibid.*

30. Bob Wagner, Girls' pro baseball league made impact," *Kalamazoo Gazette*, 28 February 1982. Reported in *TODAY'S NEWS, AAGPBL Newsletter*, May 1982.

31. Ruth Davis to Merrie Fidler 21 June 2004.

32. Pepper Paire Davis, "Good Morning All-Americans," *TODAY'S NEWS, AAGPBL Newsletter*, Fall 1982.

33. Bob Becker, "First-Ever Reunion Hatches Priceless Baseball Memories," *Grand Rapids Press*, 7 July 1982. Contributed by Jean Geissinger Harding, May 2004. Marge Wenzell emphasized that for the most part everyone checked name tags first because they had all changed considerably between the end of their playing days and 1982 and didn't recognize each other. Telephone interview with Marge Wenzell, 20 July 2004.

34. The author's sentiments as she sat in the lobby observing players reunite.

35. *TODAY'S NEWS, AAGPBL Newsletter*, August 1982.

36. Undated, unsigned letter contributed by Jean Geissinger Harding, May 2004.

37. *Ibid.*

38. Notice in front of January 1984 issue of the newsletter, contributed by Jean Geissinger Harding, May 2004.

39. Undated, hand written letter by Pepper Paire to AAGPBL members between January and February 1984 newsletters, contributed by Jean Geissinger Harding, May 2004.

40. *AAGPBL Newsletter*, October 1986.

41. *TOUCHING BASES AAGPBL Newsletter*, October 1993.

42. Jeneane DesCombes Lesko to Merrie Fidler, 10 October 2004.

43. *AAGPBL Newsletter,* August 1985.

44. Letter from Fort Wayne Convention and Visitors Bureau to Dottie Collins, 11 September 1985. Contributed by Jean Geissinger Harding, May 2004.

Chapter 15

1. Merrie Fidler to *TODAY'S NEWS, AAGPBL Newsletter*, May 1981. The author knew Jean Faut Winsch had donated Dr. Harold Dailey's Records to the Notre Dame Sports and Games Collection.

2. Sharon Roepke to *TODAY'S NEWS, AAGPBL Newsletter*, May 1981.

3. Sharon Roepke interview with Susan Johnson, 29 September 1992. Susan Johnson AAGBBL research materials collection, Northern Indiana Center for History, South Bend, Indiana.

4. *TODAY'S NEWS, AAGPBL Newsletter*, January 1982.

5. Ruth Williams to *TODAY'S NEWS, AAGPBL Newsletter*, July 1981.

6. *TODAY'S NEWS, AAGBBL Newsletter*, October 1981.

7. *TODAY'S NEWS, AAGPBL Newsletter*, June 1982.

8. *AAGPBL, Newsletter*, 40th Anniversary Reunion issue, September/October 1982. (By this time Shirley Stovroff was printing the newsletter and *TODAY'S NEWS* no longer appeared on the letterhead.)

9. "Hardball was these women's game," *Fort Wayne News Sentinel*, 22 September 1982. Contributed by Carolyn Trombe, author of *Dottie Wiltse Collins: Strikeout Queen of the All-American Girls Professional Baseball League*, Jefferson, N.C.: McFarland, 2005.

10. This gentleman's name in the newsletter was spelled "Don Rogisin." Tim Wiles, Research Librarian at the Hall of Fame identified him as a man who had written two baseball books — Donn Rogosin.

11. *AAGPBL, Newsletter*, 40th Anniversary Reunion issue, September/October 1982.

12. Dottie Collins to Merrie Fidler, 17 September 1982.

13. *Ibid.*

14. *AAGPBL, Newsletter*, undated, but content is consistent with the fall of 1982.

15. AAGPBL, Newsletter, July 1983

16. Telephone interview with Jean Geissinger Harding, 15 August 2004.

17. *AAGPBL, Newsletter*, January 1984. *EXTRA INNINGS, AAGPBL Newsletter*, February 1984. (This was the newsletter heading during the time Lavone "Pepper" Paire Davis was editor.)

18. Interview with Sharon Roepke, 27 August 2004. Carolyn Trombe, *Dottie Wiltse Collins: Strikeout Queen of the All-American Girls Professional Baseball League*, Jefferson, N.C.: McFarland, 2005, p. 168.

19. *Ibid.*

20. 1985 Reunion Committee Christmas brochure, in Jean Geissinger Harding's AAGBBL materials scrapbook, 1963 to 1986. Kelly Candaele to Merrie Fidler, 9 August 2004.

21. Janis Taylor to Merrie Fidler, 29 July 2004.

22. Dottie Collins Reunion Letter, *Extra Innings AAGPBL Newsletter*, January/February 1986.

23. *EXTRA INNINGS, AAGPBL Newsletter*, April 1986.

24. Carolyn Trombe, *Dottie Wiltse Collins*, p. 169.

25. *Ibid.* Telephone interview with Ted Spencer, 15 September 2004.

26. *AAGPBL, Newsletter,* October 1986. (When Dottie Collins began editing and printing the newsletter, she utilized a heading similar to that used by Shirley Stovroff in late 1982–83.)

27. *AAGPBL, Newsletter*, December 1986.

28. Janice Mall, "Remembering Those Girls of Summer," *Los Angeles Times*, 4 January 1987.

29. Dottie Collins to Ted Spencer, 12 January 1987, courtesy of Ted Spencer, Baseball Hall of Fame.

30. Ted Spencer interview with Carolyn Trombe, 24 February 2004.

31. Carolyn Trombe, *Dottie Wiltse Collins*, p. 169.

32. *AAGPBL, Newsletter*, October 1987.

33. AAGPBL Annual Meeting Minutes, 19 September 1987.

34. *AAGPBL*, "Official Communication to Player Members of the All American Girls Professional Baseball League Players Association," 16 March 1988.

35. Ted Spencer interview with Carolyn Trombe, 24 February 2004.

36. *Ibid.*

37. AAGPBL Board "Spring Meeting Report," 16 April 1988.

38. Ted Spencer Interview with Carolyn Trombe, 24 February 2004.

39. *AAGPBL, Newsletter*, April 1987.

40. *AAGPBL, Newsletter*, extra edition, June 1987.

41. *Ibid.*

42. *Ibid.*

43. Karen Violetta Kunkel to Merrie Fidler, 10 February 2004.

44. *AAGPBL, Newsletter*, August 1987.

45. AAGPBL Board Meeting Minutes, 19 September 1987.

46. AAGPBL Board Meeting Minutes, 16 April 1988 and *AAGPBL Newsletter*, April 1988.

47. *AAGPBL, Newsletter*, August 1988.

48. Karen Violetta Kunkel to Merrie Fidler, 10 February 2004.

49. *Ibid.*

50. John M. Kovach to AAGPBL Board, 14 September 1988.

51. Ted Spencer interview with Carolyn Trombe, 24 February 2004.

52. *Ibid.*

53. All of these quotes were taken from the *AAGPBL, Newsletter*, December 1988.

54. Telephone interview with Lou Arnold, 12 August 2004.

55. Reprinted in the *AAGPBL, Newsletter*, May 1989.

56. *AAGPBL, Newsletter*, August 1989.

57. *Ibid.*

58. *AAGPBL, Newsletter*, May 1989.

59. AAGPBL Board Meeting Minutes 29 April 1989.

60. *Ibid.*, 23 September 1989.

61. Telephone interview with Betsy Jockum, 12 August 2004.

62. Fran Janssen to Merrie Fidler, 11 August 2004.

63. Telephone interview with Fran Janssen, 12 August 2004.

64. AAGPBL Board Meeting Minutes, 17 September 1994, *AABPBL Newsletter*, September 1994.

65. *AAGPBL, Newsletter*, December 1990.

66. AAGBBL Board Meeting Minutes, 22 September 1990.

67. *Ibid.*, 8 January 1993 and 4 August 1993.

68. AAGPBL Board Meeting Minutes, 21 and 22 October 1997.

69. Fran Janssen Archives Report to the AAGPBL Board, 1 August 2000, AAGPBL Board Meeting Minutes 27 August 2000.

70. Fran Janssen Archives Report to AAGPBL Board, 5 August 2004.

71. *Ibid.*

72. Ted Spencer interview with Carolyn Trombe, 24 September 2004.

73. Telephone interview with Ted Spencer, 15 September 2004.

74. Tim Wiles to Merrie Fidler, 17 August 2004.

75. *EXTRA INNINGS, AAGBBL Newsletter*, September 1985.

76. *EXTRA INNINGS, AAGPBL Newsletter*, January 1986. .

77. *EXTRA INNINGS, AAGPBL Newsletter*, September 1985.

78. *TOUCHING BASES, AAGPBL Newsletter*, January 1997. (This new title for the newsletter was submitted and voted into existence at the 1993 50th AAGBBL Reunion.)

79. Tim Wiles to Merrie Fidler, 12 August 2004.

80. *Ibid.*

81. Ted Spencer to *TOUCHING BASES, AAGPBL Newsletter*, April 1997.

82. Ted Spencer interview with Carolyn Trombe, 24 February 2004.

83. *TOUCHING BASES, AAGPBL Newsletter*, September 2002.

84. *TOUCHING BASES, AAGPBL Newsletter*, September 2002 as reprinted from *Baseball Hall of Fame "Memories & Dreams,"* Summer 2002.

85. National Baseball Hall of Fame Press Release, 12 March 2003.

86. *TOUCHING BASES, AAGPBL Newsletter*, April 2003.

87. National Baseball Hall of Fame Press Release, 12 March 2003.

88. *TOUCHING BASES, AAGPBL Newsletter*, April 2003.

89. National Baseball Hall of Fame Press Release, 12 March 2003.

90. "Hall of Fame Education Updates," *TOUCHING BASES, AAGPBL Newsletter*, September 2003.

91. Announcement made by Dale Petroskey, Hall of Fame President, 12 September 2003 in front of the Hall of Fame Library; Jane Moffet to Merrie Fidler 29 July 2004.

92. Interview with Arthur E. Meyerhoff, 28 December 1972.

Chapter 16

1. Dottie Collins to Dr. Janis Taylor, video interview, AAGPBL National Reunion, Fort Wayne, Indiana, September 1986. This interview is the opening dialogue of Dr. Janis Taylor's documentary of the AAGPBL's recognition by the Hall of Fame entitled *When Dreams Come True.*

2. "Good News, Cooperstown 1989," *AAGPBL Newsletter*, April 1987.

3. Telephone interview with Fran Janssen, 16 August 2004.

4. "Extra Extra," *AAGPBL Newsletter*, June 1987.

5. Minutes of "Meeting called to discuss preparation for future induction into the Cooperstown Baseball Hall of Fame and related matters, May 23, 1987," contributed by Jean Geissinger Harding. Karen Violetta Kunkel to Merrie Fidler, 9 February 2004.

6. "Extra Extra," *AAGPBL Newsletter*, June 1987.

7. *Ibid.*

8. Copy of official "Articles of Incorporation," contributed by Jean Geissinger Harding, May 2004.

9. Karen Violetta Kunkel to Merrie Fidler 6 March 2004.

10. Karen Violetta Kunkel to Merrie Fidler, 9 February 2004.

11. *Ibid.*

12. *AAGPBL Newsletter*, October 1987.

13. *AAGPBL Newsletter*, August 1987.

14. *AAGPBL Newsletter*, October 1987; AAGPBL Board Meeting Minutes, September 1987 through August 2004.

15. *AAGPBL Newsletter*, October 1987.

16. *AAGPBL Newsletter*, August 1987.

17. Fran Janssen to Merrie Fidler, 2 March 2004.

18. AAGPBL Board Meeting Minutes, 19 September 1987.

19. *AAGPBL Newsletter*, December 1988.

20. *AAGPBL Newsletter*, November/December 1992.

21. Glen E. Greenfelder, attorney, to Joan Holderness, 7 January 1992, contained in Jean Geissinger Harding's AAGPBL Board Meeting Minutes.

22. *TODAY'S NEWS, AAGPBL Newsletter*, May 1982.

23. AAGPBL Board Meeting Minutes, 19 September 1987, 14 November 1987; Arleene Johnson Noga to Jean Geissinger Harding, 27 June 1988.

24. AAGPBL Board Meeting Minutes, 25 September 1992, 21 September 1996, 3–4 November 1998.

25. *Ibid.*, 2 November 1998

26. *Ibid.*, 19 September 1987, 29 April 1989, 13 October 1990, 14 April 1991, 25 October 1991.

27. *AAGPBL Newsletter*, October 1987.

28. *AAGPBL Newsletter*, October 1987; AAGPBL Annual Board Meeting Minute Lists of Offices and Committees, 1987–1993.

29. AAGPBL Board Meeting Minutes, 3 November 1995.

30. AAGPBL Board Meeting Minutes, 19 September 1987; 17 September 1988; and 22 October 1997.

31. AAGPBL Board Meeting Minutes, 19 September 1987, 16 April 1988; *AAGPBL Newsletter*, December 1988.

32. *TOUCHING BASES, AAGPBL Newsletter*, September 2002; AAGPBL Board Meeting Minutes, 22 September 1990, 21 October 1997, 2 November 1998; *TOUCHING BASES, AAGPBL Newsletter*, May 1989, January 1995, September 2002.

33. "AAGPBL Invited to the White House," *TOUCHING BASES, AAGPBL Newsletter*, September 2003.

34. Conversations with original board members Jean Geissinger Harding, Fran Janssen, and Karen Violetta Kunkel during the summer of 2004.

35. Jan Taylor to Merrie Fidler, 29 July 2004.

36. *AAGPBL Newsletter*, June 1987.

37. *Basewoman*, September 1987.

38. *AAGPBL Newsletter*, December 1987, August 1989.

39. Kelly Candaele to Merrie Fidler, 9 August 2004.

40. *Ibid.*, 18 August 2004.

41. *Ibid.*, 9 August 2004.

42. *Ibid.*, 18 August 2004.

43. *Ibid.*, 9 August 2004.

44. *Ibid.*
45. AAGPBL Board Meeting Minutes, 16 April, 7 May, 28 May, 16 September, 4 November 1988.
46. Taken from Carolyn Trombe's interview with Ted Spencer for her book *Dottie Wiltse Collins: Strikeout Queen of the All-American Girls Professional Baseball League*, Jefferson, N.C.: McFarland, 2005.
47. Jane Gottesman with Foreword by Penny Marshall, *Game Face — What Does a Female Athlete Look Like?* Random House, New York, 2001.
48. Unidentified News Article reprinted in *AAGPBL Newsletter*, August 1989.
49. AAGPBL Board Meeting Minutes, 21 September 1989.
50. Marie "Blackie" Wegman, "On the Set of *A League of Their Own,*" *AAGPBL Newsletter*, December 1991.
51. AAGPBL Annual Meeting Minutes, 23 September 1989.
52. Sandra Knipe, " 'League' filming winding down," *Entertainment*, 1 October 1991.
53. Lavone "Pepper" Paire Davis, "Our Movie Try Outs," *AAGPBL Newsletter*, April 1990
54. Jane Gottsman, *Game Face: What Does a Female Athlete Look Like?* Forward.
55. Telephone interview with Karen Violetta Kunkel, 27 September 2004.
56. *Ibid.*
57. Pepper Paire Davis, "Our Movie Try Outs," *AAGPBL Newsletter*, April 1990.
58. Peggy Mack, "A Little Tid-Bit of Information That May Interest You...," *AAGPBL Newsletter*, August 1991.
59. *Ibid.*; AAGPBL Board Meeting Minutes 7 April 1990; 6 January 1992.
60. Telephone interview with Karen Violetta Kunkel, 27 September 2004.
61. *AAGPBL Newsletter*, December 1990.
62. AAGPBL Board Meeting Minutes, 14 July 1990; 13 October 1990; 8 July 1991.
63. Marie "Blackie" Wegman, "*On the Set of A League of Their Own,*" *AAGPBL Newsletter*, December 1991.
64. *AAGPBL Newsletter*, August 1992.
65. Telephone interview with Karen Violetta Kunkel, 27 September 2004.
66. *Ibid.*
67. *Ibid.*
68. *AAGPBL Newsletter*, November/December 1992.
69. *AAGPBL Newsletter*, May 2000.
70. Phrase coined by former league manager Chet Grant in "I Managed Girl Baseball Teams," *South Bend Tribune Michiana Magazine* (Ind.), 9 July 1972, p. 6.
71. Wilma Briggs to Merrie Fidler, 28 May 2004.
72. Kelly Candaele to Merrie Fidler 9 August 2004.

Chapter 17

1. Except where otherwise noted, this section is summarized from AAGPBL Board Meeting Minutes and Annual Players' Association Meeting Minutes from September 1990 through September 1992.
2. AAGPBL Board Meeting Minutes, 13 October 1990.
3. AAGPBL Board Meeting Minutes, 22 September 1990 to 26 September 1992.
4. *TOUCHING BASES, AAGPBL Newsletter*, September 1994.
5. *Ibid.*
6. Except where otherwise noted this section is summarized from AAGPBL Board Meeting Minutes and

Annual Players' Association Meeting Minutes from September 1993 through November 1998.
7. *TOUCHING BASES, AAGPBL Newsletter*, October 1993.
8. Document in AAGPBL Board Meeting Minutes entitled "Goals Proposed by Baumgartner," 1 January 1994; *TOUCHING BASES, AAGPBL Newsletter*, May 1994.
9. *TOUCHING BASES, AAGPBL Newsletter*, January and May 1998.
10. AAGBBL Board Meeting Minutes, 16 September 1994.
11. *TOUCHING BASES, AAGPBL Newsletter*, September 1996.
12. Reg Langeman to Merrie Fidler, 16 October 2004.
13. *TOUCHING BASES, AAGPBL Newsletter*, September 1996.
14. *Ibid.*, January 1997.
15. Except where otherwise noted, this section is summarized from AAGPBL Board Meeting Minutes and Annual Players' Association Meeting Minutes from November 1998 through August 2004.
16. Letter to voting members, regarding reasons for voting for reorganization, 1 December 1997. Included in AAGPBL 1997 Board Meeting Minute Records contributed by Jean Geissinger Harding.
17. *TOUCHING BASES, AAGPBL Newsletter*, January 1999.
18. AAGPBL Board Meeting Minutes, November 1998 to March 2004.
19. Weed, Pamela, "ALL-STAR FANFEST — July 2002, *TOUCHING BASES, AAGPBL Newsletter*, September 2002.
20. Lefty Hohlmayer to Merrie Fidler, 15 December 2003.
21. AAGPBLPA Board Meeting Minutes, 27 August 2000 and 10 September 2003.
22. AABPBL Annual Association Meeting Minutes, 28 September 2002.
23. Ruth Davis to Merrie Fidler, 21 June 2004.
24. Unless otherwise indicated, this information was contained in *AAGPBL Newsletters*, September 1981, March 1981.
25. Kathleen Brady Shea, "The pilot, 71, was an athlete, entrepreneur," *Philadelphia Inquirer*, 1 October 2004.
26. Unless otherwise indicated, the following information was contained in *AAGPBL Newsletters*, July 1981, February 1983, July 1983, December 1986, April 1987, April 1987, October 1987, December 1988 May 1989, August 1989, November 1989, December 1989.
27. Dorothy "Kammie" Kamenshek to Merrie Fidler, 10 March 2005.
28. Jean Cione's induction into the Eastern Michigan University Athletic Hall of Fame was not reported in the AAGPBL Newsletter, but in the *Eastern Echo*, 21 April 1986. Ms. Cione contributed this article to the author during an interview in late May 2004.
29. *TOUCHING BASES, AAGBBL Newsletter*, September 1987.
30. *TOUCHING BASES, AAGPBL Newsletter*, September 1995, January 1998.
31. Unless otherwise indicated, the following information is contained in *AAGPBL Newsletters*, April 1991, August 1991, November/December 1992, April 1993, September 1995, January 1996, May 1996, September 1996, January 1997, April 1997, January 1998, September 1998, January 1999, May 1999, September 1999.
32. Jane Moffet to Merrie Fidler, 15 September 2004.
33. *TOUCHING BASES, AAGPBL Newsletter*, April 1991.

34. *Saskatchewan Baseball Hall of Fame & Museum Newsletter*, Vol. 8, No. 2, April 1991.

35. *TOUCHING BASES, AAGPBL Newsletter*, September 1994.

36. *TOUCHING BASES, AAGPBL Newsletter*, January 1996.

37. *TOUCHING BASES, AAGPBL Newsletter*, May 1996.

38. *TOUCHING BASES, AAGPBL Newsletter*, September 1996.

39. *Ibid.*

40. *Ibid.*

41. *TOUCHING BASES, AAGPBL Newsletter*, April 1997.

42. *TOUCHING BASES, AAGPBL Newsletter*, January 1998.

43. *TOUCHING BASES, AAGPBL Newsletter*, September 1998.

44. Delores "Dolly" Brumfield White to Merrie Fidler, 14 September 2004.

45. Newspaper articles mentioned here were reprinted in *TOUCHING BASES, AAGPBL Newsletter*, September 1998.

46. *TOUCHING BASES, AAGPBL Newsletter*, April 1997, September 1998.

47. "All-American Canucks: Canadian women honored by Hall of Fame," *The London Free Press*, London, Ontario, Canada, May 24, 1998.

48. *Ibid.*

49. From an Edison International Poster which illustrated and described the float, courtesy of Annabelle Lee Harmon.

50. *TOUCHING BASES, AAGPBL Newsletter*, January 2000.

51. Jeneane DesCombes Lesko to Merrie Fidler 12 October 2004.

52. Unless otherwise indicated the information for this topic can be found in *AAGPBL Newsletters*, January 2000, May 2000, January 2002, May 2001, September 2001, January 2002, May 2002, September 2002, January 2003, April 2003, September 2003, January 2004, May 2004.

53. *TOUCHING BASES, AAGPBL Newsletter*, May 2000.

54. *TOUCHING BASES, AAGPBL Newsletter*, May 2000, September 2000.

55. *TOUCHING BASES, AAGPBL Newsletter*, September 2001.

56. *TOUCHING BASES, AAGPBL Newsletters*, May 2002 and September 2002, January 2003.

57. *TOUCHING BASES, AAGPBL Newsletter*, January 2003.

58. *TOUCHING BASES, AAGPBL Newsletters*, April 2003, January 2004.

59. *TOUCHING BASES, AAGPBL Newsletters*, April 2003, January 2004, May 2004.

60. Sue Macy to AAGPBL Membership e-mail list, 17 October 2004.

61. Obituary, *Macomb Daily*, Michigan,, 12 September 2004, received via e-mail from Delores "Dolly" White; Barbara Gregorich, *Women at Play: The Story of Women in Baseball*, A Harvest Original, Harcourt, Brace, San Diego, 1993, p. 114.

62. Richard Goldstein, "Rose Gacioch, a Star in Women's Pro Baseball, Dies at 89," *New York Times*, 16 September 2004.

63. Unless otherwise indicated, the information for this topic can be found in *AAGPBL Newsletters*, January 1999, January 2003, April 2003, January 2004, and Shirley Burkovich to Merrie Fidler, 27 August 2004.

64. *TOUCHING BASES,* AAGPBL Newsletter, January 2003; Shirley Burkovich to Merrie Fidler, 27 August 2004.

65. *TOUCHING BASES, AAGPBL Newsletter*, April 2003.

66. Unless otherwise indicated, the information for this topic can be found in *AAGPBL Newsletters*, May 1989, January 1995, January 1996, September 1996, January 1999, April 1997, September 1998, January 2000, September 2003, and May 2004.

67. *TOUCHING BASES, AAGPBL Newsletter*, January 1996.

68. Jeneane DesCombes Lesko to Merrie Fidler, 12 October 2004.

69. *Ibid.*

70. Shirley Burkovich to Merrie Fidler, 27 August 2004.

71. Charlie Coleman to Shirley Burkovich, reprinted in the January 2000 *AAGPBL Newsletter.*

72. Unless otherwise noted, this information can be found in *AAGPBL Newsletters*, June 1987, December 1988, April 1997, May 2001, January 2003, April 2003, September 2003, January 2004, May 2004.

73. Helen "Gig" Smith, "A Trip to Hawaii to Represent the AAGPBL," *TOUCHING BASES, AAGPBL Newsletter*, September 1999.

74. *TOUCHING BASES, AAGPBL Newsletter*, May 2004.

75. Unless otherwise noted, the following information is contained in *AAGBBL Newsletters*, July 1981, August 1992, May 1994, May 1995, September 1995, June 1997, January 1999, January 2000, May 2000, May 2001, September 2002, May 2004.

76. *TOUCHING BASES, AAGPBL Newsletter*, August 1992.

77. *TOUCHING BASES, AAGPBL Newsletter*, May 1994.

78. Diana Duda to ?, reprinted in *TOUCHING BASES, AAGPBL Newsletter*, January 1999.

79. *TOUCHING BASES, AAGPBL Newsletter*, January 2000.

80. *TOUCHING BASES, AAGPBL Newsletter*, May 1995.

81. *TOUCHING BASES, AAGPBL Newsletter*, September 2002.

82. *TOUCHING BASES, AAGPBL Newsletter*, May 2004; Dolly White to Merrie Fidler, 28 June 2004.

83. Erin Schmidt to Merrie Fidler, 2 September 2004.

84. *TOUCHING BASES, AAGPBL Newsletter*, May 2004.

85. Erin Schmidt to Merrie Fidler, 2 September 2004.

86. *Ibid.*

87. Office Depot Official Press Release, Del Ray Beach, Florida, 1 March 2005.

88. Sue Macy, AAGPBL Board Secretary, to Merrie Fidler, 8 March 2005.

Chapter 18

1. See Larry Keith, "Not Every Bloomer Held a Girl," *Sports Illustrated*, 4 January 1971, p. E3, and J.K. Lagemann, "Red Heads You Kill Me," *Collier's*, 8 February 1947, pp. 64–66.

2. Z.Z. Lydens, ed., *The Story of Grand Rapids,* Grand Rapids, Mich.: Kregel, 1966, p. 631.

3. Arthur H. Cole with Dorothy Lubin, "Perspectives

on Leisure-Time Business," *Explorations in Entrepreneurial History*, 1 (Supplement 1964), p. 2.

4. Interview with Mike Moore (husband of former AAGBBL chaperone Lucille Moore), South Bend, Indiana, 6 January 1973.

5. Robert A. Divine, *Since 1945: Politics and Diplomacy in Recent American History,* New York: Wiley, 1975, pp. 7–11.

6. Voigt, American Baseball, 2:296, 303–305.

7. Discussion with former spectator Harold J. VanderZwaag, Amherst, Massachusetts, 26 January 1976.

8. D.C.P. Grant, "I Managed Girls' Baseball," *South Bend Tribune Michiana Magazine* (Ind.), 9 July 1972, p. 6.

9. Interviews with Jean Faut, South Bend, Indiana, 6 January 1973; Nancy Mudge Cato, Elk river, Minnesota, 26 October 1974; and Jean Cione, Ypsilanti, Michigan, 17 June 1974.

Bibliography

Books

"All-American Girls Baseball League." *Major League Baseball Facts and Figures*. Racine, Wisconsin: Dell, 1947 and 1948, pp. 129–160.

Angle, Paul M. *Philip K. Wrigley: Memoir of a Modest Man*. Chicago: Rand McNally, 1975.

Archibald, Katherine. *Wartime Shipyard: A Study in Social Disunity*. Berkeley: University of California Press, 1947.

Bealle, Morris A. *The Softball Story*. Washington, D.C.: Columbia, 1957.

Betts, John Rickard. *America's Sporting Heritage, 1850–1950*. Reading, Mass.: Addison-Wesley, 1974.

Bowers, Ethel. *Recreation for Girls and Women*. New York: A.S. Barnes, 1934.

Brown, Patricia I. *A League of My Own*. Jefferson, N.C.: McFarland, 2003.

Browne, Lois. *Girls of Summer: In Their Own League*. Toronto: HarperCollins, 1992.

Carey, Max. "All-American Girls Baseball League," *Major League Baseball Facts and Figures*. Racine, Wis.: Whitman, 1946, pp. 129–160.

Cavnes, Max. *The Hoosier Community at War*. Bloomington: Indiana University Press, 1961.

Chafe, William L. *The American Woman: Her Changing Social, Economic and Political Roles, 1920–1970*. New York: Oxford University Press, 1972.

Cozens, Frederick W., and Stumpf, Florence S. *Sport in American Life*. Chicago: University of Chicago Press, 1953.

Curtis, Henry S. *The Play Movement and Its Significance*. New York: Macmillan, 1917.

Diehl, Leonard J., and Eastwood, Floyd R. *Industrial Recreation: Its Development and Present Status*. Lafayette, Ind.: Purdue University, 1940.

Divine, Robert A. *Since 1945: Politics and Diplomacy in Recent American History*. New York: Wiley, 1975.

Dudley, Gertrude, and Kellor, Frances. *Athletic Games in the Education of Women*. New York: Henry Holt, 1909.

Dulles, Foster Rhea. *A History of Recreation: America Learns to Play*. New York: Appleton-Century-Crofts, 1965.

Durso, Joseph. *The All-American Dollar: The Big Business of Sports*. Boston: Houghton Mifflin, 1971.

Friedman, Bernard. *The Financial Role of Indiana in World War II*. Bloomington: Indiana University Press, 1965.

Frost, Helen, and Wardlaw, Charles Digby. *Basketball and Indoor Baseball for Women*. New York: Scribner, 1920.

Goldman, Eric F. *The Crucial Decade: America, 1945–1955*. New York: Alfred A. Knopf, 1956.

Gottesman, Jane, with Foreword by Penny Marshall. *Game Face — What Does a Female Athlete Look Like?* New York: Random House, 2001.

Gregorich, Barbara. *Women at Play: The Story of Women in Baseball*. San Diego: Harcourt, Brace, 1993.

Havighurst, Robert J., and Gerthon, Morgan H. *The Social History of a War Boom Community*. New York: Greenwood, 1951.

Helmer, Diana Star. *Belles of the Ballpark*. Brookfield, Conn.: Millbrook, 1993.

Hinshaw, David. *The Home Front*. New York: Putnam, 1943.

Johnson, Susan E. *When Women Played Hardball*. Canada: Seal, 1994.

Johnson, William O., Jr. *Super Spectator and the Electric Lilliputians*. Boston: Little, Brown, 1971.

Keenan, Marie. "All-American Girls Professional Ball League." *Major League Baseball: Facts, Figures and Official Rules*. Racine, Wis.: Whitman, 1945, pp. 129–144.

Kenney, William. *The Crucial Years, 1940–1945*. New York: Macfadden, 1962.

Kraus, Richard. *Recreation and Leisure in Modern Society*. New York: Appleton-Century-Crofts, 1971.

Lingeman, Richard R. *Don't You Know There's a War On? The American Home Front, 1941–1945*. New York: Putnam, 1970.

Lydens, Z.Z., ed. *The Story of Grand Rapids.* Grand Rapids, Mich.: Kregel, 1966.

Macy, Sue. *A Whole New Ball Game: The Story of the All-American Girls Professional Baseball League.* New York: Henry Holt, 1993.

Madden, W.C. *The Women of the All-American Girls Professional Baseball League.* Jefferson, N.C.: McFarland, 1997.

Mann, Arthur. *Branch Rickey: American in Action.* Boston: Houghton Mifflin, 1957.

Merrill, Francis E. *Social Problems on the Home Front.* New York: Harper and Brothers, 1948.

Merton, Robert K.; Fiske, Marjorie; and Kendall, Patricia L. *The Focused Interview.* Illinois: Free Press, 1956.

Mortin, Jenni. *Safe at Home: A History of Softball in Saskatchewan.* Saskatchewan: Softball Saskatchewan and Saskatchewan Sports Hall of Fame and Museum, 1997.

Neumeyer, Martin H., and Neumeyer, Esther H. *Leisure and Recreation: A Study of Leisure and Recreation in Their Sociological Aspects.* New York: Ronald, 1958.

Noren, Arthur T. *Softball.* New York: Ronald, 1966.

Ogburn, William Fielding, ed. *American Society in Wartime.* Chicago: University of Chicago Press, 1943.

Palmer, Gladys E. *Baseball for Girls and Women.* New York: A.S. Barnes and Company, 1929.

Polenberg, Richard. *War and Society: The United States, 1941–1945.* New York: Lippincott, 1972.

Rainwater, Clarence E. *The Play Movement in the United States.* Chicago: University of Chicago Press, 1922.

Rothe, Anna, and Demarest, Helen, eds. "Branch Rickey." *Current Biography: Who's News and Why, 1945.* New York: Wilson, 1946, pp. 497–500.

Sage, George H. *Sport in American Society.* Reading, Mass.: Addison-Wesley, 1970.

Sefton, Alice Allene. *The Women's Division, Nation Amateur Athletic Federation.* Stanford, Calif.: Stanford University Press, 1941.

Seymour, Harold. *Baseball: The Golden Age.* New York: Oxford University Press, 1971.

Steiner, Jesse Frederick. A*mericans at Play: Recent Trends in Recreation and Leisure Time Activities.* New York: McGraw-Hill, 1933.

Trombe, Carolyn. *Dottie Wiltse Collins: Strike-out Queen of the All-American Girls Professional Baseball League.* Jefferson, N.C.: McFarland, 2005.

Van Hyning, Thomas. *The Santurce Crabbers: Sixty Seasons of Puerto Rican Winter League Baseball.* Jefferson, N.C.: McFarland, 1999, p. 7.

Voigt, David Quentin. *American Baseball. Vol. 2: From the Commissioners to Continental Expansion.* Norman: University of Oklahoma Press, 1970.

Watters, Mary. *Illinois in the Second World War.* 2 Vols. Springfield, Ill.: State Historical Library, 1951–1952.

Wecter, Dixon. *The Age of the Great Depression, 1929–1941.* New York: Macmillan, 1948; reprint, Chicago: Quadrangle, 1971.

Periodical Articles

In addition to the articles listed below, much information was drawn from the newsletters of the All-American Girls Professional Baseball League, January 1981— September 2004, courtesy of Jean Geissinger Harding and Helen Filarski Steffes. The newsletters carried various titles, including Today's News, All-American Girls Professional Baseball League, Extra Innings, All-American Girls Professional Baseball League Players' Assoc., Inc., *and* Touching Bases.

Aceto, Dorothy. "Softball for Girls." *Recreation* 42 (May 1948): 66–67.

"All-American Girls ... Professional Ball at Brewer's Park." *The Hotel Greeters Guide of Wisconsin,* 1944, p. 19.

"All-American Sport." *Popular Mechanics,* July 1941, pp. 41–43, 172–173.

"America's Fastest Growing Game." *Popular Mechanics,* June 1936, pp. 834–837, 134A.

Anderson, A.O. "Softball Problems." *Recreation* 29 (November 1935): 406–407.

"Baseball: Babette Ruths." *Newsweek,* July 29, 1946, pp. 68–69.

"Baseball, Maestro, Please." *Time,* July 31, 1944, p. 40.

"Baseball Men Envy Her." *Seventeen,* September 1945, p. 168.

"Beauty Invades the Ball Park." *Dodge News,* vol. 10, no. 2, 1945, p. 2.

Biemiller, C.L. "Women's Prettiest Ballplayers." *Holiday,* June 1952, pp. 50–51, 75, 77–78, 80, 82, 84–85.

Black, Don H. "Belles of Baseball." *The Ashlar* (Publication of Massachusetts Mutual Life Insurance Company), vol. 18, no. 8, April 1948, pp. 4–8.

"Branch Rickey Rides Again: The Return of the Mahatma." *Saturday Evening Post,* March 9, 1963, pp. 66–68.

"Broomsticks and Boxing Gloves: The Rise and Spread of Softball." *Scholastic* 34 (May 20, 1939): 33.

Brown, John, Jr. "Softball Problems—Hearings on Present Situation." *Recreation* 28 (December 1934): 445–446.

Chamberlain, Ryan, "SABR Nine Questions," Society for American Baseball Research Bulletin, May-June, 2004.

"Chewing Gum Is War Material." *Fortune*, January 1943, pp. 98–100, 122, 124, 126, 130, 136.

"Chomp Champ." *Newsweek*, June 11, 1962, pp. 74, 77.

"The Citronella League." *Outlook and Independent*, August 20, 1930, p. 614.

Clark, Neil M. "The Low-Down on Salesmanship: An Interview with William Wrigley, Jr." *The American Magazine*, October 1929, pp. 22–23, 124, 126, 129–130.

Cole, Arthur H., with Lubin, Dorothy. "Perspectives on Leisure-Time Business." *Explorations in Entrepreneurial History* 1 (Supplement 1964): 1–37.

"Comeback at 77." *Time*, August 31, 1959, p. 39.

Creamer, Robert W., ed. "Scorecard." *Sports Illustrated*, December 22–29, 1975, p. 18.

Crichton, Kyle. "Not So Soft." *Collier's*, August 10, 1935, pp. 24, 38.

Crowell, Merle. "The Wonder Story of Wrigley." *The American Magazine*, March 1920, pp. 16–17, 180, 183–184, 187–188, 191–192, 195–196, 199.

Curtis, H.S. "New Games for the People." *Review of Reviews*, May 1912, pp. 582–585.

Cuthbertson, L.J. "Softball Field for Night Games, Girard, Kansas." *American City* 55 (January 1940): 87.

"Daring Damsels of the Diamond." *Allsports* (U.S. Rubber Company publication), July-August 1949, pp. 12–13.

Davidson, Aaron. "The Batter Half." *Collier's*, August 12, 1944, pp. 18–19, 41.

"Diamond Daisies." *Sport Life*, October 1949, pp. 72–75.

"Diamond Lils." *Pathfinder*, August 27, 1947, p. 34.

"Dotty Is a Slugger." *The American Magazine*, August 1950, p. 57.

Fay, Bill. "Belles of the Ball Game." *Collier's*, August 13, 1949, p. 44.

_____. "Bonnie's the Belle of the Ball Game." *Sport*, May 1946, pp. 26–28, 97–98.

Fischer, Leo. "Softball Steps Up." *Reader's Digest*, June 1939, pp. 134–135.

Frazier, Russ, "Helen Hannah Campbell: May '99 Booster of the Month," *Booster Chatter: The Official Angels Booster Club Newsletter*, July 1999.

Furlong, William B. "P.K. Wrigley: Baseball Magnate." *Saturday Evening Post*, Summer 1972, pp. 84–86, 110–118.

Gates, E.M. "Sports for Every Girl." *Recreation* 29 (March 1936): 603.

Gathrid, Raymond. "Softball." *Literary Digest*, September 11, 1937, p. 32.

Gibson, Ellen. "The Pay-Off." *Once a Year* (Milwaukee Press Club publication), vol. 49, 1945.

"Girls' Baseball." *Life*, June 4, 1945, pp. 63–66.

"Girls Baseball in Chicago for Hospital." *News of the Nation* (Quarterly Publication of the National Jewish Hospital), vol. IX, no. 2, p. 1.

Gordon, J. "Beauty at the Bat." *The American Magazine*, June 1945, pp. 24–25.

Gould, Ben. "Slide Nellie Slide." *Deb*, September 1946, pp. 24–25, 99, 104.

Graffis, Herb. "Belles of the Ball Game." *Liberty*, October 16, 1943, pp. 26–27.

_____. "Queens of Swat." *Click*, September 1944, pp. 48–50.

Griswold, J. B. "Rickey Starts in the Cellar Again." *The American Magazine*, May 1951, pp. 43, 107–112.

Haig, John Angus. "A Business Version of the Fuller Life." *Nation's Business* 26 (September 1938): 26–29, 78–81.

Hendriks, Gertrude E. "Play Ball! Girls' Baseball Team Boosts Milwaukee in Sports Circles." *The Torch* (Milwaukee advertising publication), June 1944, pp. 85, 111.

"He's a Chip off the Old Block." *System* 51 (January 1927): 30–31.

"In-Door Base-Ball." *Harper's Weekly*, March 8, 1890, p. 179.

"Indoor Baseball." *Time*, November 27, 1939, p. 62.

"The Innovator." *Newsweek*, December 20, 1965, p. 58.

"The Island Kingdom of P.K. Wrigley." *Forbes*, November 1, 1970, pp. 22–23.

Keith, Larry. "Not Every Bloomer Held a Girl." *Sports Illustrated*, January 4, 1971, p. E3.

Klein, Norman. "Baseball — Business Booster." *Forbes Magazine of Business*, April 1, 1947, p. 21.

Kofender, Bill. "Gals Play Ball Too." *Sports Graphic*, June 1947, pp. 8–9.

"Ladies of Little Diamond." *Time*, June 14, 1943, pp. 73–74.

Lardner, John. "Speaking of Rickey." *Newsweek*, December 9, 1957, p. 50.

Larimer, Robert. "Diamond Damsels." *Sportfolio*, October 1947, pp. 121–129.

Leo, Fred, and Seymour, Ray. "These Gals Play for Keeps!" *Moose Magazine*, July/August 1949, pp. 19, 25.

Loggiea, Marjorie Sloan. "On the Playing Fields of History." *Ms.*, July 1973, p. 63.

"The Mahatma." *Time*, December 17, 1965, p. 76.

Markey, Morris. "Hey Ma, You're Out!" *McCall's*, September 1950, pp. 40, 68, 74, 77, 80.

Masin, H.L. "No Game for Aunt Sarah." *Scholastic* 38 (February 24, 1941): 36.

"More Light on Night Baseball." *Literary Digest*, September 27, 1930, pp. 36, 38.

Moss, E.W. "Comparative Figures for Three Competing Classes of Baseball." *Baseball Bluebook*, Supplement No. 9, November 1945.

Nicholson, W.G. "Women's Pro Baseball Packed the Stands ... Then Johnny Came Marching Home." *WomenSports*, April 1976, pp. 22–24.

Noren, Arthur T. "Softball, the Game for All." *Recreation* 30 (January 1937): 508, 518.

_____. "Softball, the New American Fever." *Recreation* 34 (March 1941): 735–736, 745.

"Not So Softball." *Scholastic* 36 (March 4, 1940): 40.

Noyes, Elizabeth. "Recreational Athletics for Women." *Journal of Health and Physical Education* 7 (February 1936): 106–107, 127.

"Old Master Painter." *Time*, June 18, 1956, pp. 59–60.

"Part of Cotton Wrigley Bought Makes 6 Million Handkerchiefs." *Business Week*, May 25, 1932, p. 10.

"The Pioneers of Pro Softball: Who's Playing Where and Why." *Sportswoman*, June 1976, pp. 14–21.

Robinson, Jackie. "The Most Unforgettable Character I've Met." *Reader's Digest*, October 1961, pp. 97–102.

Saskatchewan Baseball Hall of Fame & Museum Newsletter, Vol. 8, No. 2, April 1991.

"Softball." *Time*, September 16, 1935, pp. 47–48.

"Softball for Oldsters." *Recreation* 34 (March 1941): 746.

"Softball's Head Man." *Scholastic* 42 (March 29, 1943): 31.

Spencer, Rachel, "Women's Softball League Standards." *Journal of Health and Physical Education* 9 (April 1938): 224, 259.

Stenbuck, Jack. "Glamour Girls of Big-League Ball." *Magazine Digest*, July 1946, pp. 68–71.

Suhband, Thomas. "A Man Who Made $32 Grow to $13,000,000." *System*, February 1916, pp. 181–183.

Taylor, Graham Romeyn. "Recreation Developments in Chicago Parks." *American Academy of Political and Social Science* 25 (March 1910): 90.

Tork, Patrick A. "Softball Captures a City." *Recreation* 34 (October 1940): 439–440, 453.

"TV Can Kill Baseball." *Newsweek*, June 8, 1953, p. 67.

Wharton, Don, ed. "The Case of the Moving Jaws." *Reader's Digest*, December 1947, pp. 59–62.

"What's a Ball Game Without Curves?" *Liberty*, October 21, 1944, pp. 35–36.

Wiebe, V.R. "Softball Round-up, Iowa City." *Recreation* 47 (May 1954): 292.

Wilkinson, C.A. "Softball Plus for Girls." *Recreation* 49 (March 1956): 118–119.

Wrigley, William, Jr. "I Never Make an Appointment." *System: The Magazine of Business*, July 1926, pp. 40–41.

_____, with Crissey, Forrest. "Owning a Big League Ball Team." *Saturday Evening Post*, September 13, 1930, pp. 24–25.

"Wrigley: Chews All He Bit Off." *Business Week*, November 17, 1945, pp. 80, 82–83.

Yoder, Robert M. "Miss Casey at the Bat." *Saturday Evening Post*, August 22, 1942, pp. 16–17, 48–49.

Newspapers Articles

Selected AAGBBL Articles

Camp Ellis News (Illinois), 25 May 1945.

The Chicago Daily News, 9 February, 11 May 1943; 12, 17, 18, 19 July 1944; 22 May 1945; 23 May, 6, 18 September 1947; 20 Dec. 1949.

Chicago Daily Tribune, 13, 16, 18, 19 July 1944; 8 September 1947; 17 November, 22 December 1949; 15 July 1951.

Chicago Herald-American, 12, 13, 15, 16, 18, 19, 23 July 1944; 12 May 1947; 16 March, 19 June 1949.

Chicago Sun Times, 12, 16, 18, 19 July 1944; 16 July 1947; 17 November 1949.

Chicago Tribune, 1, 2 July 1943.

Goldstein, Richard, "Rose Gacioch, A Star in Women's Pro Baseball, Dies at 89," *New York Times*, 16 September 2004.

The Michiana Sportsman (South Bend, Indiana), 14 June, 19 August, 2, 16, 23 September 1952.

New York Times Magazine, 4 August 1946.

South Bend Tribune Magazine (Indiana), 15 August 1954.

South Bend Tribune Michiana Magazine, 9 July 1972.

This Week Magazine, 26 August 1944; 31 July 1949.

AAGBBL Game Coverage

Fort Wayne Journal-Gazette (Indiana), May–September 1948, 1949, 1952, 1953, 1954.

Fort Wayne News-Sentinel (Indiana), May–September 1946, 1948.

The Grand Rapids Herald (Michigan), May–September 1949.

The Grand Rapids Press (Michigan), May–September 1949, 1953, 1954.

Kalamazoo Gazette (Michigan), May–September 1950, 1953; 1 April–2 February 1955.

Kenosha Evening News (Wisconsin), April–September 1943, 1944, 1947, 1948.

The Milwaukee Journal, June–August 1944.

The Milwaukee Sentinel, July-August 1944.

Minneapolis Star-Tribune (Minnesota), 22 June 1944.

Minneapolis Tribune (Minnesota), May–July 1944.

The Peoria Journal (Illinois), May–September 1949.

The Peoria Star (Illinois), May–September 1949, 1950.

Racine Journal Times (Wisconsin), May–September 1943, 1944, 1945, 1947, 1949.

The Rockford Morning Star (Illinois), May–September 1943, 1944, 1948, 1949.

Rockford Register-Republic (Illinois), May–September 1943, 1944, 1945, 1950, 1953, 1954.

South Bend Tribune (Indiana), May–September 1943, 1944, 1949, 1952, 1953, 1954; August 1957.

Springfield Journal (Illinois), May–September 1949.

Dissertations, Documents and Records

All-American Girls Professional Baseball League Players' Association Board Meeting Minutes, 1987–2004, courtesy of Jean Geissinger Harding and the Executive Board of the Players' Association.

Harold T. Dailey AAGBBL Records, 1943–1954: Joyce Sports Research Collection, Department of Special Collections, University of Notre Dame, South Bend, Indiana. A microfilm copy of these records is located at Pattee Library of the Pennsylvania State University, State College, Pennsylvania.

D.C.P. Grant AAGBBL Collection: Joyce Sports Research Collection, University of Notre Dame, South Bend, Indiana.

Arthur E. Meyerhoff AAGBBL Files, The Wrigley Building, Chicago, Illinois (1974). The author was unable to locate the current location of these files. Copies of some documents from these files are included in the author's research files housed at the Northern Indiana Center for History in South Bend, Indiana.

Carl Orwant AAGBBL Records: Grand Rapids (MI) Public Museum.

Pieper, Marjorie, "The Origin and Development of the All-American Girls Baseball League and Comparing Its Standards with Those of the National Section on Women's Athletics." Thesis Proposal for the University of Michigan, Spring 1953. Courtesy Jean Cione.

Ruetz, Edward J. Jr., "Play Ball" [Memoirs of an AAGBBL Bat Boy], 2001. Contributed by Jnell Ruetz, July 2004. (A copy is held by the National Baseball Hall of Fame.)

Sexton, Maria, "Implications of the All-American Girls Baseball League for Physical Educators in Guidance of Highly-Skilled Girls," Type C Project, Advanced School of Education Teachers college, Columbia University, 1953.

Yale, Judy Meyerhoff, "Arthur E. Meyerhoff Memorial Fund." Pamphlet. Biographical sketch of Arthur E. Meyerhoff and rationale for establishing a Memorial Fund in his memory for Chicago Youth Centers, Chicago, Illinois, April, 1998.

Interviews

Alvarez, Isabel. Fort Wayne, Indiana, 22 May 2004.

Armstrong, Charlotte. Video-taped oral history interview by Jon Magnuson of the Arizona Diamondbacks, courtesy of Yvonne Jacques, Phoenix, Arizona, May 29, 1997.

Arnold, Lou. South Bend, Indiana, 13 May 2004.

Baumgartner, Mary "Wimp." Kalamazoo, Michigan, 28 August 2004

Blair, Maybelle. Palm Springs, California, 9 January 2004.

Briggs, Wilma. Kalamazoo, Michigan, 28 August 2004

Burkovich, Shirley. Palm Springs, California, 9 January 2004, and Cathedral City, California, 27 April 2004.

Campbell, Helen Hannah. Fountain Valley, California, 11 January 2004 and 25 April 2004.

Cato, Nancy Mudge. Elk River, Minnesota, 26 October 1974.

Cione, Jean. Ypsilanti, Michigan, 17 June 1974, and Bozeman, Montana, 30 May 2004.

Des Lauriers, Ed. South Bend, Indiana, 6 January 1973.

Doyle, Dorothy "Snookie." Palm Desert, California, 10 January 2004, and Cathedral City, California, 27 April 2004.

Eisen, Thelma "Tiby." Palm Desert, California, 10 January 2004.

Fox, Nickie. Video-taped oral history interview by Jon Magnuson of the Arizona Diamondbacks, courtesy of Yvonne Jacques, Phoenix, Arizona, May 29, 1997.

Grant, Chet. South Bend, Indiana, 6 January 1973.

Harding, Jean Geissinger. AAGPBL Reunion, Kalamazoo, Michigan, 28 August 2004.

Harmon, Annabelle Lee. Costa Mesa, California, 26 April 2004.

Horstman, Katie. Palm Springs, California, 9 January 2004.

Hunter, Dorothy. Grand Rapids, Michigan, 3 January 1976.

Janssen, Fran. South Bend, Indiana, 13 May 2004.

Jenkins, Marilyn. Grand Rapids, Michigan, 3 January 1976.

Jochum, Betsy. South Bend, Indiana, 6 January 1973 and 13 May 2004.

Kamenshek, Dorothy "Kammie." Palm Desert, California, 10 January 2004 and 27 and 28 April 2004.

Kunkel, Karen Violetta. AAGPBL Reunion, Kalamazoo, Michigan, 25 August 2004.

Kurys, Sophie. Video-taped oral history interview by Jon Magnuson of the Arizona Diamondbacks, courtesy of Yvonne Jacques, Phoenix, Arizona, May 29, 1997; telephone interview, 17 July 2004.

Macy, Sue. AAGPBL Reunion, Kalamazoo, Michigan, 29 August 2004.

Mahon, Elizabeth "Lib." South Bend, Indiana, 6 January 1973.

Meyerhoff, Arthur E. Rancho Santa Fe, California, 28 December 1972.

Moore, Lucille. South Bend, Indiana, 6 January 1973.

Moore, Mary. 177 All-American Girls Baseball League Players' Videotaped Oral History Interviews, Recorded at Players' Association reunion sites, 1996-present, courtesy of Mary Moore and the Executive Board of the All-American Girls Professional Baseball League Players' Association, summer 2004.

Orwant, Carl. Grand Rapids, Michigan, 3 January 1976.

Ricketts, Joyce. Grand Rapids, Michigan, 3 January 1976.

Roepke, Sharon. Kalamazoo, Michigan, 27 August 2004.

Schaefer, Dona. AAGPBL Reunion, Kalamazoo, Michigan, 29 August 2004.

Schultz, John. Minneapolis, Minnesota, 19 June 1975.

Sears, Janet "Pee Wee" Wiley. South Bend, Indiana, 13 May 2004.

Sells, Ken. Video-taped oral history interview by Jon Magnuson of the Arizona Diamondbacks, courtesy of Yvonne Jacques, Phoenix, Arizona, May 29, 1997.

Sindelar, Joan. Video-taped oral history interview by Jon Magnuson of the Arizona Diamondbacks, courtesy of Yvonne Jacques, Phoenix, Arizona, May 29, 1997.

Stoll, Jane "Jeep." Video-taped oral history interview by Jon Magnuson of the Arizona Diamondbacks, courtesy of Yvonne Jacques, Phoenix, Arizona, May 29, 1997.

Taylor, Janis. 82 All-American Girls Baseball League Players' Videotaped Oral History Interviews, South Bend, Indiana, 1993, courtesy of Janis Taylor and the Executive Board of the All-American Girls Professional Baseball League Players' Association, summer 2004.

VanderZwaag, Harold J. Amherst, Massachusetts, 26 January 1976. (An informal discussion rather than a formal interview.)

Ward, Gadget. South Bend, Indiana, 6 January 1973.

Wenzel, Marge. Palm Desert, California, 10 January 2004 and 27 and 28 April 2004.

White, Delores "Dolly" Brumfield. Palm Springs, California, 9 January 2004.

Winsch, Jean Faut. South Bend, Indiana, 6 January 1973.

Zintak, Leonard. Telephone interview, 20 July 2004; personal interview, Huntley, Illinois, 24 August 2004.

Index

Numbers in **bold italics** refer to photographs

AAGBBL Allocation Board 204
AAGBBL Allocation of Players 35
AAGBBL Allocation Procedures 202, 204
AAGBBL All-Star Game 139, 208
AAGBBL All-Star Team 208; (1943) 182; (1946) *214*; (1947) *215*; (1948) *217*; (1951) *220*; (1952) *223*; (1953) *225*
AAGBBL All-Star Team Rosters 1943, 1946–1954 210–211
AAGBBL Balls, 1943–1954 *72*
AAGBBL Board of Directors, 1947 *82*
AAGBBL Car Policy 198
AAGBBL "Central Division" 74
AAGBBL Chaperones 36, 38, 59, 149, 168, 169, 270, 327; in Cuba, 1947 *175*; dress 175; duties 174
AAGBBL Charm School 60; training 36
AAGBBL Commissioners, 1946 81–82
AAGBBL Conduct Rules 36, 59, 196–198, 327
AAGBBL Documentary 250
AAGBBL Dress Code 195
AAGBBL Drinking Policy 195
AAGBBL Expense-Sharing Plan, 1947 79
AAGBBL Expense-Sharing Plan, 1949 79
AAGBBL Facility and Equipment Changes 71
AAGBBL Financial Status, factors affecting 84
AAGBBL Franchises dropped and reorganized 151
AAGBBL Fraternization Policy 198
AAGBBL League Song 341
AAGBBL Lists of Champions 342
AAGBBL Managers, 1943–1948 156
AAGBBL Managers, 1949–1954 157
AAGBBL Most Valuable Player Awards 209–226
AAGBBL Newsletter Logos, 1980–2004 *242*
AAGBBL Official League Title, 1946–1950 36
AAGBBL Player Loan Policies 202

AAGBBL Player Point Rating Chart 344
AAGBBL Player Procurement 104, 111, 133, 135, 185
AAGBBL Player Retirement 190
AAGBBL Player Salaries 199
AAGBBL Players, Age Upon First Joining the League 187
AAGBBL Players, Height & Weight Statistics 187
AAGBBL Players, Occupation Statistics 188
AAGBBL Players, Respective States/Provinces of Residence 186
AAGBBL Post Season Exhibition Tours 101, 111–124
AAGBBL Post-Season Tour, 1951 141
AAGBBL Pre-Season Tour Agenda, 1947 97
AAGBBL Pre-Season Tour, 1951 141
AAGBBL Promotional Loss and League Management Relations 121–124
AAGBBL Publicity and Promotion Compared with Seasonal Attendance, 1943–54 137
AAGBBL Rookie Rule 111, 133, 134
AAGBBL Rookie Tour 104
AAGBBL Rookie Tour, 1952 133, 141
AAGBBL Rookie Tours, 1949, 1950 105–111
AAGBBL Scholarship Series 64
AAGBBL Scorekeepers 68
AAGBBL Smithsonian Institution Display *247*
AAGBBL Smoking Policy 195
AAGBBL "Southern Division" 74, 76
AAGBBL Spring Training Tours 94–104
AAGBBL Summer Barnstorming Tours 105–111
AAGBBL Team Operating Expenses, 1948 78
AAGBBL Team Presidents, 1947 148

AAGBBL Teams at Universidad de la Habana *100*
AAGBBL Trade Regulations 202
AAGBBL Uniform Changes *199*
AAGBBL Uniforms 327
AAGBBL Waiver Procedures 202
AAGBBL "Western Division" 74, 76
AAGBBL Women Managers 161
AAGBBL World Champions, 1952 *224*
AAGBBL/AAGPBL Historical Highlights 338–340
AAGBBL/Chicago Softball League Uniform Styles 57, *58*
AAGPBL 1986 *227*
AAGPBL 2005 Office Depot Visionary Sports Award *318*
AAGPBL 50th Anniversary Reunion, 1993 241, 290
AAGPBL 60th Anniversary Reunion, 2003 266, 267
AAGPBL Archives 244, 255, 257, 261, 270, 289
AAGPBL Archives Dedication, 3/19/90 *263*
AAGPBL Baseball Cards 231, 289
AAGPBL Baseball Cards (Fritsch) 290
AAGPBL Baseball Cards (Star Series) 249
AAGPBL Baseball Hall of Fame Exhibit *259*
AAGPBL Baseball Hall of Fame Statue 292
AAGPBL California Ambassadors *309*
AAGPBL Charms, Rings, Watches 273–274
AAGPBL Commemorative Stamp 275
AAGPBL Documentary 292
AAGPBL Executive Boards 288–294, 333–337
AAGPBL First National Reunion Announcement, Chicago, July 1982 *238*
AAGPBL First National Reunion, 1982 261, 329
AAGPBL History Project *316*
AAGPBL Honorary Members of

the Canadian Baseball Hall of Fame *302*
AAGPBL Honored at White House T-Ball Game *307*
AAGPBL Lifetime Roster 257, 270, 274–275, 289
AAGPBL Logos 290
AAGPBL Managers 270
AAGPBL Marks and Logos 272–273
AAGPBL Media Center 272
AAGPBL Newsletter 261, 290, 294
AAGPBL Newsletter Newspaper Article Reprints 1982–1992 277
AAGPBL Official League Title, 1944–1945 36
AAGPBL Oral History Project 291
AAGPBL Players' Association 10, 11, 255
AAGPBL Players' Association First Board of Directors *258*
AAGPBL Reunion Support Fund 291
AAGPBL Second National Reunion, 1986 243, 254, 269
AAGPBL Shield 273
AAGPBL Statue 330
AAGPBL-PA Website (www.aagpbl.org) 2
AAGSBL Models *37*
AAGSBL, Creation of 29–49
AAGSBL, Official League Title, 1943 36
AAU 34, 59, 166
Abbot, Elliott 281
Abbott, Velma 200, 297, 301
ABC *Movies of the Week* 250, 278
Adams, Evelyn 277
Addams, Jane 16, 19
Africa 293, 310
AGABUBBLE 172
AGBL (American Girls Baseball League) 125, 131; Official League Title, 1951–1954 82
Ainsmith, Eddie 156
Akron-Westfield Community School, Iowa 315
Alabama 19, 105, 166, 184
Alabama College 300
Alberta, Canada 290
Alderfer, Gertrude (Gert) *106*, *109*, 315
All American Classic 285
"All for One, One for All" 227, 267, 330
All Star Ranger Girls 308
All-American Girls Professional Baseball League Players' Association (AAGPBL-PA) 243
All-American World Champions 157; tour stops, 1955–56 *161*
All-Americans at 2004 Fan Fest, Houston, Texas *311*
Allegan, Michigan 231, 234, 279
Allen, Agnes *128*
Allen, Betty Petryna 297, 301
Allen, Mel 141
Allentown, Pennsylvania 218

Allington, William Baird (Bill) *53*, 107, 134, 155, 156, 157, *158*, *159*, 160, 164, 222, *223*
Allington's "All-American World Champions," 1955 *159*
Allington's All-Stars 161
Allsports (U.S. Rubber Company Publication) 51
Alva Jo Fischer Memorial Softball Complex 276, 295
Alvarez, Isabel (Lefty) viii, 99, 100, 102, *103*, *106*, *109*, 115, *116*, 117, *227*, 243, 267, 298, *299*
Amateur Softball Association (ASA) 7, 20–21, 23, 24, 41, 182
American Association Baseball Club Parks 46
American College of Physical Education 167
American Dream 191
American Institute of Mining 149
American League 208
American Legion 147, 149
American Magazine 50, 67
American Samoa 314
American Stars 117
Americanas 115
Americanas y Cubanas *116*
Americans 120
Amundsen High School, Chicago 313
Anaheim, California 311
Anaheim School District Workshop 311
Anderson, Andy 92
Anderson, Janet See Perkin, Janet
Anderson, Marie Teichman (Teddy) *39*, 167, 168
Anderson, Vivian Sheriffs 305
Anderson Union High School District 8
Angelou, Maya 318
Angle, Paul 31
Annual Baseball Awards Dinner, Los Angeles 310
Apple Computer 267
Appleberry, James 256
Applegren, Amy Irene *75*, *101*, *199*, 298, 312
Arab Horse Registry of America 31
Arab Horse Society (England) 31
Arbour, Bea 315
Ardmore, Oklahoma 94
Arellano, Roman 313
Arizona 277
Arizona Softball Hall of Fame 294
Arkansas 105
Arleene Johnson Noga Grandstand 295
Armed Forces 142
Armington, Dorothy vii
Armstrong, Charlotte (Skipper) 300
Army 142
Army and Navy Bombers 182
Arnett, Jeff 267

Arnold, Louise (Lou) 211, *224*, *227*, 234, 256, 257, 260, 261, 262, 278, 283, 296, *307*, 310, 313, 315, 329
Arnold, Norene *109*
Ashe, Becky viii
The Ashlar (Massachusetts Mutual Life Insurance Company Publication) 51
Athletic Femininity 36
Atlanta, Georgia 313
Atlantidas 112
Attendance Figures 68
Austin, Helen 315
Australia 293
Avery, Arlene *227*, *235*, 236

Babb's Angels, Female Negro Softball Team 190
Badini, Jane Jacobs 298
Bajda, Dolores Mueller (Champ) viii, 92, 298, 306, 313
Baker, Mary (Bonnie) 10, *40*, 60, *128*, 141, 157, 162, *163*, 182, 192, 210, *214*, 233, 234, 277, 297, 301
Baker, Mildred 168, *175*
Balancing Committee 205, 206
Balboa, Panama 115, 120
Balfour Company 274
Ball State University 267, 292, 330
Baltimore Orioles 107
Bamburger, George 107
Bancroft, Dave *77*, 117, 155, 157, *158*
Barbaze, Barbara *78*, 301
Barber, Danielle 252, 255, 269
Barker, Lois (Tommie) 259
Barnes, Darrah viii
Barnett, Charlene *77*, 117, 301
Barney, Ashleigh 301
Barquisimita, Venezuela 115
Barr, Doris *40*, 55, *78*, 301
Barringer, Patricia (Pat) *106*, *109*, 110, 157, 169
Barts, Diane viii, 262, 264
Baseball Assistance Team (BAT) 290
Base-Ball Femenino Poster *122*
Baseball for Girls and Women 17
Baseball Hall of Fame viii, 9, 10, 80, 231, 239, 243, 244, 252, 253, 254, 255, 256, 257, 259, 260, 261, 264, 265, 266, 267, 269, 271, 274, 275, 281, 289, 300, 329, 330; Bullpen Theater 267; Educational Advisory Council 266; Electronic Field Trip (EFT) 266, 292; files 265 Women in Baseball Exhibit 9, 254, 258, 261, 264, 266, 267, 269, 292; Women in Baseball Exhibit, Nov. 5, 1988 250, *259*
Baseball, nine-inch 131, 132, *132*, 140
Baseball-Concert Campaign, Milwaukee 66
Basketball and Indoor Baseball for Women 17

Basketball Red Heads 323
Bass, Dick 156
Batikis, Annastasia (Stash) 299, 304, 305, 310, 313, 315
Battle Creek, Michigan 41, 131, 156, 157, 168, 169
Battle Creek Belles 130, 203
Bauer, Arnold 229, 234
Baumgart, Jacquelin (Jackie) Mattson viii, 305, 312
Baumgartner, Mary (Wimp) viii, *106*, *109*, 156, 162, 184, 211, *224*, *225*, *227*, *235*, 236, 241, 243, 278, 282, 288, 289, 290, *291*, 295, 298, 312, 315
Bayh, Birch 2
BBDO Chicago 70
Beardstown, Maryland 182
Beckett, Christine Jewitt 297, 301
Behrens, Catherine 168
Beirn, Ken 30
Bellman, Lois (Punky) *93*, *106*, *109*
Bend, Olive *see* Little, Olive
Bennet Pumps Division of John Wood Manufacturing Company, Inc. 149
Bennett, Catherine 297, 301
Bennett, Kay 55
Benson, Diane viii
Benson, Leigh viii
Bensonville, Illinois 216
Benton Harbor, Michigan 151
Berberich, Elizabeth (Boots) 92, *93*
Berg, Patty 34, 238
Berger, Barbara *109*
Berger, Joan (Joanie) 158, *159*, 210, *223*
Berger, Margaret (Marge, Sonny) *40*, *106*, 182, 210
Berger, Norma *109*
Bergmann, Erma *75*, *78*, 284, 296, 298, 305, 315
Berra, Yogi 108, 110
Berryman, Jack W. vii
Berryman, Ruth 92
Berthiaume, Betty *see* Wicken, Betty
Bertrand, Kathy 241
Best Buy's Children Foundation 267
Bickley, Joanne viii
Biebel, William (Bill) 92, *93*
Bigbee, Carson *78*, 156, 157, 193
Bigelow Field, Grand Rapids, Mich. 151
Billings, Josh *38*, 154, 156
Biltmore Hotel, Havana, Cuba 172
Biltmore Hotel, Los Angeles 171
Birmingham, Alabama 74
Bittner, Jaynne (Jaynnie) 192, *206*, 211, *227*, 233, 274, 295, 313
Black, John 69
Black, Mr. 133
Black Charity *see* Colored Orphans

Black Female Softball Team *see* Babb's Angels
Black Major League 42
Blaine, Joseph viii
Blaine, Mike, Pastor viii
Blair, Maybelle viii, 38, 308, 309, 310, 312
Blaski, Alice 211
Bloomer Girl Baseball Teams 17, 200, 308, 323
Blue, Merle 263
Blue Island Dianas 88; roster 92
Blue Island Recreation Commission 88
Blue Island Stadium 89–90
Blue Island Stars 88; roster 92; uniform patch *93*
Blue Springs, Missouri 317
Bluebirds 92, 200
Blumetta, Kay (Swish) *48*, *75*, *101*, *128*, 233, 260, 277
Boca Raton, Florida 308
Bockmann, Lois 92
Boeing 183
Boland, Joe vii, 7, *139*
Borchert Field, Milwaukee, Wisc. 66, 67
Boricua 114
Boss, Marilyn 92
Boston, Massachusetts 16, 20, 191, 252, 277, 293
Boston Braves 155
Boston Garden's Hall of Fame 296
Boston Red Sox 6, 203
Boston University Sports Hall of Fame 296
Bowlers Journal All American Team 296
Boyce, Ethel 301
Boyle, Ralph (Buzz) *75*, 156
Boys' Club 147
Bradley University 149, 164
Braves 305
Briggs, Rita 117, 210, 211, *223*, 233
Briggs, Wilma (Briggsie, Willie) viii, 23, 184, *206*, 211, *227*, 233, *258*, 260, 270, 282, 286, 288, 289, 304, 309, 310, 315
Broadway 32
Brooklyn, Michigan 277
Brooklyn, New York 43, 168, 277, 285
Brooklyn Dodgers 39, 99, 155
Brooks, Maggie 298
Brough-Stevenson, Mikell 314
Brown, Kelly viii
Brown, Patricia I. 181, 277
Brown, umpire 114
Browne, Lois 10, 181
Brumfield, Delores *see* White, Delores
Bryson, Marion *75*
Buckley, Jean (Buckets) 129
Buffalo Gram 286
Bunselmeier, Dale viii
Bunselmeier, Pat viii
Burdick, Bill viii

Bureau County Sports Hall of Fame 298
Bureau of Labor Statistics 21
Burkovich, Shirley viii, 23, 59, 167, 184, 267, 286, 292, 308, *309*, 310, *311*, 312, 313, 315
Burmeister, Eileen *40*
Bush, George W. 298
Bush, President George W. 275, *276*, *307*
Bush, Guy 157, 203
Butterworth Hospital, Grand Rapids, Mich. 194

Caden, Mary Lou Studnicka viii, 88, *89*, 92, 93, *94*, *201*, 300, 310
Calacito, Lou 286
Calacurcio, Doris 92
Calgary, Alberta, Canada 182, 285
California 7, 8, 70
California Girls 173
California Girls Baseball League 74
California State University at Chico 6
Callaghan, Helen *see* Candaele, Helen
Callaghan, Margaret (Marge) *see* Maxwell, Margaret
Callen, Gloria 34
Callow, Eleanor *77*, 210, 211, 219, *220*, *223*, *225*, 301
Camp Grant 52
Camp Le Jeune, North Carolina 171
Campanella, Roy 268
Campbell, Helen Hannah viii, 167, 168, 169, *170*, 171, 172, *173*, *175*, 267, 277, 308, 309, 310, 312
Campbell, Sarah viii
CAN Illinois Community Television Competition and Festival, Chicago 278
Canada 1, 15, 36, 44, 59, 80, 154, 157, 166, 167, 169, 185, 278, 293, 323, 325
Canadian Baseball Hall of Fame 262, 301
Canadian National Team 24
Canadian Players 182
Canadian Provinces 185
Canadian Sports Hall of Fame, Alberta 298
Candaele, Helen Callaghan *48*, *227*, 250, 251, 278, 301
Candaele, Kelly viii, 250, 251, 278, 279, 287, 329
Caracas, Venezuela 113
Card, Andy viii, 275, *276*
Carey, Mary *128*
Carey, Max 1, 46, *47*, 71, 80, *81*, *82*, 87, 88, 94, 96, 99, 100, 112, 113, 114, 115, 117, 119, 120, 121, 155, 156, 157, 167, 172, 200, 268, 324, 330
Carey-Cup Play-off 81
Carigy, Virginia 297
Carl, Coralyn (Corky) viii

Carlson, Phyllis 92
Carrig, Virginia 168
Carver, Virginia 211
Carveth, Betty *see* Dunn, Betty
Castillo, Ysora *see* Kinney, Ysora
Catalina Airlines 171
Catalina Island 30, 32, 70, 170
Catalina Island Yacht Club 31
Cathedral City, California 311
Catholic Social Services 312
Catholic Youth Organization (CYO) 20
Cato, Nancy Mudge vii, viii, 8, 195, 211, 214, 277, 312
Cavanaugh, Megan (Marla Hooch) 266
Cavarretta, Phil 32
CBS TV 141
Celebrity Golf Tournament Fund Raiser 309
Celina, Ohio 286
Central America 32, 112, 113, 114, 115, 121, 191
Central Park, New York 183
CFRN TV Edmonton 285
CGBL *see* Chicago Girls Baseball League
Chafe, William 62, 65, 191
Changing Roles of Women 191
Chaperones *see* AAGBBL Chaperones
Chapman, Dorothy Maguire (Mickey) *39*, *47*, *75*
Charleston, South Carolina 43
Charm 67
Charm School *see* AAGBBL Charm School
Chattanooka, Tennessee 96
Cherry Point 171
Chicago 1, 7, 8, 15, 20, 32, 36, 41, 69, 74, 87, 104, 121, 125, 126, 151, 156, 157, 168, 169, 171, 182, 192, 192, 193, 198, 200, 233, 236, 238, 248, 269, 286313
Chicago Athletic Association 31
Chicago Bears 125
Chicago Colleens 92, 93, 103, 105; (1948) *77*
Chicago Cubs vii, 6, 8, 29, 30, 42–43, 44, 71, 126, 170, 238, 267, 323
Chicago Daily Herald 286
Chicago Girls Baseball League (CGBL) 87–94, 105; official players' contract 90; rosters 92
Chicago Herald 113
Chicago Historical Society 313
Chicago Metro Fair 313
Chicago Metropolitan Girls Major Softball League 33, 121, 198, 199, 200
Chicago National Girls Baseball League (NGBL) 38, 74, 200, 201, 212
Chicago National League Ball Club 31
Chicago Old Timers Baseball Association 298, 300, 308

Chicago Old Timers Baseball Hall of Fame 304
Chicago Park Department 87, 88, 92
Chicago Softball League 57
Chicago Yacht Club 31
Chico State College 6
Childress, Cartha Doyle 276, 315
Chill Shelter 69
Choctaw, Arkansas 184, 192
Christ, Dorothy (Dottie) 296
Cincinnati 31, 36, 98, 182, 191, 285
Cincinnati Reds 155
Cinco de Mayo 172
Cione, Jean (Ci) vii, viii, *2*, 8, *53*, 72, *75*, 157, 198, 210, 267, 292, 293, 295, 313
Citizen of the Year 295
Citizen's Stamp Advisory Committee 275
Civic Theatre, Fort Wayne, Ind. 149
Clark, Dan A. *82*, 147, *148*, 234
Clark, Dee viii
Clark, Jane Forbes 267
Clark, Ken viii
Clark, Mary Jane 234
Clarke's Restaurants, South Bend, Ind. 147
Clearwater, Florida 286
Clemmer, Ron 280, 281
Cleveland 17, 36
Cleveland Indians 155
Click 50, 67
Clinton, Connecticutt 277
Clinton, Hillary Rodham 287
Clinton, President William J. 287
Coast Guard 55
Cobb, Ty 171
Coben, Muriel *40*, 297, 301
Cole, Arthur 326
Cole Lenzi Field 92
Coleman, Charlie 311
Colleens and Sallies: (1949) *106*; (1950) *109*
College of Art and Design, Savannah, Georgia 312
Colliers 50
Collins, Dorothy Wiltse (Dottie) viii, 19, *48*, 155, *227*, 235, 240, 241, 242, 243, 246, 247, 249, 250, *251*, 252, 253, *254*, 255, *258*, 261, 262, *263*, 269, 270, 271, 272, 274, 275, 278, 282, 284, 288, 289, 292, 294, 298, 301, 304, 312, 313, 314, 329
Colorado 192
Colorado Silver Bullets 265
Colored Orphans and Industrial Home 97
Columbia, South Carolina 300
Columbia Pictures 282, 284
Columbia Studio 284
Columbianas 112
Community Chest 149
Community Welfare 51, 63, 324, 326
Competition with Men 139, 140

Conduct Rules *see* AAGBBL Conduct Rules
Constable, Burt 286
Cook, Clara *38*, *40*, *47*
Cook, Donna (COOKIE)
Cook, Doris *77*, *109*, *128*, 284, 313
Cook, Dorothy 301
Cooke, Penny O'Brian (Peanuts) 301
Cooper, Joe 157
Cooperstown, New York 9, 245, 259, 266, 275, 281, 282, 293
Cordes, Gloria *see* Elliott, Gloria
Cornett, Betty 277
Coronet 67
Cosmopolitan 67
Costa Rica 115, 120
Courtney, Pat 109, 296
Coveleski AAA Baseball Park, South Bend, Ind. 256, 257
Cox, Janet 92
Cozens, Frederick 57
Crawley, Pauline (Hedy) 304, *309*, 310, 312
Crescent City, California 216
Crites, Shirley *193*, 211
Crocker, Cheryl 318
Croteau, Julie 267
Crowell, Jim 171
Cruthers, Pres 156
Cryan, Margaret Villa (Maggie, Poncho) *116*, 117, 210, 272, 312
Cuba 1, 96, 111, 113, 120, 121, 166, 172, 191
Cuban Baseball Hall of Fame 300
Cuban Girls' Baseball League 99
Cuban Tour, 1952 141
Cuban Trip 99
Cubanas 115
Cubans, Draft-proof 42
Cunningham, Bernice 92
Curtis, Henry S. 16, 20
Cvitkovich, Fran viii

Dailey, Elizabeth 169
Dailey, Harold T. vii, 7, 72, 81, *82*, 98, 123, 132, 133, 137, 150, 162, 207, 230
Damascus Steel Products Corporation, Rockford, Ill. 147
Dancer, Faye *27*, *48*, *101*, 155, 251, *258*, 270, 281, 310
D'Angelo, Jo *40*
Danhauser, Margaret (Marnie) *39*
Daniels, Audrey Haine (Dimples) *48*, 59, 166, 267, 285, 301, 310
Daniels, Bud 267
Danz, Shirley 92, *93*, *106*, *109*
Dapkus, Eleanor *see* Wolf, Eleanor
Davis, Barbara 92
Davis, Geena viii, 10, 282, 283
Davis, Gladys (Terrie) *40*, *47*, *75*, 182, 210, 301
Davis, Lavone Paire (Pepper) viii, *48*, 114, 117, 155, *206*, 211, 238, 240, *241*, 246, 251, 270, 277, 281, 293, 312, 329

Davis, Marguerite Jones 297, 301
Davis, Ruth (Ruthie) viii, *235*, *236*, 238, 248, 329
Davis Shoe Softball Team, Racine, Wisc. 168
Dayton, Ohio 151, 286
DDT 98
Dean, Jay Hanna (Dizzy) 110
Dean, Paul 110
Dearfield, Norma 309
Deb 50
DeCambra, Alice (Moose) 277
Dedeaux, Rod 281
Deegan, Mildred (Millie) *53*, 168, 233, 276, 294, 295
Degner, Betty *109*
Delmonico, Lee Surkowski 297, 301, 308, *309*, 312
Democracy 20
Denia, Puerto Rican Girls Baseball Team 114
DePauw University 312
Depression 192
Derringer, Norm 157
Deschaine, Alice Pollitt 210, 211, *220*, *223*, 315
DesCombes, Jeneane *see* Lesko, Jeneane
Desegregation 230
DeShone, Nancy *see* Dinehart, Nancy
Des Lauriers, Ed vii, 7, 65, 229
Detroit, Michigan 36, 192
Detroit Tigers 170, 300
Development and Decline of the All-American Girls Baseball League, 1943–1954 2, 230, *231*, 234
Dewar, Patricia 297
Deyotte, Anne Surkowski 297, 301
Diamond Ball 17, 21, 24
Diamond Gals 86, 249
Dierstein, Mary viii
DiMaggio, Joe 108, 110, 171
Dinehart, Nancy DeShone 262, *263*, 289, 296
Dinner and a Movie 313
Disselhorst, Jean 92
Distinguished Alumna of the Year 300
Dodge News 51
Dodger Stadium Jumbotron 308
Dodger Stadium Softball Clinic 311
Dokish, Wanita 277
Dolgeville, New York 277
Dolgeville, New York School District 266
Dominguez, Ma. E. 117
Dominiak, Dolores 92
Donahue, Terry viii, 59, *75*, 166, 212, 267, 272, 286, *295*, 297, 298, 301, 306, 308, 310, 313
"Double Your Pleasure, Double Your Fun" 70
Doublemint Twins 70
Douglas, Mary Lee 65
Douglas, Mary Lou Graham *224*

Dowler, Jean Lovell *128*, 139, 211, *225*
Doxey, Marilyn Jones (Jonesy) 211, 308, 315, *318*
Doyle, Cartha *see* Childress, Cartha
Doyle, Dorothy Harrell (Snookie) viii, *53*, 70, *101*, 112, 129, 155, 188, 191, 211, *215*, *217*, *223*, 304, 308, *309*, 310, 312, *321*
Draper Middle School, Mohonasen, NY 266
Dries, Dolores Lee (Pickles) 158, *159*, *161*, 298
Dubuque, Iowa 151
Duda, Diana 314
Duda, Jennifer 314
Dummerth, Edna Frank 296, 305, 315
Dundee High School, Dundee, Ill. 182
Dunn, Betty Carveth *53*, 72, 301
Dunn, Gertrude (Gertie) *159*, 211, *224*, 294
Dunsmuir, California 5
Dunsmuir City Baseball Park 6; grandstands 5
Dunsmuir Lions Club 5
Dusanko, Julie Sabo 297, 301

Earl, Elsie Wingrove 297, 301
Earp, Mildred 113, 210, *215*, 219
East Greenville, Pennsylvania 23
East Greenwich Athletic Hall of Fame 304
East Greenwich, Rhode Island 23, 184
East Stroudsburg University Sports Hall of Fame 296
Eastern Michigan University 2, 198
Eastern Michigan University Athletic Hall of Fame 295
Eastern Michigan University Hall of Fame 304, 305
Eastman, Jean Faut *see* Faut, Jean
Economy Homes, Inc. 127
Ederle, Gertrude 34
Edmonton, Alberta, Canada 182, 285
Educational Philosophy for Girls and Women's Sports 18–19, 21, 24, 25
Edwards, Bill 156
Eisen, Thelma (Tiby) viii, *47*, 55, 60, 70, *75*, *101*, 112, *116*, 117, *118*, 119, 120, 121, 155, 156, 161, 162, 166, 188, 191, *206*, 210, *214*, *227*, 251, 260, 270, 277, 281, 298, 306, *307*, 308, *309*, 310, 312, 313, 315
El Toro Air Base, Santa Ana, California 171
Electric Park, Tucson, Arizona 310
Elgin Sports Hall of Fame 301
Elk River, Minnesota vii
Elkins, Lee 138, 152
Elks 147

Elliott, Gloria Cordes 106, 107, *128*, 185, *199*, 210, 211, *223*, 266, 284, 298, 306, *307*, 309, 314, 315
Elmhurst College 216
Emerson, June 274, 297, 301
Emralino, Gilbert viii
English, Madeline (Maddy) *39*, 57, 59, 112, 191, 210, *214*, *217*, 260, 266, 277, *304*
English, Woody 157, *201*
Erickson, Louise (Lou) *see* Sauer, Louise
Estrellas Cubanas 117
Eureka, California 216
European U.S.O. Tour 141
Evansville, Indiana 281, 282
Everett, Massachusetts 109, 277, 304
Extramural Sports 18

Fairfield, California 277
Family Entertainment 51, 65, 324, 326
Family Togetherness 65
Fan Club, Kalamazoo, Michigan 138
Fan Clubs 152, 153
Fan Fest, Seattle 312
Fantry, Jean Faut *see* Faut, Jean
Far East Tour 142
Faralla, Lillian (Lil) *75*, *101*
Farnham, Marynia 62
Farragut Boat Club, Chicago 15
Farrow, Elizabeth *48*
Faut, Jean vii, viii, 7, 23, 72, 98, 99, *139*, 169, 188, *190*, 210, 211, 218, *219*, *220*, 221, *224*, *225*, 226, *227*, 272, 289, 291, 292, 297, 299, 304, 306, *307*, 312, *318*
Federation of Cuban Players in Exile 300
Fedoruk, Sylvia (Right Honourable Lieutenant Governor) 297
Feldman, Jay 52
Femininity 19, 51, 57, 63, 65, 324, 326, 327
Feminist Movement 20, 230, 329
Fenton, Peggy 92
Ferguson, Dorothy (Dottie) *see* Key, Dorothy
Ferguson, Sarah Jane Sands (Salty) 233, 260, 309, 310
Ferlybutt 70
Fernandez, Mirtha Marrero *77*, 102, *103*, *116*, 117, 121
Fidler, Jean 5
Fidler, Jess (Dinger) 5
Fidler, Jess William (Skip) 5, 6
Fidler, Marilyn viii
Fidler, Marshall viii
Fidler, Merrie 2, 3, 5, *6*, 11, 244, 247, 254, *259*, 274
Fidler, Robert Griffith (Bob) 5, 6
Fidler, Tressa Jean (Tress) 5
Fidler, Walter *106*
Fiedler, Marty 74

Field of Dreams Celebrity Ball Game, 1995 310
A Field of Her Own 300
Figlio, Josephine *47*
Filarski, Helen *see* Steffes, Helen
Fischer, Alva Jo (Tex) *53*, *75*, 172
Fitzgerald, Lorraine (Fitz) viii, *91*, 92, *93*
Flanagan, Marcie 314
Fleming and Weber 171
Flint, Michigan 151, 212
Florida 98, 99, 105, 113
Florida International Baseball League 224
Florida Men's League 140
Florreich, Lois (Flash) *40*, 55, 210, *217*
Folder, Rose *see* Powell, Rose
Forbes Magazine of Business 51
Ford, President Gerald R. 260
Ford, Whitey 110
Forness, Consuelito 117
Fort Lauderdale 223, 224
Fort Sheridan 52
Fort Wayne, Indiana 73, 104, 149, 156, 157, 168, 214, 239, 247, 248, 250, 269, 270, 277, 278, 279, 301
Fort Wayne Baseball Hall of Fame 301–302
Fort Wayne Basketball Association 149
Fort Wayne Chamber of Commerce 149
Fort Wayne Convention and Visitors Bureau 243
Fort Wayne Country Club 149
Fort Wayne Daisies 47, 81, 130, 131, 138, 148, 152, 162, 205, 220, 221, 231, 234, 248, 250, 278, 298, 312; Fan Club 153; infield, 1953 *193*
Fort Wayne Daisies, 1952 *206*
Fort Wayne Girls Baseball League 64–65
Fort Wayne Historical Society 248
Fort Wayne Journal Gazette 190
Fort Wayne Junior Daisies 234
Fort Wayne Junior Daisy League 64–65
Fort Wayne News Sentinel 246, 302
Fort Wayne Old Timer's Baseball Association 305
Fort Wayne Old Timer's Game 278
Fort Wayne Women's Bureau (FWWB) 230, 234, 243, 248, 281, 284, 329
Fortune Magazine's Most Powerful Women Summit 308
Foss, Anita 281, 310, 313
Foss, Betty Weaver *206*, 210, 211, 220, 221, *222*, *223*, 226
Fountain Valley Police Department, California 173
Fox, Helen Nicol (Nicki) *38*, 52, 182, 210, 298, 301
Fox, Jean Peterson 298

Fox-Movietone 141
Fox 32 Chicago 286
Foxx, James Emory (Jimmie, Double X) 10, 155, 157, *206*
Francis, Betty viii, 92, 94, *106*, *109*, *128*
Frank, Edna *see* Dummerth, Edna
Fraternal Order of Police Lodge No. 36, South Bend, Ind. 147
Frick, Grace 92
Fritsch, (?) 92
Fritsch Baseball Card Company 290
Fritz, Betty *40*
Froning, Mary *see* O'Meara, Mary
Frost, Helen 17
Frye, Zella *13*
Fusco, Christopher 313
FWWB *see* Fort Wayne Women's Bureau

Gacioch, Rose *53*, 210, 211, 211, *223*, *225*, 300, 300, 308, *308*
Gala Visionary Award Dinner 318
Gallagher, James 43
Gallegos, Luisa *78*, 102, *103*
Ganz, Lowell 280
Garcia, Adelina 117
Gary, Indiana 36
Gascon, Eileen (Ginger) viii, 31, 92, *93*, *109*, 200, 300, 306, 313
Gehrig, Lou 171
Geissinger, Jean *see* Harding, Jean
Gene Autry Museum 173
General Aurand 52
Gentry, Ruth Middleton 301
George, Gene *see* McFaul, Gene
Georges, Ann *109*
Georges, Beulah *77*
Georgeson, Murline viii
Georgia 105
Gerber, Ellen W. vii, viii, 6, 230
Gerdom, Millie viii
Gerring, Betty *75*, 168
Gilchrist, Jeanne 301, 310
Girls Clubs of America 312
Girls' Athletic Association (GAA) 19
Girls' Little League Softball World Series 304
The Girls of Summer 280
Glamour 67
Glans, Carl 129
Glasgow, Scotland 267
Glenview Park District Golf Course 305
Gloucester County Hall of Fame 296
Golden, Thelma 301
Goldsmith, Bethany (Beth, Betty) 117, 169
Gonlag, Frances 92
Gonzales, Eulalia (Viyalla) 101
Good Morning America 237, 238, 246, 284, 286
Good Night Irene 236

Gottselig, Johnny *39*, *75*, 154, 156, 157, 169
Graham, Adrienne viii
Graham, Mary Lou *see* Douglas, Mary Lou
Grambo, Thelma *see* Hundeby, Thelma
Grand Rapids, Michigan vii, 8, 34, 41, 67, 73, 79, 147, 151, 156, 157, 168, 169, 170, 193, 277, 284, 286, 313
Grand Rapids Black Sox 141
Grand Rapids Chamber of Commerce 147
Grand Rapids Chicks vii, 8, 34, 83, 93, 96, 109, 130, 131, 148, 151, 152, 152, 156, 176, 194, 201, 201, 209, 212, 217, 276, 304, 312, 328; (1952) *201*
Grand Rapids Hall of Fame 298
Grand Rapids Jets 83, 151
Grand Rapids Museum, Michigan 233, 276
Grand Rapids Public Museum, Michigan viii
Grand Rapids Sports Hall of Fame 304, 304
Grand Rapids Veterans Counseling Center 147
Grant, Chet vii, 7, 9, 146, 154, 156, 176, 177, 234
Grant, Olga 301
Grapefruit League 284
Grau, Ramón, Cuban President 101
Great Depression 22–25
Great Lakes Sports Training Center 249, 255
The Greater Akron Baseball Hall of Fame 298
Greater Flint Michigan Area Sports Hall of Fame 295
Greater Fort Wayne Chamber of Commerce 243
Greater Muskegon Chamber of Commerce 149
Greater Peoria Sports Hall of Fame 298
Green, Dorothy (Dottie) *53*, 168, 169, *223*, 274, 284
Green Bay Packers 125, 126
Greenville, South Carolina 182
Greenville Spinners 182
Gregorash, Lucille 92
Gregorich, Barbara 181, 308
Greiner, Harold 156, 157, 235, 243
Gretsky, Wayne 260
Griffin, Viola Thompson (Tommie) *47*, 72, *73*, 155, 182, 300
Griffith Stadium 108
Grube, Frances 168
Guatemala 115
The Guatemala Bulletin 115
Guatemala City 115, 119
Guilfoile, Bill *250*, 251, 264
Gunderson, Belmar viii
Gutz, Julia *78*, *103*
"Gypsy Baron Overture" 66

Habben, Carol 300
Haber, Lynn 252, 255, 269, 270
Hagan, Jerry 226
Hageman, Jo *40*, 168, 169, *175*, 176
Hager, Tina 307
Hagerstown 108
Haine, Audrey *see* Daniels, Audrey
Hall, Orline M., Second Officer 52
Hamilton, Jim 34, 43, 181
Hancock Alumnus of the Year 296
Hanks, Tom viii, 10, 283, 284
Hanna, Marjorie 301
Hannah, Helen *see* Campbell, Helen
Hannah, James Harrison (Truck) 170
Hansen, Florence *13*
Hanson, Harry *82*, 147, *148*
Harbor Springs, Michigan 277
Harding, Jean Geissinger viii, *159*, *193*, *201*, 211, *227*, *235*, 249, 255, *258*, 269, 270, 271, 274, 282, 288, 289, 292, 293, 294, 329
Harkness, N.J. (Nate) *82*, 147, *148*
Harmon, Annabelle Lee (Lefty) viii, 19, 36, *48*, *75*, *101*, 114, 115, *116*, 117, 118, 119, 155, 182, 191, *280*, 301, *303*, 309, 310, 312, 313
Harms, Dutch 92
Harnett, Ann *37*, *38*, 57, 60, 182, 200, 210
Harney, Lee *38*
Harper, Paul V. 34, 42, 324
Harrell, Dorothy *see* Doyle, Dorothy
Harrington, Darci viii
Harrington, Helen Rauner 168, *227*, 235, 243
Hartman, David 246
Harvey, Walter 10
Hatzell, Beverly *see* Volkert, Beverly
Havana, Cuba 96, 98, 99, 112, 166, 172
Haven, Kansas 315
Haverbeck, Mary Jo viii
Havlish, Jean (Grasshopper) viii, 188, *193*, 211, 277, *296*, 312, 315
Hawaii 312
Hay, Florence 92, *109*
Haylett, Alice 210, *217*, 219
Healy, Muriel 64
Heaphy, Leslie 275
Hearst Metronome News 67
Heart Association Fund Raiser 309
Heim, Barbara 92
Heim, Kay *see* McDaniel, Kay
Heim, Nyema Lindblade 92
Heinz, Tom 9
Heitmann, Jacqueline viii
Helmer, Diana Star 10, 181
Henderson State University, Arkadelphia, Arkansas 309
Henderson State University Hall of Fame 300

Hendrich, Carol viii
Herbst, Henry *82*
Hernandez de Leon, Sra. Mercedes 117
Hernlund, Vern 71, 88
Hershey, Esther *78*
Hess, Oklahoma 96, 192, 193
Heverly, Ruth Williams *128*, 162, 192, 234, 245, 257, 272
Hickey, Lillian 301
Hicks, Helen 34
Hickson, Irene (Choo-Choo) *39*, 169, 210, 259
Hill, Joyce *see* Westerman, Joyce
History Day Fair 314
History Day Regional Competition 315
Hoffman, Barbara (Barb) 211, 234, 236, *235*, 296
Hohlmayer, Alice (Lefty) viii, 169, 267, 277, 281, 293, 315, 317
Holda, Mary *40*
Holderness, Joan viii, 65, 92, 94, 282, 286, 288, 289, 305, 315, *318*
Holgerson, Margaret (Margie, Mobile) *116*, 117, 166, *201*
Holiday 50, 141
Holiday Inn, Chicago City Center 236, 237
Holiday Inn, Skokie, Illinois 281
Holloway, Marion 169
Hollywood 9, 19, 60, 279, 280, 285
Holm, Eleanor 34
Holmes, Agnes Zurowski 297, 301
Holsinger, Ros *22*
Homestead, Florida 182
Hornsby, Rogers 87, *89*
Horstman, Catherine (Katie) viii, 157, 158, *159*, *206*, 211, 250, 251, 260, 277, 278, 286, 295, 300, 309, 310, *311*, 315, *318*
The Hotel Greeters Guide of Wisconsin 51
Houston, Texas 192, 310
Howe, Murray 107
Hudson County Athletic Hall of Fame 298
Huffington, Ariana 308
Huggins, Miller 171
Hughes, Bill 281
Hughes, Ellen Roney 246
Hughes, Joe viii
Hull-House Playground 16
Hundeby, Thelma Grambo 297, 301
Hunt, Carrie *128*
Hunt, Virginia viii
Hunter, Dorothy (Dottie) vii, 8, *39*, *47*, 55, 60, *101*, 117, 168, 168, 169, *170*, *175*, 185, *225*, 277, 301, 328, 330
Huntingburg, Indiana 281
Hurt, Elaine 92
Hutchison, Anna May 80, 210, *214*, *215*, 260, 285, 310
Hyslop, H.C. *82*

Illinois 105, 185
Illinois State History Fair 313
Illinois State Normal School, Bloomington 127
Independent Team Owners 82, 128, 129, 135, 139, 142, 149, 151, 164, 165, 183, 185, 201, 202, 206, 207, 325, 327
Indiana 105, 185, 312
Indoor Baseball 15–21
Industrial Recreation 21
Industrial Softball 19–21, 24
Inglewood, California 216
Integration 42
International Association of Fire Fighters Local No. 362, South Bend, Indiana
International Base-Ball School, Costa Rica 121
International League of Girls Baseball 112, 113, 115, 121
International Softball Tournament 311
Intramural Sports 18, 19
"Introduction to the Third Act of Lohengrin" 66
Iowa 185
Ireland, Kathy 318
Irvine, California 311
It Happens Every Spring 155
Ives, Irene 168

Jack Cramer Award 298
Jackson, Elizabeth 190
Jackson, Lillian (Lil) *40*, *48*, 270, 271, 278, 285
Jackson Bowling Hall of Fame 297
Jackson County, Altus, Oklahoma Baseball Hall of Fame 295
Jackson District Library 313
Jacksonville, Florida 285
Jacksonville Florida Sports Hall of Fame Honor Roll 298
Jacobs, Helen 34
Jacobs, Jane *75*
Jacobson, Floyd 92
Jacques, Yvonne viii
Jameson, Janet *78*
Jameson, Shirley *37*, *38*, 52, *58*, 60, 182, 185, 210
Janet Lynn Award for Sports 305
Janikowski, Charlotte 92
Janikowski, Lorraine 92
Janowski, Alice 301
Janssen, Frances (Fran) viii, *106*, *109*, 184, 188, *227*, 255, 257, *258*, 262, *263*, 269, 270, 271, 274, 275, 288, 293, 296, *299*, 312, 313, 329
Japan 171
Jenkins, Amber 314
Jenkins, Marilyn vii, viii, 8, 170, *201*, 234, 274, 286, 297, 312, 313
Jewish Sports Hall of Fame 306
Jochum, Betsy vii, viii, 7, *40*, 52, 55, 192, 207, *227*, 236, *247*, 256,

256, 257, 262, *263*, 283, 296, 298, 302, 312, 313, 315, 329
Jody (?) *93*
Johnson, (?) 92
Johnson, Arleene *see* Noga, Arleene
Johnson, Cecil 245
Johnson, George 156
Johnson, Margaret *77*, 168
Johnson, Susan 10, 181
Johnson, Wilbur 150, 176
Johnson's Wax Team, Racine, Wisc. *22*
Jones, Margaret Russo (Marge) *225*, 277
Jones, Marguerite *see* Davis, Marguerite
Jones, Marilyn *see* Doxey, Marilyn
Jonnard, Claude (Bubber) *48*, 156
Junor, Daisy 192, 297, 301
Junior Girls Baseball Leagues 64
Junior Lassies, Kalamazoo, Michigan 138
Junior League Girls Baseball 87
Jr. Seau Kids Organization 309
Justra, Mary *see* Shastal, Mary

K Rations 32
Kabick, Jo *47*, *77*, 200
Kachline, Clifford 244, 245, 248, 249
Kadlec, Sheri 275
Kalamazoo, Michigan 41, 84, 127, 151, 156, 157, 168, 169, 205, 219, 230, 232, 277
Kalamazoo All-City Squad, 1954 141
Kalamazoo Gazette 141, 226
"Kalamazoo Klouters" 141
Kalamazoo Lassies 107, 130, 131, 138, 152, 162, 199, 201, 214, 219, 231, 298; (1952) *128*
Kalamazoo Stadium (CAA Field) 139
Kamenshek, Dorothy (Dottie, Kammie) viii, 31, *40*, *53*, 58, *101*, 112, 113, 115, *116*, 117, 118, 119, 121, 129, 131, 140, 153, 166, 185, 191, 195, 210, *214*, *215*, *217*, *220*, 222, *223*, 224, 225, 226, 231, 232, 238, 246, 270, 274, 276, 281, 290, 295, 304, *309*, 312, 329
Kansas 159
Kansas City, Missouri 169
Kansas State History Day Competition 315
Kappel, Shirley 64
Kaufman, Joan 246
KCET 279
Keagle, Pat (Merle) *47*, 55, 210, *214*, *331*
Keenan, Marie 46, 268
Kelley, Jacqueline (Jackie, Babe) 210, *227*
Kellogg, Vivian *48*, *101*, 156, 161,

162, 182, 233, *258*, 260, 277, 297, 305, 313, 315
Kemman, Florence *22*
Kemmerer, Beaty *227*
Kendall College of Physical Education, Chicago 168
Kenosha, Wisconsin 7, 36, 41, 48, 52, 63, 79, 125, 126, 145, 149, 157, 168, 169, 204
Kenosha Comets 52, 55, 123, 130, 145, 148, 152, 162, 185, 209, 216, 249–250, 256; (1943) *38*; (1947) *147*
Kenosha County, Wisc. 126
Kenosha County Courthouse, Wisc. 125
Kenosha Evening News 63
Kenosha News 145
Kenosha Planning Committee, Wisc. 149
Kent Country Club, Grand Rapids, Mich. 147
Kent County Family Service, Mich. 147
Kentucky 185, 285
Kerwin, Irene 200
Kessler, Eunice 168
Key, Dorothy Ferguson (Dottie) *53*, *101*, *179*, 301, 305
Keystone Steel and Wire Company, Peoria, Ill. 149
Kidd, Sue viii, 23, *106*, *109*, 184, 188, 192, *203*, 211, *224*, *227*, 298, 300
Kiekow, Lorraine 92
Kimball, Kay 169
King, Billie Jean 308
"The King and His Court" 138
Kinney, Ysora del Castillo (Chico) 102, *109*, 117, *300*
Kiska, Tim 280
Kissel, Audrey *see* Lafser, Audrey
Kittenball 17
Klabacha, Lorraine 92
Kline, Maxine *see* Randall, Maxine
Klosowski, Delores *47*
Kloza, Jack 156
Knezovich, Ruby *see* Marty, Ruby
Knights Templar 147
Knoxville, Tennessee 96, 215
Knoxville News-Sentinel 276
Koehn, Phyllis (Sugar) *38*, 72, 234, 278, 298
Konwinski, Dolly Niemiec 92, 277, 286, 298, 304, 309, 312, 315, *318*
Koopman, Dolores 92
Korean War 174
Kotil, Arlene viii, 92, 94, *95*, *109*
Kotowicz, Irene (Ike) *53*, *101*, *116*, 117, 278, 300
Kovach, John 256, 257, 329
Krauss, Vern 235
Krick, Jayne (Jaynie, Red) *201*, 300
Kroupa, Carolyn *22*

Kruckel, Marie (Kruck) 234, 296, 315
Kughn, Richard 280
Kunkel, Karen Violetta viii, 72, 249, 252, 255, *256*, 257, *258*, 269, 270, 271, 272, 277, 279, 280, 281, 282, 284, 288, 294, 306, *307*, 329
Kurys, Sophie (Soph) viii, 38, *39*, 55, 210, *212*, *214*, *215*, *217*, 274, 295, 315; base stealing statistics 213
KUSA Channel 9 286

La Duc, Neola 211
La Nueva Prensa, Managua, Nicaragua, newspaper 119
Ladies' Days 31
Ladies' Home Journal 65
Lady Bird Johnson Community Park, San Antonio, Texas 276, 295
Lafser, Audrey Kissel *48*, 277, 284, 296, 305
Lake Geneva Yacht Club 31
Lake View High School, Chicago, Ill. 167, 266
Lamers, Margaret *22*
Lamphere, Louise *13*
Lamphere, Maude *13*
Landis, Kenesaw Mountain 29, 35
Lang, Marge 200
Langeman, Reg 290, 293, 313, 330
Lansing, Michigan 212
Latin American Dances 119
Latin American Feminine Basebol League (LAFBBL) 101, 111, 113, *112*, 114
Latin American Sports Writers 120
Latin American Tour 112, 113, 121
Latin Music 119
Lawson, Mary *75*
League Board of Directors 74, 79, 80, 81, 82, 83, 84, 96, 104, 105, 111, 112, 121, 123, 124, 130, 131, 134, 136, 142, 146, 150, 162, 175, 177, 200, 201, 206, 208, 324, 325
League City Sites, Map *41*
League-Management Relations 80, 83, 123
A League of Their Own 9, 11, 70, 87, 243, 264, 266, 272, 276, 278, 279, 280, 282, 284, 285, 286, 287, 290, 291, 296, 297, 305, 312, 313, 319, 329
Leback, Jean 92
Lebanon, Pennsylvania 192
Lee, Annabelle *see* Harmon, Annabelle
Lee, Dolores (Pickles) *see* Dries, Dolores
Lee, Joseph 16, 20
Lemnius 260
Lenard, Jo (Bubblegum) *53*, *75*, 129, 210, 211, *215*, *224*
Leo, Fred K. *81*, 82, 125, 126, 133, 137, 139, 140, 141, 205, 324, 330
Leon, Nicaragua 115

Leon, Rafael 99, 113, 114, *116*, 117
Lesko, Jeneane DesCombes (Jeanie) viii, 161, *241*, 292, 293, 303, 304, 310, 312, 329
Lesko, Matthew 293
Lessing, Ruth (Tex) 10, *48*, *179*, 210, *214*, *215*, *217*, 300
Lester, Mary Lou *38*, 182
Lewis, Guy M. viii
Lewis, Suzy 241
Lexington, Kentucky 97
Liberty 50, 67
Liebrich, Barbara (Bobbie) 105, *106*, 108, *109*, 110, 157, 169, 282, 288
Life 50, 184
Lillard Brothers 171
Lima, Ohio 286
Lincoln National Life Insurance Company 149
Lincoln Park, Kenosha, Wisconsin 125
Lincoln Park, Michigan 108
Lindblade, Nyema *see* Heim, Nyema
Lionikis, Kay *109*
Lipkowski, Kris viii
Little, Alta 298, 300
Little, Olive Bend (Ollie) *40*, *53*, 210, 277, 301
Little Rock, Arkansas 184
Lloydminster 277
Lonetto, Sarah 233
Long Island University 168
Longbow Productions 279, 280, 281, 329
Look 67
Los Angeles 23, 32, 60, 74, 155, 171, 191, 277, 281
Los Angeles Angels 170, 171
Los Angeles County 192, 295
Los Angeles County Natural History Museum 313
Los Angeles Times 251, 252
Lotz, Ruth *13*
Louisiana 105
Louisville 98
Lovell, Jean *see* Dowler, Jean
Lowenstein, Ira 10, 70
LPGA 294
LPGA Ellen Griffin Rolex Award 298
LPGA Tour 188
Luckey, Lillian 296
Lucky Strike Bowling Alley, Kalamazoo 127
Luna, Betty *101*
Lundahl, Mildred 168, *175*
Lundberg, Ferdinand 62
Lundin, Linda 241
Lyons, Jeffrey 266

Macarelli, Tiffani 304
Machado, Angel E. 121
Machado, Helen (Chow) *75*
Mack, Connie 109, *147*
Mack, Peggy 260, 281

MacLean, Lucella *see* Ross, Lucella
Macy, Sue viii, 10, 181, 270, 292, 308, *318*, 319
Madden, Jack *22*
Madden, W.C. 181
Madison, Wisconsin 151, 234
Madonna 87, 281, 283, 284
Magazine Digest 50
Maguire, Dorothy (Mickey) *see* Chapman, Dorothy
Mahon, Elizabeth (Lib) vii, 7, 182, 192, 198, 210, 211, *214*, *227*, 234, 237, 257, 262, *263*, 296, 298, 329
Mahoney, Marie (Red) 92, 300, 310
Maier, Ken 92
Major League Baseball 29, 30, 33, 39, 70, 95, 96, 208, 323, 324, 326, 326; All-Star Game 208, 293; Fan Fest 292, 310; spring training camps 284
Major League Baseball, Canada 310
Major League Baseball Facts and Figures 51, 268
Malanowski, Jean Marlowe *78*, *128*, 260, 305
Mall, Janice 251
Management Administration 70, 79, 82, 83, 86, 125, 128, 130, 132, 133, 135, 138, 142, 151, 164, 165, 176, 183, 184, 185, 202, 324
Management Corporation 51, 73, 76, 77, 84, 96, 104, 113, 121, 123, 125, 204
Managua, Nicaragua 115, 119
Mandell, Babaloo 280
Mandella, Lenora (Smokey) viii, 110, 309
Manitoba 231
Manitowoc, Wisconsin 300
Manning, Martha Rommelaere 301
Mansfield, Marie 315
Mantle, Mickey 295
Manufacturers Association, Racine, Wisc. 147
Maracaibo, Venezuela 113, 115, 121
Marian Award for Girl Scouts 305
Marine Corps 171, 172, 173
Marks, Gloria *39*
Marlowe, Jean *see* Malanowski, Jean
Marquette, Michigan 277
Marquette Park, Chicago 87, 88
Marrero, Mirtha *see* Fernandez, Mirtha
Marsh, Nancy 92, *93*
Marshall, Garry 266
Marshall, Penny viii, 9, 266, 279, 280, *280*, 281, 283, 284, 285, 329
Marshall, Theda (Teke) 192
Martin, Billy 108
Martiniak, Betty 92
Martz, Ruby Knezovich 297, 301
Maryland 185

Masculine Women 63
Mason, 32nd Degree 147
Mason, Ruth 301
Massachusetts 7, 185
MassMutual/Office Depot Sports Visionary Award 308
Matt Pentathlon 212
Mattson, Jacquelin (Jackie) *see* Baumgart, Jacquelin
Mature, Victor 55
Maxwell, Margaret Callaghan (Marge) 182, *227*, 260, 301, 310
Mayaguez 114
Mayer, Charlene Pryer (Shorty) *75*, 210, 211, *220*, 285, 302, *303*
Mazier, Marie 190
McAuley, Mildred Warwick (Millie) *40*, 52, 297, 301, 308
McCall's 50, 65
McCammon, Earle E. *127*, 128, 129, 138, 162, 206, *224*, 330
McCann, Shelley viii, 241
McComb, Joanne 310
McCormack, Marie 92
McCoy, Joyce viii, 315
McCreary, Ethel *38*, *40*, 301
McCulloch, Colleen Smith 301
McCutchan, Alexandra (Lex) 168, 169, 174, 216, 283
McDaniel, Kay Heim *38*, 301
McFadden, Betty *40*
McFaul, Gene George 297, 301
McGwire, Mark (Big Mac) 304
McKeesport, Pennsylvania 110
McKenna, (?) 92
McKenna, Eddie 145
McKinley, Therese *see* Uselmann, Therese
McLean School, Potomac, Maryland 313
McLin, Donna viii
McManus, Martin (Marty) 156, *158*
McNamara Racing, Kalamazoo, Michigan 138
McNamara Trucking, Kalamazoo, Michigan 138
McNaughton, Alice *see* Hohlmayer, Alice
McNaughton, Shawn 317
Meachem, Mildred *78*
Measner, Hazel *see* Wildfong, Hazel
Meier, Naomi (Sally) *206*
Mero, Everett 20
Metallurgical Engineers 149
Metrolis, Norma *75*
Metropolis, Illinois 220
Metros, Angeline 92
Meusel, Bob 5
Mexico 111, 167
Meyer, Rita *see* Moellering, Rita
Meyerhoff, Arthur E. vii, 7, 8, 10, 34, 51, 67, 68, 73, *81*, 83, 86, 99, 102, 104, 105, 107, 108, 111, 114, 121, 123, 124, 126, 134, 146, 181, 324, 327, 330

Meyerhoff, Arthur E. Associates, Inc. 44, 51, 70, 140
Meyerhoff, Judy see Yale, Judy
Meyerhoff Files 8
Meyers, Benny 156
Miami 98
Michigan 96, 185, 269, 277, 278
Michigan Amateur Softball Hall of Fame 298
Michigan Amateur Sports Hall of Fame 305
Michigan Department of Commerce, Lansing, Mich. 271
Michigan Distributors, Inc. 147
Michigan High School Athletic Association Leadership Conference for Women in Sports 298
Michigan State Championship Team 212
Mickelsen, Darlene 38
Middleton, Ruth see Gentry, Ruth
Midland Park 300
Miller, Gertrude 22
Miller, Harriet 281
Miller Park 304
Milwaukee, Wisconsin 36, 41, 44, 46, 67, 73, 125, 156, 157, 168, 169, 293
Milwaukee Brewers 66, 107, 305, 306; Walls of Honor 305, 308
Milwaukee Brewers AA Team 67
Milwaukee Chicks (Schnitts) 55, 67, 68, 80, 155, 169, 209; (1944) 47
Milwaukee Journal 46
Mink, Patsy 2
Minneapolis, Minnesota 41, 44, 46, 73, 156, 157, 168, 169, 277
Minneapolis Millerettes (Orphans) 46, 68, 250; (1944) 48
Minneapolis Sports Hall of Fame 296
Minneapolis Tribune 46
Minnesota 159, 185
Minster, Ohio 277, 286
Minster, Ohio High School 295
Minster Hall of Fame, Ohio 295
Misas, Migdalia 117
Mississippi 105
Missouri 105, 185
Missouri Hickory 69
Mitchell, Jackie 249
The Mobile Press Register 96
Moczynski, Betty (Moe) 275, 305
Moellering, Rita Meyer (Slats) 75, 249, 272, 296
Moffet, Jane viii, 109, 266, 267, 292, 296, 305, 315, 318
Molinari, Susan 298, 299
Monahan, Kathleen (Toots) 92, 93
Montgomery, Dorothy 75
Moody, Ede viii
Mooney, Jette Vincent 211, 224
Moore, Dolores 200
Moore, Eleanor 201, 210, 225
Moore, Helen 168

Moore, Lucille vii, 7, 168, 174, 175, 234
Moore, Mary viii, 108, 168, 169, 194, 266, 291, 300, 310, 313
Moose Magazine 51
Moran, Gussie 225
Morgan, Dorothy 92
Morgan, Miss 71
Moritz, Christie 22
Moroz, Evelyn Wawryshyn (Evie) 75, 78, 210, 272, 301, 310
Morris, Carolyn 53, 70, 210, 214
Morrison, Violet Palumbo 92
Moses, Mayor, Fort Wayne, Ind. 243
Mosher, Stephen D. viii
Most Valuable Player Award 212
Mt. Hope Stadium, Cristobal, Panama 120
Mt. Pleasant, Michigan 277
Movie Royalties 289
Movietone News 67
Muckrakers 21
Mudge, Nancy see Cato, Nancy
Mueller, Bill 94
Mueller, Dolores see Bajda, Dolores
Mueller, Dorothy (Dot, Dottie) 98, 210, 211, 215
Mueller, J.L. 148, 149
Mulcahy, Anne 318
Murphy, Leo 96, 155, 156, 157, 162, 191
Murray, Margaret (Marge) 78, 92
Murrillo Orchestra 121
Musial, Stan 31
Music Maids 92, 200
Musicians Local No. 278, South Bend, Ind. 147
Muskegon, Michigan 41, 41, 149, 151, 156, 157, 168, 169
Muskegon Belles 130
Muskegon Cinema 12 Theatre, Michigan 286
Muskegon High School, Mich. 149
Muskegon Lassies 63, 84, 96, 99, 100, 146, 148, 167, 170, 171, 172, 173, 176, 201, 205, 206; (1946) 75
Muskegon Manufacturers Association, Mich. 149
Myrtle Beach, South Carolina 291
Myzon 69

Nancy Rehm Memorial Award, Fort Wayne, Indiana 295
Nashville, Tennessee 43, 182
National Amateur Athletic Federation 24
National Amateur Softball Tournament 214
National Archives, Washington, D.C. 278, 279
National Association of Sports for Girls and Women 312
National Collegiate Athletic Association (NCAA) 20
National Field Hockey Team 188

National Futbol Stadium (Soccer) 120
National High School Hall of Fame 296
National History Day Competition 315
National Lacrosse Team 188
National League 208
National League Club Owners 38
National Museum of American History 246
National Negro Baseball League 301
National Open Hearth Steel Committee 149
National Playground Association 20
National Polish-American Sports Hall of Fame 305
National Professional Baseball Clubs Associatioin 31
National Recreation Association 20, 23
National Softball Association 21
National Track Hall of Fame 295
Naum, Dorothy (Dottie) 128, 331
Navy 5
Navy Pier Band 55
Neal, Doris 78
Nearing, Myrna 38
Negro Leagues 231, 244, 265, 275, 293
Negroes 120
Nelson, Helen see Sandiford, Helen
Nelson, Stella 22
Nesbitt, Mary see Wisham, Mary
Nescopeck, Pennsylvania 192
New Agenda Conference 249
New England 108
New Jersey 105, 185, 305
New Jersey Softball Hall of Fame 276, 295
"A New Manpower Crisis, Ladies," cartoon 45
New Orleans Jax 92
New Star Theater, Grand Rapids, Mich. 284, 286
New York 20, 38, 105, 185, 231, 236, 281, 284
New York Celtics Softball Team 168
New York Giants 155
New York Mets 107
New York Times 267
New York Times Magazine 51
New York Yankees 5, 109, 110, 170, 203, 223, 304, 305
News of the Nation (quarterly publication of the National Jewish Hospital) 51
Newsome, Buck 171
Newspapers in Education 267
Newsweek 50
Newton, Joye 131
Nicaragua 115
Nichols, Nan viii

Nicholson, Phil 32
Niehoff, John Albert (Bert) *40*, 154, 156
Niekro, Phil 267
Niemiec, Dolly *see* Konwinski, Dolly
Nixon Library 173
Noga, Arleene Johnson viii, *75*, *77*, 188, *258*, 270, 274, 277, 295, 297, 298, *299*, 301, 305, *306*, 310
Norris, Donna Lee 211
Norteñas 112
North America 121, 278
North American Society for Sport History (NASSH) 231, 245
North American Stars 114
North Battleford, Saskatchewan 285, 297
North Carolina 105
North Plainfield, New Jersey 277
North Town Co-eds 88, 94; roster 92
North Town Debs 88, 92; (1948) *93*
North Town Stadium 88–90, 92
Northbrook, Illinois Park District Float 306
Northeast Indiana Baseball Hall of Fame 295, 304
Northeastern Pennsylvania Sports Hall of Fame 305
Northern Indiana Center for History (NICH) viii, 7, 264, 268, 275, 313
Northern Indiana Historical Society (NIHS) 256, 257, 262, 264, 290, 329
Northern Michigan University, Marquette, Mich. 249, 255, 257, 270, 272
Northwestern University 147, 250, 278
Northwestern University Club 147
Notre Dame Alumni Association 147
Notre Dame International Sports and Games Collection vii
Notre Dame Joyce Sports Research Collection 7
Notre Dame Library Special Collections Department viii, 7
Nun, Puerto Rican Girls Baseball Team 114

O'Brian, Penny *see* Cooke, Penny
O'Brien, Eileen *75*, 168
O'Brien, Mr. 138
O'Donnell, Rosie 283, 284
O'Doul, Lefty 171
O'Dowd, Anna Mae 92, 94, *106*, *109*, 315
Office Depot's Success Strategies for Businesswomen Conference 318
Office of War Information 30
Ogema Heritage Grandstand, Ogema Saskatchewan 295
O'Hara, Janice *38*, 182

Ohio 105, 159, 160, 192, 285
Ohio Baseball Hall of Fame 302
Ohio Northern University Athletic Hall of Fame 303
Ohio Track Hall of Fame 295
Ohio Women's Hall of Fame 295, 295
Oklahoma 96, 105
Oklahoma City, Oklahoma 192, 193, 96,
Olinger, Marilyn *77*
Oliver Family Mansion, South Bend, Ind. 262, 263
Olympic Softball Team 311
Omaha, Nebraska 157
O'Meara, Mary Froning *224*, *227*, 305, 312
Once a Year (Milwaukee Press Club Publication) 51
Ontario California Fast-Pitch Softball Tournament, Calif. 311
Ontario Fast-Pitch Softball Association, Calif. (OFSA)
Opalocka, Florida 96, 99, 104
Orange Bowl 113
Orange County, California 277
Orange Lionettes 161
Oravets, Pauline *40*
Organizational Structure of the AAGSBL/AAGPBL, 1943–1944 43
Organizational Structure of the AAGPBL/AAGBBL, 1945–1950 76
Organizational Structure of the AGBL, 1951–1954 126
Orion Film Company 279
Orlando, Florida 304
Orschel, Albert K. 79
Orschel Plan 79
Orwant, Carl vii, 8
Orwant Records 8
Oswego Art Guild, New York 278
Oswego Herland Film and Video Festival 278
Ozburn, Dolly Vanderlip *206*, 233, 312

Pace, Bill 280
Pacific Coast League 170
Padres, Johnny 268
Page, Tillie 92
Paire, Lavone *see* Davis, Lavone
Palermo, Toni *106*, *109*, 200, 310
Palesh, Shirley 312
Palm Springs, California 291
Palmer, Gladys 17, 18
Palumbo, Violet *see* Morrison, Violet
Pam Cooking Spray 69
Panama 111, 115
Panama Canal 120
Panos, Vicki *47*, 301
Paramount News 67
Parra, Manuel 112
Pasadena Tournament of Roses Parade 301

Pascagoula, Mississippi 96, 98, 99, 184
Pascale, Mat 157, 159
Pathé News 67
Patricia Stevens, Inc. 86
Payne, Barbara (Bobby) *106*, *109*, 300
Pearl Harbor 171
Pearson, Marguerite (Dolly) *see* Tesseine, Marguerite
Pechous, Doc 125
Peña, Tony 296
Peninsular Club, Mich. 147
Pennsylvania 105, 184, 185
Pennsylvania Hall of Fame 295
Pennsylvania Sports Hall of Fame 294, 305
Pennsylvania State University 8
Penny, Prudence 92, *93*
Peoria, Illinois 41, 43, 149, 151, 156, 157, 169
Peoria Association of Commerce, Ill. 149
Peoria Community Chest and Council, Ill. 149
Peoria Redwings 82, 83, 139, 140, 148, 152, 162, 164, 168, 173, 201, 212; fan club 153; (1946) *75*
Peoria Star 152
Peppas, June viii, 65, *128*, 138, 210, 211, 222, *225*, 231, *232*, 234, 235, 238, 239, 244, 245, 248, 253, 255, *258*, 261, 262, 269, 270, 274, 276, 279, 284, 288, 293, 315, 329
Perce, Joyce 92
Perez, Migdalia (Mickey) *77*, 102, *103*, *109*, 117, 120
Perkin, Janet Anderson 297, 301
Perlick, Edythe (Edie) *37*, *39*, 112, 117, 182, 200, 210, *215*, *217*
Personal Service Contract 35
Peru, Illinois 95
Peters, Marjorie *40*, 275
Peterson, Jean *see* Fox, Jean
Peterson, Ruth 168
Petras, Ernestine (Teeny) *47*, 157, 162, *163*, 169, 260, 305, 310
Petroskey, Dale 267, 268
Petrovic, Ann Meyer 285
Petryna, Betty *see* Allen, Betty
Petty, Lori (Kit) 266, 283
Philadelphia Athletics 108, 110
Philadelphia Phillies 155, 220
Philadelphia Sports Hall of Fame 296
Philatelic and Postal Services Dept. 275
Philharmonic Orchestra, Fort Wayne, Ind. 149
Philippine Tour 141
Phoenix, Arizona 277
Picture Magazine 67
Pieper, Marjorie (Marge) 230, 274
Pipp, Wally 223
Pirok, Pauline (Pinky) *38*, 192, 200, 210
Piskula, Grace 308, 315

Pitch and Hit Club of Chicago 310

Pitman, New Jersey 109

Pitman High School Hall of Fame 296

Pittsburgh, Pennsylvania 167, 184

Pittsburgh Pirates 80, 155

Player of the Year 96, 209–224

Playground and Recreation Association 20

Playground Ball 17, 20, 21, 24

Playground Movement 20, 21, 23

Playland Park, South Bend, Ind. 190

Policy and Procedure Manual 288

Polish Sports Hall of Fame 298

Pollitt, Alice see Deschaine, Alice

"Pomp and Circumstance" 66

Popular Culture Association 231

Portage la Prairie, Canada 277

Portland, Oregon 285

Portland TV 285

Post-Dispatch 276

Potaczyk, Helen 92

Powell, Rose Folder 304

Pratt, Dorothy 13

Pratt, Mary viii, 249, 250, 267, 277, 292, 293, 296

Prescott, L.A. 148, 149

Price, James 74

Prichard, Alabama 192

Pringle, Dolores 92

Printer's Ink 50

Professional Women's Bowling Association 190

Project View 267

Prune Pickers 173

Pryer, Charlene (Shorty) see Mayer, Charlene

Public Recreation Program of Greater Muskegon 63

Public School Athletic League (PSAL), New York 17, 295

Publicity Themes 51, 86, 324

Puerto Rico 111, 112, 113, 114, 115, 121

Queens 200

Quincy, Massachusetts 249, 277

Racine, Wisconsin 7, 36, 41, 49, 86, 125, 126, 147, 157, 168, 169, 209, 300

Racine Belles 55, 86, 99, 100, 101, 148, 155, 168, 169, 200, 212, 214, 256, 281, 298, 310; (1943) 39

Racine Belles Year Book (1944) 22

Racine Belles Year Book (1946) 213

Racine Cemetery Commission, Wisc. 147

Racine Elks, Wisc. 147

Racine Heritage Museum 313

Racquet Club 31

Rancho Cucamonga Quakes "A" Baseball Team 310, 311

Rancho Santa Fe, California 7

Randall, Maxine Kline 159, 206,

210, 211, 220, 223, 235, 274, 305, 315

Rapp, Nettie 92

Rauner, Helen see Harrington, Helen

Ravenswood-Lake View History Fair 313

Rawlings, John William (Johnny) 117, 119, 121, 155, 156, 157, 158, 194

Rawlins, Betsy 188

Rayner, William J. (Bill) 301

Rayson's Sports CGBL Team 94

Reader's Guide to Periodical Literature 6

Reagan, Nancy 261

Reagan, President Ronald 261

Recreation Committee of Kenosha Chamber of Commerce, Wisc. 149

Recreation for War Workers 51, 324, 326

Recreational Softball 19–21

Red Cross 53, 149, 149

Red Cross Benefit Game Flyer, 1944 54

Red Cross "Thank You" Night 67

Redding, California 5, 6

Redding Comets 6

Redlands, California 311

Redman, Magdalen (Mamie) 201, 315

Reeser, Sara 75

Regina, Saskatchewan, Canada 169, 182, 277

Regina-Moose Jaw Royals Women's Softball Team 154

Reiber, Gerry 168, 169

Reich, Gladys 22

Reid, Doris 77

Reiner, Tracy (Betty Spaghetti) 266

Reno County Museum 315

Renshaw, Mary viii

Reunion 229, 230, 231, 232

Reynolds, Mary (Windy) 75, 112, 116, 117, 157, 162, 164, 169, 210, 215

Rhode Island 185, 310

Rhode Island Scholar-Athlete Hall of Fame 304

Rhode Island's Greatest Sports Figures, 1900–2000 286

Rhoten, Agnes vii

Rhubarb at Home Plate 331

Rice, Grantland 86

Richard, Ruth viii, 115, 117, 120, 159, 210, 211, 220, 223, 225, 259, 306, 307

Richards, Ann 308

Richards, Charles (Cardo) 56

Richards, Jon viii, 275

Richards, Lucille Stone (Lou) 275, 276, 306, 307

Richmond, Virginia 43

Rick, Gladys 92

Ricketts, Joyce vii, 8, 211, 225, 234

Rickey, Wesley Branch (Branch) 39, 41, 42, 99, 126, 324

Rieber, Jerry 235

Riis, Jacob 16, 20

Rios, Georgiana 102

Risinger, Earlene (Beans) vii, viii, 8, 96, 117, 120, 192, 193, 201, 210, 225, 234, 255, 258, 267, 269, 270, 271, 284, 286, 288, 294, 295, 298, 300, 312, 313, 329

Rivera, Monica viii, 120

Rizzuto, Phil 108, 109

Roark, Mildred 169

Robinson, Jackie 42

Rochester, New York 111, 309

Rockford, Illinois 1, 2, 7, 36, 41, 43, 49, 52, 126, 147, 151, 156, 157, 168, 169, 193, 204, 277, 305

Rockford Peaches 1, 83, 84, 130, 131, 138, 148, 152, 155, 157, 176, 198, 199, 222, 224, 225, 226, 249, 276, 281, 285, 310; Board of Directors 63 Fan Association 131, 153, 225; (1943) 40; (1945) 53

Rockford Register Republic 1

Rockford Rotary Club, Ill. 147

Rockford Stadium 285

Rock-Ola Softball Team 200

Rockwell, Nancy DeShone see Dinehart, Nancy

Roepke, Sharon viii, 230, 231, 235, 244, 245, 246, 248, 249, 250, 252, 254, 255, 257, 268, 269, 270, 329

Rogers, Bill 156

Rogers Park Girls Indoor Baseball Team 13

Rogosin, Donn 246, 247

Rohrer, Kay 53

Romane, Frances 92

Romary, Gerald 65

Romatowski, Jenny 128, 188, 211, 225, 233, 234, 304, 305

Rommelaere, Martha see Manning, Martha

Roos, (?) 92

Roosevelt, Franklin D. 29

Rose, Pete 308

Rosecrantz, Charles (Chuck) viii

Rosecrantz, Tressa Fidler (Tress) viii

Rosemont Theater 305

Ross, Lucella MacLean 40, 55, 200, 277, 285, 297, 301

Roth, Elaine 128

Rountree, Mary (Square Bush) 75, 113, 114, 115, 116, 156, 161, 162, 163, 201

Royal Canadian Museum 262

Royal Ontario Museum 257

Rubenstein, Helena 60

Rudis, Mary 78, 168, 193

Ruetz, Jnell viii

Ruetz, Judge Edward J. 82, 113, 123, 125, 127, 133, 145, 146, 148, 149, 330

Ruetz, Edward J., Jr. 55, 56, 125

Rugg, George viii
Ruhnke, Irene *58*, 60, *61*, 182, 200
Ruiz, Gloria 102
Rumsey, Janet (Jan) 203, 211, *224*, 298
"Run, Jane, Run" (RJR) 234, *235*, 241, 242, 243, 246, 248, 249, 250, 270, 271, 329
Russo, Margaret (Marge) *see* Jones, Margaret
Ruth, George Herman (Babe, The Bambino) 5, 171
Ryan, Ada *38*, *48*, 168
Ryan, Margaret 169

Saddle and Cycle 31
Safeco Field, Seattle, Washington 304
Saginaw, Michigan 151
St. Aubins, Helen *see* Candaele, Helen
St. Henry High School Hall of Fame 304
St. Joseph, Michigan 151
St. Joseph, Missouri 43
St. Louis 36, 41
St. Louis Browns 42
St. Louis Cardinals 200, 296, 304, 305
St. Louis Softball Hall of Fame 298
St. Marys 286
St. Marys, Ontario, Canada 301
St. Paul, Minnesota 43
Salvation Army 147
Sams, Doris (Sammy) 96, *128*, 210, 211, 213, *214*, *215*, *220*, *223*, 226, 260
San Diego, California 267, 293
San Diego Military Baseball Team 310
San FranciscoGiants 6
San José, Costa Rica 115, 119, 120
San Juan, Puerto Rico 115
Sanders, Rudy 199, 200
Sandiford, Helen Nelson *40*, 301
Sands, Sarah Jane *see* Ferguson, Sarah Jane
Santa Catalina Island Company 171
Santo Domingo, Dominican Republic 111, 121
Saskatchewan, Canada 277
Saskatchewan Baseball Hall of Fame 295, 297
Satterfield, Doris (Sadie) *201*, 210, 211, *223*, *225*
Saturday Evening Post 67
Sauer, Louise Erickson (Lou) 210, 298, 312, 315
Savanna Ordnace Camp, Savanna, Illinois *53*
Saville-Biltmore Hotel, Havana, Cuba 98
Sawyer, Helen *40*
SBC Communications 264
Scarborough, Ros 260
Schaefer, Dona viii, 243, 270
Schaer, Marlene 92

Schatz, Joan 301
Schenck, Audrey 92
Schenectady, New York 267
Schick, Yolande Teillet 301
Schiedel, Frances 92
Schiedel, H. 92
Schillace, Clara *37*, *39*, *61*, 182, 200, 210
Schmidt, Erin viii, 315, *316*, 317
Schmidt, Violet 277, 315
Schnieder, (?) 92
Schofield, June *78*, 301
Schoolyard Playgrounds 19
Schrall, Leo 156, 157, *164*
Schroeder, Dorothy (Dottie) *40*, 117, 119, 120, *141*, 158, *159*, *206*, 210, 211, *223*, *225*, 232, 233, 272, 274, 300, 305
Schultz, John vii, 8
Schumm, Maryanne viii
Schweigerdt, Gloria (Tippy) 92, *93*, *94*, *95*, 286
Scott, Pat *78*, *206*, 211, 284, 285, 304
Scottish Band 138
Scottsdale, Arizona 239
Sears, Janet Wiley (Pee Wee) viii, 234, 256, 262, *263*, 283, 296, 310, 313, 315, 329
Seattle Mariners 304
Segregation 190
Sells, Kenneth (Ken) 10, 43, *44*, 57, 145, 146, 150, 154, 182, 198, *250*, 261, 274, 324, 330
Settlement House Playgrounds 19, 25
Seventeen 50
Sexton, Maria viii, 34, 230
Seymour, Ronald viii
Shadic, Lillian *106*, *109*
Shaffer, Bo 240
Shafranas, Geraldine *40*
Shastal, Mary Justra 301
Shattuck, Debbie 313
Shaughnessy Play-offs 86
Sheehan, Jack 71
Shepherd, Otis 57
Sheriffs, Vivian *see* Anderson, Vivian
Shero, Doris *see* Witiuk, Doris
Shiners, Ralph 156
Shively, Twila (Twi) 234, *235*, 238, 256, 262, *263*, 298, 312
Shollenberger, Fern *128*, 210, 211, *220*, *223*, *225*
Shrewbridge Field 92
Sidney, Ohio 286
Sifrer, Frances 92
Silver Bullets 310
Silverstein, M. 117
Simmons, Al *147*
Sindelar, Joan (Jo) 92, *93*, 94, *95*, *106*, *109*
Sisler, George 41–42
Skokan, Josephine *40*
Skokie, Illinois 277
Skupien, Mitch 92, 93, 94, *94*, 111, *128*, 157

Skydome 305
Slippery Rock Hall of Fame 298
Sloan's Linament 281
Sloppy Joe's Bar, Havana, Cuba *101*
Smith, Charlotte *39*
Smith, Ernest 42
Smith, Hazel 92
Smith, Helen (Gig) 306, *307*, 312, 313, *318*
Smith, Jean *159*, *201*, 211, 277
Smith, Joyce viii, 288, 289, 292, 293
Smith, Marge 200
Smith, Mr. 138
Smith, Ronald A. viii
Smith, Shirley 301
Smith, Sue viii
Smith Oil and Refining Company, Rockford 42
Smithsonian Institution 246; AAGBBL Display *247*
Smithsonian Museum of American History, Washington, D.C. 315
Social Criticism 17
Social Reform 19, 21, 25
Social Reform Movement 21
Social Values 17
Society for American Baseball Research (SABR) 231, 245, 275, 305, 312
Softball, Joint Rules Committee on 20
Softball World Champions, 1926 *22*
Somerset, Massachusetts 277
Sommer, A.H. *82*, *148*, 149
Somoza, Anastacio, Nicaraguan Minister of War 119, 120
South America 32, 112, 113, 114, 118, 121, 191, 293
South American Tour 115, 124, 194; scorecard, 1949 117
South Bend, Indiana vii, 7, 36, 41, 49, 52, 82, 107, 126, 147, 151, 156, 157, 161, 168, 169, 190, 204, 235, 238, 241, 256, 257, 261, 268, 271, 277, 285, 291, 293, 313
South Bend Blue Sox vii, 7, 55, 65, 73, 81, 83, 98, 99, 123, 130, 131, 132, 136, 137, 138, 139, 148, 150, 162, 167, 174, 176, 190, 201, 203, 207, 218, 219, 229, 234, 262, 296, 312, 329; directors 131; fan club 153; organizational structure 146; (1943) *40*; (1952) *224*
South Bend Bobbie Sox League 64
South Bend Court House 263
South Bend Indiana Baseball Hall of Fame 299
South Bend Indiana Sports Hall of Fame 298
South Bend Rockettes 188
South Bend Tribune vii, 7, 139
South Bend White Sox 296
South Carolina 105, 192

South Carolina Athletic Hall of Fame 300
South High School Field, Grand Rapids, Mich. 260
Southeastern Wisconsin Educator's Hall of Fame 299
Southern California 19, 174, 191, 278
Southern League 155
Sowers, Barbara 288, 289
Spears, Betty viii
Spencer, Ted viii, 249, *250*, 251, 252, 253, 254, 255, 259, 262, 264, 266, 269, 279, 329
Sport 51
Sport History Award 298
Sport Life 51
Sportlight Film 86
"Sports Answer Man" 142
Sports Educators of America Free Baseball Clinics 311
Sports Graphic 51
Sports Illustrated 248, 275, 286, 295
Sports Illustrated for Women 295
Sports Museum of New England Legacy Award 296
Sprayer, Alice 92
Spring Training 111
Springfield, Illinois 41, 74, 78, 156, 157, 168
Springfield Sallies 93, 94, 104, 105; (1948) *78*
Stalwart, Michigan 192
Stancevic, Marian 168, *175*
Stanton, Marion Watson *102*, 301
Star & Herald (Panama) 119
Stargell, Willie 260
Stark, Mae 301
State of Michigan Distinguished Graduate , 1946 305
Staten Island 106, 107
Staten Island Sports Hall of Fame 299
Statz, Jigger 171
Steck, Elma *109*
Stefani, Marge *40*, 169, 192, 210
Steffes, Helen Filarski (Fil) viii, *53*, 113, 156, 157, 266, 300, 310, 313
Stengel, Casey 108, 109, 110
Stephens, Ruby *78*, 113, 117
Stevenson, Emily *47*
Stevenson, Rosemary (Stevie) 192, 277, 286, 296, 312, 313
Stis, Chas. 156
Stoll, Nancy Jane (Jeep) *75, 78, 101*, 117, 210, 211, *225*
Stolze, Dorothy *75, 201*
Stone, Lucille (Lou) *see* Richards, Lucille
Stovroff, Shirley *78*, 117, 169, 176, 211, *239*, 240, 274, 329
The Strategy of Persuasion 70
Stratton Story, The 155
Stronack, Carrie *13*
Studebaker 158
Studebaker Plant, South Bend, Indiana 131

Studnicka, Mary Lou *see* Caden, Mary Lou
Stumpf, Eddie *40*, 154, 156
Stumpf, Florence 57
Stunach, Mary *13*
Success Strategies for Businesswomen Conference, 2003 308
"Suite from Carmen" 66
Sundance Producers 279
Sundquist, C.L. *82*
Sunset Haven Senior Center 309
Surkowski, Anne *see* Deyotte, Anne
Surkowski, Lee *see* Delmonico, Lee
Sutherland, Shirley 92
Svec, Polly *22*
Swamp, Rella *40*
Syracuse, New York 2

Taft, Robert (Bob) 295
Tah-Cum-Wah Community Center 298
Tah-Cum-Wah Field #2 *299*
Tah-Cum-Wah Recreation Center, Fort Wayne, Indiana 234
Talbot, Howard C. 258
"Tales from the Vienna Woods" 66
Tampa, Florida 192
Tavern on the Green, New York 284
Taylor, Cheryl viii, 264
Taylor, Janis viii, 194, 250, 278, 291, 329
Taylor, Mr. 132
Taylor-Roepke, Sharon *see* Roepke, Sharon
Teillet, Yolande *see* Schick, Yolande
Tennessee 105, 214
Tesseine, Marguerite Pearson (Dolly) *128*, 185, 207, *225*, 277, 298, 310
Tetzlaff, Doris (Tetz) *47, 77, 101, 116*, 117, 169, *206*
Texas 105, 111, 159
Texas Rangers 298
That's Incredible 238
Thayer, (?) 92
Thillens, Mel 88, 94
Thillens Stadium 92
"This Used to Be My Playground" 87
This Week Magazine 51, 67
Thomas, Mava 286
Thompson, Annabelle *39*
Thompson, Anne J. 301
Thompson, Beverly Stuhr 260
Thompson, Viola *see* Griffin, Viola
Thornton, Marion 92
Time 7, 50, 181
Times Square 32
Timm, Marie *40*, 168
Title IX 2, 19
Today Show 279
Today's News 232
Toledo, Ohio 151

Tom and Dill 69
Topa, Josephine 92
The Torch (Milwaukee Advertising Publication) 51
Torch Club 147
Toronto, Ontario, Canada 182, 267, 285
Toronto Blue Jays 305
Toronto Blue Jays' Skydome *306*
Toronto Sunday Morning Class Team 182
Towner, Bob 234
Tracy, Frank 88
Travis, Gene *see* Visich, Gene
Trezza, Betty (Moe) *48, 116*, 117, 183, 277, 284, 285, 297
Trombe, Carolyn viii, 181, 253, 266
Tronnier, Ellen *40*, 275, 296, 305, 312, 315
Trustee Administration 57, 71, 76, 77, 86, 94, 125, 128, 129, 130, 134, 135, 138, 142, 164, 181, 185, 191, 202, 204, 324
Tucker, Betty *75, 77*, 200, 285
Tucson, Arizona 285
Tulare County History Day, Wisc. 315
Turner, Rosemary 92
TV 13, Grand Rapids, Michigan 284
TV 8, 13, Grand Rapids, Michigan 286
Twamley, Ruby *13*
Twentieth Century Fox 282
Tyson, Alex 315

U.S.O. 149
United States 1, 15, 36, 44, 59, 80, 101, 102, 113, 115, 154, 157, 166, 185, 278, 323, 325
U.S. Doctors from Africa 311
U.S. Olympic Training/Education Center 249, 255
Universal Newsreel 67,
University of Chicago 42
University of Havana, Cuba 98
University of Indiana Hall of Fame 295
University of Maryland 315
University of Massachusetts, Amherst vii, 2, 6, 230
University of Minnesota vii; Saint Paul campus 8
University of Montevallo, Alabama 300
University of Notre Dame Library Special Collections Department 268
University of Pittsburgh 312
University of Southern California 281
University of Wisconsin 43, 168; Eau Clair 312; Parkside 313
Upper Peninsula Sports Hall of Fame, Mich. 296
USA Today 275
Uselmann, Therese McKinley

(Terry) 92, 275, 298, 305, 306, 313

Van Andel Museum Center, Grand Rapids, Mich. 313
Vancouver, B.C. 43, 285
Vanderlip, Dolly *see* Ozburn, Dolly
VanderZwaag, Harold J. vii, 8
Van Hyning, Thomas E. (Tom) viii, 112
Van Orman, Harold 127, 137, 138, 152, 162, 176, 205, 330
Varsity Club, Rock Hill, South Carolina 312
Venezuela 111, 113, 115
Villa, Margaret *see* Cryan, Margaret
Vincent, Jette *see* Mooney, Jette
Violet, Zonia 117
Violetta, Karen *see* Kunkel, Karen
Virginia 105, 185
Visich, Gene Travis 284
Vivian Kellogg Field *297*
Volkert, Beverly Hatzell (Bev) *109*, *235*
Vonderau, Kathryn (Kate, Katie) *206*, *225*, 288, 289
Voyce, Inez *101*, 117, *201*, 281, 310, 313

WAAC 52, 312
Waco, Ruth 168
Wadewitz, William R. *82*, 147, *148*
Wagner, Audrey *38*, 200, 210, *215*, *216*, *217*, 226
Wagoner, Betty *132*, 188, 210, 211, 219, 220, *224*, *225*, 234
Wagoner, Irene 169
Walker, Gary 270
Walmsley, Thelma 301
Walsh, Christy 5
Walters, Barbara 318
Walton Community Park 304
Walulik, Helen *106*, *109*
Wambsganss, Bill 155, 156
Wanless, Betty 200, 211
War Bond 149
Ward, Gadget vii, 7, *102*, *331*
Wardlaw, Charles 17
Warren, Nancy (Hank) *75*, 117, *206*, 211, 274
Warwick, Mildred (Millie) *see* McAuley, Mildred
Washington, D.C. 108
Washington Junior High School, Racine, Wisc. 168
Washington Senators 108
Watertown Athletic Association, 1998 310
Watson, Marion *see* Stanton, Marion
Waveland Park, Chicago 96
Wawryshyn, Evelyn *see* Moroz, Evelyn
Way, Rose Virginia *40*, 168

WBKB, TV, Chicago 86
WCUZ Radio, Grand Rapids, Michigan 286
Weaver, Betty *see* Foss, Betty
Weaver, Jean *206*, 211, 221
Weaver, Joanne (Jo) *159*, *206*, 211, 221, *222*, *223*, 226, 301
Weddle, Mary 211
Weeks, Rossey *102*, 285, 298
Wegman, Bill 282
Wegman, Carol 282
Wegman, Marie (Blackie) 98, 233, 281, 282, *283*, 284, 285
Welfare Work 21
Wenzell, Margaret (Marge) viii, *27*, *75*, *78*, *224*, 231, 270, 274, 281, 304, *309*, 312, 329
West Chester, Pennsylvania Athletic Hall of Fame 294
West Coast League 155
West Division High School, Chicago 16
West Los Angeles, California 277
West Putnam 298
West Virginia 105, 185
Westerman, Helen (Pee Wee) *38*, 60
Westerman, Joyce Hill 56, 57, 129, 166, 211, *224*, *227*, 285, 304, 305, 308, 310, 313
Western Canadian 192
Western Canadian Championship 182
Western Electric Company 276
Western League 155
Western Printing Company, Racine, Wisc. 147, 188
Whalen, Dorothy 200
What's My Line 141
Wheeling, West Virginia Hall of Fame 308
"When Diamonds Were a Girl's Best Friend" 278
White, Dee 305
White, Delores Brumfield (Dolly) viii, 19, 23, 59, 96, 166, 167, 184, 192, *193*, *206*, 111, 266, 267, 287, 292, 293, *299*, 300, 306, *307*, 308, 309, 310, 314, 315
White, Jason viii
White House, Washington, D.C. 306, 330
White Lake Yacht Club, Mich. 147
White Sox Baseball Park 286
Whiting, Betty *47*, *77*, *101*
Who's Who in American Education 296
Who's Who in American Women 296
Who's Who in Orange County, California 276, 295
WIBC Hall of Fame 296
Wichita Eagle 315
Wicken, Betty Berthiaume 297, 301
Wigiser, Margaret (Wiggy) *48*, 200, 295
Wilder, Dawn 257

Wildfong, Hazel Measner 297, 301
Wiles, Tim viii, 265, 266, 267
Wiley, Janet *see* Sears, Janet
Wiley, Pee Wee *see* Sears, Janet
William Wrigley, Jr. Company 30, 50
Williams, Jim 83, 151, 152
Williams, Ruth *see* Heverly, Ruth
Willams, Ted 171
Wills, Helen 34
Wilmington Transportation Company 171
Wilson, Betty 92
Wilson, Dolores *77*
Wilson, Kim 250, 251, 278, 279, 329
Wilson, Mildred 168, 169, *175*
Wilson Brothers 132
Wilson Elementary School Baseball Field, Medford, Oregon 302
Wiltse, Dorothy (Dottie) *see* Collins, Dorothy
Wind, Dorothy *39*, 200
Windy City 38
"Wine, Women, and Song Waltz" 66
Winger, Debra 282
Wingrove, Elsie *see* Earl, Elsie
Winnipeg, Manitoba 169, 185, 277
Winsch, Jean Faut *see* Faut, Jean
Winsch, Karl 157, 220, *224*, *225*
Winter, Joanne (Jo) *39*, 168, 182, 188, 210, *214*, *217*, *258*, 270, 274, 277, 294, 298
Wirth, Senaida (Shoo-Shoo) 113, 192, 210, *214*
Wisconsin 185
Wisconsin Old Timers Baseball Organization 305
Wisconsin Softball Hall of Fame 296
Wisconsin State Bar Association 149
Wisham, Mary Nesbitt viii, *39*, 210, 298, 315
Wisniewski, Connie (Iron Woman) *47*, 200, *201*, *209*, 210, 211, 212, *214*, 216, *217*, *220*, *223*, 226, 234, 298, 325
Witiuk, Doris Shero 301, 304
WLAV Radio 284
WMEE Radio, Fort Wayne, Indiana 234
Wohlwender, Marion 182
Wolenberg, Sally 92
Wolf, Eleanor Dapkus (Ellie) *39*, 200, 210, 214, 298
Woman of the Year 305
Woman's Day 67
The Women 141
Women in Sports Celebration, Anaheim Convention Center 312
Women Marines 173
Women's Army Air Corps 52